THE
ALL NEW
COMPLETE BOOK
OF
Bicycling

by Eugene A. Sloane

3rd Totally Revised
and
Updated Edition

Simon & Schuster
New York

Copyright © 1980 by Eugene A. Sloane
All rights reserved
including the right of reproduction
in whole or in part in any form
Published by Simon and Schuster
A Division of Gulf & Western Corporation
Simon & Schuster Building
Rockefeller Center
1230 Avenue of the Americas
New York, New York 10020

SIMON and SCHUSTER and colophon are trademarks of Simon & Schuster.
Designed by Irving Perkins Associates
Manufactured in the United States of America
Printed and Bound by The Maple-Vail Book Manufacturing Group
1 2 3 4 5 6 7 8 9 10

Library of Congress Cataloging in Publication Data

Sloane, Eugene A
The all new complete book of bicycling.
Published in 1974 under title: The new complete book of bicycling.
Bibliography: p.
Includes index.
1. Cycling. 2. Bicycles. I. Title.
GV1041.S55 1980   629.2′272   80-20298

ISBN 0-671-24967-3

Grateful acknowledgment is made for permission to reprint
from the following articles:

"Frame Repairing and Refinishing," by Otis Childress, from
Bike World (October 1977, Volume 6, Number 10).

"Tips to Inexpensive Frame Painting," by Otis Childress, from
Bike World (January/February 1979, Volume 8, Number 1).

"Exercising for Physical Fitness," by Herbert Adise, from Computer
Instruments Corporation.

"The Fallacy of Manual Pulse Taking," by Herbert Adise, from
Computer Instruments Corporation.

A small portion of the material contained in this book appeared in
The New Complete Book of Bicycling by Eugene A. Sloane.

Contents

Readers who are acquainted with the first two editions of this book will quickly see that this edition bears little resemblance to its forebears. There is so much that is new in bicycling equipment, camping gear for cycle touring and camping, places to cycle and new government regulations affecting bicycle design that I had to take a completely new approach to writing this volume. In effect, this, then, is an entirely new book, with very little of the two previous volumes used in this edition.

People I am particularly indebted to include my son Todd Sloane, who wrote much of Chapters 4, 5, 6 and 7. A great deal of his interest in and practical experience with sports medicine is particularly reflected in Chapter 6 on the health aspects of bicycling. I also wish to thank Tom Boyden of Fastab Cycles, Garland, Texas, and Gary Klein of Klein Bicycle Corporation (see Appendix) for their comments on selecting a custom frame builder. Otis Childress of Los Angeles furnished most of the section on frame painting in Chapter 16, for which I thank him and *Bike World* magazine, which published the original version.

Dave Tibbets of the Pony Shop and Lee Katz of the Turin Bicycle Shop, both in Evanston, Illinois, were most helpful with technical data, as was Ken Bostrom of the Schwinn Bicycle Company. Gene Portuesi, former U.S. Olympic bicycle team coach and owner of America's oldest mail order bicycle supply house, Cyclo-Pedia (Appendix)—who probably has forgotten more than most of us will ever know about bicycles and bicycling—was also most helpful. Cecil Behringer, who builds very fine bikes, indeed, was also very cooperative in furnishing technical data on some of the finer points of frame design and component selection.

I wish also to thank all the many manufacturers and importers of bicycle components and bicycles for their cooperation in enabling me to evaluate their products. This includes almost all the companies whose products are mentioned in this book.

I wish also to give a really big "thank you" to my editor, Pamela Diamond, for her patience, editorial savvy and gung-ho attitude which have contributed much to the intelligent organization of this book. Finally, to copy editor Barbara Grenquist, who has slaved mightily over this book to eliminate as far as humanly possible all my inconsistencies, errors and other sins of commission, my gratitude for a job well done.

One final note: The president of a large oil exploration firm told me in a recent meeting that the world's supply of liquid fossil fuel (oil) will, at the present rate of depletion, last *at best only another thirty-five years*. If you are thirty years old, by the time you are ready to retire at age sixty-five, the liquid sun will have set forever. This estimate is based upon known oil fields and all known and even foreseeable oil reserves, and includes all known primary, secondary and tertiary methods of oil recovery (drilling, water and steam injection, etc.).

Volunteer methods of fuel economy will never work, and decontrolling oil prices will only create hardships for the poor. The solution seems to me to lie primarily in alternative means of transportation—and not in mass transportation, which does not save fuel even as well as private transportation, according to recent studies.

But consider the bicycle. Not only is it virtually 100 percent fuel efficient, as compared with the automobile, in terms of use, but it takes a lot less energy to produce. A 30-pound bicycle has to take a lot less oil, natural gas and any other kind of energy to produce than does a 4,000-pound automobile; that's a ratio of 133 to 1. People laughed when I sat down at this typewriter a few years ago and predicted gasoline would cost two dollars a gallon. Now I forecast either strict gas rationing or a price of five dollars per gallon. Either way, you really should have a bicycle around as standby transportation. It may take you longer to get to work on a bike, but it *will* get you there, and you will be a lot healthier for the exercise, to boot. I also predict that once you have a bicycle, you'll ride it a lot with or without high gas prices or rationing . . . simply because it's a fun way to get places. Happy cycling!

It is a hot summer day high up in the green, thickly forested hills of southern Vermont. On a two-lane highway slicing up between two peaks in the hills, three cyclists push their finely tuned, lightweight machines ever upward, grimacing and wondering when the agonizing vertical journey will end. Out of their seats, they push down on the pedals, using their full weight to achieve one more turn of the cranks. They are quiet, intent on an inner cadence, a rhythm that will carry them at last to the end of the 3,000-foot climb. Then they are there. The quiet meditation of the endurance athlete shifts just as surely and quickly as their gears as the lead rider gives a throaty yell and the trio plunges into a fast descent that reaches fifty miles an hour. Tired but satisfied, they reap the payoff of an hour's good work. . . .

The scene changes. It is now a gray, threatening morning in late fall on Chicago's lakefront. While cars form a moving mass on Lake Shore Drive in the mad rush to Chicago's Loop, a lone figure, dressed in a sweatsuit against the cold, pedals swiftly downtown. His briefcase is strapped to his bicycle, and he pushes harder into a tough wind. He arrives in the Loop, and while cars jam up and horns create a cacophony of ugly, impatient sounds, he rides by quickly, disappears into a basement and arrives in his office minutes later. He is alert while others move slowly from the coffee maker to their desks. He is vigorously healthy, whereas many of his office mates look pale, overweight. Tonight he will ride his bike home again, completing a thirty-mile round trip. Tomorrow he will ride to work again. . . .

Now it is dawn on a steep country road just outside Seattle, in the foothills that lead to the great Olympic Mountains. Two young men in their early twenties are moving very quickly up and down the rolling hills on their road racing bicycles, their feet strapped to the pedals. One "drafts" the lead rider, riding just behind in his slipstream. They quickly shift places, with the second rider keeping the dizzying lead pace while the other rests. As they approach town on the return, they speed downhill, their faces plastered to the front handlebars for the least wind resistance. Theirs is a difficult sport, demanding superior strength and riding ability. They are hard muscled, with sinewy tissue that looks like steel rods in their thighs and calves. They are full-time bicycle racers, and this is what they do when they are not working at part-time jobs. There are only a few hundred riders who make it to the top. These two will make it. . . .

It is after dinner in suburban Atlanta, and one family is out on wheels, but not for a "Sunday drive." They are out for some fun and for exercise, which the parents wisely recognize that they need as badly as their children, perhaps more. As they ride about the neighborhood north of town, they see old friends, explore the landscape. Before a red sunset, they commune with the earth in a way they had not felt possible before, when they were trapped in the typical car-oriented world. They have sold their second car recently, and invested less than one thousand dollars in four bicycles. The father is immersed in learning how to maintain the bicycles, and he shares a new closeness with his son, who is also learning the joy of owning and maintaining a fine piece of machinery. Most blessed of all, the house stands empty while the family is out together, and the television screen, which once ruled the evening hours, is blank. . . .

For over ten years now, this generation on two wheels has been growing, and it shows signs of exploding once again in the 1980s. Lots of people try other sports first, but then so many of them join the ranks of the cyclists; they realize that cycling is an enjoyable, safe and sane exercise for the heart, the legs and the mind. If statistics do not lie, in the 1980s millions of Americans will be hitting the roads on high-quality bicycles, joining the millions more who have taken up bicycling since this book first appeared a decade ago. The bike boom has paralleled the fitness craze in general, and now bicycling is emerging once again as the sport everyone can participate in.

On the side streets, the main streets, the back-country roads, Americans push their bicycles on short rides, long rides, tours or races that last for several days. Almost half the population now owns bikes, and looking at the crowds on open roads on any sunny day, it looks as though everybody uses his bike frequently. It is only fitting, because until the advent of the automobile, bicycling was the national pastime in this country.

Bicycling is pure pleasure, whether done in groups, with a special friend or on your own. Once you buy a good bike, you will be amazed to feel yourself sailing over hills you once thought you could never even climb. This is the pleasure of adventure, of rediscovering the place where you live or exploring new areas. This is the fun and the feeling of achievement you get from cycling—being aboard a vehicle powered by you and only you.

Imagine being close to the countryside, out of the steel and glass cage of the automobile, hearing the sounds of nature, of birds and insects and the swishing of trees in the wind. Huddle against the handlebars on a quick descent of a hill, going as fast as you want, saving strength and gathering momentum to fly over the next hill without slowing down.

Bicycling gives you freedom to exercise when you want to and where you want to. It can be highly technical for those who love to tinker with fine equipment, or it can be very simple for those who do not want to bother. For the child, it is a basic means of transportation as well as fun, just as it is for the adult.

As exercise, bicycling is a way of life for many thousands of people. An "aerobic," or endurance, exercise, it increases the body's efficiency for using oxygen and in the process expands the blood vessels serving the heart. This has been proven to save lives in people who might otherwise succumb to heart disease. One of the greatest sights is surely that of a heart-attack or stroke victim vigorously pedaling his or her way back to the world of the healthy. Exercise on a regular basis reduces fat on the body, leaving less weight to carry around, and it gives a sense of well-being that transcends the physical and alters one's total attitude toward life. This is an experience recounted by cyclists the world over. The permanent sense of well-being, reflected in the energy brought to the sport and the dedication to the mechanical needs of the bicycle, is something that can enhance your life.

In this day of limited energy and deflated expectations, bicycling is also practical. We have entered the world of the late twentieth century, full of high-cost gasoline and "stagflation," a changing economy and, more importantly, change of every imaginable description in our social system. Experts in the fields of energy, the environment and economics have predicted that our very way of life is going to change. We will have to travel less, consume less, borrow less and conserve more. In many ways, we will be going back a bit on the continuum we have called the progress of civilization. To us bicyclists, this is not such an unpleasant proposition. Perhaps it is time we took stock of ourselves and began to think smaller. Maybe we ought to explore within what we have tried to expand beyond, to reestablish our roots in an increasingly rootless society.

Bicycling will play a key role in this new energy- and conservation-conscious world. Bikes use a renewable source of energy—the human body. They are a clean, energy-efficient means of transportation. They are relatively inexpensive, easy to maintain and, with the proper care, will last a lifetime. If more people take to their bicycles, as has been predicted for the next decades, the air will be that much cleaner, the junkyards that much emptier and people that much healthier. Maybe the changes ahead will not be so hard on people after all.

This is the third edition of this book, which came out for the first time with the first "bike boom." With the second explosion of interest in bicycling this book comes out again. It has been expanded again to fill the greater needs of the biking community and is designed to be an introduction to bicycling and a handy reference guide for the new cyclist. There is new material on all aspects of bicycling, including selecting and maintaining the bicycle, touring and commuting by bike, as well a history of bicycling and a look at bicycle racing, a growing sport.

Whoever you are, whether you are a new cyclist or confirmed bike nut, you will find here what you need to know about bicycling, the sport of the 1980s.

Bicycle Basics—Everything You Need to Know to Get You Going . . . Around Town, Around the World I

So You Want to Buy a Bicycle! 1

Welcome to the world of bicycling. It is a varied world, and can be as fulfilling as you would like it to be. One thing is certain, your investment of time and money will be returned many times over with the pleasures of bicycling.

Bicycling can be expensive (moderately) or inexpensive, intricately detailed or simple, depending on how involved you would like to become. If you are like many people, you may not have been on a bike since childhood, or you may be seeking to move up from your 40-pound commuter special to a lighter, streamlined touring bike. Whatever your age, occupation or interest, you are joining the second bicycling boom, and we are glad to have you with us!

The first step to enjoying the health and financial benefits of bicycling is to decide what you will be using the bike for, and to then select the most appropriate bike for that use, given monetary constraints. Worrying about the right components can come later, if at all, because most bicycles come fully equipped. Some people use their bikes exclusively for commuting to work, whereas others never ride their bikes to work for fear they will be stolen, preferring to ride at night or on the weekends.

During the past four or five years, mystique has grown up about the selection of a really good bicycle. In general, however, it can be said that, the better the bike, the more expensive it will be. There is a definite correlation between price and quality. Although at the various price levels one bike may be slightly better than another, more than price should influence your choice. Buying a bike is also a very personal decision, one that should be governed by the facts in books like this one and by road-testing yourself. Remember too that the market for bicycles in the United States has drawn the undivided attention of every bicycle manufacturer from every Western nation and even from such sources as Taiwan and Korea. Competition has already eliminated the less successful brands, and high-quality bike shops carry name brands with records of success.

Using cost as a general indicator of quality, you must decide what your price range will be and, again, your chief use for the bicycle. It simply does not make sense to buy, for example, a Masi or Fuji road-racing bicycle for toddling about town and for occasional trips to the store. On the other hand, if you think that you need more exercise and want to put

Fig. 1-1: This 10-speed Raleigh Touring bicycle is a symbol of performance for a moderate price. Like many other good-quality bicycles of moderate cost, this bicycle will provide a lifetime of exercise and cycling enjoyment.

some time into bicycling, then nothing can compare with the first experience on a fine ten-speed touring bicycle. (Fig. 1-1). A high-quality bicycle is more responsive, faster and safer than the old clunker that has been sitting out in the garage for eight years. The first trip on such a machine can be breathtaking. You simply had no idea that a bicycle could do such things. Exercise becomes more pleasurable, more interesting.

There are good-quality, responsive bicycles available at fairly low costs, low enough for the commuter or occasional bicyclist to pick up without feeling a budget pinch. Many are still under $200, a bargain at today's inflated prices. A simple look at gasoline prices and the cost of taxis, buses or trains (in the few places where these are convenient) makes bicycling to work, to the store or on shorter trips look very attractive.

Then there are the more expensive, lighter bicycles, equipped with the latest and lightest derailleurs, hubs, cranksets, seat posts, handlebars and bottom brackets. For the serious touring or even racing cyclist, these expensive bikes are a must, and a simple test ride will convince many noncyclists to become actively involved in bicycling.

Because most companies who make ready-to-ride bicycles use parts made by only a few firms such as Campagnolo, SunTour, Huret, Stronglight, and so forth, the first thing to look at is the frame, then the components, which we will also examine in that order. More detailed discussions of various parts will be found in the relevant chapters. At the outset, we will make specific selections in each price range that should help you in buying your bicycle.

A WORD ABOUT FRAMES

While we will go into much greater detail on the construction of frames later on in this book (see Chapter 2), it is important for you to understand good frame materials and construction right now if you are to choose the right bicycle. The best frame construction makes for stronger, lighter and more responsive machines and can make the difference between a fair bike and a really exciting machine.

Bicycle frames are made of a number of different kinds of steel and tubing. The garden-variety, inexpensive, coaster-brake or three-speed bicycle is usually made of seamed tubing—a strip of steel wrapped into tubular form by rollers and then automatically welded electrically into a tube. Such tubing is straight gauge, meaning that it is not reinforced where it joins other parts of the bicycle. Typically, the tubes of this type of frame are simply stuck into each other and welded at the joints. The problem with a frame of this sort is that electic welding is done at high temperatures, which causes stresses at the joints that can weaken them. Simply sticking frame members into each other and welding them makes for the weakest type of frame construction. Unfortunately, the vast majority of bicycles are made this way.

The best bicycles are made with Reynolds '531' double-butted, cold-drawn, seamless manganese-molybdenum steel, Columbus, Tange, Ishiwata or other high-carbon, chrome moly steel. This tubing combines lightness with high strength and resistance to "fatigue," and high tensility for maximum resilience with a feeling of "liveliness" in the frame.

The average cyclist cannot tell if a frame is double-butted just by looking at it. Double-butting means that the metal is thickened at both ends where maximum stress occurs, without changing the outside diameter of the metal tube. (Fig. 1-2).

You can find the type of tubing on the bike by reading the decals placed on the frame, or a good bike dealer can give you the specifications. But if it's decals you're depending on, you must learn to read them properly. For example, there are a number of different combinations of Reynolds '531' tubing, so a Reynolds decal on a frame does not necessarily mean that it is a superior bicycle.

Here is what the various Reynolds labels or decals (Fig. 1-3) mean:

The label that says "Reynolds '531' Frame Tubing" means that the top tube, seat tube and down tube are made of Reynolds '531' plain-gauge (not double-butted) steel.

The decal or label that says "Guaranteed built with Reynolds '531' plain-gauge tubes, forks and stays" means that all the tubing in the frame is Reynolds '531' plain-gauge (not double-butted) steel.

The decal that says "Guaranteed built with Reynolds '531' butted-frame tubes" means that the top, seat and down tubes of the frame are of Reynolds '531' double-butted tubing.

The label that says "Guaranteed built with Reynolds '531' butted tubes, forks and stays" means that the frame is all Reynolds double-butted. This is the most costly and best frame you can buy. But even this type of frame is not the best possible one unless it is brazed properly and finest quality, precision-made, hand-filled lugs are used.

The Reynolds manufacturer specifies that the best brazing is done by hand, using low-temperature bronze-brazing materials with a melting point no higher than 850 degrees Centigrade. Look for bicycle-frame specifications that say "all-lugged, low-temperature, bronze-brazed" or words to that effect. High-temperature brazing makes joints brittle at the point of stress, which can negate the good tensile qualities of the Reynolds steel.

A Word About Other Tubing

Really cheap bikes have frames of seamed, welded, low-carbon steel tubing with a "joined" or "yield" strength (after having been welded) of about 22,000 pounds per square inch, which seems strong but really isn't. These frames are heavy and stiff, and give a spine-jolting ride.

In the low- to medium-range bikes, frames are seamed, welded, low-

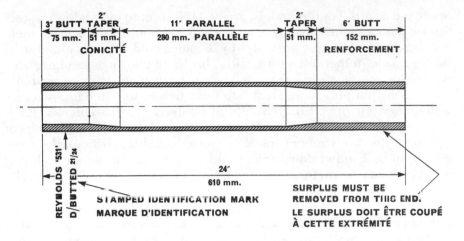

Fig. 1-2: A cross-section of Reynolds' '531' double-butted tubing for bicycle frames. This tubing is used only on the finest bicycles, and is only rivaled by the best of the chrome molybdenum tubing.

carbon steel, with a joined strength of around 32,000 pounds per square inch.

We have already discussed Reynolds '531' tubing, which has a joined yield strength of around 80,000 pounds per square inch, and contains 1.45 percent manganese, 0.25 percent molybdenum, 0.29 percent carbon and 0.35 percent silicon.

A frame metal also used on high-quality bicycles, such as the Cinelli line, is the famous Italian Columbus tubing. This is a high-quality chrome molybdenum tubing which gives a somewhat stiffer ride than Reynolds '531,' and thus is favored for track and road-racing machines. A similar metal is made in Japan and used in their top bicycles, such as the Fuji line.

Schwinn uses three different types of tubing, depending on the quality of their bicycle. The top-line Paramount series is made of double-butted Reynolds '531' tubing. Schwinn's second line, such as the Super

Fig. 1-3: '531' tubing comes in several varieties and uses. These decals will appear on various levels of bicycles, differing according to the cost and quality of the machine. The best bicycles, of course, use the last decal signifying that only top-grade Reynolds double-butted tubing is used throughout the bike.

Only the Top Tube, Seat Tube and Down Tube of a frame with this transfer are made from REYNOLDS 531 Tubing—plain gauge.

All the tubing in a bicycle with this transfer is REYNOLDS 531 — Frame Tubes, Chain & Seat Stays & Fork Blades, but it is all plain gauge tubing.

The Top Tube, Seat Tube and Down Tube of a frame which bears this transfer are REYNOLDS 531 BUTTED tubing.

This transfer signifies that the bicycle is an aristocrat, a thoroughbred — made throughout of REYNOLDS 531 tubing BUTTED for lightness with strength.

Sport and Sports Tourer models, are of 4130 chrome molybdenum steel tubing with a yield strength of around 75,000 pounds per square inch. Other Schwinn bicycles are of 18- to 20-gauge cold drawn welded steel tubing, made in their own tube mill. The 18- to 20-gauge steel explains why Schwinn lower-priced models are a bit heavier than comparable bikes; Schwinn puts more steel into their frames for strength, whereas some other low-priced bicycles are of lighter 14- to 15-gauge welded-steel tubing. When it comes to lower-priced models, as for youngsters of ten to fourteen, a stronger frame is more desirable, particularly if the bike is to be handed down from child to child in the family. I should point out that my stricture about nonlugged frames does not apply to the Schwinn chrome moly frames, which are gas welded and built up at the joints. It is also, of course, possible to build beautiful '531' or Columbus-butted frames without lugs, and without detracting from strength, and in fact some fine machines are built that way. These are usually frames tailor-made to individual order. The frames that bother me are the ones with low-carbon tubes simply stuck into each other that are machine-welded at high temperature on a mass-production line. These frames tend to be poorly aligned and weak and unresponsive.

Custom Frames

There has been a lot said and written about the hows and whys of buying custom-made frames from companies that make such specialty frames. Much is said of the frame geometry such as the rake of front fork, angle of seat and down tubes, wheelbase, and so forth, and the composition of the frame and the details of putting frames together.

But in this chapter we are concerned only with off-the-shelf bikes, and not with the more specialized custom frames. Buying such a frame entails deciding what special parts you want on it and then arranging to put it together, a process that can be gleaned from succeeding chapters of this book. See Chapter 2 for a discussion on buying a custom frame.

The Lower the Weight, the Higher the Price and Quality

Generally speaking, the more a bicycle costs, the lighter and better it will be. If you drew a curve based on weight and price, with the weight line on the bottom and the price line vertical, you would find that the curve would ascend gradually as the weight decreased from 38 to 32 pounds and then would rise dramatically for every pound thereafter. For example, you can buy a ten-speed bicycle that weighs around 38 pounds for around $150, or a bike that weighs 28 pounds for $300, or a 26-pounder for $500 . . . on up to the 22-pound or lighter bikes that cost $1,000 and up.

In the absence of price as an indicator, you should look for the quality of the components, which are also dependent on the quality of the bike. Manufacturers are not going to put top-line, ultralight parts on a balloon-tired bike. The best parts on complete-production bikes are made by Shimano, SunTour, Campagnolo, Sugino Simplex and Huret. In descending order of quality, the Campagnolo parts are:

- 4000 F Series Super Record Road Group
- 1032 F Series Record Road Group
- 2240 Grand Sport Road Group
- Valentino Extra Road Group
- Rally Gear large ratio (found on better bicycles)

The best Shimano (Japan) parts, considered by many to rival the top-ranked Campagnolo parts, are the DuraAce parts, made in a separate factory from other Shimano parts. The Shimano Crane wide-range derailleurs are also of the highest quality. The Shimano 600 road and touring components are second; the Altus-Selecta line is the mid-priced range; and the Shimano PPS, or positron shift mechanisms with a push-pull cable system for derailleurs, are specialty items.

Other companies make certain parts well, such as Sugino Mighty Compe cranksets; the SunTour GT series, a set of parts considered by some to be among the very best; the Simplex line of derailleurs, like the Super LJ and Criterium derailleurs, as well as lesser derailleurs by Simplex, such as the Maxi-Prestige, and the Huret Luxe and Super-Touring derailleurs.

The better bicycles, those costing about $600, use Campagnolo Nuovo Record or Shimano DuraAce brakes, derailleurs and other parts. Bikes that cost above $600 or so generally are fitted with Campagnolo Super Record or Shimano DuraAce parts. The frames will be hand brazed with silver and will be beautifully finished. The better bikes will also have brazed-on fittings for cables, eliminating any need to strap on such things as the shift levers, cable guides and water-bottle cage and pump hangar, which will always mar the finish.

Higher-quality touring bikes use double-butted, high-carbon, chrome molybdenum steel tubing, which is very strong, yet light, and gives a high-yield strength, as shown in Table 1-1. The yield strength of tubing

Table 1-1 Yield Strengths of Bicycle Tubing

Tubing Brand Name (or Generic)	Yield Strength in KG/MM ^{2}
High Carbon 2030	17
Durifort A35	32
Durifort E36.3	67
Vitus 172	67
Super Vitus 971	67
Reynolds 531	67
Columbus	67
Ishiwata	67
Tange	67
4130 steels	67
Rubis 888	67
Super Vitus 888	67

is that point at which the tubing will become permanently distorted, as in a crash.

The really cheap bikes use seamed electro-welded tubing, and have far lower quality components. Bicycles in the medium-price bracket use components such as Shimano 600 EX—in the upper third price bracket Shimano 600, in lower price brackets, Shimano Altus parts.

CRITERIA FOR A BICYCLE

There are several bicycle manufacturers in the United States, and large numbers of bikes are imported from England and Japan. To aid you in picking out a good-quality bicycle from the multitudes available, here is a brief analysis of what to look for. Some of the distinctions among bikes in a given price range are going to be pretty fine, but as long as you are in the market, it makes sense to get exactly what you are looking for and the very best value for your investment.

The Frame: Where frame tubes meet, they should be brazed into lugs at their joints (Fig. 1-4). Frame construction where tubes are inserted into each other (Fig. 1-5) is not nearly as strong as the lugged and brazed frame, except as noted on page 20. However, there are lugs and lugs. The very plain lugs that look like pieces of sawed-off pipe in a "T" shape

Fig. 1-4: An example of good lugging on a well-made bicycle frame.

Fig. 1-5: This frame construction is not as strong as the lugged frame in Figure 1-4.

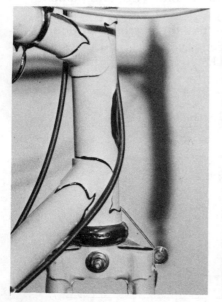

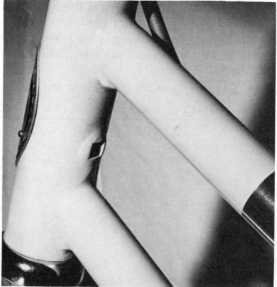

Fig. 1-6: Here is what can happen to a cheap bike frame, where tubes are simply stuck into one another and welded into place. This was a brand-new bike, barely a month old, when the owner found himself on a "collapsible bike." Note how the welds simply parted at the head tube.

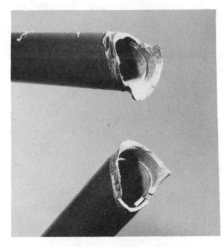

Fig. 1-7: Automatic welding by machine led to this problem with the frame construction.

Fig. 1-8: Close-up of the headset of the bicycle in Figures 1-6 and 1-7. Note that the welding is practically nonexistent on this cheap frame, another good reason to buy only a lugged frame. Only a few unlugged bicycles, notably Schwinn, are strong enough to hold up for very long under pressure.

are more than likely simply cast steel, whereas the cut-off decorative-looking lugs on the finer bicycles are forged steel—the latter being, of course, much stronger as well as lighter. The poorly welded, unlugged frame may come apart at the joints as shown in Figures 1-6, 1-7 and 1-8.

Caliper Brakes: There are three basic types of caliper "hand" brakes—side-pull, center-pull and cantilever (see Figs. 1-9 through 1-11). Cantilever brakes are used mostly in tandems, although Raleigh uses them on their new top-line touring bike described later in this chapter. Until the 1970s, only inexpensive bicycles had side-pull brakes because, until some of the new cam-action designs came out, they were considered inferior. They pulled up from one side only, and would not work as positively as center-pull designs. Cheap bikes still use side-pulls but they are not the same as the highly engineered, polished aluminum alloy brakes, such as those made by Campagnolo, Shimano and Universal, which are used on high-priced bicycles.

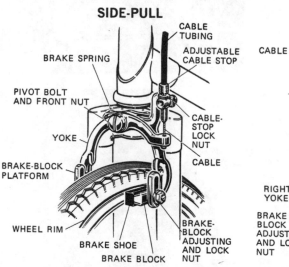

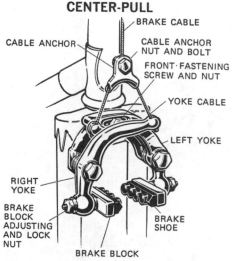

Fig. 1-9: Side-pull brakes once were found only on less costly bicycles. Now the most expensive bicycles often use top-quality side-pulls, such as those made by Campagnolo or Shimano.

Fig. 1-10: Center-pull brakes are found on medium and some high-priced bicycles.

Fig. 1-11: A cantilever brake. See discussion of brakes in Chapter 10.

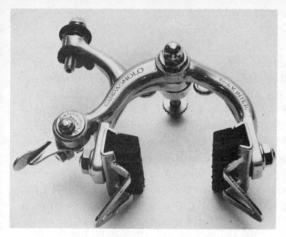

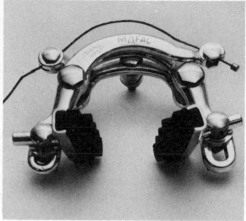

Fig. 1-12: (Above) Campagnolo side-pulls are quite expensive; they are designed for the road-racing cyclist who wants very accurate braking control.

Fig. 1-13: (Above right) Mafac center-pull alloy brakes still offer excellent fingertip stopping control. They are reliable and comparatively inexpensive.

Fig. 1-14: (Right) High-quality side-pull brakes on a Windsor Super Carrera bicycle. Note the beautiful brake bridge design on this bicycle.

Until Campagnolo came along with their expensive side-pull caliper brakes, (Fig. 1-12), the center-pull Mafac "Competition" (Fig. 1-13) was thought to be the best brake. Now Campagnolo is thought to be about the best, along with other first-rate side-pulls like the less expensive but high-quality Shimano (Fig. 1-14). But these side-pulls all cost four or five times as much as the Dia-Compe or center-pulls like the Mafac "Competition" and "Racer," Universal, the Weinmann 999 alloy brakes without working four or five times better. So unless you are looking at the highest-quality bicycle, it is just not worth it to get the more expensive side-pulls.

Chainwheels, Cranksets and Bottom Brackets: The best makers of all these parts integral to the pedaling process, and therefore crucial to the quality of a bicycle, are Campagnolo, Sugino (their five-pin crankset) and Shimano DuraAce.

T.A. also makes alloy chainsets, but I've had trouble with them due to pins that hold the cranks together coming loose, so that the chainwheel flattens irretrievably under cycling pressure. After tightening loose pins on a replacement T.A. crankset, I had no further problems, though. Nervar also makes a fairly good alloy chainset. Sugino makes a three-pin alloy crankset, but their five-pin is stronger and more likely to stay in alignment.

Headsets: The headset on a bicycle is the set of bearings, cones, top washer and locknuts that hold the fork in place and permit it to turn accurately and smoothly. Headsets on good bicycles have their maker's name stamped on them, usually on the top locknut. To check headset adjustment, lift the front wheel off the floor and turn the fork by the front wheel, feel for binding or roughness. Hold the bike down, handlebars grasped firmly, wheel on the floor, and lift handlebars to rear and front of the bike to check for sideplay looseness. Cheap headsets often have cracked lower cups, which you can't detect in the assembled bike. If in doubt, disassemble headset (see Chapter 14) and check top and bottom cups for tiny cracks and imperfections, and for shiny "galled" spots showing wear at misaligned points. Better headsets are made by Campagnolo, Stronglight and Zeus.

Stems and Bars: The best bicycles come with aluminum alloy stems and handlebars. The very best machines come with recessed stem bolt design stems (Fig. 1-15), with the stem bolt head hidden from view. This is mostly a cosmetic advantage, though the lack of a protruding stem bolt can add to safety. But you'll need a 6- or 7-millimeter Allen key wrench for the stem bolt, which is one extra tool to carry on trips you would not need with conventional stem bolt design. Recessed stems are handsome, though, especially the stem and engraved bars made by Cinelli, Dia-Compe, Sakae Ringyo, Ltd., and t.t.t.

Seat Posts: Seat posts on fine bicycles are made of aluminum alloy and have a unique microtilt adjustment (Fig. 1-16) that lets you move the saddle up or down in as small an increment as you wish, to accommodate the curves of your you-know-what. These seat posts are made by Campagnolo, Zeus, Unica-Nitor, t.t.t., and Sakae Ringyo, Ltd.

Fig. 1-15: The best handlebars on top-quality bicycles have dressier recessed stem bolts.

Fig. 1-16: A high-quality alloy seat post with microtilt adjustment of the saddle

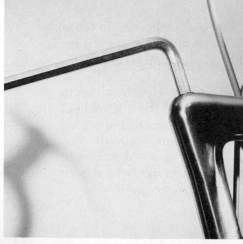

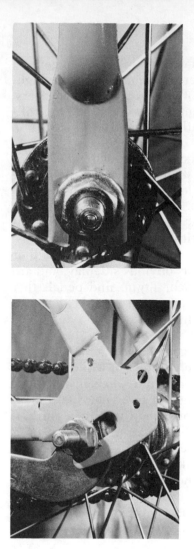

Fig. 1-17: (Left) Stamped fork dropout

Fig. 1-18: (Below left) Weak chainstay dropout of spot-welded, stamped construction

Fig. 1-19: (Below right) Forged, brazed, very strong dropout found on better bicycles

Dropouts: The slotted fitting where the wheel axle fits in on the fork blades and stays is called a "dropout," because when you loosen axle bolts or quick-release skewer, the wheel "drops" out. Cheap bikes with fairly flimsy construction use stamped dropouts, often just stuck into the fork blade and welded there (Fig. 1-17), and pressed and spot-welded into rear stays (Fig. 1-18). Compare these dropouts with the strong, forged-steel brazed-in-place dropout in Fig. 1-19.

Lugs: Lugs are the sleeve braces by which the tubes of the frame are joined together (Fig. 1-4). The trade name "Nervex" indicates high quality. Even though some lugged frames are stronger than unlugged frames, this is not always so. If lugs are simply cast-iron hunks of metal, little better than water pipe, about all they do is add weight to the bicycle, and give it the vague appearance of a more costly machine.

Hubs: There are several fine makers of good-quality hubs, and in general these are the same firms that make the other good components for high-priced bikes. Campagnolo is still the best of the European hub makers, while SunTour and Shimano make excellent, lightweight but easy-rolling models. Look for all of these brands while seeking a new bike.

Pedals: All of the better bicycles have pedals made of light, forged-aluminum alloy barrels and with alloy or steel "rattrap" sides and toe clips for inserting the foot so it won't slide off. (Accidents leading to injury and fatality have been attributed to feet slipping off the pedals resulting in loss of balance.) Cheaper bikes have rubber and steel pedals, or all-steel rattrap pedals, usually without toe clips and straps, although they can be fitted on later. Cheap pedals are wider, and either bind as they turn or are so loose that there is obvious sideplay, and are comparatively heavy, around 10 ounces each. Try to find pedals that have reflectors on them, or add them before you use the bike, because these moving reflectors can help save your life.

Kickstand: You'll never find a kickstand on a good bicycle for at least four reasons. First, if the kickstand is bolted on chainstays, it will eventually loosen and when you tighten it, you squeeze and weaken the stays. Second, if it's welded on, stays are weakened at the weld due to heat stress. Third, kickstands, even aluminum ones, add weight. Fourth, a good breeze, or a passerby, can knock over a bike propped up by a kickstand, with possible damage to derailleur, finish, brake levers, or handlebars; it's much better to *lean* the bike against a wall. And you can't conveniently chain a bike to a telephone pole or fence and still have it held up by the kickstand, and in any case the chain will hold the bike in place. So please wipe that look of dismay off your face because good bikes are "missing" a kickstand; it's a negative feature.

Safety Levers: On some bikes you'll find two sets of brake levers. One set is the standard kind that sticks up above the handlebars, on the curve of the bars. The second set is flatter, connected to the same brake lever as the first, but the lever is parallel to and just underneath the top, flat part of the handlebars. I have used these "safety levers" and in my opinion they're anything but safe. They can, in fact, mislead you into thinking you can stop when in fact you cannot. The reason is that the "safety levers" do not have the distance of "travel" the standard levers do. Thus, unless wheel rims are almost perfectly true, and brake shoes adjusted so they are no more than ⅛ inch from the rims, "safety levers" won't pull up enough to force the brake shoe against the rim for a safe stop, especially a successful panic stop. Brakes get out of adjustment easily, rims won't stay aligned forever, brake cables stretch, so a "safety lever" that stopped you safely once may not do so when you need it. My advice is to go to your bike shop and have these unsafe safety levers removed, or do it yourself by unscrewing the nut holding the safety lever, removing the spacer and replacing it with a shorter spacer (from your bike dealer) and screwing the nut back on again.

BIKES FOR COMMUTING AND/OR TOURING

In general, if all you are going to do with your bike is travel to work or go for an occasional weekend ride, then the less expensive bicycles, costing under $200, will work out well for you. You are not looking for a race, or for high-speed workouts. All you want is a dependable bike, and I have selected several respectable brands to try out. But if you want to make bicycling your pastime, then you should look for the more expensive touring machines, because nothing will stir your interest and continuing devotion to exercise more than having a responsive bicycle. Let's look at the kind of bike suitable to each general category.

If you want to join the growing legions of people who are taking the alternative to using the gas-guzzler or the crowded trains to get to work, and are bicycling to save energy, money and the cost of ill-health, more power to you. The needs of the commuting cyclist are different from those of other cyclists. The type of bike you buy will depend on whether you can store the bike indoors, where it is guaranteed to be safe (that is, chained to your desk, or in a locked room, because you never know who will steal an expensive bike), or whether it will be outdoors, exposed to criminals and the elements. It is not worth riding a flashy, well-equipped bike to work if it attracts criminals. Even if you lock up such a bike, parts can be easily removed. You can't lock up your $50 saddle, or your $75 derailleur. If you can put the bike up indoors, then you can use a good touring bike (if you want to buy one) to go to work. If you have no need for an expensive bike anyway, then buy a relatively lightweight, inexpensive, modest-looking machine.

I will discuss other accessories for commuting later on, but just let me point out a few essentials here: You should have fenders for wet weather (a telltale streak of greasy rain up your back is a sure sign of a fenderless bike), a carrier for hauling your briefcase and a good horn for offending motorists. (We will return to this subject in detail in the chapter devoted to commuting.) But let's just stick to the basic bike for now.

Unless you are going to be climbing a lot of hills on the way to work, a simple five-speed gearing system will do just fine. A good gear selection for flat riding would be something like a 48- or 52-tooth single chainwheel in the front and a 14-to-32 or -34-tooth rear freewheel.

If you have to climb hills on the way to work, I would select a ten-speed inexpensive bike with wider gears that enable you to pedal more easily over the hills, say a 42 and 52 chainwheel set (double wheel in the front, as you see on ten-speeds) and 14-to-34-tooth rear freewheel.

If you commute under five miles each way over fairly flat ground a three-speed bike will do. You are not out to break any speed records, and if you have to leave the bike out in the cold, rain or snow, you don't want to subject a more expensive bike to that kind of treatment.

I would buy a commuting bike with solid axles so you can bolt the wheels to the dropouts, those pieces that extend from the rear fork of the bike. Many bikes sold in this country have the fashionable quick-release skewers which make it a two-second job to remove the wheel for repair. But a thief can also remove the wheels quickly, putting you in the position of having to walk home carrying a heavy bike. The quick-release was originally designed for the racing community to facilitate quick tire changes. This is not essential for the commuting cyclist. The few added minutes of loosening bolt-on wheels is well worth the added protection of bolt-on hubs. You will need a wrench to remove the bolts, of course, and this you should have with you, along with other items we will describe later.

The commuting or touring bikes selected and described on the following pages can and should be used for utility riding about town, for shopping, visiting friends, and the like.

RACING VERSUS TOURING BICYCLES

If you are willing to spend top dollar for a bicycle, you will find that the road-racing models are right up there in price with the best of the touring bicycles. Any bicycle shop that carries both types of costly bicycles will know the difference between the two, but you still cannot rely on the salesperson to caution you about what you might be getting into if your heart skips a beat when you look at a pure-bred road-racing model. The shorter wheelbase, short fork rake, super high quality components, can be very appealing. The bike simply *looks* as though it wants to go fast. *Don't do it!* Do not buy the road-racing machine if you want a bicycle to tour or commute with. The short wheelbase, short fork rake, stiff frame will be super-responsive, to be sure, but will jolt your innards out on an all-day tour or even a relatively shorter commute. (Refer to Chapter 2 on frame design.) Measure the frame wheelbase, axle nut to axle nut, with a tapemeasure. If you come up with 39 inches or so (100 centimeters) forget it as a touring bike. If you find a wheelbase of 41 inches (104 centimeters) you will now have a frame that absorbs road shock and doesn't transmit it to your personal framework of bones and ligaments and muscles.

Also look for wheels that are four-crossed laced (spokes crossed over four—see Chapter 15) and have low-flange hubs (Fig. 11-17). The low-flange hubs require longer spokes. Four-cross spokes are also longer. The longer spokes absorb road shock better than the shorter spokes of a high-flange, crossed-three-spoked wheel found on some racing models. And spokes will last a lot longer on the low-flange hubs.

For the really high-priced touring bicycles, look for such niceties as loose ball bearings in the headset and crank, because caged bearing sets mean fewer balls and shorter bearing life. It takes longer to assemble a bike with loose instead of caged bearings, but longer life is worth it. You won't find many bikes that come with loose bearings (Bertin is one that does) so you can, when maintenance time comes, replace the caged bearings with loose balls yourself. Chapter 12 covers headset and crankset maintenance procedures.

A WORD ABOUT TIRES

There is still a lot of confusion in this country about tire nomenclature. There are only two types of tires in wide use today. Back in the thirties and earlier, tires were the "clincher" type, which meant that they had a bead around the inner perimeter which fit or clinched into a matching section of the rim. These tires are obsolete today. We now use what are known as "wired-on" tires on all but racing bicycles. They are called "wired on" because the tire has a wire bead sewn into the casing so that when the tire is pumped up the bead will hold the wire onto the rim. The only other tire in common use today is called a "tubular" tire, so named because the tire is actually a tube with the inner tube sewn up as shown in Figure 1-20. The rim for these tires does not have a flat inner side because the tire is beadless. Tubular tires are glued to the rim. They are quite thin and prone to flats and should therefore be ridden carefully. Avoid running over bits of glass or other sharp objects.

Tire nomenclature has since been simplified, eliminating the awkward expression "wired-on" to distinguish those tires from the tubulars. Today and throughout this book when we refer to a tire we mean "wired on." When we refer to a tubular we mean tubular tires. You can, of course, tour on tubulars, and you can buy heavier tubulars that are less flat prone. But you lose the advantage of lightness or a lower rolling resistance from the narrow profile of the tubular when you do so. In fact today we have tires that rival tubulars both in terms of weight and low rolling resistance. Such a tire is the Clement 22-622 series, with a diam-

Fig. 1-20: These tube-type lightweight tires are easier to repair than the sewn-up "tubular" type. They are heavier and less responsive than tubulars but are fine for touring.

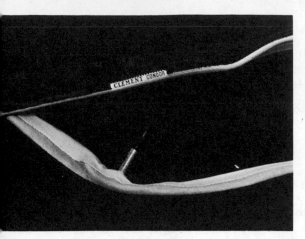

Fig. 1-21: A tubular tire is lighter and gives less rolling resistance than wider, tubed tires, but has the drawback of getting more flats. It is used on road- and track-racing bicycles more often than on touring bikes, but it is suitable for some types of touring.

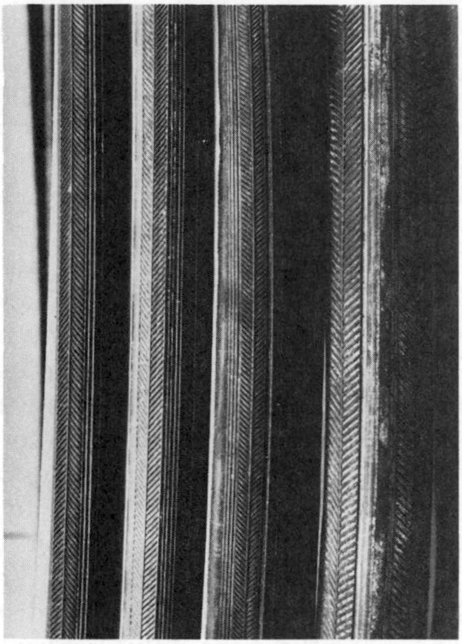

Fig. 1-22: Four types of narrow- to wide-profile tires for the touring cyclist. The narrow-profile tires have lower rolling resistance; the wider-profile tires stand up better to heavy loads and are more shock absorbent and comfortable. Left to right: the Clement "Gentlemen ¾-inch tire"; Clement 1-inch tire; Specialized Touring 700 C X 28 C (1⅛ inch); and Specialized Touring's 700 C X 32 C (1 and ¼ inch). None of these tires is a tubular.

eter of 700 centimeters and a 28-centimeter thin profile, which looks just like a tubular. Figure 1-22 shows four tires of differing tread widths. Remember, the thinner the tire, the less rolling resistance.

RIMS

The lightest rims are made of aluminum. Mavic, Weinmann, Fiamme, Ridgida, Super Champion and Milremo are all of high quality. Steel rims are found on bikes of lesser quality because they are so heavy, or on heavily loaded touring bikes.

MAKE AN ACCEPTANCE CHECK BEFORE YOU LEAVE THE STORE

It would be nice if all you had to do was pick out a bicycle, have it adjusted for your height and then leave the store with it right away. But, like an automobile, the bicycle must be finely tuned to avoid possible safety problems or difficulties with its operation later on. For this reason it is important that you purchase the bicycle from a qualified bicycling store, and then check it thoroughly *before* you leave the store. See Chapter 2 for tips on how to select the right size bike for you.

Points for you to check are:

- *Wheels:* Spin wheels. Put a finger or pencil on the frame while wheels turn; watch for out-of-roundness. Pay no attention to tire, watch rim only. Wheels should be perfectly true from both side-to-side and concentrically as to roundness. In checking display bicycles, I found that 90 percent of them had wheels way out of round.
- *Spokes:* "Pluck" spokes or "twing" them as you would strings on a guitar. Spokes should give about the same musical pitch all around, and should show about the same degree of tightness. Derailleur-equipped bike rear wheels should have tighter spokes on the freewheel side than on the left side. Even if wheels are aligned, loose spokes will cause them to go out of round soon.
- *Hubs:* Spin wheel slowly. Wheel should come to a stop gradually. If wheel stops suddenly, hub cone needs readjustment.

  Grasp wheel between fingers and, holding the bicycle frame firmly, move wheel from side to side. If wheel has side play, hub cones are too lose.
- *Brakes:* Test coaster brakes on an actual ride. They should grab enough under hard back pressure to make wheel skid.

  Check caliper hand brakes. Brake blocks should grab both sides of wheel rim squarely and evenly. When hand lever is released, brake blocks should be clear of rim sides and not rub. Test on a ride, trying front and rear brake alone. Each should show about the same degree of braking ability. Levers should be adjusted to fit your hand (cable adjustment). Brakes should stop evenly and smoothly, even when gripped tightly, should not "shudder," grip unevenly or squeal.
- *Gears:* See troubleshooting section on both hub gears and derailleur (ten-speed gears in Chapter 13). A bicycle should exhibit none of the defects listed and should operate smoothly through all the gear changes. Make sure a three-speed gear hub is lubricated before riding a new three-speeder because oil evaporates in storage and in transit.
- *Frame:* Sight down fork and frame for alignment. Check frame where fork goes through head tube; look at the paint. If paint is wrinkled slightly where top tube and steering head meet, the bicycle has been in an accident and frame has probably been bent. Wrinkled paint indicates metal movement under stress, such as collision with a brick wall.
- *Fenders:* Should be on tight and not rattle. Try a road test. In fact, on a road test nothing should rattle, and when you coast over a bumpy road all you should hear from the bicycle is the sound of the wind in your ears and the slight click of the freewheel pawls from the rear, as you coast.
- *Chainwheel and bottom bracket:* Check bottom-bracket adjustment by slipping chain off chainwheel and spinning the assembly. Chainwheel should come to a stop gradually, move easily and freely. It should not come to a stop suddenly, or "bind." Have someone hold the frame steady and push cranks from side to side. You should be able to feel or see no side play. If any of these defects are present, the bottom-bracket cone should be readjusted. Check chainwheel for alignment by rotating pedals and sighting down the side into

the teeth of the chainwheel. If the chainwheel is "wavy" it can be straightened; if wavy and a ten-speed, the chain will rub in spots on the chainwheel and front derailleur cage. If too wavy, it may jump off the chainwheel.

- *Pedals:* Should turn freely, not bind, and should have no side play.
- *Handlebars and Saddle:* Should be adjusted to fit the rider, and be tight. (See Chapter 2 for details on fitting.)

Just because a bicycle, of any make or model, is brand new, right out of a crate and you have bought it from a bicycle dealer, you have no guarantee that nothing can go wrong (or is wrong) with it.

The sad fact is that you or your bicycle dealer *must* check *every* bolt, nut, cable adjustment, derailleur adjustment, and everything else that can come loose or go out of whack, before you ride the new bicycle out of the shop. This is true regardless of *how* much the bicycle costs or *what* make it is.

Let me give you an example. I bought a fine, rather costly, derailleur-equipped bicycle expressly designed for touring. After giving it a most cursory inspection, I set off on a short trip. After a few miles, while I strained up a steep hill, the chain suddenly slipped off the center of the three chainwheels. I was mildly annoyed at the time, but if I had given it proper thought, I would have stopped cycling right there and walked home. (A chain does not simply slip off the center chainwheel! Off the smaller or larger wheel, possibly, if the front derailleur is out of adjustment. But slipping off the center chainwheel meant that something was drastically wrong.) All I did, however, was slip the chain back on the wheel (which was rather difficult because it had gotten firmly wedged between the center and outer chainwheel). About fifty feet farther, the chain slipped off again. This time I studied the chainwheel closely, and I found, to my horror, that a center bolt, spacer, and nut had fallen out entirely in two places out of the five, and the other three bolts were loose. This time the chain was wedged in firmly, and the center chainwheel was badly warped from the wedge pressure of the chain.

To give you another example, a friend of mine rode a brand-new, expensive bicycle out of a showroom, and after cycling about five miles, the rear derailleur cable slipped right out of the derailleur cable clamp. The clamp bolt had fallen out as well, which meant a long ride home over the hills in top gear. Incidentally, if you should break a cable on the road and don't have a replacement on hand, you can adjust the rear derailleur so it stays in an intermediate gear, thus avoiding having to ride in top gear all the way home.

These are trivial mechanical troubles in the showroom, but on the road, they can spoil a trip. Replacement parts can be obtained only in the bike shops specializing in high-quality bicycles. Parts for these machines are almost always made in Europe and nuts are threaded on the metric standard. So check *everything* before you leave the bicycle store.

One final word of advice. If the mechanic needs any special tools to remove the freewheel or adjust the derailleur, for example, buy the tool while you are in the shop.

FLASHY PAINT AND PALE ALLOY: A CAUTION

A glittering paint job and lightweight aluminum alloy parts such as handlebars, seat post, chainwheels and cranks, may all be a cover-up for a cheap, heavy, "dead"-feeling frame. If you think the bike you are looking at is a dud, heft it and compare its weight with some of the more expensive bicycles in the store. If the dealer will let you (and he should), take it for a test ride and compare how it feels with a bike that weighs less. Some of these heavy monsters can weigh upwards of 36 to 38 pounds.

The problem here is that the manufacturer uses inexpensive low-carbon steel tubing. To maintain strength, this tubing must have thicker sidewalls, which is where the weight and the "dead" unresponsive feel come in. This type of ride takes all the joy out of bicycling, unless of course you just want a bike for utility cycling. These bicycles have welded joints which can come apart, as shown in Figures 1-6, 1-7 and 1-8.

Check the frame label to see what kind of steel the frame is made of. It it's a cheaper bike, say under $180 or $150, look to see if the frame has lugs, because even if the frame is welded, at least the lugs will add some strength to the joints. An unlugged frame may simply have the tube ends stuck into holes in the facing frame tube and not be mitered at all. Mitering simply means that the tube end is cut or shaped to fit perfectly snugly against the tube to which it is to be joined.

Also, today, the better bicycles now use 700-centimeter wheels rather than 27-inch wheels and tires, simply because 700-centimeter tires are available throughout the world and the economics of mass production mean you can or will eventually be able to get these tires at less cost. Eventually the bicycle industry in this country will go metric and then we will all have 700-centimeter wheels on all bikes. Right now the 700-centimeter wheels are a sign of a higher-quality bicycle.

SELECTING THE BIKE FOR YOU

We now turn to selecting the right bike for you from the wide variety available in today's market. Not all of the good bikes available will be listed here, because sheer numbers make it impossible to test them all. But we made an effort to either road-test or examine many different makes in each price range and in each category of bike. We shall proceed to rate bicycles in the following categories:

- Commuting, shopping, around-town bikes
- Touring
- Road and track racing
- Bicycle motocross
- Ages 12–15
- Ages 9–11
- Ages 5–9

It should be pointed out that the prices given are as of this writing in early 1980, and can only be used as a rough yardstick of what things are costing these days. The cost of bicycles has skyrocketed in recent years due to the higher cost of materials, labor and shipping. You must check out each bicycle for its current price.

Bicycle Selections for the Commuter

Ten-Speed Commuting Bicycles
Schwinn World Sport

At the low end of the Schwinn ten-speed price line, this model (Fig. 1-23) still makes news with its lugged, brazed frame which weighs in at a remarkable light 33 pounds for a bike in this price range. In fact, when I saw the price I called Schwinn back to double check it; it seemed so low for this high-quality machine. This is a combination commuting and touring bike, although if you plan to do a lot of cross-country touring, I would opt for one of the lighter, higher-performance models found in the section on touring bicycles in this chapter. Still, the price/quality ratio is exceptionally high, so the World Sport is a very good bargain indeed.

Specifications:
Frame: 18-gauge carbon steel, brazed and lugged construction (not welded). Fork has fender eyelets.
Frame Sizes: Men's: 21, 23 and 25 inches. Women's: 19 and 21 inches
Fork: Tubular steel with fender eyelets
Crankset: Three-piece cotterless crankset with alloy cranks and steel chain-wheels with 40 and 52 teeth
Freewheel: Maeda SunTour with 14, 17, 20, 24 and 28 teeth
Hubs: Sanshin high-flange alloy rear; Sanshin low-flange steel hub rear
Derailleurs: Rear: Maeda SunTour Honor. Front: SunTour Spirit. Shift levers on stem
Brakes: Alloy center-pull with extension levers
Saddle: Black quilted narrow style on lightweight plastic base

Fig. 1-23: Schwinn "World Sport" 10-speed

Handlebars: Steel, dropped style, on alloy stem with recessed binder bolt
Rims: Tubular steel with 27 x 1¼-inch gumwall tires
Pedals: KKT rattrap with reflectors
Weight: 33 pounds
Cost: $139.95

Schwinn Caliente 10-Speed (Commuting)

Equipped with built-in kickstand, welded carbon-steel tubing frame, steel handlbars, stem, rims and crankset, this model weighs in at a hefty 37 pounds, much too heavy for touring but just fine for short-distance commuting and gunkholing around town. The positive indexing derailleurs and shifters help assure jam-proof shifting—rather important in busy city traffic when you're concentrating on the cars and trucks around you. Steel components will take road shock potholes and general banging around, and in this sense the Caliente is also a fine bike for high-schoolers and college people.

Specifications:
Frame: Electro-forged of 16-gauge 1010 carbon steel. Fork of tubular steel.
Frame Sizes: Men's: 20, 22 and 24 inches. Women's: 20 and 22 inches
Handlebars: Steel, dropped type on steel stem
Crankset: Forged steel one-piece crank with Shimano FF freewheeling FF system with 39- and 52-tooth chainwheels which can be shifted into another gear with pedaling, say at a stoplight for a faster getaway
Freewheel: Shimano FF with 14-, 17-, 20-, 24- and 28-tooth cogs
Hubs: High flange alloy
Rims: Chrome-plated steel with 27 x 1¼-inch gumwall tires
Derailleurs: Shimano Positron positive indexing rear, Schwinn-approved GT-290 front
Brakes: Alloy side-pulls with extension levers
Weight: 37 pounds
Price: $166.95

Fig. 1-24: Schwinn "Caliente" 10-speed

Huffy Avanti 10-speed Model 28009

The manufacturer does not specify the weight of this model, but from the specifications I would guess at least 36 pounds. The bike is not terribly expensive, though, and should be fine for the teenager who wants to bike to school, or the adult who needs to commute to work up to five miles one way. This model comes in the 23-inch frame size only, which means it will be too big for anyone under 5 feet 10 inches tall. (See Chapter 2 for a discussion of fitting the frame to your torso).

Specifications:
Frame: Lugged-steel frame, welded joints
Frame Size: 23 inches only
Fork: Touring angle (about 2½-inch rake) with chromed tips
Handlebars: Dropped, steel, Maes bend
Crankset: Alloy three-piece cotterless double chainwheel
Pedals: Steel rattrap
Brakes: Alloy center-pull with extension levers
Tires: 27 x 1¼-inch gumwall
Weight: About 36 pounds
Cost: $149.05

Windsor 10-speed Commuting Bicycles

Windsor makes two excellent models ideally suited to the commuter cyclist, primarily because of their high quality but relatively low cost. *Model AM-7 (Men's) and Model AM7L, Women's (Mixte), Specifications*
In case you're wondering what the "Mixte" frame for women is, this is a cross between a standard men's frame and the conventional (and heavy) sort of "U"-shaped women's model. Advantages of the Mixte versus conventional women's frame are that it is stiffer, lighter, and has more direct cable paths to rear brake and derailleur. Disadvantages are that it is still not as stiff as a men's frame by its design, and cable runs are a lot longer, extending down the down tube to the bottom of the seat tube and then up the seat tube to the rear brake. Longer cable runs mean harder cable action and greater cable stretch. Personally I see no reason for the existence of any women's frame, unless a dress is going to be worn while cycling.

Frame Sizes: Men's: 19½, 21½, 23, 25 inches. Women's: 19½, 21½
Frame: High-tensile tubing, lugged (Nervex-type lugs)
Brakes: Shimano Tourney side-pull with extension levers
Rims: Alloy with 27 x 1¼-inch tires
Hubs: Windsor alloy with solid axle and bolts
Crankset: Shimano five-pin allow cotterless
Derailleurs: Shimano Centeron RS rear, Shimano III front
Handlebars: Alloy dropped bars except on women's model, which are flat
Saddle: Leather covered, padded. Wider saddle on women's model
Weight: 28 pounds
Cost: $165

Fig. 1-25: Soma "Generation" 10-speed

Soma 10-speed "Generation"

This bike (Fig. 1-25) costs a bit more than the Raleigh "Sprite" but it weighs a few pounds less thanks to greater use of alloy components, and should therefore be easier to pedal. Also comes in a wider range of frame sizes.

Specifications:
Frame Sizes: Men's: 19, 21, 23 and 25 inches. Women's: 19 and 22 inches. Also in a boy's size of 18 inches with 24-inch wheels for the really short person (under 5 feet tall)
Frame: High carbon steel, seamless tubing with cut-away lugs
Gears: SunTour front and rear. Freewheel: 14–28 teeth. Chainwheel 14–28T. Stem-mounted shift levers
Handlebars: Steel dropped design
Chainset: Sugino steel chainwheel, 52 and 40 teeth
Brakes: Dia-Compe alloy center-pull with extension levers (remove). Quick-release to make it easier to remove wheels (fatter tire)
Hubs: High flange front and rear
Tires: 27 by 1¼ inches
Pedals: KKT steel. No clips
Weight: 32.5 pounds
Cost: $165

Schwinn Suburban 10-speed

Here is a sturdy commuter bike (Fig. 1-26) with a broad range of frame sizes down to 17 inches in the women's model. The smallest frame size of 22 inches for men is a tad too big for anyone under 5 feet 9 inches, however, so if you are shorter you will have to use the Soma or one of the other smaller models available.

Specifications:
Frame Sizes: Men's: 22 and 24 inches. Women's: 17, 20 and 22 inches

Fig. 1-26: Schwinn "Suburban" 10-speed

Frame: 16-gauge 1010 carbon steel
Fork: Tubular steel
Handlebars: Chromed steel flat
Saddle: Mattress with spring cushioning
Crankset: Forged steel one-piece with Shimano FF front freewheeling chainwheel. Freewheel is Shimano FF system with 14-, 17-, 21-, 26- and 32-tooth cogs
Chain: Shimano Uni-glide
Hubs: Maillard low-flange alloy front and rear
Derailleurs: Rear, Shimano Positron II with positive indexing. Front, Shimano GT-290. Shift levers are stem mounted
Brakes: Alloy side-pull. (Note: side-pull brakes work better than center-pull on out-of-line wheels, other things being equal)
Rims: Steel, 27 x 1¼ inches
Pedals: Union rubber pad type
Weight: 39 pounds with built-in kickstand
Cost: $169.95

Puch "Pathfinder" 10-speed

The most expensive but also the best commuting bike I can recommend, the quality shows in the weight, which is light for a machine of this price. Comes in a wide range of sizes, even down to 19 inches in a men's model, which should fit people down to 5 feet 2 inches, at least.

Specifications:
Frame Sizes: Men's model only: 19, 21, 23, 25 inches
Frame: Puch 482 nickel/carbon steel (one reason for the light weight)
Fork and Stays: Puch 482 nickel/carbon steel
Brakes: Weinmann alloy center-pull with extension levers (remove extensions)
Gears: SunTour 7 front and rear
Weight: 31 pounds
Cost: $182

Fig. 1-27: Schwinn "Continental" 10-speed

Schwinn Continental II 10-speed

A better selection of higher-priced components make the Continental II (Fig. 1-27) a good buy for general commuting and utility cycling. The frame is strong enough to carry a small child in a carrier over the rear wheel (see Chapter 5 for a recommended carrier), or a heavy load of groceries in wire panniers. The wide gear range is adequate for most hills, and the rest of the components are as foolproof as engineers can design.

Specifications:

Frame: Electro-forged of 16-gauge 1010-gauge steel. Built-in kickstand housing, welded-on cable lugs. Tubular steel fork, chrome tipped with eyelets.

Frame Sizes: Men's: 20, 22, 24 and 26 inches. Women's: 20 and 22 inches

Handlebars: Randonneur design, dropped, alloy with GB forged alloy stem

Crankset: Forged-steel diamond style heat-treated crank. 39- and 52-tooth chainwheels

Freewheel: Maillard with 14-, 17-, 20-, 24- and 28-tooth cogs with high-speed chainguard and built in dust seal

Derailleurs: Rear, Huret GT-150 with jam-free backpedal cage. Front, Huret GT-290 with jam-free chain cage. Shift levers mounted on stem

Brakes: Alloy center-pull with extension levers

Rims: Tubular steel chrome-plated with 27 x 1¼-inch gumwall tires

Pedals: Maillard rattrap

Hubs: Alloy high flange

Saddle: Vinyl covered over molded pad

Weight: 36 pounds

Cost: $176.95

Raleigh "Sprite"

This is a "best buy" all-around bicycle well equipped for commuting and utility use. (Fig. 1-28). It comes equipped with fenders, and an alloy Pletscher carrier is optional (and recommended). The steel rims can

Fig. 1-28: Raleigh "Sprite" 10-speed

handle potholes with more aplomb than alloy rims. It's a hefty 34 pounds, but again, you're not out to set speed records. And at the price, you can almost afford to have it stolen.

Frame Sizes: Men's: 21½, 23½ and 25 inches. Women's: 19½ and 21½.
   (Women's model is a Mixte frame with twin parallel downtubes)
Frame: 2030 high-tensile steel with Raleigh lugs
Fork: Raleigh tubular pressed crown
Handlebars: Alloy, flat
Stem: Alloy
Brakes: Raleigh/Weinmann alloy center-pull
Pedals: Rubber tread
Rims: Endrick 27 x 1¼ inches
Saddle: Brooks B103 vinyl top
Seat post: Chromed steel
Gears: Front, SunTour. Rear, SunTour GT. Stem-mounted shifters
Fenders: Narrow "U" section
Weight: 34 pounds
Cost: $187.95

Miyata Model 400 Commuting Bicycle

The "400" is the lightest of the commuting bicycles, and it sells at a very reasonable price indeed. It is also the only machine that has an extremely wide range of frame sizes which will fit people from 5 feet 2 inches all the way up to 6 feet 6 inches! At the price, the components are of suprisingly high quality, so this is a bike I can highly recommend for the commuter. Given the quality involved, this bike can also double as a touring machine, particularly in view of its wide gear ratios, which will make hill climbing easier.

Specifications:
Frame sizes: Men's model only: 19½, 21, 23, 25 and 27 inches
Frame: High-tensile steel tubing, lugged
Fork: High-tensile steel tubing with forged dropouts
Handlebars: Alloy dropped, Randonneur design
Gears: Front, 52–40 teeth. Rear, SunTour Pro-Compe good, 14–32 teeth
Crankset: Sakae alloy cotterless three piece. 165-millimeter cranks for 19½ and
 21-inch frames, and 170-millimeter cranks for larger frame sizes
Pedals: MKS-33, no clips
Saddle: Quilted and padded, vinyl covered, medium narrow
Rims: Steel, 27 x 1¼ inches
Hubs: Sanshin alloy high flange. Front has quick-release
Weight: 28–29 lbs, depending on frame size
Cost: $185

Coaster-Brake and Three-Speed Models

Schwinn Collegiate Tourist
This model comes both as a coaster-brake and three-speed model

Frame Sizes: Men's: 20, 22 and 24 inches. Women's: 17 and 20 inches
Frame: Electro-forged of 1010 carbon steel
Handlebars: Flat (Dropped on 10-speed)
Saddle: Spring cushion style
Crankset: One piece, with 46-tooth chainwheel
Hubs: Front: Low Flange. Rear: Bendix Coaster Brake
Rims: Steel
Tires: 26 x 1¼ inches
Pedals: Rubber block
Accessories: Built-in kickstand
Weight: 39 pounds
Cost:[1] $99.95

Soma "Generation" 3-Speed (Fig. 1-29)
Frame sizes: Men's: 21 inches. Women's: 19 and 22 inches
Frame: High-tensile steel tubing, lugged frame
Handlebars: Flat
Saddle: Vinyl padded, touring type, with springs
Crankset: Three-piece cottered design, steel
Hubs: Low flange, steel front with Shimano 3-speed hub rear
Rims: Steel
Tires: 26 by 1⅜ inches
Weight: NA (but around 34 pounds)
Cost: $155

---

[1]As a three-speed with caliper brakes, $114.95; as a three-speed coaster-brake model, $119.95; as a five-speed, $134.95; as a ten-speed, $139.95. The five- and ten-speed models use the new Shimano FF freewheeling chainwheels which permit jam-free shifting.

Fig. 1-29: Soma "Generation" 3-speed

Bicycle Selections for the Touring Cyclist

Windsor Model International AM-5 Men's and AM-5L (Women's) 10-speed

This model can also be used for touring, although it is a bit on the heavy side. It is basically the same frame and comes in the same frame sizes as the AM-7 and AM7L above, and weighs the same. Therefore I will add only those components which increase the price (and the performance) such as better brakes, hubs and cranks.

Specifications:
Frame: Tange chrome molybdenum tubing with cut-away lugs. Fork is of Toshima high-tensile steel with chromed lugs
Brakes: Dia-Compe alloy center-pull with quick-release and extension levers
Hubs: High-flange Sanshin with quick-release
Crankset: Sugino Idol Alloy five-pin cotterless. Chainwheels with 52 and 40 teeth
Freewheel: SunTour Pro Compe Gold with 14 to 32 teeth. (Wide gear range)
Handlebars: Gran Compe Allen Key Alloy stem and alloy dropped bars
Cost: $185

Azuki Gran Sport 10-speed

The Gran Sport represents one of the best buys in bicycles in the $200 price range, give or take $12.

Specifications:
Frame: Tange chrome molybdenum tubing with cut-away lugs. Fork is of Toshima high-tensile steel with chromed lugs

Frame Sizes: 19, 21, 23 and 25 inches
Crankset: Sugino "Idol" alloy cotterless. 40 and 52 teeth
Freewheel: Shimano Uniglide with 14-, 17-, 20-, 24- and 28-tooth cogs
Hubs: Front: low flange with quick-release. Rear: low flange bolt-on
Rims and Tires: 27-inch Araya alloy rims. 27 x 1-inch tires
Derailleurs: Front, Shimano "600" alloy. Rear, Shimano "600"
Bars and Stem: Alloy Randonneur. Stem, alloy with Allen bolt
Saddle and Post: Leather, racing quilted on alloy "Asp" post
Brakes: Dia-Compe center-pull with extension levers
Pedals: KKT steel rattrap
Weight: About 25 pounds
Cost: $209.95 (Mixte women's models, $211.95)

Windsor AM-3 Men's and AM-3L Women's Mixte 10-speed

This Windsor model is a very reasonably priced bike set up for touring
with wide-range gearing with a 52 x 40-tooth front chainwheel and a 14-
to-32-tooth rear freewheel. Pedals have toe clips and straps which make
pedaling safer and easier, particularly when riding uphill when feet are
otherwise apt to slip off pedals and lead to a spill.

Specifications:
Frame: High-tensile steel tubing with lugs, chrome fork tips and backstays.
   Dropouts are forged steel with set screws for aligning rear wheel
Frame Sizes: Men's: 19½, 21½, 23 and 25 inches. Women's: 19½ and 21½
Rims: 27 x 1¼-inch alloy
Tires: IRC high-pressure (100 psi) 1⅛-inch narrow profile (less rolling resis-
   tance)
Hubs: Low-flange Sanshin (low flange means longer spokes for a softer, less
   fatiguing ride) alloy, with quick-release skewers
Derailleurs: Front: SunTour Compe V Alloy. Rear: SunTour VGT wide range
   alloy
Handlebars: Dropped alloy with alloy stem. Stem has Allen key binder bolt
Crankset: Chainwheel is SR Apex 5RG2 Custom f-pin alloy cotterless, 52 x 40T
Freewheel: SunTour Pro Compe Gold, 14 x 32T
Pedals: Windsor alloy with toe clips and straps
Saddle: Leather covered and padded, narrow style, on alloy seat post
Brakes: Dia-Compe Alloy center-pull with quick-release and "safety" levers
Weight: 28 pounds
Cost: $215

Fuji Royale 12-speed

I won't give all the specs for this model because I will cover the basics
on the Fuji Model S12-S in this chapter. (See page 49.) The only difference between the two models are that some of the components of the
Fuji Royale 12-speed are less expensive and the bike weighs only a half
pound more than the S12-S (26.5 lbs.) yet costs around $80 less. The
crankset is one notch down the Sugino line from the S12-S crankset, the
pedals are steel and not alloy, hubs are one step down the Sanshin line
from the S12-S hubs, the seat post is steel, not alloy. Everything else is
the same except the price, which is $219.95.

Fig. 1-30: Raleigh "Grand Prix" 10-speed

Raleigh Gran Prix 10-speed

Here's a bicycle (Fig. 1-30) you can use for touring or commuting or general recreational use at a fairly modest price. It has light alloy equipment and a comfortable soft paddle saddle and, among other sizes, comes in a small 19¾-inch frame for people from 5 feet 4 inches to 5 feet 8 inches tall.

Specifications:

Frame: Raleigh high-tensile 2030 steel with Bocama feature cut lugs. Fork is 2030 steel with forged Vagner crown

Frame Sizes: 19¾, 21½, 23½, 25½. Also comes in a Mixte women's frame in 19½, 21½ and 23½ inches

Crankset: SR alloy 5-pin cotterless with 42/52T, slotted spider and Allen key bolts. 165-millimeter (6½-in.) cranks

Freewheel: SunTour 14 to 34 T (ultra-wide range)

Hubs: Normandy high flange with quick-release

Derailleurs: SunTour VGT rear, Comple V front with handlebar end shifters (see Raleigh Touring 14 for my comments)

Rims and Tires: Steel rims with 27¼-inch high-pressure tires

Bars and Stem: Maes alloy handlebars, SR alloy stem with Allen key bolt

Saddle and Post: Padded vinyl top on padded nylon base. Seat post is alloy, 25.4 millimeters (1 in.)

Brakes: Weinmann alloy center-pull with quick-release and extension levers. The purpose of the quick-release is to spread brake arms so the thicker section of the tire sidewall can pass, making wheel removal easier

Pedals: Raleigh design. No toe clips or straps

Weight: 29 pounds (21½-in. frame)

Cost: $234

Schwinn Super Le Tour II 12-Speed

This model (Fig. 1-31) uses some of Shimano's new and innovative components which make shifting a lot easier and more accurate, even when under high torque in hill climbing. All components are high quality.

Fig. 1-31: Schwinn "Super Le Tour II" 12-speed

Specifications:

Frame: Torch-brazed and lugged frame of 18-gauge 1020 steel with tubular semi-sloping fork crown and 6 inches of chrome on fork blades

Frame Sizes: 21-, 23- and 25-inch men's only

Crankset: Sugino Maxy alloy cotterless with 39- and 52-tooth chainwheels

Freewheel: Shimano cassette with 13-, 15-, 17-, 19-, 24- and 29-tooth cogs

Hubs: Front: Maillard alloy low flange with quick-release. Rear: Shimano low-flange alloy free hub with quick-release

Rims and Tires: Weinmann A-125 light alloy 27 x 1¼-inch rims. Schwinn gum-wall high pressure 27 by 1⅛-inch tires

Bars and Stem: SR alloy, Randonneur bend, drop style with double sleeve. SR alloy stem with recessed Allen stem bolt

Saddle and Post: Selle Royale contour saddle with leather-finish vinyl top and lightweight plastic base. Alloy La Prada 25.4-centimeter post

Brakes: Weinmann 605 Delux alloy side-pulls. Rubber-hooded alloy deluxe levers

Pedals: Maillard rattrap alloy with reflectors, toe clips and straps

Weight: 28 pounds

Cost: $249.95

Trek Model TX 311

Trek Bicycle Corporation, in Waterloo, Wisconsin, is a relative new-comer to the U.S. bicycle scene. However, they make a very high quality product indeed, at an excellent price. Frames are particularly well made. Of the fourteen or so Trek models, I have selected a bicycle in the middle price range. Other Trek bikes range from $110 to $792, and I can recommend them all. Because distribution may be limited, I suggest you check dealers by phone to find a Trek dealer, or write to the factory at 286 Jackson Street, Waterloo, Wisconsin 53594 or phone 414/478-2191.

Specifications:

Frame: Ishiwata 0265 high-tensile tubing, fully double-butted, silver brazed. (You can also buy the frame only for $110 and hang your own equipment on it. A very good buy)

Frame Sizes: 19¾, 21, 22½, 24 and 25½ inches

Crankset: Sugino NJX-1

Freewheel: SunTour Pro-Compe 12–28 teeth
Hubs: Sanshin quick-release alloy
Rims and Tires: Alloy rims with IRC 90 pound 27 by 1⅛-inch tires
Derailleurs: SunTour VX front, SunTour VXGT rear
Bars and Stem: ST custom alloy
Saddle and Post: NA
Brakes: Dia-Compe center-pull
Pedals: MKS alloy
Weight: NA but about 26 pounds
Cost: $250

Bertin C-28

As with all Bertin cycles, this touring model (Fig. 1-32) represents a fine, lightweight machine at quite a reasonable price. The frame is of high-strength tubular steel, hand brazed. With taper-gauge forks and stays for extra strength and a smooth ride, this model offers comfort and strength for touring and riding over rough roads. It comes with 700-centimeter rims with Wolber 700 by 25-centimeter tires. You can also use balloon tires on the same rims if you ride over very rough roads (such as pothole-lined city streets). The 700-centimeter rims can be interchanged with wheels equipped with tubular tires because both are 700 centimeters, without having to change the location of brake shoes.

Specifications:
Frame: Durifort light-gauge main tubes, butted Durifort forks and stays, Bocama
  lugs
Frame Sizes: 52, 54, 58 and 62 centimeters (multiply by 0.3937 for inches)
Crankset: Solida cotterless crankset. 40 and 52 teeth
Freewheel: 14 to 28 teeth. (I would switch to the Shimano 14-to-34-tooth chain-
  wheel for hill climbing)
Rims: 700-by-26-centimeter Super Champion rims with SF QR hubs with
  four cross double-butted Robergel spokes (see Chapter 15) with Wolber 700-
  centimeter Super Sport 100 psi tires. Presta valves
Pedals: Lyotard 36 with reflectors
Derailleurs: Simplex Criterium rear. Parallelogram front
Handlebars: Milremo Professional extra-wide reinforced bars, 44 centimeters
  wide, on forged alloy stem with recessed Allen stem bolt

Fig. 1-32: Bertin C-28 10-speed

Weight: 25.5 pounds
Cost: $275
Note: As Model C-28XL, this same bike comes in a 70-centimeter size (27½ inches) for the person over 6 feet 4 inches. It has heavy gauge main tubes and butted Durifort forks and stays. It weighs 28 pounds and costs $275.

Fuji Model S12-S (Men's) and S12-SL (Women's Mixte) (12-speed)

The Fuji people make some of the best bicycles to come out of Japan. Way back in 1968, when the first edition of this book was in preparation, I drooled over the first Fuji I ever saw, in a New York showroom. At that time they were not well distributed in this country, but I am glad that you can now buy Fuji's in most major cities in the USA. This model Fuji (Fig. 1-33) is a reasonably priced but fine-quality touring machine with an excellent selection of gear ratios, particularly at the low end for hill climbing.

Specifications:
Frame: Fuji chrome molybdenum 441 tubing, fully brazed and lugged. 73 degrees and 73 degrees
Frame Sizes: Men's: 19, 21, 23 and 25 inches. Women's: 19 and 21½ inches
Crankset: Sugino Super Maxy 2D, dual plateau, 42 and 52 teeth, 170-millimeter cranks
Freewheel: SunTour Mighty 6. 14 to 30 teeth (six cogs)
Hubs: Sanshin Gyromaster low flange with quick-release
Rims and Tires: Ukai alloy 27 by 1¼ inches with Silver Star 27 by 1⅛ inches
Derailleurs: Front: SunTour Comple V. Rear: Road VS-S
Bars and Stem: Nitto Olympiade B115 alloy on Nitto Young alloy stem with Allen recessed stem bolt
Saddle and Post: Fujita Road Look. Alloy stem
Brakes: Dia-Compe No. 500-G side-pull. Women's Mixte has Dia-Compe center-pull with extension levers
Pedals: MKW quill 2K alloy with quick-release
Weight: 26 pounds
Cost: $229.95

Fig. 1-33: Fuji S12-S 12-speed

Nishiki International

This is Nishiki's best true touring bicycle, with touring angles and fork rake, hand-brazed frame and alloy components that provide a comfortable and responsive ride for distance touring.

Specifications:
Frame: Hand-crafted Tange chrome molybdenum tubing with cut-away lugs. Toshiba high-tensile fork blades with speak tops and chrome tips
Frame Sizes: 21, 23 and 25 inches
Crankset: Sugino Super Maxy II allow cotterless, 40- and 52-tooth
Freewheel: SunTour Gold with 14-, 17-, 20-, 24- and 28-tooth cogs
Hubs: Low-flange front and rear with quick-release
Rims and Tires: Araya light alloy Model 20A rims, 27-by-1-inch hp tires
Derailleurs: Front, SunTour NSL. Rear, SunTour Cyclone
Bars and Stem: SR CTD alloy downturned bars with Sanshin Pro-Alloy Allen bolt stem
Saddle and Post: "Elina" padded leather saddle on S/R P-5 fluted allow stem
Brakes: Dia-Compe 500-G side-pull with drilled levers
Pedals: KKT "Top Run" alloy
Weight: About 25 pounds
Cost: $299.95

Windsor Super Carrera Model AM-10 (Men's Model only) 10-speed

At first glance this beautiful machine looks like a road racing bike because the fork rake is only 1¾ inches, which would ordinarily mean a rather stiff ride. Most touring bikes use forks with a 2½-inch rake. You can tell the difference by looking at the end of the fork. Greater curvature at the wheel end means a longer rake. However, the Italian maker (based in Mexico) uses frame angles and tubing lengths that partially compensate for the shorter fork rake. The result, a bike that's somewhat stiffer but more responsive than a conventional touring frameset; a cross between a Cinelli road bike and a softer-riding regular tourer. For me the ride is a bit stiff, but if you are under forty I doubt you'd notice the difference even after a 100-mile trip. Low-flange hubs help soften the ride.

Specifications:
Frame: Tange double-butted chrome moly tubing throughout all nine tubes. Spearpoint chrome lugs; half chrome fork and backstays; Cinelli design seat stays; forged dropouts with set screws. Fork-stiffener tangs with diamond reinforcements on bridges
Frame Sizes: 19½, 21½, 23 and 25 inches
Rims: Alloy box design, 1⅛, using 1⅛ high-pressure tires
Hubs: Low-flange alloy Shimano 600 with quick-release
Derailleurs: Front, Cyclone. Rear, SunTour Cyclone Alloy wide range
Brakes: Shimano 600 side-pull brakes. Brazed-on cable guides
Handlebars: Dropped alloy bars; alloy Allen stem
Chainset: SR Apex custom 5-pin alloy cotterless cranks with 52 × 40T
Freewheel: Pro-Compe gold with 14 x 32T
Saddle: Suede leather padded on micro-adjusting fluted alloy seat post
Pedals: Tagamex alloy quill with toe clips and straps

Weight: 23 pounds
Cost: $312

Raleigh Super Course 10-speed

The old reliable British bicycle company has come up with a moderately priced touring bicycle with a highly responsive frame design. The geometry is such that it handles nearly as quickly as a true road racing bike, with a short wheelbase and moderate fork rake, yet remains a comfortable machine for distance touring. Bar-end shifters for easier, safer shifting are unusual on a machine in this price bracket.

Specifications:

Frame: Reynolds '531' main tubes, Raleigh 2030 high-tensile steel forks. Chainstays have SunTour forged fork ends. The 21½-inch frame has a wheelbase of 39⁹⁄₁₆ inches. Frame angles are 74 degrees head, 74 degrees tube on the 21½-inch frame. Lugs are Bocama feature cut

Frame Sizes: 21½, 23½ and 25½ inches

Crankset: Raleigh/SR alloy 5-pin cotterless 42- and 52-tooth double-plateau chainwheels with Allen key bolts and 170-millimeter (6¾-inch) cranks. The Allen key makes it a lot easier to tighten the cranks onto the steel spindle, especially on a tour. You don't need a heavy special wrench for this job

Hubs: Atom low-flange front and rear with quick-release

Freewheel: Raleigh/SunTour Perfect 14-to-28-tooth cogs

Rims and Tires: Weinmann 700-centimeter alloy concave design A124 narrow section for the Raleigh narrow high-pressure tires with Presta valves

Derailleurs: Front: SunTour Compe. Rear: SunTour Cyclone GT. Bar-end shifters

Bars and Stem: Raleigh Italienne alloy on SR alloy stem with Allen key bolt

Saddle and Post: Suede saddle on SR 26.8-millimeter seat post

Brakes: Weinmann short reach alloy center-pull

Weight: 26 pounds

Cost: $330

Soma "Competition" 12-speed

Here is a really super touring machine (Fig. 1-34) with quite adequate gearing for those hills you will have to climb. This model has top components and is very handsome besides, with a leather copper-riveted saddle on a dural Allen seat post, recessed stem bolt, sparkling paint job with gold trim around lugs.

Specifications:

Frame: Hand-brazed-up chrome molybdenum single-butted tubing with Italian style cut-away lugs. Fork is high-tensile steel tubing with partially chromed blades

Frame Sizes: 19, 21, 23 and 25 inches

Freewheel (and Hub): Shimano 600 EX cassette type six-speed with 14 to 28 teeth

Crankset: Shimano 600 EX 52 x 42 teeth with 6¾-inch cranks

Rims, Hubs, Tires: Rims are Araya light alloy 27 by 1⅛ inches. Hubs (see freewheel above). Tires are IRC Roadlite narrow profile 27 by 1 inches

Saddle and Post: Leather saddle with copper rivets on SR light alloy post

Fig. 1-34: Soma "Competition" 12-speed

Derailleurs: Front and Rear, Shimano 600 EX
Brakes: Shimano EX 600 side-pull
Pedals: KKT forged alloy with toe clips and straps
Weight: NA (about 24 pounds for the 19-inch frame model)
Cost: $355

Miyata 1000 15-speed

The Model 1000 is designed for long-distance touring. It has a triple crankset with wide-range gearing, although I would still like to see a 14-to-34-tooth freewheel instead of the 14–28 furnished. The frame is hand brazed and has Miyata's long-point lugs. Small fittings such as cable stops, water bottle mount and cable guides, are all brazed on the frame, making for a vibration-proof mounting of these parts and better appearance. Unique is a 40-spoked rear wheel, which should be highly resistant to spoke breakage, especially for the heavier rider carrying a full load of camping gear. Cantilever brakes give powerful stopping. The bicycle is available with or without alloy carriers, water bottle and cage already attached.

Specifications:
Frame: Tange Champion plain chromoly main tubing with Miyata lugs
Frame Sizes: 21, 23 and 25 inches
Crankset: Sakae Super Apex-5TG triple chainwheels; 52, 47 and 34 teeth
Freewheel: SunTour Pro-Compe 14–28 teeth
Rims, Hubs, Tires: 27 by 1⅛-inch alloy, 36 spokes front, 40 spokes rear. Hubs, Sanshin Gyro-Master low flange with quick releases. Tires, 27 by 1⅛ inches
Derailleurs: Front, SunTour Cyclone. Rear, Cyclone GT
Bars and Stem: Sakae RND alloy, randonneur dropped with forged-alloy stem
Saddle and Post: Ariake Jaguar 11 padded on alloy post
Brakes: Dia-Compe No. 960 center-pull, cantilever type
Pedals: MKA quill alloy with toe clips and straps
Weight: 27 pounds (21-inch frame, heavier for larger frames)
Cost: $369.95

Puch Marco Polo 10-speed

The Styr Daimler Puch people have been making bicycles in their factory in Graz, Austria, since the turn of the century, and they produce some of the most elegant machines made anywhere. The Marco Polo model is no exception.

Specifications:
Frame: Reynolds double-butted '531' tubing in main tubes. Fork and stays are Puch 482 nickel carbon steel
Frame Sizes: 21, 23 and 25 inches
Derailleurs: SunTour Cyclone
Brakes: Weinmann Center-Pull 999
Weight: 24.5 pounds
Cost: $385

Raleigh Touring (14-speed)

Raleigh makes a top-grade bicycle in any price category, and this surprisingly inexpensive bicycle designed expressly for touring is an example of their quality. The price is reasonable and then some, considering the components and frame material and general workmanship. The seven-speed freewheel in back and the triple chainset in front deliver fourteen usable speed selections with a range of 32.9 on the low side to 108.0 on the high side. Handlebar end shifters make for safe shifting—you don't have to reach down to the downtube shift levers, momentarily going off-balance to do so. The shifters are at your fingertips at the ends of the handlebars. (My own bikes are so equipped.) This model comes equipped with front and rear alloy carriers.

Specifications:
Frame: Tange high-tensile double-butted tubes and stays with SunTour GS fork ends, and Tange lightweight professional lugs. Fork is Tange taper gauge with forged crown and SunTour GS fork ends
Frame Sizes: 21½, 22½, 23½, 24½ and 25½ inches
Crankset: SunTour Vx Cotterless triple chainset, 39 to 52 Teeth with 170-millimeter (6¾ in.) cranks
Freewheel: SunTour Ultra 7 14–34 teeth (gives you "Granny" gears for steep hills)
Hubs: SunTour Road Vx high flange with quick-release
Rims and Tires: Arraya 700-centimeter alloy rims with Raleigh 700- by 25-centimeter lightweight narrow-profile tires
Saddle and Post: Padded suede on nylon base. SR light alloy fluted post
Pedals: SunTour light road alloy Vx with toe clips and straps
Brakes: Dia-Compe cantilever with drilled levers and natural gum rubber hoods
Derailleurs: SunTour Vx-GT rear and SunTour Vx front. Bar end shifters
Weight: 28 pounds (23½-inch frame)
Cost: $390

Bertin Model C-117

A fine touring bicycle on the whole, this model has one minor European style drawback, which can be easily rectified. Ever since the bike boom hit in 1971, Europeans have been sending bikes to the U.S. designed for touring but without touring-gear ratios or derailleurs to handle them; Bertin is no exception. This model comes with a 40-to-52-tooth chainwheel and a low gear on the freewheel of 28 teeth, a combination that will not get you over a steep mountain carrying 25 or 30 pounds of camping gear, unless you're in Olympic condition. At the price, this bike is a good buy, but I would change the freewheel at least to a 14-to-34-tooth unit, and the rear derailleur to a Crane GS or Campagnolo Gran Sport that will handle the wider gear range. You could also change the 40T to a 26T chainwheel, to give yourself a super-low gear to drop down to for those super-high hills you will inevitably have to climb. Frame sizes are also limited.

Specifications:
Frame: Vitus 172 double-butted throughout, Campagnolo dropouts
Frame Sizes: 20 and 22 inches (52 and 56 cm.)
Crankset: TA 1690 Cyclo Touriste Professional alloy cotterless alloy cranks, 40 and 52T
Freewheel: 14–28 teeth
Brakes: Mafac Racer with full rubber hoods on levers. Alloy center-pull
Rims and Tires: Milremo tubular rims, SF QR hubs, 4x spokes, Milremo Cadetti 270 g tubular tires with butyl tubes
Saddle: Ideale 80, pretreated, on dural post
Weight: 22.3 pounds
Cost: $395

Schwinn Paramount 10- and 15-speed Deluxe Tourers
The Rolls-Royce of American-made true touring bicycles, the Schwinn Paramount (Fig. 1-35) is a hand-brazed-up machine with top components that will compare more than favorably with any bicycle made anywhere. This is the top-of-the-line Schwinn that took me across most of Europe, which in Germany prompted the query "Was ist das Schwinn?" because this so German-sounding a marque was not known there. It is now. The only difference between the 10- and 15-speed is the triple-plateau chainwheel set of the latter.

Specifications:
Frame: Hand-built frame of Reynolds '531' double-butted and taper-gauge 531 manganese alloy steel tubing, fully lugged with Campagnolo fork ends with eyelets. Head and seat mast angles 73 degrees parallel. Fork is Reynolds '531' taper-gauge blades and single-butted steering tube with Campagnolo fork ends with eyelets. 1¾-inch fork rake. (But a comfortable ride anyhow)
Frame Sizes: Men's: 20, 21, 22, 23, 24, 25 or 26 inches. Women's: 20 or 22 inches. Custom-size frames can be made to order at extra cost
Crankset: On 15-speed model: Campagnolo Record Strada triple-plateau cotterless alloy with 36-, 46- and 54-tooth rings. On 10-speed, with 42- and 52-tooth rings
Freewheel: Regina Oro with 14-, 16-, 19-, 25- and 31-tooth cogs on 15-speed and 14, 16, 18, 21, and 24 on 10-speed
Hubs: Campagnolo Record high-flange alloy, quick-release

Fig. 1-35: Schwinn "Deluxe Touring Paramount" 15-speed

Rims and Tires: Super Champion 27-by-1¼-inch rims with Super Record 27-by-
1⅛-inch tires
Brakes: Campagnolo alloy side-pull
Pedals: Campagnolo Super Legerri alloy rattrap with toe clips and straps
Weight: 26 pounds
Price: $885

Road-Racing Bicycles

A road-racing bicycle, although it has (usually) ten speeds, has a short
wheelbase, and is a very light and responsive machine. Fork rake is
short, around 1¼ or 1½ inches. Rims are usually small flange to save
weight and use tubular (sew-up) tires. The better models have silk tubulars and use costly thin but very strong double-butted chrome molybdenum tubing such as Columbus or Reynolds '531'. Gearing is narrow
range; typical combinations are a 13-to-21-tooth freewheel and a 42- and
52-tooth double chainwheel. Rims, hubs, bars, stem, chainwheel and
main parts of derailleurs and shifters are aluminum alloy, as is the seat
post. In other words, a road-racing bicycle is designed to be stiff for
maximum energy transfer from muscles to wheels. The more costly the
bike, the better the components, with top-of-the-line bikes using high-
precision machined hubs and ball bearings, headset, pedals and bottom-
bracket assembly to reduce friction. You *could* tour on a road bike, but
the ride would be stiff, and after a half day's ride you'd have a sore rear
end (I know I do). In selecting a road-racing bike, look for precision,
high-quality components, frame materials and design and light weight,
as well as price. The models listed below have been selected on those
criteria and are the best I can find within their price range. But touring
on a road bike . . . well, it's not quite as outrageous as using an Indy 500
race car on the road . . . but it comes close.

Windsor Model AM-6C Competition 10-speed
Specifications:
Frame: Columbus double-butted tub ̖s throughout. Same frame design as AM-
1 (see below). Chrome spear-point lugs. SunTour forged dropouts with set
screws. Fork-stiffener tanks and diamond-reinforced bridges. Brazed brake-
cable guides on top tubes

Frame Sizes: 50 to 63 centimeters in one-centimeter increments (19.685 to 24.8031 inches in 0.3937-inch increments) (13 selections of frame size)
Rims: Windsor light alloy rims with tubular (sew-up) tires
Hubs: Sanshin alloy low flange with quick-release skewer
Brakes: Universal 68 or Shimano 600 side-pull
Crankset: Sugino alloy cotterless, 42 x 52T
Freewheel: SunTour 13-21T (close ratio)
Derailleurs: SunTour Cyclone, front and rear. Shifters downtube mounted
Pedals: KKT Pro-Ace alloy, toe clips and straps
Saddle: Leather padded, with Gran-Compe alloy stem
Handlebars: Windsor alloy, dropped
Weight: 22 pounds
Cost: $385

Windsor Professional AM-1 Road Bike:

Specifications:
Frame: Same as AM-6C above. Cut-out bottom bracket, special spear-point, drilled-chrome lugs, Campagnolo dropouts, chrome plated
Headset: Campagnolo Super Record
Rims: Windsor tubular alloy, sew-up tires
Hubs: Campagnolo Record low flange, with quick-release
Brakes: Universal 77 side-pull alloy
Derailleurs: Campagnolo Record front and rear
Crankset: Campagnolo Record, 170-millimeter cranks, 44/53T
Freewheel: Regina Oro Gold, 13–21T
Pedals: Cmapagnolo Record Road pedals, toe clips and straps
Saddle: Windsor Professional padded leather on Campagnolo seat post 26.8 millimeters
Weight: 21 pounds
Cost: $646

Miyata Model 1200 (10-speed):

Specifications:
Frame: Tange Champion chrome molybdenum with cut-out lugs, hand brazed at low temperatures. Short 15⅝-inch fork stays with straight forged fork ends for strength and energy-transfer efficiency
Frame Sizes: In centimeters: 54, 56, 58 and 60. In inches: 21¼, 22, 23.6
Headset: Shimano DuraAce
Rims: Ukai 700-C with National Panaracer tubular No. 230 tires
Hubs: Shimano DuraAce low flange with quick release
Crankset: Shimano DuraAce Extra. 52 x 42 teeth. Cranks are 165 millimeters for 54- and 56-centimeter frames and 170 millimeters for 58- and 60-centimeter frames
Pedals: MKS Unique custom road, forged alloy with chrome moly spindle, toe clips and straps
Derailleurs: Shimano DuraAce front and rear, shifters on brazed-on posts on downtube
Handlebars: Sakae World Custom WS-410 alloy dropped
Saddle: YFC soft professional (super soft) on Sakea new Roal IIES II with titanium binder bolt

Fig. 1-36: Soma "Superbe" 12-speed

Weight: 20 pounds
Cost: $699.95

Soma Superbe (12-speed)

This is a superb road-racing bike for sure (Fig. 1-36) and its $800 price is one indication. From the sloped fork crown to the straight dropouts in the rear, this is a thoroughbred machine that can also double as a touring bike, although the gear ratios would have to be drastically altered for the latter purpose, as you will note below.

Specifications:

Frame: Hand-brazed chrome molybdenum steel, double-butted with Italian-style cut-away lugs and SunTour Superbe straight dropout road type fork ends. Seat stay is semi-wrapped type

Frame Sizes: 19, 21, 23 and 25 inches

Crankset: Sugino Super-Mighty with 52 and 40 teeth and 6¾-inch cranks

Freewheel: SunTour Winner-S, 13, 14, 15, 17, 19 and 21 teeth (close ratio)

Hubs: SunTour Superbe large flange, quick-release

Rims and Tires: Araya tubular, light alloy. Soyo tubular tires, Gran Prix X 350

Derailleurs: Front and rear, SunTour Superbe

Bars and Stem: Nitto No. 55, light alloy, recessed stem bolt on Nitto alloy stem

Saddle and Post: Ariake 77 NDX, seamless suede leather, alloy post

Brakes: Gran-Compe GC450 center-pull

Pedals: KKT Pro Lux, toe clips and straps

Weight: About 23 pounds

Cost: $800

Raleigh Professional MK V (12-speed)

For the professional or amateur, here is a road-racing bike (Fig. 1-37) with an extremely wide range of frame sizes that sells at a reasonable price, considering the quality of workmanship in the frame and the quality of the components hung on the frame. I toured Austria on one and can report that it held up well and was suprisingly comfortable for a

Fig. 1-37: Raleigh "Professional" 12-speed

road-racing machine with a short-wheelbase frame and low fork rake. However, you may, as a tourist, prefer a less responsive, less stiff and more comfortable ride on a true touring machine.

Specifications:

Frame: Reynolds '531' double-butted tubes, forks and chainstays, with Campagnolo fork ends (dropouts). Lugs are hand-profiled Haden lightweight lugs with window cutouts, and the fork is Reynolds '531' taper gauge with Vagner Crown Campagnolo fork ends. 73-degree head angle, 75-degree seat angle

Frame Sizes: 20½, 21½, 22½, 23½, 24½ and 25½ inches

Rims: Mavic Sprint with reinforcing ferrules

Tires: Raleigh Imperforable Seta (tubulars)

Hubs: Campagnolo Nuovo Record low flange with quick-release

Crankset: Campagnolo Nuovo Record cotterless, 42 x 51 teeth

Freewheel: 13 to 24 teeth

Chain: Regina Oro

Derailleurs: Front: Campagnolo Nuovo Record. Rear: Campagnolo Nuovo Record 12-speed. Downtube-mounted controls

Saddle: Brooks Professional Team Special on Campagnolo 27.2-millimeter seat post

Handlebars: Raleigh Italienne alloy. G.B. Biba stem, forged alloy

Brakes: Campagnolo Record side-pull

Weight: 23 pounds

Cost: $898

Schwinn Road Racer Paramount 10-speed

Not to be confused with the touring Paramount, this road-racing machine (Fig. 1-38) is the only high-quality road bike made in America, and is equal to the best of the European brands, with the possible exception of the Puch "Ultima" (see below), which costs 78 percent more.

Specifications:

Frame: Short wheel-base frame, hand built of Reynolds '531' double-butted and taper-gauge manganese alloy steel tubing, fully lugged, with Campagnolo fork ends. Head and seat mast angles 73 degrees parallel. Fork is Reynolds '531' taper-gauge round blades and single butted steering tube with Campagnolo fork ends. Rake is 1¾ inches

Fig. 1-38: Schwinn "Road Racer Paramount"

Frame Sizes: 20, 21, 22, 23, 24, 25 or 26 inches. Can be made to measure at extra cost

Handlebars: Cinelli aluminum alloy drop bar with Cinelli forged-aluminum alloy with recessed binder bolts

Crankset: Campagnolo Record Strada three-piece forged alloy double plateau with 42–52-tooth chainwheels

Freewheel: Regina Oro with 14-, 16-, 18-, 21- and 24-tooth cogs

Chain: Regina Oro

Hubs: Campagnolo high-flange alloy with quick-release

Rims: Super Champion 330 gram alloy

Tires: Campionato Del Mondo silk tubulars

Derailleurs: Front: Campagnolo Record alloy. Rear: Campagnolo Nuovo Record alloy. Both with downtube shift levers

Brakes: Campagnolo alloy side-pull

Saddle: Cinelli Unica-Nitor suede leather on plastic base, on Cinelli forged alloy stem

Weight: 23 pounds

Cost: $900

Gios Torino Super Record Strada

Campagnolo brakes, seat post, cranks, chainwheels, bottom bracket and pedals

Hand-brazed frame of Columbus tubing

Regina chain and freewheel, Cinelli bars, stem and saddle, Mavic rims with Clement tubulars and Galli toe clips

Gios also makes a Record Cross model for cyclo-cross racing

Price: $1,095

Steyr-Daimler-Puch "Ultima" (12-speed)

This road-racing machine probably *is* the ultimate in quality. It certainly is a beautiful thing to behold, and if you want a truly high-performance road-racing machine that is as responsive as the finest-tuned racing car or thoroughbred racehorse, and money is no object, this is the machine for you. I have one, and I like to leave it in my living room just to show it off. (I also ride it once in a while just to keep the feel of a fine machine between me and the road.) Components are Campagnolo's highest quality, with extensive use of light but strong titanium. The frame is a masterpiece of frame building and finishing craftsmanship, with cut-out and filed lugs, gold pin-striping around lugs, piano-finish frame enamel job in amethyst. Tubular tires are very light silk sew-ups.

Specifications:
Frame: Reynolds '531' double-butted. 74-by-74-degree angles. Fork also Reynolds '531' double-butted and engraved. Lugs are Bocama Super Luxury, cut-out and filed. Dropouts are Campagnolo. Chainstays are chromed, mounts are brazed on for water bottle cage and pump. Comes in elegant protective velvet foam case
Frame Sizes: 21, 22, 23, 24 and 25 inches
Rims: Fiamme Ergal No. 1
Tires: Clement Strada 66 (tubular)
Hubs: Campagnolo Record Strada, small flange with quick-release
Crankset: Campagnolo 4030 Super Record Strada with titanium bottom-bracket spindle. Dual chainwheels with 42 and 53 teeth
Freewheel: Regina Oro 13, 15, 17, 19, 21 and 24 teeth
Chain: Regina Oro, drilled
Brakes: Campagnolo 4060 Super Record side-pull
Derailleurs: Front, Campagnolo Record. Rear, Campagnolo Super Record
Shift Levers: Campagnolo, on brazed-on mount on down tube
Pedals: Campagnolo 4021 Super Record with Titanium axles
Saddle: Cinelli No. 3, Buffalo suede, on Campagnolo Super Record Seat Post
Weight: 21 pounds, 2 ounces with pump, bottle cage and bottle (furnished) on 23-inch frame. Smaller frames will weigh less
Cost: $1,600

Klein Road-Racing Bicycles

The Klein Bicycle Corporation makes two super-light bicycles designed primarily for road racing and criterium racing events, although the maker says they can also be used for time trialing (a solo race against the clock). Two models are available, the Team Super Frame (Fig. 1-39) and the Heavy Duty Frame. Both have the same basic components, the difference being that the Heavy Duty version has extra stiffening for the heavier rider. The lighter-weight model also uses more titanium parts, which are not used with the Heavy Duty model because of strength and stresses from a heavier, stronger rider.

Frames are of a special blend of alloys, mainly aluminum, manganese and boron, and are exceptionally stiff and strong, well in excess of even Reynolds '531' or Columbus steel tubing in terms of deflection under stress.

Bottom-bracket bearings are standard electric motor bearings, pressed in flush with the housing and retained with Locktite 601. Klein will replace these bearings if they ever wear out. Frames are finished in DuPont Imron enamel, so should be highly resistant to marring and scratching.

Specifications: (Super-Light Model): 10-speed
Frame: See above
Frame Sizes: (In centimeters. For inches, multiply by 0.3931) 51, 54, 57, 59, 16
and 64 centimeters
Crankset: Klein spindle (see above) with Campagnolo Super Record cranks.
Chainrings and crank lengths to order. (If you are going to spend this kind of
money you need to know exactly what you want. Please see Chapter 2 for data
on gear selections.) Crank lengths available are 165, 167.5, 170, 172.5, 177.5
and 180 millimeters. The bigger frames generally need longer cranks
Freewheel: Cyclo or Maillard Alloy, 13 to 19T
Hubs: He-E heavy duty front, high-flange rear, both with sealed bearings with
Pino Titanium quick-releases
Rims and Tires. Super Champion Record du Mond or comparable with Clement
Criterium Seta Extra, 230 gram
Derailleurs: Campagnolo Super Record, with brazed-on shifters
Bars and Stems: Cinelli Model 63 or 64. Specify 38- or 40-centimeter width
Stem: Cinelli Model 1. Specify length in centimeters (See Chapter 2)
Pedals: Campagnolo Super Record
Seat and Post: Avocet Racing II, padded and leather covered on Campagnolo
Super Record post
Brakes: Galli 75 Ti
Equipment: Water bottle and cage, toe clips and straps for pedals, Silca Impero
pump painted same color as frame
Headset: Campagnolo Super Record
Weight: 17.5 pounds (57-cm. frame)
Cost: $1,998 (frame only: $927)

Fig. 1-39: Klein "Super Light" racing bicycle

Klein Heavy-Duty Road-Racing Bicycle[2] 10-speed

Specifications:
Frame: See above
Frame Sizes: Same as lightweight model
Crankset: Same as lightweight model
Freewheel: Regina Oro 13–19T
Hubs: Same as lightweight model
Rims and Tires: Same as lightweight model
(Balance of specifications same as or equal to lightweight model)
Equipment: Same as lightweight model
Weight: 57-centimeter frame weighs 18.6 pounds
Cost: $1,925 (costs more than the lightweight model due to extra stiffening, greater use of titanium or stronger parts. Frameset only is $927)

Nishiki O. N. P.

Many manufacturers do not sell a completely equipped track bike because component selection is such a personal thing with racing cyclists. Thus there are a number of suppliers who make the frame only. One of them is Nishiki, which makes a very elegant frameset for around $280 retail.

Specifications:
Frame: Chrome molybdenum double-butted tubing including fork, with Cinelli-style crown. Fork crown has reinforced upper inside lug. Tange "Levin" headset is furnished. Seat stays are mitered to fit snugly. Seat stays are large diameter, mitered to back of the seat lug and brazed
Frame Sizes: In millimeters. Multiply by .0394 for inches. 520, 540, 560, 580; 600, 620 and 640 millimeters
Cost: $280 (Includes headset)

Windsor Professional AM-4 Track Bicycle[3]

An experienced European frame builder makes elegant bicycles down Mexico way, which are distributed in America via bicycle stores. The track bike above is one of two made by Windsor.

Specifications:
Frame: Columbus double-butted tubing throughout. Special spear-point-drilled chrome lugs. Campagnolo track front and rear dropouts. Chrome fork crown
Frame Sizes: 50 to 63 centimeters
Crankset: Campagnolo No. 760 49T chainwheel, 1,655 millimeter cranks
Sprocket: Campagnolo No. 763, 15T
Headset: Campagnolo Record
Bars and Stem: ttt

[2] Klein is readying a touring version of their bicycles for introduction early in 1980. Write to Klein (see Appendix) for specifications and price, not available at this writing.

[3] Windsor also makes a less expensive model, basically the same frame but with less costly components. This is Model AM-8 Track Standard, costs $375, weighs 18 pounds.

Hubs: Campagnolo Record high-flange front and rear. Track No. 1036
Pedals: Campagnolo Record Track No. 1038
Tires and Rims: Windsor tubular rims and tubular tires
Saddle: Windsor padded leather on Campagnolo 26.8-millimeter seat post
Weight: 18 pounds
Cost: $500

Schwinn Paramount Track Bike

Schwinn's contribution to the track-racing scene is a hand-brazed-up short-wheelbase track machine.

Specifications:
Frame: Frame is made of Reynolds '531' double-butted tubing throughout, fully lugged with Campagnolo track ends. Head and seat mast angle is 74 degrees. Fork is also Reynolds '531' taper-gauge round fork blades with single-butted steering and Campagnolo fork ends. Fork has a 1⅜-inch rake
Crankset: Campagnolo Record Pista 3-piece forged alloy, 50T chainwheel
Sprocket: Campagnolo with choice of 15 or 16T
Hubs: Campagnolo high-flange alloy, Record Pista
Rims: Super Champion 330-gram alloy with Clement No. 9 cotton tire. Clement No. 3 track silks available at extra cost
Bars and Stem: Cinelli aluminum alloy track drop bar on Cinelli forged-aluminum alloy track stem with recessed bolts
Pedals: Campagnolo Record Pista alloy rattrap with toe clips and straps
Weight: 20 pounds
Cost: $659

For The Smaller Rider

Short (no pun intended) of having a special frame built for you, if you're under 5 feet one or so, at great expense, my suggestion for a high-quality touring bicycle would be the Bertin Model C-32. At 18 inches (46 centimeters) you should be able to straddle the top tube if your inseam measurement is 28⅝ inches or less. This bike can be used for touring, as well as for commuting.

The problem with making a fully lugged small frame of 18 inches is that the lugs will touch at the head tube, often limiting the frame size to 19 inches or even 20 inches. Some builders fudge by using shorter seat and downtubes so the bottom bracket is higher off the ground. Because the bike size is measured from the center line of the bottom-bracket spindle to the top of the seat tube (see Chapter 2) you can fudge your way into an 18-inch frame. But the top tube is still too high for the shorter rider. Another way to fudge is to use smaller wheels, say 26- or 24-inch wheels, and this too is done. The trouble with the small wheels is that they offer more rolling resistance and a lot less shock and vibration absorbance than the larger 27-inch wheels or the 700-centimeter wheels. My recommendation is to use 700-centimeter wheels so you can use the new Elan ¾-inch narrow-width tire for low rolling resistance comparable to a tubular tire.

Bertin Model C-32:

Specifications:

Frame: [4] Close-coupled frame for quick-response steering. Bocama lugs specially designed for this frame, and a modified Wagner forged-fork crown provide adequate clearance. Butted Durifort alloy steel tubing in fork blades, steering tube (head tube) and rear triangle. Main tubes (top, down and seat tube) are of light-gauge plain steel tubing. Reinforced vertical stamped-steel dropouts are used on the rear, with an integral derailleur hanger. Dropouts have hangers for mounting carriers.

Headset: None furnished. Select your own and the distributor will install. I recommend Campagnolo or Shimano DuraAce

Frame Dimensions: 18 inches (46 cm.). Head tube angle: 71.5 degrees. Seat tube: 76 degrees

Bottom-Bracket Height: 10⅝ inches (27 cm.)

Top Tube Length: 20¼ inches (51.5 cm.)

Chainstays: 16 inches (40 cm.)

Fork Offset: 1½ inches (rake) (40 mm.)

Headset Threads: metric 25 by 1 millimeters

Bottom Bracket: metric 35 by 1 millimeters

Stem Size: 25.8 millimeters

Wheelbase: 38 inches (96.5 cm.)

Brakes: Mafac Cantilever brakes with short reach levers. Brakes are brazed on

Weight: 6 pounds (2.72 kg.). Frame only

Cost: $159.95 (frame and fork only, without headset, with brakes)

Bicycles for Ages Twelve to Fifteen

I have made a fairly arbitrary selection of bicycles for this age group. All of these bikes are sturdy, represent good value for the money and should last long enough to be handed down to other children as the current owner either outgrows his bicycle or wants to move up to one of the better touring or commuting models described elsewhere in this chapter. None of these bicycles have what I would call high performance, but then the price is not high either. Selections were made on the basis that growing teenagers tend to be careless about locking up their bikes and, in any case, ride them to school—a high-risk area for bike security in many towns. Maintenance is not always attended to carefully either, and I see many kids riding bikes with rusty chains and parts about to fall off. Not infrequently I observe bikes being dropped forcefully on the pavement at the local high-caloric-intake shop. Bicycles I can recommend for teens are:

---

[4] For this frame you will, of course, need rims, tires, spokes, crankset, handlebars, stem, seat post, saddle, freewheel, cables, chain and derailleurs. You should be able to assemble the parts needed for around $300 at the most, for a complete bike. Or cannibalize your old bike. Available at your dealer or from R. C. Hallett, 2122 Coal Place SE, Albuquerque, New Mexico 87106 (phone 505/843-9378).

Fig. 1-40: Schwinn "Boy's Collegiate Sport" 10-speed

Schwinn Collegiate Sport 10-Speed[5]

This model (Fig. 1-40) also comes in a 5-speed version for slightly less money. It's a hefty 39 pounds because the frame is low-carbon steel and so has to be thicker and heavier to stand the gaff. But the bike is sturdy.

Specifications:
Frame: Electro-forged of 16-gauge 1010 carbon steel. Built-in kickstand and welded-on cable lugs. Forged steel fork
Frame Sizes: 17, 20 and 22 inches for the boy's model; 17 and 20 inches for the girls' design frame
Crankset: Forged-steel one-piece crank with Shimano FF front freewheeling with 39–52 T chainrings
Freewheel: Shimano
Hubs: Maillard low-flange alloy front and rear
Rims and Tires: Schwinn tubular-steel chromed 26 by 1¼ inches, Schwinn Sports touring gumwall tires
Derailleurs: Front: SunTour Sprite. Rear: SunTour Seven. Shift levers on stem
Brakes: Alloy side-pull calipers with extension levers
Saddle: Messinger R1 racing style, vinyl top on forged-steel post
Pedals: Union steel rattrap
Weight: 39 pounds
Cost: $142.95

Schwinn Varsity 10-speed

The old reliable (Fig. 1-41) made by Schwinn for years and found throughout the land chained to high school and college bike racks. A reliable bike for general-purpose use, one I can recommend to take to college for speeding to and from classes and back to the dorm. Comes in men's and women's frames. Once the cables have stretched and brakes and derailleurs been readjusted to take up the slack, very little needs to

[5] The same bicycle as a 5-speed. It weighs 38 pounds, costs $136.95.

Fig. 1-41: Schwinn "Varsity Sport" 10-speed

be done to keep this bike running practically forever—beyond oiling the chain occasionally and, every three or four years, depending on use, disassembling hubs, bottom bracket and headset for cleaning and re-greasing.

Specifications:
Frame: Electro-forged of 16-gauge 1010 carbon steel with built-in kickstand and welded-on cable lugs. Forged-steel fork has chrome-finish cap.
Frame Sizes: Men's: 17, 20, 22, 24 and 26 inches (a size for just about everyone). Women's: 17, 20 and 22 inches
Crankset: Forged-steel diamond-style heat-treated one-piece crank with 39 and 52T chainwheels
Freewheel: Maillard with 14-, 17-, 20-, 24- and 28-tooth cogs. Built-in dust seal
Hubs: Maillard high-flange alloy front, small-flange alloy rear
Rims and Tires: Tubular-steel chromed rims with Schwinn Puff gumwall 27-by-1¼-inch tires
Brakes: Alloy side-pull with extension levers
Derailleurs: Front: same make and design. Rear: Huret GT-51 with jam-free backpedal cage. Shift levers stem mounted
Saddle: Narrow style with vinyl cover over special molded pad
Pedals: Union steel rattrap
Weight: 38 pounds with kickstand
Cost: $156.95

For Ages Nine to Eleven

Subteen children are notoriously hard on bikes. They leave them out in the rain, ride them up and down curbs, pull "wheelies" and practice other assorted mayhem on their two-wheelers. You want a bike that's sturdy, with good brakes, heavy-duty balloon-type tires and with components that will stay together so you aren't spending all your spare time fixing the thing. Bikes for this age group should also be inexpensive, because kids are not good about putting them away or locking them up.

So if you live in a big city, chances are the bike may be stolen sooner or later.

I'm not going into a lot of detail on the specifications—you'd only be bored. I have seen all these bikes, and I know they are sturdy, so the minimum specs herewith are offered as backup to the selections:

Schwinn Model CC1-6 has 24-inch wheels with coaster brakes and balloon tires, heavy electro-forged cantilever frame. Model CC7-6 is the same bike with 26-inch wheels and *Model CC5-5* the same machine with a 5-speed gear system and handbrakes instead of coaster brakes. I would recommend buying the 1-speed coaster-brake model because you just can't depend on kids to take care of the 5-speed system and it's going to get out of adjustment eventually. Of course, your child may be different . . .

Anyhow, the Schwinn CC1-6 sells for $136.95, as does the CC7-6. The CC5-5 5-speed goes for $169.95.

The Nishiki FFS Tourist comes with either 27-inch wheels for the taller person, or 24-inch wheels with a 17-inch frame for the child or short adult. This model also comes as a Junior Mixte in the same configuration as above. Equipment includes the Shimano front freewheeling system, which permits shifting anytime the bike is in motion, including coasting, backpedalling or even pedaling hard uphill. Cost for all models: $149.95.

Raleigh Rampar R-6AW model has a 3-speed transmission with hand brake. It features the Sturmey-Archer old reliable AW 3-speed rear hub, comes in a 13-inch frame, costs $109.95.

A bit more expensive Raleigh for this age group is *Rampar Rambler*. This is a heavyweight cruiser with twin curved top tubes, wide steerhorn handlebars, balloon whitewall tires that would probably survive collision with a truck, although I have my doubts about the rider. Has a 19-inch frame, costs $124.95.

If you want a really good bike for your subteen child, I can recommend the *Sekai 400 Junior 10*. It comes with smaller 24-inch wheels, so should be small enough to fit most kids in this age bracket. The frame is Tange high-carbon steel, with medium-grade components such as derailleurs, chainsets, saddle, bars and pedals. The frame sizes are 18 and 24 inches. This is quite a jump in frame size, but the 18-inch size with the 24-inch wheels should fit a child or short adult. This bike weighs only 30 pounds, which is light for a child's model, and costs around $170.

The Schwinn Bantam Pixie is adjustable to fit a fairly wide range of child sizes. It has a convertible top tube so you can pass it along to younger children, regardless of their sex. Has chrome-plated fenders, 20-by-1¾-inch tires, weighs 32 pounds and costs $84.95.

The Nishiki Stinger (boy's) and *Angel* (girl's) are attractive bikes for the younger set, both heavily chauvinized. The Stinger has black hi-rise bars, blue frame, black banana saddle. The Angel, a girl's frame, has the same equipment but handlebars are less macho in design and the banana saddle is flower printed. Both have a Shimano coaster brake rear hub. Cost: $89.95.

Bikes for Ages Five to Nine

For children five to nine you need a bike that's comfortable to ride, that will fit the child so he can reach the ground from the saddle or top tube in comfort or safety, yet won't penalize him with a lot of weight. There are two fine machines for this group that will let the child tag along with you on rides up to ten miles or so.

For ages five to seven, I like the Raleigh Model R-80. It has a small frame, only 14 inches, made of 2030 high-tensile steel and with lugs. Dropouts, where wheel axles fit in, are not the el cheapos you see on dime store bikes of stamped steel spot welded in place, but strong, heavy steel that will stand a lot of abuse. Comes with coaster brakes, sensible (not hi-rise) handlebars, chainguard, comfy black vinyl mattress saddle and mudguards (fenders) so your child won't come in all mud splattered when he rides in the rain. Weight only 25 pounds. Cost: $98.95

For ages seven to nine, a similar bike is the *Raleigh Model R-54* with a 16-inch frame, lighter-weight tires and three speeds with hand brakes for $129.95. At that price I would buy my child a good lock (see page 292) and teach him how to use it. Have extra keys made for when (not if) he loses one.

Exercisers for All Ages

Finally, I have included a selection of stationary bicycles for those months of the year when you cannot be outdoors pedaling around (see a discussion of exercisers in Chapter 6). First, let me say that the number of companies making these exercisers has proliferated, so it is important to know what you are looking for in a stationary bike before you go out to buy one. First, it should have a timer to clock your time on the bike, an odometer to check your pace and a precisely calibrated pressure gauge to adjust and measure the resistance against which you are pedaling. All of these should be on one control panel, so that you can easily adjust the bike while on it.

The Schwinn Air-Dyne ErgoMetric exerciser (Fig. 1-42), which retails for $395, gives both upper and lower body exercise through progressive resistance. You can either push with both legs and arms, or each of them singly. The exerciser also gives off cooling air through a "wind-vane" system which you are operating while you pedal. This is a good, readily

Fig. 1-42: Schwinn Ergo-
Metric Exerciser

available model. There is a more expensive model, too, which also has the display panel but only exercises the legs, called the ErgoMetric exerciser, with push-button controls. It retails for over $600. A reading stand is optional on both pieces of equipment.

What to Look for in A BMX Bicycle

Bicycle motocross racing is here to stay. And even if your child, from nine to fifteen, is not a BMXer racer, he will surely enjoy the responsive, fun aspect of barreling around the neighborhood and over rough terrain in the country on a BMX machine.

BMX prices, and quality, vary considerably. Prices range from around $125 to over $300. The cheaper bicycles are heavier, have welded frames of heavy-gauge steel tubing—heavy gauge because the low-yield strength must be compensated for by thicker tubing. The thicker-tubing frames, of course, weigh a lot more than more exotic tubing metals. Less expensive components add to the heft of the bike because steel is used instead of aluminum alloys.

A BMX bike for competition is made to do one thing—Win! If your child is interested in BMX racing he wants a lightweight but strong frame hand brazed of high-carbon chrome molybdenum steel tubing, strong hubs, preferably sealed against friction creating, dragging dirt and dust, and alloy bars rims.

Most BMX bikes are single-speed machines with heavy, one-piece cranksets of steel. Better BMX bikes come with alloy rims, bars, stems and cranksets. These days you can get some fairly exotic equipment for these little 20-inch two-wheelers. One component supplier, SunTour, makes a two-speed freewheel and rear derailleur combination with a special shift lever which permits the rider to start off fast in low gear, release the lever and shift into high gear. This is SunTour's Hole Shot Model RD-2900 rear derailleur, which should be used with their Model No. MF03000 two-speed freewheel and LS-2600 shift lever or LS-2700 trigger-type lever. SunTour, along with Shimano and a host of other parts manufacturers, also make BMX coaster-brake hubs, caliper brakes for BMX bikes, special tools for removing freewheels and changing freewheel cogs and cranksets. Special heavy-duty alloy seat posts, BMX rattrap pedals, anodized aluminum parts (usually black for the macho effect) rims, hubs and handlebars are also available.

Before deciding on one of the BMX bicycles we have selected in various price ranges, be sure you know what your child plans to do with the bike. If he's going to enter competitive BMX racing he'll need the best bike you can afford. Chapter 7 gives details on BMX racing and BMX racing organizations. There is also a large selection of BMX protective clothing to shield your child from bruises, abrasions and cuts in the inevitable fall or crash during BMX racing. Of course your child should wear a crash helmet; in fact, it's mandatory in official, sponsored races. Most helmets have long visors. Actually, the whole BMX racing scene is very much like motorcycle cross-country racing, including the type of clothing, the kind of helmets and even the lingo. It's a toss-up as to whether BMX racing is the best thing that's ever happened for the future of bicycling, or motorcycling. Right now it has to be bicycling . . . millions are being spent every year by BMX bike purchasers for bikes and equipment. One can only hope that this interest will project into bicycling as an adult.

How can you tell the difference between the real thing and a regular child's street bike that's gussied up to look like a BMX bike but isn't— and won't be suitable for BMX rough stuff (Fig. 1-43)? First, the kid's

Fig. 1-43: Kids give BMX bikes a really rough workout, which is why so many of them have gusseted, reinforced frames of high-tensile, strong steel tubing.

Fig. 1-44: This Schwinn Tornado is a fine child's bike, but the cantilever frame and banana saddle say that this is not a BMX bike—just to point out the difference between a small-frame bike for children and a true BMX bike. BMX bikes don't have fenders, either.

street 20-incher will have a cantilever frame with double construction (Fig. 1-44). This bike may carry a label that says, "Not for racing or stunt ruding," because the bike won't stand up to that kind of rough treatment. Your true BMX bike has a diamond frame, single (not banana) saddle, little or no rake in the fork, and the price will be way, way up there (Fig. 1-45).

Besides the well-known manufacturers such as Schwinn, Raleigh and Soma, this market has become so specialized that there are now a host of companies that make BMX bikes exclusively, mostly in California, where BMX racing was born and is the most popular, at this writing. Here, then, is our selection of BMX bikes. We've tried to give you a choice from brand names as well as from the specialized manufacturers. These bikes are listed in order of price, the lowest-priced models first.

Fig. 1-45: By contrast with the bike in Figure 1-44, here is a high-grade, true BMX bike, the Team Mongoose, which sells for $299.95.

Huffy Pro-2 This is one of five Huffy models ranging in price from $79 to $150. The Pro-2 is in between. Frame is gusset reinforced where top and downtubes meet the head tube. Handlebars are not as extreme in height as on some BMX bikes. Top tube has a plastic protector as does the handlebar cross tube. Chainset is one piece. Single speed, coaster brake, quilted nylon saddle, rattrap pedals. Uses 20-by-2.125-inch stagger block knobby tires. Has a rear caliper brake. Weight: NA. Cost: $89.

From West Coast Cycle Supply (see your dealer) comes a full line of BMX bicycles, from which we have selected a sampling in various price ranges.

The Cycle Pro Macho has a diamond, reinforced frame, MX fork, (Fig. 1-46) steel box handlebars, forged-steel stem, chrome dimpled 105-gauge steel rims, Shimano coaster brake, 20-by-2.125-inch tires, Sugino one-piece steel crankset. Weight: NA. Cost: $109.95

Raleigh Rampar R-10: Raleigh makes a number of different BMX models, from which we have selected two. The R-10 is one of them. Bike has a 12-inch frame designed for hard, competitive riding. Frame is of high-carbon steel. Bars are black or chrome with crossbar and pad. Brakes are Shimano coaster. Crankset is one-piece forged steel. Rims are rim section chrome steel. Hubs are low-flange steel. Tires are 20 x 2.125 inches. Saddle is padded, quilted vinyl. Weight: NA. Cost: $119.95

Sekai Model 250 MX: Sekai is a Japanese manufacturer of high-quality bicycles, including a line of BMX machines. The Model 250 MX "Challenger" has a mild steel frame, gusset reinforced at the head tube. Has a one-piece forged steel crankset, Shimano BMX coaster-brake rear hub, rattrap pedals and 20 x 2.125-inch tires. Wright: NA. Cost: $129.95

Fig. 1-46: Cycle Pro Macho, BMX from West Coast Cycle Supply

Fig. 1-47: B.M.X Products, Inc., Pro Mongoose

BMX Pro Mongoose: B.M.X. Products, Inc., 9621 Irondale Ave., Chatsworth, California 91311 (I give address in case you can't find a dealer) makes a complete range of BMX bikes and components. The Pro Mongoose (Fig. 1-47) main tubes of high-tensile strenth tubing heliarc welded and double gusseted for strength. Crankset is one-piece forged steel. Uses a Bendix No. 76 coaster brake. Wheels are Motomag II lightweight and rigid construction. Weight: NA. Cost: $169.95

Pro Trophy: From West Coast Cycle Supply comes this high-performance BMX machine with lugged, high-tensile, brazed-steel diamond frame. Headset is by Tange. Rims are 80-gauge alloy. Hubs are alloy, with rear hub a 16-tooth Shimano freewheel on a Sanshin hub. Crankset is one-piece forged steel. Saddle is quilted nylon base on chrome steel seat post. Pads are included for top tube and handlebar crossbar. Brakes are Shimano side-pull front and rear. Weight: NA. Cost: $179.95

Cycle Pro Trophy: Also from West Coast Supply, this model has a lugged high-tensile-strength steel frame with a Tange headset. Bars are new-style steel with alloy bend. Stem is forged-steel black. Rims are 80-gauge alloy with 20-by-2.125-inch tire front and 20-by-1.75-inch tire rear. Crankset is one-piece steel. Comes with top and handlebar pads (Fig. 1-48) and reflectors. Chainwheel has 44 teeth. Brakes are Shimano alloy side-pull front and rear. Crank, bar, stem, rims, frame and fork are powder coated with two-step process using silver undercoat. Weight: NA. Cost: $179.95

Soma Standard BMX: Frame is of high-tensile steel with cut-away lugs. Uses a SunTour BMX freewheel with 14 teeth, and a one-piece crankset with 44 teeth. Brakes are Dia-Compe light alloy side-pull design with touring hooded cover. Hubs are high-flange steel. Bars and stem are forged steel. Rims are Araya steel with 20-by-2.125-inch tires. Weight: 30 pounds, 14 ounces. Cost: $180.

Fig. 1-48: Cycle Pro Trophy, West Coast Cycle Supply

Fig. 1-49: Panda Super Cross 3T

Fig. 1-50: Schwinn SX-1000

Panda Super Cross 3T: Made by Panda Bike Company, 1450 Franquette Ave., Concord, California 94250 (in case you can't find a dealer). Has high-tensile-strength steel frame, double-gusset construction. Bars and fork are chromed as is the stem and one-piece forged-steel crankset (Fig. 1-49). Heavy-duty wheels and hubs. This model has mag-type wheels with 20-by-2.125-inch tires. (Wire-spoked wheels are slightly less expensive.) Brake is Shimano heavy-duty coaster brake. Weight: NA. Cost: $195.

Schwinn SX-1000: Here's a top-grade BMX (Fig. 1-50) at a reasonable price. Has a tubular chrome moly steel frame with reinforcing gussett. Frame is hand brazed up. Caliper brakes are on both wheels. Crankset is one-piece forged steel. Saddle is quilted nylon racing design. Weight: 28 pounds. Cost: $196.95 painted (chromed, $201.95).

Cycle Pro Duster from West Coast Cycle Supply has a high-tensile-strength steel frame, chromed high-tensile-steel fork, a Tange headset. Cranks are Sugino alloy three-piece cotterless with a 44-tooth Sugino alloy chainwheel. Hubs are alloy, rear hub has Shimano 16-tooth freewheel. Tires are 20 by 2.125 inches front and 20 by 1.75 inches rear. Brakes are Shimano alloy side-pull front and rear. All parts are anodized, chromed or painted. Weight: NA. Cost: $229.95

Raleigh Rampar Model R-9: has a 12-inch frame, of aircraft-quality chrome moly steel, heliarc welded. Form is all chrome moly steel. Bars are light alloy as is the stem. Brake is Dia-Compe alloy side-pull on rear wheel. Crankset is Sugino Mighty Mx 5-pin alloy cotterless. Freewheel is SunTour. Rims are Araya 20 x 1.75 inches flat sided with 20 x 2.125-inch tires. Saddle is special MX design on fluted heat-treated anodized aluminum. Weight: 24 pounds. Cost: $264.95

Soma High Grade BMX Lugless: Has hand-brazed chrome moly frame and fork. Uses two-speed rear freewheel with 15 and 16 teeth. Crankset is Sugino Super Maxy forged light alloy cotterless design with 44 teeth. Brakes are Dia-Compe alloy side-pulls. Bars and stem are light alloy. Stem has recessed Allen bolt. Saddle is Unimax on Dia-Compe light alloy fluted post. Rims are Araya light alloy 20 by 1.75 inches with 20-by-2.125-inch tire front and 20-by-1.75-inch rear. Weight, approximately 24 pounds, 10 ounces. Cost: $295. Soma's lugged frame is basically the same as the above, weights a bit less at 24 pounds, 4 ounces, costs $305.

BMX Products Team Mongoose: Their top-line BMX bike, this model has super-light, thin-walled chrome moly frame with alloy caliper brakes on rear wheel. Has light suede saddle on alloy stem. Cranks are Shimano's top-grade DuraAce cold forged alloy with 44-tooth sprocket. All components are either Shimano or other high-caliber top-line quality.

Weight: NA but under 24 pounds. Cost: $299.95 Figure 1-51 shows frame, available separately for $79.95.

Schwinn's top-of-the-line Sting BMX bike: Probably the ultimate in BMX machines (certainly the most expensive) is this model with all hand-brazed high-tensile-strength steel tubing frameset and fork. All components are high-tensile-strength aluminum alloy or lightweight steel. Brakes are Weinmann side-pull alloy on rear wheel. Crankset is SunTour cotterless three-piece aluminum alloy. Bars are alloy on alloy double clamp stem by Cook. Weight: about 23 pounds. Cost: $427. Figures 1-53 and 1-54 show construction details. Bicycle components, helmets, clothes, tires and framesets are available from Schwinn, B.M.X. Products, Inc., Panda BMX and Cook Brothers Racing, 1609-B East Edinger Avenue, Santa Ana, California 92705. All of these companies have parts catalogs describing literally hundreds of parts and pieces for BMX bikes. If your dealer can't supply the catalog, write the manufacturer directly.

You can also buy complete frames and build up your own BMX bike with just the parts you want on it. Besides the BMX frame shown in Figure 1-55, which lists for $80, other frames are:

- *Cook Brothers racing set:* $188
- *Schwinn Sting BMX:* $230.95 (See Figs. 1-52, 1-53, 1-54)
- *BMX Team Mongoose:* $54.95 (Fig. 1-55)
- *Sekai Model 450:* $69.95
- *Sekai Model 250:* $39.95
- *Sekai Model 380:* $54.95

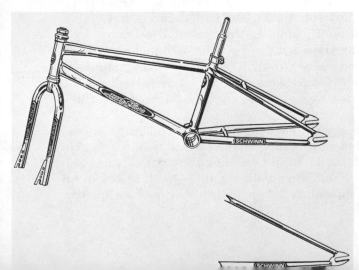

Fig. 1-52: Schwinn top-of-the-line Sting BMX frameset. Notice track-type rear dropouts, gusset-reinforced fork dropouts.

Fig. 1-53: Close-up showing details of the Schwinn Sting BMX bike.

Fig. 1-54: And here is the complete Schwinn Sting machine, probably the best BMX bike on the market.

Fig. 1-55: Frame from B.M.X. Products is their Mongoose at $54.95

Fig. 1-56: Moto-Mag wheels from B.M.X. Products. $28.95 each.

Fig. 1-57: Roger de Coster BMX fork from B.M.X. Products: $28.95

Fig. 1-58: Mongoose SS Handlebar: $17.95

Typical components you can buy are mag-type wheels, $28.95 each (Fig. 1-56); fork, $28.95 (Fig. 1-57) and bars, $17.95 (Fig. 1-58). All from B.M.X. Bicycles.

How to Select the Right Size Bicycle for You— and How to Ride It for the Most Fun and Healthful Exercise 2

In this chapter we will review the basics of selecting the right size bicycle for you, to fit you comfortably. We will also examine the selection of ready-made, off-the-shelf framesets, the components that can be hung on them and the approximate cost of the best framesets and components. Also in this chapter we will take up the more exotic subject of custom-made framesets, crafted just to fit your own measurements. And finally, because even the best bicycle will not give you the most pleasure unless you know how to ride it efficiently, we will review the basics of riding techniques as perfected by riders over the past 100 years.

SIZING THE STORE-BOUGHT BICYCLE

Bicycles for sale in stores are ready-made, like suits of clothes. And like clothing, they have to be altered and adjusted here and there for a correct, comfortable and safe fit. There are variables in a ready-made bike that can be adjusted for a better fit—and there are fixed components which, for the most part, cannot be changed or can only be changed at some expense to you. Let's look at what cannot be changed. You cannot change basic frame dimensions (Fig. 2-1). Length of frame tubes, height of the top tube from the floor, wheelbase are all fixed. Likewise, wheel diameter is fixed. Which means that a very basic step in selecting the right size store-bought bike is determining the right size frame.

This you do very simply, by straddling the top tube, with both stockinged feet (shoes removed) on the ground. You should have at least 1 inch and preferably 1½ inches between your pelvic bone and the top tube. This is important, because without sufficient clearance between you and the top tube you could be hurt when (not if) you have to come to a sudden, panic stop and come sliding down off the saddle with both feet extended, ready to hit the ground. You also need clearance just to be able to stop comfortably at stop signs and lights. A bit of extra clearance makes stopping by the side of the road on the banked shoulder to read a map a lot more comfortable. Figure 2-2 shows ample clearance between the rider and the top tube. Here the rider is wearing shoes, to be sure, but you will notice more than ample clearance in the critical

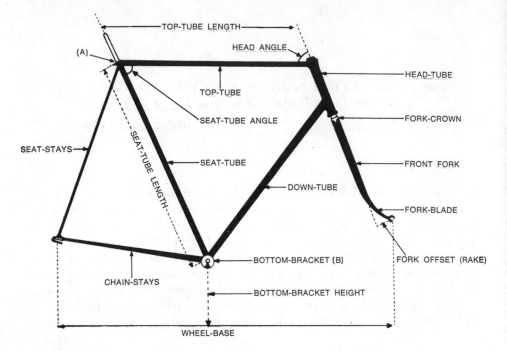

Fig. 2-1: Basic frame dimensions. Seat-tube length is the same as the frame size; i.e., if a seat tube is 21 inches, the frame is termed a 21-inch frame.

area. Table 2-1 gives your inseam measurement, as taken from the floor to your pelvic bone in stocking feet, and relates this measurement to bicycle-frame size. But no two of us are alike. People of the same overall height have different length legs, arms, torso and torso-to-shoulder height. So you can take this table as a rough measurement and ask to see bikes in the frame sizes indicated within your price bracket.

Table 2-1 Bicycle Fit *

Frame Size	Inseam Measurement From To
17″	26″ to 30″
19″	28″ to 31″
20″	29″ to 32″
21″	30″ to 33″
22″	31″ to 34″
23″	32″ to 35″
24″	33″ to 36″
25″	34″ to 37″
26″	35″ to 38″

* Courtesy of Schwinn Bicycle Company

Fig. 2-2: Clearance of about one inch between the young lady and the top tube of the bicycle is an important safety and comfort aspect of frame selection. You need the frame clearance shown for safety, because in a sudden stop you could be thrown forward and you want clearance between you and the top tube when your feet hit the ground. For safety and comfort you should have a bicycle that lets you adjust the saddle and handlebar stem at the correct height for you and yet permits sufficient metal on these components to remain inside the bike frame so they won't break off.

A Word About Frame Size

When you read the newspaper classified ads showing bicycles for sale, you almost always find the ad, if it mentions any dimensions at all, saying "27-inch man's bike" ... or "26-inch woman's bike" ... or "24-inch boy's bike." From Table 2-1 you will note that a 26-inch bicycle is fit only for a giant of over 6 feet 5 inches tall, and that this table, courtesy of Schwinn Bicycle Company, does not show a 27-inch frame at all, although they are made and are available. See the bicycle selections in Chapter 1; you'll find one or two there. What the ads are saying, of course, is that the bike for sale has wheels of a given diameter, and nothing more. The frame may be right for a 4 foot 11 inch person or a 6 foot 5 inch person.

Measuring Frame Size

To measure the frame size of any bicycle, all you need do is take a tapemeasure and check the number of inches between the centerline of the bottom-bracket spindle and the top of the seat tube, as shown in Figure 2-1, where it says "seat-tube length." Seat-tube length is the same as the frame size.

Frame sizes are also available in half-inch increments, depending on the make of bicycle. Unless you are very short or very tall, or have an unusual combination of body measurements, you should be able to find a bicycle that fits you, in a good bicycle store.

Children's Bicycle Fit

The child should be able to sit on the saddle and have both feet reaching the ground comfortably without having to lean the bike to one side. This is particularly important in the case of bicycles with a banana seat and high-rise handlebars, which do not allow for as much control as other designs. With this type of bicycle, when the child is seated on the saddle, his toes, at the very least, should touch the ground, and the handlebar grips should be no higher than his shoulders.

Variables You Can Adjust

Once you have selected the right size frame for you, and have decided on a particular bicycle, you can now proceed to make the more minute adjustments that spell the difference between comfort and pain, especially on a long, cross-country ride. At this point I would refer you to Chapter 14 to review your options as to type of saddle (mattress, semi-wide or narrow racing style) and handlebars (downturned, flat or somewhere in between). Let me just say here, though, that nothing can be more conducive to comfort, or pain, than the right or wrong type of bars or saddle.

I do recommend downturned bars, as shown in Figure 2-2. These bars can be held in at least five different positions, as shown later on in this chapter, so you can relieve stress on arms, shoulders and hands five different ways during your ride. Flat bars have only one position. Maybe two. Further, in the slightly dropped position, with your hands on the top of the bars, as in Figure 2-2, you will, when seated, be bent at an angle of around 45 degrees, not extreme at all. In this position the spinal segments are much farther apart, permitting road shock to be better absorbed both by the spine and by the arms upon which some of the body weight is resting. In the straight upright position the spine is compressed, little body weight can be absorbed by the arms and road shock is more readily, and uncomfortably, transferred to the body. You will find that the better bikes come almost exclusively with dropped bars.

As for saddles, there are three basic types, made out of a variety of leathers and plastics. The three types (Fig. 2-3) are, left to right, mattress, narrow touring and racing saddle, and lightweight racing saddle. I prefer the narrow saddle in the center, for two reasons. First, the wider mattress saddle tends to rub on the inside of the thighs when you ride in the more efficient angle position with dropped bars. Second, the springs in the mattress saddle absorb energy I would rather see go into turning the back wheel. You can find a more comfortable frame without having to use a mattress saddle. Please see the section in this chapter on custom frame design for a discussion on stiff racing and more resilient, shock-absorbing touring frames.

Since 1974, when the second revision of this book appeared, there has been a great deal of thought given to saddle design, especially for women, who up until the bike boom of the early 1970s were rarely seen on anything else but a mattress saddle, or at least one with springs, outside the racing scene. Men's saddles simply are not designed for women, so something had to be done, and it has been done. Please see Chapter 14 for details on saddle design, materials and costs. I will say that I have never seen a stock bike in a store come with a really comfortable saddle designed for women.

In addition to changing parts, there are other variables under your control in any stock bike (Fig. 2-4). These are: saddle height, saddle-

Fig. 2-3: The three basic saddle designs are, left to right: mattress, narrow touring and racing, and pure racing.

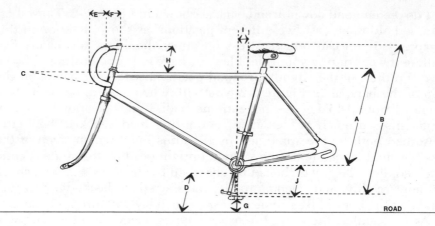

Fig. 2-4: Important frame measurements are (a) frame size, (b) saddle height, (c) handlebar angle, (d) bottom bracket road clearance, (e) handlebar throw, (f) stem length, (g) pedal-to-ground clearance, (h) handlebar height, (i) saddle position behind bottom bracket centerline, (j) crank length.

nose-to-handlebar distance, saddle tilt and saddle-nose distance from bottom-bracket-spindle centerline. These measurements are very critical to riding comfort. If the saddle is too low, you can't extend leg muscles fully, and you will overstrain your knees during part of the stroke revolution. According to orthopedic surgeons I have talked to about knee problems (see Chapter 6), this overstress can lead to serious and even permanent knee damage. If the saddle is too high, you won't be able to reach the pedals at the bottom of the stroke and so will lose pedaling efficiency. And you might also lose control of the bicycle, because with one foot dangling off the pedal you lose some upright support and the ability to maintain proper balance. You may remember as a child borrowing an older child's bike and how difficult it was to ride, as your little body bobbed up and down trying to reach the pedals.

I will describe more sophisticated methods of setting saddle height according to frame design later in this chapter in the section dealing with custom frames, but at this point, I'd like to make a few specific recommendations about the crucial matter of setting the saddle height on off-the-shelf bicycles.

First, we must consider another safety aspect of the proper saddle height. As is shown in Figure 2-5, you must have at least 2½ inches of the seat post *inside* the seat tube, or you risk breaking off the post when you are straining uphill. The post may also break off because of the extra lever effect when too much of it is left outside the seat tube. Or, the post may break from metal fatigue if it is stressed unduly with just a little in the seat tube. Note also from Figure 2-5 that the saddle is raised or lowered by loosening the binder bolt, shown just below the bottom part of the caliper ruler. This spreads the seat-post cluster and top of the seat tube that is slotted, and permits the seat post to move up and down. If

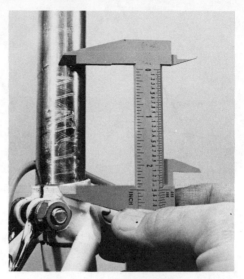

Fig. 2-5: You must have at least 2½ inches of the seat post inside the seat tube for safety, so the post won't break under stress.

the seat post sticks, grasp the saddle and twist it from side to side while exerting upward pressure. You may need to straddle the top tube while doing so, or have someone hold the bike down while you twist and pull upward.

Scientific Approach to Saddle-Height Adjustment

Experiments conducted at Loughborough University, England, illustrate the importance of saddle height to cycling efficiency.[1]

The experiments, which used well-known racing cyclists and a bicycle ergometer (a stationary bicycle) with a harness to hold the rider in position, showed that cycling energy output varies significantly with minor changes in saddle height. Tests proved that alterations in saddle height of 4 percent of inside leg measurement affected power output by about 5 percent. Experimenters also concluded that the most efficient saddle height is 109 percent of inside leg measurement.

These are average values, however, and it must be expected that some minor variations will be necessary for individual builds and preferences. But it is interesting to note that recent studies of racing cyclists reveal that the better racers tend to have their saddle height conform to this formula.

How does one adjust saddle height to 109 percent of leg length? The method is easy:

First, measure the length of your leg *on the inside,* from the floor to the crotch bone, while standing erect and without shoes.

Then, multiply this length as measured in inches by 109 percent. Let's

[1] Vaughn Thomas, "Scientific Setting of Saddle Position," *American Cycling* (now *Bicycling!*), June, 1967, pg. 12.

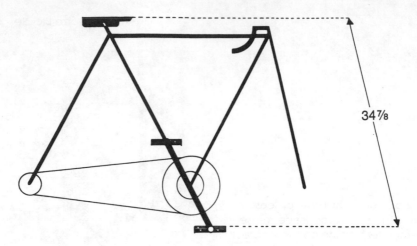

34⅞

Fig. 2-6: A scientific method of adjusting saddle height is measuring leg height from floor to crotch, on inside of leg, and multiplying this measurement by 1.09. Result should equal length from top of saddle to pedal spindle, as shown above. If leg measures 32 inches, saddle height should be 34⅞ inches, for example.

say, for example, that your leg measures 32 inches from floor to crotch. Multiply 32 × 1.09 = 34.88 inches. With the crank parallel to the plane of the seat tube (Fig. 2-6), measure or adjust the saddle so that the top of the saddle is 34⅞ inches from the pedal spindle.

Some cyclists will not want to follow this formula because they feel more comfortable at some other saddle-to-leg length ratio. But you should bear in mind that saddle height is something one becomes accustomed to, and any particular saddle adjustment is not necessarily the most efficient because it is, at the moment, the most comfortable. The beginning cyclist who adjusts his saddle according to the formula above will, in my opinion, be more likely to wind up a more efficient cyclist than the experienced cyclist who departs from this formula.

Few people are more opinionated than racing cyclists, or more concerned with the minute details of technique and equipment. Yet, when this formula for saddle-height adjustment was announced in 1967, a fierce controversy arose and many skeptics protested. The furor appears to have died down, and many professional cyclists, as well as their coaches and scientists who are interested in cycling, have adopted the formula.

Don't forget that this formula is the result of tests on 100 racing cyclists, ranging from beginners to the late world champion, Tommy Simpson. Four hundred readings were obtained at four different saddle heights—105, 109, 113, and 117 percent of inside leg measurements. These measurements were made from the top of the saddle to the pedal spindle at the bottom of the stroke, with the *crank* aligned with the seat tube.

If you find that there is a great difference between the formula height and the present height of your saddle, I would suggest that you make the adjustment gradually, in increments of one eighth of an inch, over a period of several months. This will give you time to adjust to the new setting, and give the formula a fair try. If you boost or lower the saddle height an inch or so to adjust to the formula at one time, you might find the new setting uncomfortable. Saddle height, as I said above, is something one must adjust to.

I have tried this formula on long trips. Once I had become used to the minor change I had to make, I found my cycling more efficient.

Saddle Height Affects Muscular Power Output in Cycling

Muscles have ranges of optimum stretch. They will stretch only to a limited degree. Experts say that leg muscles can exert more power as they approach the fully extended position—one reason why people who use a child's bicycle without readjusting the saddle huff and puff so ridiculously. But if leg muscles are stretched beyond their maximum capacity by a saddle that is too high, fluidity of leg movement will be disrupted.

The saddle height of 109 percent of leg measurement seems to give the best combination of maximum muscle stretch and maximum pedaling fluidity.

Saddle Tilt

I strongly recommend you tilt the saddle slightly downward, at an angle of about 10 degrees. This downward angle throws more of your weight on the broader, rear section of the saddle and keeps pressure off more sensitive areas. Further, the slight forward tilt permits you to take more pressure off the saddle and put it onto the arms, which can then act as shock absorbers.

Some saddles, such as the Avocet (see Chapter 14) need only be tilted about 5 degrees down, in my experience, or perhaps can even be left flat, parallel to the top tube. Ride each position for a week or so, change it slightly, try again until you have just the right tilt for you.

Saddle tilt on less expensive bikes is adjusted by loosening the saddle clamp (Fig. 2-7) and forcing the nose up or down and retightening the

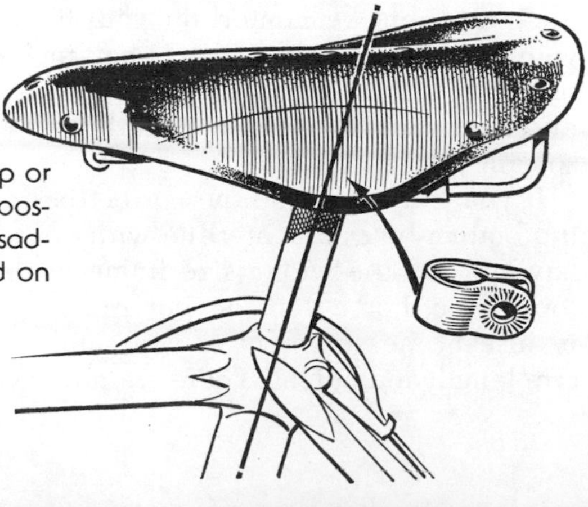

Fig. 2-7: You can tilt the saddle up or down, or move it horizontally, by loosening the saddle clamp bolt, on saddles with this type of fitting. Found on less expensive bicycles.

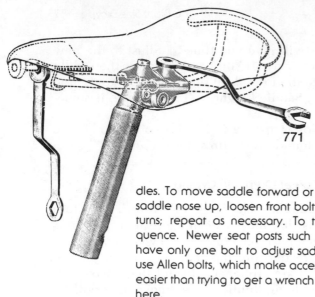

Fig. 2-8: Typical aluminum alloy micro-adjusting seat post, this Campagnolo post is adjustable by loosening the two top bolts with the special Campy No. 771 spanner (or a 10-mm. socket, which, with a ratchet wrench, is a lot easier to use). The other end of the Campy spanner is 13 mm., for taking up stretch from leather saddles. To move saddle forward or backward, loosen both bolts. To tilt saddle nose up, loosen front bolt two turns and tighten rear bolt two turns; repeat as necessary. To tilt saddle nose down, reverse sequence. Newer seat posts such as the Campagnolo Brevett Inter. have only one bolt to adjust saddle tilt, others, such as the Avocet, use Allen bolts, which make access to the seat-post adjustment much easier than trying to get a wrench way up under the saddle, as shown here.

771

clamp binder bolt when you have the saddle where you want it. On better bikes using Campagnolo-style alloy seat posts (see Chapter 14) the saddle tilt can be micro-adjusted by tightening the rear bolt to tilt up and the front bolt to tilt down (Fig. 2-8). You will have to loosen the opposite bolt to permit the facing bolt to be tightened.

Two Horizontal Saddle Adjustments

For most cyclo-tourists, the favored location of the saddle from the handlebars is where the nose of the saddle is from 2 to 2½ inches behind the centerline of the bottom bracket. Look at the "i" dimension in Figure 2-4. If you dropped a plumb line from the saddle nose, it should fall 2 to 2½ inches behind the centerline of the bottom-bracket axle (spindle).

So loosen the saddle-clamp binder bolt or the Campy-type adjustment bolts, both of them (Fig. 2-8), and slide the saddle back or forward until you find the approximate nose-to-bottom-centerline distance as shown. Leave the binder bolt or Campy bolts loose. Put your elbow on the nose of the saddle and your fingertips on the edge of the handlebars. If you picked the right size frame and the saddle is the right distance behind the bottom-bracket centerline, your fingers should just touch the bars. If your fingers are no more than a half inch or so ahead or behind the bars, move the saddle forward or backward until your elbow is on the saddle nose and your fingertips are on the edge of the handlebars. This is the so-called cubit adjustment.

If you can't combine the correct basic location of the saddle behind the bottom-bracket centerline with your "cubit" adjustment, either you have picked the wrong size frame or the manufacturer has put in too long or too short a stem, or your arms are too long or short for your height or inseam measurement or your fingers are too long or short for your arm length and height. There are now two more solutions available. But remember, it is important that you be able to reach the bars without strain or discomfort. Before we take further drastic steps, let's make one more check of this saddle horizontal location.

With someone holding the bicycle upright, sit on the saddle in a comfortable, slightly forward position. Put one hand on top of the handlebars. Swing the other arm over your shoulder, keeping it relaxed, and let this arm fall naturally onto the bars. The hands should just be able to curl around the top of the bars comfortably. If you feel strain, and the saddle can't move you far enough to or from the handlebars without moving it too far away or too far over the bottom-bracket centerline (remember, the 2- or 2½-inch saddle-nose location behind the bottom-bracket centerline lets you pedal more efficiently than if the saddle nose is right over the bottom bracket or too far behind it—within the 2-to-2½-inch range is a location right for you) then you have two more alternatives. You can twist the seat-post saddle clamp around so the clamp is forward on the seat post. This you can do by removing the clamp from the saddle and turning it so it faces forward. Or on a Campy-type seat post (Fig. 2-8) loosen both adjustment bolts, remove the saddle, loosen the seat-post binder bolt, twist the entire seat post around until the saddle-clamp section faces forward, retighten saddle-post binder bolt, reinstall the saddle and readjust saddle tilt and height. (I mark my saddle height by scratching a tiny line on the seat post so I can bring it back to the laboriously worked out correct saddle height for me, should I have to remove the saddle or post for any reason.) By reversing the direction of the saddle clamp or Campy seat post you can pick up about one extra inch of horizontal saddle movement.

A better way to adjust saddle distance from the handlebars is to replace the stock stem with a shorter or longer stem as necessary, or borrow an adjustable stem from the dealer for a week or two until you find the correct length stem for you. Figure 2-9 shows a variety of stem lengths, and at top left, an adjustable stem.

Most saddles will eventually stretch, thus altering the saddle-nose-tip-to-handlebar adjustment. The better saddles have a stretch adjustment that will restore the original saddle tension. The location of the saddle-tension adjustment is shown at the left of Figure 2-8. When you take slack out of the saddle you should readjust the saddle location horizontally, as shown above.

Adjusting the Handlebars

The handlebars, whether flat or downturned, should be set so they are about as high as the saddle. You must have at least 2 inches of the stem inside the seat tube, as shown in Figure 2-10. The 2 inches must be above the stem's split skirt, shown at the bottom of Figure 2-10.

To raise or lower the handlebars, loosen the stem bolt (Fig. 2-11). The stem-expander bolt is beveled and is inside the stem. As you tighten the bolt, the beveled bolt expands the stem in the split-skirt area and holds

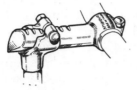

Fig. 2-9: A shorter or longer stem can be used to adjust the distance of the saddle from the handlebars. Seven stems of different lengths are shown and, at top left, an adjustable stem.

the stem in place inside the head tube (Fig. 2-11). In some stems, when you loosen the expander bolt (either with an Allen wrench or spanner, depending on the stem) the stem is still tight. In that case, tap the expander bolt with a plastic mallet to push the bolt down. The problem is that the bolt bevel is still tight inside the stem.

Fig. 2-10: To prevent handlebar stem from breaking under stress, always have two inches of the stem above the split skirt, as shown below, inside the head tube below the head set locknut.

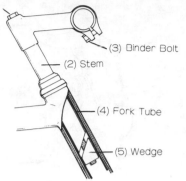

(1) Stem Expander Bolt

(3) Binder Bolt

(2) Stem

(4) Fork Tube

(5) Wedge

Fig. 2-11: You can raise and lower the stem by loosening the stem expander bolt. Note that the expander bolt is a wedge that, when tightened, forces the split skirt of the stem against the fork (head) tube. *(Drawing courtesy Soma Bicycles)*

If, as noted earlier, you wish to install a new stem in an existing bicycle, please refer to Chapter 14 for detailed instructions on stem removal and installation.

I like the handlebars, the downturned kind, with the drops (bottom handles) at about a 10-degree angle. That's right for me. You may want them at some other angle, say 5 degrees. In any case, the drops should have a slight downward tilt (Fig. 2-2). To tilt the bars, loosen the binder bolt at the stem head (Fig. 2-11), adjust bars, retighten binder bolt. Some binder bolts, in better bikes, have recessed Allen heads, and use a 5- or 6-millimeter Allen wrench.

BRAKE LOCATION

On downturned handlebars, the brake levers should be where you can reach them quickly and safely, without strain or imbalance. The normal location is about midway on the curve of the bars, as shown in Figure 2-12. To move the levers to another position, remove handlebar tape,

Fig. 2-12: Brake levers should be located at the rise of the bar curve, as shown, where they are convenient for hand resting points as well as for braking. *(Photo courtesy Dr. Clifford Graves)*

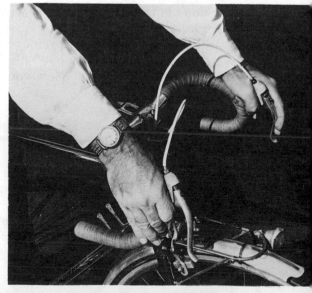

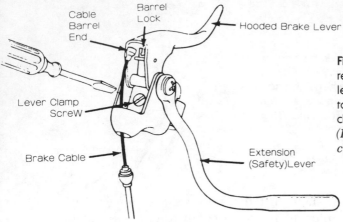

Cable
Barrel
End

Barrel
Lock

Hooded Brake Lever

Lever Clamp
Screw

Brake Cable

Extension
(Safety)Lever

Fig. 2-13: To move brake levers, remove handlebar tape, loosen lever clamp screw, move levers to new location, tighten lever clamp screw, rewind bar tape. (*Drawing courtesy Soma Bicycles*)

loosen the brake lever (Fig. 2-13) with a screwdriver (or a 5- or 6-millimeter Allen wrench if it's one of the newer Campy or Shimano levers) and move the levers to where you want them.

I would also remove the extension levers, the so-called safety levers (Fig. 2-13), because they do not have nearly the distance of travel of the bar-mounted levers. Squeeze the bar levers as tightly as you can. They should not come all the way to the handlebars. If they do, the brakes need adjustment (see Chapter 10). Squeeze the extension levers. They will usually come right to the bars, touching them. What this means is that the extension levers will stop you under conditions where mild braking ability is needed but won't work well in a panic stop situation. Their limitation is amplified by the fact that cables stretch, and if you don't take up the slack (see Chapter 10) the extension levers will be almost worthless. Yet, because they are in such a convenient location, right under the flat of the bars, you come to depend on them and could from habit reach for them in an emergency, and not be able to stop. If you don't have these levers, you won't become addicted to them. Your bike dealer can provide a shorter, replacement axle. All you do is unscrew the side binder bolt, remove and throw away the safety lever, remove the old axle, replace it with the shorter one and screw the side binder bolt back in place. Now you are saved from the "safety" lever addiction curse.

ALL ABOUT GEAR RATIOS

If you pedal on flat terrain only, and at most five or six miles at a trip, you don't need gears at all. Any single-speed gear within a moderate gear ratio (see below) will get you there and back.

But if you plan to ride longer distances over hill and dale, through flat country, into varying wind conditions, you will need a wide range of gears. The broad selection of gears, say from ten to eighteen gear selections, will let you compensate for the incredible variations in cycling conditions you will encounter on any cross-country trip. Gears are particularly important when you cycle tour and carry thirty or more pounds of camping gear on your bike.

To use an automotive analogy, your car's engine needs only three gears (four or five if it's a tiny four-cylinder) because the engine can provide power under a wider range of conditions. The human body, on the other hand, can cope with only a narrow range of resistances such as hills of varying percentage grades, wind conditions of varying directions and velocities and your own level of energy at any given time. The latter is a factor you need to recognize. If you could draw a curve for how much energy you have to expend during a day-long bike ride, I am sure you would find that you have a lot from 8 AM to around 11 AM, when you start to fade away till noon. After lunch, from 1 PM to 3:30 you do fine, then from 3:30 to camping time, around 5 PM, your energy level drops off again. And there are other factors that affect health and energy such as your physical condition. So your relatively narrow-range engine, your body, needs a wide range of gears to cope with the myriad of resistance factors you will need during a day's ride.

When you buy a bicycle from a dealer, you are stuck with the gears that come with it. You don't have to keep them, however, if you want a wider gear range. For example, a ten-speed bicycle often comes with gears something like this: front double plateau chainwheel with 40 and 50 teeth, rear five-cog freewheel with 14, 17, 20, 24 and 28 teeth. The low-gear combination using the 40-tooth chainwheel and the 28-tooth rear cog is not what I would call a low low gear at all, and certainly would not have gotten me up many of the hills I hit in Vermont and in Europe, where I met grades up to 15 percent. Unless you are in top physical condition and under thirty-five, you will need a combination of front and rear cogs that will give you a "Granny" gear ratio. For example, a 32-tooth rear freewheel cog and a 24-tooth front chainwheel will get you up just about the worst hill I ever encountered, the 15-percent-plus Route 101A into Calvin Coolidge State Park in Vermont. Even the American Youth Hostel kids were walking their bikes up that one. I had a fully equipped reasonably lightweight touring bike loaded with about thirty pounds of gear (tent, sleeping bag, food, clothes, cookware, etc.) along with everybody else. Yet my "Granny" gear of a 32-tooth rear cog and 24-tooth chainwheel got me up the hill sitting down on the bike. Not any faster than anybody else who was walking up, or not much faster, but a lot more comfortably. I'd rather pedal than walk any day.

Before we get into specific recommendations for gear selections, let's first become acquainted with what gear ratios and gear "inch" tables are all about, a subject you should at least have a nodding acquaintance with.

Gear ratio is simply the number of times the rear wheel will turn for every turn of the chainwheel up front. For example, my touring bike has a low-gear combination of 32 teeth on the freewheel cog and 24 teeth on the chainwheel, as noted above. That's a negative gear ratio, and extremely low. To find the gear ratio, simply divide the number of teeth on the chainwheel by the number of teeth on the freewheel. In this case $^{24}\!/_{32}$ = .75. This means that the gear ratio between the chainwheel with 24 teeth and the freewheel cog with 32 teeth is 1 to 75 (1:75). Translated into action it means that for every revolution of the chainwheel 24-tooth ring, the rear wheel only turns ¾ of a revolution, which is why it is a negative gear ratio.

Going to the other extreme, my fifteen-speed bicycle has high gears of 50 teeth on the front chainwheel and 14 teeth on the freewheel cog in the rear, which gives a ratio of: $^{50}\!/_{14}$ = 3.57, which means that for every turn of the chainwheel the rear wheel turns over a bit more than 3½ revolutions. So at a constant pedal cadence I am crawling in the low low "Granny" gear and going like mad in the high gear (if the road is flat and there's a thirty-mile-an-hour wind behind me). See discussion of cadence below. But first let's discuss the archaic term "gear inches," still in wide use. I would prefer the more meaningful concept of gear ratios instead of gear inches, but custom is a powerful inhibitor to progress. Besides, once you understand and get used to what gear inches means, you develop a feel for the relative differences between different gear (inches) combinations and so will speak bicyclese to other bike experts.

EQUIVALENT WHEEL SIZE AND "GEARS"

If you will refer to the history of bicycling (Chapter 8), you will note that the bicycle evolved from a pedal-driven front wheel with both wheels of about the same size, to one with the rear wheel quite small and the pedal front wheel quite large, 54 inches or so. This means that you could increase the speed you can pedal either by making a pedal-driven front wheel bigger, or by gearing up a chain-driven rear wheel. The effect, as far as speed is concerned, is the same either way. As high-wheeler bicyclists of the 1880s soon realized, the larger the front wheel, the faster they could ride, up to a point beyond which the wheel became too big (i.e., the gear ratio too large and the pedals too far away) for them to pedal. The high-wheeler (Ordinary or Penny Farthing, as it was called) thus set the standard for gearing used today. You will hear modern cyclists on ten-speed bicycles talk about "the gear I'm in" or "what gear do you use to climb hills?" and if racing is involved, the "gear" the racer is using for a specific event. The "gear" shown in Table 2-2 (computed by your author) is simply a conversion table which converts gear ratio to the equivalent high-wheeler front-wheel diameter in inches. This is something like converting the thrust of an aircraft jet engine into the horsepower of a piston engine to find our how much power the aircraft has . . . sort of roundabout, to say the least. But the gear chart is in wide use, cyclists use it to compare gear ratios, so there it is and we're stuck with it.

Table 2-2   Gear Chart (27- and 700-centimeter wheels only)

Number of Teeth
in Chainwheel

		24	25	26	27	28	29	30
Number of	12	54	56.2	58.5	60.8	63	65.2	67.5
Teeth in Rear	13	49.8	51.9	54	56	58.2	60.2	62.3
Sprocket	14	46.3	48.2	50.1	52.1	54	55.9	57.9
	15	43.2	45	46.8	48.6	50.4	52.2	54
	16	40.5	42.2	43.9	45.6	47.3	48.9	50.6
	17	38.1	39.7	41.3	42.9	44.5	46.1	47.6
	18	36	37.5	39	40.5	42	43.5	45
	19	34.1	35.5	36.9	38.4	39.8	41.2	42.6
	20	32.4	33.8	35.1	36.5	37.8	39.2	40.5
	21	30.9	32.1	33.4	34.7	36	37.3	38.6
	22	29.5	30.7	31.9	33.1	34.4	35.6	36.8
	23	28.2	29.3	30.5	31.7	32.9	34	35.2
	24	27	28.1	29.2	30.4	31.5	32.6	33.8
	25	25.9	27	28.1	29.2	30.3	31.3	32.4
	26	24.9	26	27	28.0	29.1	30.1	31.2
	27	24	25	26	27	28	29	30
	28	23.1	24.1	25.1	26	27	28	28.9
	29	22.3	23.3	24.2	25.1	26.1	27	27.9
	30	21.6	22.5	23.4	24.3	25.2	26.1	27
	31	20.9	21.8	22.6	23.5	24.4	25.3	26.1
	32	20.3	21.1	21.9	22.8	23.6	24.5	25.3
	33	19.6	20.5	21.3	22.1	22.9	23.7	24.5
	34	19.1	19.9	20.6	21.4	22.2	23	23.8

Table 2-2 Gear Chart (continued)

Number of Teeth
in Chainwheel

		31	32	33	34	35	36	37	38	39	40
Rear	12	69.7	72	74.3	76.5	78.7	81	83.2	85.5	87.8	90
Teeth	13	64.4	66.5	68.5	70.6	72.7	74.8	76.8	78.9	81	83.1
	14	59.8	61.7	63.6	65.6	67.5	69.4	71.4	73.3	75.2	77.1
	15	55.8	57.6	59.4	61.2	63	64.8	66.6	68.4	70.2	72
	16	52.3	54	55.7	57.4	59.1	60.8	62.4	64.1	65.8	67.5
	17	49.2	50.8	52.4	54	55.6	57.2	58.8	60.4	61.9	63.5
	18	46.5	48	49.5	51	52.5	54	55.5	57	58.5	60
	19	44.1	45.5	46.9	48.3	49.7	51.2	52.6	54	55.4	56.8
	20	41.9	43.2	44.6	45.9	47.3	48.6	50	51.3	52.7	54
	21	39.9	41.1	42.4	43.7	45	46.3	47.6	48.9	50.1	51.4
	22	38	39.3	40.5	41.7	43	44.2	45.4	46.6	47.9	49.1
	23	36.4	37.6	38.7	39.9	41.1	42.3	43.4	44.6	45.8	47
	24	34.9	36	37.1	38.3	39.4	40.5	41.6	42.8	43.9	45
	25	33.5	34.6	35.6	36.7	37.8	38.9	40	41	42.1	43.2
	26	32.2	33.2	34.3	35.3	36.3	37.4	38.4	39.5	40.5	41.5
	27	31	32	33	34	35	36	37	38	39	40
	28	29.9	30.9	31.8	32.9	33.8	34.7	35.7	36.6	37.6	38.6
	29	28.9	29.8	30.7	31.7	32.6	33.5	34.4	35.4	36.3	37.2
	30	27.9	28.8	29.7	30.6	31.5	32.4	33.3	34.2	35.1	36
	31	27	27.9	28.7	29.6	30.5	31.4	32.2	33.1	34	34.8
	32	26.2	27	27.8	28.7	29.5	30.4	31.2	32.1	32.9	33.8
	33	25.4	26.2	27	27.8	28.6	29.5	30.3	31.1	31.9	32.7
	34	24.6	25.4	26.2	27	27.8	28.6	29.4	30.2	31	31.8

41	42	43	44	45	46	47	48	49	50
92.2	94.5	96.7	99	101.3	103.5	105.7	108	110.2	112.5
85.2	87.2	89.3	91.4	93.5	95.5	97.6	99.7	101.8	103.8
79.1	81	82.9	84.9	86.8	88.7	90.6	92.6	94.5	96.4
73.8	75.6	77.4	79.2	81	82.8	84.6	86.4	88.2	90
69.2	70.9	72.6	74.3	75.9	77.6	79.3	81	82.7	84.4
65.1	66.7	68.3	69.9	71.5	73.1	74.6	76.2	77.8	79.4
61.5	63	64.5	66.0	67.5	69	70.5	72	73.5	75
58.3	59.7	61.1	62.5	63.9	65.4	66.8	68.2	69.6	71.1
55.4	56.7	58.1	59.4	60.8	62.1	63.5	64.8	66.2	67.5
52.7	54	55.3	56.6	57.9	59.1	60.4	61.7	63	64.3
50.3	51.5	52.8	54	55.2	56.5	57.7	58.9	60.1	61.4
48.1	49.3	50.5	51.7	52.8	54	55.2	56.3	57.5	58.7
46.1	47.3	48.4	49.5	50.6	51.8	52.9	54	55.1	56.3
44.3	45.4	46.4	47.5	48.6	49.7	50.8	51.8	52.9	54
42.6	43.6	44.7	45.7	46.7	47.8	48.8	49.8	50.9	51.9
41	42	43	44	45	46	47	48	49	50
39.5	40.5	41.5	42.4	43.4	44.4	45.3	46.3	47.3	48.2
38.2	39.1	40	41	41.9	42.8	43.8	44.7	45.6	46.6
36.9	37.8	38.7	39.6	40.5	41.4	42.3	43.2	44.1	45
35.7	36.6	37.5	39.3	39.2	40.1	40.9	41.8	42.7	43.5
34.6	35.4	36.3	37.1	38	38.8	39.7	40.5	41.3	42.2
33.5	34.4	35.2	36	36.8	37.6	38.5	39.3	40.1	40.9
32.6	33.4	34.1	34.9	35.7	36.5	37.3	38.1	38.9	39.7

Table 2-2   Gear Chart (continued)

Number of Teeth
in Chainwheel

		51	52	53	54	55	56	57	58	59	6
Rear	12	114.8	117	119.2	121.5	123.7	126	128.3	130.5	132.7	13
Teeth	13	105.9	108	110.1	112.2	114.2	116.3	118.4	120.5	122.5	12
	14	98.4	100.3	102.2	104.1	106.1	108	109.9	111.9	113.8	11
	15	91.8	93.6	95.4	97.2	99	100.8	102.6	104.4	106.2	10
	16	86.1	87.8	89.4	91.1	92.8	94.5	96.5	97.9	99.6	10
	17	81	82.6	84.2	85.8	87.4	88.9	90.5	92.1	93.7	9
	18	76.5	78	79.5	81	82.5	84	85.4	87	88.5	9
	19	72.5	73.9	75.3	76.7	78.2	79.6	81	82.4	83.8	8
	20	68.9	70.2	71.6	72.9	74.3	75.6	77	78.3	79.7	8
	21	65.6	66.9	68.1	69.4	70.7	72	73.3	74.6	75.9	7
	22	62.6	63.8	65	66.3	67.5	68.7	70	71.2	72.4	7
	23	59.9	61	62.2	63.4	64.6	65.7	66.9	68.1	69.3	7
	24	57.4	58.5	59.6	60.8	61.9	63	64.1	65.3	66.4	6
	25	55.1	56.2	57.2	58.3	59.4	60.5	61.6	62.6	63.7	6
	26	53	54	55	56.1	57.1	58.2	59.2	60.2	61.3	6
	27	51	52	53	54	55	56	57	58	59	6
	28	49.2	50.1	51.1	52.1	53	54	55	55.9	56.9	5
	29	47.5	48.4	49.3	50.3	51.2	52.1	53	54	54.9	5
	30	45.9	46.8	47.7	48.6	49.5	50.4	51.3	52.2	53.1	5
	31	44.4	45.3	46.2	47	47.9	48.8	49.6	50.5	51.4	5
	32	43	43.9	44.7	45.6	46.4	47.3	48.1	48.9	49.8	5
	33	41.7	42.5	43.4	44.2	45	45.8	46.6	47.5	48.3	4
	34	40.5	41.3	42.1	42.9	43.7	44.5	45.3	46.1	46.9	4

61	62	63	64	65	66	67	68	69	70
137.2	139.5	141.8	144	146.2	148.5	150.7	153	155.3	157.5
126.7	128.8	130.8	132.9	135	137.1	139.2	141.2	143.3	145.4
117.6	119.6	121.5	123.4	125.4	127.3	129.2	131.1	133.1	135
109.8	111.6	113.4	115.2	117	118.8	120.6	122.4	124.2	126
102.9	104.6	106.3	108	109.7	111.4	113.1	114.8	116.4	118.1
96.9	98.5	100.1	101.6	103.2	104.8	106.4	108	109.6	111.2
91.5	93	94.5	96	97.5	99	100.4	102	103.5	105
86.7	88.1	89.5	90.9	92.4	93.8	95.2	96.6	98.1	99.5
82.4	83.7	85.1	86.4	87.8	89.1	90.5	91.8	93.2	94.5
78.4	79.7	81	82.3	83.6	84.9	86.1	87.4	88.7	90
74.9	76.1	77.3	78.5	79.8	81	82.2	83.5	84.7	85.9
71.6	72.8	74	75.1	76.3	77.5	78.7	79.8	81	82.2
68.6	69.8	70.9	72	73.1	74.3	75.4	76.5	77.6	78.8
65.9	66.7	68	69.1	70.2	71.3	72.4	73.4	74.5	75.6
63.3	64.4	65.4	66.5	67.5	68.5	69.6	70.6	71.7	72.7
61	62	63	64	65	66	67	68	69	70
58.8	59.8	60.6	61.7	62.7	63.6	64.6	65.6	66.5	67.5
56.8	57.7	58.7	59.6	60.5	61.4	62.4	63.3	64.2	65.2
54.9	55.8	56.7	57.6	58.5	59.4	60.3	61.2	62.1	63
53.1	54	54.9	55.7	56.6	57.5	58.4	59.2	60.1	61
51.5	52.3	53.2	54	54.8	55.7	56.5	57.4	58.2	59.1
49.9	50.7	51.5	52.4	53.2	54	54.8	55.6	56.5	57.3
48.4	49.2	50	50.8	51.6	52.4	53.2	54	54.8	55.6

The gear chart is derived very simply by multiplying the gear ratio by the diameter in inches of the rear wheel, which then converts the rear-wheel diameter to the equivalent diameter of a "high-wheeler." Take a low gear of 34 teeth rear, 36 front: $^{36}\!/\!_{34} \times 27 = 28.6$, or, this gear is equal to riding a high-wheeler with a pedal-driven front wheel of 28 inches diameter. To find out how *far* one turn of the chainwheel with this gear combination (or one turn of the front wheel on the "high-wheeler" equivalent) would take you, multiply the equivalent "gear" by pi, or 3.1416. In this case, one turn of a 36-tooth chainwheel connected to a 34-tooth rear gear ($^{36}\!/\!_{34} \times 27 \times 3.1416$) would cause the rear wheel to move forward 89.81 inches, or almost 7½ feet. You can check the "gear" for any combination of rear and front gear teeth by checking the chart. For example, find 14 teeth on the chart under "sprocket size" at left. Move along that line to the right to the 54 T column and you find 104.1, which multiplied by 3.1416 (*you'll* have to do it) tells that you will travel the 327 inches we came up with above (or $^{327}\!/\!_{12} = 27¼$ feet).

HOW TO SELECT YOUR OWN GEARS

We've talked a lot, up to now, about gear ratios, gear inches, cadence and speed. Maybe you looked at your bike and discovered that the reason you couldn't make those hills was not advancing age, but simply because you did not have low enough gears. That's my excuse, anyway. But you have decided you want to change your gearing. What gears should you select is now the question.

Well, unless you're pretty good at math, coming up with a good selection of gears for where you live, your physical condition and the kind of cycling you do can be a difficult task. All I can do to help you is offer some rather general suggestions.

For example, you can conceive of a gearing system or combination of gears on a bike to fall within three groups, as shown in Figure 2-17. There's the low range, the intermediate or cruising range and the high range. As a general rule, you should take the low range, for hill climbing, in fairly large steps. You don't want to have to change through a bunch of gears to get to the low low on a steep hill. You need to change down as you approach the hill, not when you're climbing it. Otherwise, under high torque, gears change noisily, slip, or don't change at all but hang up on top of a cog or chainwheel tooth. When you're in the cruising range, on the flats or a moderate hill, or into a fairly strong wind on the flats, you need a wider selection of gears in smaller increments, clustered around the gear you normally use. And when you're tearing down a hill or riding fast before a high wind, you want a wide change between high gears, which you seldom otherwise use.

The curves in Figure 2-17 represent a selection of gears for an eighteen-speed bicycle. Table 2-3 represents the same selections in numerical format.

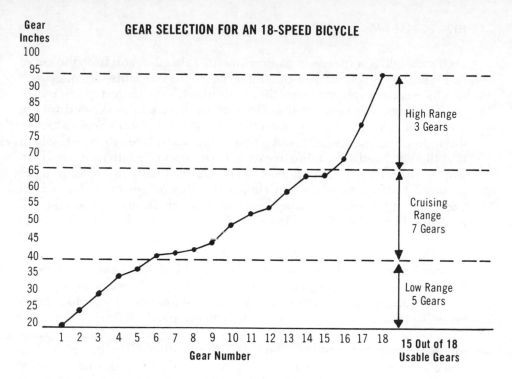

Fig. 2-17: Gear selections for an 18-speed bicycle. Low range has five speeds in larger increments. Intermediate range has seven speeds in closer increments and high range has 3 gears in still larger increments (than low range). Three gears are unusable, 8 and 9 because they are at extremes of the gears and 14 because it duplicates 15.

Table 2-3 Gear Combinations for an 18-Speed Touring Bicycle

Gear No.	Number of Teeth in Freewheel	Number of Teeth in Chainwheel	Gear, Inches
1	32	24	20.3
2	26	24	24.9
3	22	24	29.5
4	32	40	33.8
5	19	24	34.1
6	16	24	40.5
7	26	40	41.5
8	32	50	42.2
9	14	24	46.3
10	22	40	49.1
11	26	50	51.9
12	19	40	56.8
13	22	50	58.7
14	16	40	67.5
15	19	50	67.5
16	14	40	77.1
17	16	50	84.4
18	14	50	96.4

Of the eighteen speeds in column one in Table 2-3, and from the curve in Figure 2-17, you can see that three gears are unusable—two, gears 8 and 9, because each combines the smallest with the largest gears, which put the chain at a very great angle, that is, the chain is skewed way to the left in gear 8 because it is on the largest front chainwheel, which is the right-hand chainwheel, and on the largest rear freewheel cog, which is at the left-hand side of the freewheel. The opposite situation occurs in gear 9. Either way, with the chain skewed drastically, there is going to be much faster wear of the soft aluminum alloy (expensive) chainwheel and even of the steel freewheel cogs and the chain itself. And you will probably hear a lot of noise from the front derailleur because it's going to be hard to keep the chain from rubbing on the inside of the front-derailleur side plates at these extreme chain angles.

Gear 15 is unusable because it duplicates 14. So out of eighteen gears (six-speed freewheel, triple chainwheel, 6 × 3 = 18) we wind up with fifteen usable gear selections, combinations of freewheel cogs and chain-wheels. This is not at all bad for this many gears. Even a twelve- or fifteen-speed gear has two unusable combinations because of extreme angle of chainline, and one close gear duplication. The idea here is to select those gears that give you a quick downshift to the lower-lower gears without shifting through a lot of other gears along the way. Most of the total number of gear selections on a bike are in closer increments in the mid or cruising ranges in which you will usually by pedaling, and are farther apart as you move upward to higher gear ranges (for when there's a tail wind, or you're going downhill, or a dog is chasing you, etc.).

Figure 2-17 clearly shows that the basic criteria for gear selection are reasonably well met. I would probably opt for perhaps a wider spread in the lower ranges, but if you look at the curve you will see that the low and high ranges are fairly steep and that the cruising ranges are closer together. There are five usable gears in the low range, six in the cruising range and three in the high-speed range, which to me is a good combination for distance cyclo-touring. Again, gears 8, 9 and 14 (or 15) are not usable, as a practical matter.

HOW TO TELL HOW FAST

All of these arithmetical shenanigans are fine, but they won't tell you how *fast* you are moving. We have to factor in another figure, which is the number of *times* you move the chainwheel one revolution in one minute. The formula to derive miles per hour at a given crank rpm (or chainwheel, or rear wheel rpm, it's all the same) is gear ratio times crank rpm, 3.1416 × 60 divided by 63,360. All this work is saved for you, however, by the cadence chart (Fig. 2-14), which was kindly pro-grammed on an IBM computer by Sam Rhoads of Boise, Idaho, who recognized the limitations of the conventional cadence chart.

Fig. 2-14: Handy computerized speed chart tells you how fast you are going, if you know your gear inches and your cadence (crank rpm's).

```
THE SPEED IN MPH EQUALS PI TIMES THE GEAR        TIMES THE CRANK RPM TIMES 60 DIVIDED BY 63,360
                              REVOLUTIONS PER MINUTE OF THE CRANK ARM
```

60	70	80	90	100	110	120	130	140	150	160	
4.64	5.41	6.19	6.96	7.73	8.51	9.28	10.06	10.83	11.60	12.38	MPH
4.82	5.62	6.43	7.23	8.03	8.84	9.64	10.44	11.25	12.05	12.85	MPH
5.00	5.83	6.66	7.50	8.33	9.16	10.00	10.83	11.66	12.49	13.33	MPH
5.18	6.04	6.90	7.76	8.63	9.49	10.35	11.22	12.08	12.94	13.80	MPH
5.35	6.25	7.14	8.03	8.92	9.82	10.71	11.60	12.49	13.39	14.28	MPH
5.53	6.46	7.38	8.30	9.22	10.14	11.07	11.99	12.91	13.83	14.76	MPH
5.71	6.66	7.62	8.57	9.52	10.47	11.42	12.38	13.33	14.28	15.23	MPH
5.89	6.87	7.85	8.84	9.82	10.80	11.78	12.76	13.74	14.73	15.71	MPH
6.07	7.08	8.09	9.10	10.11	11.13	12.14	13.15	14.16	15.17	16.18	MPH
6.25	7.29	8.33	9.37	10.41	11.45	12.49	13.54	14.58	15.62	16.66	MPH
6.43	7.50	8.57	9.64	10.71	11.78	12.85	13.92	14.99	16.06	17.14	MPH
6.60	7.71	8.81	9.91	11.01	12.11	13.21	14.31	15.41	16.51	17.61	MPH
6.78	7.91	9.04	10.17	11.30	12.44	13.57	14.70	15.83	16.96	18.09	MPH
6.96	8.12	9.28	10.44	11.60	12.76	13.92	15.08	16.24	17.40	18.56	MPH
7.14	8.33	9.52	10.71	11.90	13.09	14.28	15.47	16.66	17.85	19.04	MPH
7.32	8.54	9.76	10.98	12.20	13.42	14.64	15.86	17.08	18.30	19.52	MPH
7.50	8.75	10.00	11.25	12.49	13.74	14.99	16.24	17.49	18.74	19.99	MPH
7.68	8.95	10.23	11.51	12.79	14.07	15.35	16.63	17.91	19.19	20.47	MPH
7.85	9.16	10.47	11.78	13.09	14.40	15.71	17.02	18.33	19.63	20.94	MPH
8.03	9.37	10.71	12.05	13.39	14.73	16.06	17.40	18.74	20.08	21.42	MPH
8.21	9.58	10.95	12.32	13.68	15.05	16.42	17.79	19.16	20.53	21.90	MPH
8.39	9.79	11.19	12.58	13.98	15.38	16.78	18.18	19.58	20.97	22.37	MPH
8.57	10.00	11.42	12.85	14.28	15.71	17.14	18.56	19.99	21.42	22.85	MPH
8.75	10.20	11.66	13.12	14.58	16.04	17.49	18.95	20.41	21.87	23.32	MPH
8.92	10.41	11.90	13.39	14.87	16.36	17.85	19.34	20.82	22.31	23.80	MPH
9.10	10.62	12.14	13.66	15.17	16.69	18.21	19.72	21.24	22.76	24.28	MPH
9.28	10.83	12.38	13.92	15.47	17.02	18.56	20.11	21.66	23.20	24.75	MPH
9.46	11.04	12.61	14.19	15.77	17.34	18.92	20.50	22.07	23.65	25.23	MPH
9.64	11.25	12.85	14.46	16.06	17.67	19.28	20.88	22.49	24.10	25.70	MPH
9.82	11.45	13.09	14.73	16.36	18.00	19.63	21.27	22.91	24.54	26.18	MPH
10.00	11.66	13.33	14.99	16.66	18.33	19.99	21.66	23.32	24.99	26.66	MPH
10.17	11.87	13.57	15.26	16.96	18.65	20.35	22.04	23.74	25.44	27.13	MPH
10.35	12.08	13.80	15.53	17.25	18.98	20.71	22.43	24.16	25.88	27.61	MPH
10.53	12.29	14.04	15.80	17.55	19.31	21.06	22.82	24.57	26.33	28.08	MPH
10.71	12.49	14.28	16.06	17.85	19.63	21.42	23.20	24.99	26.77	28.56	MPH
10.89	12.70	14.52	16.33	18.15	19.96	21.78	23.59	25.41	27.22	29.04	MPH
11.07	12.91	14.76	16.60	18.44	20.29	22.13	23.98	25.82	27.67	29.51	MPH
11.25	13.12	14.99	16.87	18.74	20.62	22.49	24.37	26.24	28.11	29.99	MPH
11.42	13.33	15.23	17.14	19.04	20.94	22.85	24.75	26.66	28.56	30.46	MPH
11.60	13.54	15.47	17.40	19.34	21.27	23.20	25.14	27.07	29.01	30.94	MPH
11.78	13.74	15.71	17.67	19.63	21.60	23.56	25.53	27.49	29.45	31.42	MPH
11.96	13.95	15.95	17.94	19.93	21.93	23.92	25.91	27.91	29.90	31.89	MPH
12.14	14.16	16.18	18.21	20.23	22.25	24.28	26.30	28.32	30.34	32.37	MPH
12.32	14.37	16.42	18.47	20.53	22.58	24.63	26.69	28.74	30.79	32.84	MPH
12.49	14.58	16.66	18.74	20.82	22.91	24.99	27.07	29.15	31.24	33.32	MPH
12.67	14.79	16.90	19.01	21.12	23.23	25.35	27.46	29.57	31.68	33.80	MPH
12.85	14.99	17.14	19.28	21.42	23.56	25.70	27.85	29.99	32.13	34.27	MPH
13.03	15.20	17.37	19.55	21.72	23.89	26.06	28.23	30.40	32.58	34.75	MPH
13.21	15.41	17.61	19.81	22.01	24.22	26.42	28.62	30.82	33.02	35.22	MPH
13.39	15.62	17.85	20.08	22.31	24.54	26.77	29.01	31.24	33.47	35.70	MPH
13.57	15.83	18.09	20.35	22.61	24.87	27.13	29.39	31.65	33.91	36.18	MPH
13.74	16.04	18.33	20.62	22.91	25.20	27.49	29.78	32.07	34.36	36.65	MPH
13.92	16.24	18.56	20.88	23.20	25.53	27.85	30.17	32.49	34.81	37.13	MPH
14.10	16.45	18.80	21.15	23.50	25.85	28.20	30.55	32.90	35.25	37.60	MPH
14.28	16.66	19.04	21.42	23.80	26.18	28.56	30.94	33.32	35.70	38.08	MPH
14.46	16.87	19.28	21.69	24.10	26.51	28.92	31.33	33.74	36.15	38.56	MPH
14.64	17.08	19.52	21.96	24.39	26.83	29.27	31.71	34.15	36.59	39.03	MPH
14.82	17.28	19.75	22.22	24.69	27.16	29.63	32.10	34.57	37.04	39.51	MPH
14.99	17.49	19.99	22.49	24.99	27.49	29.99	32.49	34.99	37.48	39.98	MPH
15.17	17.70	20.23	22.76	25.29	27.82	30.34	32.87	35.40	37.93	40.46	MPH
15.35	17.91	20.47	23.03	25.58	28.14	30.70	33.26	35.82	38.38	40.94	MPH
15.53	18.12	20.71	23.29	25.88	28.47	31.06	33.65	36.24	38.82	41.41	MPH
15.71	18.33	20.94	23.56	26.18	28.80	31.42	34.03	36.65	39.27	41.89	MPH
15.89	18.53	21.18	23.83	26.48	29.13	31.77	34.42	37.07	39.72	42.36	MPH
16.06	18.74	21.42	24.10	26.77	29.45	32.13	34.81	37.48	40.16	42.84	MPH
16.24	18.95	21.66	24.37	27.07	29.78	32.49	35.19	37.90	40.61	43.32	MPH
16.42	19.16	21.90	24.63	27.37	30.11	32.84	35.58	38.32	41.05	43.79	MPH
16.60	19.37	22.13	24.90	27.67	30.43	33.20	35.97	38.73	41.50	44.27	MPH
16.78	19.58	22.37	25.17	27.97	30.76	33.56	36.35	39.15	41.95	44.74	MPH
16.96	19.78	22.61	25.44	28.26	31.09	33.91	36.74	39.57	42.39	45.22	MPH
17.14	19.99	22.85	25.70	28.56	31.42	34.27	37.13	39.98	42.84	45.70	MPH
17.31	20.20	23.09	25.97	28.86	31.74	34.63	37.51	40.40	43.29	46.17	MPH
17.49	20.41	23.32	26.24	29.15	32.07	34.99	37.90	40.82	43.73	46.65	MPH
17.67	20.62	23.56	26.51	29.45	32.40	35.34	38.29	41.23	44.18	47.12	MPH
17.85	20.82	23.80	26.77	29.75	32.72	35.70	38.67	41.65	44.62	47.60	MPH
18.03	21.03	24.04	27.04	30.05	33.05	36.06	39.06	42.07	45.07	48.08	MPH
18.21	21.24	24.28	27.31	30.34	33.38	36.41	39.45	42.48	45.52	48.55	MPH
18.39	21.45	24.51	27.58	30.64	33.71	36.77	39.84	42.90	45.96	49.03	MPH
18.56	21.66	24.75	27.85	30.94	34.03	37.13	40.22	43.32	46.41	49.50	MPH
18.74	21.87	24.99	28.11	31.24	34.36	37.48	40.61	43.73	46.86	49.98	MPH
18.92	22.07	25.23	28.38	31.53	34.69	37.84	41.00	44.15	47.30	50.46	MPH
19.10	22.28	25.47	28.65	31.83	35.02	38.20	41.38	44.57	47.75	50.93	MPH
19.28	22.49	25.70	28.92	32.13	35.34	38.56	41.77	44.98	48.19	51.41	MPH
19.46	22.70	25.94	29.18	32.43	35.67	38.91	42.16	45.40	48.64	51.88	MPH
19.63	22.91	26.18	29.45	32.72	36.00	39.27	42.54	45.81	49.09	52.36	MPH
19.81	23.12	26.42	29.72	33.02	36.32	39.63	42.93	46.23	49.53	52.84	MPH
19.99	23.32	26.66	29.99	33.32	36.65	39.98	43.32	46.65	49.98	53.31	MPH
20.17	23.53	26.89	30.26	33.62	36.98	40.34	43.70	47.06	50.43	53.79	MPH
20.35	23.74	27.13	30.52	33.91	37.31	40.70	44.09	47.48	50.87	54.26	MPH
20.53	23.95	27.37	30.79	34.21	37.63	41.05	44.48	47.90	51.32	54.74	MPH
20.71	24.16	27.61	31.06	34.51	37.96	41.41	44.86	48.31	51.76	55.22	MPH

CALIBRATED BY AN IBM 360 AND PROGRAMMED BY SAM RHOADS

Here's how to use this very convenient cadence chart. Let's say you're pedaling at 70 crank-revolutions per minute and your chain is on the small 14 T rear gear and the largest 54 T front gear. First, find your *gear* from the gear chart on pages 95–99, which will be 104.1. Then from the cadence chart, find 104 under the gear column (left) and, moving to the right under RPM of the crank arm of 70, you'll find you're moving at 21.66 miles per hour, which is a pretty good clip for anybody much over thirty. In the low gear combination of 34 T rear and 36 T front, we have a *gear* of 28.6. From the cadence chart, at a *gear* of 27 (we fudge a little) you will travel at 5.62 mph (which is not fast but better than walking up a steep hill).

An easy (but not quite as accurate) way to figure speed is to use the speed chart (Fig. 2-15). To find speed, first find your gear from the gear

SPEED IN MILES PER HOUR

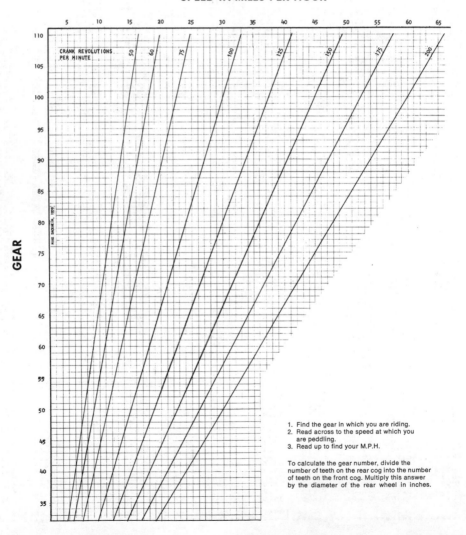

1. Find the gear in which you are riding.
2. Read across to the speed at which you are peddling.
3. Read up to find your M.P.H.

To calculate the gear number, divide the number of teeth on the rear cog into the number of teeth on the front cog. Multiply this answer by the diameter of the rear wheel in inches.

Fig. 2-15: Another way to compute speed is to use this nomogram, following instructions at the right of the graph.

chart on pages 95–99 and, knowing your crank rpm, follow the gear line to its intersection with the crank rpm line. For example, you're in a 100 gear at 75 crank rpm. Reading to the right from 100 intersection with curve 75, and upward to the speed line, you will be doing almost 23 mph. This chart has limitations in crank rpm selections and jumps up in fairly large chunks, but it's handy to copy and take along on the road.

One more point. You can use a stopwatch fastened to your handlebars to keep tabs on crank rpms. But this means you have to take your eyes off the road momentarily to look at the stopwatch, hardly a safe procedure. A better way is an ingenious little transistorized metronome, which costs about half the price of a good stopwatch, and which you can carry in your breast pocket. It weighs only nine ounces, has a neck strap, and can be adjusted from 40 to 208 beats per minute. The click is audible enough to hear above normal street traffic even when the unit, called a Mininome, is in your breast pocket. The Mininome is available from Hartley Alley's Touring Cyclist Shop (see Appendix and also Figure 2-16).

It's also a good idea to make up a cadence chart for your own particular combination of gears, so you always know how fast you are traveling at any crank rpm (see Table 2-4). This is one way to train yourself to work harder at pedaling, for better health. Also, because you can accurately predict how fast you can pedal (once you find your limitations), you can be quite accurate in estimating arrival times (but don't forget to consider hills).

Fig. 2-16: A handy guide to training yourself to maintain a steady cadence, shifting gears so you can hold it comfortably, is a cigarette-pack-sized transistorized metronome, called the Mininome. It has a range of from 40 to 208 beats a minute, with adjustable volume, and weighs nine ounces.

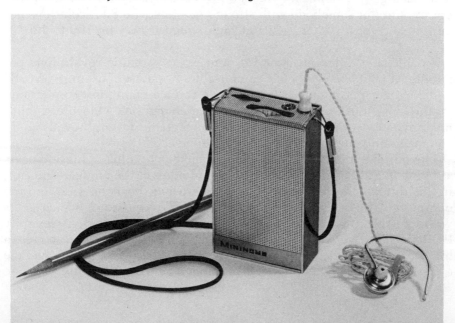

Table 2-4   Sample Individualized Speed Chart*

| | Number of Teeth in Rear Sprocket | | | | |
	14	17	22	28	34
Chainwheel T 54					
Gear (Inches Eq.)	104.1	85.8	66.3	52	42.9
MPH Speed	21.45	17.88	13.8	10.83	8.8
Chainwheel T 49					
Gear (Inches Eq.)	94.5	77.8	60.1	47.3	38.9
MPH Speed	19.35	16.8	12.5	9.8	8.0
Chainwheel T 36					
Gear (Inches Eq.)	69.4	57.1	44.2	34.7	28.6
MPH Speed	14.9	11.89	9.2	7.1	5.9

* Based on 72-rpm cadence. You'll probably be going a lot faster downhill, so you may want to gradually increase the cadence for fast runs downhill or before the wind. Or you can make up several charts, say one for a cadence of 72, one for 80, one for 85, etc., so you can pull out a 3 x 5 card for every road condition. And you may be pedaling a lot slower than 72 rpm up steep hills. Because the gear inches did not correspond exactly to the cadence chart, we made our own interpolations, which is why the speeds,or some of them, don't correspond exactly to speeds on the cadence chart.

THE MEANING OF CADENCE

First, let's establish what cadence means. Cadence is the pedaling or turning of the crank arm at more or less constant revolutions. It is important to understand this concept, because a regular cadence is necessary for smooth long-distance cycling. You should try to pedal at the same rate of crank revolutions per minute all the time, varying your gear ratio to suit wind and road-grade conditions. For example, let's say you establish that a good cadence for you is between 60 and 75 turns of the crank per minute (for somebody with strong legs it may be 80 revolutions per minute and for a racing cyclist at high speed it may be 100 to 120, or more).

We all have different natural cadences, or pedaling revolutions per minute, at which we feel most comfortable. For most of us, from 65 to 85 pedal strokes per minute is the pace we can maintain most comfortably for the longest period. The reason for gear changes on a bicycle, then, is not only to help you climb hills or go down grades faster; they also help you maintain your natural pedaling cadence at all times.

The mistake most beginning cyclists make is to think of bicycle gears as being like automobile gears, with their bodies as the engine. The fault in this thinking is that whereas you can advance gears on a car and the engine will push the car faster, on a bicycle, you can advance gears without getting much speed at all. As an engine your body is severely limited. And if you are thinking that you can travel faster and longer in high than low gears, then you are wrong, at least if you are an average cyclist and not a trained racing champion. You would actually penalize

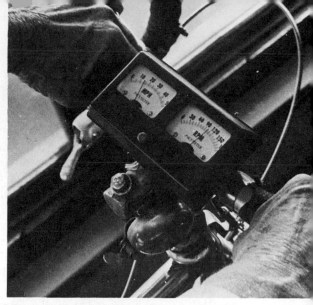

Fig. 2-18: A unique electronic speed-ometer and cadence counter is com-puterized to tell you how fast you are going and how fast you are pedaling in any gear. The Pacemeter by Eris-man is available in bicycle stores. It uses magnets on wheel and cranks, so there is no pedaling resistance, un-like speedometers and odometers.

yourself by riding in high gears for long distances; although you might be able to maintain your natural cadence for a short time, you would find your pedal revolutions per minute slowing down bit by bit until you were literally forcing your feet around the pedaling arc and making your body wobble from side to side with the effort.

Cycling should be fun, not strenuous. Find your natural cadence and shift gears only to maintain it.

As soon as it becomes work to maintain good cadence, shift down. When you find your feet zipping around the arc without resistance, shift up. Beginning cyclists should stick to the lower gear range until they find their natural cadence. On a three-speed bicycle, stay in low or sec-ond gear. On a ten- or fifteen-speed bicycle, stay in the next to lowest gear ratio for the first 100 miles. This will establish and help you to get used to your natural cadence pedaling rpm. Then you can change gears when necessary, according to the vagaries of wind velocity, road grade, your current physical condition, or a load you may be carrying.

Do not change through the whole ten gears at once. Shift from one gear range to the next until you feel comfortable at your natural cadence.

How to Shift Gears and Other Riding Techniques

To begin at the beginning, I am going to assume that a ten-speed bike is something you are not familiar with. So let's just run through the steps in correct shifting, starting with the basics. There are two shift levers, because there are two shift mechanisms on ten-speed bicycles. On five-speed bikes, there is just one shift lever, on the right, that controls the derailleur, or shift mechanism, on the rear wheel. On ten-speed bikes there is also a shift mechanism on the chainwheels. The gear-shift lever on the right (as you face toward the front of the bike) controls the rear derailleur. As you move the rear derailleur lever, the cable connecting this lever to the derailleur tightens or loosens, depending on which way you shift. I suggest you hang the bike from the basement or garage ceiling to check how these gears work. *You must always be pedaling while you change gears.* (The only excepton is the new Shimano Front Freewheel Systems [FFS], where the chainwheel or the crankset is the freewheel. The FFS System is used only on less expensive bikes, not the kind I would recommend for touring.) So, with the bike hung from the ceiling (or with someone holding the bike so the rear wheel is off the ground) push the right side gear-shift lever all the way toward the front of the bike while at the same time you turn the pedals to keep the rear wheel turning. With the right derailleur all the way forward, you will now see that the chain is on the smallest rear cog, or gear, which is the highest-speed gear. Now, with the rear wheel off the floor, again twirl the pedals and move the right shift lever slowly toward the rear of the bike. As the shift lever moves you will see that the cable pulls the derailleur inward toward the bike frame, causing the chain to move to each next bigger cog. Finally, with the shift lever as far toward the rear of the bike as it can go, the chain should now be resting comfortably on the biggest rear cog, which is the lowest gear. Going through these five gears in this manner is very much like shifting a car, if it has five forward speeds. The difference between the car and the bicycle in shifting is that the car shift is very precise. There is never any doubt as to which gear you are in. But on a bicycle, unless you risk looking back at the rear wheel to check, you can only tell which gear you are in by how easy it is to pedal. Actually, that's the whole point of all these gears. It really isn't important *which* gear you are in so long as you feel comfortable in that gear.

It makes little sense to struggle in an uncomfortably high gear, for example, which causes you to crank the pedals over slowly and laboriously. This type of pedaling is terribly hard on the knees and is very inefficient. Ideally you should pedal at a fairly fast cadence, at least as fast as you are comfortable with, and strive to twirl at a faster and faster cadence as your physical prowess and cycling skill increase. I'd say a minimum of 65 crank rpm's is a good starter.

Okay, so you have seen how the rear derailleur works. Now, again with the bike off the floor, twirl the pedals and move the *left* gear-shift lever all the way forward. You will now see that the chain has moved or is on the smallest front chainwheel, which is now the lowest gear. This may be confusing, but the engineering of the gear setup is that the smallest of the rear cogs is the highest-speed gear and the smallest of the front chainwheels is the lowest-speed gear. Just remember those facts: little cog in the back, highest speed (if you have the muscle, there's nothing automatic about it, *you* are the engine); little chainwheel up front, lowest speed.

You can select any one of these ten-speed gear combinations that you wish; and as I have said, it's not important which one you do select so long as you twirl the pedals as fast as you can within the limits of comfort, and at the same time feel that you are exerting yourself. If you select too low a gear you must pedal too fast to attain a reasonable speed. If you select too high a gear, as I said earlier, you spin over the cranks agonizingly slowly and with great effort. The secret in selecting the correct combination of front and rear gears is simply to be in the gear that lets you spin the pedals fairly rapidly and within the bounds of your physical ability. For example, as you approach a long, sloping, upward climb, one that increases in severity as you go up, you will need to start changing gears just before you start to climb. As you go up the hill, or mountain, be aware of any change in grade or change in your own reservoir of stamina. If you wait until the hill actually becomes steeper in grade, and then attempt to shift as you strain on the pedals just to keep forward momentum, you may well find it is too late, that the strain on the gears will keep the derailleur from shifting. If this ever happens to you, do not succumb to the temptation to turn back and forth from side to side of the road to lessen the strain while you shift, because you might find yourself wandering around in the stream of traffic, or across the flow of traffic, and that's dangerous. As a last resort you should stop, lift the rear wheel off the ground, twirl the pedals and shift up. This may seem as though it takes three hands, and it does, but you can do it with two hands, with patience and practice. Just pull the right gear lever back a bit, twirl the pedals, and perhaps, if you can, nudge the derailleur over with your knee. It would have been much better if you had shifted *before* the hill got too steep, *before* the going got too rough and before you had to apply a *lot* of pressure to keep moving forward.

The lowest combination of gears is operating when the chain is on the smallest chainwheel and on the biggest rear cog. This would be your steep-hill-climbing gear. In my discussing of gear ratios, I pointed out that for touring you need what I called a "Granny" gear, which to the racing cyclist in top physical condition would be ludicrously low, and quite properly so. But for the average cycle tourist, carrying 28 to 36 pounds of camping gear, a low low gear with 32 or 34 teeth on the rear biggest cog and 26 to 36 on the smallest chainwheel is a good "Granny" gear that will get you over most mountains.

Going the other way, as you shift up for more speed, you pull the left lever back and push the right lever forward. Remember that the proper sequence in shifting up or down is to shift one rear gear first, then as you need another gear, to shift the front gear, and as you need still another gear, to move the gear at the rear. Consider the front gear as a halfway gear between each of the rear cogs. Of course, if you come upon a really steep hill you will need to shift right down to your lowest gear and not bother with this sequence. And as you crest the hill and start down the other side, it's okay to shift right up to your biggest gears. But don't, in either case, try to shift through all the gears at once. You will still need to shift carefully and reasonably slowly, because if you try to pull the right shift lever all the way back to get into a low gear quickly, you will more than likely hang the chain up crossways on one of the rear cogs, and it will be jammed and you will have to stop and unjam it, getting your fingers greasy as you try to move the chain, unless you have a screwdriver. You can shift up to a higher gear a lot faster than down to a lower gear, though, because it's so much easier to control pedal pressure. Easing off on pedals, but still pedaling, helps make gear shifting a lot smoother and easier. And remember, as I have illustrated elsewhere, that due to chain-angle changing as you shift, you will have to make slight adjustments of the front derailleur as you move up and down through the rear gears, to keep the chain from rubbing on the inside of the derailleur cage. Such chain rub is perfectly normal and natural, but avoidable. Get in the habit of listening to the chain as you shift, and be aware of any clicks or rubbing sounds. If the noise comes from the rear, the gears are telling you that the chain is too close to an adjoining cog, or is riding up on top of the cog. In either case, a slight adjustment of the right shift lever, one way or the other, will move the chain to the correct position on the cog and the noise should cease. Listen for a noise from the front. If you see a long, clear traffic situation up ahead, look down quickly and you will see that the chain is rubbing on one side or the other of the front derailleur cage. A slight adjustment of the left (front) shift lever will move the cage so the chain no longer rubs and the noise disappears.

All of the above is predicated on the assumption that the derailleurs are correctly adjusted and cable slack, due to cable stretch, has been removed. I give adjustment instructions in Chapter 13.

Perhaps Figure 2-19 will help explain how gear combinations can be

A

B

Fig. 2-19: Possible gear combinations for a 10-speed bicycle

G

F

E

D

C

obtained. A and B in this illustration are the smallest and largest chain-wheels. C through G are the rear-wheel cogs. Here is the gear sequence, starting with the lowest (slowest) gear combination. Remember that you don't necessarily start off in the low gear and shift up to high gear as you start off, as you do in a car. That's not the point of bike gears at all. It's perfectly okay to start off in any gear that's comfortable for you and stay in that gear all day, if you feel no undue strain and your speed in miles per hour meets your approval. Bike gears are such a personal thing—for the tourist, now, not the racer—that I hestitate to give any hard-and-fast rules about which gear you *should* be in. I will say that you should be able to average at least 10 and better still 12 miles per hour without undue strain, even if your physical condition is just average. If in doubt, though, get a clearance from your physician.

Now, let's turn to the gear combinations, which are not strictly sequential, but nearly so. Please refer to the discussion on gear ratios in this chapter and the gear table, Table 2-2. These gears are based on a double chainwheel with 52 and 40 teeth and a five-speed freewheel with 14, 17, 21, 26 and 32 teeth:

Gear Number	Freewheel	Chainwheel	Gear (from gear table)
1	C 32	A 40	34
2	D 26	A 40	42
3	C 32	B 52	44
4	E 21	A 40	51
5	D 26	B 52	54
6	F 17	A 40	64
7	E 21	B 52	67
8	G 14	A 40	77
9	F 17	B 52	83
10	G 14	B 52	100

Note that in going from the low gear to the high gear you start out with a combination of the largest chainwheel and the largest freewheel. But to get to the next highest gear you would use the next smallest freewheel (26T) but stay with the small chainwheel (40T). Then, to get to the third gear, you would shift down or back to the biggest (32T) freewheel but move up to the biggest chain wheel (52T). The rest of the shift table speaks for itself. Just remember that this gear-shift sequence does not necessarily apply to *your* gear setup. To discover your own bike's gear sequence, you need to refer to the gear table (Table 2-2) to find the gear that each combination of front and rear gears works out to. Then the correct sequence for shifting, or at least the sequence of successively higher or lower gear combinations would be the progression of "gear" numbers as shown in column four in the table above.

Shift Only When Pedaling

Let me reiterate this point. *You must never shift derailleur gears unless you are pedaling. The cranks must be moving when you shift.* If you stop pedaling, change gears, then start pedaling again, you might tear up the chain or the teeth and possibly damage the derailleur mechanism.

A good ten-speed derailleur-equipped bicycle is still enough of a novelty to tempt itchy-fingered young children (and some adults) to play with the gear shift levers, if you park your bicycle where they can get at it. If someone has moved your gear-shift levers from the position they were in when you parked your bicycle, and you unsuspectingly climb on and start to ride, you may also damage gears and derailleur, just as if you shifted gears improperly without continuing to pedal. So, always, after you have left your bicycle unattended for a while, start riding very gingerly, applying very gentle pressure to the pedals. If the gear levers have been moved, very gentle pedaling will at least permit the derailleur to function without tearing up the works. Another technique is to hoist up the rear wheels by the seat with one hand and twirl the crank with the other. This will let the chain move to another position without damaging it. Then you can mount, ride, and return the chain to the gear combination you prefer.

How to Change Gears—Three-Speed Hubs

To change gears on a three-speed internal rear hub, such as the Sturmey-Archer, ease off pedaling, pedal gently, and snap the gear quickly into the new gear. You can change gears at a stoplight, going to the lower gear for a quicker getaway. If you change gears when the bicycle is stopped, rest the weight of your foot on the higher pedal (at the two-o'clock position) while you make the change. This will allow the internal gears to rotate and change easily.

Riding the Straight and Narrow

Part of correct riding is to be able to ride and steer accurately. With a little training and attention to correct riding technique, you should be able to steer right down a yellow dividing line (a path about four inches wide) and stay on it. This is important to safety, as we have already discussed.

Meanwhile, remember that good riding is easy riding. You should ride relatively relaxed, without your muscles being all knotted up.

Tips for Easy Cycling

There are six positions (Figs. 2-20 to 2-25) for riding bikes with dropped handlebars; shifting from one to another will help you beat fatigue on a long trip. In particular, notice Figure 2-25. Here hands are on the lowest

Fig. 2-20: There are six basic positions for placing hands on handlebars, which you can vary from time to time to change cycling position on long rides. In this position, hands are at top of handlebars, next to stem. This is also a good position to use when hill climbing with your bottom in the saddle; it permits you to brace against the effort put out by strong leg and back muscles.

Fig. 2-21: In the same position as in Figure 2-20, but with thumb and forefinger extended downward.

Fig. 2-22: Base of thumb and forefinger rest on brake levers, providing support for forward weight of upper torso. This is a particularly restful position to adopt on long downhill "coasts," with the added safety factor of allowing you to reach brake levers quickly and conveniently. This is also the position to use when "honking" uphill, climbing with bottom out of the saddle.

part of the handlebars. This is the position that's safest on speedy downhill "slalom" runs, particularly where you have to steer around potholes or debris. I also strongly recommend that the inside of your wrists be locked tight against the handlebars, just above the brake levers, on the sides of the bars. In this position you can help prevent front-wheel "shimmy" from starting; once shimmy starts it's almost impossible to stop it, and you should brake to a stop as soon as possible. (See Chapter 5 for a discussion of front-wheel shimmy and its causes.)

On tours, do not try to be the first in line, unless you're in top physical

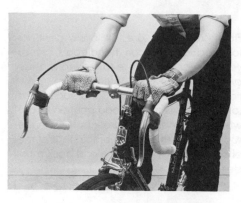

Fig. 2-23: An alternate position frequently used when "honking" uphill. Here the hands are grasping the top of the handlebars firmly; arm muscles are helping "honk" up a steep hill.

Fig. 2-24: This position is used frequently when the going is hard, as on an uphill climb. This is also a position which reduces wind resistance.

Fig. 2-25: On high-speed downhill runs, especially over a bumpy road, it is possible, for any of a number of reasons, for a bicycle to develop a front-wheel wobble or shimmy which could lead to disastrous loss of control. In the position held here, front-wheel shimmy possibility is minimized by the way the handlebars are locked into position between the inside of both forearms, as well as held firmly by the hands. This is the recommended position when riding a camping-gear-laden bike at high speed, downhill especially.

condition. If you stay behind the leader, or behind two or three other riders, they will "break the wind" for you, and you will be able to ride farther before tiring. This technique is called "drafting," and to do it safely you should never get right behind and in line with the person in front, but stay behind and two or three inches to one side. Then if the rider in front suddenly brakes or slows down, you can go by without running into him. I've had following riders run right into me with their front wheel jamming between my right chain stay and derailleur, bending and ruining the derailleur. (If I seem more concerned about damage to the bike than to the rider, I am not. It's so obvious that chain hang-up and resulting wheel lock, or being run into from the rear, can cause you to lose control and hit a passing car or the curb that I prefer to tell you what can happen to your bicycle. *Any* type of equipment failure is an invitation to an accident.)

Watch yourself as you ride. Make sure you do not wobble from side to side, or bend your back up and down as you pump. Learn to use your stomach, back, ankle, thigh and leg muscles as a team to help you cycle smoothly, without tiring.

I have spent hours watching highly trained road and track cyclists riding their bicycles, trying to learn their technique. These cyclists are a symphony of effortless motion. They ride true as an arrow, with absolutely no side wobble, legs pumping like smooth-functioning pistons, and the ankles and feet like wrist pins. It looks so easy, until you mount your bicycle and try to fall in behind them. You discover that the racing cyclist may look as though he is just loafing along, but he is actually pedaling away at about twenty to twenty-five miles per hour, and you will probably not be able to catch up to him, or, if you do, not for long.

I am not trying to make a racing cyclist out of every overweight adult American, though. I am just simply showing you how proper technique will make cycling more fun, even if learning this technique takes practice. Once these good riding methods have become a habit, cycling will really be a joy for you, and perhaps someday you will surprise all your friends by doing the century (100-mile) tour in a single eight-hour day. There are hundreds of others—fathers, mothers, grandfathers, grandmothers—who do the century run regularly every year.

Mounting

I prefer cleated cycling shoes (Figs. 2-26 to 2-28) and toe clips because they increase pedaling efficiency about 30 to 40 percent, but you might not like them. Whatever you prefer, if you do use rattrap pedals with straps, you will have to learn how to mount the bicycle and how to insert one foot into the pedal quickly and safely. Once underway, you won't have time to fuss and look down, trying to fit your foot into the pedal; you must keep your eye on the road. You should practice slipping your free foot promptly into the pedal.

Try this mounting technique. Straddle the bicycle, put one foot in a toe-clip pedal, and pull the pedal up to the one-o'clock position. One foot is in a pedal; the other is on the ground. Use the foot on the ground to shove you off and get you moving, while in one graceful, quick motion you pull yourself up into the saddle by pushing down on the other pedal and hoisting yourself up by pressure on the handlebars. The foot that pushes down the pedal should get you 90 percent of the way into the saddle and, at the same time, get you going forward quickly. Hold the pedals still a moment while you insert your toe and then your foot into the empty pedal. Practice this technique until it's as easy as rising from

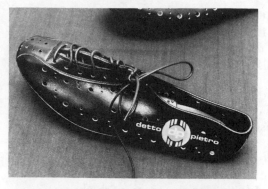

Fig. 2-26: One of the best bicycle shoes you can buy, this Detto Pietro Italian-made shoe has a steel plate in the sole to absorb pedal shock. Hard cycling can put over 1,000 pounds per square inch on tiny metatarsal bones of the foot, so a steel support in the shoe is important to comfortable cycling.

Fig. 2-27: The Detto Pietro cycling shoe also has built-in two-way adjustable cleats. The cleat slot fits over the rear frame member of the rattrap pedal. When you tighten toe-clip straps, you can pull up with one foot and push down with the other at the same time, for far greater pedaling efficiency. Cleats are adjustable sidewise and front to rear, in two planes, by loosening the two screws on cleat, shown.

Fig. 2-28: Another approach to cycling shoes is a less expensive shoe with reinforced sole and serrated sole design that grips both ends of pedal cage so you can pull up with one foot, down with the other. Not as efficient as the Detto Pietro shoes in Fig. 2-25, but plenty good enough for casual cycling and touring.

a chair to walk around the room. Mounting your bicycle this way will distinguish you as an experienced cyclist, at least to other experienced cyclists.

CLEATS AND BICYCLING SHOES

I also recommend using shoe cleats (Fig. 2-29). Cleats give you more cycling efficiency because they fit firmly into the pedal and let you pull back and down without allowing your foot to slip out of the pedal. You should also consider investing in Italian or Belgian cycling shoes (Fig.

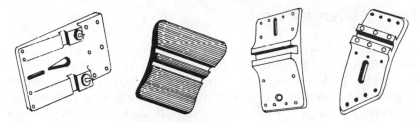

Fig. 2-29: Shoe cleats, for use only with road- or track-racing shoes made for this purpose. Cleats fit into rattrap pedals, permit you to pull pedals up and push them down, and keep feet from sliding off pedals. Shoe cleat at left is for cyclo-cross racing; next, a leather model used for touring; third, a track cleat, and on the right, a road cleat.

2-26). They have long, built-in steel shanks, which keep the steel pedal and your innersole apart, allowing you to put more even pressure on the pedals.

Rattrap pedals and cleat-equipped shoes (Figs. 2-32 and 2-33) are a "must" for cycle touring, in my opinion. If you learn to ankle (Fig. 2-31) properly, you will find that on hills, particularly, without shoe cleats your feet will slip off even rattrap pedals as you apply pressure, especially in the four- and seven-o'clock positions. Pedal straps should be tight enough to keep the shoe cleats in position. If you pedal in city traffic, or as you approach a rest stop, you can bend over from the saddle and loosen the straps slightly so that you can lift your heel up and pull your feet out of the pedals quickly. Cycling shoes, built with steel shanks and shaped for this special use, are ideal for touring. You can carry a pair of slip-ons for off-bicycle use; cleat shoes aren't practical for walking about. I especially want to warn you against cycling with sneakers—they don't offer much protection against the surface of rattrap pedals. If you don't use cycling shoes, at least use flexible leather loafers. But cleats are preferable because they will keep your feet from sliding off the pedals.

Fig. 2-32: Bike shoes with a steel shank under the leather sole protect metatarsal bones against the pressure of rattrap pedals.

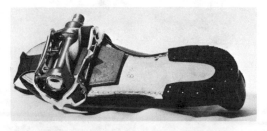

Fig. 2-33: Bike shoes with cleats that fit over the rattrap-cage bridge let you pull up with one foot while you push down with the other, make cycling about 40 percent more efficient, keep feet from sliding out of pedals. In traffic, loosen toe straps so you can pull feet out quickly.

TOE CLIPS, A SAFETY FEATURE

Toe clips are both an important safety feature and a major contributor to cycling efficiency. Clips with straps (Fig. 2-30) will keep your feet from sliding off the pedals when you need to accelerate quickly, or keep them from sliding off accidentally at any time, causing you to lose control of the bicycle. Toe clips also permit you to pull back and up with one foot while you are pushing down and forward with the other. This can increase your cycling efficiency about 40 percent.

For the beginning cyclist, the major concern about toe clips that are tightened with straps is that he will not be able to pull his foot out fast enough if he has to stop quickly. Let me say that no cyclist should ride with straps tightened firmly in city traffic anyway, but you can pull your foot off the pedal, with or without straps, if you have to stop fast and support yourself.

It is important to get the right size toe clips. Toe clips come in three sizes—small, medium, and large. The toe of your shoe should not touch the inside edge of the clip; if it does, it could cause uncomfortable chafing, which could be troublesome, especially on a long trip. If toe clips are too long, the top edge will hit your shoe tongue and chafe the top part of your foot. In general, men who wear American shoe sizes from six to eight should use the small-size toe clips; shoe sizes from eight and a half to ten, the medium size; and over ten, the large clips.

Because my feet are broad, I have found that conventional cycling shoes, even Belgian shoes, pinch just behind my toes, especially when I wear extra-heavy ski socks in cold weather. I solved this problem by wearing shoes a size larger, which moves my foot back away from the toe of the shoe, so I can wiggle my toes inside the shoe in comfort and pinching is eliminated. But then I found that to keep the ball of my foot in the proper position on the pedal, the toe of the larger shoe hit hard

Fig. 2-30: Toe clips are essential for any kind of distance riding, particularly for cycle touring. Only with toe clips and rattrap pedals can you ankle efficiently through 360 degrees of the pedal movement. Keep toe straps tight when touring, but loose in city traffic so you can draw foot out quickly when stopping for any reason.

against the toe clip, and I was already using the large-size clip. I then used a spacer of ½ inch wide by ⅜ inch thick aluminum, with holes drilled for toe clip bolts, longer bolts being required. This positions the ball of the foot correctly on the pedal.

"ANKLING" TECHNIQUE

One important first step in learning to cycle efficiently is to "ankle" correctly (Fig. 2-31). Ankling simply means efficient pedaling. If your bicycle is a conventional three-speed machine with rubber pedals, start by cycling *only* with the ball of your foot. *Never* place your arch on the pedals; you'll never be able to use your leg muscles effectively that way. When you use rattrap, all-steel pedals and toe clips, you have no choice; the toe clips keep the ball of the foot on the pedal correctly.

To learn how to ankle properly, ride your bicycle someplace where you can watch your ankles as you ride, without having to beware of traffic or obstructions. A bicycle exerciser is an excellent way to practice ankling. Or a country road or school parking lot will do.

Fig. 2-31: The "ankling" technique taught to racing cyclists permits more efficient pedaling because muscles can be used more efficiently. At the beginning of the downward stroke, at twelve o'clock, the foot is flat and remains flat until the six-o'clock position. As it passes six o'clock, the heel is pulled up slightly as leg and foot muscles pull the pedal upward to twelve o'clock, at which point the foot becomes flat again. If you don't use rattrap pedals, toe clips, cleats and straps, however, you can vary ankling by pushing down with the toe, the foot pointing slightly downward, on the down power stroke. The heel can be at more of an angle on the upward stroke, which, without cleats and straps, etc., won't go much beyond the eight-o'clock position in any case.

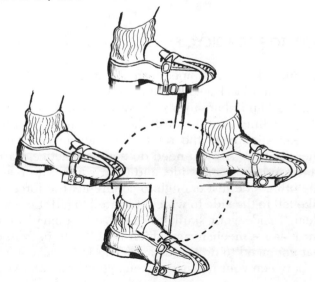

The foot should be flat at the top of the stroke and remain flat all the way down on the downward power stroke. At the bottom, or six-o'clock position, of the power stroke, the heel should be slightly downward. This permits, on the down power stroke, the use of leg and foot muscles more efficiently. The tendency is to pull the heel up on the downward power stroke, which leads to using the toe part of the foot during this stroke, which does not provide as much thrust as the flat position. Toes are weaker than leg muscles, and with toes down, leg muscles aren't used as effectively. As you pass six o'clock, a slight lift of the heel upward permits pulling the pedal up to the twelve-o'clock position, at which point the foot resumes a flat position. This is the "ankling" technique taught to racing cyclists.

Ankling or stroking should not be jerky. You should apply a steady pressure from the top of the stroke all the way to the bottom of the forward stroke. Try ankling with one foot only. Racing cyclists wear shoe cleats that fit into the steel pedal and are held on by toe straps, and they ankle "around the clock." As the pedal passes the six-o'clock position, the heel is up slightly, the toe down, and, with shoe cleats, toe clips and straps, you can actually *pull* the pedal back around to the ten-o'clock position.

Racing cyclists, wearing toe clips (Fig. 2-30), straps and shoe cleats (see Figs. 2-28 and 2-29), can also continue ankling around the clock by pulling the foot straight upward from the six- to the twelve-o'clock position.

Practice ankling correctly until you do it automatically, and you will find cycling much easier and more enjoyable. A good way to practice is to put the gears in the lowest ratio so that the pedals move as quickly as possible to perfect your ankling technique. If you wear straps, keep them tight, but not fully strapped, so you can release them quickly, if necessary.

LEARNING HOW TO RIDE A BICYCLE

Hop up on your bike, with someone holding the bike by standing in front with the front wheel wedged between his legs and with both his arms holding the handlebars firmly. Now you should be able to sit on the bike without falling over. Lean slightly to the left. The bicycle leans to the left. Lean slightly to the right. The bicycle leans to the right. That's all there is to it. All you need do now is practice learning *when* your bike starts to lean to one side, and train yourself to react instantly to lean to the other side just enough to counteract the forces tending to make the bike fall to the side to which it started to fall. Let me make this perfectly clear. Inside your skull, buried inside a small hunk of solid bone, is your balance mechanism, which I shall refrain from describing further. What you need to do to ride a bicycle is to make a lot of neural connections between your balance system, your brain and your muscles so you can react instantly and just enough to counteract by your own weight those forces of gravity that are pushing the bicycle over to one side or the other. The bike leans one way, you lean the other. You learn to ride by realizing it's mostly a balancing act, with the bike one pendulum, and your body another, both neutralizing each other. The shifts in leaning or balance you need to make to stay up are very minute, perhaps an inch or two lean one way or the other to keep upright. I've seen trained racing cyclists with fixed gear locking wheels immovable, balancing upright on their bikes, which is a lot harder to do than if you're moving forward. Of course, when you first step out on a bike, someone should run alongside for a couple of hours (ten minutes at a time) until you get the hang of it. This applies also to a child. I don't think "training" wheels help a child to learn how to ride as much as they keep him from having to learn how to ride. Training wheels are a poor excuse for a parent not taking the time to teach his child by offering him the moral and physical support he or she needs while learning.

Cornering

The beginning cyclist approaches a corner with the urge to slow down. This tendency is at least a safe procedure, but often unnecessary. But let's discuss the *kinds* of corners we will be facing. City street corners, corners or gentle curves on flat country lanes, corners at sharp angles going downhill at high speed, corners on country roads intersecting with other country roads. All of these kinds of curves or corners require different techniques if the turn is to be made safely and without losing too much speed or having to brake excessively (and dangerously).

Cornering on City Streets
First, let's consider city or suburban street corners. These are right-angle turns. You must be able to take them without swerving into the line of oncoming traffic. If you approach the corner too fast, you won't be able to stay in your own lane, but just to stay up you will have to swing wide into or near the oncoming lane. As with all cornering, you should apply brakes before you turn, or be traveling at a safe speed to make the corner. *Do not apply brakes as you turn!* Braking as you turn, especially if you do not apply brakes evenly, can cause loss of control and a fall, possibly into the path of a following or oncoming car. As you approach the corner, if it is unobstructed, look into the street you want to turn into, to check traffic.

Country Roads
On flat roads in the country, curves are usually gentle and you can even see what's ahead around most of the curve—at least for some distance ahead. If you have a slight downhill run with a following wind you could be going 20 miles per hour, so you should be able to take the turn without slowing down. But keep to the right-hand side of the road, don't

let the bike take you out into the opposite lane. Anticipate what the bike is doing, make gradual, careful braking to keep speed control, but don't slow down any more than necessary to keep from swinging left into oncoming traffic lanes. Make those slight shifts in body weight of head and torso, and slight handlebar turns that keep steering control as accurate as possible.

Sharp Curves Downhill

When you are going at a fast clip downhill, say 40 miles per hour and you come to a sharp curve, not as sharp as a city street corner, but a fairly tight turn, remember to slow down *before* you reach the curve, keep in the right side of the right-hand lane, be aware that you can't see around the corner so you don't know what's ahead and have both hands on or near the brake levers, as shown in Figure 2-22, so you can stop quickly if you find a cow crossing the road, a car coming up in your lane, gravel strewn over the road from preceding auto traffic, someone in front who has fallen over on a bicycle or some other obstruction. I've faced them all and so far have managed to stop in time. It *was* a bit disconcerting, though, when I once came upon four or five huge bulls who had wandered away from a local slaughterhouse, right there in the highway around that sharp bend. They looked as formidable as army tanks to me.

Intersections

On country roads, county highways intersect with dirt roads every few miles, at least. Be prepared to stop at these junctures, because country folk tend to think of the highways off their dirt roads as extensions of their driveways, and often don't even begin to stop as they drive out onto the highways, (even though there may be stop signs). Look for a cloud of dust on the dirt road ahead, indicating approaching traffic from right or left at the intersection.

Techniques for Safe Braking

I am going to assume that your brakes are properly adjusted, all cable stretch taken up, brake shoes ⅛ inch away from rims and rims straight. If not, please refer to Chapter 10 on brakes and Chapter 15 for wheel truing and make these adjustments. Nothing I can tell you about safe braking maneuvers will work if your brakes won't stop you.

Normal Braking

Going around town, pedaling on city streets, seldom requires much expertise in braking. You usually are not going faster than 10 or 12 miles per hour, at most, and if the brakes are good ones (Chapter 10) and are adjusted properly, they should stop you for any conceivable situation. Panic stops, however, are not your usual braking maneuver. If a dog, a child or a car in front requires you to stop as quickly as possible, there are methods for doing so safely and effectively. First of all, in city driving, your hands must always be near the brake levers so you can grab them quickly. Riding on the lower flats of the bars or toward the stem on the tops of the bars is not conducive to quick stopping; hands will be too far from the brake levers when split seconds are vital to stopping in time. To make an emergency stop, bend down and extend your rump as far back on the saddle as you can and at the same time squeeze brake levers hard. Pushing your weight over the rear wheel will help distribute weight evenly and keep the wheels from skidding.

You should practice panic stops; learn to come to a halt with the bike under control. Wheels must not skid, because a skidding, locked wheel throws you out of control and usually results in a fall. Practice stopping until you know how your brakes work. If you have a new bike, with a different make of brake, get used to that particular brake because different makes of brakes have different braking characteristics (see Chapter 10 for details).

Fast Downhill Braking Techniques

Going down a steep mountainside at high speed can be a thrilling experience. Speed can build up quickly to 45 miles per hour or even more. There's really no problem in high-speed downhill runs, per se, if the road is straight and you can see for miles ahead. But if, like most mountain roads, there are curves to maneuver, you need to be able to keep speed under control, slow enough so you can take them safely, without having to swerve out into an oncoming lane to keep from losing control and falling. And if at the bottom of the hill there is a sharp turn, speed control is absolutely vital.

The main problem in keeping speed control on fast downhill runs is heat. As the brake shoes rub on rim sides, friction generates heat, which is transferred to the air in the tubes inside the tires. As the air heats up, it expands, and if it gets too hot, it expands too much, and the tire can blow out. A blowout at high speed can be very hazardous. At the least you can lose a lot of skin, break bones, get a collection of bruises. At worst you can get killed, especially if you're not wearing a helmet (see Chapter 5 for helmet information). Heat blowouts are particularly liable to occur with tubular tires, because they are under a lot of pressure to begin with. But ordinary tires are not immune to heat blowouts either. I have seen the new 700-centimeter narrow-profile tires blow out just from the bike being left out in the hot summer sun while the owner went into a store to buy the makings for lunch while on tour. The sound of an exploding tire under the hot sun is guaranteed to get your instant attention.

To brake so as to minimize heat buildup on high-speed downhill runs, try not to use both brakes at once. Apply the rear brake to keep speed control for a moment, then go to the front brake and let the rear rim cool off, and vice versa. Better yet, don't let speed build up to the point where you have to brake severely to keep control. Hard braking at high speed builds up a lot of heat quickly, and if the sun is at the right angle and heating up your tires, and if tire flex at high speed adds to the heat gain, hard braking could be enough to cause a blowout. The next time you are going downhill and have to brake, stop after braking and feel the rims. You'll get the picture.

Earlier, and throughout this book, I have taken every opportunity to urge you to remove the so-called "safety" levers, extension or auxiliary levers which come with less expensive bikes. Even with exact adjustments of brakes and rims true, extension levers have a shorter distance of travel than regular levers, and just won't stop you in time if you have to panic stop. Chapter 10 tells how to remove them.

Hill Climbing

If you have the proper "Granny" gears, you should be able to climb any hill without standing up. If you have to stand and "honk" your way uphill, you lose about 30 to 40 percent of pedal power, because it's difficult to ankle your way around the clock while standing up. The idea is to push down with one foot and pull up with the other (which you can do if you have toe clips and straps on pedals, a really necessary item for distance touring). Standing and honking uphill creates a lot of downward pressure, but it takes a real expert to pull upward when you're off the saddle. Also, remember to shift down *before* you hit a sharp rise.

And, finally, don't be ashamed to get off and walk if you can't make a hill. I'd rather see you walking up the hill than weaving from one side of the road to the other trying to cut down the grade of the hill. Weaving is dangerous if there is any traffic in either direction.

ALL ABOUT FRAMESETS

If you fit a standard bicycle sold in bicycle shops, you can fit a standard bicycle frame, some of which are sold in bike stores, others of which need to be ordered directly from the maker. The only reason you might want to buy a frameset alone (bear in mind that these are already made and cannot be tailored to you any more than a complete bicycle can) is that the frameset may have some special characteristic that you find desirable. For example, some of the more exotic European and American frame builders have a top name that, on a bicycle, is one to be envied. That's an ego trip for you.

Or, you may have all the component goodies already hung on a frame, but you have wrecked the frame, outgrown it, or simply have changed your type of riding from, let's say, racing to touring . . . or you may want a highly specialized racing frame for a specialized type of race, such as criteriums, time trials or stage races like the Tour de France. Of course, in the Tour de France, riders have specialized bicycles for the different stage events such as hill climbing, sprints, time trials. If the day is going to be over cobblestones, yet another, stronger bike is needed.

Store-Bought Frames

Here, then, are some of the better framesets available off the shelf. First, detailed specifications on framesets are not always available, nor are prices. If I have listed these framesets, it is because the maker has a fine reputation for quality that should carry over to his framesets. Unless otherwise stated, all framesets come with headset and fork already installed.

Sekai Framesets

Model 4000 Professional: For long road races but also built with clearances for fenders or standard tires (not tubulars—to repeat, in this book all tires are the wired-on type unless called tubulars).

Model 2700: For long-distance touring. Frame is double-butted tubing with forged steel dropouts and Italian-style lugs, hand built of low-temperature brazing material.

Model 2500: A lower-cost double-butted frameset for touring and commuting bikes, available in six sizes.

Model 2400: For all-around use, road racing or touring, frame is Tange "High Tensile" single-butted low-temperature brazed. Model 1000 is similar except that it comes with brazed-on eyelets for fenders or carrier racks. The Mixte 1000 is the same except that it is a double downtube women's configuration in 19-, 21- and 23-inch sizes. And the Model 500 is a good enough utility frame to be a low-cost way to replace a wrecked frame using old components. For prices on these and the 5000 series super-light framesets, write Pine Street Cycle, 611 E. Pine St., Seattle, Washington 98122 (206/325-1958).

Nishiki O.N.P. Framesets

These are designed for high-speed road racing, yet have the stability and strength for safe handling down steep mountain passes. Tubing is chrome molybdenum double-butted, including front fork with Cinelli type sloping crown. Fork has reinforced upper inside lug. Tange

Table 2-5 Standard dimensions for O.N.P.

A	B	H	F	G	$f°$	$s°$
105	545	520	584	52	73°30′	74°
115	550	540	586	60	73°30′	74°
135	555	560	589	60	74°	74°
155	565	580	598	60	74°	74°
175	575	600	609	60	74°	74°
185	580	620	617	70	73°	74°
205	585	640	623	70	73°	74°

"Levin" headset is included. Caution: These are highly responsive frames that would be fatiguing for long-distance touring. Vertical rear dropouts indicate high-quality workmanship (alignment is a lot tougher with vertical than with conventional dropouts). These are beautiful frames indeed. Dimensions in centimeters are given below. Price: $280.

Gios America Torino Frames

For road racing, track racing or cyclo-cross (specify which) Gios has some of the finest frames made in Europe. Without the fork, price is $350. With frame kit consisting of fork, seatpost, stem, chainwheel, bottle, jersey and hat, price is $460. Available through better bicycle stores catering to the racing fraternity.

Trek

Trek Bicycle Corporation, a newcomer to the U.S. bicycle and frame making scene, makes top- to good-grade frames at very reasonable prices. All Trek frames include as standard equipment a brazed-on chainstay cable stop and a downtube underside cable clip stop, so you won't have to mutilate the finish, clamping these stops onto the tube. Additional braze-ons are available at extra cost. See your dealer or write Trek Bicycle Corporation, 268 Jackson Street, Waterloo, Wisconsin 53594 (414/478-2191). All frames machined to Campagnolo 1039 Record road headset specifications:

Model 510: Ishiwata 022 tubing $175
Model 710 Reynolds '531' tubing $215
Model 910 Columbus SP/SL tubing $235
Model 530 Ishiwata 022 tubing $230
Model 930 Columbus SP/SL tubing $255

Raleigh Framesets

Raleigh makes a full line of good-quality framesets out of Reynolds '531' butted tubing. To decide which frame you need, see your Raleigh dealer, who can help you select the type you should have for touring, road racing, time trials or track. Prices are around $430 for Reynolds '531' double-butted tubing and $540 for the new Reynolds '731' ultra-light double-butted tubing. Frames are all hand brazed and are built in ½-centimeter increments from 52 to 62 centimeters (20.5 to 24.5 inches).

The above framesets are just a few of the many good-quality sets available from U.S., European and Japanese builders. Space does not permit me to list all of them; those that are listed should give you an idea of the price range and types available.

All About Custom Framesets

Earlier in this chapter we stated that most people come in fairly standard sizes and implied that, were this not so, the clothing industry would still be in the cottage-industry stage, or at best in a mess, or perhaps we would all be wearing one-size-fits-all togas or dashikis or Arabian Nights robes. But not all of us come in standard sizes.

If you are short—under five feet—you will definitely need a custom frame, because stock bikes just do not take your size into consideration. Sure, the standard tables matching frames to the human body that bicycle manufacturers make up (see Table 2-1) may include you in them. But you will often find that the top tube is still too high for you to straddle comfortably—that the tube presses uncomfortably against your crotch when you stand over it with both bare feet on the floor. The frame may be listed as 17 inches (length of top tube from center line of bottom-bracket spindle to top of tube). The frame is not, however, a true 17-inch frame. The tube may be 17 inches, but this length was achieved by simply shortening the tubes and moving the bottom bracket higher.

In addition to having too high a top tube, smaller stock frames may well have a top tube too long for your arm reach, and nothing, not even a shorter handlebar stem, or moving the saddle to the far forward position, will compensate for the superfluous length. In this case you will find such a bicycle to be painful to ride over long distances because you will be forced into an uncomfortable position.

Let me give you an example. Gary Klein, head of Klein Bicycle Corporation, who makes very exotic, super-light bicycles out of aluminum, mostly for racing, says: "If someone has short legs, short arms and a long torso, and is considering a smaller frame, he will find the top tube too short for his torso and arm length, and will also probably find the handlebars too low for his longer torso (more vertical height) and shorter arms (less vertical drop). In general, he will require almost the same frame (for the same type of riding) as the long-legged person of the same height. Using myself as an extreme example—I am 6 feet 1 inch, with a 37-inch inseam and a 35-inch sleeve length—I raced on a 25-inch frame for two years, and finally realized that it was too large for me. After experimenting with several frame sizes, my best results have been a 23.5- to 24-inch frame. From Table 2-1 you will note that a 37-inch inseam calls for a frame size of 26 inches, instead of the 23.5-inch frame that's comfortable for me."

Gary has a formula he uses to compute frame size, which you may find useful. It is, for a racing frame: $.3937 \times height - 5.118$. In my own case, I am 69 inches tall, so this works out to $.3937 \times 69 - 5.118 = 22$ inches. For a racing frame, the formula gives me $.3937 \times 69 - 4.724$ or a 22.4-inch frame. But my torso is longer than my inseam, so in fact I am more comfortable on a 21-inch frame. However, Gary points out that this formula applies only to people of his own dimensions, so all is forgiven. Which is why all your significant bodily frame dimensions are required by a custom frame builder.

What to Tell a Custom Frame Builder

Before we discuss how to find a reliable, talented and suitable frame builder for your personalized frameset, let's discuss what such a builder needs to know before he can put his time, talent and tools to work for you.

First, please refer to Figure 2-34, a simple sketch of the human body's basic dimensions. Frame makers need to know the distance from the tip of the shoulder (the acromion process) to the knuckles, tip of the hip (the greater trochanter) to the ground, overall height, inseam measurement from crotch to floor while standing in bare feet and the arm length from tip of shoulder to tip of the fingers. In addition, it is well to provide the frame builder with your weight, because a 5-feet-6-inch, 250-pound person needs a different (stronger) frameset than would a 5-feet-6-inch, 125-pound person who does not need the extra weight of frame reinforcement or heavier-gauge tubing.

Next, the frame builder wants to know what kind of bicycling you will

Fig. 2-34: To order a custom frame, send body measurements as noted above to frame builder.

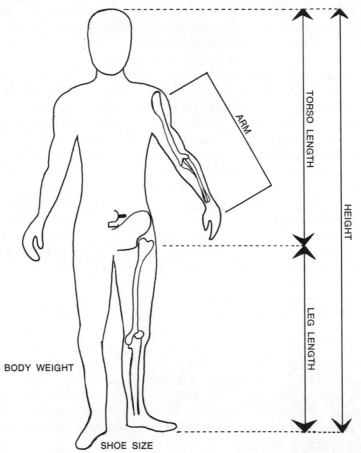

be doing. Are you a cyclo-tourist? Do you want a bicycle for racing, and if so, what kind of racing? A track bike is nothing like a cyclo-cross bike, of course. The track machine is designed with a very stiff, responsive frame and minimum wheel clearances, with no brakes, for riding only on a smooth surface; the cyclo-cross is designed to go over very, very rough terrain, including logs, rocks, creeks, mud, swamps and whatever else lies in the way across open country.

I would recommend fenders (mudguards in Europe) if you will be touring in any wet season anywhere. So you will need to tell the frame builder to braze on eyelets for fastening down fenders. In fact, now is the time for you to carefully consider just exactly what you do want brazed on the frame. After the frame is built and painted is no time for second thoughts. I hate to use metal clamps for anything on a good frame. They spoil the finish, the appearance, and often come loose. The one thing you don't want to happen on a long tour is to have the carriers come loose and spill your camping gear and camera all over the road. Besides, loose equipment can be dangerous if it gets into the spokes. Mainly, though, you are going to pay a fairly hefty sum for a tailor-made frame, so you might as well go all the way and have everything that you need brazed on. I would include (and I give sample prices for this work from several frame builders):

Table 2-6

Chainstay stop	$ 4.50
Bottom-bracket left- and right-hand guide	3.00
Water-bottle mounts	7.00 (per set)
Downtube stops for bar-end levers	7.50 (pair)
Rear-rack mounts (carrier mounts)	10.00 (pair)
Top-tube cable guides	10.00

I would also have a pump holder brazed on the underneath side of the top tube, just underneath the saddle—the bottom of the pump can fit where seat and downtubes meet. This fitting is a simple piece that looks like a sawed off nail measuring $\frac{3}{16}$-inch in diameter and about ¼ inch in length. You will then need a Silca pump the proper length for your seat tube. Any good bike shop can fix you up with such a pump. Many of the better custom frame builders can supply you with this pump painted the same color as your frameset. Use a Silca pump with Campagnolo ends.

Above all, listen to what the builder has to say about such things as frame angles and reinforcements. Don't try to second guess him on frame angles especially. You may like a friend's bike, and it may have 74-degree angles that would be all wrong for you. Frame angles depend on frame geometry, which in turn is related to the use of the bike and the size of the frameset. Dictating angles to a builder will put severe limitations on him that may work against you. A good frame builder will accept your angle requirements only if they happen to meet the geometry he designs for you. Some builders will build anything you ask, and at most will put up only a feeble argument against what they know would not be right for you. That kind of a builder you don't need. Would you tell a doctor how to do an appendectomy on you? Most builders will not build you anything drastically wrong. For example, they won't build you a 27-inch frame if you are only six feet tall.

None of these adjurations will stop people from sending builders detailed specs on the frame of their dreams. For example, a magazine article in one of the bicycle magazines had an article on frame casters, and Tom Boyden, who is a top frame builder under the name Fastab Cycles, in Garland, Texas, had a lot of people ask him what caster he uses. The problem is that no two frames have the same caster. There are subtle differences or characteristics that make the caster a bit different on most frames, depending on what the frame calls for (or what the human configuration and end-use requirement of the owner are).

Again, Tom Boyden cautions: "Beware of the latest fad in frame angles. You may see a bike someone else has and want a frame just like it. You may also see a suit on someone else, but would you want one *exactly* that size? You would expect sleeve length, cuff length and waist circumference to differ somewhat, at the very least. The same holds true for frame angles, a function of tube geometry."

Back to brazed-on fittings. I would also have a lamp mounting brazed onto the frame front and rear, if you intend to ride at night.

Don't ask a builder to send you names of people for whom he has made frames. Most builders won't provide this information because it is usually a customer irritant and invasion of privacy.

For Physical Problems

Skilled bicycle builders, such as those listed in the Appendix, can often make a bicycle, or a tricycle or quadricycle, for the handicapped. Because the bicycle has been amply demonstrated to be the most efficient transformer of human muscle power to locomotion ever devised, it's highly attractive to the physically handicapped. I think the most appealing aspect of bicycling is the freedom it gives, and if even with limited use of muscle or limb you can move about on your own, this, then, has to be the real attraction of cycling for the handicapped. What I recommend is that you visit a good frame builder, review your physical limitations with him, and take his suggestions and drawings to your doctor to see if they are practical for you. I have one caveat here, though, and that is that your doctor should be dedicated to outdoor exercise. He should, in fact, be a sports doctor and not the type who tells you not to exercise if he feels you are not up to it. Seek out several doctors, but do try to find one who is himself or herself well versed in sports physiology; this is a special mind set you won't find in every physician, unfortunately.

For those with limited leg use, Cyclo makes a left- and right-hand crank with articulated pedal action. This is suitable for a rider with slight or partial knee action (Fig. 2-35).

Fig. 2-35: Articulated pedal for those with limited knee action.

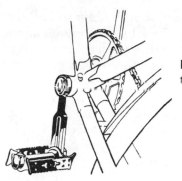

Fig. 2-36: Short cranks for those with one leg shorter than the other.

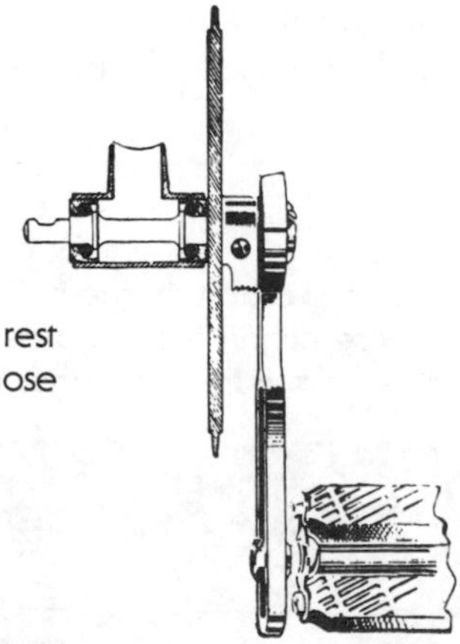

Fig. 2-37: Freewheel crank so you can rest one leg and pedal with the other. For those who can only use one leg.

Fig. 2-38: The special spindle required for the crank in Figure 2-35.

If you have one leg shorter than the other, Cyclo also makes a special shorter crank (Fig. 2-36). And if you have a stiff limb or an artificial leg, Cyclo makes a free-wheeling crank arm that permits one leg to remain stationary while the other leg does all the work (Fig. 2-37). The crank in Figure 2-37 requires a special spindle, (Fig. 2-38) which, unfortunately for weight freaks, is cottered. Cyclo products are available through your Raleigh dealer, or were the last time I checked. If you can't find them, please write to me % my publisher and I will search out a local supplier for you.

How to Select a Custom Frame Builder

The better custom frame builders have been in business for years. They have a sizable investment in machinery, jigs, fixtures, paint and finishing equipment and other tools (Figs. 2-39 to 2-41). The twice-a-year frame builder with wooden jigs or Rube Goldberg fixtures cannot guarantee accuracy of alignment.

In fact, alignment can vary all over the map, from builder to builder, depending on his experience and equipment. Talk to your builder about what tolerances he can hold. Don't let him tell you that his frame is perfect and that there is no need to worry about tolerances. Everything has a tolerance of some sort within which you must stay. Bike frames have fairly loose tolerances in terms of high-precision industrial standards. Still, better builders will hold a tolerance of frame angles to plus or minus one half a degree, fewer still can hold to a tolerance of .03 of a degree, which is excellent. Tom Boyden of Fastab Cycles notes: "In building any frame with any tooling concept, the angles and dimensions of any frameset will vary slightly during the process of heating the frame up for tube assembly for the brazing process. The builder with the tooling that holds the best tolerances should be given favorable consideration. Dimensional tolerances of plus or minus two millimeters are fairly common in the industry, and plus or minus one millimeter is excellent."

Fig. 2-39: Experienced custom frame builders use accurate jigs and fixtures to assure correct and accurate alignment of frame members. Here top frame builder Matt Assenmacher silver solders front fork ends in a special fork jig.

Fig. 2-40: Cable ferrules are brazed on by hand. Note that the frame is held in a special fixture. *(Photo courtesy Schwinn Bicycle Company)*

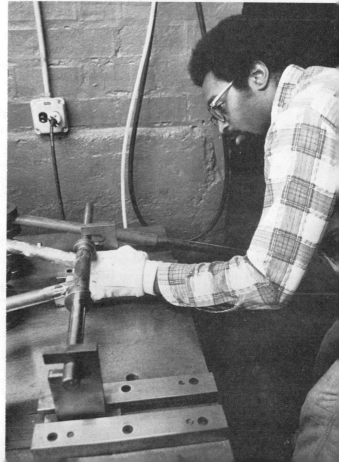

Fig. 2-41: Steering head tube alignment is accurately positioned in this fixture. *(Photo courtesy Schwinn Bicycle Company)*

Fig. 2-42: Some custom frame builders, notably in Europe, "eyeball" frame alignment. Notice the absence of jigs or fixtures in this European frame builder's plant.

Many builders are not terribly willing to show you their tooling, which may be considered proprietary. The end result, after all, is what counts. But most builders use some sort of jig or assembly tool to assemble framesets. Boyden notes that some still follow the old British tradition of clamping the bottom-bracket shell in a vise and putting the tubes into place, lining them up by eye and putting the torch to them (Fig. 2-40). That does not generally produce the best quality or the highest accuracy. Tooling is essential, but, again, it's not how fancy the tools are, it's how well and how accurate the frame is made that counts.

Many builders provide literature on their work. Study it carefully. Boyden suggests you look for versatility in design. That is, you want to look for a builder who can fit anybody from a midget to a giant and everybody in-between, as shown in Figures 2-43 and 2-44. Finally, look for a builder with a warranty. Some guarantee their framesets for a year, some forever. Somewhere in-between is average.

A builder who uses only one of the three brazing techniques is probably not as versatile as one who can use all three—brazing with brass, nickel silver and silver alloy (silver solder). Boyden advises, and I agree, that you should talk to your builder about what he recommends, because often a combination of these three brazing materials, each of which has its own brazing technique, is often required to build the frame you need. Silver solder assembly is a bit more expensive because, by the time a complete frame is assembled, more costly brazing material has been

Fig. 2-43: One of the smallest bicycle frames made, a true 18-inch frame is ideal for the shorter rider. Uses 27-inch or 700-centimeter wheels, yet top tube is close to the ground. Shown is a top-line Model C32 Bertin extra small 46-centimeter frame bike.

Fig. 2-44: One of the largest bicycle frames made, this high-grade Bertin Model C-34 is a huge 70-centimeter (27½-inch) bicycle.

used. In addition, silver solder brazing requires strict metal cleaning because cleanliness is much more critical with this brazing material.

It is not the best idea to tell the builder which of the three brazing materials to use, because the builder's own experience will dictate which is best. Some builders prefer the silver solder because it requires a lower brazing temperature and thus less risk of compromising the heat treatment of the tubes. Others feel that the higher-temperature brazing materials make a stronger frame.

I would also leave the choice of lugs, bottom-bracket shell and fork crown up to the builder. In general, however, I prefer investment cast lugs because, although they do cost more, they offer much greater precision and are easier to work with and finish. Excellent investment cast lugs are made by Cinelli and Roto. The fork crowns I prefer are made by Haden, Cinelli and Zeus.

Variables That Determine Frame Size

Earlier in this chapter, I cautioned against specifying frame dimensions and angles, or even drawing up your own frame design and insisting that the builder build such a frame. A good builder won't do it if you are all wrong, at least not the U.S. builders. European builders tend to build anything you ask for.

For example, the seat-tube length is a function of your leg length. The top-tube length depends on the length of your arms and torso. The angles of the head and seat tube are a function, largely, of tube lengths and the use to which you will put the bike. A racing bicycle may use 74-degree head- and seat-tube angles and have a 39-inch wheelbase, whereas a touring bike may have 73-degree angles and a 40-inch wheelbase.

I have a beautiful, custom-made touring bicycle made by Alex Singer of Paris, France. I visited his booth some years ago while attending the annual bicycle show in Paris. He took my measurements and made a touring bicycle as only the French know how, which is to say, superbly. Below I compare the measurements of this bicycle to my own frame measurements, and to the measurements of a good compromise bicycle, the Soma Competition (see Chapter 1), which offers a bit more quick response with a bit less comfort so it can be used for road racing as well as for touring.

After extensive riding of the Soma (I have traveled all over Europe with the Singer) I can report that the Soma corners more quickly and accurately than the Singer and that it is a more fatiguing bike to ride on a long tour (for me, at least) because the frame is stiffer and more responsive. The Soma's stiffer frame, shorter wheelbase and steeper angles translate into faster getaway in sprints, faster cornering, as noted, and about three pounds less steel to carry around. The Singer's longer wheelbase, longer fork rake and springier construction make it ride like a Rolls-Royce, corner like one (versus a racing car) and tote more steel around. For me the more comfortable ride of the Singer is worth the extra money, and I am not going to race a touring frame in any case. Here are the comparative specs:

My own measurements:
- Weight: 150 pounds
- Height: 69 inches
- Cubit (elbow to fingertip): 18 inches
- Tip of shoulder to knuckles: 24 inches
- Hip to floor: 49 inches
- Hip to shoulder: 20 inches
- Inseam: 31 inches

You will note that according to Table 2-1, I should be riding a 19-inch frame, yet I am perfectly comfortable on the 22-inch Singer as well as on the 21-inch Soma. I have 3½ inches of seat post showing on the Soma and only 3 inches on the Singer, which would seem odd because the Singer is a one-inch larger frame than the Soma. But I am using a Campy seat post on the Singer and a SR Laprade seat post on the Soma, a Brooks Professional saddle on the Singer and an Avocet Touring I saddle on the Soma (the latter is not what comes with the Soma), and these components have different dimensions. The point here is that the builder should know what you intend to hang on the bicycle he is going to make for you, so he can plan accordingly.

Specifications of these two bicycles are:

	Soma Competition	Alex Singer
Saddle nose to centerline of handlebars:	18½"	19"
Top-tube length	21"	22"
Fork rake	1½"	2"
Downtube length	24½"	25"
Seat-tube length	21"	22"
Chainstay length	15"	15½"
Seatstay length	18½"	20"
Drop (distance from bottom bracket to ground, inches)	10½"	10½"
Stem length	3¼"	3"
Saddle-height setting (from centerline of bottom bracket to stop of saddle measured parallel to seat tube)	27½"	28½"
Wheelbase	39½"	40½"

Clearly, from the table above, the 109-percent multiplication of inseam measurement to determine saddle-height setting (noted earlier) has to be considered at best a beginning yardstick, because, from my own inseam of 31 inches, a 1.09 increase would show a 33-inch saddle height, which is too high for me. So let the builder select all frame dimensions, and just concentrate on giving him accurate body measurements. Better still, if you can, visit the builder and let him take your body measurements. Then there can be no room for error.

Here is yet another way to tell the builder about your body measurements. This method is used by Tom Boyden of Fastab Cycles, 2706 S. Glenbrook, Garland, Texas 75041, one of the country's top frame builders.

As shown in Figure 2-45, Tom wants you to hold a piece of pipe straight overhead, with your arms fully extended but not stretched. Take all measurements in your stocking feet. He wants height from floor to top of the pipe, floor to crotch (inseam), floor to top of *both* shoulders (two measurements) and, sitting, from center of arch of back to front of knee, as shown in the drawing. You should stand erect but do not thrust shoulders back.

Tom also wants to know what kind of bike, by brand name and model, you now ride, how many miles you ride weekly, dimensions of the seat tube, top tube and stem (see Fig. 2-1).

He also wants to know your age, sex, weight and shoe size, and whether you intend to use the frameset for general riding, training, racing, road racing, criterium racing, time trials, touring, local or extended touring.

If you are ordering a tandem frameset, your rear rider (the stoker) will also have to send in his or her dimensions.

Fig. 2-45: One way to obtain all the measurements you need for ordering a custom frame: Holding pipe above head, in stocking feet, measure from floor to centerline of pipe. Measure from crotch to floor, shoulder to floor (both shoulders) and top of head to floor. Seated, measure from back of chair to tip of knee, as shown.

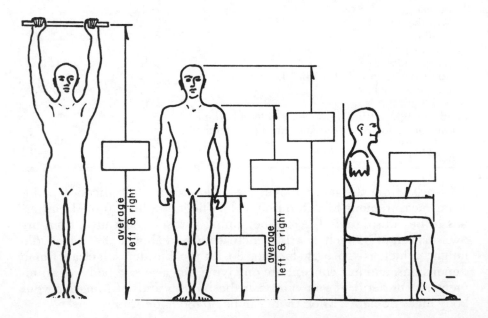

About the Frame Finish

Whether to paint or chrome finish the frame may be a question for you. If so, you should know that it is with everyone, and most frame builders with whom I have discussed chrome-finished frames agree that there is is a definite hazard involved. Chrome finishes are highly scratch and scar resistant, do a good job of protecting the tube metal from rust and are easy to keep clean and highly polished; however, in the process of chrome plating the tubing is subject to hydrogen embrittlement, which simply means that free hydrogen ions penetrate the tubing and result in a steel that is more brittle than the tubing manufacturer designed it to be. That is, it is brittle enough to have a tendency to crack. With some trouble and extra expense, it is possible, says Boyden, to reduce the propensity to crack by applying a specialized heat-treating process after the chrome plating process. If you still want a chrome-plated frame— and they are undeniably handsome—talk to your builder about post- chrome heat treatment. If he does not know what the proper heat treat- ment should be, I would advise against chrome plating. Some builders refuse to chrome plate for fear of risking later frame failure, and I don't blame them one bit.

I had one chrome-plated frame which snapped off at the head tube. Of course I did subject it to cruel and unusual punishment by running into the back of a parked car at around 15 miles per hour. The accident was probably my fault, because, as I recall, I was daydreaming, but actually a driver zoomed around me, pulled into the curb, slammed on the brakes and parked, all in one fell swoop. I had little chance to stop, but if I had been more alert I could have perhaps swerved out into the road. The point is, however, that I rammed the rear fender of this humongous Cadillac, at which point the expensive bicycle departed this world for- ever by snapping its neck off at the junctures of the head tube, down and top tubes. About ten years earlier I had a similar accident (it takes time to learn these things) with a similar high-quality bicycle, only this one was painted. The frame survived fine, though the fork decided to beat a strategic retreat for about an inch, at the steering head. Judicious straightening, cold, revived the fork and I am still riding this old-timer.

There are fads in paints for bicycles just as there are fads in frame angles. Currently the fad seems to be for Dupont Imron, a very tough finish indeed. Your builder should be able to supply you with a good color chart from which to select the color of your choice. I am inclined to leave the type of paint up to him, because he works best with what he knows. There is more than one good brand of paint in the world.

Custom Frame Cost

Every custom builder I know requires a deposit with your order, all or most of which is nonrefundable should you change your mind about accepting the frame within a certain period of time. The builder is justified in keeping at least some of the deposit, because prior to touching metal on your behalf he spends a considerable amount of time designing a frameset just for you. A lot of work goes on paper before the frame is built.

But you should make sure that the price agreed upon with the builder is the price you pay upon delivery. Some builders—and the British are notorious for this—deliver framesets at the price in effect at the time of delivery rather than the price quoted when you placed your order.

Costs do vary somewhat from builder to builder. As an example, Dennis Bagenstos of Aquila Cycles, Colorado Springs, Colorado, delivers a frameset for anywhere from $275 to $325 for fairly standard frames. If you want a lot of brazed-on fittings, the price could go up to $400 (this is for the frame and fork only).

For custom tandem frames, you are looking at a layout of $550 to $600, depending on what you ask for. Aquila includes a custom rear stem and cantilever brake sets on the tandem frameset.

Which Steel to Use

There are a great many very fine sets of steel tubing, with differences in flexibility, strength, weight and yield strength after brazing (see Table 1-1 in Chapter 1). The choice of steel tubing should be left up to the builder, because only he can really decide. He may use a combination of tubing—for example, Columbus for the fork blades, Reynolds '531' for the main tubes. Unless you want a super-light racing bike, he won't use the new Reynolds '753', which is not recommended for touring. Reynolds '753' is used when you want great rigidity and lightness as a combination. Reynolds won't even ship '753' to a builder unless they know he can braze it successfully. They send the builder a sample set of tubes, he brazes them together, sends them back to Reynolds and if his joints meet their tests he gets on their approved list to use '753'. The reason for this is that '753' is thin, only .020 inches in the unbutted section, .024 inches in the butted section, as compared to .024 and .036 respectively for Reynolds '531.' Even though thinner, '753' is considerably stronger at 134,000-pounds-per-square-inch yield strength. Frames of '753' are used for pursuit races among other types.

How to Judge the Finished Product

Types of tubing, methods of tube brazing, brazing materials, frame angles and wheelbase variables aside, the only true test of a frameset is performance. It should fit you perfectly, be very comfortable, and once you have made the necessary saddle and stem-height adjustments (see Chapter 1) the bike should feel like an extension of your body as it flows smoothly down the road.

From the standpoint of appearance, here are some examples of good workmanship: Figure 2-46 shows a handmade Carleton frame (which is

Fig. 2-46: Raleigh hand-made Carleton bicycles show top craftsmanship. Notice brazed-on brake-cable fitting and brazed-on brakes.

entirely chrome plated, by the way). Notice the brazed-on brake-cable stop, where the cable fits, the brazed-on brakes which are very responsive, and the neat appearance of these joints. Figures 2-47 and 2-48 show, respectively, a really artistic job of brazing front and rear dropouts. Notice how the fork blades and chainstays are scalloped out—a lot of hand work. Figure 2-49 shows what a good frame should *not* look like. Here the frame has just been brazed, and has not been cleaned prior to painting. The arrows show a poor mitering job and gaps between the top and downtubes and the steering head tube. Joints must be mitered to fit perfectly, because the brazing compound, be it brass or silver, is not strong enough to substitute for the steel of the tube.

Figure 2-50 is a beautiful illustration of very high-quality framework, put together by Gary Klein, of Klein Bicycle Corporation. This is a handmade aluminum frame for racing. Figure 2-51 shows the Carleton approach to fork dropout brazing. Figures 2-52 and 2-53, respectively, are a good example of off-the-shelf framework, by DBS Oglaend, Norway, showing the head-tube lug work and the seat-tube cluster. Figure 2-54 is a finished product of a custom frame built by Assenmacher. And Fig-

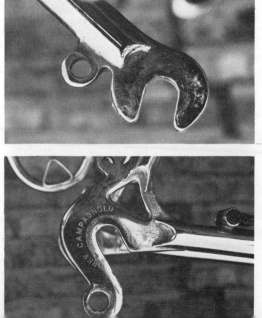

Fig. 2-47: The fork dropout in a handmade Alex Singer French touring bicycle shows careful workmanship, much hand finishing.

Fig. 2-48: Rear dropouts in the chainstays of an Alex Singer hand-made frame show scalloped stays, beautiful brazing job. At right, on right-hand chain stay, is the rear end of a rubber strip which keeps stay clean of grease and oil spatter from chain.

Fig. 2-49: Not all hand-brazed frames are equal. In this lugless frame, a photo of which was taken just after brazing, before cleaning, arrows point to gaps where top and downtubes meet head tube. Because brass or bronze or silver solder is weaker than the steel of the frame tubes, depending on the brazing compound for structural strength leads to frame failure. Note also poor mitering of top and downtubes, which do not butt closely up to head tube. It takes expensive machinery and sometimes time-consuming hand work to make a closely fitting mitered joint, but that's the hallmark of a skilled and conscientious craftsman.

Fig. 2-50: Gary Klein, of Klein Bicycles, is an artist in aluminum frame building. Here is one of his lugless aluminum frames, designed for the racing bicyclist. He plans to make touring bicycles in 1980.

Fig. 2-51: Fork dropout in a Raleigh Carleton handmade frame shows rugged and beautiful work. Dropout eye is for fastening a fender or front carrier, and is threaded for a metric bolt.

Fig. 2-52: A factory-made frame, this DBS Oglaend top-of-the-line bicycle shows fine detail and craftsmanship in lug work around top tube.

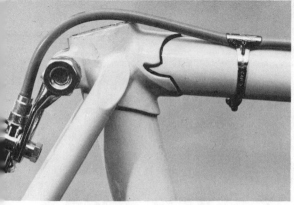

Fig. 2-53: Seat stay cluster of DBS bike shows painstaking brazing and lug filing.

Fig. 2-54: Here is a finished Matt Assenmacher custom-built, handmade frame bicycle. This is a road-racing design, as you will note by the small fork rake, close-ratio gearing and general get-up-and-go appearance. This bike looks as though it's aching to take off.

ure 2-55 is my very own Alex Singer, my pride and joy. (Figs. 2-56 through 2-58 show examples of its quality workmanship.) I saw an Alex Singer clone of this bike for sale recently at $1,250, used. It's worth the price.

Fig. 2-55: Here is my very own Alex Singer bicycle, made to order by this top French custom touring-bicycle builder in Paris. This machine has super-wide range gears, with emphasis on the low side ("Granny" gears). This bike costs upwards of $2,000.

Fig. 2-56: Bottom-bracket shell on my Alex Singer, showing reinforced lug points on the shell, where downtube, seat tube and chainstays meet.

Fig. 2-57: Bottom of bottom-bracket shell on Alex Singer bike, showing brazed-on fittings for derailleur cables.

Fig. 2-58: Top-tube and head-tube lugwork details on my Alex Singer bicycle. Notice that the lug has been built up with brazing compound for added strength, and that much hand work is in evidence in the smooth, sculptured appearance of this joint. This bike is five years old and has seen much use on long tours in this country and abroad. Underneath the top tube is a brazed-on brakecable clip. This bicycle uses Mafac cantilever brakes.

A Word About Lightness

Some racing cyclists, and a few touring cyclists, drill out everything possible on the bike to save a few ounces. I can understand the need for weight saving as far as a racing cyclist is concerned, because hundreds of thousands of dollars in prize money can be at stake for professional racing champions (once a phenomenon only in Europe and now also in this country). Racing is a growing sport in America, and I hope it continues to grow for it contributes enormously to the art and science of cycling in general. Racing cyclists have access to expert mechanics who know when to stop drilling to preserve the strength in frame and components necessary for the human power of the particular rider. Such components as the derailleur cage plates (Fig. 2-59), the brake arms and head tube (Fig. 2-60) and brake levers (Fig. 2-61) are often drilled out. Cutouts are made in the bottom-bracket shell, which admit dirt, by the way. I have also seen the crank arms and chainwheels drilled out to the point where they look like some sort of coarse lacework. Cyclo-tourists should definitely *not* cut out anything, especially on a custom frameset. You would be second-guessing the builder, who has designed and made you a frameset with maximum strength and comfort built into it. Drilling out parts on a touring bike can often lead to disaster on the road. See Table 2-7 in this chapter for parts-weight comparisons.

Parts to Hang on Your Custom Frameset

Normally most builders give you the option of letting them supply certain components with the frameset. Since the builder knows the relevant dimensions and thread cuts of the bottom-bracket shell, headtube and seat tube, I would strongly recommend you select whatever parts you want and let the builder install them. An alternative would be to make sure all parts are English threaded so you know what threading to order on components if installing them yourself. But I do urge you to let the builder install these components of your choice: crankset (spindle, crank arms and chainwheels); headset, seat post and stem. Stem length is a factor of frame design anyway, and the builder knows what length stem you should have, because he already has your body dimensions. The same holds true for the crank arms, which come in different lengths (see Chapters 13 and 14).

On page 149 are my recommendations for components, which I have, in fact, on my own touring bicycle. The price of $1,049.16 is well within the limits for a top-quality touring bicycle available off-the-shelf in the better bike stores, and you have the advantage of having a bike that fits you and has just the equipment you want on it. For brazed-on fittings you might add another $100 maximum. Still a good buy.

In the next chapter, we will explore the joys of two-up tandem cycling, and delve a bit into tricycles.

Fig. 2-59: Some folks will do anything to shave a few ounces off their racing bicycles. Here the rear derailleur cage plates are drilled out.

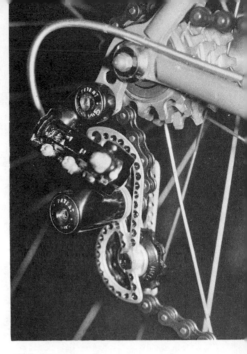

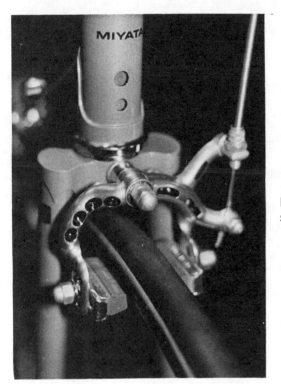

Fig. 2-60: Drilled-out brake arms save a half ounce or so.

Fig. 2-61: Drilled-out brake levers may save something under a half ounce. The top-line Campagnolo levers come predrilled. I would squeeze these levers very, very carefully. Note drilled-out head tube, out of focus, in background.

Table 2-7 Weight Versus Cost

Superlight Part	Part Name	Weight (grams)	Cost	Weight Savings (grams)†	Comparable Part Name	Weight (grams)	Cost
Brakes:	Galli Ti	450	$ 75.00	159	Campagnolo	609	$ 89.98
Chain:	Regina Titanium	255	135.00	169	Regina	424	8.75
Alloy and Titanium Kit*		113	45.00	147	Steel Parts	260	15.00
Crankset:	Avocet	810	107.90	115	Campagnolo	925	119.98
Freewheel:	Cyclo Alloy	205	60.00	202	Steel five-speed	407	8.98
Headset:	Avocet	145	40.00	48	Campagnolo	193	27.98
Hubs:	Avocet Mod. III Titanium	395	125.00	106	Campagnolo Low	501	55.98
Pedals:	Campagnolo Super Record	260	108.00	169	Campagnolo Steel Road	429	46.98
Seat:	Avocet Racing	260	35.00	315	Ideale	575	23.98
Seat Post:	Avocet	215	21.95	100	Campagnolo	315	24.98
Stem:	SR Extra Super Light	210	16.98	37	Cinelli	247	19.50
Toe Clips:	Avocet Alloy	28	5.98	35	Steel	63	2.98
Water-Bottle Cage:	Avocet Alloy	47	6.98	43	Steel	90	4.50
Totals:		3,393	$782.79	1,645		5,038	$449.57

* Stem bolt, binder bolt for rear derailleur, seat binder bolt, brake center bolt, brake nuts, alloy washers for shift levers, bottom-bracket ring, crank arm bolts, chainwheel bolts.

† Selected parts total weight minus total weight of comparable parts.

Note: Most of Table 2-7 came from the excellent 1979–1980 catalogue published by Palo Alto Bicycles, P.O. Box 1276, Palo Alto, Calif. 94302 (415/328-7411).

Table 2-8 Component Selections*

Part	Manufacturer and Model Number	Cost
Crankset, complete †	Avocet Triple, 24–40–50 teeth	$ 117.90
Freewheel	SunTour New Winner Ultra Six, 14–16–19–22–26–32 teeth	15.98
Chain	SunTour Ultra (compatible with freewheel above)	7.50
Hubs	Phil Wood low flange	59.95 (pr.)
Hub skewers	Campagnolo	22.00 (pr.)
Tires	Specialized Touring 700 by 25 centimeters	15.00 (pr.)
Rims	Super Champion 700 by 25 centimeters	22.00 (pr.)
Tubes	Palo Alto lightweight 700 centimeters with Presta valve	7.00 (pr.)
Brakes	Campagnolo Record side-pull	90.00 (pr.)
Brake shoes	Matthauser	14.00 (pr.)
Spokes	D.T. stainless, heavy duty (74) (for 36-hole rims, 2 extra. With nipples)	21.60
Headset ‡	Avocet sealed	49.95
Handlebars §	Cinelli Model 64 Giro d'Italia	
Stem	Cinelli road, Model 1/A	19.50
Saddle	Avocet Touring III	37.95
Seat Post ''	Avocet	21.95
Front derailleur	SunTour Cyclone G.T. with wide-range adapter (for triple chainwheel)	15.00
Rear derailleur	SunTour Cyclone G.T.	21.98
Shifters	SunTour Bar end shifters	12.98
Pedals	Phil Wood sealed bearing	55.00 (pr.)
Bottle	Avocet	1.98
Bottle cage	Avocet	6.98
Toe clips #	Avocet	5.98 (pr.)
Toe straps	Avocet Mod. III	6.98 (pr.)
TOTAL:		$ 649.16
Frameset: (Estimated)		400.00
Total bike (excluding shipping costs)		$1,049.16

* Available from your local bicycle shop or from Palo Alto Bicycles.

† Specify crank length and threading (Lengths are 170, 172.5, 175 mm, bottom-bracket threads are cut English, Italian or French).

‡ Specify English, French or Italian threads.

§ Specify 38- or 40-centimeter width.

'' Specify diameter (25, 25.4, 25.8, through 27.4 in 2-mm increments).

Specify small, medium or large (for varying shoe sizes).

Alternate parts are made by Campagnolo, Shimano, Dia-Compe, Brooks Pro saddle, Ideale Pro saddle, Hi-E rims and hubs. Specify top-of-the line only.

All About the Joy of Tandems and Trikes for Grown-ups

Tandems have fascinated cyclists since the days when the old song said something about how sweet Daisy would look on a bicycle built for two. There is something about a tandem that no single bike can have, and that is the shared intimacy of riding within constant earshot of your partner. You are both riding the same steed, sharing the out-of-doors, the healthful exhilaration of sweeping down the open road.

A fine tandem is a lot easier to pedal than a fine single bike. For one thing, the tandem only weighs about 40 pounds, so you chop off about 8 pounds right there, if you figure two single bikes weigh 24 pounds each (and that's a conservative figure). Two wheels offer less rolling resistance than four. A tandem can go up a hill more easily than a single bike, if both riders pull their weight and pedals are out of sync. (All bets are off if one rider is substantially weaker than the other, and about as heavy.) We discuss out-of-sync pedaling pros and cons later on in this chapter.

A tandem (Fig. 3-1) is a lot steadier in a side wind because there's more weight on the wheels and so it resists being blown off course better than a single bike. Even if one partner is somewhat weaker, the stronger one can compensate for the other, making it possible for them to ride together. You can go longer and farther with a partner who panics at any ride over ten miles, because a tandem is far less tiring. Speaking of gender remainds me that in my old copies of the *Wheelman*, circa 1899,

Fig. 3-1: Typical high-quality tandem. Drive train is cross-over, with front-to-rear crankset on left side, rear bottom bracket to rear freewheel on left side.

the woman was always up front and the man in the rear. It used to be that you would never see a tandem in a club ride. Today not only are tandems in wide use, but the single bikes, according to tandem owners, are languishing in the basement. Tandeming is still somewhat of a novelty, though, and for that reason is a fun thing to do. The stoker (the rider in back) has life a lot easier, too. With no responsibilities beyond being aware of what the captain is up to, the stoker can relax and enjoy the scenery, take pictures, navigate, make turn signals, and spray dogs with Halt (see Chapter 5).

With two reasonably strong riders, even seasoned cyclists on single lightweight road-racing bikes have trouble keeping up with a good tandem. Cycling into a headwind, the singles can easily be left behind. In most cases it still takes a very strong cyclist to draft or keep just behind a pair of strong tandem pedalers.

THE CAPTAIN

We've talked about the stoker, now what about the person up front, whom most tandem riders refer to as the captain. The captain's responsibility is to help the stoker get both feet into pedal toe clips on the takeoff. I might note that because both sets of cranks are connected in the transmission system, any unforeseen reverse pressure on pedals will throw the other rider off stride and make for an unbalanced and temporarily cooler relationship.

The captain should advise the stoker about upcoming potholes or railroad tracks that can't be avoided so the stoker can get some of the weight off the saddle to ease the bump. The stoker needs to know when a turn is going to be made so he can signal it from the rear and both riders can lean into the turn gracefully. If the stoker leans the wrong way at the wrong time the tandem may take a nosedive.

A tandem frame is an irrevocable thing. I see no reason why the woman should not be up front, but if you're going to order a custom frame, you must specify which end you want the small size on. Otherwise you know who will be back in the rear saddle again.

I have mentioned the rear saddle at least twice now, and it's time to point out that one drawback to the stoker's position is that of the derriere over the rear wheel. The captain's bottom is about in the center of the long tandem frame and is far less subject to road shock because the frame absorbs a lot of it. The stoker sits right over the rear wheel, or close to it, and *does* absorb a lot of road shock. So the stoker needs the best saddle money can buy. I would recommend the Avocet WI or WII for a woman stoker, or the same version in a narrower men's saddle, wherever the male sits. In any case, keep your stoker happy, don't skimp on the rear saddle. Oh yes, and the captain can lean forward over a bump, taking a lot of it in his arms. The stoker can too, but to a far more limited extent than the captain. The captain should, of course, always warn about an upcoming stop, and the stoker can keep the captain informed about oncoming cars and other traffic hazards.

Some tandems have three brakes: two caliper brakes, one on each wheel, and a drum brake. The drum-brake control is often worked by the stoker, and should not be used by the stoker without conversation with the captain, who should decide when and how much to brake. On fast downhill runs, for example, it will mostly be up to the stoker to use the drum or disc rear brake to keep speed control and to avoid heat of friction buildup on rims from hard application of caliper brakes. If rims get too hot, air in the tubes can expand and cause a blowout. It happens too often not to emphasize this point.

ABOUT TAKING OFF

Taking off, or starting from a dead start, is a problem that plagues all new tandem riders and is particularly acute for the novice stoker. There's no problem for the captain, who can anticipate when the bike is moving fast enough to safely coast for the second or two it takes to get the other foot into the toe clips. Not so for the stoker, who has to wait for the captain to coast and who will always be lagging behind the captain in getting the other foot into the clips. Sometimes pedaling must be resumed before the other foot is in the toe clips because momentum is lost and the tandem starts to weave.

One way to help the stoker get his feet in the pedals is for the captain to hold the bike up, from a straddled position with both feet on the ground, while the stoker gets *both* feet in the toe clips. Then both can take off. When stopping, the captain should rest both feet on the ground and hold the bike up, while the stoker gets his feet out of the pedals. The stoker may have a brief moment of panic when the tandem stops and leans over to the side a bit, but there's really no danger of it falling over. In fact, even a little 250 cc motorcycle weighs 250 plus pounds, yet you will notice that when the motorcycle, *with* passenger, stops at a stoplight, the passenger always keeps both feet on the pegs while the driver balances the motorcycle. I've seen 98-pound women do that with a humongous Harley Electroglide that weighs in at 900 pounds, *without* the passenger. It's merely a question of balance.

TANDEM RIDING WITH CHILDREN

Between the ages of two and a half and eight, a child simply cannot begin to stay with adult riders; there is no good equipment available for small children and most of them have neither the strength nor the required stamina—at least, certainly not below the age of five. But because it is fun to take the children out for a bike ride, I offer two solutions. The first is a small trailer designed for use with a bicycle, and with a proper hitch. Cannondale Corporation introduced the first sensible bike trailer way back in 1971, and thousands found their way to the back of America's bikes for shopping, touring, and carrying the kids around. Now Cannondale has introduced a much improved version of their original model Bugger, called the Bugger III, which is lighter, has somewhat less rolling resistance, excellent carrying capacity (up to 80 lbs.) and a greatly improved trailer hitch mechanism (Fig. 3-2).

The quick-connect safety hitch dampens road shock and attaches to any size bicycle seat post without tools and without removing your bike carrier. The original version would not fit Campagnolo and similar sizes seat posts, and would not fit over carriers, so the new design is good news indeed. The Bugger III has a tough, molded plastic one-piece chassis with a lower center of gravity than the old model, so it corners better. The 20-inch wheels have sealed-bearing hubs that roll easier and reduce hub maintenance. The trailer has a tie-down harness system which lets you carry two small children safely, and which also doubles as a hold-down for carrying groceries, camp gear or whatever. And an accessory tonneau cover of waterproof pack cloth should keep your load dry and clean, an important feature when you're on a camping trip and run into a summer rain shower.

I think a trailer is a good idea on a camping trip because you can load it up with camping gear for four (clothes, tents, sleeping bags, utensils,

Fig. 3-2: You can tow children along in this Cannondale trailer.

food, etc.) and eliminate the expense and inconvenience of carriers and panniers. If you travel as a group in mulitples of four, a trailer really should be considered. With a trailer, for example, four cyclists can switch off pulling it, since the trailer is quickly detached and remounted. Or, if one rider is a lot stronger than the other three, he or she can pull the trailer. When you arrive at the campsite, you can pull the trailer right to where you want to pitch the tents. And you can go fetch five gallons of water, shop for food without loading up the bike. You will always need lots of water at the camp, and a plastic five gallon container with spigot is very useful for coffee, dishwashing and personal hygiene. I am not too happy about loading up a fine bicycle frame with carriers that stress the frame and scratch the finish, and unless I am cycle camping solo or with one other person I would opt for a trailer. Sure, this trailer weighs 25 pounds, about five pounds less than the original model Bugger, and you are carrying this extra weight. But deduct from this 25 pounds the weight of the carriers and panniers you will not need and you approach about the same weight of these items. So the trade-off of trailer versus carriers and panniers for four bicycles comes close to even in terms of weight. The Bugger III sells for $189.50, the optional tonneau cover for $19.95. From The Cannondale Corporation, 35 Pulaski Street, Stamford, Connecticut 06902.

The second solution makes life easier still and costs a lot less. This is a bolted-on bottom-bracket assembly on the rear stays, and up high enough so even a three-year-old can reach the pedals (Figs. 3-3 and 3-4). This arrangement puts the child in the active stoker role, and as Chuck Harris, who makes and originated the idea of the rear-view mirrors that fasten on glasses, said, "It's like adding a little lawnmower engine." Instead of 40 or 50 pounds of weight, you now have a real little assistant back there who will be much happier in the more active role.

Fig. 3-3: Conversion bottom bracket has been mounted on the rear downtube so a child can be the stoker. An excellent way to carry a child from five years of age and up. *(Photo courtesy "Chuck" Harris)*

Fig. 3-4: Close-up of another conversion unit for a child stoker. Note homemade carrier for a smaller child over rear wheel. *(Photo courtesy "Chuck" Harris)*

Gear the rear cranks so that the stoker/child can match your cadence (see Chapter 2 for gear data). Be sure to use toe clips and straps on all pedals as they are good insurance against feet slipping off pedals and unseating the child, especially on uphill runs. You can still have wide-ratio gearing and fifteen speeds with the child-assist higher bottom bracket.

You can buy a special attachment (bolt-on bottom-bracket set) to convert the tandem for your child from Andrew Hague Cycles, 1 Kipling Grove, Beaumont Leys, Leicester, England, for around $45. The conversion unit comes assembled and fastens onto the rear seat tube. The unit is supplied with chainwheel, cranks, freewheel, boss and Allen keys. It can be used with children from two and a half years up, is adjustable as to height because it can be fitted on the seat tube at the correct height and can move down as the child grows up. It's advisable for pedals to be in phase, according to some tandem riders who have ridden with children, although I do not see why, because you should be able to hold the bike upright while your child gets both feet in the toe clips before taking off. If I had a small child I would experiment with out-of-phase cranks. They should work better than in-phase cranks, because, as noted earlier, out-of-phase cranks smooth out torque delivery, and with a child you can use every bit of smoothness you can get. Figure 3-5 shows Chuck Harris, of Ultralite Shop, Brinkhaven, Ohio, with yet another adaptation of a tandem, this one with a plywood "running board" so the kids can mount more easily and by themselves, and a child carrier over the rear wheel. I'm waiting for Chuck to come up with yet a third bottom bracket for the rearmost stoker. It's not impossible.

TANDEM CLUB

There are now so many tandems on the road that a tandem club has been formed. You can join with other tandem owners on club rides, share information about tandem riding, safety, maintenance and other techni-

cal data. To join, send $3.50 (for your tandem team) to: Malcolm Boyd, Editor, Tandem Club of America, 179 S. Sierra Madre Blvd., Pasadena, California 91107. A copy of the club bulletin can be obtained from Beth Zeichner, Secretary, Tandem Club of America, C-5 West Drive, Princeton, New Jersey 08540. The newsletter has a swap/sell column and is bimonthly.

WHAT TO PUT ON THE TANDEM

After years of tandem riding and looking at new products to hang on my own Schwinn Paramount tandem, I have selected a group of products that experience has proved work well and stand up under the extra stresses of a tandem.

Brakes

First, the brakes. I doubt that anything is more important to safety on a tandem than brakes, unless it is the proficiency of the riders and their own good judgment.

A tandem with two riders weighs about 350 pounds—and more if laden with camping gear. On a steep downhill run a tandem can quickly get up to really frightening speeds, easily to 50 miles an hour and greater. So it's vital that you control speed within the limits of your capability, and consider the nature of the road, its turns and curves and twists, its surface. If you have a straightaway drop, say of five miles on a 5- or 6-percent grade, you know there are no intersecting roads for ten miles and that you are descending into the desert or a sparsely populated rural area, and you are experienced tandemists, let 'er rip. But the usual descent involves winding mountain roads; and around the next bend may be a gravel-strewn road, an overturned truck-trailer, a child weaving around on a small bike, or even a herd of cows crossing the road! I've come upon all of these and so far have been able to stop in time to avoid a collision, because I had kept the tandem under enough control to be able to do so immediately upon making the curve.

The major problem in braking the tandem is heat. Friction generated by brake pads rubbing on wheel-rim flats can blow out tubes and tires with no difficulty at all.

You could use alternate front and rear caliper brakes to keep speed control, but the time will come when you must use both brakes, and then you could be in trouble. My solution is to use a good hub brake. The best brake I have found to date is made by Phil Wood (see Chapter 10), weighs one pound and costs $132, each. I use two. The heat of high-speed runs is dissipated in this brake's disc. So far I have had no problems with brake fade, a phenomenon that affects auto disc and drum brakes, and is due to heat squeezing some of the ingredients out of the lining which then turns into a lubricant. Letting brakes cool usually brings them back to normal. With the Phil Wood brakes I feel much more secure and confident during downhill runs, and when I see a straightaway run I usually let the tandem get up to 45 to 50 miles per hour. We have passed some pretty startled motorists. The $264 for two Phil Wood brakes is a lot of money, but the security is worth it to me.

To use the Phil Wood brake you must use a special Phil Wood hub designed for the brake. Schwinn uses these hubs on its Paramount tandem and sells the Phil Wood brake as an optional extra.

You could use just one Phil Wood on the rear, and use Mafac cantilever brakes fore and aft as well or, better yet, Phil Wood brakes on both wheels. The Phil Wood can be controlled by the stoker, while the captain uses both brake levers up front for the cantilevers.

Shimano makes a drum brake (their Radiax), but it's on a low-quality steel hub, obviously intended for the youth market. Braking quality is excellent, though. It costs around $35, per brake, in your bike shop. Before considering it, measure the inside flats of your dropouts to make sure the Shimano hub will fit. The rear hub is 124 millimeters wide. The dropout-flat-to-dropout-flat widths on most of my one-up bikes is 124.5 or 125 mm, so the stays can be stretched that little bit or spacers can be used to receive this hub. However, there is no Shimano front-wheel hub for their drum Radiax Brake (see Chapter 10) so it can only be used on the rear wheel. I don't like the hub you have to use with this brake. It's steel, weighs 16.9 ounces, and is nowhere near as precision made and free spinning as Shimano's high-quality DuraAce aluminum hub, which weighs 10.8 ounces. I also don't like the fact that the Radiax brake weighs a good 20.8 ounces. So my overall objection to the Radiax is that it looks as though it belongs on a less expensive child's bike, uses an inexpensive hub and, in short, does not seem to me to be the kind of high-quality item that I would like on my tandem. This brake does not, as of this writing, come on any bicycle made in the United States.

I should point out that a hub brake, because it is enclosed, offers far better stopping power than a caliper brake. The same is true, but to a slightly lesser extent, of disc brakes. In the rain, discs take a few seconds to heat up enough to dissipate moisture, before full braking power is available. But discs are a vast improvement over caliper brakes in wet weather.

Bottom Bracket

The bottom-bracket assembly of cones, lock nuts, bearings and spindle takes a beating on any bicycle. On a tandem the beating is doubled. It's not unusual for a bottom-bracket set to wear out in three or four thousand miles of hard use. The Phil Wood bottom-brackets sets, thus far, seem to hold up well; and they have the added advantage of being sealed, so there is one less component to worry about on a trip. The spindles come in 40- and 48-millimeter widths.

Hubs and Spokes

Tandems are hard on spokes. On a trip the problem of spoke breakage can be a real headache, especially because you have to remove the freewheel when a spoke breaks on that side. Most spokes seem to break where they bend out of the hub, at the radius of the spoke under the head. One way to relieve stress at this critical point is to use a wider hub, one with wider flanges. Phil Wood hubs have such a flange (no, I am not a stockholder) and better yet, you buy them drilled for forty-eight spokes. Rims with forty-eight spokes are also available, so if you have had spoke problems, there's your solution! Five-cross lacing with forty-eight spokes is a good combination (see Chapter 15).

I don't like quick-release skewers on tandems: too apt to come loose, or not hold the rear wheel on tightly enough, so the wheel sometimes cocks to the left and rubs on the left chainstay. Yes, you can use dropout fittings to hold the axle where you want it. But it's safer to use a solid steel axle and bolt the wheels in place. And a solid axle is stronger than the hollow axle you need with quick-release skewers.

Handlebars

Use any high-quality bar for the front. There's some disagreement about what's best for the stoker. I would opt for dropped rather than flat or slightly curved flat bars because there are more places to put the hands, and so more ways to avoid fatigue and pressure.

Tires

The narrow-profile tire and the tubular tire can be used for tandem touring. But I prefer a slightly wider tire, such as the Schwinn Le Tour, 27 by 1¼ inches or 700 centimeters by 25 millimeters wide, or the

Michelin T53 27 by 1¼ inches with a tread designed for varied terrain. This is a fairly heavy tire, at 510 grams, versus the Elan's 300 grams, but the difference really is minimal when you consider the added comfort and reliability of the wider-tread, tougher tire. Another excellent tire is the Michelin T54 which comes in both 27-by-1¼-inch and 700-centimeter-by-25-millimeter width. These tires range from $5 to $6 each. Another excellent tire is the Specialized Touring Tire in both 700 centimeters by 25 millimeters or 27 by 1¼ inches. It offers low rolling resistance plus a heavy tread for reliability and comfort. Its cost, around $7.50. You can also get a light folding tire (remember, when I say "tire" I refer to wired-ons, a "tubular" is a sew-up) to serve as a spare, that weighs only 235 grams, in the 700-centimeter or 27-inch size, for $12.50 from Specialized Touring Tire. If it's not available in your bike store, you can order it from Palo Alto Bicycles (see Appendix). Carrying a folding tire saves space, and if you blow a tube on a tandem it's not safe to patch it. It's much better to install a new tube.

The Super Champion rim, in either the 700-centimeter or 27-inch diameter, comes in a 40-hole drilling, which I would use for the front wheel, crossed-three lacing. This rim costs around $12. The Super Champion is also available with 48 spoke holes, which I would use on the rear, as I noted earlier. These drillings are not in wide demand as yet, so you may have to have your bike store order them from the wholesaler; or try shopping by phone first. See Chapter 15 for wheel-lacing instructions.

Derailleurs and Shift Levers

Since you should have wide-range gearing on your tandem, you will need a derailleur that can handle that range. I have tried all the super wide range derailleurs on the market and much prefer the Shimano alloy Crane GS, which has a long cage for handling up to 34 teeth on the rear cog. Shimano also has a new wide-cage front derailleur, their top-line DuraAce EX, Model EA-210, with a trapezium movement that makes shifting smoother and permits wider spacing design of the front derailleur cage. The wider spacing frees you from having to make minute readjustments on the front derailleur when you shift a rear gear (usually needed because the chain angle is altered as it moves from one rear cog to another and the new angle causes the chain to rub on the derailleur cage unless such adjustments are made). The EA-210 weighs but 3.6 ounces. If you order a custom frame, you can have it fitted to a special Shimano braze-on. This fitting permits the front derailleur to be bolted down. A groove in the fitting gives the derailleur vertical adjustment, should you change the outer chainring. (The derailleur cage should be about ⅛ inch above the largest chainring.)

I prefer bar-end shifters because you can shift while still holding the handlebars, and you do not have to lean down to reach the levers on the downtube. Levers on the stem are strictly a hazard because you can snag a vital part if you come barreling down the top tube in a sudden stop and hit a shift lever. Up till now, the problem with bar-end shifters on a tandem is that no one made cables long enough to reach the rear derailleur. You need extra-long cables as it is for bar-end shifters on a single bike. I used to tie cables together and then solder the knot, a workable but ugly solution. You can now get extra-long cables from one California bike shop that specializes in tandems, tandem parts and supplies: Bud's Bike Shop, 217 W. First St., Claremont, California 91711. Bud also sells tandem framesets, and he reports that a new tandem frame builder, Santana, is doing a fine job, but so far only sells through that shop. If you have a tandem problem you might want to phone either Bill McCready or Darryl Le Vesque at their shop, 714/626-3285. They will even take calls on a Tuesday until 10:00 PM Pacific time.

TANDEM FRAMESETS

The better custom frame builders (see Appendix and Chapter 2) will make special sizes of tandem frame front and rear combinations, for about $500 a frame, minimum. Allow up to six months for delivery. Off-the-rack framesets by the English frame builder, Bob Jackson, may be ordered from the better of your local bike shops. The Bob Jackson touring tandem, with fork and headset, will run you about $500.

From surveying the better custom frame builders, I can recommend among them a few who build very fine tandems. They are:

• Tom Boyden, Fastab Cycles, 2706 Glenbrook Drive, Garland, Texas 75041
• Caylor Frames, P.O. Box 1793, Modesto, California 95354
• Colin Laing, 3454 N. First Ave., Tucson, Arizona 85719
• Bill Boston Cycles, P.O. Box 114, Swedesboro, New Jersey 08085

As for components to hang on framesets, I would leave this up to the builder, for two reasons. First, he knows what works best with his frames. Second, he knows how to put them on, what brazed-on fittings are needed. If you do much touring I would advise fenders, fifteen-speed wide-ratio gearing (see Chapter 2) and brazed-on fittings for panniers fore and aft. Two riders really will need front carriers and panniers as well as rear carriers and panniers, if you do cycle touring via the camping route (see Chapter 4). Fifteen speeds are necessary because you are lugging the weight of two riders plus a 40-pound frame plus whatever else you carry. The fifteen speeds let you change into a wider selection of gears to cope with an infinite variety of wind speeds, road grades, and the physical condition of front person and stoker.

You have two choices of crankset configuration, though: the cross-over type (Fig. 3-6) or the same-side type (Fig. 3-7). The cross-over distributes pedaling forces more or less equally on each side, so bike balance is easier. That is, the torque or force of pedaling is on the left side of the

Fig. 3-6: This fine Bertin tandem (see specifications in this chapter) has a very wide gear range necessary for touring. Note that the transmission is cross-over design (front drive chain on left, rear drive chain on right).

rear bottom bracket and on the right side of the front bottom bracket, thus equalizing the power strokes and reducing forces that tend to flex the frame in one direction or the other.

The second of the two crank configurations is your choice between synchronized cranks, where right and left pedals are always in the same o'clock position (Fig. 3-8)—and where these pedals are out of sync, as in Figure 3-9.

An advantage with the sync crank arrangement is that it is much easier to mount the tandem and take off than when pedals are out of sync. For example, both right-side pedals can be at the two-o'clock position (Fig. 3-8) ready for take off. Captain and stoker each put their right foot in the pedal, push down with the foot and at the same time get into the saddle,

Fig. 3-7: Schwinn mid-price-range tandem, Deluxe Twinn Sport 10-speed. This model has a transmission all on one side. Note chain tensioner just behind front chainwheel. More expensive models do not need a chain tensioner because chain slack on front drive is taken up by an offset bottom bracket which can be adjusted so that, in effect, bottom bracket is moved fore or aft as necessary.

pump three or four times, coast long enough to get the left foot into the pedals and continue cycling.

With pedals out of sync, it's a lot more difficult to get going if the right rear pedal is at 9 o'clock when the right front pedal is at 11 o'clock (Fig. 3-9).

One disadvantage with the sync position is that there's a dead spot or null point in pedal power when zero or little torque is being applied to the rear wheel—when cranks are vertical to the ground, as in Figure 3-10. In this position, on an uphill climb, the tandem can lose momentum, and in fact will alternately surge forward and slow up as the synchronized pedals are at 12 o'clock on the same side at the same time. On the other hand, when out-of-sync pedals are used, the pedals are never at a dead spot at the same time. When rear pedals are at the noon and six-o'clock null position, the left front pedal is completing its power stroke (Fig. 3-11). And as the right front pedal comes around to *its* zero torque position, the right rear pedal begins *its* power stroke. So with out-of-sync cranks, pedal power is applied much more evenly throughout the 360 degrees of pedal rotation, and you should find hill climbing easier. Also, with power being applied more smoothly, you don't have two riders putting maximum torque or pressure on the bottom-bracket bearings at the same time, at the same side of the bottom bracket, as in Figure 3-8. Tandem owners who use the out-of-sync pedal arrangement report longer bottom-bracket life. That's been my own experience as well.

How to "Out-of-Sync" Your Pedals

To move your pedals to the more efficient pedaling position where they are out of sync is simplicity itself. On a good tandem you do not have a front chain tensioner. Instead, chain tension is adjusted by an offset bottom-bracket fitting. All you do is loosen the bolts holding this fitting, rotate it until the chain is loose enough to slip off one of the front chainwheels, rotate one set of cranks until they are out of sync and readjust the front bottom bracket for proper chain tension. Now when the right front pedal is at 2 o'clock, the right rear pedal should be at 12 o'clock.

On the less expensive tandems without an adjustable front bottom-bracket assembly, front chain tension is taken up by a chain tensioner (Fig. 3-12). In this case just loosen the chain-tensioner jockey wheel where it slides in the fitting, slip the chain off the front chainring, and move the pedals to the out-of-sync position as shown above. Readjust the tensioner so there is about ¼- to ⅜-inch chain slack, at most.

TANDEM SELECTIONS

I don't have space to list all tt manufacturers' specs on tandems, but here is a list of manufacturers who have been making fine-quality tandems for many years. You should be able to find their tandems in at least

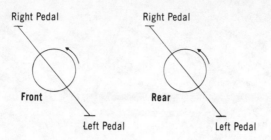

Fig. 3-8: When cranks are synchronized, pedals remain in the same relative position. When front right-side pedal, for example, is at ten o'clock, rear right-side pedal will be at the same position. This makes it easier to take off from a standing start.

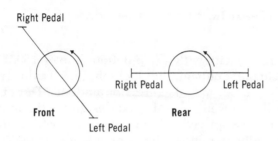

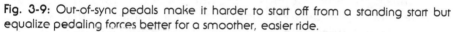

Fig. 3-9: Out-of-sync pedals make it harder to start off from a standing start but equalize pedaling forces better for a smoother, easier ride.

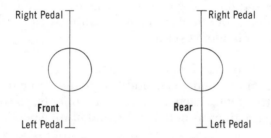

Fig. 3-10: In-sync cranks have a power "dead spot" during which little or no power is applied to the rear wheel, making for a loss in tandem forward momentum until pedals get past the 12-o'clock position.

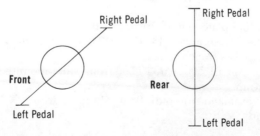

Fig. 3-11: Out-of-sync pedals do not have the "dead spot" of power transmission shown in Figure 3-10 because when the rear right-side pedal, e.g., is at the dead or zero torque transmission spot as shown, the front right-side pedal is at the power stroke at 2 o'clock. Pedaling is smoother.

Fig. 3-12: Schwinn Deluxe Twinn Tandem five-speed

one bike store in any city with a population of over 150,000. These are Urago, Follis, Gitane, Pohliagi, Bob Jackson, Jack Taylor and Schwinn.

There are many other manufacturers of tandems. Out of these I have selected a few as representative of good design for the money. We start off with the two lower-priced Schwinn tandems, which are a bit heavy for serious tandeming but fine for beginning tandem fun. You can always sell these units and move up in quality. The problem is that there's a quantum leap in price between the mid-range Schwinn tandems that we start with here and the really top-quality tandems. You can also buy less expensive tandems, but they are heavy, cumbersome, and guaranteed to take the joy out of tandem cycling.

Schwinn Deluxe Twin Sport Tandem 10-Speed (Fig. 3-7)[1]

Schwinn makes three tandems in addition to the Paramount lightweight, which are pretty much alike except for components, so we will list them all here, with variations as noted at the end of the specification table.

Specifications:
Frame: High-tensile steel lugless construction
Frame Sizes: 22 inches front, 19 inches rear
Handlebars: Dropped alloy front, flat rear, on steel stems
Saddles: Padded vinyl on steel seat posts
Crankset: Alloy dual plateau with 39 and 52 teeth
Freewheel: Tandem design with 14, 17, 20, 24 and 28 teeth
Hubs: Alloy, 36 spokes front and rear
Derailleurs: Shimano TT 500 rear, TT290 front, stem-mounted shift levers
Pedals: Steel rattrap
Brakes: Front, Weinmann side-pull. Rear, Maillard drum
Weight: 52 pounds
Cost: $375

[1] Five-speed version (Fig. 3-12) uses semi-hi-rise bars front and rear, has one-piece steel cranks, weighs 64 pounds, costs $239.95. The coaster brake one-speed model (Fig. 3-13) weighs 64 pounds, costs $219.95

Fig. 3-13: Schwinn Tandem, coaster brake, single speed

Soma Prestige Tandem 15-speed

Here's a fine tandem at a relatively modest price. Uses top-grade Japanese components throughout to wind up with a very light, responsive machine. Note that you can get frame-size choices to your order.

Specifications:
Frame: All hand-brazed double-butted chrome moly steel tubing. Chrome moly fork tubing with Cinelli-style fork crown
Frame Sizes: To order. Just about any combination. Allow 120 days for delivery
Handlebars: Light alloy dropped bars front and rear, on forged alloy stem front, steel tandem stem rear
Saddles: Ariake New Jaguar 2 on alloy seat posts
Crankset: Sugino Super-Maxy Tandem with 32-, 46-, 53-teeth chainwheels
Freewheel: SunTour Pro-Compe 14–30 teeth (combination of 32 front and 30 back give a low "Granny" gear for hill climbing)
Hubs: Shimano high flange, alloy with quick-release on front only. Rear-wheel axle has bolts. 36 spokes front and rear in 4X pattern, 14-gauge steel. Rims are Araya alloy, 27-by-1¼-inch tires
Derailleurs: Front, SunTour SL, bar-end shifters. Rear, SunTour VS
Pedals: KKT Pro VIC2 light alloy with toe clips and straps
Brakes: Mafac cantilever-type tandem brakes on front and rear *plus* Dia-Compe alloy center-pull on rear
Weight: 39 pounds
Cost: $1,000

Schwinn Paramount Touring Tandem 15-Speed

Schwinn's top-line tandem. Ranks with the best made by anybody anywhere. Light, responsive, a joy to ride (Fig. 3-14).

Specifications:
Frame: Hand-brazed frameset of 4130 chrome moly steel. 4130 steel has the same ultimate tensile strength and yield strength after brazing as Reynolds '531,' Columbus, Ishiwata, Tange, or any of the other high-carbon, chrome moly tubing used on fine bikes. The fork is 4130 steel, taper-gauged tubular, reinforced for the stresses of tandem riding

Fig. 3-14: Schwinn 15-speed Paramount tandem

Frame Sizes: [2] Paramount touring tandems have men's front, Mixte-style rear. Two sizes: 22-inch front, 19-inch rear; 24-inch front and 22-inch rear. (See Chapter 2 for sizing data)

Handlebars: Front, Cinelli alloy drop. Rear, GB alloy all-rounder style on Cinelli forged alloy front stem and heavy-duty forged steel bracket, rear

Saddles: Cinelli Unica-Nitor suede leather top on plastic base on alloy seat posts

Crankset: Campagnolo Record Strada three-piece alloy 15-speed with 36-, 46- and 54-teeth chainwheels with tandem cross-over drive

Freewheel: Heavy-duty tandem design with 14-, 16-, 19-, 25- and 31-tooth cogs

Hubs: Phil Wood stainless steel heavy-duty tandem hubs with sealed bearings adaptable for disc brakes. Forty-eight holes, laced with TD .080 stainless steel spokes into Super Champion alloy rims with 27-by-1¾-inch tires

Derailleurs: Front, Campangolo Record Alloy. Rear, Maeda SunTour VGT alloy wide range, with Maeda ratchet bar end shifters

Pedals: Campagnolo Super Leggeri alloy rattrap with toe clips and straps

Brakes: [3] Front, Mafac cyclomoteur. Rear, Weinmann Vanquer. Both front and rear equipped with Matthauser brake blocks

Weight: 43 pounds

Cost: $1,395

Bertin Model T-2 Tandem 15-speed (Fig. 3-6)

Bertin tandems, like all Bertin bicycles, are made in France by a former cycle-racing champion, André Bertin, and are designed for rugged use over the cobblestone roads of Northern France and Belgium. The frame and components are designed for comfort, to take up road shock.

To be able to climb steep hills, this tandem has wide-range gearing with the low end a 36-tooth chainwheel front and a 32-tooth cog rear.

Specifications:

Frame: Lugless construction of special Vitus 172 tandem series tubing. Head tube is 38 millimeters in diameter rather than the standard 32 millimeters, so

---

[2] Also comes in men's front and rear in 22–22 and 24–24 inches. Special sizes can be made on request—as for a very short stoker and tall front person—at extra cost. See dealer for details.

[3] As of this writing, Phil Wood disc brakes are optional and cost extra.

a stronger, oversized butted steering tube and stronger tandem head set bearings can be used. Top and down tubes are 38 and 30 millimeters, respectively, rather than the usual 26- and 28-millimeter tubes. These tubes, along with a 49-millimeter oval bottom tube, eliminate the need for extra bracing, resulting in a lighter frame. Forks are extra-large round-oval design

Frame Sizes: 21½-inch front, 19½-inch rear man-man and 22.8-inch front and 21½-inch rear, man-man. Check supplier for other size availabilities

Handlebars: Milremo pro 420 millimeters on forged alloy stem

Saddles: Avocet extra-light with alloy frames on Milremo micro-adjusting seat posts

Crankset: TA 1690 triple plateau with 36-, 48- and 56-teeth chainrings

Freewheel: Special cyclo-tandem heavy duty, 14 to 32 teeth

Hubs: Maxi-Car tandem hubs with 140-millimeter flanges rear with 40 extra-heavy tandem spokes. Front, Maxi-Car tandem. Super Champion 700-centimeter rims with Wolber Super Sport tires. Hubs have friction-free labyrinth seals

Derailleurs: Huret Duopar

Pedals: Maillard black alloy with toe clips and straps

Brakes: Rear, 130-millimeter drum brake rear, Mafac Cantilever front and rear

Weight: 40 pounds

Cost: $1,695

ADULT TRICYCLES

If you're beyond the age when you think you can learn how to ride a bicycle, or if, for some reason, you cannot or should not balance yourself on one, adult tricycles might be the answer for you.

There is a wide variety of these tricycles, however, and it's important to get a good one, because with these bikes, the best costs so little more. In this market, you're paying a larger price because of the small demand and limited production.

Actually, a good tricycle isn't much less efficient than a good bicycle. In England, there have been racing events in which tricyclists have attained speeds of forty miles an hour or better.

The real difference between a bicycle and a tricycle of equal quality lies in the greater maneuverability of the two-wheeler and the consequent greater skill it takes to ride one.

Still, rather than give up the joy of outdoor pedaling, a tricycle can be an excellent compromise. One sees great numbers of tricycles in retirement areas.

Three Types of Tricycles

There are three basic types of tricycles available. One is a rather heavy (around 65 pounds) unit with 26-inch tires, complete with detachable rear wire utility basket; a trike conversion unit so you can convert a reasonably good ten-speed into a fairly lightweight (38 pounds or so)

Fig. 3-15: Schwinn Tri-Wheeler adult tricycle with differential transmission

ten-speed trike; and a tailor-made tricycle with any gear ratio you wish, made of Reynolds '531' butted tubing and also with ten speeds.

If you want a tricycle because you have a balance problem and feel more secure on a trike, I recommend the Schwinn Tri-Wheeler as the best of the domestic models (Fig. 3-15). This model has a differential transmission system, which means that the trike will corner more accurately because the rear wheels rotate at a differential speed, depending on the degree of turn. You can power this tricycle into a turn with less tendency to wheel lift, and if the wheel does lift it won't be the power wheel, unlike a conventional trike with direct chain drive.

If balance is not your problem, however, and you want a tricycle for winter use over snow or ice, or just for the fun of it, I can recommend a conversion unit that lets you change your lightweight ten-speed bicycle into a lightweight tricycle, with either direct drive (pedals turn as long as the trike is rolling; there's no freewheel) or ten-speed. I prefer direct drive because I can back up as well as go forward.

How to Make Your Own Lightweight Tricycle

I like to use a tricycle. It's fun, particularly in winter when the roads are ice covered and really too slippery for a two-wheeler. You can convert an old bike, or even a good bike, to a tricycle and reconvert it back to a two-wheeler in an hour or so.

There are two or three conversion kits on the market to transmute a two- to a three-wheeler. I like the one made in England by Ken G. Rogers, 71 Berkeley Avenue, Cranford, Hounslow, Middlesex. TW4 6LF, for about $75, including U.S. duty. I converted an old Schwinn Super Sport lugless frame (a fine frame, by the way) into a trike for winter use (Fig. 3-16). To make the conversion:

STEP ONE: Lace up whatever wheels you want on the special hubs furnished (see Chapter 15). You must use these hubs, because they are made to fit a tapered axle. I would suggest Super Champion 700-centimeter-by-25-millimeter rims with narrow-profile tires (which are definitely not the type on my tricycle, but I was using up old parts at the time).

STEP TWO: Remove the rear wheel and derailleur from the old bike, as well as the seat binder bolt.

STEP THREE: Find extra links for your chain or install a new, longer chain. You will need about four extra links, the same make as your chain.

STEP FOUR: Remove the space bar between the cage of an old front derailleur, and install a jockey wheel from an old rear derailleur, for use as a chain tensioner. I did not use this setup in the trike shown in Figure 3-16, until I figured out why the chain kept jumping off the rear cog: too loose. There's absolutely no way you can adjust chain tension otherwise.

STEP FIVE: Adjust the tensioner to your chainline, leave a bit of slack on the chain.

STEP SIX: You do have your choice of using a five speed freewheel or a single gear on the rear. If you use a five-speed freewheel you will, of course, not have to worry about chain tension, because the rear derailleur automatically takes up the slack. Personally, though, I prefer a fixed gear on my trike, as noted earlier. This way I can back up as well as go forward, which shakes up motorists no end as I move back and forth while waiting for a stoplight, or back up out of a diagonal parking slot.

Fig. 3-16: A conversion of a two-wheeler to a lightweight, fixed-gear tricycle

The terrain is flat around Chicago, so I don't need multi-gears. You can, of course, also use the two- or three-plateau chainring setup on your existing bike so you can have the same number of gear changes you are used to. My conversion added 12 pounds to the Super Sport, which, as a trike, weighs in at 38 pounds, or around the weight of one of the less expensive two-wheelers. Since there's only one brake on the Super Sport cum trike (there being nowhere to fasten a rear brake) I like the direct drive (pedals turn when the bike moves, no freewheeling). I can get more aerobic exercise by putting back pressure on the pedals when I want to stop. In fact, I almost never use the front brake, which is now a drum brake (not shown).

STEP SEVEN: Okay, now you are ready to fasten the adapter unit onto the bike. The unit slides into the rear dropouts (Fig. 3-17) and is bolted in place there.

STEP EIGHT: Now you fasten the two reinforcing stays, supplied with the conversion kit. The upper part of the stays fastens onto the seat post binder bolt, and it may have to be a longer bolt than the one that came with the bike. The lower end of the reinforcing stays is clamped onto the axle housing of the adapter unit (Fig. 3-18).

STEP NINE: Make sure the chainline is accurate (Fig. 3-19). You have some leeway in chainline by using spacers on either side of the rear cog or freewheel.

The Rogers kit is very clean-cut and makes a very good-looking trike. You could, with some ingenuity, fasten a wire basket on the rear. For a ten-speed conversion, Rogers supplies an adapter which slips into a mounting fitting on the conversion unit, to which you can attach a rear derailleur (Fig. 3-20). Rogers also makes lightweight trike frames, in case you are interested in one for touring, or for racing, or for just plain high performance. Send for his latest price list.

Oh yes, the Rogers conversion unit weighs 7 pounds (3½ kilos), so whatever your bike weighs now, add 7 pounds, plus the weight of the spokes, rims, tires and tubes. As I said, I added about 12 pounds to my own Super Sport, including the weight of the rear wheels and the front drumbrake, and it is a lot of fun. Somehow the conversion looks racy, which is fine by me.

A Tandem Trike

If you put a Ken Rogers special trike conversion unit on your tandem you can combine the features of tandem togetherness and comradely cycling, working in harmony close enough to hold a conversation, with

Fig. 3-17: Conversion unit slides into rear dropouts.

Fig. 3-18: Two reinforcing stays or braces run from conversion unit drive shaft housing to the seat post binder bolt.

Fig. 3-19: When installing conversion unit, make sure chainline is accurate. This is especially important for single-speed, fixed gear. Not shown is a front derailleur with old rear-derailleur jockey wheel, installed on chain stay, used to take up chain slack. Keep chain under proper tension so it does not jump off cogs.

Fig. 3-20: There is a brazed-on boss on axle housing, just to right of the U-shaped cog bend, to fasten a derailleur if you want a five- or ten-speed tricycle.

the features of a tricycle—stability, no problems balancing, more relaxed cycling. I did and it makes tandeming, especially on wintry, snowy streets, much safer and, for me, more fun. One word of caution, though. Adding the Rogers trike adapter means, as noted, you have no brake on the rear wheel, and so braking must be done only on the front wheel, which cuts braking power in half. If you have enough fork clearance, and brakes with long enough caliper arms (they come in different lengths), you may be able to put a double set of caliper brakes on the front wheel, one set in front and one behind the fork. Or you can put a drum brake on the front wheel, plus the caliper brake that grips the rim. You'd better have a strong fork, though, because stresses in stopping with a hub brake plus a caliper brake can bend the fork. You can't put caliper brakes on the rear wheels because there's no place to attach them, and you can't substitute a drum brake on the rear wheel because you can use only the hub that comes with the trike adapter unit, and drum brakes are integral with their own hub. The same applies to a disc brake, used on some of the child "Chopper"-style bikes.

You might experiment with a Shimano disc brake next to a fixed rear cog on the adapter unit. I haven't done it myself, but it might just work.

How to Ride a Tricycle

Tricycles can be dangerous! Yes, *very* dangerous, if at first, without due caution, you just climb up into the saddle and take off. I have let dozens of people of all ages and strengths try my tricycle, and, without exception, each one would have run into a tree, or a bush, or even lost control right out in traffic, had I not started them off in the center of a huge school yard on a Saturday. I'm not clear in my own mind exactly why even highly seasoned cyclists have such trouble coping with a three-wheeler. I know I did. My first ride on a trike was in Central Park in New York City, and the first thing I did—ridiculously, I thought at the time—was turn and hit a tree. I just couldn't control the thing. I got on again, and ran right off the sidewalk into the middle of the street. Fortunately, it was on a weekend, a day when only muscle-powered vehicles are allowed on Central Park roads, so all I did was imperil myself and a few other skilled bicyclists who maneuvered, muttering, out of my out-of-control way. It took about fifteen or twenty minutes for me to realize I was doing at least two things wrong. First, I was afraid to turn the handlebars to avoid a tree for fear I'd fall over, as I would have on a bike if I had turned that sharply. Second, I tried to avoid going the wrong way by leaning in the opposite direction, which for some reason (that escapes me) only makes the trike obstinately go the wrong way, only more so. Finally, after hours of practice, I realized that the only way you can safely make a turn at slow or moderate speeds is to lean slightly *away* from the direction of turn, instead of, as on a two-wheeler, *into* the direction of turn. In other words, on a trike, to turn right, you lean left a bit, and to turn left, you lean right, so that your weight is *always* on the outer wheel that wants to lift off the ground. It's a bit more vital to lean on the left wheel, and somewhat more heavily, when you turn right, because in most trikes, as in mine, that's the driving wheel, and you need traction when it's slippery

One final note of caution: When you're learning to ride a trike, a particularly dangerous thing to do is to ride on the sidewalk over a driveway that's on an incline into the street, as are most driveways. As you ride across the incline, the trike will try to turn into the street, and if you are afraid to simply force the wheel back so that you go straight, for fear you'll fall over, you *will* go out into the street, right into traffic. It happened to me, and it has happened to several skilled cyclists I let try my trike. Now I advise anyone who wants a trike to bring the machine to a large vacant parking lot or school yard and, very slowly at first, ride around until you have trained yourself to lean *against* the direction of turn, retrained your sense of balance not to send danger signals when you make sharp turns to keep from going off in an unwanted direction and learned how good your brakes are.

About Winter Riding on the Tricycle

Many city streets are slanted to the right for drainage purposes. In any weather the slant on some streets requires a bit of left lean on your part to keep the trike on the straight and narrow.

In winter, the problem is exaggerated by slippery ice and snow. You need to practice control of the trike on slippery streets before venturing very far. I have found that without a lot of leftward lean the trike will just slide into the curb on the right. Sometimes the trike will just sort of drift over to the curb and to get it back I have to pedal hard and lean hard to the left. For a two-wheel cyclist, a trike can be a strange beast indeed, but, as I said, it's fun.

UNICYCLES

Strictly in the gimmick and toy area is yet another cycling variation, the unicycle (Fig. 3-21). This is a one-wheeled cycle with a banana seat, which children seem to be able to ride with great facility for short distances, and with a lot of fun and enjoyment. Personally, I'd rather try a delayed parachute fall—at least I'd have a chance for an easy landing.

But, if your child wants a unicycle, I'd recommend a Columbia or Schwinn unicycle. Columbia furnishes a four-page instruction manual on how to ride the thing, which may ease the pain of the learning process. The Columbia model also seems to be the best made and comes in

Fig. 3-21: Schwinn unicycles

a 20-inch or 24-inch wheel size, the choice of which depends on your child's age, or your own size, if you're the one who wants to learn this circus trick. The manufacturer calls this "A new fun fad . . . ," which I suppose it is.

Bicycle Commuting, Touring and Camping— a Fun Way to Travel the World

Perhaps historians will someday point to the summer of 1979 and say, "That's when it all started." That was when thousands of people from the steaming hot gas lines that wound around blocks in Southern California gave up in disgust and bought bicycles. It was the time when gasoline and construction costs forced a decline in new-car sales, and another startling jump in bicycle sales. It was when the bicycle once again became the vehicle of the future, an odd irony of our modern age.

At a point in history when travel is becoming prohibitively expensive and the idea of a long-distance car vacation seems a hazardous undertaking to many people, the bicycle, the simple, unsophisticated bicycle, which doesn't go from zero to fifty in four seconds or impress dates with mag wheels, is taking over again.

Although their numbers are still relatively small (for reasons we will look at shortly), several hundred thousand Americans ride their bicycles to work. If you add students, the numbers climb into the millions. And although statistics are very hard to come by, many thousands of Americans are taking that vacation on two wheels. They are learning that bicycling is a cheap, healthy and, in the case of commuting, surprisingly quick mode of transportation. In this day of diminishing expectations, the bicycle is an anomaly. There is virtually no limit to its potential as a means of transportation or a pleasure-giving machine. You can ride almost anywhere for as long as your body will push the bike, and you do not have to stop for gasoline or oil. A few tools and accessories are all you need.

In this chapter we will consider traveling by bicycle in a variety of ways, broken down into two larger categories: commuting and touring. These are essentially different uses of the bicycle, and both serve to demonstrate why the bicycle is to become one of the dominant means of transportation in the late twentieth century.

COMMUTING BY BIKE: SAVING TIME AND MONEY WHILE AVOIDING STRESS AND HEADACHES

It was not so long ago that the person who bicycled to work was considered rather odd. People safely ensconced in their warm autos would stare at the cyclist cruising by the traffic jam-up as though he were a circus freak. Maybe it wasn't so much wide-eyed amazement as blank, uncomprehending awe. A half generation later things are quite different. People don't stare at bicyclists anymore (who would, with all of the bikers, joggers, roller skaters and unicyclists on the trails these days). There *are* bike paths in many places, and more frequently there are bike routes or separate bike lanes. But government and business have been slow to react to the need for bike-related facilities, and this has slowed the growth of commuting. With the burgeoning movement toward bike commuting, things will just have to change.

Witness some of these developments:

—With an advanced system of bike paths and routes, and the very important involvement of departments of the federal government in the area, greater Washington, D.C., has an estimated 70,000 persons who commute regularly by bike.

—In Denver, where the bicycle has long been a part of city traffic and transportation planning, 25,000 commuters use extensive paths and bike routes to get to work. There, too, industry and business have taken care to provide some services to biking employees. The city has also provided bike racks that are thief-proof.

—In Oregon, the state ensures that part of the state gas-tax revenues be plowed back into building local bicycle lanes; and the city of Portland has taken full advantage of the money to build a city-wide system of bike routes that extends from the downtown area out into the Willamette Valley.

—In state after state, cities are designing bicycle routes to facilitate bike movement to downtown, using the bicycle in the transportation plans as one of the main means of getting around town.

—The city of New York has added special bike lanes on some major thoroughfares and on the well-traveled Queensboro Bridge linking Queens to Manhattan. Commuters now come daily by bicycle from all five boroughs, and the numbers are just beginning to rise. The city has also installed bike racks in train stations and parking garages, as well as in some municipal buildings, and has purchased metal bike lockers to lease to bike commuters.

—In San Diego, where the city transit service installed bike racks on buses, the gas crunch caused a 500 percent increase in ridership by cyclists.

These are only a few examples of how pressure from bikers on city hall or federal government agencies has produced some reaction. In the private sector, with some notable exceptions, business and industry have not made much in the way of concessions to the bike boom. The largest problems include bike racks (the need for them), showers (the lack of them) and the absence of storage for the cyclists' personal effects. This lack of attention to bikers' needs is surprising. Business leaders seem to be interested in physical fitness—many companies sponsor sports teams and encourage their workers to get exercise on a regular basis—but fail to provide the facilities that their workers would need to ride their bicycles to work. We will return to this problem and propose some solutions in the sections that follow.

For now, you will want to know how to go about becoming a commuter. Riding your bike to work is very simple, which is the beauty of it. First of all, you must decide that this is what you really want and need to do—it is much easier to chuck the whole thing and get back into the car every morning. But if you need exercise and feel that bicycling provides good exercise, then commuting may be for you. Bicycling to work will probably take no more time than using any other means of transportation, and you'll get exercise while you do it. Various studies have compared the time it takes to commute by car and by bicycle. One such study in Chicago showed the average commuting distance to be 6.9 miles, and the average speed to be 22 miles per hour for the car, a trip of roughly 19 minutes, whereas the trip for the bicycle at 12 miles per hour is 34 minutes. Thus, the car *seems* much faster. But consider that a car must be parked, often involving some minutes of delay at garages, and that the car must be started, warmed up and must sit in long traffic tie-ups. The bicycle gains much, if not all, of the time back, because it is so easy to park. Furthermore, if you need more convincing, the upkeep of the bicycle is less than one penny a mile (in fact, two-tenths of a penny), whereas the car runs you about twenty-five cents a mile. The train or bus will be much cheaper than the auto, but at a dollar fifty for a round trip or more, the train is still expensive. In some areas the bus will be a bargain, but it will also be much slower than the bicycle when you consider the agonizing time spent waiting for it to show up.

Once you have decided to pedal to work, you should make sure that there is a safe place to store your bicycle, preferably within the building in which you work. If you use a high-quality touring bicycle, the bike should, of course, be in your sight all day or secure in a locked room at all times. Many office buildings have storage space in the basement. If you have to lock the bike out of doors, be sure to carry a good case-hardened metal chain and a heavy security lock (see Chapter 5 for a discussion of locking the bike). Lock the bike in an outdoor place where there is plenty of pedestrian traffic so a thief does not have any time by himself to work on the lock.

What about the bike you ride to work? Well, it can be the finest ten-speed you can afford, if you have a secure place to keep it—or, if you ride mostly on the flats, a cheap five-speed or even a three-speed bike will do for up to five or six miles one way. (There's more on inexpensive bikes for commuting in Chapter 1.)

In early spring and late fall you will, if you are a nine-to-fiver, ride during the dark of the dawn and of the evening. You will need lights and, to make you visible from all sides, reflectors. (Please see Chapter 5 for more details on lights to see by and to be seen by.) Never, but never, go out at night without lights of some kind. On brightly lighted city streets you will need brighter lights that stand out as contrast against existing light.

Because tubular tires (Chapter 9) are thin and flat prone, they aren't reliable enough over rubble- and glass-strewn city streets. In general, reliability is what you need in a commuting bike so you can get to work on time. Of course, carry a spare tube and tire irons just in case, for your regular tires.

Planning the Route

More years ago than I care to think about, when I started commuting to my office from Grosse Pointe to downtown Detroit, I used my car to plan a route that combined low traffic, directness and safety. I went through streets with the signs in my favor and parked cars dotting the curbs en route so I would not be scrunched over to the curb by cars and trucks. There's always a three-foot lane between parked cars and moving traffic, and that's all I needed. You must watch out for car doors suddenly opening, though. A rearview mirror (Chapter 5) is very helpful in assessing the volume of traffic behind you, but, because it's monocular, not the speed at which cars are catching up. But at least you can tell in your little mirror clipped to glasses or helmet whether or not it's safe to swing out into the car lane to avoid an opening car door . . . a dog . . . a child chasing a ball . . . a car backing out of a driveway, or any of the other myriad avoidance situations that call for evasive action on your part.

Back to route planning. If you work downtown, you will, of course, eventually have to cope with a lot of traffic. My advice is simply to learn to be steely-nerved about traffic. For the first week you will be rigid with fright. I was. Every car around me reeked of lethality. Soon, however, my faith in the American driving public was almost restored as, miracu-lously, I kept arriving at work on time, unscathed and in daily growing health. Common-sense rules like keeping to the curb at stop signs and stoplights, not trying to rush things, letting the pack of cars behind clear the intersection first so you don't compete as you cross, things like that, you will learn in a few days. Cars move slowly in congested streets, meaning you can move at least as fast, or faster. Just watch out for cabs and buses. Neither give way to you. Be resigned and let them go, i.e., stay away from them, it's an unequal battle.

In a city new to me I use a detailed city-street map to chart my way, at first, marking attractive routes in red. Then I drive over them and finally bicycle down them. Sometimes the route seems devious, but going a little bit out of the way avoids high-traffic roads and streets. Use bike lanes if available, but be aware that signs that say "Bicycle Path" or

"Bicycle Route" soon become invisible to motorists and will not make life easier for you. I would prefer to go a mile or so out of my way to use a bike trail alongside a lake or through a park if by so doing I get away entirely from city traffic. But be aware that at night, at least in large cities, hoodlums may infest secluded bike lanes. During spring and fall, when it's dark, I prefer the relative safety of well-lighted city streets. I have also found that the post–World War II emphasis on high-speed suburb-to-downtown expressways is a real boon to us cyclists. These highways relieve secondary roads of traffic, and there are lots of them paralleling freeways into town, with all the stop signs in your favor.

Check your local bicycle club. They may already have plotted a route downtown. For example, the Harrisburg, Pennsylvania, Bicycle Club has published a booklet entitled *62 Tried and True Bicycle Routes*. Any bicycle store can tip you off about local bike clubs.

Trying the Route

For the first few weeks, until you build up muscles and have memorized the location of every pothole, hidden intersection and pit stop (if you drink a lot of coffee at breakfast, as I do), take it easy. You can comfortably pedal at eight miles an hour no matter what your physical condition may be, short of being an absolute invalid. So plan accordingly. You'll find as you cycle to work regularly that, within a few weeks, what took an hour now takes forty-five minutes. Every day you will cut a minute or two off your time. If you can leave your bike safely *inside* your office, there's no need to ride it home every day. Try alternating your old way of getting to work (if there is public transportation, or if you can share a ride) with cycling.

Carry a light rain suit (See p. 242) in case of a downpour en route. Learn about dressing for cold weather and don't let anything down to 20 degrees Fahrenheit and over two inches of snow or ice on the road stop you from cycling to work. You will make your own summer as you cycle during the winter, by creating body heat through use of muscles. Your heart will know the difference!

Some of you who have been using a company car or government-owned vehicle may be able to be reimbursed for not using it to get to work. In 1977, Robert duVall, a California state employee, won the right to be reimbursed for not using his government-owned car. The state did not pay him for the actual cost of using his bicycle instead (which would have been minuscule in any case), but he did get some money for not using a state car. And the Association of Pennsylvania State College and University Faculties actually reimburses employees at the rate of four cents per mile, for cycling to work. Isn't it ridiculous that these should be isolated cases? Here we are, at the beginning of what seems to be a permanent fuel shortage—in a country where everyone from the chief of state and corporate presidents on down emphasizes health through vigorous exercise—and nothing, or very little, is being done to encourage bicycle commuting. Yet commuting to work by bike saves energy . . . promotes health . . . unclogs city streets and parking areas . . . and gets you to work all in one fell swoop. Industry supports costly executive health plans, gives business leaders time off to exercise, yet makes almost zero effort at making it possible to maintain physical fitness in the most practical of ways, by using the time otherwise wasted riding to work in a car or train. I find that I plan my day's activities as I cycle to work, so even during this period I am on the job, so to speak.

What's needed is permission to bring the bike up the elevator to the office, at least via the freight elevator. Or down to a basement secure bike parking area. Lockers and showers, on the European co-ed principle, would be ideal, because you could get to work invigorated, shower, and change into laundry-fresh clothes ready to give your all during the day. I did that for years, but I was probably the only business executive in the Chicago Loop who was so lucky. Many's the day I would take the elevator up from the basement locker/shower area I shared with building maintenance personnel, and be standing in the elevator obviously just out of the shower, in a nice white shirt, neatly pressed suit, no coat or hat, feeling refreshed, to be stared at by already tired office workers, wearied from the crush of traffic, the crunch of public transportation and the chill wind of a cold winter day. (Every Saturday I drove downtown to replace my wardrobe.)

Bike Storage

There are several makes of bicycle-storage lockers on the market that can be closed and locked just like their smaller counterparts, the coin-operated locker at railroad, bus and airport depots. There's lots of room for them in odd corners of auto parking garages. But you never see them installed. In Europe, where cycle commuting is a way of life, there are guarded bike facilities in cities and secure bike racks in factory parking lots. But not in America—not yet, anyway. To try to park your bike in a car parking lot or garage is, for the most part, to invite stares and often rude remarks about where you can park it.

A few years ago I wrote a letter to the editor of one of the major Chicago daily newspapers asking for an expression of interest about starting a bicycle commuter's club. The thought was that it would operate out of a store, perhaps, or an old warehouse, where we could have showers, a concierge-cum-guard and lockers. Jogging was in its infancy then, but mostly joggers responded to the letter. I would guess that today such a club would be more viable. I queried local health clubs, but no dice. No place to put the bikes. Ditto local YMCAs.

There are, to be sure, more and more bike racks being installed outside office and factory buildings these days, but not nearly enough to handle the bike traffic. And bikes really aren't secure out there. My advice, if you park outside, is to leave your really heavy chain and lock on the bike rack so you don't have to lug it back and forth, and to ride a cheap "banger" bike.

About Bikeways and Bike Paths and Trails

There has been some commitment from federal, state and a few city governments to funding construction of separate bike paths or trails. But these seldom are in the direction you want to go to get to work, being designed mostly for recreation. And on most of them you will find joggers, walkers, children weaving all over the place on hi-rise bikes, roller skaters and broken glass. In some cities you will find a curb separating the bike lane from city traffic, which is a really great idea. Some city fathers, have marked out a bike lane with a two-inch paint strip, over which cars freely drive and in which they stubbornly park. In Europe, curbs for bike lanes are often used, and even paint strips are reasonably well honored and enforced by the police.

Yet I still find bikeways in cities obviously designed by noncyclists, forcing cyclists to use sidewalks terminating in three inch curbs with no asphalt ramps, a drop which could cause a bike accident. If you have to stop and ease over every curb, that's not a bike path, that's an obstacle course!

Any bikeway must meet some of the following requirements: It should be away from major thoroughfares, where serious accidents and delays due to traffic and pedestrains may occur; it should be on a well-surfaced street to avoid road shock and blowouts on tires; it should be well lit at night; it should, if it is a bike lane or path, be at least five and possibly eight feet in width to allow for one cyclist to pass another or for two-way traffic; it should have eight to twelve feet clearance under overpasses; it should be curved and graded based on average expected bicycle speed (the higher the speed the gentler and wider the curves should be to allow for making manuevers).

Those lobbying for a particular type of bikeway should remember that others have done this before, and they should work on the models of the past. Washington, D.C., has adopted a comprehensive bike bill, as have Portland and Denver. The state of California in 1972 conducted and released a major study of bike routes in both urban and rural settings. It included the experience in Europe, where bike paths and routes have long been established and where bike commuting is the order of the day. It dealt with all kinds of bike systems for engineers and with planning and getting community involvement for planners and for persons advocating a bike system. Printed copies of this study are still available from the Division of Highways, State Dept. of Public Works, 1120 N. Street, Sacramento, California 95814.

Proponents of the bike system should work directly with the city council or county board, the mayor's office and the parks and recreation department, as well as the city engineer. It will help to know generally what you want first, so you should study maps and be able to recommend routes for bikeways when you first approach a government official.

To get locker and storage facilities in public and private places, you should first remember that organization and thorough research are the keys to a successful drive for such neccesities. If you work for a large firm, you should survey the membership to find out how many ride to work and form a committee or organization to research where storage and shower facilities could be placed, how much this would cost and who in the company supports such a move. Don't forget to try and involve the firm's management in the process and make sure they know how many employees are interested in the improvements. Bike lockers are becoming more and more accepted as a good way to safely store a bicycle where it cannot be watched by a security guard. These should be advocated for every large or small business. One way to encourage the purchase of such lockers is to guarantee they will be all rented out to company employees for a small fee, which will help in the long run to offset the initial expenditure. If bike lockers are too expensive, you should ask for guarded racks. The kind of straight pipe racks that allow for only the front wheel to be easily locked can and should be replaced by straight pipes anchored in cement with a hardened metal ring on top through which a chain or lock can be hung. Many places in Europe have racks where bikes can be stored by being rolled into racks and securely locked vertically (see Fig. 4-1). These have the advantage of locking all of the bikes at once.

Fig. 4-1: A view of a small part of the bicycle-parking facility at the Monarch Crescent bicycle factory in Varberg, Sweden. Note that these are all coaster-brake or three-speed bikes: strictly utility commuting bikes.

Fig. 4-2: Whether you just ride your bike to the train station or go all the way to work, bicycle commuting is an eminently practical, health-giving and energy-saving way to commute. Note that this rider is crossing the railroad tracks at the correct angle to prevent bike wheels from getting trapped in the tracks.

TOURING BY BIKE

Using your limited vacation time to travel by bicycle is quite different from cycle commuting. In fact, your conception of a vacation—lolling around in the sun for days on end, or jetting off and renting a car to "really get close to the land"—may become radically altered.

On an extended bike tour you almost *have* to be in intimate contact with nature and with the people you meet as you pedal by. On a bicycle, you feel invigorated and alive, with the fresh wind in your face. Your heart, lungs and circulatory system are functioning at their peak—you simply are happy to be alive. Contrast cycle touring with any other mode of travel—car, bus or plane. With other vehicles you are immobile, sitting inside the glass and metal box, remote from the countryside. On a bike you can stop and admire a view, talk easily to people, go off on side trips wherever your whim takes you and still have energy to dine and to dance, or whatever you want to do. You are outside as you would be on a beach, you are still getting that tan, but you are also staying healthy and really enjoying yourself, instead of yawning at the slap-slap of the waves.

I think this capsule description of a trip by bike I remember vividly, through Germany, Belgium, and that made-for-bicycle-touring country, Holland, will illustrate the joys of cycle touring. I went to Cologne, Germany, in September 1972 (after most of the tourists had left and the countryside was turning into autumn colors) to attend the International Bicycle Show. I brought my bicycle along so I could cycle later from Cologne to Amsterdam. After the show, I packed my panniers and put away my knit suit for a track suit more suitable for the chilly weather. I said goodbye to Cologne's ancient, magnificent cathedral and its modern city Centrum with miles of flower-laden pedestrian shopping malls, and cycled out of the city toward a country road that would take me to Euskirchen, about 50 miles away on the other side of a "Natur Park," with some small hills of about 500-feet elevation. Natur Parks are fine, deep, dark Valkyrian forests. Some of them are more scenic than hilly, and some are as hilly as scenic, with small mountains of about 1,500- to 2,000-feet elevation, a moderate hill climb. I remember the Natur Park between Nideggen and Gressenich, over the Hurten Wald. The *Generalkarte* map showed the twisting, snaky route with the words "Scenic View" in the legend, and it was all of that. Pine-fringed mountain tops parading in the distance, spectacular vistas of plunging valleys and mountain streams, and rural charm. One always begins a first trip through mountainous country with some misgiving, and it is a rewarding accomplishment to be able to climb mountains, or, as cyclists say, "storm" or "honk up" them. I noticed a lot of building walls pocked and chipped with the effluvia of various weaponry, and for the first time it came home to me that here, right here, in Nideggen and in Aachen and Heimbach, the wars had raged. It's hard for Americans to realize what it must have been like for parents with small children, with a war raging right up to their doorstep; the fear and insecurity and helplessness that prevailed when bombs dropped, shooting began, and great tanks rumbled past the front door. Somehow, as I cycled past these modest dwellings, the horror of war came home to me, who had spent World War II as a civilian in the U.S.A.

I cycled down the winding Moselle River Valley to the softly beautiful old Roman town of Trier, and across the Moselle back north again to Heimbach, on the Rhine. Here the Rhine was narrow and fast and deep, mysterious and black. My hotel was perched on the Rhine Valley just underneath an ancient and ruined castle, and dark woods filled the valley all around. I half expected a band of Nibelungen dwarfs to come storming out of the hills, and Siegfried and his warriors, dragging a slaughtered dragon, to meet and wage war with them.

In the small rural villages of Germany I had trouble paying for my noonday meal of wurst and beer, where, when curiosity overcame the natural reserve of the natives, they would crowd around my table and talk about me, my bike, my trip, and about America. More than once I staggered out of a noonday meal, replete with good food and much beer, an hour behind schedule but full of warmth and good cheer. How else can you get so close to these delightful folk; certainly not by driving through at 50 miles an hour.

I did not look forward to unloading my panniers at border checkpoints, so it was with some dismay that I saw a long line of cars backed up at the Belgian border, just outside Aachen, Germany. But as I cycled past the string of cars up to the checkpoint, a Belgian customs official ran out into the road and waved me on, with a cheer I can only interpret as "Hurray,

Eddy Merckx." Fortunately, I had stopped in a bike store that morning in Euskirchen, and bought a bicycle cap with Eddy Merckx's name on it. These are light, inexpensive cloth caps with a small visor, worn by racing cyclists. It just happened that Eddy Merckx is a national folk hero in Belgium, in Holland, and in Europe generally (professional racing cyclists can earn upward of $100,000 a year in Europe), who a few months earlier had for the fourth successive time won the grueling Tour de France, a several-thousand-mile bike race through the French Pyrenees, with climbs up 6,000-foot mountains a frequent occurrence. I was also cheered on past Customs into Holland, still wearing my Eddy Merckx cap, and wondering whether Customs thought I was Eddy's father, trainer, or perhaps a member of his team. Certainly my fifteen-speed, laden, chrome-gleaming touring bicycle could not be mistaken for a stripped racing machine, and the gray-haired rider would appear as anything but that.

Passing through small villages I was transported back to the Middle Ages, as I cycled down narrow cobblestone streets, past thatched-roofed houses so old no one knew who built them, with farm animals sharing quarters with inhabitants, and definitely no fender clearance for Cadillacs.

Holland was a surprise. I had thought this tiny country to be jam packed, with little or no room for more housing. But Holland, as you enter it from the southeast corner, proved to be entirely rural, with gently rolling hills traversing forests and farmland. Most of the twelve million Hollanders seemed to be packed away in cities—in Rotterdam, The Hague, Amsterdam, Utrecht and Eindhoven (home of Phillips Electronics). Beside every road, usually in a physically separated lane, there's a paved trail only for cyclists (Fig. 4-3). Even the main arteries, the four-lane separated superhighways, have bike trails that parallel them, but usually far enough away, and separated by a green barrier of trees and shrubs and lawn, for cars and trucks to be heard or seen only at rare intervals. Many of Holland's bike trails (marked on the map as are the roads) take you far from any roadway, through farmland, fields of tulips, avenues of tall, waving corn, along canals filled with barges from which fly the day's wash for the family that lives on them. Cycle touring is, indeed, the best way to see a country, savoring the land and the people slowly and deeply, as you would a vintage wine. After a cycle tour, you'll find memories of the land and the people engraved in whatever portion of the mind pleasure resides.

Making Plans for a Two-Wheeled Trip

Touring by bicycle is a different world from touring by car or plane. The bicycle tourist is concerned not with getting from place to place, but with what happens during the trip. The act of touring on a bicycle is a means and an end for the bicyclist. Communing with nature and with people in places near and far is his goal; getting on to the next city is

Fig. 4-3: We need more lovely bike trails like this one in Holland. The trail is nice and wide, and separated from the highway by a green strip plus concrete posts. This couple was out for a Sunday ride while your author was on his way from Cologne to Amsterdam.

merely a byproduct of a week's enjoyment of the countryside. It is with this spirit that the novice bike tourer should approach a bike tour, just as the veteran biker does.

The bike tour must be planned in meticulous detail with regard to the equipment you will use, and you should have a good idea of what general area you plan to be in, because you will need a good map of every place you visit. You must, of course, decide first of all where to go, how you will accommodate yourself and the tour overnight, and how long you want the tour to last. The kind of equipment you pack is very dependent upon how you spend the night: whether camping, in motels or in private homes. If you stop at motels, then you need a minimum of gear. If you camp, you must be very rigid about what you bring and leave behind. Or, if you have a sagwagon, which is an accompanying van or truck to hold camping gear and spare parts, and which can serve to transport tired or injured riders, then you need carry only a water bottle and perhaps a handlebar bag. Sagwagons cost money to operate, and you have to have tour members who are willing to donate time to drive the vehicles. They are, however, very handy on larger tours. Most tours run by American Youth Hostels—the large, national organization which has tours and lodges that have become famous with the bike boom—have sagwagons.

American Youth Hostels regularly schedule trips of various distances and duration from most major cities. There are AYH chapters almost everywhere, which you may join even if you don't live in a particular city. Or, you can be a member at large, and select the group you want to travel with. Don't let the word "youth" fool you. American Youth Hostels members are of all ages, although, naturally, the majority of cyclists are under thirty. The AYH maintains hostels all over the United States, and as a member, you will be entitled to a list of them. All you have to do to use the facilities is to bring with you your own sheet or a sleeping bag, or both. Contact the national AYH group by writing to American Youth Hostels, Inc., Delaplane, Virginia 22025.

A big advantage of joining the AYH cycle-touring group is that you will be under the watchful eye of an experienced bike-tour leader, who will make sure that the day's journey is within your physical capacity, and that you can handle the average speed of the group. Some AYH groups bring along bike-repair experts for the larger tours. At least, there is someone who knows his way around a bike on most AYH tours.

The *North American Bicycle Atlas* published by the AYH contains detailed routes and maps of bicycle tours throughout the United States and Canada. These tours are graded by length and difficulty. Easy trips are rated from 8 to 15 miles over fairly flat terrain, whereas rugged trips may contain hard mountain passes, unpaved roads, and go up to 100 miles a day. The atlas is a handy and complete touring guide and can be bought from your nearest AYH chapter.

The League of American Wheelmen is another old cycling club, whose members include some of America's most dedicated cyclists. The LAW has chapters in most large and medium-sized cities, and chapter members are usually quite willing to aid travelers and fellow members. The LAW also has numerous tours prepared by local member groups. These are very well planned, with the routes worked out in painstaking detail by members who have local knowledge. With this group you will find yourself among an older set than that at AYH and can be assured of having enough bike enthusiasts on hand to fix anything that could possibly go wrong with your bike, short of a busted frame. Local clubs also provide evening and weekend jaunts, and you can share knowledge and experience. Many clubs have seminars on cycling safety and maintenance that can be of great help to you. As a league member, you will receive the monthly LAW Bulletin, which gives dates and details on bicycle trips throughout the nation that are sponsored by the local clubs. Of all of the cycling publications, the LAW's is, to me, among the most valuable, and it is free to members. You also receive a membership roster, which can be quite useful if you are stuck somewhere north of Boise and need help.

There are other planned tours. In fact, they have proliferated in the past year to the point where it is difficult to keep track of all of them. Many are listed in the Appendices. A few include those led by Dr. Clifford Graves, a surgeon who is president of the International Bicycle

Touring Society, and one of our most prominent and experienced cycle tourists. These tours cover Europe and North America. Many businessmen, housewives and professional people join him on these tours, which are fairly deluxe trips, with most meals eaten in restaurants and with evening layovers in hotels.

Other cycle-touring groups that tour abroad include The Cyclists' Touring Club of England, based in England, which has a club magazine called *Cycle Touring*. This group has tours all over the world.

Getting on an organized tour is advisable, especially on your first tour with a bike, when you may not have much mechanical experience with the machine. The tours are usually well run: You do not have to start out carrying everything you need for the trip, and you can sit back and really enjoy the scenery and the people without worrying about losing your way or getting a reservation at a hotel. You can also learn a lot from these tours, in terms of mechanical know-how and how to conduct a tour of your own later.

Someday, however, you will probably want to go off on your own or with family and friends for at least a weekend trip. Once you have decided the area you want to cycle in, and how long the tour will take, you may consult local bicycling organizations (which you should join) such as AYH or LAW, state governments, counties, and most importantly a good large bookstore to see what publications are available that include established bikeway maps and descriptions. With a good map, you can plan out an excellent route combining hill climbs and flat stretches with riverside paths and rides through interesting towns.

The next important decision is whether to stay in hotels or motels and eat prepared food, or to cycle-camp. Personally, I prefer cycle camping, which permits you to stop where and when you like. I have found that it's helpful to phone ahead to the next campground and check with the camp management about space. Campgrounds, be they federal, state, county or city, are automobile oriented and provide space to park, usually, next to the campsite (called "getting away from it all"). On a bike you don't need a car parking space, so what the authorities have designated as parking space for one campsite can usually accommodate two or three cycle campers. You can usually find a corner, even a "filled" campsite, to park your bike and pitch your tent. Just be good at wheedling the camp management. You can always plead, with justification, that you have pedaled umpteen miles that day, are too tired to travel to the next campground and really need only a teensy, weensy little space for yourself.

Some small towns have camping facilities not published in camping directories. In a pinch you can usually get permission from the police to camp overnight in the local park (small towns only) and even police protection. But don't use these facilities without an okay from police.

I have found county parks to be far less crowded and located in more scenic areas than many state parks, at least in the midwest and in Wisconsin in particular. County campgrounds often have better facilities, such as showers, nice beaches and campsites, than federal or state parks.

Never camp by the side of the road, on a deserted stretch of beach or private woods. In these places you don't have the protection of the authorities or people around you, and you are asking for trouble. I suppose camping on the long beaches of Oregon, or empty stretches of rivers in the wilds of Maine or Canada is okay. I just feel more comfortable with some people around at night. My kind of people, that is. In bear country . . . well, what can I say?

Do your shopping before you hit the campsite. Leave room in your panniers for food for dinner and breakfast. This is why I recommend front as well as rear panniers (see the section on recommended bike bags later on in this chapter.)

I like to shop, and I have found from experience that it's best to hit the local store around five. In the backwoods of Vermont you will find gourmet foods, even fresh lobsters and cold duck, but don't count on such delicacies away from the East Coast. You can carry dried munchies for day use, but remember, you are not backpacking in the wilderness so you do not have to be totally self-sufficient as far as food is concerned. Where there are roads, there are towns, and in those villages there are stores. There are even wayside stores at road intersections, but don't count on finding them. Plan your stop at the first town before your campsite. Of course, if you are crossing the western deserts or taking some such isolated trip, you might have to carry food overnight, but those are rare situations. So count on buying whatever you like for dinner and breakfast each night. Just enough fresh meats, vegetables and salad stuff, eggs, bacon and fresh milk. Freeze-dried foods are for backpackers and the birds; they're very expensive and not as nourishing or tasty as the real thing.

Campground Notes

Just because you are in a public campground with people around is no guarantee that your bike's safe from theft. I know one couple whose bikes were not even safe in Alaska! They left bikes parked on a road to walk off to view the scenery and came back to find nothing but a severed bike cable. Lock bikes, yes, but don't leave them unattended for very long.

Do not park near public restrooms, or near Winnebagoes, or next to the public water supply or pump. After all, you want peace and quiet, especially at night. Check your radio for a weather report every night. If you have to, ditch your tent (dig a small channel around the tent) to divert water away from you if it rains. The tent fly or opening should face away from the road or other campsites. Choose a smooth, flat or level area to pitch your tent. Police the ground for rocks, sticks and anything else that could stick into you or puncture the tent floor. Pitch as far away as possible from campers with dogs—dogs seem to want to howl or bark a lot at night.

If you must pitch your tent on a slope, do it so your head is a bit higher than your feet. Make sure the tent fly or fly screens are closed at all times to keep the tent insect-free. Get in the habit of stowing stuff in the same place each night so you don't have to search for shoes, flashlight or morning clothes. And memorize the location of the restrooms for late night use.

Touring Abroad

European bike touring is a marvelous, slow-paced way to see the country, meet and enjoy the people there and really savor the new experiences you will encounter every mile you pedal your way through history.

American bike trippers are by now pretty well understood in Europe, although back in 1971 when I began traveling extensively, I was somewhat of a novelty. In fact, on one sponsored tour in Austria, our group was trailed by a mini-cam van from the Austrian-National TV, and we made it big on the TV screens there for about a week. In fact, I somehow got ahead of my group and stopped on Sunday afternoon to watch a soccer match. I was alone, but the spectators noted my strange (to them) ten-speed and my cotton shell that said "Illinois" on the back, and they took up an old Austrian folk song that has the word *Raddel* in it, which is Austrian slang for "bicycle". I was cheered by the goodwill gesture. Cycling through Germany and stopping in small towns was a treat because of the camaraderie and the trouble I had paying for my own beer and wurst. And everybody in rural Germany seemed to have a cousin in Milwaukee.

In Europe, bikes are mostly coaster-brake utility monsters that last forever and are used to get you to work or to the store—the equivalent of a few miles each day. Bike trippers on expensive ten-speeds are still a novelty there, so you will have trouble finding parts or tires. If you're stuck for a part—say a chain or derailleur or a tire—look for a bike shop that caters to the racing trade. And by all means do not use tubulars because of the flat problem with them. Use 700-centimeter-by-25-millimeter tires, the European standard. You'll have trouble finding 27-by-1-inch or -one-and-a-half-inch-tires in Europe, although you can use tubes that size in the 700-centimeter tires in an emergency.

As I cautioned in Chapter 1, do *not* buy your bike in Europe. There are so many fine bikes made in this country, or sold here, and so many really excellent bike shops that can fine-tune your steed, that it just does not make sense to risk a European purchase. You won't save much money, you may not have a bike that's well set up, and you will have to de-bug it on the road. If it breaks down far from the dealer, forget about the warranty. Know, yourself, that your bike is as mechanically sound as possible before you set off on a European tour.

Packaged Tours

The appendix lists a host of packaged bike tours led by experienced cyclists, with sagwagons included for carrying luggage. These tours are a good idea because they have leaders who speak the language, know where to stop, what to see, and can take care of medical emergencies or bike breakdowns. Best of all, you have the company of fellow cyclists during the day and evening, with whom there is lots to discuss about the trip.

Even on an organized trip you need route maps for the day's ride. People bike at different speeds and, without a map, you could find yourself alone and lost. (A compass is also very helpful.) So make sure you know where you are going each day by way of a map.

If you travel alone, plan each day's ride in advance, at least in general terms. Personally I am not a planner, though I like to have a rough idea of where I will wind up each night, and feel more comfortable if I have phoned ahead and have a reservation. But I like to be open-minded about the route. Many times I have found an attractive country lane that the map said would get me to the hotel and taken that route instead of the one I had charted for myself.

Camping

There are far more campgrounds per mile in Western Europe than in the U.S.A. Each village, for example, seems to have its own local campground in a scenic location. I have biked from Paris to Nice, mostly down the Rhône, and found lots of bike camps—small, some of them—on the river. You can also use Youth Hostels, but make sure you have your own sheet, blanket and towels. I travel in Europe in September and October, when camps are uncrowded. During those months you should also have no trouble with hotel reservations. Bed and Breakfast places, very modest in price, are particularly reasonable in Ireland and Scotland. Small hotels in Europe provide a European breakfast, which comes free with the room, but the coffee and toast or bread is not enough for me. For a bit extra you can have eggs, bacon and cereal in the same hotel.

Shipping Your Bike by Air and Rail

For those bike tours that start at a place too distant to ride or drive to, you must ship your bicycle along with you on planes or railroads. Although it is not nearly as much trouble as it used to be, it can be a hassle, especially on overseas flights; but with a few tips from an experienced bike traveler, you can get by.

The increased flow of passenger traffic on airlines and the growing numbers of bike riders have forced all major airlines to have a standardized system of dealing with bikes. The problem is that bicycles have many projecting parts such as derailleurs and chainstays and brake levers which can be damaged in a baggage compartment and which can cause damage to other baggage or even the plane itself. So all major airlines now require protective covering for the bicycle, usually a bike box or plastic bag made from heavy-gauge plastic. Many sell these at the baggage check-in point, but the tools for adjusting the bicycle are not made available. In addition, at smaller airports, they often don't even have bike bags or boxes. Call your airline in advance and see if they provide them. If not, you can purchase bike bags and boxes at a bicycle supply store. Most airlines require that the handlebars be turned parallel with the frame and the pedals removed and either put back in on the opposite side of the crank or stored elsewhere. Experience shows that the best thing to do is to adjust the bike accordingly, remembering to bring along an Allen wrench if you have a recessed handlebar stem bolt or a proper regular wrench if you have an exposed bolt head. Then either box the bike at home or at the airport if they provide boxes on your airline. United Airlines provides boxes for free, and American Airlines provides a heavy-gauge plastic container for around $3.50 (Fig. 4-4). Braniff provides a box for $5, as do TWA and Pan Am.

Some airlines will allow you to simply protect the handlebars and pedals with styrofoam or heavy plastic, but this invites damage to the bike frame and working parts. The bike should always be neatly contained in a heavy bag or preferably in a free bike box.

As for shipping charges, some airlines, such as Braniff and American, charge $10 to $12 for domestic flights. But most airlines treat the bike as

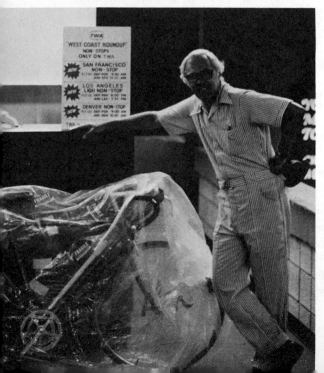

Fig. 4-4: American Airlines provides a plastic bag for carrying your bike on their planes. It's reusable, as long as it lasts. Note that pedals have been removed, along with pump. Both are in my panniers as carry-on luggage. Security always wants to know what the pump is, as though they had never seen a tire pump before, so have your story ready.

Fig. 4-5: What the well-dressed bicycle will wear on a cycle camping trip. Weight is evenly balanced between front and rear, making bike easier to handle, reducing or eliminating problems of spoke breakage in the rear wheel.

normal luggage, and do not charge extra unless you already have two large bags in addition to the bike. Then you will have to pay an excess charge on one piece of luggage, $12 or so, on some airlines. United will allow the bike free, and two other bags as well. On international flights, however, the picture changes—you can bring the bike on, and carry two very small bags measuring only 44 inches, all free. But if you have a larger bag or two larger bags, then one of the bags becomes excess baggage, a charge of $41. If you go from one European city to another on a separate flight on a different day, you pay another international charge of $41, and you will pay $41 more on the way home, a large amount of money altogether. It is best to travel extremely lightly to Europe, as I do, so that the excess charges are not levied.

Once you are at the airport, always check in, and then tell the agent you are taking the bike personally to the baggage room, because the bike does not fit onto regular conveyers. If you are going on to another city after the first stop on a different airline, always check the bag to the first city only (if you have time) and then bring the bike to the next airline baggage room yourself. The bike is too expensive to be handled any other way.

Airline representatives point out that you should pick up extra travel insurance to cover the bicycle for the duration of the trip. As a piece of baggage, the bike comes under the usual remuneration rules for damaged or lost baggage, which means you can only collect a few hundred dollars for a lost or damaged bike. The travel insurance will save you from this fate.

About Customs

If you take a foreign-made item from the U.S. overseas, such as a bicycle, tools, camera, watch, panniers or whatever, and don't declare it to U.S. Customs *before* you leave this country, you may have a tough time convincing customs officers on your return that you did not buy it overseas. You can avoid this hassle by declaring in advance everything foreign made you are taking out of the country. You must take everthing you are to declare to the customs officers at the airport or in the city, and they will fill out and sign Form 4457 (Fig. 4-6). You must have serial numbers on all items that are declared.

On your return from Europe, the stewardess on the plane will hand you a form for declaring what you bought overseas, if your total purchase exceeds $100. If the purchase is under this figure, you do not have to itemize, but I keep a running tally of whatever I buy overseas no matter how small or inexpensive. I have found that the more detailed the list, the less likely you are to be delayed by a officer checking out your luggage. If you're carrying a lot of stuff, and your bike is crated so you have to carry that, too, you should quickly grab one of the wire carts (like supermarket carts) that are in the customs area for tourists to use free. Go get your luggage, load it on the cart, look for a short line at a customs

Fig. 4-6: On an overseas trip, never leave the U.S. airport without finding the customs office, filling out a form like this one and having it signed by a customs officer. Predeclare everything that's made outside the U.S.A. you are taking abroad, or you will very likely have to pay duty on it again when you return. Declare the bicycle, if foreign made, any items of clothing, optical equipment, watch, anything else foreign made. Show this form when you return and pass through customs. Make sure customs also stamps the date on the form.

THE DEPARTMENT OF THE TREASURY
CERTIFICATE OF REGISTRATION
BUREAU OF CUSTOMS

Form Approved
O.M.B. 48–R0394

Number

Name of Owner

Address of Owner

Description of Articles

I certify that the information shown hereon is true and correct to the best of my knowledge and belief.

Signature of Owner

Port

Date

Signature of Customs Official

Customs Form 4457 (3/71)

counter and get in line. If you have a choice of counters, look for a youngish customs officer, preferably one with a beard; he will be more understanding about your bicycle, although by now all customs people have seen them on tour and should be used to them.

By Train

Amtrak, the nation's passenger rail system, is a bicycle disaster. When you board a train, you should have your bicycle boxed, using the $5 boxes Amtrak provides. Charges for shipping the bike vary according to your destination, but there is a minimum charge of $7.50. Like the airlines the trains allow you to substitute your bike as one of the three pieces of luggage you are allowed. The problem is that the railroads are less used to seeing bicycles and are not as smooth at handling them. You must, of course, carry the bicycle out to the train, and put it on the train's baggage car yourself so that you can watch how it is disposed of. Be sure it is tied down to something so that heavy objects will not fall on it. You can't rely on railroad people in the United States to be at all solicitous about passengers and their belongings.

In Europe, it is different; a cyclist's delight. In Holland every through passenger train (Fig. 4-7) has a baggage car for bicycles, and although you have to hoist it up yourself, the porter will give you a lift, and show you where to tie it down. A rubber shock cord will secure your bike to a rail. You can then walk from the baggage car to the nearest passenger car

Fig. 4-7: You can carry bikes in railroad baggage cars in Europe. All you do is get a ticket at the station, find the baggage car, hoist the bike into the car and tie it with a bungee cord to anything handy, as the author did on this train from Eindhoven to Utrecht, Holland.

and forget about your bike till arrival, although it would be a good idea to lock the bike to the stanchion as well as tie it down. Other European railroads also have bike cars with handy tie-down fixtures. And the trains are fast, clean, comfortable and usually uncrowded, except in Italy and Spain, and at rush hours. If the train is crowded, buy a first-class ticket so you will get a seat. You will need a ticket for the bike, which you usually get at the baggage counter. It's also a good idea to put your name tag on the bike, and keep it on.

On the Bus

Bus companies are a little better than trains, but they do not provide boxes, which can leave you high and dry on occasion in small towns. It is handy that you can see the driver put the bike into the baggage area, which is usually so stuffed that you will have no worry about the bike banging around. The bike goes free on buses, as long as you are a passenger, of course, and it is very cheap to send bikes; but I don't recommend sending a bike when you are not accompanying it. At every stop of the bus, take note of the bicycle, and make sure that it is still on the bus. When you change buses, take the bike with you. Don't rely on anyone else to do it.

On Arrival

The traffic in most major European cities is horrendous. During the rush hour (which seems to be all day), on roads designed for wagons, the congestion from these airports can cost you a bundle while the taxi meter clicks on. I have put my bike together right at the luggage section, attached panniers, and cycled off, to arrive at my hotel a full hour before others in my party arrived. I found that cycling from the airport is a good way to dispel at least some of the jet lag. But you will still need a good night's sleep or a good day's rest on arrival.

Get a city map while still at home and mark out the route to your hotel from the airport. That way you should have no trouble finding your hotel. Most of us arrive in Europe around 10 AM (4 AM EST), so you will have lots of daylight time to bicycle to your hotel.

A word of warning about England! Traffic, as you know, is reversed in England. Ride your bike very slowly and carefully until you get used to traffic coming at you first from the right and then from the left, and car doors opening at you from the left instead of from the right side of the road. Look first to the right and then to the left at intersections.

In Rome—ah, in Rome—use side streets exclusively. Italian drivers are macho madmen, and if you are tired and cycling from the airport, try to be doubly alert. The same is true in Mexico City and in most cities in Spain.

Overland European Travel

Use finely detailed section maps, such as the Michelin maps, and stick to what would in this country be county roads. In France, for example, there are "A" routes (super highways, with no speed limits); "B" routes (like our state highways) and "C" routes, like our county roads. In more prosperous European countries such as England, France, the Scandinavian countries and Germany, the back roads are beautifully paved, cover scenic routes, and are relatively traffic-free. However, in more impoverished nations such as Spain and Portugal and many parts of Italy, back roads are often impossibly rutted, and in the rain become muddy paths, so you will have to stick to the secondary road systems.

You will note on Michelin maps that some roads are marked with little chevrons, or sideways "V's", and if you look at the multi-language description of route markings, you will see that each chevron stands for a 5-percent gradient. Three chevrons means a 15-percent road grade, which is a very steep hill indeed. Unless you have Granny gears (see Chapter 2) I would avoid anything greater than a two-chevron road. Sometimes you will see little marks that look like chicken tracks which indicate scenic areas, usually mountains. But you need not learn how to

Fig. 4-8: Part of a scenic bike trail in Cape Cod National Park. Bikes can be rented in the park, so if you visit, beware of bikes careening downhill and around curves— they will be heavy coaster-brake jobs.

Fig. 4-9: A quiet road in Holland, just outside Amsterdam, on the Amstel River. The cyclists are natives.

read terrain maps if you watch out for chevron marks. In England there are ordinance survey maps (Barts) which will show every footpath, cow trail and just about every turnstile in every country. These are great for cycle touring.

In England, cycle camping has always been big. In fact, there is a magazine devoted to it called *Cycle Touring*, at 69 Meadow, Godalming, Surrey, England, that can help you with tours there.

About Languages

If you don't know the language where you tour, at least learn "right," "left" and "straight ahead," so you can understand directions. I would also learn how to count to 100 fairly fluently, and acquaint myself with the currency system in order to avoid being overcharged.

A new angle to the language problem is a fairly expensive hand-held computer made by Lexicon that lets you punch in your word or phrase in English and see on the screen the foreign language translation or approximation thereof. I haven't used one but it seems like a good idea. They're sold in major department stores for around $225 with a card programmed for one language, $65 each for additional cards, and are available in all European languages including Russian, Greek, Norwegian and Swedish. African languages are coming up.

More About Route Planning in the U.S.A.

If you plan to tour the Midwest, East, far West, Northeast or some regions of the South, county maps are a must. In some areas, major interstates and many other main roads, such as state routes, do not allow bicycles. In any case, county roads and residential roads provide some of the best touring there is in this country. Find out what counties your general route will pass through and write the county government asking for a map, or write the state department of tourism (or transportation) asking for all of the county maps on the tour. By writing the county, you can get some information that you won't get from the state, such as more recent information on lodging, but you must specifically ask for this. County maps show you each road no matter how small; they even indicate where buildings and landmarks in small towns are located. In the western mountain regions, county maps are less important, because you will have to take larger state or interstate roads anyway to get from place to place. County roads in the West are often not well paved because they are so infrequently traveled, and where there is a good county road system, the roads are often in disrepair. Of course in the far West there are more people, and better secondary roads.

Even better than county maps are those put out by the United States Geological Survey. These are maps of quadrangles of various sizes, rated according to detail and size of area covered. USGS maps are assembled from special aerial photos, and the most detailed show every house, every piece of open land, every creek and every hill. They have contour lines showing elevation of certain roads. The key for the cyclist is to choose the roads that cross the fewest contour lines. A USGS map tells you where the hills are, how steep they are and how to avoid them. Conversely, they show the steepness of the downhills and even the location of dangerous intersections. The maps tell what intervals are used for elevations, so that when you have crossed one of the lines, you have gone up either 20 feet or 40 feet, or whatever.

Bicyclists use what are known as 7½-minute, 15-minute, and 1:250,000 maps.

The 7½-inch maps are incredibly detailed, so detailed that they can only cover 7 by 8 miles. The 15-minute maps, which are now being replaced by the more detailed 7½-minute maps, show an area four times as large. For all but the most expert trip planner who seeks great detail, or for mountain and large-hill climbers, the 1:250,000 maps are the best. You can carry ten of these maps covering a trip 1,000 miles or longer. In the case of the 1:250,000 maps, one inch on the map equals four miles on the ground, with each map covering 80 by 120 miles of terrain. At this ratio, detail on individual houses is lost, and the intervals of elevation are 100 feet, a fairly rough demarcation. Yet all roads are shown, all creeks, all landmarks. For maps and information on how to read them, write: (west of the Mississippi River) U.S. Geological Survey, Box. 25286 Federal Center, Denver, Colorado 80225 *or* (east of the Mississippi) U.S. Geological Survey 1200 South Eads Street, Arlington, Virginia 22202.

From these maps you can create your own route, and you can even make your own route maps, making sure you keep to scale. The reason for making your own set of maps is to avoid having to pack loads of maps. If you're leading a tour you should make copies of your route maps, to distribute to tour members. This is important should any tour members become separated from the pack. It's also a good idea to hold onto copies of the county or U.S. maps in case there is a detour or another kind of problem, and have the original map on hand, should you decide you want to make a side trip.

However independent you want to be (a noble desire), you still should look up bike routes in your selected geographic area before deciding to plan an entire trip on your own. It does not hurt to build upon the experiences of thousands of veteran bike tourers. Consult the AYH or the LAW chapters in your area for this information.

Cycle Touring Gear

If you're touring alone, or with a group too small to afford the luxury of a sagwaon, you will either have to carry all your gear with you, or do as we did on one IBTS trip through the Lincoln country of Illinois and Indiana, and "stage"-advance all cars, or one car. Every morning we'd pack luggage, suitcases, and so forth, into one car. One of the trip members would then drive to the next motel stop, leaving late enough and driving slowly enough to be able to pick up any stragglers or riders with mechanical or physical trouble. (The latter can happen; one member of our tour began to have appendicitis pains on his bicycle, and wound up having an appendectomy in a local hospital.) An alternate approach was also used, in which the sagwagon driver on this trip drove early and fast to the next stop, carrying his own bike, and spent the rest of the day cycling around the area, and phoning in to the motel from time to time during the day to check as to whether any of the group needed to be picked up. A third approach was also used. Because most of us drove to the starting point and did not want to cycle back the 350 miles or so to pick up our cars, and there was no convenient public transport back to the start, we would have the day's sagwagon driver drive us back the 50 to 90 miles to the day's starting point and we would drive our cars back to the evening's stop. I don't recommend this latter technique except in an emergency; after a day in the saddle, a 150-mile-plus round-trip car ride isn't the easiest way to spend an evening, or the most enjoyable. It's moot as to which is easier, though, and it seems strange that the prospect of a 350-mile, seven-day bike ride is more enjoyable than a four- or five-hour car ride would be to go back to pick up your car; but that's cycle touring for you. Fun!

Riding a Loaded Bicycle

If you've never ridden a bicycle loaded with camping gear (Fig. 4-7), take it easy the first day out until you get the feel of things. You'll find you can't bank steeply around sharp corners at high speed without risking a spill. Also, you must shift down sooner going uphill, and you must use brakes sooner to avoid speed buildup, unless the downgrade is straight, smooth, and relatively free of traffic.

A word of advice about downhill rides. We've talked about wheel shimmy, brake fade, tire roll-off, and other hazards of high-speed downhill rides elsewhere in this book. There is one more point having to do with your comfort. On some very long hills, which can be five or ten miles or so of steady uphill pedaling, and another five or ten miles down the other side (if you're lucky), you will arrive at the crest of the hill in a sweat, with perspiration streaming from your brow, even though at the top of the hill the air temperature is only 50 or 60 degrees. Even if it's 70 or 80 degrees, remember that your body is bathed in sweat and your shirt may be wringing wet. If you go right on over the hill and start down, with a sigh of relief that you're about to cool off, you'll find you can cool off much too fast and arrive at the bottom quite chilled, so much so that you will be lacking the energy you may need to attack the next climb. On a fast run downhill, your body will lose heat very rapidly in two ways. First, the latent heat of evaporation as moisture dries will rob your body of heat. Second, heat will be lost by convection to the 40-mile-per-hour rush of air passing over your body. That's why you'll see in races over mountain country, as in the Tour de France, spectators passing newspaper, magazines, anything the cyclist can stuff in his shirt front as he's about to go downhill to avoid debilitating, excessive body heat loss.

I know it's tempting to go right down that hill, but I can assure you one freezing, miserable ride following a sweat-filled mountain "storming" will see you stopping and spending the forty seconds it takes at the top of the next hill to pull out a light nylon windbraker from your front bag to keep warm, and removing it when you start the next climb. Or you can simply wrap the windbreaker around you middle if you're facing a repeated series of hills. You'll find, too, that cycling in hill country is mostly uphill; it may take an hour to climb a long, gradual incline to the top, and fifteen minutes to get down the other side; never long enough to rest up for the next climb, but long enough so you can make it, and make it, and make it, once you're in condition.

WHAT YOU SHOULD KNOW ABOUT BICYCLE BAGS

Bicycle bags have come a long way during the past ten years. When I first began bike tripping, there were the good bags produced in limited quantity by the then new Touring Cyclist Shop and a lot of heavy, cumbersome and nonleakproof canvas bags sold by American Youth Hostels and some European producers. During the past decade, a lot of talented people who are experienced cyclists have designed an incredible array of bike bags for every conceivable type of bicycle use from month-long tours in the back country to day trips or for commuting to work. There are dozens of companies making these bags now, and from these I have selected a few dozen bags of various types I can recommend to you.

Some of the bags (see Table 4-1) cost a lot more than others, and for that reason I have injected a figure for cost per cubic inch into the table. You will note, however, that whereas a rear pannier may have a cost of around two cents a cubic inch, a handlebar bag will cost upwards of six cents or more a cubic inch. This is simply because these bags require a lot more work to produce. A bar bag has small sewn-in pockets, a plastic sewn-in map case (usually), and many times an aluminum-alloy or steel-handlebar mount. It needs more reinforcement at wear points than the pannier, and often has leather reinforcements at critical wear points.

I have noticed that articles in bicycle magazines urge you to try out panniers and bar bags before investing in them, to check their durability, ease of installation and removal and stability under rough road conditions. This is an admirable idea, but I doubt very much that a bike store is going to let you borrow a brand new set of expensive panniers to take out on the highway. A more practical approach is to review the experience of others with these bags, (see Table 4-1) along with prices, and make your decision accordingly. The various types of bags used in Table 4-1 are rated for ease of mounting and removal, stability under rough riding conditions, durability and water repellency. I haven't attempted to break out or group similar kinds of bags (all rear panniers, all handlebar bags, etc.) because I prefer to keep a manufacturer's line grouped in one area. You will note quite a price range, from the low low of Bellwether to the high of Touring Cycle Shop or Kirtland. You get pretty much what you pay for in bags, and if you want an inexpensive set of bags that will hold up for a couple of years, and you will take the trouble to pack in plastic bags anything that can be damaged by water, the Bellwether is a low-priced solution.

Stability

But the difference between $30 and $50 is not that great, and the middle of a long-planned vacation, far from the madding crowd, is no time for panniers to start coming apart. I have had even expensive rear panniers fly off the rear carrier and fall out into the street. Once, cycling from the Louisville, Kentucky, airport over to the University of Louisville with a $900 Hasselblad camera in one of my two rear panniers, I hit a pretty good bump, and the bag with the camera fell off and rolled around in the street. With traffic coming up behind me, I set a world's record for getting off the bike, dashing into the street and retrieving the bag before the Hasselblad was run over. I'm not going to say whose bag this was because the mounting system has been vastly improved and I doubt that the new bags would come loose from my carrier under like conditions. But certainly the mounting should be a first checkpoint.

Look for a generously sized set of dual-alloy or steel hooks that go over the carrier frame, along with heavy elastic with strong hooks that attach the panniers to the dropouts or to a mounting point on the carrier (more about carriers later).

As I review each of the manufacturers' lines in this section you will see illustrated some good examples of stable mountings that not only secure the bag on the carrier but also prevent the panniers from sliding back and forth, causing your heel to hit the bag. The mounting system should also prevent side sway, which causes the panniers to hit the spokes, a situation guaranteed to wear a hole in the bags very, very quickly, and frazzle nerves in the process. The bags must also be kept from the tires (plural because these admonitions apply to front panniers as well). Watch out for worn shock cords, they can cause an accident if they break and get caught in the spokes. Check them where they are fastened on the bag and on the bike.

The better panniers use some sort of stiffener to keep the bag's shape when loaded. If the stiffener is an aluminum sheet, be careful in handling the bags as you take them off and put them back on during the trip; the stiffener can bend to the point where the bottom of the bag will hit the spokes and wear a hole in the bag. This is not a serious problem, but one you should be aware of.

Some panniers use a foam-type plastic sheet for a stiffener. I prefer something more substantial, such as a tough plastic or metal frame. Plastic sheets just won't work. I've tried them and I hate them with a passion because the bags get all bent out of shape on a trip, you can't stand them up on a camp table and pretty soon they look like something sewn by a beginning student in home-ec.

About Closures

Zippers keep out more water than Velcro closures or tie-down flaps. Zippers with a rain-flap cover keep out more water than zippers without such flaps. Bags with a combination Velcro and zipper closure, such as bar bags, are handier because you can use the Velcro tabs during the day when you are likely to be fishing something out of the main compartment such as a snack, camera or wallet. If you hit a rough road or it starts to rain, you can close the zipper. Zippers should have pull tabs, preferably leather, and double pull tabs if they go around corners.

For zippers, look for the nylon-coil, self-repairing kind. All zippers should have a rain flap over them, as noted above. Zippers should be double stitched on both sides and triple stitched at the ends.

Durability

As I stated above, bike bags should be reinforced at all wear points. Some bags are made of a coarse, heavy nylon fabric; however, with the coarser-fabric weave waterproofing tends to break down earlier than with finer weaves. For a good bag I like densely woven Parapac nylon oxford, waterproofed with a double coating of K-Kote.

Table 4-1 Bicycle Bag Selections and Comparisons

Make and Model No.	Cubic Inch Capacity	Pockets	Material	Closures	Type Bag	Weight (ounces)	Shoulder Straps or Handles	Map Case	Ratings*				Cost Per Cubic Inch	Total Cost
									A	B	C	D		
Bellwether 1202	1,200	4	Cordura nylon	Velcro & zipper	rear pannier	20	no	NA	8	8	9	7	$.02	$24.00
Bellwether 1203	2,200	3	Cordura nylon	zipper	rear pannier	28	no	NA	8	8	9	7	$.0155	$34.00
Bellwether 1204	540	3	Cordura nylon	zipper	bar	8	yes	yes	8	7	8	7	$.0277	$15.00
Bellwether 1200	180	1	Cordura nylon	zipper	seat	6	no	NA	6	8	7	6	$.0388	$ 7.00
Bellwether 1201	632	2	Cordura nylon	zipper	bar	11	no	yes	8	8	8	7	$.0284	$18.00
Cannondale B037	750	4	Urethane coated nylon	zipper	bar		yes	yes	10	10	8	9	$.0526	$39.50
Cannondale B041	2,400	10	Urethane coated nylon	zipper	rear pannier		yes	NA	10	10	9	9	$.0290	$69.50
Cannondale B027	580	2	Urethane coated nylon	zipper	bar		yes	yes	8	9	8	9	$.0413	$24.00
Cannondale B040	1,800	4	Urethane coated nylon	zipper	rear pannier		yes	NA	8	8	8	9	$.0275	$49.50
Cannondale B031	275	1	Urethane coated nylon	zipper	seat		NA	no	8	7	9	8	$.043	$11.95
Cannondale B017	420	1	Urethane coated nylon	zipper	bar		yes	yes	10	8	9	9	$.0379	$15.95
Cannondale B045	390	1	Urethane coated nylon	zipper	rear		NA	no	7	7	9	9	$.0332	$12.95
Eclipse Nomad	680	2	7-ounce nylon	zipper	rear pannier	19.84	yes	NA	10	10	7	6	$.0478	$32.50
Eclipse Superlite	450	2	8-ounce Cordura	zipper	rear or front pannier	17.6	no	NA	10	10	8	7	$.0888	$40.00
Eclipse Standard	805	4	8-ounce Cordura	zipper	rear pannier	24.64	yes	NA	10	10	8	9	$.062	$50.00
Eclipse Trans-continental	1,075	12	8-ounce Cordura	zipper	rear pannier	34.24	yes	NA	10	10	9	9	$.079	$85.00

Eclipse Professional	610	8	8-ounce Cordura	zipper	bar	23.52	yes	yes	10	10	9	$.0754	$46.00
Eclipse Nomad	450	2	5-ounce nylon	zipper	bar	15.2	no	yes	7	9	5	$.0533	$24.00
Eclipse Standard	540	3	Cordura nylon	zipper	bar	21.5	no	yes	8	9	8	$.065	$35.00
Kirtland Vagabond 3	1,296	3	Cordura nylon	zipper	bar	24	yes	NA	9	7	10	$.0153	$19.95
Kirtland Vagabond 1	905	2	Cordura nylon	zipper	front pannier	19	yes	NA	8	7	10	$.0314	$28.50
Kirtland Century 100	270	1	Cordura nylon	zipper	seat	4	no	NA	6	7	10	$.0426	$11.50
Kirtland Century 100 U	100	1	Cordura nylon	zipper	seat	2	no	NA	6	5	10	$.08	$ 8.00
Touring Cycle Shop	1,751	8	8-ounce super Parapac with Super K-Kote	zipper	rear pannier	37	yes	NA	10	9	10	$.0377	$66.00
Touring Cycle Shop	611	4	8-ounce super Parapac with Super K-Kote	zipper	bar	16	yes	yes	10	9	10	$.09	$55.00
Touring Cycle Shop	921	4	8-ounce super Parapac with Super K-Kote	zipper	front pannier	28	yes	no	10	9	10	$.0477	$44.00
Touring Cycle Shop	223	1	8-ounce super Parapac with Super K-Kote	zipper	day trip	28	no	NA	7	9	8	$.071	$16.00
Velocipac Fox V-1	567	3	8-ounce super Parapac with Super K-Kote	zipper	frame pak	6	no	NA	5	7	9	$.0387	$21.95
Velocipac V-3	492	4	8-ounce super Parapac with Super K-Kote	zipper	bar	11.5	yes	yes	7	8	9	$.0558	$27.50
Velocipac V-4	789	6	8-ounce super Parapac with Super K-Kote	zipper	bar	14.5	yes	yes	7	8	9	$.0475	$37.50

Table 4-1 Bicycle Bag Selections and Comparisons

Make and Model No.	Cubic Inch Capacity	Pockets	Material	Closures	Type Bag	Weight (ounces)	Shoulder Straps or Handles	Map Case	Ratings* A	B	C	D	Cost Per Cubic Inch	Total Cost
Velocipac V-5	1,306	4	8-ounce super Parapac with Super K-Kote	zipper	rear pannier or front	30	no	no	9	8	8	9	$.031	$39.95
Velocipac V-6	2,032	8	8-ounce super Parapac with Super K-Kote	zipper	rear pannier	36	no	NA	9	8	8	9	$.027	$55.00
Velocipac V-7	2,632	10	8-ounce super Parapac with Super K-Kote	zipper	rear pannier	38	no	NA	9	8	8	9	$.0227	$59.95
Velocipac V-9	126	1	8-ounce super Parapac with Super K-Kote	zipper	day trip	3	no	NA	7	8	8	9	$.079	$ 9.95
Kangaroo F/R	1,200	6	8-ounce parachute pack cloth, waterproofed	zipper	front/rear pannier	NA	no	NA	6	8	8	9	$.0395	$47.50
Kangaroo Cross Country	2,200	6	8-ounce parachute pack cloth, waterproofed	zipper	rear pannier	NA	no	NA	7	8	8	9	$.0318	$69.95
Kangaroo Lightweight	1,700	4	8-ounce parachute pack cloth, waterproofed	zipper	rear pannier	NA	no	NA	6	8	8	9	$.0235	$39.95
Kangaroo Bar	290	1	8-ounce parachute pack cloth, waterproofed	zipper	bar	NA	no	no	6	5	8	9	$.043	$12.50

Kangaroo Bar	650	4	8-ounce parachute pack cloth, waterproofed	zipper	bar	NA	yes	yes	8	8	8	9	$.0460	$29.95
Kangaroo Tool	90	1	8-ounce parachute pack cloth, waterproofed	zipper	seat	NA	no	NA	7	8	7	9	$.083	$ 7.50
Kirtland G/T	2,400	8	8-ounce pack nylon urethane coated	zipper	rear pannier	46	no	NA	10	9	9	10	$.0368	$88.50
Kirtland S/T	2,000	8	8-ounce pack nylon urethane coated	zipper	rear pannier	38	yes	NA	9	9	9	10	$.0368	$54.00
Kirtland L/T	1,100	6	8-ounce pack nylon urethane coated	zipper	rear pannier	30	yes	NA	3	9	9	10	$.0490	$54.00
Kirtland Century 600	1,476	6	8-ounce pack nylon urethane coated	zipper	rear pannier	30	yes	NA	9	9	9	10	$.0318	$47.00
Kirtland Century 200	905	2	8-ounce pack nylon urethane coated	zipper	front pannier	24	no	NA	9	9	9	10	$.036	$32.50
Kirtland S/T Bar	680	6	8-ounce pack nylon urethane coated	zipper	bar	28	yes	yes	10	10	9	10	$.0735	$50.00
Kirtland L/T Bar	600	3	8-ounce pack nylon urethane coated	zipper	bar	24	yes	yes	10	10	9	10	$.0700	$42.00
Kirtland Century 600	381	2	8-ounce pack nylon urethane coated	zipper	bar	20	yes	yes	9	9	8	9	$.075	$28.50
Kirtland Vagabond #5	1,700	4	8-ounce pack nylon urethane coated	zipper	rear pannier	30	no	NA	8	7	8	9	$.0294	$50.00

Fig. 4-10: One way of mounting handlebar bags. *(Velocipac)*

All structural seams should be double stitched with nylon thread of at least 12 pounds tensile strength, and there should be triple bar tack stitching at all stress points. Webbing used for mounting or reinforcement should be of the nylon strapping type that has over 300 pounds tensile strength. Needless to say, all hardware should be rustproof.

Safety

Besides mounts that hold the bags securely, and shock cords that won't break and catch in wheels, it's a good idea to use reflectors on all sides of the bags. A few makes come with a reflector on the front bag. I would mount them all over. As far as color is concerned, you can get bags in a number of colors, but I prefer yellow for visibility. Bar bags make it difficult, if not impossible, to use a Freon bar-mounted power horn with the mount that comes with the horn. I tape mine to the stem instead.

Handlebar Bags

Bar bags these days generally come with a mounting bracket included in the price. They are a bit tricky to mount, something like a Chinese puzzle at first until you get the hang of it. Figure 4-11 shows the Velocipac method; Figure 4-13 shows the Eclipse approach.

As I mentioned earlier, there's a lot more work involved in making a bar bag than a pannier. The ideal bar bag opens from the rear so you can reach in and take things out while on the bike. There should be a transparent plastic map case on the top, so you can check your route. If you're tempted to scan the map while pedaling, make sure the road ahead is clear before you take your eyes off the scene. It's always better to stop while checking the map.

Bar bags should have two side pockets, not necessarily closable, into

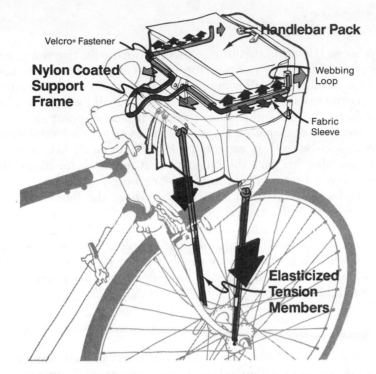

Velcro® Fastener

Handlebar Pack

Nylon Coated Support Frame

Webbing Loop

Fabric Sleeve

Elasticized Tension Members

Fig: 4-11: Another handlebar mounting system that is very stable. Tension members fasten to dropout ears. *(Eclipse)*

Fig. 4-13: A better way to distribute the load is to use front panniers and a large bar bag, virtually eliminating spoke breakage, leaving room for grocery shopping at night and making for a safer-handling bicycle. *(Touring Cyclist Shop)*

which you can stick thin, flat things such as postcards, tire irons, letters, extra maps. A larger front pocket, zippered, in addition to the main compartment, is handy for smaller items; and two longer, narrower zippered rear compartments are useful for carrying Halt, small tools, loose change, toothbrush, toothpaste and smaller items. The bag support should keep the bag from rubbing against the front tire, even when heavily loaded. The problem of bag rub is especially acute with small bike frames, 21 inches and under, because the bags are that much closer to the tire. It takes just a few minutes of rubbing to wear a hole in the bag.

Support places are areas of high stress. Where the bag is supported, and underneath, I like to see double or triple layers of material, or leather, plus lots of stitching, because this is where the bag will fail you on the road. Bag support should not sag appreciably when you carry a camera—I will have more to say on that point later (see page 243)—because cameras, expecially single-lens-reflex types, are not designed to tolerate much vibration.

Front Panniers

I like front panniers. It's important for both safety and convenience that the load you carry be balanced, and not concentrated entirely on the rear. Figure 4-12 shows an unbalanced load condition; Figure 4-13 shows an ideal balance between front and rear. You might think that with a fifteen-knot wind from the side there would be more "windage" or sail pressure if you're riding with the front panniers. Not so in my experience, which covers thousands of miles of cycle touring with front

Fig. 4-12: An overloaded, unbalanced condition. Note that all the weight is over the rear wheel, putting lots of stress on spokes. This is one reason rear-wheel spokes break on tour.

Fig. 4-14: Yes, you can get lost on a bike tour. The Silva compass shown here fastens to a special mounting loop on the handlebar bag. *(Touring Cyclist Shop)*

panniers. True, I might have to lean a bit into the wind for balance if the breeze is stiff from one side, but you do that without any panniers at all. I prefer the balanced condition, with weight distributed more or less evenly fore and aft.

With an even distribution of weight you will also find far fewer instances of spoke breakage than with all the weight, including much of your own, concentrated over the rear wheel. And spoke breakage on the rear wheel is a nuisance, especially when the spoke breaks on the free-wheel side, because then you have to remove the freewheel to get at the spoke.

There are two more advantages to balanced weight distribution. On a fast downhill run, with all the weight over the rear wheel, the front wheel tends to jump when it hits a bump. If, in addition, there is more weight on one side than on the other side of the bike, you could have a dangerous front-wheel "shimmy" or oscillation from side to side that no amount of firm gripping can stop. In fact, once shimmy starts, every oscillation increases in frequency and severity, so that the only solution is to stop as soon as possible. Of course, shimmy can also be due to a bent fork blade, loose front wheel or headset bearings or an out-of-round front wheel. But don't ask for trouble by riding with an unbalanced load.

Front panniers also mean extra room for groceries. Lots of times when I toured without these panniers, I found after stopping for groceries in the town nearest to my campsite that I had little room for any purchases in the rear panniers. It's very disheartening when you can't find room for groceries and instead have to pedal on another five to ten miles to the camp, unload, set up the tent and pedal back to the grocery store with an empty pannier after a day's riding when you are hungry and the "bonks" are coming on. (The bonks is just another name for a low level of blood sugar in your body when you are a pooped pedaler.) Front panniers also give you room for souvenirs purchased en route—at least room enough to mail them from the next post office. No point in lugging a lot of souvenirs around until you get back.

Seat Bags

I don't like seat bags, as a general rule. They bounce back and forth and somehow always manage to hit the backs of my legs. I prefer to mount a small carryall on top of the carrier. Of course, if you put a carryall in that position you don't have room for a tent, which is another good reason for using front panniers. For casual cycling, I recommend a carryall such as the one made by Touring Cyclist Shop, which mounts quickly over the rear carrier.

Rear Panniers

All of the data I have given on stress reinforcement apply in spades to rear panniers. Points of attachment should be especially reinforced. Zippers should have rain flaps. Panniers with a lot of pockets let you stow small items so you don't have to fumble and waste time looking for them. It's nice to be able to find toilet paper, razor, detergent, salt and pepper, film, toothbrush and toothpaste, lotion, the first-aid kit, matches, cookware and stove, without having to paw through clothes and other stuff. A sensible approach to packing can only be done with a many-pocketed set of front and rear panniers and bar bag.

Wrap items like honey jars in plastic, and carry lots of extra small plastic bags just in case something breaks that can smear and make a mess. Watch out for spare flashlight or radio batteries! I didn't once, and the terminals of a nine-volt radio battery hit a knife blade, shorted out and burned a hole in my pannier. Put tape over battery terminals.

Panniers should be reasonably water repellent. But repellency does not mean that things will not get wet in a hard rain. Water will find its way into the tightest of zippered compartments. If I see rain coming, my solution is to wrap items such as film, papers, wallet and watch in the kind of plastic bags you can seal, the kind that have a locking, zipperless seal. You should also carry a few heavy-duty, large leaf bags along. They weigh practically nothing, but they can keep tents and especially sleeping bags dry in a hard downpour. A wet sleeping bag, especially a down-filled bag, is a mess. You can't use a down-filled bag it it's wet; but you can wring enough moisture out of a synthetic-down bag to retain body heat. More about sleeping bags later.

Attachability and detachability in a pannier is vital. At a campsite it's convenient to lock the bike to a small tree and move the pannier to the tent or picnic table where you have access to it. If you cycle tour the motel or hotel route, you can't always bring the bike into the room, so quick detachability is important.

Panniers should also clip or zip together to make one unit, and the unit should have a shoulder strap for ease in carrying aboard an airplane. If the panniers have a handle, preferably leather for comfort, they can be clipped together over the carrier top for added anchorage, should one come loose on a hard bump.

I mentioned the need for stability earlier, and I would like to repeat that rear and front panniers *must* be firmly pressure anchored to the carrier, and should not bounce around. I will review the various pannier-mounting features of specific makes below. You may think that loading down the panniers will hold them on; not so. A good bump will lift the heaviest load upward and, if not anchored, off and downward as well. Dragging a pannier down the highway behind you is not conducive to safety or a healthy outlook on life. And if the pannier falls off entirely, an oncoming car or truck may not be able to avoid running over it. Now let's look at specific makes of bike bags and their features. In Table 4-1 I cover each manufacturer's product. What I want to do first, however, is to spell out the basic construction features unique to a particular manufacturer, to help you make up your own mind about which one to purchase. You can get by, for example, with a smaller rear-pannier set, say 1,700 cubic inches, if you use a front pannier. There will be some minor weight savings with smaller panniers, but I would say rather minimal. You should keep your total load well under thirty pounds, though, and if you will review the list of items that I recommend you carry (Table 4-2) you can do so. If you travel in Europe, add on a decent-looking suit or dress for evening use. Europeans are more formal in their dress codes that we are, and if you like good food in a fine restaurant, you really should wear a suit, tie and shirt. Fortunately synthetic fabrics are available that do not require pressing and spring back to life after unfolding. I sometimes combine business, such as attending bike shows, with a bike trip through Europe, so I really need to have some decent dress-up clothes along. When I'm through with business and on the road, I wrap the fancy duds in a plastic bag and put them at the bottom of the rear carrier main compartment.

Bellwether: 1161 Mission Street, San Francisco, California 94103 415/ 863-0436

Bellwether does not go in for innovation and experimentation; their bags have not changed much over the past five or six years, so costs are relatively low. In fact, their bags are among the least expensive made. They don't have the good mounting and detachment features of other bags; you can't snap them or tie them on and off quickly. If fast attach and release features are what you want, Bellwether doesn't have them. But their bags are sturdy enough and the Model 1203 with 2,200 cubic inches should be of ample size. The company does not make a front

Table 4-2   Bicycle Camping Equipment

	Weight * (oz.)
Fastened to the Bicycle	
Water bottle	2.25
Bottle cage	3.5
"Halt" with clip	4
Pump	5.5
Pannier bags	35
Metal pannier carrier	28
Front handlebar bag	7
Saddle bag	5
Subtotal, pounds:	5.64
Sleeping Gear	
Down-filled sleeping bag	40
Half-length foam pad	14
Tent (2 person)	27
Subtotal, pounds:	5.06
Cooking Gear	
Brillo pads	2
Paper towels	4
Bowie knife	4
Plastic water bottle, 2 gal.	1.5
Liquid soap	6
Cook stove	9
Fuel bottle, aluminum	4
Nesting pots and pans, aluminum	26
Fork, knife, spoon set	1.5
Four 6 x 12-in. poly bags	8 (all)
Two 9 x 18-in. poly bags	4 (all)
One 18 x 30-in. poly bag	2
Pot lifter	3
Plastic mug	1.4
Four plastic squeeze bottles	8 (all)
Subtotal, pounds:	5.83

Staples	Weight (oz.)	*Staples*	Weight (oz.)
Matches	2	Mustard	3
Salt (small containers)	2	Coffee	4
Sugar (small containers)	3	Margarine	6
Pepper (small containers)	1		
		Subtotal, pounds:	1.62

* Average weights

Table 4-2 Bicycle Camping Equipment (continued)

Clothing	*Weight (oz.)*
(besides what you wear)	
Knit jeans	17
Shoes, loafers (or sneakers)	20
Socks, one pair	1.6
Underwear, one pair (top & bottom)	6
Shirt, polyester & cotton, one	4
Shorts, cycling, one pair	5
Light sweater or sweatshirt	5
Rain jacket	10
Subtotal, pounds.	4.29

Personal Articles	*Weight (oz.)*	*Personal Articles*	*Weight (oz.)*
Toothpaste	4	Razor	2
Toothbrush	1	Comb	½
Soap and soap box	3		
		Subtotal, pounds:	.656

Miscellaneous	*Weight (oz.)*	*Miscellaneous*	*Weight (oz.)*
Flashlight	19	Wallet	6
Batteries for above	2	First aid kit	8
Bug spray	4	Combination lock & cable	9
		Shock cords (four)	6
		25-ft. nylon cord	5
		Tools (Table 4-2)	63.5
		Subtotal, pounds:	8.4

Optional Items	*Weight (oz.)*	*Optional Items*	*Weight (oz.)*
Small AM-FM radio	12	Playing cards	5
35-MM camera (miniature)	12	Pocketbook	5
Film, 35 MM, four rolls	4	Fly-fishing outfit	16
Mini-binoculars	9	Extra eyeglasses	2
		Subtotal, pounds:	4.06

Cold-Weather Clothing	*Weight (oz.)*
Down coat, with outer detachable shell	44
Knit warm-up suit	32
Thermal socks, two pair	14 (all
Ear flaps	1.5
Cycling bootees	30
Down sleeping bag, 15° to 25°	56
Subtotal, pounds:	11.09
less 25° bag	− 2.50
	8.59

pannier, and the rear models are too big for up-front use. Figures 4-15 through 4-18 show their basic line.

Cannondale: 35 Pulaski Street, Stamford, Connecticut 06902 203/359-1705

Cannondale was one of the early designers of bike bags and related equipment and their line has shown steady improvement each year. Today the bags (Fig. 4-19) are sturdy, mount quickly and firmly and have a high degree of water repellency. The B037 bar bag is tops for ease of mounting, durability, capacity, number of compartments and general utility use. Their bags feature double stitching, nylon web, nylon coil zippers with easy-to-grasp lace loops through all pulls, pull tabs on zipper handles and shoulder straps. Panniers can snap together to make one legal carry-on bag for air travel. Cannondale prices are very competitive. All rear bags come with mounted reflector, as do bar bags. Their B041, with ten compartments, is one of the most convenient to pack and use of any set of rear panniers and it has the most overall capacity at 2,400 cubic inches. Check Table 4-1 and compare price per cubic inch.

Eclipse, Inc., P.O. Box 7370, Ann Arbor, Michigan 48107 313/761-1170

Eclipse's mounting system for rear and front panniers is the best on the market, both in terms of quick attachment and removal and stability.

Table 4-3 How Much You Should Carry*

Category	Weight in Pounds
Staples	1.62
Clothing (warm weather)	4.29
Personal items	.656
Miscellaneous (with tools)	8.40
Carried on the bike	5.64
Sleeping gear (warm weather)	5.06
Cooking gear	5.83
Total, basic camping gear	31.496 lbs.
With: cold-weather items	8.59
	40.086 lbs.
With: Optional items:	4.06
	44.146 lbs.

* From items in Table 4-2, subtotals. Try not to carry more stuff than this. Don't count daily food items you shop for; you don't carry them very far, on the bike. I would never carry more than 32 pounds. If you are traveling as a pair, cut the tent, optional items and miscellaneous weights in half. Tent now becomes 13.5 ounces, optional items 32.48 ounces and miscellaneous 67.2 ounces. So deduct all these items, which total 113.18 ounces (7.07 lbs.) and you come up with a maximum weight of 24.426 pounds for your warm-weather camping gear (basic gear from above, 31.496 lbs. − 7.07 lbs. = 24.426 lbs.). That's pretty light camping indeed! An ideal figure to aim for. A good reason not to travel alone.

Fig. 4-15: Bellwether handlebar bag mounts with Velcro strips.

Fig. 4-16: Rear pannier mounts over carrier. *(Bellwether)*

Fig. 4-17: Larger pannier with room at the top for sleeping bag or small tent. *(Bellwether)*

Fig. 4-18: A larger bar bag with map case at top. *(Bellwether)*

Fig. 4-19: Cannondale handlebar bag and rear panniers on a 14-speed Raleigh touring bicycle. Note ample heel clearance.

Fig. 4-20: Unique carrier with slots or grooves on either side into which panniers fit. Four plastic buttons keep panniers in place. *(Eclipse)*

You do have to use their carrier (Fig. 4-20) or an Eclipse adapter (Fig. 4-21) for your existing carrier if you use their front or rear panniers. The Eclipse carrier weighs 21 ounces and costs $25. The slide-mount adapter costs $5. Eclipse also makes a unique mount (Fig. 4-22) that permits the use of attachment-bar carrier at both the front and the rear of the bike, allowing you to treat your pannier as either a front bag or a seat bag. This is a good idea, because it removes my basic objection to seat bags: that they rub on thighs. With this mount the seat mounting is far enough back to clear your legs and thighs. The mount costs $10. All carriers are aluminum alloy.

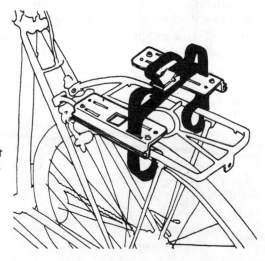

Fig. 4-21: A slide-mount adapter kit for use with conventional carriers. *(Eclipse)*

Fig. 4-22: An adapter permitting use of a handlebar bag or a seat bag, which keeps either far enough back so they do not rub on rider's thighs. This idea has to come from a cyclist of experience. (*Eclipse*)

The Eclipse system uses a slide mount (Fig. 4-23) plus tough plastic snaps that hold the panniers in place and keep them from sliding back or forward. This is the most stable mounting system I have seen, as noted earlier.

Handlebar bags mount in a fairly conventional way, using a handlebar mount. Like the Cannondale bar bags, the Eclipse bar bag (or "seat" bag, if it's attached at the rear) also has two elastic shock cords (Fig. 4-24) that fasten below to dropout ears. This method provides a very stable mount that keeps the bags from bouncing up and down on rough roads. So, properly cushioned, a small camera tucked inside a bar bag should survive a trip.

With the Eclipse adapter, you can use their 450-cubic-inch Superlite panniers on the front. The largest Eclipse rear pannier, the Transcontinental, is only 1,075 cubic inches, or about half the size of the biggest Cannondale rear pannier set. But with the Superlite up front and the Transcontinental in back, along with the quite large 610-cubic-inch Professional bar bag, you get a grand total of 2,135 cubic inches and 22 pockets or compartments. None of the bags I have seen is really big enough to carry a tent, and a sleeping bag would be a tight fit. So with all these pockets you should be able to do a really intelligent job of stowage. You might even make a stowage map, number each pocket, type out what's in each pocket on a 3-by-5 card, have the card sealed in plastic and keep it in your bar bag map case for ready reference. I cannot overemphasize how important it is to be able to lay your hands on just what you need, when you need it. You are traveling with a mini set of kitchen shelves, dresser drawers, bathroom cabinet and clothes closet, all in one small package.

Eclipse also makes a pannier rain cover which fits tightly over any of the Eclipse panniers. The rain cover protects against water infiltration, which is going to occur with the best-made pannier, especially at the seams. You may also have some condensation inside the panniers, which rain covers will not prevent, but this has never been a problem for me. The rain covers also keep road grime off your new panniers. They weigh 3.84 ounces and cost $12.50 a pair.

Fig. 4-23: Slide-mounting method of attaching a rear pannier. Note plastic buttons on bag that fit into receptor buttons on carrier to keep panniers from sliding backward and forward. *(Eclipse)*

Kangaroo Baggs: 29 North Garden Street, Ventura, California 93001 805/653-0431

All of Kangaroo's bags are well made and sturdy, with a hook mounting system and tie-downs that keep bags stable under rough road conditions. Extra large, plastic-coated hooks grip the carrier for a secure attachment, yet the bags can be off-loaded quickly. The rear-pannier tie-downs are adjustable for different-size bike frames. Panniers can be hooked together to make one carry-on luggage bag. An optional shoulder strap adds to ease of toting aboard airplanes. Bags are made of 8-ounce parachute pack cloth with a waterproof coating inside. By the way, one way to tell if a bag does have such a coating is to look inside. If the inside surface looks a lot shinier than the outside, it's coated.

The Cross Country panniers with 2,200 cubic inches and twelve pockets, plus the front panniers with 1,200 cubic inches and four pockets (both), and the Touring Bagg with 650 cubic inches and six pockets, give you 4,050 cubic inches of space and twenty-two pockets. There should be lots of room left over for groceries and souvenirs.

Fig. 4-24: This adapter shows how handlebar bag can be mounted behind the saddle and still clear rider's legs. *(Eclipse)*

Kirtland Tour Pak: P.O. Box 4059, Boulder, Colorado 90306 303/449-8080

All Kirtland panniers have a three-position adjustment to compensate for varying sizes of bike frames. You need this feature because if you have a small bike frame, the tie-downs won't be stressed enough for stability. Adjustment is a simple matter of repositioning hooks. Heavy steel hooks curve over the carrier's top bracket to hold the pannier down securely.

Velocipac: 2300 Central Avenue, Boulder, Colorado 80301 303/443-4690 (Figs. 4-27–4-31)

Another producer of very high-quality bicycle bar bags and panniers, Velocipac makes the largest-capacity system on the market. The Big Horn V-7 panniers at 2,632 cubic inches have more carrying capacity than any others made. Add to these the Caribou V-5 front panniers at 1,306 inches, and the V-4 Handlebar Pack, and you have a total of 4,727 cubic inches. You can add still more capacity by using Fox V-1 Frame Pack, with 576 cubic inches, for a total of 5,303 cubic inches. A frame pack fits inside the "V" framed by the top, seat and downtubes, fastens to all three tubes and still leaves room on the down tube for a water bottle. It's designed for frames that are 22 to 25½ inches. For smaller frames, Velocipac has a 491-cubic-inch version of the frame pack. Compartments for the total system are: nine for the bar bag, ten for the rear panniers, four for the front panniers and two for the frame pack, or a total of twenty-five compartments or pockets. That's an awful lot of stowage space. You could add a seat bag and carry another 450 cubic inches for that kitchen sink you left behind. You should be able to squeeze a sleeping bag, a tent and a foam pad or air mattress into the rear pannier, however, so you would instantly fill up two of the main compartments plus one of the medium-sized ones. But you would have everything under one roof, so to speak.

Fig. 4-26: The mounting brackets on these panniers permit adjustment for frames of different height and wheelbase length. *(Kirtland)*

Fig. 4-27: Large-capacity rear panniers. *(Velocipac)*

Fig..4-28: Handlebar mounting bracket supports bar bag at bottom. *(Velocipac)*

Fig. 4-29: Handlebar mounted on bar bracket. *(Velocipac)*

Fig. 4-30: Front panniers provide extra carrying capacity, help balance load. *(Velocipac)*

Fig. 4-31: Attachment method like this makes for quick, easy and secure attachment of rear pannier to carrier. Shock cords fasten to dropout ears. *(Velocipac)*

All Velocipacs are made of 8-ounce Parapac double urethane-coated nylon oxford, rather than the coarse-weave nylon some makers use. Zippers are Number 5 Ykk nylon coil, self-repairing. Two-way zip slides on large main compartments make it easier to open them. Zippers have a 1-inch rain flap over them, and bags are sewn with a 12-pound tensile-strength nylon thread, with all seams double stitched. Nylon reinforcement webbing on packs has 350 and 750 pounds tensile strength. Hardware is nickel plated for corrosion resistance. The bar bag map case is of ultraviolet-resisting 10-millimeter clear vinyl plastic. The suspension system is a heavy-duty double wrap ¼-inch shock cord as reliable as and lighter than steel springs.

Yet another adjustment is for the fore and aft position of the panniers on the carrier—to get the panniers back far enough for your heel clearance and to keep them there. The pannier springs can be adjusted at an angle (Fig. 4-26) that provides additional back holding tension. And the carrier hooks can be repositioned either forward or back by using other bolt holes in the stiffener. Just unbolt the hooks, move them fore or aft as needed and rebolt in place.

All Kirtland panniers snap together to form one piece of luggage. A leather handle facilitates carrying.

Touring Cyclist Shop: P.O. Box 4009, Boulder, Colorado 80302 303/ 449-4067

If by now you have noted that Boulder, Colorado, must be the bike bag capital of the country, you are right. And the Touring Cyclist Shop is where it all started, in 1971. Proprietor Hartley Alley and wife, Jean, can truly be said to be the parents of the bike bag industry, which began when they were planning for a bicycle trip to Europe, and found no decent bags—lightweight, water repellent, multi-compartmented—that were suitable for bike touring. That was when they designed their own, and they have been at it ever since. TCS bags are not inexpensive, but they're well worth the money, if you want super-convenience, stability and durability. Actually, on a cost-per-cubic-inch basis, they are less costly than other comparable makes.

TCS's handlebar bag has an incredible eleven pockets, three of which are inside for loose change, billfold and even a slot for a pen. It's the only bar bag with a loop for carrying a compass (Fig. 4-14). Outside pockets have Velcro closures to make it easy to get at them, and the main compartment can be held closed with a Velcro fastener for quick access, or with a flap-covered zipper. The bar bag fastens to the bar-support bracket with three Velcro snaps, making it easy to remove the entire bag for when, say, you go to a restaurant.

You must, however, pay extra for the bag support: $5. Unlike other makes TCS does not include the bag support with the bag. The TCS bar bag has a sturdy swiveled snap-hook-attached shoulder strap for ease of carrying, and when not in use as a bar bag, it makes an excellent photo gadget bag or utility bag for sports use, such as fishing, or for long plane or train trips.

All TCS bags are of 8-ounce waterproof nylon and are sturdy and easy to attach and remove (Figs. 4-32 and 4-33). Their panniers have an aluminum sheet stiffener. They can be zipped together to form one carry-on. Optional shoulder straps ($2.50 each) with a black rubber shoulder pad ($2.25 each) make carrying more comfortable. I use these straps on all panniers and bar bags, and they can be used on other makes as well. Order the pad and the strap together ($4.75 for both).

You won't find TCS bags in your bike store, as they are sold only by mail order from TCS in Boulder. Their catalog also lists other convenience items such as tools, clothes for cycling, helmets, rearview mirrors for glasses, compasses, gloves, Blackburn and other carriers, tires and tubes, bag-seam sealers and many other items. I can recommend TCS products as being among the very best. Figure 4-13 shows what the well-dressed touring bike will wear, with the complete TCS line installed. Note the large rucksack-type bag on the rear carrier. The rollstand is also a TCS product. Figure 4-32 is a close-up of the TCS rear pannier. Note that the large outside pocket is at the rear, so these, like all such panniers, are right- or left-sided and can't be used with the big pocket forward or you won't have heel clearance. Note the generous-sized zipper pull tabs.

PANNIER CARRIERS

About five years ago the only lightweight pannier carrier was the old and well-known Swiss Pletscher. I have found this carrier to be unreliable. The stays simply buckle under any real load. To be fair, the Pletscher was really not made for that application, but that was all we had available to us, unless we wanted to carry a heavy steel carrier around, one that would succumb to rust. Things are different today. There are now two very fine carriers indeed, on the market: the Eclipse, mentioned earlier, and the Blackburn carrier, made by *Jim Blackburn Designs, 1080 Florence Way, Campbell, California 95008, 408/379-3110.*

The Blackburn carriers are made of aluminum rod, Heli-Arc welded for strength and durability. The struts are triangular in shape, for rigidity (Figs. 4-34 and 4-35). I have toured extensively with these carriers and carried some fairly heavy loads on them. In fact, I recently carried an eighty-pound boy, seated on a cushion, his feet in panniers to either side, for about ten miles over rough roads. The panniers held up fine, which is more than I can say for yours truly.

Blackburn carriers weigh only 14.81 ounces (420 grams) rear, and 10.23 ounces (290 grams) front. A new, adjustable carrier (Fig. 4-35) weighs in at 15 ounces (425 grams). The nonadjustable model comes in two sizes for different-size bike frames, Model C-SS-3 for 18- to 20-inch frames and Model C-SS-2 for 24- and 26-inch frames. For 22- to 28-inch

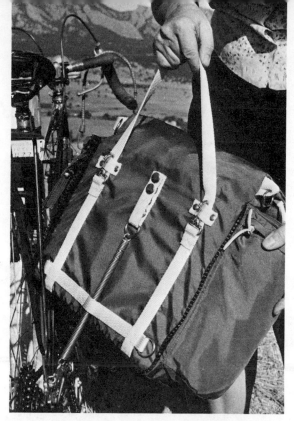

Fig. 4-32: This method uses a heavy-duty steel spring and tough nylon webbing to secure panniers to carrier. Note carrying strap, and outside zippers that permit the two separate rear panniers to be joined as one for carry-on luggage on airplanes, where only one bag is permitted as on overseas flights. *(Touring Cyclist Shop)*

Fig. 4-33: Well-designed rear panniers have ample heel clearance, many pockets for convenience, leather pulls on zippers, rain flaps over zippers. *(Touring Cyclist Shop)*

Fig. 4-34: These very strong, light-weight aluminum alloy strut-braced carriers are heli-arc welded and fasten to dropout ears. (*Jim Blackburn Designs*)

Fig. 4-35: Front carrier similar in design to rear carrier in Figure 4-36. (*Jim Blackburn Designs*)

Fig. 4-36: Aluminum carrier with adjustable stainless-steel mounting tongue that compensates for varying sizes of bike frames so carrier can remain level. (*Jim Blackburn Designs*)

Fig. 4-37: Coated clamps for mounting nonadjustable aluminum alloy carrier on seat stays. (*Jim Blackburn Designs*)

frames, use the adjustable model C AR 2. These carriers are available in smooth polished aluminum or smooth anodized black, which are most attractive. Blackburn used to make carriers for custom frames, but with the adjustable model now available, they have discontinued this line. Add 10 percent to the list price for black carriers. The adjustable model has a sliding steel extender which gives you 1¾ inches horizontal adjustment, so the carrier can be adjusted level. The other two models either bolt onto brazed-on fittings or are held on by special Blackburn coated seat-stay clamps (Fig. 4-37). Figure 4-38 shows front and rear Blackburn carriers in place on a bike frame. The rear carrier is the adjustable model, and as you can see, it fastens to the rear brake bridge, on the brake bolt. The front model fastens to the front brake bolt. All models fasten to either dropout fender ears, or, with special fittings supplied by

Fig. 4-38: Alloy carriers mounted on bike frame. (*Jim Blackburn Designs*)

Fig. 4-39: These fittings permit carrier mounting on Campangolo dropouts without "ears" on dropouts. (*Jim Blackburn Designs*)

Blackburn, to the triangle (Fig. 4-39) in the rear dropout. Front dropouts come with fender eyes.

Blackburn also makes an elegant, light water bottle cage (Fig. 4-40) which can either be used with brazed-on fittings found on more expensive or custom-built bikes, or clamped onto the seat or down tube.

Blackburn carriers are around $22.50 for the front FR-1 carrier, $24.50 for the SS-1 and SS-2 carriers and $24.50 for the adjustable carrier. Add about $3 for the black anodized models. The bottle cage is $7 in clear, $8 in black. Prices may vary from dealer to dealer. The bottle case weighs 1.58 ounces (45 grams).

Figure 4-41 shows a close-up view of the Eclipse carrier (described in the section on Eclipse bags) which will help you understand how it works. The standard Eclipse Professional Slide Mount Pannier Pack costs $25 and weighs 21 ounces. The Slide Mount Adapter costs $5 and weighs 8 ounces.

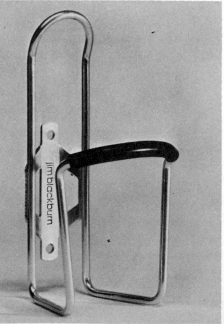

Fig. 4-40: Lightweight alloy water-bottle cage, drilled for mounting on brazed-on fittings on custom bike frame. Can also be clamped on. (*Jim Blackburn Designs*)

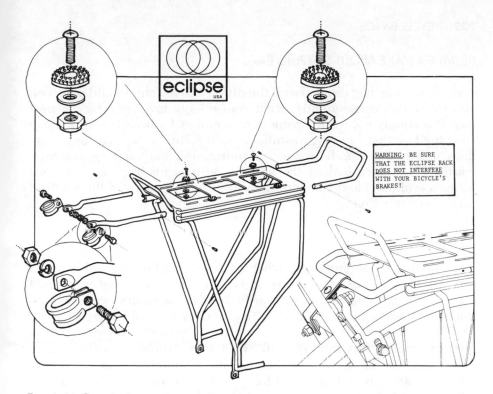

WARNING: BE SURE THAT THE ECLIPSE RACK DOES NOT INTERFERE WITH YOUR BICYCLE'S BRAKES!

Fig. 4-41: Detailed view showing how slide-mount carrier works. *(Eclipse)*

A WORD ABOUT COMPASSES

You can get lost on a bike trip. Even with a map. You may think you travel too slowly ever to need a compass direction. Wrong! A compass can save you hours of frustration, if by doing nothing else than confirming that you are headed in the right direction. I have been thoroughly lost in unfamiliar country, and wished earnestly at the time for a compass bearing, for just such reassurance. Once, in Holland, I saw an attractive road, totally free of traffic, wending its way through farmland. I did have a compass, and so felt free to abandon my planned route for the day with the knowledge that I was at least headed in the general direction I wanted to go. I wound up at my destination pretty much on time, but I had the fun of departing from plan, on the spur of the moment, and finding much more scenic routes as a reward. A compass fastened to your bar bag can be a big comfort indeed. Touring Cyclist Shop has a fastening point on their bag for a compass, and even sells the compass (Fig. 4-14) for $11.75. This is a Silva Huntsman precision, Swedish-made compass which weighs only one ounce. In the TCS mounting position, the compass is far enough away from the bike to avoid needle deflection and wrong readings due to bike-frame attraction. It is also useful for walking tours in foreign cities not laid out on a grid pattern. As for winding country roads, a compass, as noted, is just about a "must."

BE WIDE AWAKE ABOUT SLEEPING BAGS

A good sleeping bag can make all the difference in comfort and how well you sleep and, consequently, what your energy level will be the next day. It is simply not worth trying to save money by investing in a cheap sleeping bag that's heavy, unstuffable into a stuff sack, that lumps up, does not have a durable cover or lining and that can't be machine washed. Now let's look at the assorted fillings for bags, and the bag designs available, and compare the pluses and minuses of the kinds of fill and construction.

Filling

The filling in a sleeping bag is what insulated you from the cold around you. Your body loses heat in three ways: by convection, that is, by cold air currents carrying heat from your body as it passes over you; by conduction of heat when warm flesh is in contact with a cold object, such as a metal zipper, ice or snow, or water which is chilling you by evaporation (you experience this kind of chill effect as moisture evaporates when you step out of the shower); and by radiation. Radiation heat loss occurs when you are exposed to any surface colder than you are. For example, when you stand next to a single glazed window on a cold day, you will feel a chill as radiant heat waves from your body pass into or are absorbed by the colder window glass.

With that background, you can appreciate how important the fill in a sleeping bag can be. Let's compare the three popular types of fill. First, though, the more expensive bags use either down or DuPont Dacron® Hollofil™. Cheaper bags use solid polyester fiber such as Fortrel or Insul.

Goose Down

Pluses

- More insulating value for weight than any other fill
- Greater "loft" or bulk with lightness
- Better stuffability (into your stuff sack)

Minuses

- Tends to migrate inside the bag unless the bag is constructed of compartments to minimize this tendency
- Impossible to use when wet, takes a long time to dry out, mats when wet
- Expensive

You can toss the down-filled bag into a laundromat dryer on the road, if it gets wet, but that's not much help when it's time to camp and you find the bag is wet.

Down is a hollow-core type of natural fiber that traps a lot of air and so has excellent insulating value, as noted.

DuPont Dacron® Hollofil™

From now on I will refer to this fill material as DDH for convenience. DDH is a synthetic fiber with the unique characteristic of having a hollow center in the polyester fiber yarn, making it similar to goose down in that respect.

Pluses

- Excellent insulation for weight
- High "loft"
- Soft, very stuffable
- Less tendency to migrate than down
- Less expensive than down
- Machine washable and dryable
- Can be used when wet by squeezing out excess moisture. Does not mat when wet, still have insulating value when wet

Minuses

- Costs more than solid polyester fiber
- A bit heavier than down, takes more to achieve same temperature rating

Solid Polyester

Another fill is solid polyester fiber, found in less expensive bags.

Pluses

- Cheap
- Machine washable

Minuses

- Not for cold weather
- Heavy
- Not usable when wet
- Can bulk up into uncomfortable bumps
- Poor insulation against ground cold

Types of Sleeping Bags

Whatever the material and construction, sleeping bags come in three general configurations:

Mummy: a tapered design that hugs the body closely, conserves body heat, is used for extreme cold weather. The problem is that you may feel trapped in a bag that is so close fitting, but if it's cold outside, say 10 degrees Fahrenheit (What are you doing bicycle camping in such cold!), you can get used to the mummy approach quickly. Personally I prefer more room to turn around in, and I feel confined when my feet have no room to spread. Can be used to −10 degrees.

Modified Mummy or Taper Design: roomier, but still somewhat constricting. For temperatures down to 20 degrees, depending on fill material.

Rectangular: for milder temperatures, say down to 35 or 40 degrees, the kind you are more likely to encounter while bicycle camping, the rectangular-shaped bag offers many advantages. First, you have room to squiggle around in, which I find necessary for my comfort. I can shift body position without finding myself restricted by a tight-fitting shell around me. The ideal sleeping bag for bike touring is rectangular in shape, weighs overall no more than 3 pounds, has a goose-down or DDH fill, a nylon ripstop outer shell of 1.9-ounce fabric, an inner shell of soft-feeling nylon taffeta and features left or right zippers. If you buy one left- and one right-sided zipper location you can zip the bags together for togetherness.

You don't really need the head covering, which the −10-degree bags come with, but you do need *some* sort of head covering. Heat can escape from an uncovered head very quickly and lead to a lot of discomfort. I use a Navy wool watch cap, sometimes pulled down over my ears, and in cold October days in the Midwest, or even in Scandinavia, that was sufficient. If you're going to Polar Bear it, you do need a mummy bag, which is designed for low temperatures.

Sizes: You can buy most sleeping bags in at least two lengths. For example, the 83-inch length fits people up to 6 feet tall, the 89-inch length up to 6 feet, 6 inches.

Loft: I've mentioned "loft" in several places. Loft is simply how high the fill will puff up. The greater the loft, the more the insulating value. For example, a 6-inch loft with DDH fill is found in 20-degree bags, an 8-inch loft in −10-degree bags.

The Cover: The cover, for durability, should be 1.9-ounce ripstop nylon. Cheaper bags use 100-percent cotton sheeting, which won't last long. A bit more expensive bags use nylon oxford, which is more durable but not ripstop, so when (not if) you tear the cover, the rip can spread.

Lining: The better bags use nylon taffeta, which is soft to the touch and very durable. Cheaper bags use flannel, which, although soft, is not very durable.

Zippers: Polyester zippers don't get cold to the touch. Better bags use them. Aluminum zippers do get cold, and will wake you up out of a sound sleep if you brush against them on a cold night. Better bags also have flaps or draft tubes over zippers to keep air leaks away from you. Zippers of any kind will leak air. Zippers should be pullable from inside the bag.

Pillows: Some physicians recommend that you not use pillows at any time, to keep your back straight and avoid back problems. But if you want something under your head, a few bags come with a built-in pillow. I use a folded down jacket.

Pads: A pad under your sleeping bag is an absolute necessity, both to keep you away from bumps in the ground, and, more importantly, to keep ground cold and ground moisture from seeping into your bag and body during the night. I recommend a pad even if you sleep on a tent canvas floor. There are several approaches to a pad. Touring Cyclist Shop sells an Ensolite pad of closed cell foam that cannot absorb water, good to 5 degrees Fahrenheit, is 42-by-18-by-⅜ inches and fits in a stuff sack with room to spare. $6.50.

For $21.95 you can buy a full-length air mattress that weighs only 13 ounces. It has six separate air chambers inflatable by two breaths each. It is made of urethane-coated nylon and comes in a tote bag with a patch kit. *From Stebco Industries, 1020 W. 40th Street, Chicago, Illinois 60609.*

Early Winters, a mail-order sporting equipment house, *110 Prefontaine Place South, Seattle, Washington 98104* has a similar pad, either 56 or 73 inches long, for $14.95 for the shortie and $17.95 for the full-length model. The shortie weighs 11 ounces, the full length 14 ounces. A stuff sack for either pad is $3.47 with dust flap and toggle. It will not absorb water, is highly resistant to tearing or gouging and it is not affected by ozone, sunlight or extreme cold. Both sizes are 22 inches wide. This is my choice for a pad.

Sleeping Bag Selections

Without getting into a lot more detail, and based on many many thousands of miles of cycle-tour camping in all sorts of climates from desert to mountain in Europe and America, here are the sleeping bags I prefer:
Campe 7 Arete: designed for cycle touring. Warm down to 14 degrees Fahrenheit, has 2.5 pounds of goose down (check to make sure you are not allergic to down) and is compressible. A large stuff sack for home storage and a stuff sack for cycle touring are both supplied. Joinable (order left and right sides). 1.7-ounce nylon ripstop nylsilk cover. The regular size for up to 5 feet, 11 inches weighs 2 pounds, 5 ounces, costs $150. The long size for up to 6 feet, 6 inches weighs 2 pounds, 8 ounces, costs $160. These are modified mummy bags.

If you will be camping during summer months and do not plan on stopping somewhere near the treeline of mountains, a lightweight bag will do. The Camp 7 Pioneer uses a synthetic polyester fill, is rated down to 45 degrees Fahrenheit, is made of 1.9-ounce rip stop nylon and can be used as a cover for another sleeping bag to increase warmth. Regular size weighs 2 pounds and costs $49; long size weighs 2 pounds, 4 ounces and costs $54—quite a reasonable price for a high-quality bag. Both bags are available from Touring Cyclists Shop or your sporting goods store.

The Coleman Model 585 Peak 1 sleeping bag is a more comfortable rectangular shape, weighs 40 ounces and costs $37.50. It has a 2.5-pound DDH fill and will keep you toasty down to around 40 degrees. Construction is very high quality, with a double quilt, stagger seam to prevent migration of fill. It is joinable, machine washable, uses two-way polyester zippers and comes with a nylon stuff sack.

There are hundreds of other sleeping bags on the market within these general specifications and price ranges. Look for the bag that suits you best that fits these specifications. I really can't recommend your spending a bankroll on Arctic-type sleeping bags when you are not going to be touring in really cold weather. Of course, if you're planning an all-season, round-the-world tour, you should be prepared for the worst of conditions. In that case, I can recommend the − 10°F Cannondale Great Northern, a modified mummy bag with DDH fill with an 8-inch loft. Available in regular and long lengths that weigh 92 and 99 ounces, respectively, it costs $95 with stuff sack. This sleeping bag is joinable, machine washable, has a contoured hood that covers your head, a full length draft column over the zipper, 1.9-ounce ripstop outer shell, nylon taffeta inner shell and sandwich method insulation construction.

ABOUT TENTS

There are a number of very lightweight tents on the market, ranging from little more than a one-person pup tent to a two- or even three-person tent.

The ideal tent—and I speak from experience—should "breathe" so as to prevent moisture from condensing on the inside of the tent. Even on a rainless night, if the moisture gets down below the "dew point" (the point at which the surface of the tent gets cold enough to condense out moisture from your body and breath), I have had tents that literally "rained" on me. And on a cold, windy, wet and rainy night, to brush against the inside of the tent is to release a small Niagara of condensed moisture.

If by chance your tent does accumulate moisture at night, you *must* turn the tent inside out, dunk it in detergent sudsy water and wash off the moisture. Otherwise, the next night will find you with a tent that smells awful.

The ideal bike tent should have a full "bathtub" floor (a floor with sides that go up about two inches all around), a rear window with mosquito covering and be openable from the inside. A small outer vestibule in which to stow gear is a deluxe and most appreciated feature. Some small tents have one built in, others offer an optional vestibule or small "front porch" that will contain the bike (with wheels removed), panniers and bags, and keep them safe from roving animals, both two- and four-legged. A vestibule gives you lots more room in the tent and adds very little weight to the tent itself.

A front fly, zippered and openable from both sides, with a nylon insect screen is also vital.

A tent that can be quickly erected by one person is ideal. Tent pegs and peg nylon loops should be at all four sides in the middle of each side. The pegs should really dig into the ground and resist pulling out. Tent guy lines should have a friction catch for length adjustment. No tent should depend on nearby trees for support—you can't rely on your campsite to have trees where you need them.

Unless you're going over the Rockies in the fall, you won't need an insulated tent, which can get fairly heavy.

Carry your tent and sleeping bag in water-resistant sacks. Most small tents and sleeping bags come with a sack, but these sacks are closed with a drawstring, which will definitely admit water in a hard rain. You could close the tent or bag in a plastic leaf bag, as noted earlier. I like the Cannondale C902 stuff sack for sleeping bags and their A004 stuff sack for a tent. They are made of urethane-coated nylon, have web handles, top flaps and cord locks and are more durable and a lot better-looking than plastic bags. The C902 costs $6.95, the A004, $7.95. If you have a larger sleeping bag, or one with down fill, I'd use the A004 instead of the C902.

Tie the tent and sleeping bag on top of your rear carrier, or better yet, if you don't use a bar bag, but do use front panniers, put the tent on the rear carrier, and the sleeping bag up front. If there are two of you, you only need one tent and one set of cookware and one stove, and you can split the load between you. On a trip especially, two bodies are a whole lot better than one.

Here are My Tent Selections

The Cannondale Susquehanna Model C895 can sleep two and in an emergency three persons, has a vestibule and rear awning, weighs 7 pounds 2 ounces. It is made like a thermos bottle with 6 inches of dead air space around the sleeping area that insulates as well as stops condensation. A coated bathtub-type floor extends up to 12 inches inside the inner walls all around. This is a feature you will appreciate if you camp in a hollow where water puddles can turn into a small pond and you aren't permitted to shovel a narrow drainage ditch (called "ditching") around the tent. It's disheartening to awaken in a pool of water inside the tent. I know.

Ventilation is controlled by one set of zippers which drops both screen and front door, and another set which drops only the door, so you can control ventilation from inside. The aerodynamic shape resists wind. From Cannondale or their local dealer, costs $195.

This tent is fairly heavy, but if two of you split the load, the other person can carry both sleeping bags and ground pads, and perhaps the

Fig. 4-42: One-person "Pocket Hotel" is light, strong, ideal for solo touring. *(Early Winters)*

stove and cooking gear as well. I find the added comfort of a good tent conducive to a good night's rest and worth the extra weight and cost.

The Pocket Hotel™ from Early Winters is probably the ultimate in a high-quality, super lightweight tent for the solo cyclist camper. It's made of breathable Gore-tex fabric that minimizes the condensation problem, sets up quickly, is tough, durable and comfortable. It even has a small vestibule (Fig. 4-42). It weighs but 2 pounds and costs $99.95 (may be more by the time you read this book).

The *Light Dimension*™, a two-person model (Fig. 4-43), weighs 3¾ pounds, has a small vestibule and costs $238. *The Winterlight*™, a

Fig. 4-44: The Gore-Tex tents in Figures 4-42 and 4-43 are expanded in this version of a deluxe two-person tent with large vestibule. *(Early Winters)*

Fig 4-43: Lightweight two-person tent has a small "vestibule" which is very convenient, makes for lots more room in sleeping area. *(Early Winters)*

tougher and lot more deluxe two-person tent, weighs 4.5 pounds and costs $274 (Fig. 4-44).

Coleman's Peak 1 Model 838 two-man tent has a wet-weather fly and outside framework with spreader bars. The spreader bars are a good idea, because no matter how taut your guy lines, any tent will sag some, and when it does you lose living space. It features double-lap felled seams, with chain and lock stitches. Stress points are reinforced with extra material or nylon webbing. Tent walls are breathable nylon taffeta. Floors are waterproof urethane coated and wrap up to 10 inches on sides and ends. Door thresholds are above ground level to keep water out. (If you have done much camping, you will appreciate this feature. Water can run in rivulets in front of the tent, and if the door "frame" sags some of that water can run right into the tent.) It's a helluva good foul-weather, lightweight tent that weighs 5 pounds, 10 ounces, sleeps two and, in a pinch, three. This is Coleman's Peak Number 1 top-line small tent. Costs $110.

CLOTHING

The proper clothing to wear while cycling obviously varies with the weather. Consequently I will talk about clothing for moderate weather (June to October in the so-called "Temperate Zone"), wet weather in any season, and cold weather.

Warm-Weather Clothing

Here are a few general tips and precautions about clothing for the June–September season. First, the don'ts:

• *Never wear 100-percent synthetic fiber anything.* Nylon and the like won't absorb moisture, you will sweat profusely and you and your clothes will make a billy goat blanch. I know synthetics keep their shape, dry fast and wash out easily. That's the best I can say about them.

Gore-Tex™, by the way, is the only fabric that violates my no-synthetic adjuration about bicycle clothing. This is because Gore-Tex™ is a laminated fiber that "breathes"—lets moisture through but keeps out water. In other words, the fabric is permeable to water vapor but not to liquid moisture. Gore-Tex™ is also a very tough fabric which resists tearing and abrasion. So anything made out of Gore-Tex™ has my blessing—parkas, jackets, raingear, tents, bootees, whatever.

• *Never wear a short-sleeved non-V-neck shirt.* Any shirt that is closed up to the neck will be super hot. You need air flowing over your neck to keep your head cool. A button shirt is better than a zipper one. Zippers going down a mountain at high speed will get cold.

Some do's:

• *Forget about style and concentrate on comfort.* Wear loose-fitting clothes. Shorts are particularly important—you don't want them to bind *anywhere.* You need at least a full inch of air between your thighs and the lower edge of the shorts. I like the L.L. Bean walking shorts or the Feather River Shorts from Early Winters made of 100-percent cotton. The Early Winters shorts are around $18.50 a pair, but are worth it.

Another idea I have found helpful is to wear a long-sleeved denim work shirt, the thin cotton kind, on those chilly mornings. Once you get going and the sun warms things up you can take it off. You'll be amazed at how useful one of these shirts can be, how much protection it offers.

After you have climbed a steep hill or spent an hour laboring up a mountain road under the hot sun you will be, well, sweaty. The first time you go downhill at speed after such a climb you will find yourself getting really chilled as all the moisture that you have accumulated on your body and in your clothes begins to evaporate and carry away body heat in the process. Even the work shirt won't be enough to keep you from being chilled. Here is where a cotton Windbreaker or pullover comes in really handy (Notice that all the clothes I recommend are light and very compact). Any sporting goods store should have them, but I have found cotton pullovers or even cotton/synthetic-blend Windbreakers or pullovers extremely scarce. Most sporting-goods stores seem to go for chemical clothes. One excellent shell is sold by Early Winters (110 Prefontaine Place South, Seattle, Washington 98104). Send for their catalog. I refer to their Eye Of The Wind model. Shells should not have knitted wristlets. You don't need and won't want all that much protection in mild weather.

About Socks

If you're lucky you can find all-wool or a blend of wool and nylon or heavy cotton socks in an army surplus store or one of those back-pack specialty stores. Mostly, though, I rely on mail-order houses because it saves me an awful lot of time searching through endless shelves in stores trying to find exactly what I need, in my size. I like the Thousand Mile socks from Early Winters. They are nine parts Merino wool and two parts nylon wrapped around an elastic Lycro core—very stretchable and comfortable. They are not cheap at $7.50 a pair, but you only need two pairs if you wash them out each night, as you should if you camp. If you tend to get blisters, use a sock liner such as Early Winters Qiana, $3.25 a pair.

Shorts, etc.

If you tend to get saddle sores, you might use chamois-lined wool cycling shorts such as those made by Protogs, Inc. (55 Ludy St., Hicksville, New York 11801, 516/935-8830), available from your bike store or write Protogs. These are elegant and fairly expensive ($31.50) all-wool shorts, but they will wear for years. I also like other Protog all-wool clothes such as their short-sleeved cycling jersey ($49.90) and their two-piece long pants and jacket cycling outfit, $78. All Protog gear is, by the way, made of 100-percent Merino wool, which is super soft and won't itch. I have used these clothes and, unlike other wool garments I have worn that are made for cycling, these are good to my itch-sensitive skin. The wool fabric used is termed "Superwash" because these clothes can be tossed into a washer and dryer without shrinking to baby size, unlike some other wool fabrics I inadvertently treated that way.

The nice thing about wool is that though it seems as though it should be too warm for hot weather, the opposite is the fact. If it gets hot out you sweat no matter what you wear. If the sweat evaporates quickly you cool fast but lose a lot of body fluid. Wool is like a wick, or a sponge, absorbing and holding body moisture and letting it evaporate more slowly, thus enhancing the natural evaporative cooling effect.

When It Rains

Sooner or later into every tour some rain must fall. If you have packed everything in sealed plastic bags in anticipation of the rain (which is one good reason to carry a small radio), all is fine except for your body. In warm weather the rain can be a blessing, a coolant. Eventually, though, you will want some protection against the wet. I can recommend a rain cape, which fits over the handlebars (Fig. 4-45) such as the one made by Bellwether ($20) and a rain hat ($5), also by Bellwether. But for cooler weather when you're cycling in a hard, driving rainstorm (personally I like the cozy warmth of a tent on these days and that's where you'll find me when it's pouring cats and dogs outside) you can wear what Velocipac calls its Thunderwear, an anorak plus rain pants made of Gore-Tex™. The anorak lists for $73.50 and the pants for $49.95. The anorak has a hood. Velocipac can be reached at *2300 Central Avenue, Boulder, Colorado 80301*.

Fig. 4-45: For rainy weather, one solution is a rain cape. *(Bellwether)*

Cold-Weather Cycling

I like riding in cold weather. When it gets below 32 degrees, Fahrenheit, and down to around 10 degrees plus, I put on thermal underwear top and bottom, a thick cotton long-sleeved shirt, a heavy wool sweater, heavy wool slacks or, better, wool cycling pants or a wool warm-up suit. On top of all this, a down jacket. Sometimes the wind-chill factor can get down to well below zero, but with all this stuff on I soon get overheated and have to stop to remove a layer. And that's what cold-weather clothing is all about. It should be in layers, so as you warm up you can remove one layer at a time. I've been out on really cold days, around 15 degrees when people were waiting for buses, shivering with the cold, and I've been warm to the point of sweating. It's a nice feeling, to know that what you are really doing is making or creating your own summer, so to speak, and can virtually ignore the cold around you.

Your feet are the most cold-prone part of your body. Way down there they don't get enough circulation, and they are, so to speak, at the low end of the totem pole of body-heat output. You need warm socks, such as Polar Socks from Early Winters. These are made of a heavyweight, worsted wool yarn that Early Winters says will absorb more than 30 percent of its own weight in moisture without feeling wet. That's one of the good things about wool. They cost about $8.45 a pair. Similar socks should be available in stores that cater to the cross-country skier. You can put liner underneath the socks, such as the Early Winters Qiana mentioned earlier, or Damart Thermawear. No doubt you've seen the many ads placed by the Damart Thermawear, Inc., in sports and bicycle magazines, showing people encased in what look like thick long johns.

Well, the company sent me some, and I am pleased to report that they do work. The fiber is a knitted one that lets out perspiration but keeps heat in. I never thought I'd be comfortable in a male version of panty-hose, but I am and feel no threat to my alleged masculinity. Damart, Inc., will be glad to send you their catalog if you write them at 1811 Woodbury Avenue, Portsmouth, New Hampshire 03805. These are soft, warm clothes that do not bind, so they are great for cycling.

For shoes, I wear some type of medium-high, lined, lightweight boo-tee. There are so many shoes like that on the market, I suggest you check with your favorite sporting-goods store. Look for a bootee that will bend, that will be flexible as you pedal, that will fit into your rattrap pedals. Keep the shoes waterproofed with neat's-foot or mink oil, or some kind of water repellent. If you wear a wool track suit, the cuffs should be elasticized and fit snugly over the tops of your shoes, to keep cold air from your ankles.

Your hands are, next to your feet, the most cold-vulnerable part of your body. I have found a two-piece leather mitten with a wool glove liner to be the warmest for me. The mitten keeps the cold breezes away and the liner retains body heat. Use the kind of mittens that have a knitted, snugly fitting wristlet that comes well up under any outerwear. If you feel mittens are too clumsy, try the three-fingered kind. Early Winters has a pair made of Gore-Tex™ for $12.50. These have neoprene palm pads and are sized to fit over a light woolen underglove. You'll have to buy the underglove separately somewhere else, as they are not sold by Early Winters. Remember, for cold-weather comfort, dress in layers, use fairly loose-fitting clothing that does not restrict blood flow, and keep on cycling!

ODDS AND ENDS

Carrying a Camera

Nothing shakes the innards of a fine single lens reflex camera like con-stant road-vibration shock. If you use a fine camera, you should protect it from day-long vibration. You can, of course, use one of the camera restraints (Fig. 4-46), distributed by C&J Supply, Box 806, Marion, In-diana 46952 or obtainable from a photo store. This may be an okay solution for a short day trip, but a fairly heavy camera dangling from your body all day is not exactly the most comfortable wearing apparel on a long-distance bike trip. A far better solution is a Sima air inflatable cam-era carrier or pouch into which your camera fits. I have one and it really works. Your fine camera will be protected and cushioned and sealed from dust in this pouch. You can also buy from your photo shop a film pouch with lead laminations that protects your film from damage by airport X-ray machines, and don't let the airport personnel or any signs delude you to the contrary. *Any* exposure to X-rays is going to fog your

Fig. 4-46: This way to carry a camera on a bike, protected against road shock, is fine for short day trips but no good for long tours. (*C&J Supply*)

film to some extent, and this applies in spades to the new high-speed color positive film. Camera and film pouches distributed in the U.S.A. by Sima Products Corp., 4001 W. Devon Avenue, Chicago, Illinois 60646.

Stoves

Finally . . . in America, we have a Svea Swedish-type stove, only a lot, lot better. It's the Coleman Peak I® Model 400. This has been out for a while but the 400 is the latest version. The 400 weighs only 2.85 ounces, holds 10 ounces of fuel, burns for a full hour and 15 minutes wide open, 3.5 hours on simmer. The stove (Fig. 4-47) puts out full performance in two minutes, uses nonleaded gas. The stove will work even in a high wind, which is sure more than you can say for the Svea. And everything you need is attached to the stove, unlike the Svea, which had a whole support system of keys, pot supports, wind shields and generator cleaners which you had to lug along and which, being small, were easy to lose.

I urge you to bring some sort of stove along if you plan to cook much outdoors. About ten years ago, in a fit of misery over the load of gear I was carrying up and down Vermont hills, I shipped everything I thought I didn't need back home, including the stove. That was a major mistake. Firewood in campgrounds is hard to come by at best, is usually damp to begin with and nobody in the camp has any newspaper or charcoal to spare. So we spent literally hours every day coaxing a fire along to the point where it was hot enough to cook by. That was a frustrating experience. Even though as a former Boy Scout and country boy from rural Connecticut I knew all about foraging for dry twigs in the deep woods.

Fig. 4-47: Here's a great little stove that pours out the heat, safely. It's light, uses nonleaded gas. *(Coleman Co)*

They *are* there, and burnable even after a hard rain. And we really were not into making the idiotic huge, roaring fires so many novice campers seem to feel are required. A small, hot fire is all we wanted, and it was not that easy to manage. A good, small, compact stove with readily available fuel would have been a Godsend—but I had shipped mine home. Don't leave home without one.

There are lightweight propane-fueled stoves available. They work well and deliver a hot, clean flame. But replacement fuel cartridges may not be available, so I prefer the Coleman. You can always buy lead-free gas. A few ounces will do you. The Coleman Peak I stove costs $30.

Cooking Gear

Any sporting-goods store has aluminum, nesting cookware that works well with the Coleman stove. Avoid aluminum or metal coffee cups, though. The hot coffee makes them too warm to handle or drink from. I prefer plastic cups. A collapsible plastic water bottle takes up little room in your pannier when empty and can save innumerable trips to the camp pump. I like the two- or five-gallon model with spigot.

Bring along a couple of copper or stainless-steel scrubbers for the fry pans, and a small jar of liquid detergent for everything else, including clothing.

Candles

Candles can be a valuable addition to your camping gear, particularly when flashlight batteries fail and you need to find something in the dark. You can read by candlelight (George Washington did), play cards, just talk. You can make a candle wind shield out of half a coffee can. To halve the coffee can, use a pair of tinsnips. (Do this before you leave for your trip.)

Bring bug repellent—a small container of Cutter will do—and a first aid kit. You might read up on the indigenous snake population where you're going, and at least know the poisonous ones by sight. And what to do if bitten.

Don't use heavy glass containers for anything. Glass breaks, and if you carry sticky goo like honey, you have an interesting and lethal combination of honey and glass shards if the container breaks. Use plastic squeeze bottles for things like honey, ketchup, margarine and anything else that will flow. I also use plastic jars with screw tops for all other foodstuffs. Actually you should not be carrying any food other than non-perishables. You can shop for breakfast and dinner food every day, and pick up lunch stuff en route.

Tools

You should be prepared for every type of minor mechanical disaster that can befall your steed, both in terms of having the right tools to make the repairs and in knowing *how* to make the repairs. Here's a recommended list:

- Spare spokes to fit front and rear wheels. Two spokes per wheel, with nipples. (total, 4; 1 oz.)
- Spoke wrench (3 oz.)
- Two spare tubes and one patch kit (12 oz.)
- Two tire irons (1.5 oz.)
- Freewheel remover (3 oz.)
- Small adjustable wrench (3 oz.)
- Two brake blocks (1 oz.)
- One brake cable, long enough to reach the rear brake. You can cut to fit the front brake (½ oz.)
- One rear derailleur cable (½ oz.)
- One foldable lightweight tire such as the Michelin Elan, particularly important if you use 700-centimeter tires not readily available in small-town bike stores, the usual hardware stores or auto-parts stores that sell bikes (11 oz.)
- Small screwdriver (2 oz.)
- Chain lubricant (4 oz.)
- Hub lube (if you do not have sealed bearings) (2 oz.)
- Allen wrenches to fit rear derailleur, seat post binder bolt, stem (if Allen bolt fitted) (3 oz.)
- Chain rivet remover (chain "breaker") (4 oz.)
- Four spare chain links (same make as your chain) (2 oz.)
- Set of hub wrenches (unless sealed bearings) (4 oz.)
- Spare rim tape (1 oz.)
- Roll of black electrician's tape (a patch-all you will not appreciate until you need it) (2 oz.)
- Set of lightweight box wrenches 8-, 9-, 10-, 11- and 12-millimeter sizes (3 oz.)
Total 63.5 ounces = 3.97 lbs.

Bikecology, and probably your local bike shop, has a lightweight set of tools handy consisting of three tire irons, 5-, 6- and 7-millimeter Allen

wrenches, spoke wrench, three open-end wrenches from 6 to 13 millimeters, and a 6-inch crescent wrench, two headset adjusting tools (won't
fit new Shimano DuraAce headsets), tire patch kit, chain rivet tool, all in
a zippered case for $12.88. Bikecology, P.O. Box 1880, Santa Monica,
California 90406. This is item TL8. The entire kit weighs only 1 pound.

About Those Emergency Repairs

Because the sections on various bike parts and their maintenance, adjustment and/or replacement are quite complete I won't duplicate this
information here, except to list the kinds of things you might expect to
go wrong on the road. Please refer to the specific chapter involved for
repair data:

- *Flat tires.* Of course. Chapter 9
- *Broken spokes.* Preventive maintenance can pretty well eliminate them. Chap-
  ter 15
- *Broken chain links.* Replace the old chain before you go on tour. Chapter 13
- *Broken, frayed cables.* Ditto. Chapters 10 and 13
- *Wheels out of true.* Align first, before the trip. Chapter 16
- *Brake blocks worn.* Replace beforehand. Chapter 10
- *Sand or dirt in the wheel hubs.* Listen for grinding. Spin wheels of upside-
  down bike each day, especially if you have traveled over dirt or sand-covered
  roads. If you hear gritty sounds, disassemble, clean, repack, and readjust hubs.
  Better yet, install Phil Wood, Avocet or Durham sealed-bearing hubs before
  you leave. Chapter 11
- *Gritty sounds from bottom bracket.* Follow the same procedure if you hear
  gritty noises from the bottom bracket. Slip chain off first. Spin cranks. Listen.
  If you hear gritty sounds, you have trouble unless you brought along a set of
  bottom-bracket spanners and crank puller. But be of good cheer. This is a fairly
  rare occurrence. You could install an Avocet, Phil Wood or Durham sealed-
  bearing bottom-bracket assembly before leaving home. Chapter 13
- *Gritty sound from freewheel jockey and idler wheels.* Clean and relube if
  necessary. Better yet, install a set of Durham sealed-bearing derailleur wheels
  beforehand. Chapter 13
- *Loose carriers.* Check every day. Tighten nuts and bolts as necessary. This
  chapter
- *Loose headset. This is serious.* Check by gripping handlebars, keeping bike
  steady (use a helper if necessary to hold the bike) and feel for looseness or
  "play" in headset. Lift front wheel off ground, turn the handlebars with one
  finger. They should turn easily. Remember, a loose headset can flatten headset
  bearings and score bearing races, because tremendous pressures are exerted
  in this small area due to road shock, weight of rider and his belongings, and
  the bike itself. A loose headset can also cause or contribute to high speed
  "shimmy," especially on downhill runs, which can cause loss of control, definitely not a healthy situation. Chapter 14
- *Loose cranks.* Grip crank at pedal, try to move laterally, from side to side. If
  loose, retighten. The crank is aluminum, the spindle is steel. A loose crank
  will soon wear the beveled flats inside it, and you will need a new crank. On
  the road this is guaranteed disaster unless you are lucky enough to find a bike

shop with a spare crank that fits your bottom-bracket spindle and is threaded to receive your pedal. Well, sure, a French threaded crank can be rethreaded English. On a new bike, or if you have removed the crank for bottom bracket maintenance, the cranks should be tightened every fifty miles for three or four sets of fifty miles. After that the crank should be well seated and need no further retightening. Before a trip, check it anyway. If you are lucky enough to have one of the new Shimano cranksets that goes on and off with one Allen wrench, you can save a pound of tools, such as a spanner and a crank puller. Well, a half pound anyway. Chapter 13

- *Check hub-cone adjustment* by gripping the wheel with both hands on opposite sides and move gently from side to side. If you feel looseness, remove wheel and readjust hub cones. Better yet, remove the wheel and spin the axle between thumb and forefinger. Axle should spin freely, without binding. Holding the axle the same way, try to move it from side to side. There should be no sideplay. Readjust as necessary. Chapter 11
- *Make sure the seat post and stem are inside their respective tubes.* Chapters 2 and 5
- *If you get dirt in the freewheel,* or have used too heavy a lubricant (use chainlube, or a *very* light oil) the pawls can hang up (they are spring loaded) and the freewheel will rotate but you won't. The bike will stay put. If you're lucky and can get to some kerosene or other nonexplosive solvent, try pouring some on the freewheel. Do not get any on the tire! Solvents eat tires. If this doesn't free up the freewheel, remove it and soak it in solvent, spinning at the same time, holding it from inside, where it threads onto the hub. Of *course* you brought along a freewheel remover, didn't you, and a wrench to fit it? See Chapter 13

CARRYING YOUR BIKE ON YOUR CAR

Few of us are fortunate enough to live where we can conveniently start right out on a scenic bike tour. Most of us travel by plane to where we want to start, or drive. If you drive, it's important that you carry your bike on your car on a properly designed carrier. The homemade carrier described below works pretty well. It even breaks in your saddle for you, because the saddle rests on one of the cross members of the carrier. On a long car trim, the minute vibrations from the road are transmitted to the carrier and from the carrier to the saddle. The saddle gets a slight but high frequency "bounce" for as long as you drive. My leather Brooks Pro saddle is broken in beautifully as much from transporting the bike by car as by riding the bike—but only, I hasten to add, because I live in the Chicago area, which is a good place to get away from by car but if you try to do it by bike you eat and breathe a lot of exhaust fumes for the first two or three hours, at least. And so I escape to the verdant countryside by car for the first fifty miles. I don't think Chicago is that much different from New York, or Philadelphia or Boston, for that matter, or any other major metropolitan complex of fume-filled streets.

After looking at a dozen or so bike carriers I can say that most are pretty junky, and in fact will contribute in no small measure to the demise of the paint job on your nice bike, if indeed the bike stays rooted to the carrier in the first place.

There are exceptions. I like the Atkins-Graber line. Someone at that company must be a bicyclist and a skier, because their carriers are made with care, consideration and good design built in. The company makes both rear-bumper-mount carriers or roof carriers. I prefer the roof carrier. I just don't like the idea of my bike being back there where it's vulnerable to being hit. And you can use the roof carrier for other things such as luggage, skis, a canoe or two, whatever.

I think, though, that my favorite carrier is the Altra, Inc., unit, various models of which fit any domestic or foreign car with or without rain gutter, including hatchbacks. You attach one part of the carrier to the bike with straps supplied, lift the bike up, slide it into the roof-mounted section, clamp the bike in place with a wing-nutted vinyl-coated clamp and off you go. Figures 4-48 through 4-50 show various aspects of this carrier. Schwinn dealers sell it and prices range from $29.50 to $61. Accessory trays are available for luggage, skis, boats, kayaks, canoes and a lockable luggage carrier. This is a truly beautifully designed and very versatile carrier, with lots and lots of accessories for ski poles and what not. Some models can carry up to five bikes. Remember the bikes are up there, so don't drive into a garage or a motel staging area where there's an overhang. It's been done. Not by me, but it's been done.

Fig. 4-48: One of the best car-top bike carriers and general convenience toters made. It's aluminum, light, strong, quick to mount and detach. This is a five-bike model. Smaller versions are available. (*Altra, Inc*)

Fig. 4-49: Another way to mount the carrier in Figure 4-50. *(Altra, Inc)*

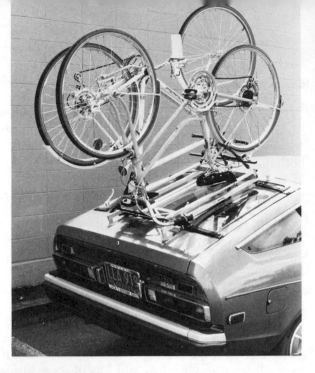

Fig. 4-50: There's room for two plus a canoe. *(Altra, Inc)*

How to Make Your Own Carrier

Anyone can easily make his own rooftop bicycle carrier with a little ingenuity and effort. Start with any ordinary pair of metal bar roof carriers, the kind that clamp to rain gutters or bolt to the roof, *not* the suction-cup type, which can come loose.

L. L. Bean (see Appendix) carries an aluminum alloy load bracket with drip eave clamps and carriage bolts for your own wood crossbar, costing about $15 for a set of four (Fig. 4-51). These are made by Quik-n-Easy Products, Monrovia, California.

"Chick" Mead, a bicycle dealer in Marion, Massachusetts, has designed a fine homemade carrier. His instructions, which follow, are simple (Fig. 4-52). They call for:

1. One set of brackets, L. L. Bean "Quick-N-Easy," or Sears Roebuck rain-gutter type
2. Two 9-foot two-by-fours
3. One quart wood preservative
4. 12 carriage bolts ¼ by 1⅝ inches
5. 12 feet of ⅜- or ⁷⁄₁₆-inch aluminum round (stock) for pegs
6. 64 one-inch-wide rubber bands, made from old tire tubes
7. Two pieces of ⅛ by 1 by 32-inch aluminum flat or ¾-inch angle stock for adjustable struts (total 62 inches)
8. One pint weatherstrip adhesive to glue on padding
9. Scrap ends of thick felt or carpeting for padding
10. One quart exterior-grade preservative finish paint, such as Rustoleum
11. One quart liquid Neoprene for waterproofing top of pad

If you can't scrounge old inner tubes from a gas station, try a foreign-car dealer, such as a Peugeot garage, where inner tubes are used with radial tires.

Plans should be self-explanatory. An unexpected side benefit was the fact that after about a thousand miles of driving, the slight bouncing up

Fig. 4-51: Brackets for homemade bike carrier. (*L.L. Bean*)

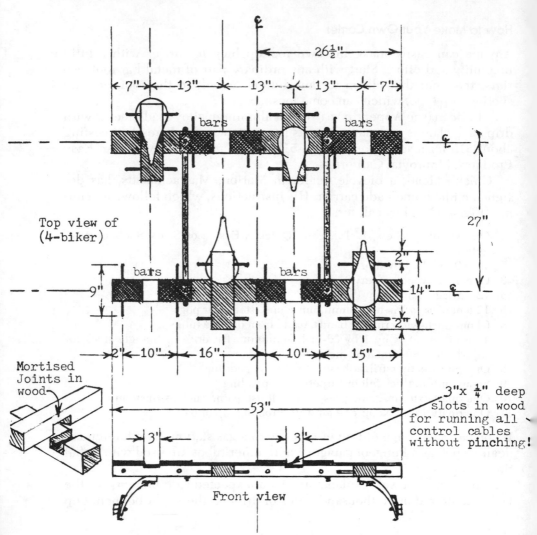

Fig. 4-52: Design for a homemade bicycle carrier holds four bicycles. *(Chick Mead)*

and down movement thoroughly broke in all our saddles! Note that the adjustable struts of aluminum flats or angles permit saddle position to be changed to conform to wheelbase of bicycle.

The nine-inch dowels of the aluminum rod should stick out about two inches from the two-by-fours.

Allowing thirteen inches apart for each bicycle, you will be able to carry up to four bicycles on this carrier. Be sure to pad the two-by-fours liberally with old hose or other soft but durable material, to avoid marring the handlebar finish.

When ready to tie down the bicycle, use the rubber holders (or leather straps) to tie both sides of the handlebars and the seat to the carrier.

Fig. 4-53: Finished homemade carrier. Note that hold-downs are from old tire tubes. *(Chick Mead)*

Stagger bicycles on the carrier, as shown in Figure 4-53. And make sure the carrier is securely fastened to the car roof!

I made one of these "Chick" Mead carriers myself, and I am able to carry four bikes on my car (Fig. 4-54). My expenses totaled about $25 for everything, and the result is a very useful and practical carrier indeed.

Incidentally, the "Chick" Mead bike carrier is also very handy for transporting luggage and other miscellany. The aluminum rod tiedowns are very convenient for securing almost anything. My carrier is always fitted to my car, though it could be removed quickly and easily.

Fig. 4-54: Finished carrier mounted on car. This is the homemade model. Total cost about $20, not counting your time. *(Chick Mead)*

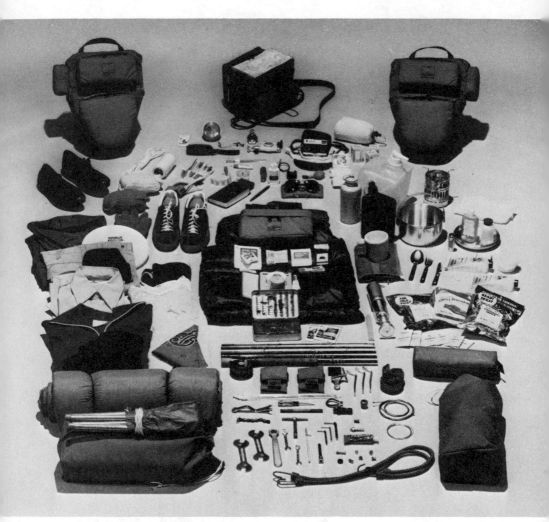

Fig. 4-55: Here's a layout of the kind of items you might consider on your next bicycle camping trip. Unless you're going to camp where you can't shop for food for dinner and breakfast, you won't need the dried food in the right hand side of this picture. But it is a good idea to lay everything out on the floor like this, make sure you have all you need and then devise a packing plan so you know where each item is stowed in the panniers and handlebar bag. (*Eclipse*)

How to Ride Safely—Sensible Tips for Everyday Riding 5

Americans are gradually becoming more safety conscious on their bicycles, according to statistics on bike usage and accidents, but they still have a long way to go. The number of bikes sold has risen steadily, and the use of bikes by those who own them has gone up sharply over the past decade; but at least one statistic—the number killed in accidents with motor vehicles—has remained static, about 1,000 to 1,100 a year. All told, there are over one million cycling accidents of one sort or another (most of them minor) each year in the United States. You need not become a statistic if you follow the rules and suggestions in this chapter.

Most bicycling accidents do not involve a motor vehicle, but most fatal accidents do. Current estimates provided by the government and by the National Safety Council indicate that slightly more than one in ten accidents involve an automobile. Just under half come from simply falling off the bike; the remainder are caused by running into fixed objects such as trees or occur while riding the bicycle (for example, the feet may slip out of the pedals and the rider fall forward onto the top tube, injuring his crotch area).

Although the median age of persons involved in serious accidents has risen due to the increased ridership among young adults and older persons, most bicycle accidents, indeed fully three quarters of them, involve children. Most of the accidents incurred by children result from abuse of the machine, such as riding double, riding a poorly maintained bicycle or colliding with a car after darting out from a driveway, side street or alley.

Two thirds of all reported bike accidents (and many go unreported) are treated at physicians' offices, and one third require emergency-room visits. Most of the injuries are to the face and head, and most of these are lacerations; fractures of the shoulders, arms and hands and wrist sprains rank high on the injury list.

Most studies on bike safety still cite children's lack of knowledge about riding safety as the root cause of bike accidents. Children, and most adults, think that riding a bicycle in a forward motion is all they need to know about bicycle safety. Safety programs have been in existence for many years under the auspices of school districts, and special police programs are now standard in most large towns and cities. The

National Safety Council, for one, has been developing and distributing literature to youngsters. It is also helpful for parents to become active in such programs, and to make sure that from the very first time a child gets on the bike he knows about proper riding.

But for now the problems continue. In collisions with motor vehicles, the cyclist is said to be at fault in four out of five accidents. In motor vehicle–bicycle collisions involving children the chief causes are darting into the stream of traffic from a side street or alley or the failure of the child to stop at an intersection. Among adults, one of the major causes of accidents is a car overtaking the cyclist, especially at night, and rear-ending the bicycle because the cyclist did not have proper lighting on the bike. Another major problem area for young adult and adult riders is riding on the wrong side of the street, which many people wrongly assume is the safe place to ride their bikes.

An additional area of concern which also can be remedied by proper attention to safety is mechanical defects in the bicycle, which account for at least 15 percent of all accidents, and one in five collisions with motor vehicles. Such defects may be faulty parts, such as brakes, derailleurs or pedals. Or, it could be that the bike simply was not well maintained by the owner, a common state of affairs with children's bikes. Parents should know enough to at least take the child's bike in to be repaired, or they should work on basic items such as brakes and pedals with the help of this kind of book. There is no excuse, and certainly no question of collecting for damages with a bicycle that is imporperly maintained.

TIPS THAT COULD SAVE YOUR LIFE

Public officials, including the police, look upon bicycles as motor vehicles, and more and more frequently hand out tickets to cyclists who ride hazardously. Common sense dictates that if you are riding a bike you should consider your actions the way you do while driving a car, because otherwise, the chances increase that you will cause an accident—and the one hurt will not be the overweight codger in the block-long Buick.

Certainly, it is tempting to run a stoplight or ride on the wrong side of the street, leaving a line of cars behind as you wend your way down the next block. But accidents have proven that this is a hazardous undertaking; you simply cannot tell when a car might shoot out of a hidden intersection, alley or driveway and come barreling down the street toward you. A bicycle, although it is a responsive vehicle, cannot move out of the way fast enough when a car suddenly appears at the side. And if you are run into after having violated a traffic regulation, you will have a mighty tough time collecting on the other guy's insurance!

Here are some cycling safety tips:

—Always ride *with* the traffic, never *into* the traffic. Riding with the traffic reduces the relative speed differential between you and the moving traffic, and thus reduces the impact if an accident should occur. You'll feel a bit nervous at first with all that traffic behind you, but you will get used to it. If your city requires bicyclists to ride the wrong way (into the traffic) then you and your fellow cyclists had better work to have that law changed quickly. A law that endangers cyclists should first be ignored and then repealed.

—Never ride on a city street where parking is not allowed! There is simply no room for you between the traffic and the gutter on streets where car parking is prohibited. Such through streets have a high volume of traffic, and cars might drive you right into the curb, or drive right behind you honking madly because you are moving too slowly. As a corollary, always ride on streets where car parking is allowed and, in fact, where cars are actually parked. By law, moving vehicles are supposed to leave from 30 to 36 inches, up to a full 3 feet, between themselves and parked cars, to allow for the doors of parked cars to open easily. If you are a reasonably skilled cyclist and can ride straight, 30 inches will be enough space, and you will even have some room to spare.

—On a bike, you are not the same size as a car. Don't ride as if you were. Many drivers fail to see anything smaller than a car on the road, because they are not used to looking for anything smaller. A friend of mine wound up with a two-month stay in bed from severe internal injuries because he assumed that an elderly female driver saw him. She and he were coming in opposite directions on a narrow street on which cars were parked. She was in the middle of the road and he assumed she would move over as she approached. She did not, and later she said she never saw him, despite his brightly colored clothing. There are excellent older drivers about (just as there are many good older cyclists); nevertheless elderly drivers are to be considered dangerous to cyclists. They often have bad vision, poor depth perception, confused color discrimination, slow reflexes, and they frequently are terrible drivers to begin with. Too many states do not require stiff annual physical examinations of drivers over sixty-five.

—Approaching an intersection calls for judgment. If it's a suburban through street with a stop sign in your favor, do not assume that traffic will stop because of the sign. Sometimes drivers will barrel up to stop signs, slow to a running crawl, and then barrel off again, even though you as a cyclist have the right of way and are already in the intersection. Male teenage drivers are particularly untrustworthy in this respect.

I have found that the safest procedure to follow upon seeing a car waiting for me to pass through the intersection, whether the car is to the left or right, is to move over to the center of the road as I approach the corner, provided there is no traffic behind me. In this position I have a better chance of swerving to either side to avoid a collision if the driver at the intersection decides to force his way through. From the center of the road, I have room to turn the corner right or left as necessary to avoid being hit. If I were to go through the intersection next to the curb, it would be impossible to turn at the sharp right angle necessary to escape collision. Get into the habit of starting up with the traffic as the light changes, so a vehicle is on your left to run interference for you. I also like to cross all intersections with a vehicle on my left; it's good protection, so long as you are sure the vehicle isn't going to turn right, straight into you.

Cultivate the habit of cycling in an absolutely straight, unwavering line at all times, and continue to do so while you quickly turn your head (or use a rearview mirror) to check traffic behind you. Accurate steering is vital in city cycling, because the clearance between traffic and parked cars is ample only if you can cycle straight, without weaving from side to side.

—Making turns on a bicycle is different from doing it in a car, so learn how. If there is traffic around, you should, of course, signal the turn. A left turn from a busy street or at a busy intersection can be made in two ways. The safest method is to cross the street to the other side of the intersection, stop and wait for the light to turn, and walk across with pedestrians. This is the way children should be taught to cross. Never attempt to make a left turn from the right curb position; this is as bad as trying to make a left turn in a car from the right lane of a four-lane highway.

I prefer to make my left turns by moving to the center of the road as I approach the intersection, signaling my intention, and making sure traffic will permit this move. I either make my left turn at once, if oncoming traffic will permit, or I wait at the intersection until the traffic clears. If the traffic is extremely heavy, I go to the far side of the intersection, wait until traffic clears, and then turn left in the pedestrian cross-lane. Letting a truck run interference is a good protective measure.

—When it is wet outside, remember to take extra care. As with autos, bicycle brakes don't work as well when they are wet, so be extra careful to start braking early and ride slowly and cautiously to eliminate the need for panic stops.

—In downhill cycling, especially at high speeds, brakes can get hot. To prevent hitting slower cyclists or obstructions and to maneuver down curves, you have to brake on long downhills. When brakes are constantly applied with this much friction, the metal rims can heat to the point where the glue that holds tubular tires on the rim can be melted soft and cause the tire to slide off. In the case of wired-ons, the rim can get hot enough to cause air in the tube to expand and blow the tube out.

To prevent the buildup of rim heat on downhill runs, brake with rear and front brakes alternately and lightly; try to keep speed under control so you do not have to brake hard. Sometimes, if the tire doesn't come off the rim entirely, it will simply slide around on the rim, so the valve is ripped loose and you get a flat. Sometimes this will happen slowly, other times there will be a blowout. Always be prepared for a blowout downhill in any case. You never know what your tire may have picked up earlier that could cause a blowout at high speeds—another good reason for holding onto the handlebars properly, which we shall now describe.

—Watch for the wobble. Downhill cycling can bring you to speeds as high as 55 miles an hour. While you are going this fast, you may experience front-wheel wobble or "shimmy," where amplitude and frequency of a side-to-side swing increase to the point where you feel you might lose control any second. The solution is to brake and stop as quickly as possible.

The wobble can still be terrifying, and the best way to handle this is to learn by experience that panicking will only make it that much worse. In the Greiner Wald section of Austria, I was descending a fairly steep hill at about 50 miles an hour, when my front wheel suddenly began shimmying. To my right was a straight, unguarded drop-off of about 2,000 feet; to my left, a dense forest of unfriendly hard trees behind a ditch; to my rear thirty-nine other cyclists careening downhill equally fast; and ahead a heavily laden oncoming truck. I consider myself very fortunate in having been able to react fast enough, at about the third widening shimmy, to be able to stop. My initial tendency was to fight the shimmy and keep on, which in the experience of others would have caused me to crash, and probably veer to the right where the lake at the bottom of the 2,000-foot drop would have been cold comfort as a shock absorber. . . .

What causes high-speed wobble? A number of things contribute: a tubular tire glued on crookedly; spokes too tight on one side and too loose on the other (as when you try to correct for a flattened section of the rim caused by hitting a curb or similar obstruction); a bent fork; a loose headset cone; unbalanced front or rear panniers; possibly even a loose front-wheel hub cone. My shimmy was due to a bent fork blade. You can avoid bent fork and stays by blocking them with wood or with a dummy axle bolted on both sides of dropouts when shipping via airline or railroad.

—Cycling in a high wind can be as dangerous as sailing in one. I distinctly recall one frightening ride from my office in downtown Chicago to my suburban Evanston home twelve miles away during a windstorm of hurricane proportions. I was riding on a fairly wide two-lane major city street during the rush hour. The first thing I noticed were pieces of debris, such as plywood sheets from building sites, pieces of paper, and various other items flying through the air, but I was not injured. Then I began to be blown over to one side and found myself leaning about fifteen degrees to the right just to be able to keep upright. But then the wind would shift and I would have to jerk the bike over to the other side to keep up. If you must ride in the wind, remember that in the cities, large buildings can alter wind patterns, making it more gusty, so that you will have to pay strict attention to what you are doing; be prepared for unpredictable, violent and sudden changes in wind direction and velocity so that you are not blown all over the street, into the traffic.

WATCH OUT FOR . . .

—*Car doors opening in front of you on streets with parked cars.* Discourteous drivers have whipped in ahead of me, parked their cars, and opened the door on the driver's side, all in one swift motion, forcing me to veer out into the stream of traffic to avoid hitting them or their car doors. As you ride on streets with parked cars, keep a close watch on the cars as far ahead as you can see. I have trained myself to watch parked cars for a block ahead, and to notice what's going on in all the parked cars on that block.

In particular, watch through the rear windows and look at the side-view mirrors of parked cars. These will help you know if a driver or passenger is about to open a door. You may notice a driver who appears immobile and waiting, but I have found that this does not mean that he won't suddenly leap out of his car. Some cities and states have ordinances that make the driver liable for any accidents caused by his opening a door on the traffic side, but you will still be better off if you can avoid running into a car door anytime. Watch out especially for children in cars, for they are always unpredictable.

The whiplash protector above car seats can hide the actions of a driver who may be about to open a door, because it covers much of his head area. So be doubly careful; assume that any car in which you cannot see the driver's side has an occupant who is about to open his car door in front of you.

—*People and animals darting out into the street in front of you.* This usually means children, who have a tendency to dart into the street after balls or pets. Just as you must look out for the child's safety while driving a car, the cyclist must also be vigilant in this area. But the cyclist must also worry about himself, because he will also hit the ground in such a pedestrian collision.

Adults also get in your way, as when they don't see a cyclist coming (in other words, they are listening, rather than looking, for an approaching vehicle), so you should use a horn or shout at them when they start to make their move. The same goes for drivers who are leaving parking spaces and who are only looking for speeding cars, not for you, the cyclist.

—*The Sunday driver.* Drivers who don't drive regularly can be dangerous to cyclists. Whenever I hear behind me the squeal of power brakes and wheels being turned rapidly, usually followed by a horn blowing, it almost always seems to be an inexperienced driver who cannot decide what to do about me. Watch for these people at intersections. They may appear to be waiting patiently for you to pass, but they seem to be unaware that an experienced cyclist in good physical condition may be coming at 15 to 20 miles an hour, and they will come uncomfortably close when they try to pass.

While cycling in the city, you should have your hands on or next to the brake levers at all times, so that you can stop instantly if you have to. Also keep toe straps loose. I'll never forget the time I forgot to loosen my toe straps on a city ride. It was during rush-hour traffic at a major intersection in Detroit, and I came to a traffic light with cars all around me. I stopped quickly, but with my feet strapped tightly in the pedals, I toppled slowly and ingloriously to the side. I was wearing shoe cleats.

Apropos of motorists' attitudes, there seems to be a curious relationship between the time of day and the attitude of the driver toward cyclists. For example, I used to cycle from my former home in Grosse Pointe Farms to my office in downtown Detroit, a distance of twelve miles. The route took me through the car-factory area, and I found that if I cycled before 8 A.M., motorists were quite discourteous and careless about my well-being. When I left home after 8, however, I found everyone quite courteous. During evening rush hour, however, there are no holds barred and courtesy to cyclists doesn't seem to exist.

—*Friday and Saturday night drunk drivers.* If you want to ride at night on weekends, you should find out which streets are least used and ride on them. Avoid main drags because these are often populated by teenagers showing off to friends or by drunk drivers.

—*Pedestrians.* They have the right of way at *all* intersections. Remember that cars on your right have the right of way also. I would advise you to give the right of way to anyone who wants it. You are not in a position to fend everyone off while on the bike.

—*Cars next to you that want to turn right.* As you approach a stoplight, watch out for cars left of you that want to turn right. Although it infuriates drivers, I veer left into the traffic line if the traffic light turns red as I approach it, to prevent motorists from pushing me to the curb. Because there are no parked cars at intersections, right-turning cars tend to hug the curb at stoplights, or as they approach intersections. Once you have stopped, you can move out of the way to let traffic by when the light changes. Be especially careful about buses. Bus drivers must pull over to the curb to let passengers on and off. If you are following a bus, remember that it may stop at any corner, and it is definitely unsafe for you to be between the bus and the curb at a corner. Stay behind a bus, even if its diesel fumes tempt you to take chances on passing. You can watch your opportunity and pass the bus between intersections or, if traffic permits, you can pass it on the left while it is stopped. Do this slowly and carefully, watching out for cars and pedestrians who may suddenly appear in your path from in front of the bus. Once you have passed a bus, you should be able to stay ahead of it. Occasionally, you can use a bus or a truck as interference for crossing an intersection, if you are in the right lane and the large vehicle is in the left lane of a four-lane street.

—*Child cyclists*. Children on bicycles usually weave from side to side, turn unpredictably without signaling, and cannot be counted on not to run into you even when you are passing them. I watch children on bicycles very closely as I approach them from the front or the rear, and I am ready to take evasive action at all times.

—*Storm-sewer grates*. Storm sewers with grated street covers are a little recognized but very real hazard in city cycling, particularly in suburbs. Many makes of these drains are designed with sufficient width between the grates to permit a bicycle wheel to drop down between them (Fig. 5-1). Some of these gratings are round, and it would be a simple matter to have them all turned with the grating perpendicular to the curb. This danger should be pointed out to the city-street or road commissioner.

If the grating is not round or square, and the openings are parallel to the curb, the best thing to do is inform the police or fire department, or

Fig. 5-1: Watch out for sewer- and catch-basin drain covers! They are wide enough to catch your bicycle wheel and bring you to a sudden stop that could cause a serious accident. Some bridges have this type of open grating where expansion joints meet.

whichever agency handles bicycle licenses, that the danger exists, so that new cyclists can be officially warned about the city's hazard. A cyclist can be seriously injured if his front wheel drops into such a grating.

—*Bridge expansion-joints.* I found myself in a predicament similar to the situation with the sewer grating on my first trip over the bridge between Detroit and Windsor, Canada. I didn't notice it when I first went over the bridge because I had a head wind and was going very slowly. But on the way back, with a strong tail wind, a steep hill and the bridge arched down to meet the land, I barely had time to swing my wheel to the slight angle needed to avoid dropping the wheel between the bars of a grated expansion joint, where two sections of the bridge met. Afterward, Gene Portuesi, former Olympic team cycling coach, told me that on the day the bridge opened many years ago, unsuspecting cyclists were thrown and hurt when they passed over this grating at high speeds. So, watch out for expansion joints on bridges, especially suspension bridges over wide rivers. These joints usually run the entire width of the bridge.

—*Dogs and other small animals.* Of course, this goes without saying, because the dog has long been a headache for cyclists and runners. We will return to a thorough discussion of four-legged creatures later.

—*Railroad, street- or trolley-car tracks.* Like sewer gratings and bridge expansion joints, you should cross railroad or trolley-car tracks at a right angle. Most of these steel tracks run *across* the road, so all you need do is hit the tracks straight on. But sometimes you will find tracks that run at an angle or curve across the road; in this case alter your angle of approach so that you hit the tracks at a right angle, in other words perpendicularly. I like to alter my approach to an angle slightly off-perpendicular, but this may be my own personal foible. The idea, in any case, is not to let your bicycle wheel get caught in the tracks.

Also, of course, do not try to get around crossing gates that are down; and if there are no crossing gates keep a sharp lookout for oncoming trains, from *both* directions.

SAFETY TIPS FOR YOUNGSTERS

The following tips could save your child from serious injury or worse. Insist that he or she learn these rules and observe them without exception:

- Ride only on streets where cycling is permitted, never on streets where signs say cycling is not allowed.
- Never ride on a street unless there are parked cars in evidence, and then watch out for car doors opening in front of you.

- Never ride at night without a good headlight and a good taillight. The rear light should be visible to motorists from two to three blocks away. Your bicycle should also be equipped with a two-to-three-inch-diameter reflector at the rear and front and in the wheel spokes, and small reflectors on the spokes.
- Brakes should always be in good working condition.
- Always signal your turns. Left arm straight out with index finger straight out means left turn; left arm straight up means right turn.
- At street intersections, give everyone the right of way, including cars, trucks, buses, and people.
- Never turn left, while mounted, at a *busy* intersection, or at one where there is a stoplight. *Always* dismount, walk to the far side of the street, across the intersection, wait till the light turns, and *walk* your bicycle across in the pedestrian lane.
- Obey all stoplights, stop signs, and other road signs, just as though you were driving a car.
- *Never* try to hitch a ride by holding on to a truck. You never know which way the truck will turn or how suddenly it will stop. Trucks often have air brakes that enable them to stop so fast that you would not be able to hold on. If the truck stops that quickly, there is probably an emergency reason which would also apply to you. The truck driver may not realize you are hanging on, and brush you against an object such as a parked car.
- Never ride two on a bicycle unless you have a tandem. Riding two on a bicycle built for one makes it hard to see where you are going, hard to stop and easy to spill.
- Always go *with* the traffic, not against it. When you ride along with the traffic, you give the drivers of cars behind you a better chance to steer out of your way, and they're more likely to see you than if you unexpectedly appear in front of them going the wrong way.
- Steer straight; don't weave all over the street; stay close to parked cars at all times.
- *Don't fool around on a bicycle.* Many boys and girls think it's fun to rear the bicycle back on the rear wheel and go off down the street with the front wheel off the ground. Fun and games and trick riding on a bicycle can be dangerous if you are thrown off balance into the path of a car, or if you fall and strike your head on a concrete curb. You can have fun on small-wheeled bicycles, because they're so maneuverable, but I would advise playing bike polo or bike hockey only on a school parking lot—and *never* pull "wheelies."

COUNTRY RIDING

Never, but never, ride on freeways, toll roads, or major arterial highways. I know there are a number of touring cyclists who argue that it is perfectly safe to cycle on interstate highways because the shoulder is broad enough to keep them away from the main traffic stream. No doubt this is true—the shoulder is wide enough, and it is paved. The trouble is that should an accident occur anywhere near you at the fifty-five-mile-an-hour-plus speeds common to interstate routes, you could be involved. At those speeds, it would take only a passing brush by a motor vehicle to send you spinning off into the wild blue yonder. Also, highway shoulders are frequently littered with broken glass and other hazardous material. Large trucks push a "bubble" of air in front and leave a vacuum behind. This "push-pull" effect can knock you off your bike.

There are other tips on country cycling in the chapter on touring. Here, let me just say that you should plan your route using roads parallel to main routes. You will be amazed at how well paved many of the less used back-country roads are, and these roads have little traffic and almost all the beauty. In general, avoid any road bearing a state or federal route number. Many states have cross-state bicycle routes, which are simply hand-picked, well-paved roads bearing little motor traffic.

If you have to ride on dirt roads, be very careful about cornering on sandy or pebbly surfaces, watch out for potholes that can send you sprawling and bend a wheel, and keep your eyes and ears open for oncoming traffic.

Country riding does have one special hazard: People who habitually drive on back-country roads are almost never alert for cyclists, or, for that matter, for any other traffic. Consider the sight of a silo or a barn to be a danger signal, and be alert for a truck or tractor to come right out on the highway from a hidden intersection, without regard for oncoming traffic, including cyclists. Farmers seem to regard the roads in front of their homes as their personal driveways, and they are prone to drive in and out of their property as though no other traffic exists.

On any country road, whether paved or not, keep your ears open for traffic coming in either direction. It's quiet in the country, and you can hear motor vehicles coming from at least a mile away. And on dusty dirt roads, you can often see as well as hear evidence of approaching traffic. Rural drivers may be on any part of the road as they approach you, so if you have just rounded a corner and you hear a car coming up fast behind you, either stay on the far right side of the road or ride well to the left, on the shoulder, to let the car by. If you're cresting a hill, keep alert to traffic behind you. After you pass the crest, if there is no oncoming traffic, cross to the left side of the road for a block or so, so upcoming cars won't zoom over the hill into you, because your presence cannot be observed below the crest.

Rural Intersections

Where two rural roads meet, any stop signs generally are not observed, so be prepared to stop as you approach intersections. Be aware, at all times, of the surrounding territory so that you will know the best place to go to steer yourself out of trouble.

For example, if as you approached an intersection a car suddenly shot out at you from the right, where could you go? There's usually a ditch at these intersections, with little or no shoulder. Or, if there is no other traffic, you could cross the lane or even make a 180-degree turn.

If you're with a group of cyclists, it's wise to have an experienced rider at each end of the line. The rear cyclist can listen for and size up potential hazards from oncoming traffic, and the lead rider can analyze the situation from up front, such as intersections, approaching traffic, curves and hills.

If you're cycling in mountainous terrain, or plan such a trip, double check the maintenance of brakes. Be sure your brake cables are in good shape, brake blocks are fresh and new and brakes properly adjusted, with levers where you can grab them quickly.

RADIOS NOT RECOMMENDED

Because ears as well as eyes must be used in any type of cycling, I definitely do not recommend listening to a radio while cycling. I have seen cyclists pedaling along with a tiny earpiece plugged into one ear, completely oblivious to the sound of traffic around them. A radio takes away from cycling enjoyment, in any case. In the country especially, how can one possibly enjoy the sound of the wind and the birds, or simply the wonderful silence, when a radio is on?

USE THESE—GLASSES AND REARVIEW MIRRORS

Just as on a motorcycle, it is imperative for cyclists to wear protective eye covering if they can. Hurtling down hills at better than 30 miles an hour exposes you to getting an insect or piece of dust in your eye, which can be disastrous if for even just a moment, you can't see out of that eye. Although it may not be as important to cover the eye during city riding at a slow pace, on tour it is essential.

Those lucky souls who do not have to wear glasses normally, can, of course, purchase sunglasses or protective goggles. But let me inject a note of caution about the kind of sunglasses that remove the glare from objects on the road: Although such glasses are handy for reading road signs or for seeing detail in the harsh sunlight because they cut down the reflection from a glittering object, they also take away a key warning sign that something metallic or glass is in your way and should be avoided. Regular sunglasses are still the best.

The size and shape of the glasses are also important. The kind of thick plastic rims that are common today, especially where the top rim rides low on the nose, can obscure what is ahead on the road. Cyclists by habit and by the position they are forced to sit in often look at the ground in front of them more than they look far ahead. Having low, thick rims further obscures the picture. Get glasses with large lenses and thin frames that have either a strap at the back or a fitted end which wraps behind the ear.

Should the glasses be made of plastic? Great advances in shatterproof glass have been made. Glass is also more scratch resistant than plastic, but plastic is lighter. Plastic lenses are preferable for cycling, but there

Fig. 5-2: This tiny rearview mirror clips onto your glasses as shown, can be a lifesaver that tells you whether the road behind is all clear or not, when you need to veer out into traffic to avoid an opening door in a parked car. Saves you from having to look over your shoulder, gives you more "look ahead" time, does not obstruct forward view. Models available for wire-frame glasses and for mounting on your helmet. From Ultra-Lite Shop, P.O. Box, Brinkhaven, Ohio 43006, or your local bike shop. $3.50

is certainly no taboo against glass lenses, if they have some guarantee of being shatterproof.

While we are considering glasses, here is the proper place to consider rearview mirrors. First, they are essential for touring when you are on highways or county roads with fast-moving traffic. In the city, they are also very important because you cannot be looking over your shoulder all of the time while ignoring the vehicular madness in front of you that is so typical of large cities.

Rearview mirrors (Fig. 5-2) wrap around the side of the glasses and are relatively unobtrusive. They are important because, just as in a car, on a bicycle you have to look behind you as well as ahead while making a maneuver. A handlebar mirror is a safety hazard, first because one spill over the bars brings you in quick contact with the mirror and its holder. Eyeglass-mounted mirrors offer an adequate view behind while not creating a blind spot in front (or much of a blind spot). Handlebar mirrors force you to lean over to look behind—a dangerous lapse of cycling vigilance during which you could hit a car.

There are now many fair brands of eyeglass-mounted mirrors on the market, but the original and still the best model I have seen is from the Ultra-Light Shop, Box 308, Brinkhaven, Ohio 43006.

I should add that a rearview mirror is used by only one eye, which does not give proper binocular depth perception. You still should glance behind you to check the *speed* of oncoming traffic.

USE YOUR HEAD, WEAR A HELMET!

Mr. A. C. Prone went tearing down a hill one day, he and his bicycle picking up speed rapidly. As he rounded a curve at 35 per, he skidded on gravel in the road kicked up by cars and trucks that had come too close to the gravel shoulder on the turn. Old A. C. bit the dust, hard, as his bike went out from under. His head hit the tarmac first. He was out for about twenty minutes, finally came to and proceeded slowly down the road, thankful his head was not fractured. A day or so later he went into convulsions and died before he could be taken to the hospital.

What went wrong? Well, first, of course, he should have been wearing one of the excellent helmets now on the market designed specifically for bicyclists. Second, when his noggin banged on the pavement, he suffered a concussion which had later results and caused his sad demise. What happened was that his brain, which normally floats inside the skull, was smacked against the bone of the skull and w..s bruised. Later, the bruise brought a mass of blood and fluid that built up inside the skull and caused a clot, called a hematoma, which built up enough pressure to cause a deep coma and later death. A. C.'s accident was in two parts. First, his skull hit the deck. Second, his brain hit the inside of his skull. Something like kicking a football with a baseball inside it.

This short scenario can take place even if, while on your bike, a car knocks you to the ground. How serious the blow is to the skull is a function of how hard you hit, and what you hit. If you are lucky and hit soft ground covered with grass, the impact may be spread over a larger surface of the head and the result may be no worse than a headache for a couple of hours. Or, you may strike a sharp object, such as the edge of a curb. Or a sharp part of a car. The problem is you never know when you might fall, and you can't control *what* you might hit. I began wearing a helmet after two serious accidents that resulted in no more than a sprained wrist in one case, a dislocated shoulder in another. I figured that from now on the odds were in favor of my hitting my head in the next accident. The first two were hard enough to break off the top tube from the head tube, ruining two good frames.

The few bucks you spend for a helmet are cheap insurance against the kind of head-smashing injury that's all too easy to come by. People I know have been killed on bikes when a dog smashed into a front bike wheel, causing loss of control . . . losing control on a downhill run . . . being hit by a car and thrown off the bike . . . having a blowout going downhill at high speed . . . running into sewer drains . . . and by a myriad of other situations that can seldom be anticipated, or, if foreseen, avoided. It's just too easy to be seriously injured in an accident that involves the head; the old brain box is just terribly vulnerable even to what may seem to be a minor impact.

Kinds of Helmets

Before helmets for bicyclists appeared on the market, we were forced to make do with what was available. Most racing cyclists wore what they referred to as a "monkey hat," which was no more than soft leather wrapped around rubber sponge (Fig. 5-3). When more and more bicyclists took to the roads, and the accident statistics involving bikers were

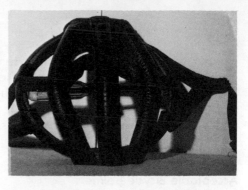

Fig. 5-3: This "monkey hat" is the ancestor of today's bike helmets, and it's still in wide use by the racing fraternity. Made of leather sewn over foam rubber. Offers minor impact protection, zero penetration protection, is of more psychological than actual safety value. Not recommended.

finally compiled, it became clear that head injuries were the leading cause of death in such mishaps. Gradually the message got across to some of us. When I looked around for a helmet in 1973, after my last serious bike-busting accident north of Seattle, all I could find, besides the monkey hat, were kayak, hockey and football helmets (Figs. 5-4 and 5-5). Motorcycle helmets, of course, were also available, but we had to rule them out because they were impossibly hot and very heavy, though unquestionably they offered the most protection. Most of us settled, in those days, for a hockey helmet and, as we discovered them, many of us switched to a kayak helmet. Few wore football helmets, because they were heavy, hot and uncomfortable.

The problem with the hockey helmets, it turned out, was that they offered some impact resistance but were poor protection against penetration. But then you don't expect a hockey player to hit a projecting curb, rock, tree stump, a sideview mirror or the sharp edge of a curb. The hockey player needs protection against the impact of a hard rubber puck coming at 80 miles an hour, a resounding swipe from a hockey stick or a head-on collision with the rounded or flat side of the rink walls or the ice. Impact resistance. Football helmets have the same shortcoming. Kayak helmets are even worse, they are thin plastic shells with very little inside lining to absorb shock, and the shell does not offer much protection against penetration.

Fig. 5-4: Motorcycle helmets are far too cumbersome, hot and heavy for use by bicyclists and impair hearing so the sounds of oncoming traffic are not clearly audible. Hearing is a vital defense sense for cyclists.

Fig. 5-5: Inside view of a motorcycle helmet. Excellent protection against impact and penetration, but, again, hot, heavy and impairs hearing to a dangerous degree.

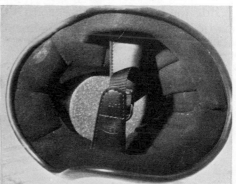

What was needed was a helmet that would absorb shock on impact, cushion the blow to the head and, itself—rather than the wearer's head —take the dents on impact. And the helmet had to offer high resistance to penetration by a relatively thin or sharp object, such as the chrome and metal on a car that Detroit calls style, the edge of a curb or the branch of a tree.

Acceptable Bicycle Helmets

Of the four helmets designed excusively for bicyclists, I like the Bell best, because in my opinion it offers the best combination of impact absorption and penetration resistance, is lightweight and provides adequate ventilation (it gets hot enough out there under the broiling sun as it is).

I am torn, for my next choice, between the MSR and the Pro-Tec. At the bottom of the list for overall protection, though at the top in weight and ventilation, is the Skid Lid.

I should note that none of the four helmets discussed here obstructs hearing, which cannot be said of the hockey, kayak or motorcycle helmets I have used. In fact, I had to cut away the plastic kayak shell around my ears so I could hear traffic around me. Hearing is a vital defense mechanism on a bike, essential to detecting traffic coming up from behind, if nothing else.

Perhaps the only major drawback to all of these helmets, except the Pro-Tec and Bell, is that none are made for kids. You can pad out the MSR, to be sure, but this won't be what you call scientific distribution of padding to the vulnerable skull, and a too-loose helmet can come off under sudden deceleration.

Let's look at these four helmets. I dismiss the monkey hat (Fig. 5-3) as slightly better than a silk top hat, and an equestrian helmet as stylish but funny-looking for a cyclist to wear and with little impact or penetration protection compared with three of the four helmets below.

The Bell helmet (Figs. 5-6 and 5-7) weighs about one pound. It has scientifically designed air scoops which offer reasonably good ventilation. In fact, I have used this helmet on some very hot summer days and never felt uncomfortable when honking up steep hills, slowly. The Bell helmet has a ventilated Lexan shell with a one-piece polystyrene liner. The helmet comes with soft foam pads that can be affixed to eight spots inside the helmet (Fig. 5-8) so that the helmet can be adjusted to your particular skull shape. The helmet also comes in popular adult head sizes. I must have an average skull, the 7⅛ size fits me without sliding around. Newer models have a quick-release on the chin strap. Price is around $34. The outside of the helmet has two front-to-rear reflective stripes to add visibility protection. The liner (Fig. 5-8) is ¾-inch thick except at the deepest protrusion of the vent scoops, where it is .220 inches. But these areas are supported by the thicker lining right next to them. I have helmet serial number 64, so there may be minor changes in

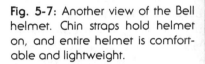

Fig. 5-6: This Bell helmet offers excellent penetration and impact protection. Ventilation is provided by air scoops.

Fig. 5-7: Another view of the Bell helmet. Chin straps hold helmet on, and entire helmet is comfortable and lightweight.

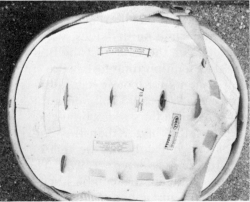

Fig 5-8: Inside of Bell helmet, showing shock protection. Velcro tabs hold foam pieces on inside to tailor the helmet to your head configuration.

Fig. 5-9: The MSR helmet offers greater penetration resistance than the Bell, but is slightly heavier.

Fig. 5-10: Inside of the MSR showing shock-absorbing straps at top and foam padding around lower perimeter.

the current models. Retention straps are adjustable only under the chin. Fore and aft straps hold the helmet in place, preventing it from sliding off to either side or front or rear.

The MSR (Mountain Safety Research) helmet weighs slightly less that the Bell (Fig. 5-9) and also has holes for ventilation, as shown. This helmet is a modification of MSR's top-grade, excellent mountain climber's helmet, which is designed for penetration resistance, such as by rocks falling from above. There isn't any meaningful hard data comparing helmets, but I suspect that the MSR has a higher penetration resistance than the Bell. Bell's own comparative test report does not mention brand names, but it does state that one helmet tested had "a six point web" attached to the shell with deformable metal clips, a shell of polypropylene-vinylchoride and a ½-inch thick ring of Styrofoam around the inside of the shell. This would fit the MSR to a T (Fig. 5-6). Bell's tests show comparable impact and penetration resistance on the sides, but the Bell outperforms the MSR when struck on the top of the helmet and gives similar protection on the crown. That is, the Bell seems to offer greater protection against blows to the top and crown areas and about the same on the sides, when compared with the MSR. A hockey helmet given the same tests by Bell was proved to be totally inadequate. The deceleration time tests were similar to that called for by ANSI Z90 requirements for motorcycle helmets. Motorcycle helmets, by the way, have a thick, heavy shell and a thick foam padding inside which traps heat, though offers more protection. From a standpoint of retention, I like the MSR better than the Bell because it has two-way adjustable straps that not only can be tightened under the chin but can also be adjusted for head length as well. The MSR also comes with self-adhering "bumps" of foam that can be stuck in appropriate places on the inside of the helmet for a better fit, and a Velcro holding, removable suede leather-on-foam sweatband in the front. The MSR sells for around $26.

The Pro-Tec PTH 3000 bicycle helmet (Fig. 5-11) is a newcomer to the U.S. bicycle scene. It comes with ventilation holes which offer surprisingly good air flow, considering the thickness of the one-inch foam liner

Fig. 5-11: The new Pro-Tec helmet does not offer as good all-around protection as the Bell or MSR, but it's lighter and feels more comfortable. It also comes in child sizes.

Fig. 5-12: Inside the Pro-Tec, showing removeable liner held in place by Velcro tabs. Liner is washable.

which, by the way, is held in place by Velcro tabs and so is removable for washing (Fig. 5-12)—a feature unique to the Pro-Tec. (The small bumps or tabs of Bell and MSR are removable, to be sure, but that is hardly the entire inside of the helmet). The Pro-Tec weighs about 18 ounces, lighter than either the Bell or the MSR. When I first laid eyes on the Pro-Tec samples shipped to me for testing, I was somewhat taken aback by the form-fitting appearance of the liner (Fig. 5-13) and by the way it hugged my head when worn. However, when I got on the bike and used the helmet for a couple of hours I noticed that the tight fit wasn't so tight any more. Something like a motorcycle helmet. When you buy a motorcycle helmet, the dealer, if he knows motorcycling, will insist on selling you a size you think is one size too small. The fit *should* be snug, that's one way to keep the helmet from falling off on impact; but more importantly, in a properly fitting helmet your head will not bounce around *inside* the helmet on impact. What you want is a helmet that both spreads impact shock and absorbs it. This the Pro-Tec would seem to do by nature of its design. The Pro-Tec people say theirs is the only helmet shaped like the human head. I've seen bullet-shaped heads,

Fig. 5-13: The Pro-Tec with liner in place.

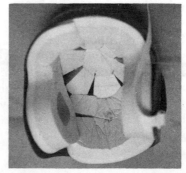

Fig. 5-14: The Skid-Lid is better than the "monkey hat" in Figure 5-3, but offers far less impact and penetration protection than the Bell, MSR or Pro-Tec helmets. Notice the open design at the top. This helmet is the lightest, most comfortable and coolest to wear of all the helmets tested, but you pay with less protection.

round heads, some almost square, so I don't know about that. I think what they mean is that the foam lining inside shapes itself to whatever configuration of head dimensions within a given size range it fits onto, and yet when removed the foam springs back to its original shape. I can't really give the Pro-Tec high marks for penetration resistance; the plastic shell is less than half as thick as the MSR's, and bends a lot easier. But it does offer a compromise among weight, comfort and protection. In fact, the form-fitting liner is comforting—something like a security blanket. The Pro-Tec costs around $21.

The Skid-Lid. The last of the four, I must confess, worries me. This helmet, if indeed it can be called that, is okay if you happen to fall where it fits. (Fall lightly, if that's possible, which I doubt, and do not hit a sharp object.) The helmet is open at the top, something like an open-face Dutch apple pie (Fig. 5-14). Inside is a moderately hard ½-inch thick liner. I would put this helmet a small notch above the monkey hat, but not much more. It offers virtually no protection against impact, because the four top prongs bend inward easily and there's nothing to hold them back except your head. You get some impact and penetration resistance around the crown, since it does go all the way *around* your head. It comes with self-adhering bumps for attachment inside and a chamois sweatband which is tucked in and removable from between the liner and the shell. The Skid-Lid is certainly a lot lighter, around 10 ounces, than the other helmets above and offers a lot more ventilation, but then what is lightness and coolness worth if your head is less well protected? The Skid-Lid costs around $28.

As I said, the Pro-Tec as well as the Bell comes in sizes for children. Model PTH 2500 is in fact *called* a Child's Bicycle Helmet. Like the adult models it is the only helmet that protects around the ears, (without interfering with hearing). By the way, Bell and MSR would like the helmets back if you have an accident. You may have lost protection by way of damage to the helmet, and they want to make sure you get a free new helmet!

Emergency Steps for a Head Injury

I'd like to talk about what to do about head injuries if they happen to someone else (you won't be conscious enough, most likely, to do anything about yourself at the time) and what you should know about head injuries if they happen to you, in terms of later on—hours, days or even weeks after the accident.

I am assuming that someone else has fallen and struck his or her head, or has fallen and you *think* he may have had a head injury. If the injured person is unconscious for more than twenty minutes, is bleeding from an ear, suffers a bad headache, vomits, is nauseated, seems confused, has blurred vision or speech, or lapses again into unconsciousness, he has had a concussion. Do not move the victim. There may be the possibility of a broken neck and if you move him you could sever nerves that will cause permanent paralysis. Do not try to slap him awake, you may only add to the injury. Make sure the person can breathe, that airways are clear. Check to see that breathing is reasonably normal; if not, apply mouth-to-mouth resuscitation. You or *someone* in any group of cyclists going on a tour should know the basics of artificial respiration and cardiopulmonary resuscitation. See your local Red Cross, hospital or fire department; they probably offer a free or inexpensive course.

If the victim is bleeding, stop the bleeding by applying pressure. Make a tourniquet out of a shirt or sock, if necessary, or a bungee cord. Be careful about the tourniquet, though, there is a fine line between a fatal loss of blood pressure and depriving a limb of blood to the point of damage. Keep the victim still and level, give no medicines or liquids. Get the patient (note change of status from cyclist to victim to patient) to a hospital quickly.

If you are the victim and recover from a head blow that knocked you out for less than twenty minutes, do make sure you get to a hospital within a few hours. You should be under medical observation because you could have a concussion that repeats the scenario at the beginning of this section on helmets. Be especially aware of the fact that if you suffer bleeding from an ear or the nose, if your head aches and feels sore, you are experiencing the effects of having been unconscious, and you could be on the road to a blood clot (hematoma), which can build up a fatal pressure inside the skull and must be medically relieved through surgery.

Remember especially that you *cannot tell* whether a head impact has caused the brain to bang on the inside of the skull, possibly causing a clot and the buildup of pressure later on. Again, be on the lookout for later symptoms of concussion such as continued headaches, nausea, vomiting, fainting or feeling that you are about to faint. If any of these symptoms occur, even within weeks after the accident, get yourself to the hospital emergency room as soon as possible (have someone else drive you and call your doctor).

I hope by now you are scared—aware enough of the risk of head injury to go out and buy a helmet, and, just as important, wear it at all times. I wear my helmet on the bike trails around Chicago, even off the highway. A couple of years ago kids on small bikes, couples arm-in-arm and joggers were the major hazards. Now it's also roller skaters, for the most part wobbling unpredictably down the tarmac. Hit one of them and I could easily have a head injury from being knocked off the bike, even at a slow speed.

WHAT YOU SHOULD KNOW ABOUT LIGHTS—SEE AND BE SEEN

If you drive a car, you know as well as I do that you just can't see a bicyclist on a dark street. You may just see the bike in time to avoid an accident if you are both on a brightly lit city street. At high speed on country lanes, a cyclist without a light is just death warmed over. At the legal speed of 55 miles an hour a car is coming up behind you at 80.6 feet per *second* ($55 \times \frac{5,280}{3,600} = 80.6$). Without lights or reflectors, the driver of the car going 55 miles an hour has—at the most—two or three seconds to see and avoid hitting the cyclist. If the driver has poor vision, has had a few drinks, is tired and so has slow reaction time, then goodbye bicyclist! That may sound awfully flip for such a serious subject as death or permanent injury, but when I see the vast number of people out at night on bikes without lights and sometimes even without reflectors it makes me wonder how seriously they take their *own* lives. I think the problem is basically one of not taking bicycling serious enough. Despite all the millions of bicycles sold since the bike boom began in 1971, all the people who ride bikes today, at least 85 percent of the bikes I see on the road are without lights. Now maybe these people don't ride at night. I am talking about all the bikes I see, day and night. I particularly don't see lights on bikes ridden by children, a safety hazard I have to blame on parents. The kids may not use the lights, but at least the parents should see that lights are available for use, and insist that they be used. A simple rule to remember is: *Never* ride at night without a light!

Europeans take bicycling seriously. They have had laws requiring lights on bikes at night for years. And not just any lights. The front light must meet standards for both brightness and road coverage, and the rear light has specific standards for brightness and visibility. You won't last long in Europe on a bike without a light—the police will haul you in. In England, be prepared to switch the location of the rear light to the right side of the bike, bearing in mind that the British drive on the left side of the highway. And their laws are specific about the placement of the rear light.

Lighting As a Defensive Art

It's a lot more important as a cyclist that you been seen by motorists than that you be able to see the road ahead. Ideally, bike lights should do both: be bright enough, cover a wide enough section of the road, far enough ahead of you, to let you see potholes in time to avoid them, and have some side visibility so that motorists coming at you from the side, as from a driveway or street intersection, will have some chance of seeing you. And the light shining ahead should light up some of the road shoulder, so you can see where you can ditch at night in the country to avoid a car, or see a dog in time to make a move. In the city, seeing the curb area can be helpful because you may have to swing into the curb, and it's nice to know whether you have to ride over a lot of broken glass, to get there or have the option of avoiding these puncture items.

There is only one bicyling lighting system that meets all of the above criteria. This system is powerful, shines well ahead of you, does a great job of alerting oncoming motorists that you are there, and, more importantly, does an equally good job of alerting any cars from behind you as to exactly where you are in the road, far enough in advance to avoid hitting you (assuming, of course, that the driver is sober).

I have never had trouble seeing where I was going at night. In the suburbs, streetlights, however dim, did a good enough job of lighting potholes for me to see and avoid them. Besides, I already know every inch of the roads I use frequently and am aware of anything in the roads that might make life difficult for me. I don't ride on country roads at night. Period. I wouldn't ride after dark on country roads, be they remote county roads, state highways or whatever, unless in dire emergency. When I go cross country on bike trips, usually camping my way, I make sure I have stopped well before dark, and if there's anything I forget, I do without. I just feel safer that way. Country folk may well be used to cyclists by now, but I remain unconvinced. In the big city I do ride at night a lot, because in late fall and early spring it often is dark out at both ends of my commute, so lights are important to me, just to be seen. I don't really need to see, because city streets are well enough lighted for me.

Details about Bike Lights

You can buy generator-powered lights, battery-powered lights and a combination of generator/battery-powered lights. Generator lights alone, for the most part, do an inadequate job of lighting up the road ahead, and taillight visibility is pretty dismal, but a lot better than nothing. When you are stopped, as at a stoplight, the generator is not generating, and you have no light. This is not terribly important on a brightly lighted city street, if, when you stop, you pull well over to the curb so a driver who wants to turn right at the light can do so. Oncoming traffic will either be stopped or going very slowly if the light is red. Still, I feel happier with a visible light when I am stopped. The combination battery/generator light sets do not put out adequate light from either power source, so I can't recommend any of them. All but one of the purely battery-powered lights put out barely enough light to be seen, and totally inadequate light to see ahead. Still, in terms of being visible to the motorist, they are an inexpensive safety aid and a lot better than no light at all.

The only battery-powered lighting system I can recommend whole-heartedly puts out light comparable to that of a motorcycle or at least a moped. And that's a lot of light, indeed, especially for a bicycle. This system does weigh a lot, over 1½ pounds, and costs as much as some inexpensive bicycles. But in terms of lifesaving insurance, the price is well worth the protection.

The battery lighting system I like is made by Bicycle Lighting Systems, and can only be purchased from this organization, located at 718 North Vermont Street, Arlington, Virginia 22203 (703/527-4164).

For the front light, BLS uses a new 4½-inch diameter halogen-sealed beam light (Fig. 5-15) which throws a powerful and wide beam. The halogen light is 40 percent brighter than comparable sealed-beam conventional incandescent headlights, yet uses no more power. For example, the GE sealed beam lamp number 7613 puts out 400 candlepower, the Halogen number 7551 emits 550 candlepower. BLS also offers a more powerful halogen light which gives 850 candlepower.

For a taillight, BLS uses a 7-inch-diameter flashing yellow light (Fig. 5-16) similar to those you see on street barricade markers. The idea here is not so much to make the motorist understand that there's a bicycle up ahead as it is to warn him that he may be approaching a big hole in the road or some other fairly lethal obstruction. The psychology is that of self-interest, rather than an attempt to create concern for you, the cyclist. The driver is far more likely to be aroused and cautious when he thinks he may be about to hurt his car, or himself. Or both.

BLS also provides a red flashing rear light (Fig. 5-17), but the boys in blue might not appreciate such an encroachment, so better check this one with your police department. You can also have a steady yellow or red light. As an auxiliary to the flashing lights you can have a steady red light, a small one about two inches in diameter. But vivid.

About Flashing Lights

Legality aside, the idea behind flashing lights is to alert the motorist. But if the light only flashes thirty times a minute, that may not be fast enough for your safety. Consider: at 35 miles an hour a car travels 51 feet a *second* ($35 \times \frac{5,280}{3,600} = 51.3$). Every other blink of the flashing light gets the driver 51 feet closer to you; you could get hit between blinks. I hear you protesting, "but I'm not standing still, I'm moving at 10 miles an hour." So, okay, subtract 10 from 35 = 25 = 36.6 feet per second ($25 \times \frac{5,280}{3,600} = 36.6$). Better, but you could get zapped inside a wink. And if the driver is going 45 miles an hour, that's 66 feet every second that two-plus tons of iron is gaining on you. So don't buy any blinking lights that

Fig. 5-15: The powerful halogen front light of a BLS bicycle lighting system throws a strong beam that lets you see what's ahead and lets motorists see you. Comparable to a motorcycle headlight. See text for more details.

Fig. 5-16: The taillight of a BLS lighting system for bicycles. Similar to a flashing road-obstruction blinker.

Fig. 5-17: This BLS bike light system also uses a small but powerful red blinking light (also available with a steady red or yellow light).

wink less than sixty times a minute. BLS's large flashing lights blink at around sixty times a minute. This adaptation of a road construction barricade light is highly visible from 500 to 1,000 feet away.

To power these lights you need some fairly hefty batteries, or a good generator, or both. BLS offers standard six-volt lantern batteries that will be dead soldiers in about ten hours and need replacing at $2.50 each. Or you can buy a BLS rechargeable nickel cadmium battery for $23 that will power both head and taillights for around two hours, give or take twenty minutes. Which means that if you cycle to work and back, both ways in the dark, you had better make the round trip in under two hours. Of course, you can buy a charger from BLS for the nickel cad batteries for around $7, keep one at both ends, and recharge the battery at work and at home. I did this double charging for years in Detroit, when I made my own lighting system out of a motorcycle headlight, complete in housing, and a motorcycle wet battery. The problem with the wet lead auto battery was that it ate away at my clothes and rusted bike tubes where the acid fumes hit. I can't recommend a lead auto battery. The connections were always getting corroded and needing to be cleaned.

Adding up the options from BLS, you can buy the halogen headlight in a housing, with switch, for $15. Extra lamps are $5 and you should buy two when you order. BLS's best, most powerful nickel cad battery will power all lights for 480 minutes, as opposed to only 140 minutes for the least expensive nickel cad battery noted above. That's eight hours. So buy the battery that will get you there and back. The 140-minute unit costs $18. The biggest 480-minute job is $45 and weighs 25 ounces, versus 8 ounces for the 140-minute battery and, as noted earlier, a charger is $7. If you want such a system, I suggest you tell BLS how you will mount both front and rear lights (on bars, on stays, wherever) so the proper clamps come with the system. Adding cost of two rear lights means you can spend upwards of $150 for their best system and add a couple of pounds to your bike. Or you can opt for the least expensive

Fig. 5-18: The Ampec Belt Beacon flashing strobe-type light puts out a bright white light. Available in models that emit either 40 or 60 blinks per minute. The 60-blink model is better. Fastens to belt or bike.

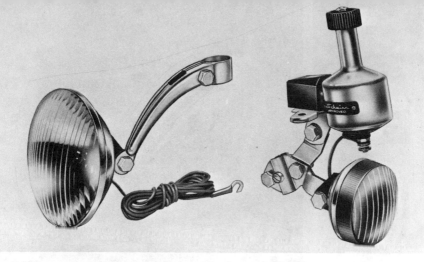

Fig. 5-19: The best of the generator light sets, available in any Schwinn shop as the "LeTour" light set, or in other stores under the Mitsuba label.

system and spend around $35 if you don't mind buying a non-rechargeable battery every week or so. I suggest the rechargeable route as the least expensive in the long run. There are other options involving less expensive batteries. Check with BLS and ask for their price list and literature.

Down the line from the BLS systems, I can recommend the Schwinn approved LeTour generator set, available from Schwinn stores for $15.95 and consisting of a six-volt, six-watt generator, powering a headlamp and taillight (Fig. 5-19). This unit throws a reasonably powerful beam forward and has a bright red taillight. Because it's powered by a generator, you have no light when you aren't moving, but you never have to worry about batteries, either. Carry spare bulbs for front and rear lights, though. If a Schwinn store is not accessible, the Mitsuba version is virtually identical.

Block generators, where the headlight and the generator are one unit and both are mounted at the side of the bike next to the front wheel, offer very little light compared with the Schwinn or Mitsuba unit above. Block units are very light, however, so if all you need is the comfort of having some light, just in case, the block generator may do. But don't use it if you bike at night a lot. The odds against you start to mount every time you go out without adequate lights at night.

Generator lights do create resistance, some more than others. The three above give minimum drag. After about 3,000 hours, though, the inner workings of the generator lights start to stick together from lack of lubrication and drag a lot, so I replace them. If you commute 10 miles round trip and average 10 mph, however, that's 300 days use out of the generator. Fifteen dollars a year isn't a bad price to pay for safety.

The French make a small battery-powered light called a Wonder Light. It emits a rather weak light, and under the blaze of city streetlights and traffic the light is not terribly visible. On a dark road, though, a

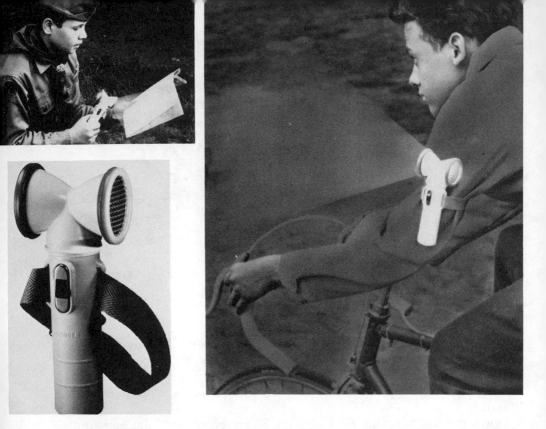

Fig. 5-20: The arm- or leg-mounted light puts out a white light front and a red light rear. Leg mounted, the light moves up and down and is an attention grabber. But the light power is weak and when in the midst of city lights or car lights, is not enough "see me" protection.

cyclist can be seen as a white pinpoint of light from the front and a red pinpoint of light from the rear. At around $4.50 per light, that's cheap light but low visibility.

An even weaker light is a strap-mounted leg light, to be strapped (Fig. 5-20) to the left leg above the calf. Though weak, it does have the attraction of being a moving point of light as you pedal. Both the Wonder Light and the leg light can double as a camp light.

There are three strobe lights on the market, none of which are particularly powerful. Ampec's Belt Beacon, (Fig. 5-18), comes in two models, M3B at forty flashes per minute and M3B60 at sixty flashes a minute. The M3B costs around $8.95, the M3B60 slightly less. The M3B60, which is the one I would use, requires a $1.79 alkaline battery that lasts about fifty hours. With battery, the unit weighs about 10 ounces and can be clipped to a belt or fastened to a bike. I would not depend on this light for my sole protection from the rear, but it does a good job as an extra added attraction to a generator light and gives you some protection when you stop, and the generator light is out. Fasten one to the handlebars for front protection, as well as using one aft.

A few years ago, in a trade magazine, I read about a unique road workers's reflective vest that was equipped with transistorized circuitry and bright flashing strobe lights on the front. I bought one, for about $40 and moved the lights to the rear. Now I had two diagonal lines of bright flashing tiny strobe lights running down my back. I can report that as I cycled down a busy main street in Chicago with this outfit I was nearly run down by motorists eager to come close to investigate this newest arrival from outer space. Too much is enough. I haven't worn the vest since, don't even know where it is. If you want one, try Aquador Plastics, Inc., P.O. Box 221, Lyndhurst, New Jersey 07071. Ask for the Flaro-Vest and when it comes, move the six strobe lights on the front to the two already on the back. Or wear the vest backwards. Comes with a battery pouch, but no batteries. Pouch holds four "C" cells, and has a switch.

Another strobe light is made by Bolo. Like the Ampec Belt Beacon, the maker claims a one-mile visibility. On a dark night, can you see forever? I haven't used the Bolo, so I don't know how well it works. At $4.25 postpaid from Bolo, P.O. Box 601153, Miami, Florida 33160, it weighs about 6 ounces, so it may be worthwhile tucking one away when you go on a trip. Could double as a flasher if you get a flat.

Did you ever take a photo strobe light out in a dark street and trigger it? I have, and it lights up the block. Now a tinkerer and photo equipment repair person has come up with a variation of a photo strobe that throws a powerful flash at fifty times a minute from a 6-volt alkaline battery which reportedly lasts eight to nine hours. With battery, this unit weighs about 8 ounces. From ZTS Photonetics, P.O. Box 262, Loveland, Ohio 45140. The strobe has been recently redesigned and now is about 200 times as bright as a good flashlight. Price: $35. Oh yes, it can also come with a nickel cad battery that holds up for three and a half hours. The charger for it is built into the light unit itself.

SOMETHING TO REFLECT ON

Reflectors on bicycles are a vital adjustment to a total-visibility system for night riding. *They by no means can replace lights*, but because they can add visibility, especially from the side, they should be used. Since you can't depend on children to use lights, if they ride at all at night, reflectors are an automatic, ever-present, passive life protector.

On pedals, reflectors add good visibility as the pedals move up and down. On wheels, reflectors fastened to spokes look like pinwheels of light as the wheels turn. (Fasten reflectors on the opposite side of the wheel from the valve stem to achieve some modicum of balance.)

Consumer Products Safety Commission regulations now require all new bicycles to be equipped with reflectors that light any side of your bicycle when a headlight beam falls on them. Reflectors must meet CPSC standards for size and reflectivity. Even super high priced bikes, in the $1,000 category, must be equipped with reflectors, which may make some of you wince at adding these things to your beautiful Imron-painted frameset and expensive hand-laced-up wheels with Campy hubs. But safety is not child's play anymore, just as your fine bike is no longer a toy for children. There are just too many cars out there on the highway to risk doing without reflectors, and you never know when your lights might decide to quit.

The 3M people also make reflective cloth tape you can sew on clothing and on bicycle bags or backpacks (Fig. 5-21) that glows in the dark when struck by light. 3M says its retro-reflective cloth tape is 200 times brighter than white paint. You can of course also use reflective self-adhesive 3M tape on bicycle tubing itself (Fig. 5-22), but I don't know what this will do to the finish.

Besides lights and reflectors, you can also use a triangular-shaped reflective plastic flag on a long pole mounted on the bike (Fig. 5-23). I have heard of instances, though, of the pole getting caught in tree branches, or being grabbed at by people in passing cars, to the injury of cyclists. No doubt the flags do attract attention, but they may also attract the wrong kind of attention. If you live in a nice, treeless suburb these flags may be okay, but be warned.

You can also buy a backpack for cyclists that has an entire rear reflective surface . . . a bicycle safety vest like the kind used by street crossing guards . . . fluorescent glowing arm bands . . . a solid fluorescent day-glo vivid red vest for daytime visibility—all from Safety Flag Co. of America, 390 Pine Street, Pawtucket, Rhode Island 02862. Send for their catalog.

Fig. 5-21: Reflective tape on a small backpack can be daytime as well as nighttime protection.

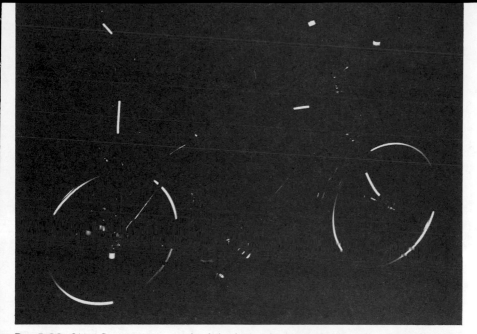

Fig. 5-22: 3M reflective tape on the bike helps the motorist spot your movements at night.

Fig. 5-23: Bike-mounted bright day-glo flag tells the motorist there's a bike up ahead, even if he can't see you in the traffic up front.

ABOUT HORNS

Bells or horns for bicycles, at least the more traditional type of mechanical horns such as the ones with a bulb that you squeeze to make the sound, are by and large not worth having. They make too little sound to alert a motorist, and are only worth the trouble if you ride along paths with joggers or other bicyclists who can hear the noise. Under such circumstances, it is more advisable to have a small bell than to have a Freon-powered horn.

But if you want to have some impact, either on major streets where there is a lot of noise or to startle dogs who might attack, then it is good to have a Freon-powered horn. The miniature Freon-powered horn, which weighs but a few ounces and makes a lot of piercing noise, comes with a clip for handlebar mounting and is widely available in sporting-goods or bicycle stores. A typical horn, called the Super Sound, sells for $5, with the clip. It gives about a hundred blasts, certainly enough for long usage (Fig. 5-24). Freon horns do not work much below freezing.

If you really want noise that will rattle a hoodlum or the most vicious dog, try a Freon-powered boat horn, available from boating supply stores. I used to have one mounted in a bottle cage on the handlebars. It sounded rather like a diesel freight train coming down the highway. One night, when I was foolish enough to ride along the trails of a park in Chicago, a pack of hoodlums got in my path, ready to do some dirty work. I accelerated right at them, then, with about ten feet to go, let go with a blast from the boat horn, sending the youths fleeing. By the time they realized they had been had, I was ten feet on the other side and speeding away. In another instance, I was between a squad car and the curb, and the blast from my horn caused the squad car to leap forward with dome light flashing. But you do not need a large horn; in general, it's far better to be alert at all times to what's happening around you and be prepared to take evasive action than it is to count on a horn to get you out of trouble. Remember you are on a bicycle, which cannot compete with automobiles in a confrontation or mishap. *You* must take the evasive action.

Fig. 5-24: Small but powerful Freon-powered bike horn is great for alerting other cyclists, cars, pedestrians, joggers and skaters that you are coming up from behind. Ideal for noisy street conditions. Use judiciously in quiet areas, because it's so loud it frightens, and the fear quickly turns to anger.

CARRYING A CHILD SAFELY

There are two basic designs for carrying children on adult bicycles. One is a trailer hitched to the seat post which has as an accessory a molded plastic seat and a restraining strap in which you can put two youngsters and even have room left for groceries. The other is a standard child's seat mounted on the bicycle, with special footrest and leg shields to keep the child's feet out of the spokes. Do not carry a child on your front handlebars or over the front wheel, because this makes for an unbalanced and dangerous situation.

The mounted child's seat, like the one in Figure 5-25 which sells for around $20 causes the least problems in maneuvering through city traffic. You do not have to worry about balancing the bike around turns or about going through busy intersections. All models should have a restraining strap as well as the wheel cover. They weigh less than 3 pounds and should be available from your local bike store or from a mail-order house (see Appendix).

But the most convenient method for carrying a child, or even two or three, if they are small enough, is in a trailer. Such a trailer (Fig. 3-2), made by Cannondale Corp., 35 Pulaski St., Stamford, Connecticut 06902, should be available from a local bike store. The trailer also comes with a zippered nylon cover for completely covering a week's load of

Fig. 5-25: This child carrier by Troxel is padded. Straps hold the child in place. Leg shields keep feet from spokes. The best of the child carriers. Available from bike stores.

groceries for a family of four, or for camping gear. The trailer hitches easily onto the seat post, with a safety wire cable hitch (but the car carrier must be removed). My Cannondale trailer also serves double duty as a yard carryall for plants, leaves or anything I used to use a wheelbarrow for. And children consider riding in this trailer about as much fun as going to the amusement park. First time I took it out on the street I had every kid on the block begging for a ride.

When towing in city traffic, do be careful about cornering and slow down for all turns. Remember you have added weight, so brake sooner than usual. And keep the trailer safety belt fastened!

ABOUT DOGS AND OTHER ANIMALS

A dog may be man's best friend when both are afoot, but there's something about a man on a bicycle that brings out the worst in a dog. For years I have been wondering what it is about a man on a bicycle that turns friendly dogs into snarling beasts. Perhaps the bicycle emits some infuriatingly high-pitched sound that only a dog can hear. Or it may simply occur to the dog that he has a human being at a disadvantage.

Whatever the reason, you should always be on the alert for an attack by a dog of any size, shape, and description, at any time, in any place. I find myself reacting instantly to the tinkle of a dog collar and watching shrubbery and front yards in the suburbs and farmyards. All dogs are potential enemies. In the country, you can usually outride a dog, which is the best advice I can give you, if this is possible. But if the dog comes at you from the front, or cheats by cutting across a yard as you round a corner, you might be in for a bad bite.

The dog problem is a serious one for cyclists, and it occupies a lot of space in bicycling magazines published in both this country and abroad. Reviewing the experience of a number of cyclists, the best defense, if you are not able to get away, seems to be a slender whip fastened to the handlebar stem, somewhat like an old-fashioned buggy whip. A cyclist can have it in his hand in an instant. One quick blow across a dog's nose will make even the most vicious animal think twice about further pursuit.

Other types of protection I have seen used include a standard bike water bottle filled with liquid household ammonia and equipped with a spray nozzle from an old bottle of window cleaner; a standard oil spray can, clip mounted to the stem and filled with ammonia; and a starter's blank pistol, which seems to scare dogs away.

You can also buy a small aerosol spray can of "dog repellent" for about $3.50 from some bike stores, which can shoot a thin stream of chemical about ten feet. The active ingredient in the spray is Oleoresin Capsicum, a pepper derivative. The trouble with this protection is that by the time you fish the can out of your pocket, aim it and press the button, you could already be bitten. But if you have time to stop, and the dog is close enough, the spray will discourage him from any further interest in you. Incidentally, although the effects are potent, there is no permanent damage done to the animal. The Capsicum is called Halt and if you can't find it, you can order cans by mail from the manufacturer, Animal Repellents, Inc., P.O. Box 168, Griffin, Georgia 30220. Be sure to ask for the plastic clip so you can fasten this little aerosol can to your stem or fork stay.

A word of caution about using Halt. Do not use this spray if you are cycling into the wind and another cyclist is behind you. On one trip I was on a cyclist did just that, and sprayed into a 20-mile-per-hour head wind, missed the dog completely, but succeeded in having the wind whip the spray up and deflect it right into the eyes of a female cyclist behind him. It took three full water bottles to wash out her eyes, and a lot of love to get that woman back on her bike.

Sometimes, with smaller dogs, you can intimidate them by growling at them viciously as you approach them, even swerving your bike right at them. I have had some dogs turn tail and run in front of me in fright. Finally, after a few blocks, they collapsed in fear in the gutter. But don't try this on a German shepherd police dog, or a weimaraner. I sprayed a German shepherd with Halt once, and I think he laughed and swallowed the spray like a child gulping down a piece of candy; if I'd thrown the can at him he'd have eaten it, Halt and all, for dessert. Perhaps the worst thing about dogs, other than the fact that their bite can put you in the hospital, is their tendency to throw themselves at, or under, the front wheel of a bicycle. Even very small dogs try to bite the front wheel, and have caused a cyclist to run into the dog, lose control and crash. A number of cyclists have been killed this way. Some ardent cyclist dog haters carry a starter's pistol loaded with 22-caliber blanks and report the loud discharge scares dogs away; frankly, I'd rather rely on more positive measures and not risk a bite for a bang.

Don't Use Weapons

Other cyclists I know have come so close to serious injury because of dogs, especially in the country, that they are seriously thinking of carrying a small 22-caliber pistol, or a CO_2 pellet gun. I strongly advise against taking these steps: first, because in most states they're illegal to carry as a concealed weapon without a license; second, the dog owner may fire back if he hears or sees you; third, it's extremely difficult to aim accurately from a moving bicycle and you may hit a fellow cyclist. You can make an effective defense out of a 30-inch piece of electric conduit, or a section of an old metal fly rod.

A problem to be aware of with dogs is that they tend to attack the first cyclist who passes by. If this cyclist is at the head of a family group, or a stream of ten or more cyclists, chances are good that the dog, concentrating on the first cyclist, will get in the way of following cyclists and cause a domino-type accident, with cyclists crashing into one another. I have even had two dogs chase a lead cyclist and almost cause a crash as following cyclists tried to get out of their way. As a leader, you can stop, dismount, and keep the dog interested in you until your group is safely out of range. The dog, however, will attack you the second you sling one foot over the top tube. So it's best, in this situation, to get the dog close enough to spray him with Halt and *then* jump on your bike and get underway fast.

The old adage that barking dogs don't bite cannot be trusted, I have found, but be doubly suspicious of the dog that comes up to you silently and stands there looking at you. He's just waiting for you to get back on the bicycle so he can get you at a disadvantage. A friend of mine who is an experienced cyclist spent two months in the hospital because of just such an incident. One evening she was cycling alone about thirty miles from home. A snarling dog chased her down a dead-end street, where she dismounted. The owner of the dog was in his yard nearby, but made no move to call the animal back. The dog waited until my friend had climbed back on the bicycle and, as she was mounting sank his teeth in her calf, penetrating all the way to the bone, through heavy jeans. Not realizing how serious the bite was, my friend rode home and attempted to treat it herself. By the time she got to her doctor, the wound was so badly infected that she not only had to be hospitalized for two months, but she has suffered minor but permanent impairment of leg movement, which affects her riding ability.

My heart goes out to children who are chased by dogs and badly frightened—or bitten. Most cities do not permit dogs to be at large anymore; they have to be either tied up or penned in the yard. In the country, of course, farm dogs are seldom tied and are almost always ready and willing to attack the passing cyclist.

What to Do If Bitten

To avoid a painful series of rabies inoculations, if you are bitten, remember to try to find out who owns the offending animal. Your child should be instructed to do the same thing if he is bitten. A dog will usually run home after an assault, and if you can manage it, and there is no one in the immediate vicinity who can tell you who owns the animal, try to follow it home. You can then warn the owner to keep the dog locked up for the period of time recommended by your doctor. If at the end of that time the dog has not developed rabies, you or your child will not need rabies shots.

If you are in the country and are bitten, and you cannot follow the animal to its home, try to memorize what it looks like: the size, shape, markings, and general appearance. A neighbor in the vicinity may recognize your description and help you locate the dog and avoid rabies inoculations.

In any case, if you are bitten by a dog, *always* get immediate treatment as soon as possible from a doctor. Then call the dog warden and your lawyer, in that order. You have all the legal redress in the world, because people should keep a dog that will attack a cyclist under restraint. Even if you yourself aren't bitten, you will be doing a favor to the rest of the cycling fraternity if you take note of the address where the chase began as the probable home of the animal, and call the area dog warden as soon as you get home. I think a dog attacks out of a sense of duty, feeling that the territory around its house is its exclusive property.

Other animals sometimes bite, too, though more rarely than dogs. Squirrels, woodchucks, and raccoons, if they think they are cornered, or are crazed by rabies, will bite. If you're bitten, it's important to capture the animal, if at all possible, so it can be held for observation to see if it develops rabies. Don't kill it, because rabies may be in the undetectable stage. The World Health Organization states that if you're bitten by an animal that *cannot* be held for observation for rabies development, you *must* undergo rabies inoculations, which is an ordeal.

If you camp out on a bicycle tour, observe all the usual precautions about snakes and other animals. Keep a simple first-aid kit with you. If you fall, clean your scratches and cuts with tap water from a canteen or flask, and apply antiseptic ointment. Then bandage lightly. If the cut did not cause a lot of bleeding or sever a muscle, there's no need to end the trip or wait for the wound to heal. If you want to cycle-tour, you'll have to get used to a few bumps and bruises and take them in stride.

Your Rights with Respect to Canines

States seem to fall into two basic categories with respect to their approach to liability for dog bites. The first type, by far the most common, is the common-law approach, under which an owner is not liable for his dog's actions unless he had prior knowledge of the dog's tendencies. In other words, you have to prove that the owner knew the dog could attack you. Such factors as whether the dog was trained to attack can make this task easier, but it still is a difficult process.

Many other states, including Illinois, Florida, Michigan, Ohio and New Jersey have adopted strict state laws that make the owner liable in *all* cases, unless the dog was protecting against an unwanted trespasser. Unwanted, that is, by the dog's owner. Most of these laws also cover loose dogs who, by their actions, cause an accident, a category called mischievous dogs. You must see what the law provides in your area.

Localities have adopted criminal laws for having dogs loose on public property, and if there is no such law in your area, you should make sure pressure is brought to bear for a leash law and for a strict liability statute (at state level).

When you are bitten, in whatever state, you should hire an attorney who can handle all of the intricacies of the local laws. You should sue to collect damages and compensation when you are injured and your bike is badly damaged. The system of contingent fees for lawyers (who collect a percentage of the money awarded, plus a small retention fee) makes it easy for you to file suit in dog attack cases. If suing sounds dramatic, think of how many times people have been injured by contact with a dog, either directly or indirectly (such as when the dog forces you to fall or get hit by an auto).

LOCKING YOUR BICYCLE . . . DON'T LEAVE IT FOR LONG!

Although having a good bike lock has little to do with bicycle safety, it does have quite a bit to do with saving your bike. As we all know by now, bicycles are one of the prime targets of theft in this country, partly because so few people understand about how to lock up properly.

Many of the bicycles we recommend in this book are high-quality machines, and they look like high-quality machines. Such jewels of engineering and design should not be left out for thieves to have at with such sophisticated techniques as freezing locks with Freon-22 and then snapping the shackle with three- to six-foot bolt cutters. Thieves are adept at such tricks as cutting the lock or cable you have around the bike with a cutter contained in a paper sack with a hole in the bottom and then returning to ride off on the bike while the owner is absent.

The rule to follow here is this: Do not leave an expensive bike for much longer than it takes to steal it, given the quality of your protection. If you have a fine Citadel or Kryptonite lock which resists most attacks, don't leave a derailleur bicycle long enough to have parts stolen. If you must leave your bicycle for all day outdoors, make sure you buy a bike that thieves will not be drawn to, that is, an inexpensive three- or five-speed. Even with a cheaper bike, lock it securely with a steel lock with hardened shackle.

Don't lock your bike to anything that can be stolen or from which the bike can be lifted. It does no good to secure your bike to a parking meter, when all the thief would have to do is lift the bike over the top of the meter. Similarly, locking the bike to a thin, sheet metal sign or a chain-link fence will make it easy to cut the sign or fence and get at the bike.

Lock more than just the wheel of the bike to the bike rack or telephone pole. Most bike racks, for one thing, are inadequate in that all you can lock is the front wheel, and, if you have a long chain, the frame as well. If you lock just the front or rear wheel, the thief merely takes that wheel off and shoves the bike into a waiting van. If you have a quick-release skewer, take off a wheel and lock it with the frame and rear wheel to the object you are locking the bike to (Fig. 5-26).

If you must lock your bike, I recommend either Citadel or Kryptonite U-shaped all-alloy steel locks (Fig. 5-27). The Citadel stands up to all types of attack, such as hammering, hacksaw and bolt cutters. It is not a cable lock, which can be easily defeated with a hacksaw in minutes. It is a relatively small, yet extremely strong extra-hardened all-alloy lock. It retails for around $25, with the vinyl mounting bracket adding about $2 to the cost. The Citadel weighs just 1.9 pounds and has a tubular key to resist picking. A straight key version of this lock, which weighs slightly

Fig. 5-26: A lock offers only time protection. This one would give a professional about five minutes' work, but would deter the novice.

Fig. 5-27: This hardened stainless-steel bike lock with a pick-resistant interior offers maximum protection, but is not invulnerable. Fine for locking inexpensive bikes to a school bike stand. No lock is good enough for a really expensive bike, if you depend on it 100 percent.

Fig. 5-28: Here's another high-protection lock that will deter the amateur and give a pro a lot of grief. If you can't bring your bike inside the office or keep it in your basement, this is the type of lock to use.

more (2.3 pounds) is the Tech-Lock, (Fig. 5-28) which retails for $18 to $20. A similar lock made by Kryptonite, which is slightly vulnerable to a hacksaw attack but is much stronger and thief resistant than other types of locks, retails for $22.

If you don't opt for the Citadel or Kryptonite because they are small and do not fit around trees or large objects as well as the frame and wheels, you may want an extra-heavy, all case-hardened steel chain, locked with a case-hardened shackle lock. By case hardened, I mean that it has a thin shell over softer metal that resists sharp blows. The chain must be at least ⅜ of an inch thick. Good chains are sold by a variety of major lock companies, with Master Lock and American being two prominent names.

The padlock for this chain should be hardened steel. Remember first, though, that such padlocks can all be defeated sooner or later. The padlock should have a thick, hardened shackle (the thing that closes around the chain); it should have a double-locking shackle, which means both ends of the shackle are locked within the frame of the lock to prevent attack with a padlock "popper" and it should use a tubular key. Ideal Security makes a double-locking, tubular key lock, as do American and Master Lock companies. Ideal's "Boss" padlock is relatively inexpensive and very effective (Fig. 5-29).

Other points to remember include:

—Register the serial number of your bike with the local police. Register also with the International Cycling Association, which has a three-year registration program tied into local police organizations, with computer registration for quick, nationwide identification. As the ICA program expands, more bikes will be recovered. As it stands, however, the recovery rate is dismally low.

—Make sure your bicycle is covered by your renter's or homeowner's insurance policy.

—With an electric engraving unit, engrave your Social Security number

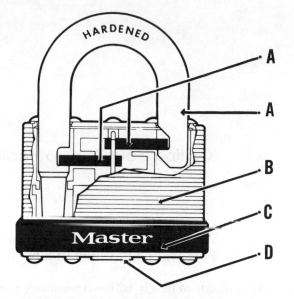

Fig. 5-29: Padlocks and chains are also a good combination, but heavy. Leave the lock and chain at one end of your trip, or a set at each end. Use a padlock with hardened shackle with internal locking at each end of shackle (A), case-hardened steel, abuse-resistant steel case (B), resilient bumper to keep lock from scratching or marring (C) and a pick-resistant pin tumbler locking mechanism (D).

on small parts of the bicycle, such as the rims, hubs, stem, seat post, bottom bracket and handlebars (under the tape).

There are several things you can do to slow down anyone trying to make off with your bicycle. The first, and easiest, is to take off your front wheel if you have a quick-release skewer. Or, you can jam a coin or washer into the brake lever to hold the brakes locked. Other handy tactics include tangling rubber shock cords in the spokes, slipping the chain just slightly off the freewheel or putting the derailleur out of gear.

When you are staying at a hotel or visiting a restaurant while on tour, you may not want to drag a heavy metal lock or chain with you. If the bicycle is somewhere in sight while you are inside, use a lighter, thin steel cable lock with a small combination padlock to at least deter potential thieves, as well as employing one or more of the tactics that I noted above to make it difficult to steal. Speaking of hotels, many inns will not want a bicycle brought into the rooms, especially if it is dirty or wet. You should not lock the bike outdoors under any circumstances, because the bike is your means of transportation and your most important possession on tour. Leave it in a baggage storage area, and, if you are in a large hotel, get a receipt for it.

Cycling Your Way to Health

You are probably already convinced of the many rewards of cycling for the body and the mind. You want to become or remain an active, alive and vital person, and you are willing to work just a bit at it to achieve that result.

Yet if you are like millions of newly active Americans, you may not be aware of what it takes to arrive at a proper level of fitness, and how to stay in shape while avoiding needless injuries. You may not even know how often you need to cycle to attain a specific level of cardiovascular conditioning, nor how long or hard to cycle each time you get on the bike.

Although cycling offers the freedom to exercise whenever the urge strikes (often, I hope!), it is still important to work out a general exercise program that you can stick to to ensure that your cycling is doing your body good. This chapter will aid you in planning such a training program.

HOW TO AVOID STRESS INJURY

There are many other aspects of staying healthy through cycling, including a general knowledge of how to limber up for riding, and how to cool down after a strenuous workout. Cycling is one of the safest of all sports; nevertheless a knowledge of preventive medicine for the average cyclist can save weeks and months of inactivity due to pulled or sore muscles and joints, just as knowing how to ride safely avoids accidents. For those who do suffer an injury, we will look at some of the common complaints of cyclists, and explain how to adjust your cycling program to aid recovery and avoid repeats of the injury. With an overview of the health aspects of cycling, you can be on your way to years of injury-free riding, and a constant state of pleasant good health.

ACHIEVING THE "TRAINING EFFECT"

Bicycling is unique among popular sports in that it does not take weeks for the previously sedentary person to become involved in regular workouts. Even for the most out-of-shape individual, a gradual buildup of an exercise plan can start immediately upon buying a good bike, as long as caution is not thrown to the wind. Cycling takes little skill for the tourist, and just a small amount of practice will enable the health seeker to get going right away. There is only a small note of caution which ought to be heeded: All adults who have not been involved in regular exercise, who are over the age of thirty-five and out of shape, or who have a history of heart, lung or circulatory disease ought to have a "stress test" before embarking on a prescribed exercise format. Persons over fifty should have an examination by a physician, whatever their fitness level if they are returning to regular exercise after a prolonged absence. A stress test, (Fig. 6-1) is performed by a physician experienced in exercise physiology and involves electrocardiogram and blood-pressure analysis at the height of physical exertion. Usually the subject works out on a treadmill or a stationary bicycle. The point of the procedure is to determine the patient's level of fitness from which the doctor can write an "exercise prescription"—a workout schedule that will not cause potential harm. The doctor may suggest less initial activity than you would like, but it is important to start things out slowly, and not join the growing ranks of people who tried to do too much too soon, out of a mistaken belief that they could "handle it." A stress test is not inexpensive, but is an excellent measure of your state of health.

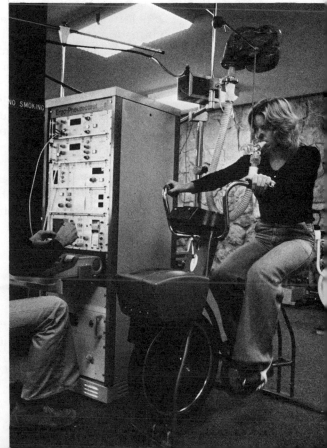

Fig. 6-1: This stationary cycle is used in hospitals during "stress test" evaluations of the cyclist's ability to engage in heavy exercise. It monitors blood pressure, heart rate and oxygen consumption during the height of exertion.

KNOW YOUR PHYSICAL LIMITS

The key to achieving a "training effect," or an increased level of cardio-vascular fitness based on a regular diet of exercise, is to discover your current phsyical limits, and then slowly but surely work to push them ever higher. Again, avoid pushing things too quickly, or the "overuse syndrome" will overtake you very soon. Yet you must still push hard enough to get positive results. To achieve this balance, you must learn to "listen to your body," a trick accomplished by most endurance athletes. This means keeping in tune with your inner vital signs such as heart rate, air intake and muscle tone. Learn what your limits are and learn to take hints such as cramps, aching joints or low energy levels and decide whether you are working too hard. This is not a skill that can be taught through words alone. It is something you must learn to hear from within yourself.

There are, of course, slightly more scientific methods for determining how much exercise you are getting for the time you are putting in. Leading experts on "aerobics" (basically, endurance exercise) give general guidelines for anyone who wants to become involved in regular exercise or who wants to increase his aerobic capacity. The key is achieving a heart rate that will expand the blood flow to the muscles and will increase the lung's capacity to absorb oxygen, thus avoiding heart and lung disease. The general estimate of the maximum-exercise heart rate is arrived at by subtracting your age in years from a heart rate of 220 beats per minute. As people age, the maximum attainable heart rate goes down. It is suggested that any endurance exercise must be kept up for thirty minutes and the biker's heart rate should be kept at about 60 to 85 percent of the maximum, easily calculated by taking the difference between your resting heart rate and the suggested maximal rate and multiplying it by .60 to .85, the measure of how much you should be working your heart.

Even for an athlete training for a big race, the heart rate, according to experts, should never exceed 90 percent of the maximum. For most people, the heart rate should be kept in the range of 150 to 170 beats per minute while working out. You'll be hearing more about how to monitor your heartbeat later on in this chapter.

A PROGRAM FOR EXERCISE

Many exercise experts swear by long riding at a moderate speed as the basis for fitness. For most of you who simply seek to be in shape, this kind of cycling should make up the bulk, but not all of your outings. Each day, or every other day at the very least, you should cycle at the best steady pace you can maintain for over a half hour. If you live in an area with mixed terrain, you should practice going up hills, and work out on flat surfaces, to utilize the different muscle groups. On one or two workouts a week, you should push yourself just a little above the normal cadence in the same gears for a specified period of time, mixing this with short "breathers" of slower pedaling. This faster pace may, in turn, become your "normal" pace in just a few months, and you will be pushing yourself to a pace you never thought you could keep up in the very near future. Push yourself just a little bit, because the chances are you need to attain a better pace for your everyday cycling. But always remember to "warm down" from bursts of speed by cycling slowly to release the buildup of lactic acid, which is the agent that can cause tight, cramped muscles. The warmdown also slows the heart rate gradually to avoid fatigue.

But, the remainder of the average exercise program should be made up of long distances cycled at a level of at least 65 percent of maximal effort. Many people will have to spend weeks or months of building from just a mile or so of riding to a "beginner's" program we describe below. They must get their orders from their doctor before embarking on the more ambitious and strenuous schedules that the reasonably fit person should follow. The following are some sample schedules for beginning and intermediate cyclists (competitive cyclists may refer to the chapter on racing for their regimens), which may aid you in establishing your own training schedule. These are only suggested sample programs and are based on the needs of the average cyclist. For a "close-enough" check of cycling speed, see the gear ratio tables and pedal cadence data in Chapter 2.

Sample Schedule 1: For Beginners of All Ages

WEEK 1: Monday, ride 4 miles at a steady pace for 24 minutes, or 6 minutes per mile, keeping the heart rate at least 65 percent of the maximum (see above). Rest Tuesday. Wednesday, ride five miles at the same pace, or for 30 minutes. Rest Thursday. Friday, repeat Monday's workout. Saturday, do a longer ride, about 10 miles, but at a slightly slower pace, finishing in under 70 minutes. Rest Sunday.

WEEK 2: Repeat week one, adding another day of 4 miles in 24 minutes if you feel you can handle this.

WEEK 3: Monday, ride at a faster pace, about 5 miles in 25 minutes. Not too fast a pace considering that champion runners can cover 26 miles *on foot* this fast. Keep up the effort for the distance. Rest Tuesday. Wednesday, try 6 miles in 36 minutes, a slower pace. Rest Thursday. Friday, ride 6 miles in 36 minutes again. Saturday, do your long workout, but increase the speed and distance, riding 12 miles in 72 minutes, if your heart is not unduly taxed. Rest Sunday.

WEEK 4: Repeat week 3.

WEEK 5: Boost your mileage and speed this week. Monday, ride 7 miles in 35 minutes, a 5-minute-per-mile pace. Rest Tuesday. Wednesday, ride 8 miles in 48 minutes, a slower pace. Rest Thursday. Friday, again ride 7 miles in 35 minutes. Saturday, cap off the week with a 15-mile ride at a 6-minute-per-mile pace, or riding continuously for 90 minutes. Rest Sunday.

WEEK 6: Repeat week 5.

WEEK 7: Monday, ride 8 miles in 40 minutes, keeping up the 5-minute-per-mile pace. Rest Tuesday. Wednesday, ride 10 miles in one hour. Rest Thursday. Friday, repeat Monday's 8-mile ride in 40 minutes. Saturday, try a long, slow ride of 20 miles, cycling at a 6-minute-per-mile pace and finishing in 2 hours or so. Rest Sunday.

WEEK 8: Repeat week 7.

If this schedule is too strenuous, you will know very quickly that you should cut back to a certain percentage of the effort described, in keeping with your body's signals. Keep up Schedule 1 for a few months, and then you will be ready to progress to a harder training routine if you want the exercise. For most people, the first step will be the only one they need to take to live a healthy life. For hardier souls, a suggested schedule for slightly more demanding workouts follows.

Sample Schedule 2: Intermediate, for Those in Good Shape

WEEK 1: Monday, ride 10 miles in 60 minutes, a moderate pace. Tuesday, begin what is called interval workouts, riding 4-minute miles, followed by 1-to-2-minute warmdowns, repeating this for 40 minutes. Rest Wednesday. Thursday, repeat Monday's effort. Friday, ride 10 miles in 50 minutes. Saturday, ride 20 miles at a comfortable pace, trying to finish in less than 2 hours. Rest Sunday.

WEEK 2: Repeat week 1, adding interval training on Friday in place of the quick, steady workout pace.

WEEK 3: Monday, ride 10 miles in 50 minutes. Tuesday, ride 2 miles in 8 minutes, followed by 2-to-3-minute warmdowns at a slower pace, repeating this procedure 3 times, then adding a 5-to-10-minute warmdown before getting off the bike. Rest Wednesday. Thursday, ride 12 miles in 1 hour, repeating this workout on Friday. Saturday, ride 25 miles in 2½ hours. Rest Sunday.

WEEK 4: Repeat week 3.

WEEK 5: Monday, ride 12 miles in 1 hour, at a steady pace. Tuesday, do intervals for 1 hour, riding 2 miles in 7½ minutes, followed by short warmdowns lasting no more than 3 minutes. Also, try for the first time riding at 90 percent of full effort for ½ mile or so, covering the distance as fast as you can. This works wonders for weak leg muscles. Rest Wednesday. Thursday, it's back to Monday's workout, at a steady pace. Friday, do it again. Saturday, ride at the 12-mile-per-hour pace for 2 hours. Rest Sunday.

WEEK 6: Repeat week 5.

WEEK 7: Monday, ride 10 miles in 40 minutes—a fast pace—keeping the speed steady. Rest Tuesday. Wednesday, do intervals of 1 mile in 3½ minutes, followed by a 1 minute warmdown, for 45 minutes. Rest Thursday. Friday, ride 15 miles in 1 hour. Saturday, ride a long, slow distance, covering 40 miles in 3 hours and 20 minutes. Rest Sunday.

WEEK 8: Monday, ride 15 miles in 60 minutes, a fast pace. Rest Tuesday. Wednesday, ride intervals for 1 hour, either 1 or 2 miles very fast, followed by a short warmdown. Thursday, ride 10 miles in 50 minutes, a slower pace. Friday, ride 12 miles in 1 hour. Saturday, try a half-century, a 50-mile ride. This will take a lot out of you, so carefully follow instructions on riding in the heat and carry lots of fluids and some food with you. (See section on diet in this chapter.) Rest Sunday.

As you can tell, these sample schedules for training provide a mix of hard interval workouts with long-distance rides of varying duration and pace. It is good to follow several hard weeks of effort with an easier week, and to rest at least one day a week. No cycling expert advocates daily training because the wear and tear on the body from such sustained workouts can actually reduce your fitness level.

From experience, you can eventually set your own regular cycling regimen, because you will soon begin to define your own level of fitness and your exercise needs.

By the way, there's finally, a quiet cyclometer on the market.

A resettable trip mileage counter cyclometer has been recently introduced by Huret that runs off a rubber belt from a pulley attached to the front wheel (Fig. 6-2). This method of attaching eliminates the noisy click, click of the striker found on conventional cyclometers. The unit costs around $12.50.

Fig. 6-2: New Huret belt-driven cyclometer is quieter than conventional cyclometers.

WHEN YOU CAN'T CYCLE—A GUIDE TO ALTERNATIVE EXERCISES FOR CYCLISTS

You do not have to exercise every day to keep in condition, but it is recommended that you perform cycling or some other form of aerobic exercise three to four times a week. By endurance, we do not mean such stop-and-go sports as basketball, handball/racquetball, tennis or weight-lifting. These sports do exercise the muscles and give you a good work-out, but they do relatively little for the cardiovascular system as compared with cycling, running and swimming.

Aerobics is continuous activity, activity that forces the muscles to use oxygen in the process of converting glycogen (blood sugar) to expended energy. Stop-and-go sports do not use oxygen, and cause the buildup of lactic acid and pyruvic acid in the muscles, leaving them tight and sore on occasion. Endurance exercise is the best exercise for the cardiovascular system—in other words, for the heart and the lungs. But endurance exercise must be practiced regularly for it to do you any good.

Those who live in the "great snow belt" (which seems to get larger every year) are now asking "How do I get out in three feet of snow, with a wind-chill factor of minus 15 degrees Fahrenheit and ride a bicycle?" The answer is that, unless you are really crazy, you cannot, and you may take the time to do a little maintenance on your machine. Now, you say, how can I maintain a level of fitness when I can't bicycle? You are learning what many experienced cyclists and soccer/football players already know, that you ought to have a second sport to practice in the off-season when you cannot bicycle.

The best alternatives to outdoor cycling are those that exercise the same muscle groups as cycling while giving you the maximum aerobic conditioning. Since cycling is somewhat on the expensive side of sports, another criterion may be that the alternative sport be less expensive. Four activities best fill the need, in my opinion:

Stationary Cycling

Many racers and expert tourers practice their sport in the winter either on the new popular rollers, which simulate actual movement on the street, or on stationary bicycles, which have been popular with the general public (including the current Pope, John Paul II) for many years. Both use the same muscles as outdoor cycling, and you can even simulate the normal training regimen when not on the street.

Advantages: You can read a book or watch television while on the stationary bike, (Fig. 6-3) to avoid getting bored by the lack of scenery. On the rollers (Fig. 6-4), even though you must balance (a trick we will describe) you can and ought to listen to music to help you maintain the pace.

With stationary bicycling you can also monitor your heartbeat. There's

Fig. 6-3: One of the many varieties of stationary bicycles for home use during long winter months when you cannot bicycle out of doors, this Schwinn Air Dyne ErgoMetric Exerciser retails for $395.

Fig. 6-4: Many racing enthusiasts and veteran tourers use "rollers" in off-season to keep up their physical conditioning.

Fig. 6-5: Electronic pulse-rate monitor

a gadget on the market which you hold in your hand that will give you a digital readout of your heartbeat rate. The problem with digital units is that you cannot get an accurate readout between numbers, and that the eye does not readily, quickly, and accurately intepret these numbers. Sometimes a digital unit responds to quirks or instantaneous changes in heartbeat that are not indicative of the true, ongoing heartbeat. I much prefer the point type of heart-rate indicators, and I like to use one to monitor my own cardiac stress as I exercise either on a set of rollers or on a bicycle exerciser.

Manual pulse measurements, the kind you take by feeling the pulse in your wrist or throat and checking this reading with the second hand of a clock, are prone to broad error, and, of course, are not practical to make on any kind of continuous basis as you exercise.

One pointer type of automatic, electronic pulse counter I like is made by Computer Instruments Corporation, 100 Madison Ave., Hempstead, New York 11550 (Fig. 6-5). It costs about $200 and can be attached to a bicycle or bicycle exerciser (Fig. 6-6). This model uses a light-beam sensor that measures the optical opacity changes caused by each squirt of blood pulsed by the heart, which *is* your pulse rate or heartbeat rate. This photo-optical readout can be seen on the pointer dial, and if you wish, a switch lets you decide whether you see a blinking red light or a beep sound at the same time.

It's important that you keep track of your pulse rate, and keep it within your target zone. I am indebted to the scientists at Computer Instruments for the medical data on heart rate and health:

Medical authorities (see references) use the term "target zone" to describe the amount of activity which is enough to achieve fitness but not too much to exceed safe limits. This target zone is the level of activity which produces a heart rate of from 70 to 85 percent of the maximum attainable heart rate during an all-out effort. In other words, your own pulse can be used as a "speedometer" that tells you how much exercise your body needs for optimum physical fitness.

But before you can begin exercising in the target zone you must know your own maximum attainable heart rate which, of course, is different for each indi-

Fig. 6-6: Pulse-rate monitor mounted on a bicycle exerciser.

vidual. Therefore, BEFORE STARTING ON ANY EXERCISE PROGRAM YOU SHOULD CONSULT YOUR PHYSICIAN AND SUBMIT TO AN EXERCISE STRESS TEST. He will then be able to prescribe your own exercise target zone and exercise program.

Based on many studies, medical authorities have established the "average" maximum attainable heart rates shown in the chart (Fig. 6-7).

This chart shows that, on average, as we grow older the highest heart rate which can be reached during an all-out exercise effort falls, as does the corresponding target zone heart rate. The average 25-year-old man has a maximum heart rate of 200. His target zone would then be 140 (70%) to 170 (85%) beats per minute heart rate; the average 65-year-old man with a maximum attainable heart rate of 153 beats per minute would have a target zone of 107 (70%) to 130 (85%) beats per minute.

HOW TO USE THE TARGET ZONE

The crucial part of your workout is the length of time you stay in the target zone, the length of time you exercise with sufficient vigor to keep your pulse rate in the 70% to 85% range of maximum heart rate.

The typical exercise pattern should begin with a 5 to 10 minute warmup of moderate exercise in which the heart rate gradually builds up, followed by more vigorous exercise to bring the heart rate up to the target zone and maintain it there for a period of from 20 to 30 minutes. The 70% level is sufficient to promote fitness; the 85% level is an upper limit which may be sustained if a more intense workout is desired. Exercise in the target zone should be followed by a 5 to 10 minute cool-down in which the exercise intensity is gradually reduced before it

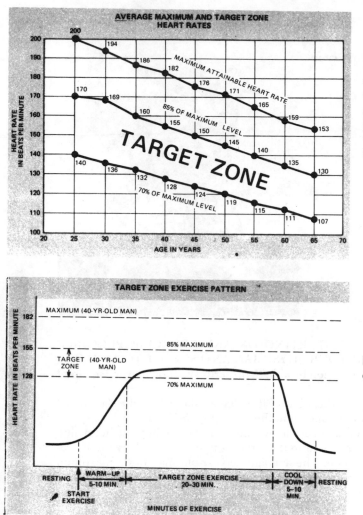

Fig. 6-7: Check your maximum heart rate. For example, if you are 40 years old you should be able to get your heart rate up to a maximum of 186 beats per minute but keep it within a target zone of 128 to 155 beats per minute.

Fig. 6-8: Target-zone exercise pattern

is stopped completely. The chart (Fig. 6-8) shows the typical target zone exercise pattern for the average 40-year-old man.

Optimum physical conditioning will result from the performance of this exercise pattern three times weekly with no more than two days elapsing between workouts.

CYCLING YOUR WAY TO PHYSICAL FITNESS

Any stationary exercise bicycle which is equipped with a Pulseminder will enable you to conveniently and safely perform the target zone exercise pattern for optimum physical conditioning by providing you with a continuous indication of your heart rate at all times. Manual pulse measurements cannot do this.

ADJUSTING THE BICYCLE

Before you begin exercising on your stationary bicycle the seat height and handgrips should be adjusted to enable your leg muscles to function most efficiently and your activity accomplished without fatigue. Adjust the seat height so that with your toe on the pedal, there is no more than a small bend at the knee when the pedal is in the full down position. Adjust the handlebar height and angle so that when grasping the handgrips the upper part of the body is leaning only slightly forward and relaxed, with little body weight supported by the arms. Mount the Pulseminder on the handlebar at an angle for easy viewing of the meter dial; loop the finger clip coiled wire around the handlebar to take up the slack so that the weight of the wire does not pull against the clip when it is on the finger. Grasp the handgrip lightly when taking heart rate measurements with the Pulseminder to insure accuracy or, optionally, release this grip and rest the forearm on the handlebar, leaving the hand free.

The typical workout—with the Pulseminder finger clip in place (set the high alarm of your Model 7830 Pulseminder at 85% maximum rate as a safety measure) and the bicycle resistance knob set at its loosest position, the warm-up portion of the exercise pattern is started by pedaling at the rate of about 50 to 60 pedal turns per minute (about 1 per second). This should be kept constant throughout the workout. Increase the resistance setting while maintaining the pedaling rate. Observe the rate of heart rate increase on the Pulseminder and adjust the resistance setting so that the heart rate rises gradually about halfway to the target zone after about 3 minutes of pedaling and continue to the lower end of your target zone after about 5 minutes of pedaling. This completes the warm-up phase of your exercise pattern.

Maintain the constant pedaling rate of 50 to 60 revolutions per minute while adjusting the resistance knob so that the heart rate stays within the target zone for at least 20 minutes. When starting the exercise program, your legs may tire sooner than 20 minutes. Do not force yourself to continue but start the cool-down phase of the exercise pattern at that point; your legs will grow stronger in time and you then will be able to pedal for the full 20 minutes or even 30 minutes at the target heart rate. Don't push yourself too fast, particularly if you haven't been normally active in the past; exercise first at a lower target zone and build up gradually to your proper target heart rate: DO NOT CONTINUE EXERCISING IF ABNORMAL HEART ACTION, PAIN, DIZZINESS OR OTHER DISTRESS IS EXPERIENCED. CONSULT YOUR PHYSICIAN.

Once you have completed the time of exercise in the target zone, you start the cool-down phase of the exercise pattern by gradually decreasing the bicycle resistance level. You will see your heart rate begin to decrease and continue to decrease as resistance level (and pedaling rate, if you wish) falls. After about 5 to 10 minutes of cool-down your heart rate should be approaching your normal resting rate. Usually the resting heart rate and normal breathing should be reached within 15 minutes after the end of the cool-down period. If not, then reduce the level of exercise at the next workout and gradually build up again to the target level over a period of weeks.

REFERENCES
Zohman, L.R.: "Beyond Diet . . . Exercise Your Way to Fitness and Heart Health," CPC International Inc., 1974.

American Heart Association, Committee on Exercise. *Exercise Testing and Training of Apparently Healthy Individuals:* A Handbook for Physicians, New York: American Heart Association, 1972.

American Heart Association, Committee on Exercise. *Exercise Testing and Training of Individuals with Heart Disease or at High Risk for Its Development: A Handbook for Physicians.* New York. American Heart Association, 1975.

Disadvantages

The disadvantages of stationary bicycling include the fact that you seem to tire more easily on the motionless bike, and it is harder to concentrate on a book or television while trying to engage in heavy exercise. One tip for those who do use this kind of exercise: Buy a cheap fan to simulate the effect of wind, or else you will have to stop before you have gotten sufficient exercise because of all the perspiration you've built up. Using the fan can actually double the time you spend on the machine.

Rollers, a heavy contraption involving a metal frame and three separate rollers, are most often used by hard-core cyclists who like to be able to use their own bikes while simulating roadwork. The problems include the fact that it takes a lot of work to stay up when you start out. Learning how to ride rollers is like learning how to ride a bicycle all over again. If the rollers you use don't have small stands on each side to help you get on, place two boxes, one on either side of the middle of the rollers, where your bike seat is (making sure the boxes will not slip away, of course.) Stand on the boxes, straddling the bike, then place one foot in a pedal. Try pedaling once and then quickly place the other foot in its pedal, and, with the front tire squarely in the middle of the front roller, start riding slowly. You may slip off once or twice, but don't worry. People do not usually get seriously hurt using rollers. Maintain a steady pressure on the handlebars to keep the bike in the middle of the rollers, placing the hands on the upright portion of the bars. You must keep very upright on the bike, and don't swing from side to side as many people do while pedaling on the street. Mastering the rollers can make your street cycling more efficient by reducing the drag of side-to-side movements. All energy must be spent pedaling directly up and down, eliminating awkward swings in the cadence. You can also learn to ride rollers by placing the unit in a doorway.

Many people make rollers, but the ones I like cost only around $100 and are made by State Aluminum Foundry, 15532 Illinois Avenue, Paramount, California 90723. I have been using these rollers (Fig. 6-9) for a couple of months now and can report that they are quiet, durable and light. The frame is adjustable for various lengths of bicycle wheelbase. This is important because the front wheel hub axle should be centered on the front roller for correct stability. These rollers use 4.5-inch steel drums, weigh around 26 pounds and will adjust from 40 to 54 inches. Ends of the drums are aluminum.

Using rollers will improve your outdoor skills, because riding them is so difficult that you increase your efficiency in using available energy

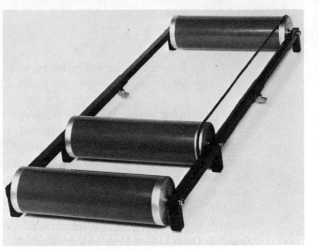

Fig. 6-9: High-quality rollers for around $99.95 a set

stores, if you keep up an active program on the rollers. But many people will also find stationary cycling somewhat boring on a routine basis, and will seek other forms of endurance exercise for the winter months. Let's look at the best of these.

Running or jogging: Whatever you call it, this sport has several advantages for the cyclist, and can even improve cycling performance. Running, although for many a boring activity, is more aerobic than cycling, increasing the cyclist's cardiovascular conditioning. Even good cyclists become winded when starting out on a jogging program, but a few weeks of work can lead to some excellent benefits.

The initial investment for running is small, involving a pair of well-built running shoes (Nike, New Balance, Tiger, Adidas and Brooks companies all make excellent, well-supported running shoes) with good arch and heel support to ward off injuries from the constant pounding. You don't need any new clothes—a good biking suit for cold weather should do well for limited running. In summer, wear light gym shorts. Indoor tracks are good for running in the winter if you do not want to be outdoors in the cold.

You should run two to five miles a day three times a week or more, at a slow pace of about eight minutes per mile, resting occasionally if need be, but trying to cover miles at a faster than quick-walk pace. Bear in mind that running at a pace half as fast as you cycle will give the same results in terms of conditioning, and you do not have to run as many miles as you would cover while cycling. A good twenty-minute run will usually suffice to keep up winter training for the touring cyclist.

Speed Skating: This sport is highly touted by racing enthusiasts because the same muscle groups are used as in cycling. It is very good aerobically at the proper pace, but its disadvantages are a shortage of tracks for real endurance workouts and the problem that very few people skate well enough to get good exercise in this manner. Merely getting out on a pair of skates and going around a local pond just doesn't do the trick unless you are up early and can use a relatively empty area for speed work.

Learning how to skate effectively is a different matter, and I can only point to skating publications for such advice.

Cross-country skiing: This is perhaps the best of all the alternatives to cycling during winter months in terms of time expended, if you have easy access to a park or open country. This is the most strenuous of all endurance sports, and one of the most enjoyable. If there are any local hills, it is a fun and exciting pastime, which uses many of the same muscles as bicycling. With a simple lesson from a friend or equipment dealer, you can be on your way, without costly investments of time and money for lessons. Many local outdoor stores have weekly sessions on waxing the skis and on how to put one ski in front of another, and these are almost always free. Attend one, and chances are you will be hooked.

The equipment, which includes a pair of thin skies, two poles, shoes and bindings, is not nearly as expensive as downhill equipment, and currently will not run you more than $200. Most stores will sell sets for much cheaper than that. You can locate excellent trail information from most sportiong goods stores or from local travel guides. In many areas, running paths are transformed into cross-country trails as soon as the snow falls. Also, many state and national parks are virtual havens for cross-country enthusiasts.

BEFORE YOU WORK OUT—LIMBER UP

So you now have an idea of how often to exercise each week and what sports can support your growing cycling program. Now, let us turn to the individual workout for some tips on how to really prevent injuries from occurring.

Often forgotten by the millions of active Americans is that all forms of exercise tighten muscles. That's what exercise is, in one way: a tightening of soft, out-of-shape muscles. Exercise shortens muscles through constant pulling and tugging. Therefore, before and after each workout, it is necessary to loosen up the major muscle groups which are tightened by cycling. These include the quadriceps, those bulky muscles on the front of the leg; the lower back; the hamstrings, which are behind the quadriceps (on the other side of the thigh bone or femur); and finally the calfs. One or two exercises for each will suffice, but always stretch out these groups.

Two rules to remember: Never, *never* "bounce" while you stretch, and always hold the stretch for as long as you can, at least thirty seconds. You may have noticed athletes trying to stretch by moving their legs back and forth, and bouncing repeatedly. Exercise physiologists cringe at the sight. Bouncing only further tightens muscles while giving the illusion of stretching, setting back exercise programs for months by occasional torn muscles. Let's look at the best stretches used by athletes.

1. Hamstrings and back: Lie on your back, legs together and

Fig. 6-10: Stretching the hamstrings and back. Remember to hold all stretches for at least half a minute, and do not "bounce."

stretched out (Fig. 6-10). Slowly bring your legs up and place them behind your head, balancing with your arms either behind your head or in front, flat on the ground. Try to touch your toes behind your head, with the legs *straight*. Hold the legs as far back as you can for 30 seconds to 1 minute, and then relax. Repeat two times.

2. *Quadriceps:* Kneel on the floor or a mat, with your feet straight behind you (Fig. 6-11). Placing your hands behind you, lean back until your buttocks touch your heels (or as close as you can get) and hold this for 30 seconds to 1 minute. Repeat two times.

Fig. 6-11: The quadriceps stretch. Keep feet behind and not to the side.

Fig. 6-12: The wall push-up. This stretches the calfs and Achilles area.

Fig. 6-13: Another good quadriceps stretch

3. *Calves:* While standing, place your hands against a wall or fence as if you were doing a wall push-up (Fig. 6-12). Then move your feet out as far as you can with your feet flat on the ground. Hold this for 30 seconds to 1 minute and repeat once.

4. *Quadriceps:* Sitting on the floor, place your left leg in front of you (Fig. 6-13). Lean over toward the toes until you can feel your tight muscles. Hold the position for 30 seconds. Relax. Do the same exercise with the right leg. Repeat.

Next, do some aerobic exercises to warm up your muscles and get the heart pumping a bit, such as push-ups, leg lifts, sit-ups, or pull-ups. Then, go for a bike ride, but build slowly to pace over the first mile or so. Ride for as long as you like, then cool down for the last mile or so, pedaling more slowly to release the buildup of lactic acid in the muscles. Finally, try to do one or more of each of the main stretches shown here so that the next time you get on your bike you won't feel so many tight muscles, and cycling will be more pleasurable than ever.

COMMON COMPLAINTS OF CYCLISTS

Although cycling is a safe, sane and refined sport, no cyclist should be unaware of the possible pitfalls on the road to better health. This section is not intended to scare you but to teach prevention first and then the proper care for bicycle-related injuries.

Before looking at specific problem areas, let us stress that no one outside the medical profession should diagnose and treat serious injuries. All cyclists should consult physicians knowledgeable about cycling. In fact, the doctor should be a sports enthusiast himself. No doctor who is out of shape and unconcerned about his own health should be caring for cyclists. The reason for this is that athletes have different problems from the sedentary multitudes. The cyclist's physiology is special because the problems he/she has must be remedied by changing some aspect of the cycling program, not by being told to stop activity in order to relieve a specific pain. The medical solutions must come from a knowledge of the types of injuries unique to cycling, which means direct experience with this area of sports medicine. When you need a doctor, consult your local bike club to see whom other cyclists go to with their problems. Who knows, there may be doctors in the club riding at the front of the pack!

Accidents Will Happen

Even the most conscientious cyclist will have an occasional "spill." No amount of safety knowledge will help when you head toward the pavement, but there are a few tips to lessen the resulting damage. Besides wearing a helmet, some racers advocate the "tuck and roll' method after starting a fall over the handlebars, a common occurrence after a run-in with a farm dog you missed with the spray. The "tuck" means flexing the neck and using forearms and shoulder in a curled position to prevent any extremity from taking the full brunt of the fall. But you may find yourself reflexively using your hands when the moment comes, thereby succumbing to one of the common cycling injuries. These include broken collarbones, shoulder separations, broken scaphoids or some form of head injury. When such an injury occurs to a rider all you can do is keep the person comfortable and warm while you pedal to get a doctor.

On every long-distance ride away from the city, you ought to carry a small first-aid kit. Not the large, boxed variety you find for autos, but a smaller kit made for campers or backpackers. It need only include a few bandages of different sizes, some kind of adhesive tape, bacitracin or some other form of antibiotic, a small bar of soap, a roll of cloth for serious bleeding injuries and fractures, some pain killer (probably aspirin) and a small pair of scissors or a knife for cutting the tape and cloth. The bandages should include large pads (gauze) for large scrapes and burns caused from falls. And that is it, unless you want more protection on long trips.

The only real advice on accidents is to prevent them by watching constantly for objects in the road, learning how to handle dogs and staying alert. (Please see Chapter 5 for specific information on dealing with animals.)

The Wobble, the Snap and the Pop—on Knees, Hips and Ankles

The proper method of pedaling, which has already been described in detail, involves straight up and down motions of the legs at the proper angles, as defined by the positioning of the seat, the cranks and the handlebars. It involves the upstroke and the downstroke, during which three major "mechanical" movements take place in the leg. From the top, these include the extension and flexing of the thigh from the hip joint, the extension of the calf at the knee and the extension of the foot structure at the ankle (ankling). This set of movements occurs thousands of times a day on tour and explains why frequent problems arise in these areas to annoy or immobilize bikers. Let's look at each problem area, in descending order of threat to the rider.

Knees: The knee (Fig. 6-14), that immensely complex structure so fundamental to cycling, is a fixation for many racers and expert tourers. Although a few seem never to have problems, most distance riders find that their knees can break down in a variety of ways. Often strange pains can come and go without warning, leaving the helpless rider fearful of their recurrence.

The knee consists of the femur, or thigh bone; the main lower leg bone, or tibia; the smaller leg bone, or fibula; the rotating bone called the patella (kneecap); and an overlapping blend of cartilage, ligaments and muscle tissue. The power of the knee to thrust downward is in the

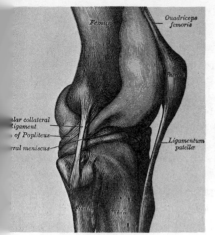

Labels on figure: Femur, Quadriceps femoris, Patella, ular collateral ligament, of Popliteus, ral meniscus, Ligamentum patellae

Fig. 6-14: Lateral view of the knee, a particular trouble spot for cyclists. Proper stretching exercises and attention to correct pedaling will avoid visits to the doctor. One major trouble spot is in the cartilage surrounding the bone structure, which is subject to degenerative conditions.

overlapping tissue in the quadriceps muscle in the front of the thigh, the patellar tendon and the tibia bone. Ligaments on the exterior of the knee at the side and the rear and key muscles behind the knee help to provide support and restrain lateral movement. Both the ligaments and the cartilage that support the patella and control all lateral movement are prone to injury during cycling, especially as a result of awkward pedaling.

Bursitis, or inflammation of the fluid sacs that facilitate movement in the knee, and inflammation of tendons and ligaments that surround the patella cause the most concern. Both of these injuries are a result of either the overuse syndrome—doing too much riding without a gradual buildup of the program—or from irregular movement of the legs while pedaling. Pain in the middle of the knee, directly under the kneecap, is often from bursitis. Treatment includes draining fluid from the knee, surgery or the injection of steroids to relieve this condition. But the best medicine is to realize you have done too much riding and to let up a bit on the duration and the intensity of the rides. Check your gearing and see if you are riding in too large or too small a gear for the terrain, and check your pedaling to see if there are any untoward motions.

Tendinitis or ligament strain in cyclists is usually found on the lateral side of the kneecap, and the symptoms are a grinding pain that feels as if the patella were being scraped by another bone, or a single sore spot in this area. Experience has shown that taking a day or two off from all activity and then returning to the bike with a smaller gear can reduce the pain. If this does not work, consult a sports-oriented orthopedic surgeon to see what he suggests. If it is chronic, he may tell you to lay off for a time until the pain goes away, a bitter pill for any serious cyclist.

A relatively common and potentially very serious condition can build up through stress on the joint behind the patella bone, a degeneration of the cartilage called chondro-malacia. Using too large gears and riding excessively in mountainous areas can contribute to this condition, but the exact causes are not known. This can also lead to a grinding sensation in the joint while riding. When it first comes on, see a specialist. In addition, consider using smaller gears for a time, cut back on your mileage and avoid riding over hills whenever possible. It is possible to arrest this degenerative condition if it is caught early.

The doctor may recommend lifting weights to strengthen the knee and upper leg while you rest from riding. If he doesn't, you ought to ask him about this. He may also advise surgery to remove some of the damaged cartilage if this condition is advanced. Many current cyclists and competitors have had this kind of operation and returned to ride distances again.

One of the alterations in the stroke of pedaling that should be made comes when you have a wobble in the knee at the top of the stroke. This exerts a force on the knees, the hips and the ankle that can cause immediate problems. If you have knee or leg pain, have someone observe your stroke and see if this is not the mechanical problem you have been looking for. One way to make sure the problem is taken care of is to buy a set of cleated shoes to cut down on lateral movement. The wobble may also be an indication of a leg-length imbalance, when one leg is actually slightly shorter than the other, a fairly common phenomenon. This problem can be solved by shortening the crank length on the opposite side of the short leg, in proportion to the leg length in balance. The local bike shop can assist you in obtaining such a crank. For a discussion of shoe cleats, rattrap pedals and straps, see Chapter 14.

As I advocated earlier, always stretch the knee out prior to a ride. While you stretch, you can relieve the knee area further through massage to loosen up the muscle mass. The same goes for the entire leg, concentrating on the ankles, the hips and knees, working your way down or up the leg.

Hips: More rarely, the cyclist will discover he has hip pain beyond the normal problems of tightness and soreness that accompany touring and commuting for long distances. The leg-length imbalance can cause more pain in the hip than the knee in some persons, as can the wobble. This pain is often centered right on the main front leg muscle, the adductor magnus, which is attached near the hip joint in the front of the pelvic structure. Improper pedaling will impede this muscle, causing strain on the ligaments that surround the joint at the hip. Hip problems can be more debilitating off the bike than on, because hip pain really impedes walking. The instructions for treatment of the hip are much like those for the knee, but the best post-injury treatment will not correct pedaling and mechanical leg problems, which must be set straight at some point before the rider can return to full activity.

The Back: Two areas of the back can cause discomfort for cyclists on long rides, regardless of the state of the back at rest: the shoulder and the lower lumbar region. Aching muscles are the root of the pain and are made painful by staying in one position too long. A good trick is to shift position of the arms constantly to alleviate corresponding pressure points on the back. Another solution is to check the position at which you are forced to sit by the angle of the seat and the handlebars. It could be that for you the normal drop bars just do not give you enough places to comfortably put your arms to avoid back pain. You must then experiment with different types of bars (see Chapter 14).

Persons with back pains in the lower lumbar region may also have pains while riding their bikes, but physicians who write on bicycling topics have noted that although no formal studies have been done, the indications are that major back pain is more often relieved rather than aggravated by cycling. Score another one for exercise!

Some neck pain is common in cyclists after long rides, as is lower back pain. Acute pain should go away with massage and sleep, and if necessary with a few days off, but chronic stiffness should be discussed in detail with a sports doctor.

Ankles and Ankling: A very common complaint in cycling is called Achilles tendinitis, a painful affliction of the tendon connecting the cyclist's powerful calf muscle to the ankle. Tendinitis is the inflammation of this sinewy material, which unfortunately does not heal very quickly. Tendons have less blood circulating in them than the connecting muscle tissue and are very inelastic and hard to stretch out. It is thus a very frustrating ailment, and the bane of some racers. It is also a very good sign of the overuse syndrome. The best cure is to wait it out, while trying to maintain some form of limited riding.

One "problem" that has no treatment and usually causes no pain is the snap or pop that can often issue from the joints of the hip, knee or ankle. This is not a sign of degenerative disease. It is as harmless as cracking your knuckles, a simple movement of fluid through the joint. It will not lead to arthritis, but it can be aggravating when riding in a group. The best advice is to ignore it, and keep cycling.

The Numbs

Cycling involves long hours spent with the rear in the saddle and hands on the handlebars, weight and pressure being forced on both places. Some cyclists complain of numbness in the hands and in the crotch, a sensation that does not go away overnight. Many claim it gets so uncomfortable that they must stop cycling until the numb feeling disappears, a process that can take anywhere from hours to several days or more. The problem is that in both places bones are directly over nerves that are compressed and shut off by long hours in one position. The solutions range from shifting position to changing bike equipment in order to cut down on the pressure.

Numb hands: Cyclists with drop handlebars usually ride with arms straight in front, hands wrapped around the bar, exposing the median nerve of the hand to the constant pressure of the full weight of the upper

Fig. 6-15: Here are the three basic types of turned-down handlebars: Left, Randonneur; center, Maes; and right, Pista. Randonneur is favored for cycle touring because it offers more hand positions.

body. The simplest remedy for the resulting numbness is to shift the hands around the bar, trying to keep weight on the two fleshy portions of the hand just below the thumb and across the palm on the pinky side. Another trick is to use well-padded rubber tape on the bars, available at most bike shops.

"Randonneur bars," (Fig 6-15) downturned bars which turn up toward the rider at the end of the bars, provide a place where the cyclist can place his hands without putting all of his weight on them. These can be obtained from some well-stocked bike shops, but for many people this may be a bit of a hassle. Mail-order houses may have them. These bars are worth a try if the numbs have gotten the best of you.

Numb feet: The same problem that causes numb hands occasionally occurs in the foot. The metatarsal bones of the feet are over nerves that run through the feet. Sometimes the pressure of rattrap pedals and great force over long rides can result in numbness. The solution involves incremental shifts in positioning of the clips, loosening the clips or even getting new pedals which place the pressure on a different area.

Numb crotch: In the crotch area, pressure on the nerves running roughly underneath the large bony areas on the underside of the pelvis can cause numbness in the entire area, a major discomfort for some riders. In numb crotch, the nerves are actually pressed between the bony points, which are called ischial tuberosities. If this condition occurs you should stop riding until feeling returns. When you're ready to ride again you should adjust the position of the seat just slightly, tilting it forward, to enable you to sit on the back portion of the seat. You may also move the seat forward on the clip that holds the saddle or you can raise the handlebars slightly to shift the pressure off the region. Each time the numbness recurs, tilt the seat forward just a few degrees to shift pressure to another part of the crotch. Another idea is to just buy a wider seat—there are so many models available. The wide-bottom Brooks B17 has worked well for sufferers from this problem. I especially recommend the Avocet WI or WII saddle (Fig. 6-16) for women.

A related problem is sore crotch caused by vertical compression of the soft tissue directly under the ischial tuberosities. This is similar to the pain felt when you have fallen asleep in a chair in one position and

Fig. 6-16: The Avocet women's saddle has a wide rear portion better suited to some women than traditional racing saddles for men. It can also help riders of both sexes who suffer from sore-crotch problems.

awake to find pain emanating from the crotch up to the lower back. Again, the solution involves shifting the saddle just slightly (not more than a few degrees) in either direction each time the pain increases. A hard saddle that has been broken in but still has a firm support through the middle of it is ideal, because you do not want to have too soft a saddle.

Saddle Burns

Speaking of saddles, another painful but common problem is saddle burn, which is caused by friction and pressure from many rides. Sweating increases the glide of the crotch over the saddle, and bunched undershorts can scrape the area raw, leaving it vulnerable to infection. The problem is made less of a burden by the use of Vaseline or some other slick substance that will allow clothing to shift but will not allow it to scrape against the skin. Also, Vaseline-type products guard against sweat getting into the infection and rubbing it raw. But remember if you have a case of raw legs, take the Vaseline off at night, because infections need air and dryness to heal quickly. The best cure here is prevention—use Vaseline before the inflammation occurs and wear the proper clothing which will inhibit chafing.

Cycling shorts are far from perfected but the kind to look for should have a crotch made of seamless cotton or chamois and should fit well over the legs to prevent bunching while on the bike (as discussed in Chapter 3). You need absorbency for sweating, but the material must still glide over the skin. This is a very individual problem, and what fits well for one cyclist may not fit well for another. Look for snug shorts that have a good feel when you put them on, and make sure there are no seams along the side of the crotch. It can be murder on the road if there are seams. For most people, finding the right shorts is a process of trial and error. Some people have even designed their own shorts, with extra padding in the crotch. If you are handy with a sewing machine, give it a whirl, using the general guidelines discussed above.

WEATHERING IT OUT—CYCLING IN HEAT, COLD AND POLLUTION

Those who live in extremes of climate like those in the Midwest, the East and near the mountainous regions, where there are hot, humid summers and dry, cold winters, know that cycling can sometimes become a bit more complicated than just stepping out for a fifty-mile ride. There are certain precautions that must be taken when going for any long-distance ride in very hot or very cold weather; and all cyclists should have a rudimentary knowledge of what these precautions are.

In the Heat—Drink, Drink, Drink

Cyclists are fortunate in that, during summer months, the action of cycling stirs up a breeze to cool them off. It is not the action of sweating that cools a rider off, after all, it is the evaporation of that sweat. Cyclists are unlike other athletes in that they can carry the proper amounts of water, other replacement fluids (ERG, Body Punch, Gatorade, etc.) and energy-producing foods with them as they ride. But to stay cool over long periods on the road, you still must sweat, and you lose valuable fluids and electrolytes (minerals, salts for metabolic processes) in the process. The biker should be aware of exactly what he needs to do to keep riding safely in the heat.

During days of high heat and humidity (over 50 percent humidity) sweating does not help in losing heat because evaporation slows down drastically. Heat exhaustion can come about as the body begins to build up heat because not enough is being released. The body then just shuts down, and the rider, feeling very tired, is forced to stop all activity.

Exercise physiologists recommend that you drink small amounts of fluids repeatedly throughout the ride. Another good idea is to drink one to two cups of water shortly before the start of a ride, allowing perhaps twenty minutes for digestion. On the ride you can carry one bottle of water and one of some commercial or home-prepared solutions with replacement salts and minerals, plus a small amount of glucose or fructose for energy. No more than 5 percent of the mixture should be a sugar. It doesn't do any good to drink replacement solutions unless you can digest them easily before the point at which you run out of steam. You need to *prevent* exhaustion, so if you do carry replacement fluids with you, drink them fairly early on. Then concentrate on keeping the body hydrated with good old H_2O, and worry about replacing lost minerals, salts and sugars later.

On hot, humid days, wear light-colored, soft and absorbent clothing. Don't wear synthetic fabrics, try to find light-colored cotton. Keep a shirt on, even if it is just a mesh shirt, because the harsh sunlight is then reflected off the back. Wear a peaked, mesh cap on the head, because the sun can heat your exposed head and neck quickly if you are not protected. Use some form of sunscreen on the uncovered parts of the body, not traditional tanning lotion.

Finally, on the hottest days, don't try to kill yourself by riding without rests (unless you are in a race). Rest often, and drink water when you do. Athletes have been known to sweat *gallons* on hot days, so you need to constantly replace what you have lost.

Cold-Weather Cycling

In the winter, or in late fall and early spring, cold air and winds serve to take heat away from the body. Cycling in such weather increases the wind chill, so the primary concern of the cyclist is dressing for the weather. Covering the extremities is especially important.

As most outdoorsmen know, it is better to dress using layers of light-weight clothing than to wear one huge coat. Coats are bulky and obstruct movement. Layers allow you to have enough to wear while warming up and to maintain body heat better because there are more layers to trap heat next to the body. Layers of wool and cotton are excellent. Another advantage is that if you should become overheated, you can remove and store one or more layers until you feel just right. On very cold days, then, you might cover the bottom half of the body with a pair of undershorts, a pair of wool or cotton long underwear, and a pair of long cycling pants or a sweat suit. On top, you might have a cotton T-shirt, a cotton flannel shirt, a sweat shirt and perhaps a down-filled jacket as well.

The extremities must be well covered. The head is the spot through which most of the body heat can be lost, so wear a wool cap under your crash helmet, along with a separate pair of earmuffs. On the feet, wear one pair of lambswool or some other thick-piled sock, and under this wear a thin wool sock. Make sure the shoes are not too tight, or else proper blood flow and heat will not be maintained. The action of pedaling will also help keep the feet warm. For the hands, the best pair of thick wool or lined mittens you can find should be worn at all times.

Dress well, but don't overdress. Wet clothing, as you may have found out, conducts heat up to twenty times as well as dry clothing, releasing heat at an extremely fast rate. Don't dress so well that you sweat too much, or the extra clothing will just become a burden.

If you do become wet and tired, don't stop to rest outdoors. Stop riding and find someone who can get you inside right away, where you should remain until you are warm and dry. Hypothermia comes on when you are not moving about and when you run out of fuel for producing heat. On cold rides, you should always have plenty of food on hand and be warmly dressed. Never stop and rest for prolonged periods. Because carbohydrates are the first foodstuff digested by the system during exercise it is important to eat this kind of food *before* you get hungry and cold. By the time you're cold it is too late to eat, digest and go on riding. Digestion and renewed heat production take too long.

Pollution

The bicycling revolution in the United States has taken place everywhere in the land. Wherever you are you can look out and see people cycling their way to health. But most of the cyclists are not cycling the majority of their miles up and down scenic slopes in Colorado or cruising the lonely stretches of the coast highways of the west. Instead they are pushing their way to work in downtown Los Angeles, exploring the streets and paths around city parks in Chicago and New York or cruising the wide lanes of Atlanta. In short, they are following time-honored cycling routes in major cities, some of these well traveled by motor vehicles.

The problem is that our major cities are polluted by noxious chemicals such as unburned hydrocarbons, lead and sulphur from autos, and a vast array of industrial pollutants. When you breathe these in on a daily basis, you stand a great risk of becoming an urban statistic, a casualty of the huge increase in heart, lung and circulatory disease. When you exercise heavily in this air, snorting the auto emissions from cars directly in front of you, you put yourself in a precarious position. There isn't much you can do about pollution, but there are a few things you can do to lessen its impact on you as a cyclist.

First, try not to ride on crowded major city arteries. This is dangerous for reasons other than the high concentration of auto emissions, but these pollutants are an extra insult. Stay on side streets in quiet neighborhoods or in wide-open spaces where they are not so many cars. Large inner-city parks are ideal, as in San Francisco's Golden Gate Park, Chicago's Lincoln and Grant Parks or New York's Central Park.

Cycling at non-rush-hour periods is also very helpful, and avoiding industrial park areas is crucial at all times. On days when the ozone levels are very high or smog covers the city with its thermal blanket of pollutants, stay inside and restrict bicycling to a quick workout. Air quality has improved in some cities around the country in the last ten years, and we can only hope that any fuel shortages will leave the cities with air as fresh as that of the countryside.

A DIET FOR EXERCISE

One of the best adjuncts to your cycling program is a proper diet. Without eating the foods that give you the nutrients and energy you need, cycling would be arduous indeed. Active people have different food requirements than sedentary types, needing more carbohydrates and more food bulk in general than persons who do not burn calories in large amounts. It is important that you come to know about the "exercise diet."

The major food groups are proteins, as found in meat, eggs, milk, fish, poultry and dark green leafy vegetables; carbohydrates, such as whole grains, fruits, vegetables; and fats, like nuts, meat and raw dairy products. The first rule for any person is, of course, to eat a diet selected from foods from each group to ensure that you get the proper amount of all essential nutrients. An athlete burns 60 percent fats, 30 percent carbohydrates and 10 percent protein during a workout; however, it is important to remember that carbohydrates provide immediate energy because they are metabolized first during exercise. When you are cycling, the same carbohydrates that Americans have cast off as producing too much fat become your life blood.

Protein is almost negligible as an energy source, instead it makes up the building blocks of tissue and assists in metabolic processes. But meats, fish and poultry, which make up too large a part of the daily diet of Americans, are foods that cannot easily be worked off by cycling. This is the reason why many Americans are still overweight and why fat buildup in the arteries is killing so many people. A small amount of meat, plus milk or cheese should suffice for this part of the diet. Vegetarians need only eat dairy products for fats and proteins.

Carbohydrates come as starches, cellulose and sugars. Starches and sugars are major sources of energy for humans. Cellulose, or bulk, is offered in fruits and vegetables; starches in grains, potatoes, dry beans and peas. Sugars are found as cane or beet sugar, sweets from fruits, honey and syrup. A good mix of these should be the basis of any good diet.

Fats contain twice as many calories as either proteins or carbohydrates and provide a large amount of vitamins such as A, D, and E. Both saturated and unsaturated fats should be part of the daily diet, obtained from such varied sources as nuts, butter and avocadoes.

The daily or competitive cyclist must recognize that a heavy meat diet does not give him the material he needs for his workouts. The best diet for the heavy cyclist is lots of breads, rice, cheese and pasta for quick energy; oil, butter or salad dressings for fats, and a limited amount of protein from some form of meat or milk. The increased caloric needs of the cyclist, who can burn off up to 800 calories in one hour, should be filled with carbohydrates primarily, then with lesser amounts of proteins and fats. Just because you are cycling a great deal does not mean your body craves lots of meat and desserts, which will not be easily used up during exercise.

For those who want to lose weight through cycling, you have come to the right place. But you must beware of the constant energy needs of a fit person. Eating only once a day to save on calories will be self-destructive. You should have three meals, each one well-balanced from the food groups we have just described. Each meal may be less on total calories, but it is important not to become depleted at any point in the day in essential nutrients. Eat well enough to support the increased caloric usage that comes with cycling.

Vegetarians among cyclists should be most aware of the nutritional lessons, eating a balanced diet of fruit and nuts, dark, leafy vegetables, yellow vegetables and especially protein foods like milk, yogurt and cheese. Excellent discussions of nutrients, vegetables and diet are found in *Diet for a Small Planet* (Friends of the Earth, 1969) and *Laurel's Kitchen* (Bantam Books, 1976).

VITAMINS AND TRACE ELEMENTS

What about vitamins, those awful-tasting little pills that athletes pop by the thousands? Cyclists ought to have the proper amounts of vitamins B-Complex, C, D and E. Vitamins play a large role in the release of energy from foods, the building of tissue and the functioning of tissue and nerves. Vitamin A is important because of its role in the growth of cells, keeping skin and the inner lining of the body healthy and resistant to infection. This vitamin is found in meat, particularly liver, and in milk products. Vitamins in the B group aid in the release of energy from food, and also aid in appetite and healthy skin. Vitamin C is crucial for preventing colds and helps to keep cells together and also builds bone structure. Vitamin B can be obtained from eating milk and liver. Vitamin C is found in fruits and dark green leafy vegetables.

Should you take vitamin supplements? If you are eating fresh vegetables and fresh foods from all the major food groups, then you probably don't. But for those of us who don't spend a great deal of time cooking and thinking about our menus, a few vitamin pills every day certainly don't hurt. Cyclists should consider taking vitamins C, B-Complex and D if they think they are not getting them in their food.

Trace elements, a new rage in the health food business, are mainly found in foods in the normal diet. The body needs such minerals as calcium (found in milk, cheese), iodine (sea foods, iodized salt), and iron (dark, leafy vegetables and liver). Cyclists in particular need a few other elements such as phosphorus and magnesium for using energy. Phosphorus is found in a wide variety of foods. Magnesium is found in several vegetables, nuts and whole-grain products.

NOTHING SHOULD KEEP YOU FROM CYCLING

One of the common misconceptions about exercise which the activity boom of the 1970s and 80s has dispelled is that vigorous exercise should be left to the young and the physically strong. Thousands of people who formerly would not have attempted any form of endurance exercise are now working out and participating in such sports as cycling, swimming and running. Even heart-attack victims, senior citizens, pregnant women and diabetics are now finding the advantages of a healthy body and mind. Physicians are actually ordering patients out to exercise.

Everyone who has a disability and wants to cycle should consult his physician and have a closely monitored stress test before embarking on a cycling career. It is not wise just to get out and start bicycling with a serious disability. Only a doctor has the experience to decide if you are capable of sustained exercise. But increasingly doctors are getting involved in the bike boom and many more are looking to cycling as the first step toward returning to good health. Cycling is easy on the body if done slowly and it allows the most out-of-shape person to start building up a program from day one.

Healing Hearts

All across America and the world, heart-attack and stroke victims are returning from their attacks to become veritable jocks. Cardiologists and internists have become aware of the need to return their patients back to health through exercise to avoid the risk of a second attack, an attack that could be fatal. They ask their patients to get stress tested, and then they write exercise prescriptions based on the results. They often advocate carefully supervised running or stationary cycling before going on the road, but many patients start out riding the first day. The usual caveat is to expand the cycling program ever so slowly until you have built up aerobic capacity and have opened up narrowed arteries.

The advantage of cycling for the heart-attack and stroke victims is that cycling is very aerobic, and aerobic exercise opens up arteries in much the same way as unclogging a jammed fuel line in a car increases engine efficiency. Although exercise does not repair tissue destroyed during a heart attack, it does reduce the chance of that second attack. This is a crucial psychological as well as physiological plus for the heart patient, who typically may lose his self-esteem and assertiveness because of the disease.

Both stroke and heart-attack victims must rigorously follow the caveats on cycling in the heat and on keeping fluid levels in the blood high enough for sustained exertion. Learn your limits and push them over so gently.

Diabetic Athletes

Over the last two decades, diabetics have joined the legions of cycling addicts, usually without complications. Exercise is an excellent means toward a better life for diabetics, but meticulous medical supervision is necessary to maintain the proper level of blood sugar in the diabetic athlete. Insulin has the effect of lowering blood sugar at specific times during the day; however, blood sugar is also extremely important during exercise to keep you going and avoiding passing out while on the bike. Insulin is crucial in the chemical process of transporting glucose from the bloodstream to the working muscle. So the proper balance of insulin and sugar must be vigilantly maintained in the diabetic who exercises.

Most doctors favor smaller doses of insulin taken several times during the day for athletes, so as to avoid insulin shock. Discuss this with your doctor and make sure he agrees with this philosophy or has a good reason not to. On your rides, always carry some form of sugar to give you a quick source of energy. A candy bar or sugared water are good examples.

Hypertension

For the millions of people who have high blood pressure, cycling can be a lifesaver. It has been proven that regular aerobic exercise can lower blood pressure over the long run, although the mechanisms for this are not known for certain. It is known that obesity contributes to hypertension, and cycling forces weight loss. In any case, many people who exercise and compete have high blood pressure, and with a few simple guidelines, all but the most seriously afflicted can join their ranks as cyclists.

Doctors encourage people with high blood pressure to avoid all forms of salt not needed for normal bodily functions. That is, if you have a normal American diet, change it. Don't oversalt food, and don't eat overly processed foods. Yet some anti-hypertension drugs rob the body of potassium salts through excretion, so if you are taking one of these drugs, you should seek out potassium supplements for use while riding. Consult a doctor on this one, though.

Asthmatics

Asthmatics have been among the best athletes for years, and in all but the most severe forms, asthma does not stop any sufferer from cycling. Caution against overexertion at higher altitudes is stressed by physicians, and medication such as inhalers should always be at hand in unusual weather conditions.

The one problem some asthmatics have on occasion is hyperventilation after a long workout, but there is medication available to correct this problem.

Pregnancy

Although by no means an ailment, pregnancy presents some special problems for women cyclists, the solutions to which should be ironed out between the woman and her doctor. In general, the woman who has previously cycled and who has not gained a significant amount of weight can continue to exercise at a moderate pace up to the third trimester, at which time only a very slow cadence can be maintained over shorter distances.

Morning sickness can be debilitating, and doctors interested in cycling suggest that liquid intake should be increased at all times to avoid dehydration from cycling. During the latter months of pregnancy, when the protein requirements of the baby increase, common sense requires that food intake increase that much more if you are exercising.

Adolescents—Special Considerations

Cycle racing by youngsters, including the new phenomenon of bicycle motorcross, has raised the question of whether adolescents should be motivated by their parents to engage in a full-blown competitive sport in the early teen or pre-teen years. Proponents point to studies showing that endurance exercise in the early teens leads to better aerobic capacity later in life. Some argue that because muscle capacity develops the most in the formative period, youngsters should be encouraged to push themselves toward later athletic prowess. Many current superstars of the international cycling community started intense competition when rather young.

But there is a second body of thought that holds that children should not be pushed into intensive competition at too young an age. For one thing, youngsters trying to compete are hampered by incompletely developed muscles, and although they may have sufficient aerobic power, they do not have the capacity to withstand the punishment of distance training or touring with hard riders.

A 1975 French study of endurance athletes showed that under age twenty, the athlete cannot use fats for energy very efficiently, meaning that once glycogen stores are depleted during a long workout, lactic-acid accumulation hampers the youngsters' ability to continue. Not many world-class bike racers are teenagers, just as few top runners are very young.

Teenagers also produce greater heat and more sweat while exercising, increasing their need for water and food while cycling. These are not available in races, and food should not be gulped down at all during a race.

Finally, there is a psychological problem with having youngsters compete, and that is the potential for hurting their future careers through boredom with the sport. Long hours of practice during formative years may leave the athlete feeling "burned out" by his prime years. Just looking at the dropout rate among young runners between high school and age twenty-five tells us enough about this problem. When racing no longer seems important, the competitive edge is lost.

This is not to say that teenagers and pre-teens should not race; they should. But moderation and not excess should be the rule. Let us avoid the Little League syndrome in cycling and wait until the children have developed physically and mentally before they are exposed to high-level competition, especially with adults.

Bicycle Racing: a New Look at an Old Sport 7

Bicycle racing is enjoying a revival in America. In the old days of professional cycling, crowds thrilled to track races ranging from a fraction of a mile to marathon six-day races. American stars Major Taylor, A.A. "Zimmy" Zimmerman and Barney Oldfield excited fans during the first "bike craze" of the 1890s and early twentieth century. Several of Taylor's records outlasted him by more than seven decades. Yet by the time of the 1970s revival of biking here, America lagged far behind European countries at all levels of competition. In the past several years, however, both amateur and professional racing are again on the upswing.

This is a fascinating sport, combining courage, speed, physical stamina and skill with the mental agility and bluffing ability of a poker buff. After the first few minutes of an auto race, such as the Indianapolis 500, the contest seems like a noisy, inhuman exercise in insanity, but a bike race is different. It takes place right in front of you, the riders are easy to see and the physical and mental effort involved in outfoxing the field and winning are all there for everyone to observe. On the last lap, when the cyclists break and sprint (Fig. 7-1) for home at close to 40 miles an hour, the excitement at the track is tremendous.

Famous track and road stars in Europe command public attention and large sums of money just as professional basketball and baseball players do in the United States. Past and present stars like Jacques Anquetil, Eddy Merckx and Bernard Hinault are household names in Europe, and the classic races such as the World Championships, the Tour de France and the Tour of Sardinia resemble itinerant circuses with the large numbers of fans lining the routes.

For the uninitiated, the variety of types of bicycle racing can be overwhelming. There are road races of varying lengths and strategies, some lasting days. There are track races for two riders up to many, individual and team races. Then there are a few assorted specialty races, such as cyclo-cross (combining running and cycling over fields and roads) and bicycle motocross, which has gotten very young kids into racing. A quick review of the variety of races will put this exciting and complex sport into perspective, and may entice you to either join racing or become an informed spectator.

Fig. 7-1: A sprint during the ten-mile point race at a National Championship match in St. Louis. Jim Rossi, six-time U.S. champion in spring competition, is at far left; he came from twelfth place to finish second. *(Bicycling Magazine)*

SOME RECORD TIMES

But first, to give you a rough idea of how fast the great stars can ride, here are the current records, as of this writing, for various kinds of races:

The professional time-trial record for one hour riding on the track was set by Eddy Merckx of Belgium in Mexico City's rarified air in 1972. Unpaced by a car or motorcycle, Merckx, considered by many experts the greatest professional rider of all time, cycled 30.7 miles, not a bad pace to keep up for that long. The 24-hour road record (unpaced) was set by Teuvo Louhivuori of Finland in 1974. He covered 515.8 miles, a pace of 21.5 miles per hour for 24 consecutive hours!

Riding a giant-geared bike in the slipstream of a souped-up Chevy, Dr. Alan Abbott of San Bernardino, California, reached a speed of 140 miles per hour on the Bonneville Salt Flats in Utah. Imagine riding downhill on the steepest grade and then try to imagine going *twice* that fast! Abbott, who won the prize money for the fastest human-powered, unpaced vehicle in 1979, also rode his modified bike 48 miles per hour without the aid of a pacing vehicle. Few single-rider vehicles of any kind have attained that speed without an engine.

There are also some amazing times recorded for road trips, including the transcontinental Los Angeles to New York journey, covered in just 13 days, 5 hours and 20 minutes by Paul Cornish. Other "racers" have circumnavigated the world by cycle and boat, covered the course from the southern tip of the Americas to Alaska and climbed mountain trails with rugged three-speeds.

So, you tourists, take heart from these riders. If they can zip off 169 miles in just over seven hours, we should all be able to do a good 75 miles a day with camping gear or 100 miles if the sagwagon carries everything.

Road Racing

Racing takes place either on specially-designed tracks (called velo-dromes) or on the road. Road racing (Fig. 7-2) is especially popular in Europe, and the most famous race in the world, the Tour de France, is a stage road race. Road races vary from short, massed-start races on the flat to long, varied stage races covering thousands of miles over mountain roads.

Time Trials

In general, a time trial is a race against the clock, not other opponents. A rider starts out alone, with a minute's space between him and the next man, so that no matter how many participate in a given race, the man with the best elapsed time wins. Because time trials need open roads, you'll find them starting very early in the morning, like at 7 A.M. on a Sunday.

There are four types of time trials:

—10, 25 and 30 miles

—50 and 100 miles

—12 and 24 hours

—Hill climbs, between 300 yards and 3 miles, depending on hill gradient

As of this writing, the record for a 25-mile time trial is near 50 minutes, which means an average sustained speed of around 27 miles per hour for one hour.

Massed-Start Racing

This is an exciting form of racing, where cyclists start together and the first one across the finish line is the winner. Often these races are held on circular or figure-eight courses closed off to car traffic, in which case

Fig. 7-2: This is a typical scene for a stage race, this from the annual Tour of Sardinia. Here riders make their way around a hairpin turn on the mountainous island as the race nears Sassari. Cycle racers from Italy, Belgium, France, Holland and Switzerland are competing in the race, which is the opening of the Italian bicycling season. *(UPI)*

Fig. 7-3: Here is a look at the pack in a road race. Notice how the group is bunched up. In particular, you will see that the man in the foreground, at left, is closely followed by another cyclist. In this way the cyclist to the rear forces the front rider to "break the wind" for him. This technique saves the rear rider's strength until a strategic moment arrives when he can "jump" the pack at high speed and take off to win. *(Ray Boldt)*

they're referred to as criterium races. On such courses, spectators can see many parts of the race by walking from one side of the course to another. They may also be held on open courses, where riders have hills or even mountains to climb before the final sprint for the finish. These are called open road races. Spectators can see the start of such races and then drive to the finish.

In either type of massed-start race, there are exciting maneuvers such as "breaks" or surges, where the front riders will break away for a sprint, then try to resume a fast pace to keep other riders back in the pack. There are also "team efforts," where several riders will move off the pack on a break while other team members block the road to keep the pack in check. Each team will have specialists in hill climbing, sprinting, blocking and "stayers," who help plan the strategy but are not expected to win.

Staged Races

The most grueling of road races is the staged race, (Fig. 7-2) which covers several days or weeks and different kinds of terrain and races. The famous Tour de France involves some time trials, some flat point-to-point courses and long, hilly climbs through the Alps and Pyrenees mountains. This race takes place over four weeks and covers 3,500-plus kilometers, over 2,000 miles! It has been won five times each by two riders, Jacques Anquetil of France (between 1957 and 1964) and Eddy Merckx of Belgium, who won four straight (between 1969 and 1972). He won his fifth in 1974, and has since retired.

CYCLO-CROSS RACING

A variation of massed-start racing is real he-man stuff—cyclo-cross racing. Cyclo-cross is a combination of road racing and cross-country running, using special bicycles with high bottom brackets, chainwheel guards to keep the mud out, and special knobbed tires for high traction.

Most events are one or two miles long, but some are as long as eight miles, over open fields and streams, through bogs of mud and sand and even wooded areas. Part of the time the cyclist is riding, other times he is running, and sometimes he is carrying his bicycle.

If you like to wallow in mud, slither through grass, grope your way through dense woods, ford streams, climb cliffs, and do all this with a bicycle on your back at maximum physical effort, then cyclo-cross racing is for you.

Track Racing

Tracks for bicycle racing are built to very rigid specifications, and few cities have them because they are so costly. There are fine tracks in the United States, however, in Encino, California (near Los Angeles); San Jose, California; Portland, Oregon; Northbrook, Illinois (near Chicago); St. Louis, Missouri; New York City, at the old World's Fair Grounds; Kenosha and Milwaukee, Wisconsin; and in Shakopee, Minnesota.

Track racing is unquestionably the most complex of all the forms of bicycle racing; to understand it takes some study and real dedication on the part of the spectator. But it is an exciting sport and well worth learning about. There are various types of track racing.

Handicaps

These are short-distance races, from a quarter mile to a half mile. Riders are handicapped by ability, with space between riders at the start according to the handicap.

Sprint

One of the most exciting types of racing, the sprint, takes two forms. Match-racing, used in the Olympic Games, involves only two or three racers per race. Usually sprint races are over 800- or 1,000-meter courses, or two or three lengths of a specific track. The last 220 yards or 200 meters only are timed, with the rest of the race used for tactical maneuvering.

In major championship races, most of the riders will be evenly matched physically, so that the only way to win is by outsmarting the opponent. One tactic is to jump to speed before the other rider is aware that you are sprinting to speed and before he can ready himself to keep up.

Another method is for one rider to give the impression that he is going all out, when actually he has considerable reserve power. This involves going around the track at a fast but comfortable pace, luring the opponent into following you closely and, at the last stretch, jumping to speed before the rearward rider can recover and try to catch up.

Another tactic is the attack from the rear. The attacker comes from behind and reaches the last banked turn before his opponent. Then he boxes him in until, in desperation, the trapped man eases back to try to pass, at which point the leading rider jumps to sprint speed.

Pursuit Track Racing

A pursuit track race is one in which two riders start on opposites sides of the track and try to catch each other over a standard distance, usually 4,000 meters. Because riders are usually evenly matched, they rarely do catch each other, so the race is decided on time, with the winner having covered the distance in the least amount of time.

Team pursuit races involve teams of four men, starting on opposite sides of the track. Each rider takes a turn at the lead, sheltering the others behind him. Smooth change of pace is essential to keep the pace and avoid breaking the chain of closely spaced riders. Time is called on the third member of each team as he passes the finish line.

An Australian pursuit involves teams of up to eight riders spaced out at equal distances, with any riders who are caught eliminated. An Italian pursuit involves two or more teams of three, four, or five riders, in which teams are equally spaced around the track and each team drops off one rider from the race each lap of the track. The last man in each team with the best time wins the race.

Other Types of Track Races

Scratch races are any races where all competitors start together, usually over a three-, five-, or ten-mile course.

Miss-and-out eliminates the last rider over each lap until at the last lap the remaining racers sprint to the finish line.

Unknown distance is a race in which the riders go on until a gong signals the last lap, at which point they sprint to the finish. If the field is solidly packed, the best attacker will usually win.

Point-to-point involves any number of competitors up to the capacity of the track for a specific distance or number of laps, with sprints at each lap or half lap for points. Points are given to the first man over the line, or to the first two or three men over the line. The winner is the racer with the most points at the end of the race.

Madison takes its name from the old Madison Square Garden (New York City) six-day bicycle races. The original version was a fairly bloody, barbarous event, in which riders staggered around the track for six days, frequently falling. Although the race was finally banned, a version of it, in which teams of two riders pair up in a race, one rider racing while the other rests, is popular today. In Europe, the Madison is a very popular six-day race, although it can be any length, from thirty minutes to six days, or any distance. An exciting aspect of this race is the entry of a relieving rider into the melee, in which he is thrown by a grasp of the hand and a push on the bottom as a tired rider leaves the group. Variations of Madisons are point-to-point competitions, where the disadvantage for the spectator is that in order to make sense out of the race, he has to keep count of all points made by all riders as they are accumulated.

Paced riding is usually done behind a motorcycle, attaining speeds of

Fig. 7-4: In high-speed track racing, cyclists sometimes stay absolutely still. "Jockeying" is the technical term for this maneuver. This photo was taken at the start of a heat in the Grand Prix of Arhus.

fifty miles an hour tearing around a small track, with the cyclist staying glued behind the motorcycle as it breaks the wind. This type of racing is rarely seen in the United States, because it requires a specially made track that is properly banked and very smooth. The motorcycles used for these events have a small roller projecting from the rear to make sure the cyclist behind can't touch the motorcycle wheel and cause a wreck. If he catches up and contacts the motorcycle, the cyclist's front wheel merely spins against the roller without effect. The idea is to permit the cyclist to obtain a uniform "shield" from the motorcycle he's following by maintaining distance behind it.

A *"repechage"* literally means a "second chance." This is a race in which riders who are eliminated in a heat get a second chance in the form of another heat, usually with four or five other riders (only one or perhaps two who finally qualify), to qualify for the quarter- or semi-finals of one event.

TIPS FOR ASPIRING RACERS

The following tips for would-be racers were taken from a tape recording made by Gene Portuesi of Cadillac, Michigan, some years ago, which he sent to members of his team before the Olympic Games in Tokyo:

If you're in training, keep a day-to-day record of track and wind conditions, how you feel, your times, hours of sleep per night, everything and anything that bears on your performance. At the end of the year you'll have a vivid picture of your performance and what affected it.

Proper rest and diet are extremely important. Use general good sense and stick to a basic diet of good meat, lots of vegetables, and milk.

In selecting gears, the mistake most novices make is to find out what the champions are using, and then strain on these gears. This makes about as much sense as to enter a weight-lifting contest and strain to lift a weight just because this is what the champ can lift. To select your gears, use a stopwatch and a little arithmetic. Trial and error will teach you what is possible with different gear ratios in terms of your own physical conditioning, and how to apply these ratios to a race of any kind, be it a hill-climb, sprint, time trial, or break-away. For example, a top-notch sprinter who covers the last 200 meters or a race in 12 seconds, using a 24 x 7 or a 92.6 gear [see page 92 for a complete explanation of gear ratios], would spin his cranks an average of 135 revolutions per minute.

Check your own cadence at the gear you can sprint best. For example, if you ride a 25 x 8 gear, in the last 200 meters of a race your crank revolutions per minute will revolve 31 times; with 23 x 7 gears, cranks will revolve 29.5 times; with 24 x 7, 28.2 times and 25 x 7, 27 revolutions. The factor determining gear selection, as stated before, has to involve a combination of your physical condition with the mechanical factors of gear selections. It makes no sense to ride a big gear like the champions, if you're not ready for it. [Note: Mr. Portuesi refers to one-inch pitch racing chains and gears instead of the usual one-half inch standard pitch. To relate the gears he's quoting to road or touring gears, multiply his figures by two.]

About Training

Many cyclists start their training in the spring, but for those of us who live in cold northern climates, this is not soon enough. The power you can get into your muscles is directly related to your heart and respiratory system. To begin training in April after a four-month lay-off and expect to get in championship condition in ten to twelve weeks is not practical. A winter program is essential. Many cyclists take up speed skating, or some indoor athletic program. Anything that makes the heart and lungs work hard will keep these organs in superior condition and permit you to enter racing training in reasonably good condition.

Weight lifting is a good winter training activity. Weight lifting, or weight training, keeps the heart and lungs in top condition, and increases muscle power, in particular, conditioning the muscles of the upper torso to a far greater degree than is possible by cycling alone.

Let me give you an example of the importance of winter training. When Nancy Neimann of Detroit was National Women's Champion, and rode for the first time on the famous Herne Hill Track in London, England, she used a gear that had won her the national championship. [Mr. Portuesi was Nancy's coach.] In what was then the fastest field of girl track riders, she spun her gear wide open. In trying to use the bigger ratios, Nancy found that she was not able to open up to top speed because the power required from her back and shoulder muscles to equalize the thrust from her legs simply wasn't there.

We instituted a winter training program for Nancy designed to improve the muscles in her upper torso, and as a result, she was able to improve her time by a half-second in the critical last 200 meters, and was able to beat the top women sprinters of England and Europe, and officially equal the then women's world record. The following year she beat the world record many times in the flats while training at home. What I am saying is that powerful legs will not give full thrust into the pedals unaided by equally powerful back, arm, and shoulder muscles.

What do I mean by weight lifting? For women, try 10 repetitions of fifty pounds in arm exercises and 100 pounds in squats. For men, some variation is permissible according to build. For example, a man of 150 pounds should stay to a maximum of 100 pounds in arm exercises and 160 to 180 pounds for squats, ten repetitions of each. Do all exercises quickly, with rapid motion and deep breathing. Work out every third day or twice weekly. Start the program in the late fall and gradually build up the weights lifted. Put emphasis on the areas of your greatest weakness, then as soon as the good weather rolls around, forget the indoor training and hop on your bicycle.

Spring Training

For your first ride in the spring, go about 25 miles, and keep in low gear (23 x 40 will do). Dress warmly, keep your legs covered with skating tights and seat pants, and use light layers of warm clothing for your upper torso. Put a sheet of newspaper between your last two outer garments to keep your chest warm against the cold wind.

Don't loaf along in low gear. Once you get warmed up, try to keep your cadence up over 100 revolutions per minute. Use your stopwatch and count your pedal action over a 30-second period. In other words, do something with your miles and time besides sitting in the saddle and just pedaling.

After you are well warmed up, try a couple of one-mile time trails, with a slight rest in between. Then try a few jumps from almost a dead stop. First take off with the right foot, next take off with the left foot, and so on. Keep your action smooth. You will find this is very hard with a low gear, but the better you can coordinate yourself with a low gear, the more you will get out of a big one.

After about two weeks or 300 miles of low-gear riding, move up about 7 or 8 points on your gear. Pick a 5-mile course and see how much faster you are with the 69 than with a 62. Keep practicing your jumps from almost a dead stop. The gear is too small to go into it from a rolling start. Concentrate on using your straps. The top of your arch should hurt from having pulled up after a good workout. Stay smooth. Stay in a 69 for about 200 miles, then move up, just like your weight-training program. Keep a record of how fast you time-trial with each gear before you move up. Put it in the book. It will be something for you to improve next year. After the girls get into a 76 and the men into an 80 gear, go back to using your 62 a couple of times a week for a 25-mile workout. It's a good idea to work out on your low gears the day after a specially hard ride. Get at least two days of rest per week. Try to vary your riding so it's hard, but not fatiguing. Work out hard, but don't run yourself into the ground.

Now, with girls on a 76 and men on an 80, start timing yourself over a 200-meter, marked flying start. Try for five or six good times over a period of a week. Then move up two points on your gear and repeat. This is one reason I prefer the use of a half-inch pitch chain. You'll find that fewer changes in sprockets are required, and gears can be moved up in smaller graduations.

When the men and boys start getting into the 86 and 88 gears, some will find that a 4-point jump is too much. As you can see, this system allows you to feel your way up into your racing ratios as your physical condition improves. And, as the gears get higher, the graduations are smaller. Also, you will find that when you start using those speeds on your road-racing bike, you will know what to expect from every ratio on your bicycle.

Keep a weekly check on your body weight. Loss of weight can mean not enough rest, improper diet, or too many hard miles. Use a little common sense and try to correct what you think is wrong. If you must make changes in your routine, don't make too many at a time, because then you will not be able to attribute any change in performance to that which was directly responsible.

Gene Portuesi should know what he's talking about. Twice Michigan state champion himself, he coached Doris Travani, four times national champion woman cyclist; Robert Travani, formerly on America's Olympic team; Nancy Neimann, four times national champion, who tied the world's record; and Joanni Specken, national champion. He served as coach of the 1964 United States Olympic Cycling Team, and runs a national bicycle and parts business from his Cadillac, Michigan, headquarters.

TRACK VERSUS ROAD-TRAINING TECHNIQUES

Bill Kund, a racing cyclist, offers some practical advice to track and racing cyclists as to the different types and methods of conditioning each should engage in:

I have found that the best way to gain endurance is to ride. I spend from two and a half to three hours on the road daily, usually riding in a small gear, 62 to 70 inches (46 x 20 to 47 x 18), at a fairly comfortable pace. If I am feeling good I will include some hills in the ride, or go into higher gear, 88 to 94 inches, and ride hard for five to ten miles. If I am feeling especially weak or stiff I will still ride for three hours, but at an easy pace in a small gear.

I also do speed work three times a week, and on Tuesday evenings, I go to the track and do interval training. This consists of about ten repetitions of 500-meter sprints at seven-eighths speed, with a one-mile rest between each one. The whole work-out, including fifteen minutes of pacing to warm up, lasts about an hour. This is a very tiring work-out, and I would not advise doing it more than once a week. On Thursday evenings I do four to six 300-meter sprints with long rests between. The emphasis on these sprints is speed, not fatigue. I usually get together with one or two other riders when doing this, and we take turns leading out the sprints. On Fridays, I incorporate at least one hour of hard motor pacing (30 to 35 miles per hour) into my three-hour stint on the road.

It is only through balanced training of this type that a rider can develop to his fullest capacity. Races are won with both speed and endurance, not with only one or the other. A sprinter who is unable to sustain his speed to the line is as worthless as a roadman in a bunch sprint who is consistently last.[1]

ABOUT THE RACING BICYCLE

Track-racing bicycles are very special machines indeed. The wheelbase is shorter, the fork rake is fairly straight, and rear dropouts are open to the rear so wheels can be bolted in place and can't come out under the stress of powerful racing cyclists. The track bike has fixed gear and no brakes, and weighs at most 18 pounds. Special-design bicycles are built for specific types of track races. Chain-stay diameter varies according to preferences of track racers, the heavier cyclists preferring stays as thick as ⅝ inch, with ½ inch for lighter racers. The idea is to minimize power-wasting "frame whip" and arrive at a stiff frame. For pursuit racing, the very lightest Columbus tubing can be used, but for track sprints or road racing, heavier tubing is needed to withstand greater stress. Professional cyclists in Europe have several bicycles designed specially for each type of race.

For races involving steep banks or turns, a racing bicycle can have a 75-degree head angle, 73-degree seat angle, fork blades with a ¼-to-½-inch rake, extra-short wheelbase and thicker rear stays.

Road-racing machines and better touring bicycles have 72-degree parallel head and seat tubes. Taller bicyclists, if having a custom frame built, can order a 73-degree head and 71-degree seat tube or let the frame builder select the angles.

---

[1] Bill Kund, "Speed + Endurance = Victory," *American Cycling* (now *Bicycling!*), April, 1966. Page 17.

Fig. 7-5: A track-racing bicycle. Notice the single fixed gear and the lack of other equipment such as brakes. Notice also the straight front fork. (*Schwinn*)

DIET AND RACING

We have already discussed a diet for active people in Chapter 6, but there are a few more tips for the racing cyclist in particular. First, because the racing cyclist is on the road and track for long hours, the food consumption must increase directly with the time and energy expended. Food should be eaten in the proper proportions as described in Chapter 6, but the extra food needed for long workouts should be made up of larger amounts of carbohydrates than the less active cyclist would need. Remember that hard cycling can use up to 850 calories per hour, so a long day in the saddle means you can afford to stuff it in at night, as long as you don't eat prodigious amounts of meat or fatty foods.

Much discussion in the cycling world revolves around a more exotic form of good consumption for endurance rides and stage races. Called "carbo-loading," this diet plan is not designed for everyday use, but for serious, one-time marathon rides lasting many hours (or days). The idea behind this is that by first starving the body of carbohydrates and then loading up on them, you increase your capability of utilizing such foods for energy.

Research on athletes has proven the effectiveness of carbo-loading over the years, and most top athletes use this to give them the energy they need to compete. Carbo-loading can increase the stores of glycogen for energy by up to 20 percent and put off the use of stored fats (which causes some discomfort) for a longer time during the ride.

Carbo-loading can be approached in a variety of ways, but the key is to first deplete the body of most carbohydrates, subsisting on protein and fats for two to four days while exercising heavily, and then rest while gorging on the likes of potatoes and butter, sweets, rice, pasta and very little else.

On race week or before a century ride, you should begin carbo-loading seven days in advance. Start the first day (call this Monday) by riding long and hard in the morning. By the time you stagger in, it is time to eat a breakfast of steak and eggs, with toast and butter and milk. For lunch, feast heartily on a roast beef sandwich or avocadoes, plenty of cheese or nuts and a salad with a mayonnaise base. Ride before dinner, sticking to meat and vegetables afterwards. Keep the vegetables light, and drink milk again. Repeat this procedure on Tuesday, and again on Wednesday, and if you are still with us on Thursday, you can put the meat away, and start on the carbo-loading diet. Start the day with another ride, but eat cereal, toast and milk. At lunch, have cheese, sandwiches and milk, and add corn or potatoes. Have a light evening workout, and return to a heaping plate of potatoes or pasta or vegetables and rice. Add very little sauce or butter, because these fats will fill you up and take away from your goal of storing energy food. When the ride is over, you can go back to your sauces and garnishings, but these are not part of carbo-loading. For dessert, eat a pie à la mode or some other sweet carbohydrate food.

By Friday, it is time to quit riding, but stick to the carbo diet. Saturday eat heartily and eat late, so that you won't be hungry and depleted come race morning. If you wish, wake up a few hours early, stuff down some cookies and go back to sleep. When you awake, have only a light breakfast of lightly buttered toast and coffee, avoiding fats or protein. Then go for your ride.

When on the ride, remember to carry some form of energy-producing food, such as a candy bar or fruit slices. Don't overeat, but eat small amounts throughout the day. And drink fluids before you become dehydrated.

THE QUESTION OF DRUGS

It is virtually unheard of for anyone on the United States cycle-racing teams to take drugs. In the first place, in this country the sport comes under rules governing amateur athletics. There are no professional bicycle racers. In Europe, however, where bicycle racing is a national obsession akin to baseball or football here, professional bicycle racers can earn over $100,000 a year. Pro racing competition is keen, and most racing athletes are fairly evenly matched physically, thus leaving only technique or drugs to decide who wins. The taking of drugs, either by injection into the bloodstream or orally, has long been a real problem in bicycle-racing circles abroad. Authorities prohibited all forms of stimulants long ago, and athletes are tested for drugs either by a spot check or by a careful physical checkup.

Taking drugs is a dangerous practice for athletes because it masks true symptons of fatigue that, when ignored, can cause heart failure. Drugs have killed more than one racing cyclist, and have "burned out" many more athletes before their time. In fact, during a Tour de France road race, a world-famous cycling champion died shortly after toppling off his bicycle. At first, death was attributed to sunstroke, but a later examination showed that he had taken a stimulant which permitted exertion to the point of heart failure.

European cycling pros who take drugs follow a typical cycle of racing success. Generally, a cyclist who takes drugs can remain in peak form and condition from eighteen to twenty-four years of age, but during this period he will build up a tolerance for the drug, and will require progressively larger doses. After the age of twenty-four, he cannot continue taking drugs without becoming addicted and endangering his life. A racer will drop out of active competition for from two to four years until his body throws off the effects of the drugs he has been taking. And, at twenty-six or twenty-eight, he will be found again in the championship ranks until, after an even shorter period of drug-stimulated racing, he either drops out for good, goes through another "cure," or becomes permanently addicted.

Cyclists don't carry small containers of pressurized oxygen which they could sniff from time to time to make up for the oxygen deficiency caused by physical stress. Pure oxygen isn't much help because racing cyclists undergo physical stress that is sustained longer than in most other sports, and their training is rigorous enough that they should be able to oxygenize blood by means of normal respiration. Also, the few times a racing cyclist would be able to inhale a fractional cubic foot of oxygen during the heat and intense mental and physical strain of a race makes oxygen-sniffing impractical.

BICYCLE MOTOCROSS

During the late 1960s and early 1970s, teenagers and children began to mimic the popular motorcycle cross-country races on the hills near where they lived. Racing down fire hills in southern California on their "stingrays," the kids invented a sport that has captured the imagination of hundreds of thousands of children the nation over.

Called bicycle motocross, or BMX for short, this sport is now practiced at hundreds of "tracks," (Fig. 7-6) which vary from well-built enclosed rectangular structures to outdoor courses through wooded countrysides. The typical track is between 700 and 1,300 feet long. The riders start with a ramp jump leading into a course containing such hazards as jumps, berms (a wall of dirt on the outside of a turn), turns and whoop-de-dos, a series of small jumps.

The sport is now so entrenched that major bicycle firms are concentrating their sales operations on BMX bikes and equipment. Sanctioning bodies control races in local and even national competition and award points for each rider so he can be compared against riders across the

Fig. 7-6: BMXers mix it up at a outdoor track similar to those used by motocross racers. Notice the jerseys they wear signifying their team memberships.

country. Top riders, while still in their early or mid-teens, have become something of celebrities within their regions, and they are rewarded with "license plates" for their track bikes which indicate that they are top dogs.

Such national organizations as the National Bicycling Association, the American Bicycle Organization, the National Bicycle League, and the California-based Bicycle Motocross League are in the forefront of sponsoring races and establishing the system by which participants in different areas can be matched against one another.

It is not unusual to have up to 500 riders at a national meet of one of these organizations. The top riders find their way into publications covering racing and several magazines specializing in BMX. (See Appendix for organizations and publications.)

At competition on local tracks, there are races for groups of different ages and abilities, ranging from novice to "pro" riders. At indoor competition, the riders are frequently of "national" class and the competition is tough. Riders here compete fiercely for prestige for themselves and local teams, which are affiliated with bike shops. Some bike shops, in fact, are now almost totally devoted to BMX, because of the numbers of kids involved in the sport. Bike shops form the support for the sport by providing clubs that hold races and fielding teams of their best riders in the various age groups. At club competitions, the teams are selected from the very best riders; and being chosen for a top team can do wonders for a child's self-esteem, just as winning one of the trophies that are handed out at most major races can give the BMXer a real lift.

Fig. 7-7: A BMX racer "bunny hops" a "whoop-de-do," or small jump, on an outdoor course in California, where bicycle motocross got its start.

To get a child involved in BMX, first find the local track and attend a race as a spectator. While there, find out what the local organizing body is, when the races are held, how to sign up and what the rules and regulations are. Also try to determine what gear ratios are being used on the track.

Next, the equipment should be purchased. If the child has a BMX bike, make sure he gets safety equipment, including a motorcycle-style crash helmet (for there are numerous falls), goggles and face guard, elbow pads, heavy-duty motorcycling boots and gloves. If the bike has not been purchased, read on. Handlebar cushions are a definite must, because many BMX bikes have cross bars between the raised bars, creating an obstacle in a head-forward fall.

No BMXer should go for a race without having practiced riding around obstacles, trying a ramp dropoff, or having ridden enough to stand the strain of racing. Watching a few races should show kids what they have to look forward to in BMX, and what the competition is capable of. One way to get involved slowly is to join a club at a bike shop, if there is such a club, and ride with the racers for a while before going into heavy racing.

About the BMX Bicycle

BMX bikes are adaptations of the old stringray bikes, but are far more sophisticated. They are built with light, strong frames to give them the speed necessary for competition and the sturdiness to hold up in the first collision. The diamond-style frame is the most popular frame design. Chrome-moly tubing is very popular now, but double-butted tubing has been used. Some say double-butting is not strong enough, and it is doubtful whether it will be more popular. The forks are usually made of tubular chrome-moly with no rakes to maximize strength and responsiveness.

In national competition, thirty-six spoke wheels with aluminum alloy or steel rims are the most common. Tires are studded blackwall or gumwall, and rosin is used for traction on indoor tracks. Racing saddles are used on BMX, with special seat posts and clamps. Handlebars are "low high risers" with a crossbar to increase their strength. Brakes are rear caliper, or back-pedal coaster brakes, used in less expensive BMX bikes

Fig. 7-8: A BMXer decked out in full armor. Note the padded pants, the motorcycle helmet, the padded gloves and elbow pads and the mouth guard.

or those with "mag" wheels. Alloy three-piece cranks are used in BMX high-level racing, but the steel one-piece cranks are popular in lower-class racing.

And, of course, there is also the colorful clothing used by teams to promote the bike stores or manufacturers: The jerseys, leathers and helmets are varied and well decorated.

HIGH-SPEED "BIKES" AND THE FUTURE OF TRANSPORTATION

Racing and touring bicycles haven't really changed all that much since the early 1900s. Certainly, bicycles are stronger, lighter, more responsive. There have also been large advances in component technology, improving speed and braking. Yet the basic bike design remains pretty much the same.

Since 1975, however, American inventiveness and ingenuity have been focused on the bicycle. A combination race and design show called the International (Human) Powered Speed Championship, held annually in southern California, has bred an astonishing array of novel human-powered vehicles. Few of these vehicles would do well on the open road. Some, specialized only for speed, can travel in a straight line only, and need a crew of helpers to get the riders in and sealed up in the streamline shell. Others, however, with little ambition for speed records, race and show innovative vehicles intended eventually for road use. Some of these vehicles may one day change the nature of commuting to work, because their speed can cut down on the time it takes to cycle from point to point.

The race format now includes three events. The 200-meter flying sprints, using bicyclelike vehicles enclosed in aerodynamic shells, continue to be the focus of the championships because new speed records are established each year. The current world record for a single rider is just about 50 miles per hour. The multiple-rider record is better than 57 miles per hour, and it climbs higher every year. The one-hour time trial for bicycles is a world standard, and vehicles have established records here too. Because the first two races tend to encourage highly specialized vehicles, a 30-kilometer road race rounds out the championships by requiring the vehicles to maneuver through corners and the riders to start out, Le Mans style, running to their vehicles.

Many of the speed vehicles are "recumbents" (Fig. 7-9), which require the rider or riders to sit back or lie down in a prone position, and some recumbents have hand as well as foot pedals. The speed vehicles are designed strictly for short-term speed, and the lowered frontal area of recumbents gives this speed. Most of the longer-distance bikes are upright, and all longer-distance records are held by more conventional machines.

The standard racing bike puts the body in the worst position in terms of aerodynamic drag, but in the best position in terms of power output.

Fig. 7-9: "Recumbent" vehicles may someday be used by the mass public for transportation. They offer the stability and the speed for slightly longer efforts than the vehicles designed merely for speed on the straightaway. *(Greg Hill)*

The answer to this dilemma is to retain the upright position, but to place a fairing, or a motorcyclelike windscreen, in front of the rider. But the problem of wind resistance under the fairing has resulted in bikes with three and four wheels to allow the fairing to be placed as low as possible. In some vehicles the bottom of the fairing is covered completely, leaving only small slits for the wheels, in order to reduce air flow through the inside of the fairing.

Machines with linear drives, in which the rider makes reciprocating rather than circular motions with the feet (and/or hands) are frequently proposed as alternatives to the standard bicycle. Though none have yet met with commercial success, there is some logic behind the claims of improved efficiency. The average person, untrained in the specialized technique of circular pedaling, can more easily adapt to and efficiently ride a machine with the stair-stepping motion of linear drive.

The problem with linear drives is that the pedal must stop and reverse at the end of each stroke. The way in which this reversal is accomplished seems to be what distinguishes the best of the linear drives. Linear drives, which continuously vary the drive ratio, using cams and cables driving one-way clutches and connecting rods driving a standard crank, have increased the effective gearing at the end of the stroke to stop the pedal, using all the momentum of the leg and producing a smooth motion throughout the stroke.

Multi-rider machines designed for speed along have so far produced the speed necessary to break the 55-miles-per-hour barrier (in 1979, when the barrier was broken, a prize of $3,000 was at stake, offered by Dr. Alan Abbott, who set the single-rider, standard-bicycle speed record of 48 mph) but have not altered the picture of the standard bicycle as the best mix of power and position. The record for speed is held by designers at General Dynamics Corporation, whose four-wheeled, three-man prone vehicle went 57.07 miles per hour.

Top speeds will continue to increase, but the future of these high-speed rigs is on the road. The principal problem with recumbents is that even those that are comfortable for long rides and are very fast on flat ground do not climb well. One of the unique advantages of the standard bicycle is the many body positions that are available to suit the conditions.

The problem of building a human-powered vehicle that will climb like a bicycle and go on the flat like a streamliner is a difficult one. Yet already, designers stimulated by the spirit of human power are turning to this problem; and their solutions, possibly involving hand and foot drives, linear pedaling and streamlining, could revolutionize bicycling and even transportation in general. Our energy-conscious society awaits new developments.

CROSSING THE CHANNEL BY "AIRCYCLE"

Bicyclist Bryan Allen got a "flying start" in his bicycle-powered contraption (Fig, 7-10) to establish a record for human-powered flight. Pedaling like crazy across the English Channel in the *Gossamer Albatross*, built by Dupont engineer Robert Macready, Allen thrilled the world by crossing the channel in just under three hours. The lightweight craft, weighing just seventy pounds, was made mainly of carbon filament tubing sheathed in a transparent material called Mylar, and needed only one-third horsepower to run. Pedaling pushed a crank system which turned a rear propeller.

Although human-powered flight is not likely to replace driving an automobile to the grocery store, it may one day become a sport for daring enthusiasts. The interesting fact is that you must be a bicyclist to ride in such a craft.

GLOSSARY OF RACING TERMS

Road Races

- *Criterium*—A road race held over a fairly short closed circuit, closed off to traffic. Known in Europe as a Kermesse.
- *Australian Pursuit*—Slowest groups of riders start first, spaced at intervals, with faster riders up to the very fastest starting last.
- *Stage Race*—A long-distance race, staged over a number of days, such as the Tour de France. Rider with the best time per day is the winner.
- *Individual Time Trial*—Based on a predetermined distance, winner is the rider completing that distance in the shortest time.

Fig. 7-10: California's Bryan Allen, all 137 pounds of him, sweats away aboard the first human-powered plane to cross the English Channel. Seen here just short of the French coast, Allen pushes the 70-pound **Gossamer Albatross**, which hovers just a few feet above the water. It took only one-third horsepower to power the propeller of the plane, which was linked to a chain driven by Allen's pedaling. *(UPI)*

Track Races

- *Course des Primes*—Involves a large number of riders, over a distance of three to five miles, with the winner amassing the most points on sprints held every other lap.
- *Paced*—Riders follow a small motorcycle called a "Derny" which "breaks the wind."
- *Miss and Out*—Each lap eliminates a last rider and narrows the field down to three, after which a sprint for the finish determines the winner.
- *Handicap*—Slow riders start a predetermined distance ahead of faster riders.
- *Madison*—Two-man teams compete over a fixed distance, usually 100 kilometers (62.14 miles). While one man rides, his partner circles slowly around the track and, at fixed intervals, takes the active partner's place. Winners of sprints that take place during the race amass points, determining the ultimate winning team.

- *Motor Paced*—Racers ride behind a specially built motorcycle on a specially designed bicycle with the front wheel smaller than the rear wheel, mounted on a reversed fork to enable the rider to keep close behind the motorcycle. See *Paced.*
- *Omnium*—Omnium means "all" in Latin, and this is a race of all types, with the winner the rider who has the most points gained from each type of race.
- *Italian Pursuit*—A team race, involving teams of four to six cyclists who start across from each other, one team on either side of the track. Slowest rider drops out each lap, the number of riders starting determine the number of laps.
- *Team Pursuit*—This is the same as an individual pursuit race but involving teams of four riders.
- *Scratch*—A handicap sprint race in which the slowest rider starts first, the fastest, last.
- *Time Trial*—A 1,000-meter (3,280.3 feet, or .62 mile) race, in which the rider attempts to cover this distance in the shortest possible time.

Bicycle Motocross

- *Berm*—A wall of dirt or gravel on the outside of a turn.
- *Bunny Hop*—When a rider approaches a jump or whoop-de-doo, he pulls on the front of the bike, hopping over the obstacle without touching it.
- *Cookin' or Smokin'*—Riding very fast on the straightaway.
- *Dropoff*—A sheer dropoff of at least 6 feet of dirt on the race course.
- *Bite it or eat it*—To fall hard.
- *European*—A kind of jump in which the ground drops off two to three feet from under the rider during the jump.
- *Hole shot*—Racer gets off to the best start during the race, dusting his competitors.
- *Kick Out*—Putting the weight on the front of the bike, leaving back tire light; then shifting weight to one side, making back wheel leave the ground and go to the side.
- *Moto*—Where four to seven riders complete one loop of the course.
- *Rad, or Radical*—Good form while riding.
- *Squirrel*—Very fast racer who is also wild in his riding style.
- *Whoop-de-doo*—Small jumps about 1 foot high and up to 10 feet apart.

The Fad That Lasted— a Short History of Bicycling ⑧

When Baron Karl von Drais introduced his "Hobby-Horse" to the citizens of Karlsruhe, Germany, in 1816, he started a love affair with man-propelled wheels that has persisted to this day.

The Hobby-Horse, or "Draisene," (Fig. 8-1) was a monstrously heavy affair, consisting of a wooden frame, wooden wheels and a most uncomfortable-looking saddle. The rider straddled the Draisene and propelled himself forward by pushing with his feet—the result was something like riding a kiddie-car.

Costly and cumbersome though it was, the Draisene was immediately accepted by the wealthy and the more enterprising middle class of the day. Within a few years, playboys of Western Europe were pushing their way up and down the boulevards of major cities on the hobby-horse. Draisene owners formed clubs and held races and sporting events.

Obviously, the Draisene was only suitable for the young and sturdy. Also, because it was so heavy and cumbersome, it could not be pushed very far or fast. Therefore, there was great incentive to find a way to make this form of propulsion more efficient.

One of the earliest attempts at mechanizing the hobby-horse was made by an Englishman, Lewis Gompertz, who in 1821 devised a rack-and-pinion arrangement that enabled the rider to pull the handlebars back and forth. By pushing with his feet and pulling with his arms, he could

Fig. 8-1: The original Hobby Horse, invented by Baron Karl von Drais, in the museum at Breslau *(The Bettmann Archive)*

Fig. 8-2: The 1862 "Boneshaker". We need say no more.

presumably go faster and farther. How he steered this contraption at the same time has not been recorded, but most likely it was inaccurately.

Bicycling really began to take over the streets and countryside when an enterprising Englishman named Kirkpatrick MacMillan put foot pedals on the front wheel of the hobby-horse in 1835. By the mid-1800s, it was truly the fad of the century. Young people found bicycling a good way to get out from under the stern eye of their parents; society saw the bicycle as an expensive and exclusive toy and pastime; and sporting enthusiasts of all ages adopted one of the thousands of variations of the two-wheeler for their activities.

As the bicycle improved, more and more people began to ride and even to go on picnics in the country and take short tours. At last man was free from the horse and wagon. A bicycle never needed daily cleaning and currying; it didn't eat, and it did not use an expensive harness that took time to put on and take off. One could jump on a bicycle and quickly be away from home. The impact of the bicycle was almost as great, in fact, as the advent of the Model T Ford. Much to the indignation and consternation of their elders and the ministers of the day, young boys and girls could ride out into the country together. Women's fashions changed to suit the bicycle. Clothes became less confining; the Gibson Girl on her bicycle, with her voluminous bloomers and leg-of-mutton sleeves, set a new style (Fig. 8-5).

Fig. 8-3: Close-up of pedals on the "Boneshaker," shown in Figure 8-2

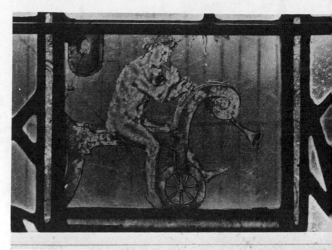

Fig. 8-4: The famous window in a church at Stokes-on-Poges, England, circa 1637, would seem to date a version of the Draisene well before the Hobby Horse introduced in 1816. *(Pierre Maisonneuve)*

Fig. 8-5: This old photograph shows an early female bicyclist in the clothing fashion of the day.

Fig. 8-6: The bicycle fad at its peak. New York Michaux Cycle Club. (*The Bettmann Archive*)

The exhilarating new freedom of mobility which the bicycle brought to the common man was undoubtedly the cause of what was truly a bicycle mania in the 1800s. An early form of this velocipede was introduced to the United States from England in 1869. This machine had iron-rimmed wooden wheels, for which it was nicknamed the "boneshaker." The front wheel was equipped with pedals.

The velocipede became so popular that riding academies with indoor rinks were established where would-be cyclists were taught, and where feats of riding skill were performed before enthralled audiences. Cycling clubs were formed in large cities across the nation by social sets, and were soon very exclusive indeed. The Michaux Cycle Club of New York (Fig. 8-6), for example, was housed in an elegant three-story brownstone mansion. Its riding rink was well lighted, and ladies and gentlemen could watch riders drill from balconies, while waiters brought them food and drinks.

The five-foot-high "Penny-Farthing," which emerged in England in 1872 (Fig. 8-7), was an outgrowth of the boneshaker, and an attempt at achieving more speed. It wasn't long before an enterprising engineer figured out that the bigger the wheel with the pedals, the faster the bicycle would go (up to a point, that is). Eventually, the wheel diameter became too big for even the strongest human to push. It would seem that bicycles developed backward for a while, until the Penny-Farthing or "ordinary," as it was called in the United States, eventually became a dangerous thing to ride, with its sixty-inch-diameter front wheel and tiny rear wheel. The ordinary was very unstable—if the rider hit a pothole, he could easily be thrown over the front wheel from a height of more than five feet, and possibly at a speed of six to ten miles an hour. There were a good many fatalities and cracked heads associated with it. Only the novelty of cycling and the freedom of movement it gave to riders accounted for the continued growth of the sport when this machine was in its heyday.

In 1876, Colonel Albert A. Pope of Massachusetts began to import these high-wheelers from England, and in 1878, he began to manufacture them in Boston. At this time the ordinary weighed around sixty pounds and cost $150, which would be about $1,800 today.

Prominent men of the day—one might call them the forerunners of our "jet set"—biked around the country on ordinarys. Well-known social figures made headlines by touring from coast to coast, from Chicago to

Fig. 8-7: Man taking a "header" off a Penny-Farthing during a race

New York, and New York to Boston. British nobility in the 1880s rode bikes around their estates, and even the Prince of Wales attended the bicycle races of the day. Bicycle clubs grew and became ritualized and institutionalized as the bicycle became improved mechanically.

In 1885 the high-wheeled ordinary gave way to the "safety bicycle," invented by an Englishman, J. K. Starley. This bicycle had a chain-driven rear wheel, and wheels about thirty inches in diameter, with solid rubber tires. Three years later, an Irish veterinary surgeon produced an invention without which the automobile could never have flourished. Dr. J. B. Dunlop of Belfast, Ireland, gave a hard-tired tricycle to his son, Johnny, who reported that his new present was quite uncomfortable and very hard to pedal. Dr. Dunlop liked to tinker in his spare time, and one of his hobbies was fabricating his own gloves out of canvas and rubber. From these he devised a set of "gloves" that could be filled with air for his son's tricycle. From rubber sheeting and strips of linen from one of his wife's old dresses, he built an air-filled tire, thus the first pneumatic bicycle tire.

Dr. Dunlop continued to make improvements on his tire until one day his friend, William Hume, president of the Belfast Cruiser's Cycling Club, persuaded him to make up a pair of tires for his racing machine. With his new tires, Mr. Hume easily beat the crack cyclists of the area in a race on May 18, 1889. After this, Dr. Dunlop was in business, and soon pneumatic tires were being manufactured by a number of firms in the United States. By 1891, the pneumatic tire was an accepted bicycle feature. The fad continued to flourish and spread.

During the 1890s, the bicycle population grew by leaps and bounds —by 1896, there were over 400 bicycle manufacturers in the United States alone. The bicycle craze even alarmed businessmen in major cities for a while. They thought the bicycle would bring the nation to economic collapse, and there were a number of compelling statistics to

Fig. 8-8: View of Oldreive's tricycle, or the new iron horse, with a woman inside. (*The Bettmann Archive*)

bear them out. The bicycle was not only a status symbol of major importance; it was the only way the average person could move about, unless
he owned a horse and carriage. By 1896, the watch and jewelry business
had fallen almost to zero, piano sales had been cut in half, and book sales
had dropped disastrously. Apparently, no one stayed home and played
the piano or read, and instead of buying jewelry, people bought bicycles.

Also, most people must have been too tired or too broke at night to go
to the theater, because attendance at theatrical performances also fell off
drastically during the 1890s. The song that would have reached the top
of the hit parade, had there been one in 1896, was about a girl named
Daisy and her "bicycle built for two."

There were also plays written about bicycling. *The Bicyclers,* by John
Kendrick Bangs, was a farce published by Harper & Brothers in 1896. It
opens in the drawing room of Mr. and Mrs. Thaddeus Perkins, at their
home in New York's Gramercy Square. It is early evening.

The bell rings and Mr. Perkins, attired in a cycling costume of knickers
and socks, answers the door. His friend, Ed Barlow, is at the door, attired
in evening dress. There follows much good-humored banter, during
which Ed asks Thad if he might speak to his father. It seems that up

Fig. 8-9: American wheelmen reposing in the woods, ca. 1890 (*The Bettmann Archive*)

until the bicycle craze only children wore knickers. Ed's wife, it is revealed, is en route by bicycle from the Barlow home in the upper Seventies, a distance of some eight miles from Gramercy Square.

While waiting for the arrival of Mrs. Barlow, Thad Perkins brags about his new "Czar" bicycle. He says, in answer to Ed Barlow's question about whether he's had any riding lessons:

"None yet. Fact is, just got my wheel. That's it, over by the door—pneumatic tires, tool-chest, cyclometer, lamp—all for a hun. The only thing they gave me extra was a Ki-Yi gun; it's filled with ammonia and it shoots dogs. You shoot it into the dog's face; it doesn't hurt him, but it gives him something to think of."

While Mr. and Mrs. Perkins and Ed Barlow await the arrival of Mrs. Barlow, the phone rings. It is Mrs. Barlow, in great agitation, phoning from a police station. She has been arrested for riding without a light. Ed Barlow, in his concern about his wife, forgets that he's had no riding experience, and jumps on Thad's bicycle. The play ends with Barlow's voice, off-stage, louder at times, then fainter, as he circles around and around the block, not knowing how to steer properly, or how to stop.

Much of the dialogue in the play is devoted to the merits and shortcomings of various makes of bicycles. Certainly, bicyclists of the 1890s had a good many machines to talk about, just as car owners do today.

Fig. 8-10: 1897 Sterling tandem with woman's seat in front, while man steers and pedals from behind. It was considered more polite to have the woman in front.

Among the bicycle manufacturers of the era were many famous names —Henry Ford, Wilbur and Orville Wright, Glenn Curtiss, and Charles Duryea. United States manufacturers alone produced and sold 2,000,000 bicycles in 1897, when the population was 72,189,000—that is, 27.7 bicycles were sold per 1,000 people. It wasn't until 1947 that bicycle sales exceeded 2,000,000 and by that time the population was 146,093,000, so the 2.8 million bicycles sold in 1947 amounted only to 19.17 bikes per 1,000 population. By contrast, in 1972 an estimated 13.5 million bicycles were sold in the U.S., when the population was 208 million, so bicycle sales amounted to 64.9 per thousand, a new all-time high, and an increase of 419 percent over 1968. Sales in 1979 were around 10 million.

The following description of the bicycle business in the February 1896 issue of *Outing* magazine resembles an article in today's *Business Week*. Cycling in those days was a sport of the wealthy. *Outing* was devoted to the leisure time of the moneyed class.

The cycle trade is now one of the chief industries of the world. Its ramifications are beyond ordinary comprehension. Its prosperity contributes in no small degree to that of the steel, wire, rubber, and leather markets. Time was when the spider web monsters, now nearly extinct, were built in one story annexes to English and American machine shops; now a single patented type of a jointless wood rim, one of the minor parts of a modern bicycle, is the sole product of an English factory covering over two acres of ground. A decade ago the American steel tube industry was unprofitable. The production of this most essential part of cycle construction has, during the past two years, been unequal to the demand, and even now every high-grade tube mill in this country is working night and day on orders that will keep them busy throughout the year. Nearly every season since 1890 has witnessed a doubling of the number of our factories and a multiplication of the product of a large proportion of the older ones. Yet the supply from the opening of last season to mid-summer was unequal to the demand, and although preparations of astounding proportions have been and are being made to meet with a multiplicity of models of the most approved designs and best workmanship, the demands of '96, the prospects are that the field offers reasonable prosperity to all makers of high-grade products. The present prices are quite reasonable, considering the quality of material and workmanship involved. Prices will be very generally maintained, and the number of riders, of both sexes, will be at least doubled.

It might interest some of our readers to review the specifications of a few of the safety bicycles of the 1890s. For example, the new 1898 line of Columbia bicycles, made by Pope Manufacturing Company, had a split crankshaft. Model 40 Columbia "light roadsters," selling for $100, had a "23-inch frame, 10-inch steering head, 28-inch wheels, 1⅝ pneumatic 'Hartford' tires, detachable sprockets, improved self-oiling chain, 6¾-inch patent round cranks, 5-inch tread, 3 ⅝-inch pedals, reversible handlebars, tubular seat rod, 66-inch gear and weighed 24 lbs."

Reviewing the specifications of these early bicycles points up the fact

Fig. 8-11: An 1896 Victor shaft-drive bicycle, using "worm gear" system inside closed shaft, was very popular around the turn of the century, but too heavy to be practical.

Fig. 8-12: The 1895 Cleveland Safety Bicycle, a forerunner of the modern bicycle. It had one speed.

that gearing was low, which was necessary because there were no gear-shift mechanisms in popular use at the time. In addition, the metallurgy of the bicycle frame and parts was far inferior to that of today's higher-quality bicycles. Gene Portuesi has told me that racing cyclists of the day could reach fantastic crank speeds. Zimmerman, a racing champion of the 1890s, could wind up to 140 crank revolutions per minute, which he had to do to get any speed out of the low gear ratios used even on the best racing bicycles of the day, A powerful modern racing cyclist would literally tear apart a racing bicycle of the 1890s, according to Portuesi.

Reviewing the names of the bicycle manufacturers of the 1890s, which seemed to be located in every major city, made me somewhat nostalgic The Columbia line was popular up until the late 1920s or early 1930s. Some readers will remember the Spalding, Iver Johnson, Rambler, Remington, Waltham and Singer bicycles.

Most of the better bicycles produced during this period had turned-down handlebars. One bicycle of 1896 even had an all-aluminum frame. It was manufactured by the Lu-mi-num Company of St. Louis, Missouri, and was successful enough to be licensed for production in England. You can buy all-aluminum bicycles today, much improved, of course, over those of yesteryear, made by Hi-E Engineering Co., Nashville, Tennessee, and a new bike introduced at the 1973 Paris Bicycle Exposition, the tubing for which is provided by Super-Vitus of France.

The introduction of the "safety" bicycle, complete with chain drive and 28-inch wheels and brakes, did not guarantee safe cycling, however. A review of early cycling hazards makes cycling today seem safe, despite the density of urban motor vehicle traffic.

There may have been no automobiles back in the 1890s, but the roads were full of potholes, except for main arteries in and near major cities. And dogs attacked cyclists just as they do now. In those days, they were not restrained as they are today in cities.

Also, the general populace resented cyclists, just as many people were against the early automobiles. Farmers took personal delight in blocking the narrow roads of the day with their wagons, and they went as slowly as possible just to aggravate cyclists behind them. Country bumpkins took great delight in thrusting sticks between the spokes of cyclists' wheels to knock them off their seats. When people were riding the "Penny-Farthing" in the early days of cycling, a stick between the spokes of the high wheel brought disaster to the cyclist and guffaws from pranksters. One of the reasons the early cycling clubs were formed, aside from social purposes, was to provide protection against wanton attacks on cyclists. Horse-drawn vehicles, in addition to blocking the roads, were often deliberately sent careening into groups of cyclists, which injured the riders as well as harmed their machines.

In England, at this time, restaurant and tea-shop owners refused to serve cyclists, particularly female riders who wore what the owner of one restaurant described as "outlandish and shocking costumes."

The world's first nationwide cycling club, the British Touring Club, organized for political as well as for social reasons, was formed in England in 1878. It was an amalgamation of a number of small regional cycling organizations, and soon began publishing its own magazine, *The Bicycling Times*. In 1883, the BTC's name was changed to its present title, the Cyclists' Touring Club. The publication became known as *The Gazette* and is now *Cycle Touring*.

The Gazette was an outspoken and fearless defender of cyclists and cycling in England. In fact, its early pronouncements must have been fairly vitriolic, because in 1898 the editor was denounced for his outspokenness at one of the club's national meetings by some of the members, some of whom were the representatives of bicycle manufacturers. At the same meeting, George Bernard Shaw, who was an ardent cyclist and lifetime member of the Club, arose to defend *The Gazette:* "Do you want it to contain fact or fiction?" he said. "You already have plenty of fiction in the advertising pages . . . I want to raise a strong protest against what has been said as to raising the tone of *The Gazette*. What we want above all things is an abusive *Gazette*. If I wish to read a nice complimentary cycling paper, one that has a good word for everybody, for every dealer and seller, and every sort of kind of invention—I can easily buy one for a penny at any news shop. But we want something quite in the opposite direction and we get it in our *Gazette,* even if that publication does sometimes refer to a lady's article as piffle." (Roars of laughter.) "In my view the gentlemen who object to ladies having to stand the same treatment as is meted out to men are the same people who object to ladies cycling altogether, and therefore, I do not think they need be taken very seriously."

The hostility of the noncycling public seemed to be universal, so throughout the Western world, Europe and America, cyclists banded together into clubs such as the CTC to protect their status. In England, the Highway and Railway (Amendment) Act of 1878 referred specifically to bicycles, and gave county authorities power to regulate their use. Many of the laws passed by local authorities were unreasonably restrictive. In some instances, cyclists were forbidden to use public highways, or had to pull over and stop whenever a horse-drawn vehicle appeared on the horizon. Within ten years, however, the CTC had grown enough in size and importance so that it was able to push through Parliament what became known as the Magna Carta of Bicyclists. The Local Government Act abolished the power given by the Highway and Railway Act to local county governments to regulate bicycling. This signaled further successes for the club, which was able to push through other laws that provided for the improvement of highways, the safe carrying of bicycles on railroad baggage cars, and recourse against the antagonisms of the general public against cycling.

A landmark case occurred in 1899 in Surrey, England, when Lady Harbeton, an influential member of the CTC, was refused service in the coffee room of the Hautboy Hotel. They offered to serve her in the bar parlor instead. The club jumped to Lady Harbeton's defense, and the hotel's owner was indicted for "wilfully and unlawfully neglecting and refusing to supply a traveller with victuals." Lady Harbeton showed the court a picture of herself, which was described as portraying "an elderly lady, wearing a pair of exceedingly baggy knickerbockers reaching below the knee, and a jacket which came well over the hips and opened sufficiently to reveal the silk blouse underneath."

In the summer of 1880, a group of American cyclists visited the CTC's headquarters in Liverpool, and returned to the United States to form the League of American Wheelmen, in Newport, Rhode Island. By 1898, membership in the League of American Wheelmen had soared to its all-time high of 102,636. But thanks to the horseless carriage, it dwindled to 8,629 by 1902.

In 1964, the league was reactivated, this time in Chicago, under the leadership of Joe Hart. With its membership exceeding 12,000, the LAW today, as it was before the turn of the century, is dedicated to the needs and interests of the ardent cyclist. To the tourist traveling across the land, an LAW membership roster is a sure guarantee of welcome in every community where the league has a chapter.

In the days before road maps, the LAW published its own maps, lists of accommodations, condition of roads and other vital information which was otherwise unobtainable. To embark on an extended tour without an LAW touring bureau itinerary was unthinkable in those days. By 1890, the LAW had a chapter in virtually every town big enough to have a hotel.

During its heyday, many famous men and women were LAW members, among them Orville and Wilbur Wright, Commodore Vanderbilt and even Diamond Jim Brady. The organization was a political force to be reckoned with, more because of the influence of its wealthy members than for the size of its membership. During the early days of its existence, the league faced many of the same problems as did its counterpart in Great Britain. Cyclists were denied the right of way in America, excluded from public parks, and horsemen and, later, early motorists deliberately crowded them off the highways. The LAW first flexed its political muscle around 1884, when it dealt with the Haddonfield (N.J.) Turnpike case.[1] The turnpike authorities refused to permit cyclists on the turnpike. At that time, turnpikes were simply cross-state roads used by horse-drawn vehicles. There were no automobiles yet. The turnpike's ruling caused a furor among cyclists. If this was allowed it would set a precedent, which could restrict cyclists to cowpaths, or worse. With the backing of the league, the Philadelphia chapter brought a test case, which resulted in the turnpike authority's rescinding its no-cycling stricture.

Before this landmark decision in 1879, the New York Board of Commissioners had decided that bicycles in New York City's Central Park

[1] *American Cycling* (now *Bicycling!*), August, 1965.

were an eyesore and a menace to the citizenry. Shortly after the league was formed, it took this case to the courts and, after an eight-year fight, was successful in getting the governor of New York to revoke all restrictions against bicycles. After this ruling, cyclists were free to ride on any public roadway in the state of New York, which set a precedent in other states which granted cyclists the same privileges. Today, New York's Central Park is the exclusive province of cyclists on weekends, and weekdays from 10–3 and 7–10 PM during the summer, when no automobiles are allowed in the park at all.

Under joint backing of the LAW and the Bicycle Institute of America (an organization formed by United States bicycle manufacturers to promote cycling generally), bicycle paths are now being laid down by a number of cities and states throughout the country. Today there are a number of fine bicycle paths and trails. Chicago, for instance, has a cycle path that extends nearly the entire 20-mile length of the city, along Lake Michigan. Wisconsin has a trail across the state from LaCrosse to Kenosha (a distance of 350 miles). It traverses much of the state's most scenic spots. Fifty miles of it is over an abandoned, cinder-tracked railway that is restricted to bicycles, and far from any road. Milwaukee, Wisconsin; Clearwater, Florida; Arlington, Virginia; and many other cities also have good trails and paths now. There are also, or will be soon, bikeways in many of our national and state parks, including the Indiana Dunes National Lakeshore, Sleeping Bear Dunes National Park in Michigan, Cape Cod (Mass.) National Sea Shore, and Fire Island National Seashore in New York. I should point out that cross-state bicycle trails are also used by automobiles for much of the way, at least. However, these trails are carefully chosen back roads, which traverse scenic areas that bear little traffic and have a good black-top or concrete surface. Efforts are now being made to link cross-state trails so that cyclists can ride all the way across the nation.

These wonderful new bikeways might, and should, tempt you to take extended touring and cycle camping trips, but long-distance touring was a far different situation back before the automobile. The first man to cross the United States by bicycle was Thomas Stevens, who in 1884 rode a high-wheel "ordinary" from Oakland, California, to Boston. "Rode" is hardly accurate—Mr. Stevens carried, pushed, shoved and dragged his seventy-five pound steed across mountains, deserts, streams and fields. His journey took him 103½ days. In comparison, in 1954, Richard Berg of Northbrook, Illinois, cycled from Santa Monica, California, to New York City in just over 14 days.

Mr. Stevens had a horrendous task. He rode an ungainly high-wheeler over roads that were largely uncharted (where they existed at all), and public accommodations were chancy all the way. Also, the attitudes of the people he met ranged from scornful indifference to downright hostility.

Let's take a look at the kind of bicycle Stevens rode. It had a high front wheel, about fifty inches in diameter, and a small rear wheel, about seventeen inches in diameter. The frame was like a curved backbone, topped by a saddle just aft of a pair of flat handlebars.

The high wheel was not very maneuverable. Stevens was wedged right up against the handlebars, so steering way was limited and sharp turns nearly impossible to make. He had to sit almost over the centerline of the front wheel, which made even slight uphill runs a matter of hard pedaling. Coasting downhill was precarious, for a small chuckhole in the road, or even a pebble, could upset the delicate balance of the rider and send him toppling headfirst toward an unyielding roadway. In fact, Stevens used to practice taking headers, and his skill at it probably contributed as much to his survival as did his cycling proficiency.

It was quite an eventful trip. Much happened to Tom Stevens, including being made to perform for a bunch of rowdy cowpokes who shot bullets around him as he rode in and around pool tables, being pursued by packs of coyotes, crossing a railroad trestle in the Rockies and discovering halfway across that a train was coming (he hung onto the side of the trestle, seventy-five-pound bicycle and all), fording rivers swollen to flood stage, riding down the Rockies at breakneck speed, with his metal brake spoons heated red hot, and being cursed at by boatmen on the Erie Canal, whose mules reared and balked at the sight of him. He was feted from Chicago on, and in Boston received the magnificent reception he deserved.

If you are interested in reading the complete account of this unusual trip, you might try to find a copy of the two-volume story of his adventure, *First Across America by Bicycle,* which was published in 1887. Original copies are rather hard to come by, according to Dr. Irving Leonard, who has published an excellent shorter version of his book which you may obtain for around $5.95 from Bear Camp Press, South Tamworth, New Hampshire. Copies of the original book are currently going for $50 or more!

Fine collections of old bicycles have been made by private collectors, such as Roger Johnson of Hadley, Massachusetts; and excellent museum collections are at the Smithsonian Institution, Washington, D.C.; Museum of Science and Industry, Chicago; Greenfield Village (Ford), Dearborn, Michigan; Carillon Park Museum, Dayton, Ohio; Franklin Institute, Philadelphia; New York Historical Society, New York; Ponderosa Museum, Quarryville, Pennsylvania; Pioneer Village, Minden, Nebraska; and the Technical Museums of London, England, Milan, Italy, and Vienna, Austria.

There have been other cross-country and even around-the-world trips by bicycle, many of which make fascinating reading for the experienced cycle tourist who has been through similar adventures. In 1894, a young American girl named Annie Londonberry set out one July morning to tour the world, which she succeeded in doing. She left without a penny, and earned over $2,000 en route from publicizing her cycling exploits. Another famous woman traveler was Fannie Bullock Workman, who spent ten years touring the world, accompanied by her husband, William. Mrs. Workman was the wealthy daughter of a governor of Massachusetts, and her husband was a physician. Old photographs show Mrs. Workman mounted on her trusty Rover safety bicycle, clad always in a high-necked blouse, a voluminous skirt, and a pith helmet.

The Workmans made an unforgettable trip over the Atlas Mountains to the Sahara, in 1895. One can only marvel at their fortitude. They published at least three lengthy volumes on their trips, which, if you are lucky, you might find in your public library or an old bookstore.

Mr. Richard Berg's record-breaking fourteen-day trip across the United States in 1954, which we mentioned earlier, was not without incident. Berg, an experienced, twenty-three-year-old racing cyclist, rode a bicycle stripped down to the essentials, an eight-speed machine with tubular sew-up racing tires. He carried no luggage, not even a toothbrush or shaving kit. He made concessions to safety and comfort only; a rear light for night travel and a water bottle.

Berg left Santa Monica's City Hall, bound for New York, with speed his main concern. He crossed the Mohave Desert at night, as he had planned, and rode twenty-four hours a day more than once during this trip. Coming down the eastern slopes of the Rockies he often hit better than sixty miles per hour, as he was told by incredulous motorists after he passed them.

Berg stayed at any motel he came to, when he was tired from the day's exertions. If he could not find a motel, he would pull off into the nearest field for the night. His biggest problem was flat tires. It seems that out West, where the cactus grows, there are two-sided pronged thorns waiting in ambush on all roads. He used to spend his evenings repairing his sew-ups, and reports having had as many as thirteen flats in one day until he hit the plains of Kansas. Incidentally, he told me he would still use tubular sew-ups if he were to make the trip again, because he believes that thorns will pierce any tire, and tubulars make cycling much easier.

Fig. 8-13: Bicycle racing in the 1890s—an unusual action shot *(The Bettmann Archive)*

RACING BEGAN AT ONCE

Starting with the Draisene, and as each improved version of the bicycle became popular, stripped-down models were used in racing events. The first bicycle race in America—at least the first officially sanctioned race—was held in 1878, over a one-mile course. It was won by Will R. Pitman in three minutes and fifty-seven seconds of what must have been arduous exertion indeed. His machine was heavy, crude, and even more cumbersome than the racing bicycles of the 1890s. In 1895, the fastest racing cyclist beat the fastest race horse for the first time, when E. F. Leonert pedaled one mile in one minute and thirty-five seconds. At this time, also, cycle racing turned professional. Six-day bicycle races held at Madison Square Garden in New York drew thousands to view this murderous and bloody spectacle. The first six-day race, held in 1891 at the Garden, was won by William "Plugger" Martin, who pedaled 1,466 miles and four laps during the six days. The nonstop six-day race has been discontinued; however, a less gory version called the "Madison" is still run in Europe.

Perhaps the greatest bicycle racer of all time was A. A. Zimmerman. Zimmerman, a professional racer, was king of the wheel in both the United States and Europe, and is still talked about by racing cyclists today. In 1891, Zimmerman pedaled to a new world record for the half mile—on the seventy-pound high-wheel "ordinary"—in 1 minute, 10¾ seconds.

Zimmerman violated all the laws and rules of training, going out with the boys and drinking and carousing, while his teammates slept. In one notable instance, he climbed on his trusty safety bicycle, after having attended an all-night party and pedaled a paced mile in 1 minute, 57⅖ seconds at the annual LAW meet in Asbury Park, New Jersey. But what seemed to gain Zimmerman the most notoriety was the fact that he never attempted to beat a record or win a race by any more effort or speed than was necessary. There is no record of how long he lived.

Until the advent of the automobile turned America's interest from bicycle to auto racing, many professional bicycle racers became wealthy from their winnings. In 1895, there were over 600 professional racing cyclists in the United States alone, and more than that in Europe. Today there are *no* professional racing cyclists in this country, although there are hundreds in Europe who have earned a lot of money from the sport. In Europe, bicycle racing has always been the principal national sport of many countries, such as Italy, France, Spain, and Belgium. The average low income of the European worker, plus the high price of gasoline, helped keep the bicycle popular; although, with the rising standard of living of the past few years, bicycling has decreased somewhat there. In the meantime, the sport has grown in popularity in America.

Early track records are mighty impressive today, when one considers the crude bicycles on which they were made. In 1895, the long-distance track record (made in Paris on September 8 and 9 by Constance Huret) was 529 miles, 585 yards, in 24 hours. This was a sustained average of about 22 miles per hour. By contrast, in 1968, Beryl Burton, England's then top female cyclist, made 100 miles in three hours and fifty-five minutes and five seconds, at an average speed of 25.4 miles per hour. In 1899, Charles "Mile-a-Minute" Murphy pedaled a record mile in 57.8 seconds, following a train over a boarded-over section of the Long Island Railroad. It wasn't until 1905 that a car beat this record, when Barney Oldfield did a mile in 55.8 seconds in Henry Ford's "999."

Things got really fast later on. On May 17, 1941, Alfred Letourner zipped to 108.92 miles per hour behind a racing car at Bakersfield, California. Letourner rode a gear of 256.5, combining a microscopic six-tooth rear gear with a fifty-seven-tooth chainwheel which equals $12\frac{9}{14}$ ½-inch pitchgear (1-inch pitch). On July 19, 1962, Jose Meiffret of France reached a fantastic 128 miles per hour behind a car on Germany's Autobahn.

ANSWERING THE COUNTRY'S CALL

There is one development in the history of bicycles we haven't mentioned so far. At one time, bicycling was threatened with incorporation into the army. The military mind of the 1890s clearly visualized the bicycle as an invaluable tool in advance scouting, for outpost duties, patrols, convoys and to enable officers to make quick observations.

Harper's Weekly's special bicycle issue of April 11, 1896, carried this notice: "It is in rapidly moving considerable bodies of infantry that the bicycle will find its highest function in time of war. Fancy a force of infantry, independent of roads and railroads moving in any direction, forty or fifty miles in one morning, and appearing on a field not weary and exhausted as after a two-day's march, but fresh and prepared to fight . . ."

The Italian army was the first to adopt the bicycle. In 1870, four bicy-

Fig. 8-14: The use of bicycles by the military. In this photograph, two soldiers carry early collapsible bikes on their backs. *(The Bettmann Archive)*

cles were furnished to each regiment of infantry, "grenadiers, sappers and miners, engineers and cavalry. The machines are provided with a brake, lantern, knapsack, rifle support and a leather pouch for orders." I suppose the first folding bicycle was made with a soldier in mind, for, in 1896, the French army had one with a hinged frame. This machine weighed only twenty-three pounds and could be carried slung over a soldier's back. In 1885, Austrian soldiers, carrying full field kit, made 100 miles per day with bicycles during field maneuvers, outdoing what the cavalry could do on horseback.

In America, the first branch of the military to use bicycles was the National Guard of Connecticut. Eventually, the U.S. Army Signal Corps and other divisions of the military used the bicycle as a direct weapon of war. The army bolted two bicycles side by side and mounted a "mountain-cannon" between them. A military tandem was equipped with rifles and revolvers as well as a field pack, and a duplex (tricycle) was rigged with a machine-gun. Another tricycle was equipped with a Colt rapid-firing machine-gun mounted on the headstay and handlebars.

Between 1890 and 1900, large numbers of soldiers learned how to ride, drill and deploy on bicycles. New methods of using the bicycle were continually studied by an organization formed for this specific purpose. The United States Military Wheelmen, a volunteer auxiliary adjunct to the National Guard, trained soldiers in the use of the bicycle. Lieutenant Whitney, of this association, stated in 1896: "The balance of power is so nicely adjusted that the chances in the coming conflict will be governed by efficiency in detailed preparation. The bicycle will weigh in the scale. We are told somewhere that for want of a horseshoe nail a battle was lost. In the next war, for want of a bicycle the independence of a nation may be forfeited."

Over the past 150 years, we have seen the bicycle evolve from a wealthy man's toy to a vehicle of precision and beauty, with an infinite variety of uses. There are faster ways of getting places but few more enjoyable than this ever-growing sport.

Preventive Medicine for Bicycles—a Complete Shopping, Maintenance and Repair Guide   II

Before we get into the specifics of which type of tires, rims and tubes are best for the kind of cycling you do or plan to do, let's clear up one semantic issue—that of tire nomenclature. You will find in bicycle mail-order catalogs and other bicycling literature numerous references to "clincher tires," "wired-on tires" and "tubular tires." All these have one thing in common. They are indeed tires and they are bicycle tires. But there has been confusion about which is which, because the terms "wired-on" and "clincher" have been used interchangeably. In fact, they are very different.

Figure 9-1 shows a wired-on tire. You will note that there is a steel wire in the bead of this tire, hence the name "wired-on." The "clincher" tire does not have a wire bead, rather a rubber bead that fits into a groove in the rim. The clincher tire is all but obsolete, has not been used on bicycles sold in this country for years and I for one will be happy to forget that it ever existed. So now we are left with wired-on and tubular tires. The tubular tire (Fig. 9-2) is, as its names implies, tubular in that it is sewn up with the tube inside. It is used for racing, primarily, although a lot of us toured on them until the new lightweight, narrow-profile

Fig. 9-1: Cross-section of a box-type rim and conventional wired-on tire, showing the wire bead cutaway. Note how the bead seats in the rim. As the tube is expanded under air pressure, the tire bead is held firmly in the slanted rim section, keeping the tire in place. The box-type rim is one of the strongest made.

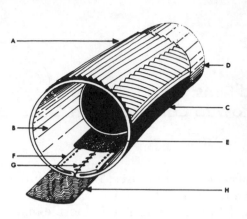

A. Tread.

B. Casing, made of fabric.

C. Outside of casing, between bottom of tread and base tape, is called the "wall."

D. Inner tube.

E. Chafing tape, to prevent inner tube from puncture by rubbing on tire stitching.

F. Hems of casing are made by gluing back the edges of fabric to the inside. In some tires, hems are folded to the outside.

G. Stitching. When repairing, use a simple hand-over-hand stitch.

H. Base tape protects stitching and provides seating for entire tire.

Fig. 9-2: A tubular tire is dissected in this sketch. You will note that the tread, bottom, is a separate part of the tubular, unlike conventional beaded tires, and that the tube is sewn up inside the tubular. Other names for tubulars are "tubs" and "sew-ups."

wired-on tires appeared a few years ago. But back to nomenclature for a moment. The International Standardization Organization (ISO) has declared that henceforth wired-on tires shall be called just "tires" and that tubular tires shall be called "tubulars." From here on in, then, I use "tire" to refer to a wired-on tire and "tubular" to refer to a tubular tire.

With that said, which type of tire (oops) which type of rubber thing around bike wheels should you use, a tire or a tubular? In general, tubulars are lighter, have a narrow profile, are higher pressure than tires, and so have lower rolling resistance. I doubt very much whether the average nonracing, commuting or touring cyclist can tell the difference in rolling resistance (ease of pedaling) between a mid-weight-tubular and a narrow-profile tire. The major differences between tires and tubulars, as far as the average bicyclist is concerned (and here we are speaking again of mid-weight tubulars and narrow-profile tires) is flat proneness, ease of flat repair and cost.

Because tubulars are quite thin compared to tires, and the tube in particular is even thinner, they are far more likely to get punctured than the thicker casing of the tire and the thicker tube. Once punctured, the tubular is a real pain to repair, because you have to cut the stitching, lift out the tube where you hope the puncture is located, patch that spot, resew and remount the tubular on the rim. To fix a flat tire, you do not even need to remove it from the rim, if you are sure you know where the puncture is located. All you do is pry away the tire from the rim, pull out the tube, patch it, push it back in, reseat the tire and pump it up. There's more to repairing both types of rubber things around rims, but more on this subject later.

As to cost, the best tire costs about one third the price of a good silk tubular, and lasts a lot longer. I should also add that tubulars, because they should be pumped up to around 100-pounds-per-square-inch pressure or more and are narrow profiled, do not take kindly to bumps and stones, so you'll jar more with tubulars than tires. I have traveled successfully many thousands of miles in this country and in Europe on tubulars, however, and have had little problem with flats. But I was both lucky and careful in avoiding puncture-causing road debris, and I made it a practice to brush the tire with my gloved hand every time I thought that I *might* have run over something sharp.

A WORD ABOUT ROLLING RESISTANCE

Rolling resistance has to do with at least four factors:

1. *Weight of the tire and rim.* The heavier these components, the more rolling resistance, due to the "flywheel" effect, and the harder it is to brake.
2. *Amount of rubber in contact with the road.* The less in contact, the lower the rolling resistance.
3. *Tire pressure.* The harder the tire, the less "flex" as the tire rolls and so less energy is used by the cyclist in turning the wheel. "Flex" is dissipated as heat in the tire casing; however, the harder (more pressure) the tire, the harder the ride. You need a tire somewhere between a rock-hard tubular at 125-psi pressure and a soft tire at 65 psi, for touring comfort on any bike.
4. *The weight on the tires.* This is a function of your weight, the bike weight and what you are carrying (loaded panniers, etc.).

AN OUNCE OFF THE WHEELS IS WORTH TWO OFF THE FRAME

I am indebted to the technicians at Bikecology for the following engineering explanation as to why weight saved in wheels is worth double the weight saved on the frame or what you carry on the frame. Of course, the best place to save weight still remains your own human frame. I digress, so back to why lightweight tires and tubes save around 2½ pounds, which is equal to a very hefty savings of five pounds on the frame:

As a bicycle moves, all parts (rider included) possess translational kinetic energy, $K_T = (½) MV^2$, where M is the mass of the part, V is the velocity of the bicycle. In addition, rotating parts (e.g., wheels, cranks) possess rotational kinetic energy, $K_R = (½) lw^2$, where l is the moment of inertia and w is the angular velocity in radians per second (to compute w, just take the revolutions per second and divide by 6.28).

For a small object or a hoop in circular motion about a fixed axis, $l = MR^2$, where M is the mass of the object and R is its distance to the axis. Both a hub and a rim rotate, but the rim (and tire), with its greater radius, contributes far more to the rotational energy of the wheel than does the hub. Likewise, the pedal contributes more to crank assembly rotational kinetic energy than does the small-radius crank spindle. In general, outer-radius weight (tires, rims, pedals) is more important than inside-radius weight (hubs, crankspindles). The relevance of all of the above physics is that, because of the rotational kinetic energy, removal of weight from wheels and crank assemblies (including pedals) is more effective than equal weight removal from frame or handlebars or saddles. For the tires and rims, the angular velocity is given by V/R, where V is bicycle velocity and R is wheel radius, then $K_R = (\frac{1}{2}) MR^2 (V/R)^2 = (\frac{1}{2}) MV^2$, or as much as the translational kinetic energy of the tire and rim.

Therefore, at a given speed, each gram of tire on rim weight will have twice as much kinetic energy as each gram of saddle of frame weight, demonstrating the validity of "an ounce off the wheels is worth two off the frame."

Bikecology Mail Order

Because tire pressures are tested at double the rated pressure, you can reduce rolling resistance by increasing tire pressure, and do it safely. I use 115 psi on my 700 centimeter by 1-inch tires, for example. The ride is a bit stiffer, but I use a long wheelbase touring frame with low flange hubs laced four cross, so the slight increase in road shock is no problem for me at all.

NEW TYPES OF TIRES

Later on in this chapter I will discuss some of the problems and their solutions in changing over from tubulars to tires. However, because most bicycles sold in this country that are suitable for touring already come with tires (isn't this getting a bit silly?) and not tubulars, the problem is moot at this time. But your new or relatively new bike may have, and in fact is very likely to have, the wider-profile tires that should not be pumped up over 90 psi, and which do have a high rolling resistance. I can sure tell the difference between a 27 x 1¼-inch wide profile tire and a 27 x 1-inch narrow profile tire. The narrower tire weighs around 300 grams (10.58 oz. or .66 lb.) and the conventional gumwall 27 x 1¼-inch tire weighs a hefty 570 grams (20.1 oz. or 1.26 lbs.). There's more than a half pound difference between the two tires. That's a full pound for two tires. Because the tube for the lighter tire is also lighter, you can save upwards of 20 ounces, or well over a pound in weight, by switching to the newer, lighter, narrower-profile tires. Experienced cycle-tourists, like backpackers, go to great lengths to reduce their load, so a pound plus of weight savings can mean a lot on a long trip. Plus there is the fact that the lighter tires, with substantially lower flywheel effect and amount of rubber on the pavement, offer such little rolling resistance that cycling is easier. I will not recommend that you go the limit and use Michelin T55 "Elan" tires which weight 300 grams, however, because under a heavy load these tires just don't hold up well on a tour. I prefer the slightly heavier IRC T52 tires at 340 grams or the Specialized Touring Tire, 27 x 1⅛ inches at 325 grams. See Table 9-1 for a selection, weights and prices of tires I can recommend for touring. All should be available in your local bike shop. I also recommend the 700-centimeter versions of these tires. In fact, I prefer 700-centimeter tires, as I have noted in

Chapter 4, for touring, especially in Europe, where they are standard and where the 27-inch tires are hard to find. Furthermore, if you have been using tubulars, and switch to another set of wheels with 700-centimeter tires and rims, you won't have to relocate brake shoes because both 700-centimeters and tubulars use the same diameter rim.

Tubes for Lightweight Tires

You can use a 27 x 1¼-inch tube in 27 x 1¼-inch and 27 x 1⅛-inch tires and in 700-centimeter tires in both widths. However, for the 27 or 700-centimeter x 1-inch super-lightweight tires, I recommend you use only the 27 x 1-inch tube for a correct fit that resists being blown off the rim. You should be able to buy a lightweight tube for either tire for around $3.50. I prefer rim tape to rim strips, as it is much easier to use, does not bunch up under the valve area, and makes tires easier to mount.

Rims for Lightweight Tires

If you elect to use the super-lightweight Michelin Elan or another 27 inch or 700 centimeter x 1-inch tire, I recommend the Mavic Elan aluminum alloy rim. It weighs 410 grams, costs around $10 and is made especially for these tires, with their narrow profiles. This rim is built like a tubular rim and has ferrules for spoke nipple hole reinforcement. It comes in 27-inch or 700-centimeter diameters. Another excellent rim is the Super Champion (Fig. 9-1) or the similar box type of construction rim (Fig. 9-3) Rigida ALU, both for around $11. The Weinmann model A129 concave rim, also with a box construction for extra strength, is available in 36, 40 or 48 holes, the latter being ideal for tandems. I would use this rim on the 27 x 1¼-inch or 1⅛-inch tire. The Japanese also make a very high-quality rim, the Arraya Model 16 A(2), for 27 x 1¼-inch or 1⅛-inch tires (not 700C). Summing up, I prefer the box construction rims (Fig. 9-3) as they are much stronger than conventional rims. This construction is found in the Mavic Elan, Weinmann A129, Rigida ALU and the Super Champion rims.

Fig. 9-3: Another view of a box-rim construction, made by Super Champion in both 27-inch and 700-centimeter sizes. You will see that there is a roll-over section of the side wall, just above the box, leaving a slight groove into which the tire bead fits.

Valves

You can buy tire tubes with Schraeder (Fig. 9-4) or Presta (Fig. 9-5) valves. I prefer the Presta valves because the valve core is permanently in place. The Presta head Silca pump (Fig. 9-6) is vastly superior to any Schraeder head pump, and it's just a lot easier to pump air into a Presta valve. If you choose the U.S. Schraeder valve, the kind on U.S. car tires, you will need rims with a larger valve hole. Yes, you can drill out a Presta valve hole to fit a Schraeder valve.

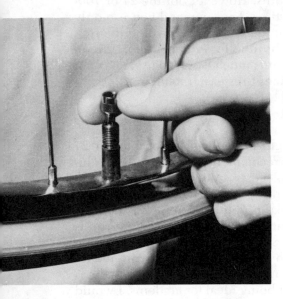

Fig. 9-4: Schraeder valve, used on U.S. auto, motorcycle and bike tubes, has a removeable valve core.

Fig. 9-5: Bicycles imported from Europe, and some U.S. made bikes, may have tubes with a thin Presta valve shown here. These valves require a special pump to fit them, although you can screw on an adapter so you can use an American Schraeder valve pump. Presta valves are easy to break and snap off if you aren't careful about removing the pump.

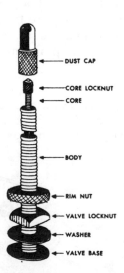

DUST CAP

CORE LOCKNUT
CORE

BODY

RIM NUT

VALVE LOCKNUT

WASHER

VALVE BASE

Fig. 9-6: When inflating a Presta valve, hold the pump firmly on the valve without wiggling, to prevent damage to the valve body.

Tires on Tubular Rims

You can't mount tires on tubular rims, except in the direst of emergencies. If while touring you blow a tire and have no spare, with 700-centimeter rims and some rim cement, you can mount a tubular (if you can find someone who will lend you one) that will get you home or to a bike shop, if you take it easy.

Table 9-1: Lightweight "Tires" *

Make and Model No.	Weight (Grams)†	Size	Retail Price
Specialized Touring	325	27" x 1⅛"	$ 7.50
Specialized Touring	325	700C x 1⅛"	7.50
Specialized Touring	345	27" x 1¼"	7.50
Specialized Touring	345	700C x 1¼"	7.50
Ultra Light	275	27" x 1⅛"	6.98
Ultra Light	275	700C x 1⅛"	6.98
Ultra Light	265	27" x 1"‡	6.98
Ultra Light	265	700C x 1"‡	6.98
Ultra Light	220	700C x 1"‡	7.50
IRC Skinwall	340	27" x 1⅛"	5.88
Michelin Elan	300	27" x 1" and 700C‡	6.88
Michelin 50	470	27" x 1¼" and 700C	4.99
IRC	510‡	27" x 1¼"	4.88
Specialized Touring Folding Turbo	235§	27" x 1⅛"‡ and 700C	12.98
Specialized Touring Folding Turbo-S	195§	27" x 1" and 700C	12.98

* Not tubulars.

† To convert to ounces, multiply by .03527.

‡ Not recommended for tandems, or extensive touring if you and your baggage weigh over 200 pounds. But fine for short trips, day trips and use around town.

§ Not for tandems or extended touring, but great as a spare tire that will get you to the next town if you destroy a tire, as, for example, by ripping the casing by running over a large piece of broken glass, or letting a German Shepherd bite a chunk out of it.

Figure 9-11 shows a folding tire.

Mounting Lightweight Tires

First of all, the new 27-inch or 700-centimeter x 1-inch tires are not mountable on any but the rims made for them (see above). The wire bead of these narrow-profile tires will not seat securely in the wider rims, and you are likely to have a blowout that will put a large hole in the tube and ruin it. If you are lucky, you won't lose control of the bike if this occurs. It has happened to me.

Different rims have different depth sides, from five to seven millimeters, so be careful about seating any narrow-profile tire, even the 1⅛-inch-wide tires. I have found that the best way to seat these tires is to pump them up to about five pounds, run my hand all around the bead area, or the sidewall area, and make doubly sure the tire is well seated, especially around the valve. If the rim strip is double thick at the valve hole, you may not be able to seat the tire at all, in which case, use rim tape instead of the rim strip. Pump the tire up to around 20 psi and check seating again. Finally, blow it up to 100 psi, which is the pressure I like, or even to 115 psi to get the lowest possible rolling resistance. Ride the newly mounted tire for a few blocks, stop and recheck the tire seating. The bend should be well into the rim all the way around on both sides. Bicycle Research has a tire-pinching tool that can help seat these tires (Fig. 9-7).

Be particularly careful when seating the new foldable lightweights,

Fig. 9-7: This tool helps seat the new lightweight, high-pressure tires on the rim. The tire bead must be seated in the groove (see Fig. 9-3).

Fig. 9-8: Comparison of a conventional thin lightweight tube, right, and a thorn-resistant tube, left, which is as heavy as it looks. I would rather fix four or five punctures a day than use one of these tubes, but if I had more flats than that, I think I would use the heavier tube.

such as the Michelin Elan TS. This tire uses a fiberglass instead of a wire rim bead, which is why it is foldable. The fiberglass bead resists seating more than the conventional steel wire bead and is far more likely to pop out.

One note of caution about rims: The Schwinn Super Record tires will not fit on Mavic rims.

Thorn-Resistant Tubes

I am told by a reader, Tom Schipper, of Greeley, Colorado, that the thornproof tubes (on his advice, now called thorn-resistant tubes) do not prevail against the Greeley Goat Head thorns which "must be bigger and longer than any thorns you have ever seen." I believe Tom, and suggest that his solution, the use of Hai! tubes plus a liquid tire sealer, is what works. I think the super-thick thorn-proof tube (Fig. 9-8) should do the trick, though. If you plan to cycle through cactus country, don't say I didn't warn you. True, thorn-proof tubes defeat anything you might do to make wheels lighter, because they weigh more than the light-weight tire. You might just carry along one of these tubes, or two, if you go through Arizona, Western Colorado or any other cactus state. Local bike shops in these states will have them.

Another solution is to dispense with tubes altogether and use an air-less insert (Fig. 9-9). These are heavier still, but you will never get a flat, ever again. You might also never ride your bike, ever again. I think these inserts, as made by Airluz Tire Corp., P.O. Box 218, Port Hueneme, California 93041, are swell for the industrial type bicycle used by ven-dors, *which are never ridden* very fast anyway, and for kids who bike

Fig. 9-9: This tire has a solid rubber in-sert, with no tube as such. Therefore it will not get flat. The tire would be de-stroyed first.

Fig. 9-10: This tire also has a semi-pneumatic, valveless insert. Not even poking a screwdriver through it will cause a flat. Great for industrial bikes that have to run over sharp debris on a factory floor.

fast but don't always see glass on the road. Airluz is coming out, or will have come out by the time you read this book, with inserts for 27 x 1-inch tires and for 2.125 BMX tires. You can poke a screwdriver right through the side wall of a tire (Fig. 9-10) without getting a flat, because the insert is a hollow-core, heavy rubber piece of tubing. Also available for 26 x 1⅜-inch tires. The cost, around $19.95 per insert.

About Pumps

For Presta valves, there is really only one pump I can recommend and that is the Silca Impero fitted with a Campagnolo steel head, for around $10.50. This pump comes in two models, the non-frame-fit type, which requires an umbrella clip (the Campagnolo clip costs $3.98) or the frame fit, which does not require the umbrella clip. I don't like to clip anything to a good bike that will spoil the finish, so I prefer the frame fit. To order the correct size pump (Silcas come in different lengths) to fit your frame, measure the distance between the bottom of the top tube and the top of the downtube where it joins the bottom bracket shell (Fig. 9-12) and bring this measurement to the bike shop. If you have a custom frame with a pump clip brazed on the underneath of the top tube, you should use the non-frame-fit pump if it is long enough to fit your bike. Otherwise, use the frame fit. The frame fit has a contour head and bottom that is shaped to bike tubes and is held in place by compression. When pump

Fig. 9-11: Top, a foldable tubular; bottom, a foldable lightweight conventional tire with a plastic instead of a steel wire bead

Fig. 9-12: Silca pumps come with curved heads that fit the frame, so do not require an umbrella fitting. Measure your frame as shown and order a pump of a length that will fit snugly.

To order: measure this distance in INCHES. Warning: this is NOT frame size!

head parts wear out you can order replacements such as the replacement rubber air chuck gasket.

For Presta valves, you can also use an adapter fitting, (sold in any good bike store for around fifty cents) that will take a Schraeder pump. These little adapters do leak, however, and you can now buy a butyl seal called an Air Nut that fits onto the Presta valve stem and can remain on the stem for future use. The Schraeder adapter fits over the butyl seal for an airtight conversion that makes it far easier to pump. You do have to remove the Air Nut when removing the tire. If your dealer does not have them they are made by Air Nuts, Jason Tech, New York, New York. You might also scout around for a small rubber gasket or seal in your local hardware store that will do the trick. Since it only takes 45 to 50 strokes to fill up a bike tire, it's best that you not use a conventional gas station pump as you're likely to blow out the tubes that way. With care, though, it can be done.

For Schraeder valves I like the Zefal high-pressure frame pump that locks onto the valve for easier pumping. It costs around $9.50 and requires an umbrella clamp. This pump is also available for Presta valves at the same price. I note that some bike catalogs sell the Silca pump with Campy steel head, the frame fit kind, for $14.88, others for $10.50. As far as I can tell, this is the same pump. Pays to shop around. For another $12 a new version of the Zefal pump comes with adapters so you can use it on either Presta or Schraeder valves.

You will find a floor pump handy for starting out on a day trip from the house. A floor pump is faster and easier to use and can pump up to greater pressures than the frame pump. For Presta valves the model in Figure 9-13, fitted with a Presta head, pumps up in about 45 strokes at most; it costs $25. Personally I never use a tire gauge, although the times I have checked my pressures with a gauge I noted around 115 psi. I do it by feel. I like my tires rock hard, so that hard pressure with a finger makes almost no depression on the tire. Or no depression.

For tires with a Schraeder valve, a compound pump with pressure gauge (Fig. 9-14) for around $15, does a great job and can also be used on your car or on a motorcycle or moped. There's also a new compound pump on the market designed by Zefal that gives an accurate readout of

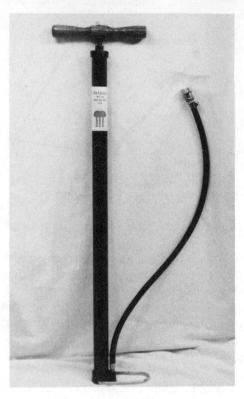

Fig. 9-13: This hand pump will inflate a tubular or conventional tire quickly.

Fig. 9-14: A better pump, with a built-in gauge, is this compound model. (*Schwinn*)

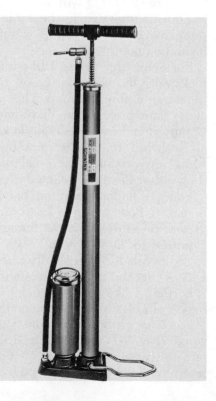

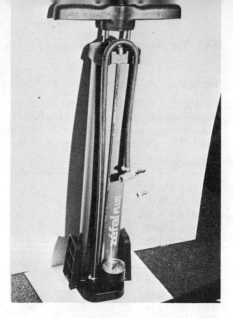

Fig. 9-15: Tires are easier to pump with this two-stage pump with pressure gauge.

tire pressure as you pump, and makes pumping much easier (Fig. 9-15). It sells for around $45.

Another approach is a pump you can plug into your car cigarette lighter (Fig. 9-16) made by Coleman that operates on 12 VDC. It weighs around 5 pounds, costs $39.95, and comes with a 13.5-foot power cord and a 3-foot air hose, with extensions for both as optional extras. The pump can inflate up to 150 psi. Not for rubber rafts or other high volume items, it can be used on air mattresses and tires, footballs, basketballs or air shocks. You can check pressure as you pump, if you have a gauge.

TIRE PRESSURE

Probably the most neglected aspect of tire care is air pressure. Use this tire chart as a guide to correct minimum tire pressure, increasing pressure according to the weight of the rider and any extra load carried. For

Fig. 9-16: Coleman's Inflate-All™ 150 is a reliable air supply that travels with you. It will pump up to 150 psi in minutes and operates off your car battery, drawing only 5.2 amps. Fits any 12-volt cigarette lighter outlet. Includes a 13.5-foot power cord, 3-foot air hose and two air chuck adapters.

Table 9-2 Air Pressure

In general, these are the air pressures you should use with various types of tires. Remember that if you are a bit heavier than average, you should add about five pounds more pressure. If tire bulges markedly, you are too heavy for the pressure used. Tire should not bulge, or at most, bulge very slightly when ridden.

Tire Size	Air Pressure (in lbs. per sq. in.)
12 in. x 1⅜ in.	30–40
16 in. x 1⅜ in.	30–40
18 in. x 1⅜ in.	35–45
20 in. x 1⅜ in.	45–50
24 in. x 2⅛ in.	35–45
26 in. x 1¼ in.	45–50
26 in. x 1⅜ in.	45–50
26 in. x 1¾ in.	30–35
26 in. x 2⅛ in.	35–45
27 in. x 1¼ in.	85–100
700 cm. x 1⅛ in.	85–100
700 cm. x 1 in.	85–100
27-in. tubular tires	Tracks with very smooth surfaces: rear wheels, 100–140; front tires, 90–120
	Tracks with uneven surfaces: rear tires, 90–100; front tires, 90
	Road racing: rear tires, 90–100; front tires, 90, depending on road conditions
	Touring: rear tires, 85–100, depending on load and road conditions; front tires, 85–90

tires used on tandem bicycles, increase above pressures from 10 to 20 pounds per square inch to handle the extra load safely.

NOTE: On cool days one can inflate tires to maximum pressures safely. However, on very hot days, with temperatures in the eighties and higher, it is safer to reduce pressures by 3 to 5 pounds under the maximum to avoid heat buildup. Air expands as it heats, and on a hot day, you could experience a blowout if your bike stands exposed to the sun.

HOW TO REPAIR TIRES

Why Tires Go Flat

Underinflated tires put more tire tread on the road and use up more energy by flexing and creating heat, which makes the bicycle considerably harder to pedal.

An underinflated tire cannot take bumps and stones, and ordinary contact with pavement roughness can be sufficient to force the tire casing inward far enough to pinch the tube against the metal wheel rim. This can cause a blowout and might even bruise the tire casing beyond repair, causing a flat spot on the rim that cannot be pulled out. Here are some common types of tire damage and how to avoid them.

Glass damage causes knifelike cuts on the tread or the sidewall. To avoid running over glass and similar sharp objects, watch the road just in front of you as you ride. If you ride at night, ride only on roads with which you are familiar and know are not likely to have glass, and use a good light to detect glass as far in advance as possible to give you time to swing out of the way. (Watch out for passing cars—swing right instead of left if you can to avoid glass.)

Blowouts can be caused by overinflation (Fig. 9-17), underinflation, and tire-casing damage such as glass cuts. A glass wound (Fig. 9-18) will open and close as the tire casing flexes and will eventually pinch a hole in the tire tube. This is why you should always look for the *cause* of a flat after a patch has been applied to the tube.

Nails and other sharp objects such as fine pieces of wire will cause a flat by piercing both tire and tube. Be sure to remove the nail before reinstalling the tire and tube. If the nail is still in the tire when you go to repair it, it will be a good guide to the location of the leak in the tube.

Ruptures (Fig. 9-19) are *always* a sign of abuse, barring accidents. Riding up and down curbs, into sharp stones and curbs, is a sure invitation to ruptures and a very short tire life.

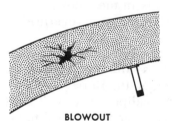

BLOWOUT

Fig. 9-17: Puncture due to overinflation

STAR BREAK

Fig. 9-18: Star break in tire casing caused by riding over stones or other sharp objects. May not be visible from outside, so always check inside of casing when repairing a flat.

RUPTURE

Fig. 9-19: Slit type of damage to tire caused by jumping curbs, hitting sharp objects at high speed, forcing casing against rim.

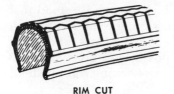

RIM CUT

Fig. 9-20: Rim cuts caused by underinflated tires. Cuts are evidence of excessive flexing.

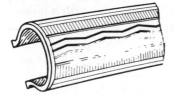

UNEVEN TREAD WEAR

Fig. 9-21: Uneven tire wear caused by skidding brake stops, uneven rims. (*Figs. 9-17 through 9-21 courtesy Schwinn Bicycle Company*)

Rim cuts (Fig. 9-20) are long, thin-looking cuts in the sidewalls and are caused by riding an underinflated tire, rusty rims, or an overloaded bicycle.

Uneven tread wear (Fig. 9-21) can be due to crooked rims, quick stops that grab and lock the wheel (otherwise known as skidding to a stop for kicks), or out-of-adjustment caliper brakes that grab the rim. Out-of-true rims also cause excessive tire wear because the caliper brake will grab at the out-of-true spot. It is a good idea to look far enough ahead to be able to avoid sudden stops, for your own as well as for your tires' longevity.

Other common kinds of tube failures or punctures include:

When the tire is under-inflated, the tube can slide around the rim and pull the valve stem out of the seat, as shown. This could also be a manufacturing defect. Always check new tubes for defects before leaving the store (Fig. 9-22).

Blowout. This is what happens to the new lightweight tires, especially the one-inch diameter sizes when used on a too large rim or not seated properly in the rim. (Fig. 9-23).

Failure at the joining (Fig. 9-24). This is a manufacturer's defect and if found, get your money back.

A genuine puncture. Looks as though it was caused by a nail (Fig. 9-25).

When you pinch the tube with a tire iron, you can cause a slit such as the one in Figure 9-26.

Fig. 9-22: Arrow points to ruptured valve. This is what happens when the tire is underinflated, permitting the tube to slide around the rim.

Fig. 9-23: Blow-out caused by sudden departure of the tire from the rim. Improperly seated tires will lift out of the rim groove, permitting the section of the tube nearest the point of lift-off to protrude and blow out. Illustrates the importance of being earnest about tire-bead setting when mounting a new tire. Older tires have stretched some, are easier to mount so beads drop into rim groove.

Fig. 9-24: Failure where the tube is joined illustrates a manufacturer's defect. Get your money back, or a new tube.

Fig. 9-25: This is a puncture, very likely by a nail.

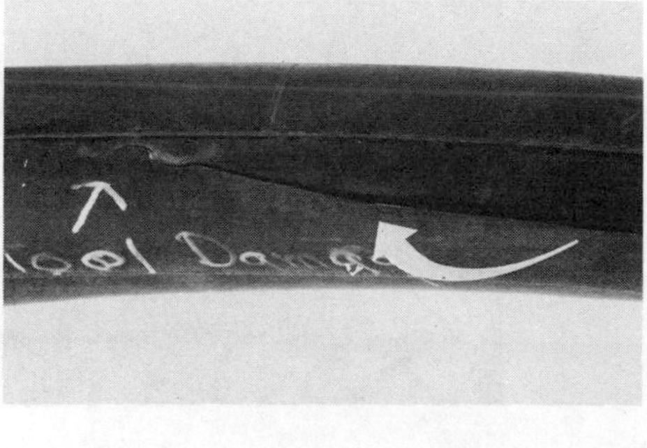

Fig. 9-26: If you are not careful when replacing tire on rim, it's very, very easy to puncture a slit like this into the tube with whatever you are using to pry the tire back on the rim, particularly at those last few mean old stubborn inches. Watch that you don't pinch the tube between the tool and the rim. This is where this type of pinch damage occurs. Use tire irons, not a sharp-edged screwdriver.

Fig. 9-27: Again, an underinflated tire will permit tube to slip around rim. Because valve is in the rim hole, when the tube slips the valve stays more or less in place until torn loose, as shown. The solution: keep tires inflated to maximum permitted pressure, plus four or five more psi.

An underinflated tire can move around on the rim and tear the valve out. Check your tires frequently. If valve becomes cocked to one side, deflate and move tire on rim until valve is straightened. Figure 9-27 shows this type of damage.

Steps in Tire Repair

STEP ONE: If the tire goes flat overnight, you may have either a tiny puncture or a slow leak through the valve. You can check for a valve core leak by removing the valve cap (Figs. 9-4 and 9-28), inflating the tire to normal pressure, and putting a bit of soapy water in the valve. If the valve leaks, you will see bubbles. In this case, all you need to do is tighten the valve core. If the valve still leaks, replace the valve core with a new one. You will need an old-fashioned metal valve cap to tighten or remove the core. This is available from any bicycle shop and most service stations.

STEP TWO: To repair a tube puncture you will need two flat-end tire levers, or two dull-edge, broad-blade screwdrivers, to pry the tire off and put it on. First, remove the valve core from the valve, with a valve cap. If there is a locknut on the valve stem, remove it from the stem. If a Presta valve, unscrew the valve and depress to deflate.

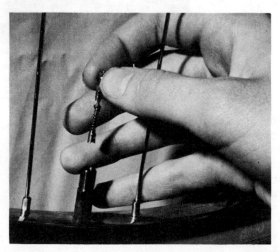

Fig. 9-28: Schraeder valve cores can be removed to get all the air out of a slow-leaking tube so you can pry the tire off the rim, or partially off the rim to get at the tube to install a patch.

STEP THREE: You usually do not need to remove the wheel if you're on the road and touring. Even with saddlebags or carriers in the way, you can attack the repair by removing the tire in the vicinity of the puncture, pulling out the tube, and patching it as described below. Otherwise, remove the wheel and, with the two tire levers, pry one side of the tire away from the rim until one side is loose enough to pull all the way off. Remove the tire by hand from the other side of the rim.

STEP FOUR: Inflate the tube and rotate it near your ear until you find the location of the puncture by hearing the hiss of escaping air. Draw a circle around the puncture with a piece of chalk. If you can't find it by listening for escaping air, immerse the tube in a tub of water and watch for bubbles as you rotate the tube in the water. Hold your finger in the puncture area while you dry the tube off thoroughly. Mark the puncture with a piece of chalk.

STEP FIVE: With a piece of sandpaper or the metal abrader that comes with tire repair kits, scrape the tube around the puncture and put a thin layer of rubber cement around it, extending outward about a half inch in all directions. Let the rubber cement get tacky, pull the paper backing off the appropriate-sized tube patch, and press the patch firmly down onto the coated area over the puncture. Be careful, in handling the tube patch, not to finger the patch over the coated area where you have removed the paper covering. Hold the patch carefully by the edges until you have pressed it into place over the puncture.

STEP SIX: While the rubber under the patch is drying, check the outside of the tire carefully and pry out any embedded glass, nails, and the like. Remember, *something* caused that tire to go flat, and that something is most likely still embedded in the tire. Then, spreading the tire apart as you go, check the inside walls for any breaks. Breaks, if not too bad, can be patched with a tire patch. However, if the tire has bad cuts or bruises, discard it and buy a new one. Check for loose spokes, and tighten them. Remove the rubber strip inside the wheel and check to make sure all spokes are flush with the spoke nipples. File down any protruding spokes to prevent a later puncture, and replace the rubber strip. Realign the rim, if necessary, as discussed in Chapter 15.

STEP SEVEN: Install the tire on the wheel. First, make sure most but not all the air is out of the tube. Tuck the tube carefully back into the tire. Put the valve into the valve hole in the rim. Next, starting at the valve, with hands on either side of the wheel, push the beaded edge of the tire all the way around until one side of the tire is on the rim. Then push the other side of the tire on the rim in the same manner. You should not need to use the tire levers to install the tire. But if you do use them, make sure that when you have the lever pushed up under the tire, you do not pinch the tube between the lever and the rim and cause a puncture. Inflate the tire and check for leaks before remounting the wheel. To make sure the bead is set, before inflating, shove down on the valve stem so it will seat. Then inflate to around five pounds. Remove the pump and rotate the wheel to make sure the bead is seated all the way around. Any bulges should be removed by deflating the tire and reseated by pushing the bead in.

TIRE AND WHEEL ALTERNATIVES

When the bike boom began and fine European bicycles began to be in demand in the United States, we all quickly found out that we were really getting road-racing machines with short wheelbases, low fork rakes (e.g. 1–½ inches) and wheels with tubulars. Somehow we learned to demand bikes that would be more suitable for touring, ones that would absorb road shock and yet be reasonably light and efficient. So around 1973 bicycles were built with longer wheelbases and longer fork rakes for comfort, but nothing was done about the tires until a year or two later, when the new lightweight tires began to replace tubulars. Meanwhile, millions of us got stuck with tubulars on our touring bikes. I recommend you switch to the new lightweight narrow-profile tires, of course, and abandon tubulars altogether for touring, for reasons already stated. You can scrap the tubular rims, cut the spokes with cutting pliers and, using the old hub, lace on rims suitable for the lightweight tires, as noted earlier in this chapter.

Another alternative is to simply keep the old tubulars and tubular rims and hubs intact and use them for day trips on country roads. For touring you can then buy a complete tire, rim and hub, ready to install on your bicycle. If you're going to be doing a lot of touring, I would recommend the complete wheel with a sealed-bearing hub such as the Avocet, Phil Wood, Durham or Hi-E. You should be able to get a set of wheels made up with hubs and using Robergel high-tension spokes for around $80 to $90, depending on the hub. You can get 48-spoke tandem wheels made up for around $120 each. For stronger wheels, specify Robergel 3 star spokes. These are stainless steel finish, double-butted.

What's New in Tubulars

For those of you who use tubulars, either for racing or touring, there have been a number of new types of tubulars introduced in recent years. These include:

The Wolber Liberty. I don't have a price on this tire, it's so new. Check with your dealer. It's made of Egyptian Cotton and has an internal coating that's claimed to be airtight. It has no tube and can only be repaired from the outside, which, believe me, when you see the rigamarole you have to go through to repair conventional tubulars, is a real advantage. The tire will fit only tubular rims and weighs 260 grams, fairly light. To repair, you use a special metal tube that has a hollow needle which is to be inserted in the puncture. A key in the needle is turned which releases sealing material. It's all fairly simple and about a thousand percent faster than repairing conventional tubulars. The only problem I can see is finding a pin hole leak. You will have to remove the wheel, and with the tire still on, dunk it in water until you find bubbles (inflating the tire at the same time, of course). Tubeless tubulars are not new. They were the only tire around on bikes in this country until around 1935 or so, and we repaired them by removing the valve core, pouring in sour milk and letting it harden, while simultaneously rotating the tire. This was fine for tiny punctures. Bigger ones we fixed by plugging the hole with rubber bands dunked in rubber cement. Tire repair in those days was a mystique and we all had our favorite sealants. Mine was sour condensed milk.

Puncture-resistant tubulars are made by Clement and Vittoria. The Clement has a latex tube which has sufficient elasticity to stretch when penetrated by a sharp object and not puncture. The tube can stretch up to one inch when sharp objects, such as nails, penetrate it. The Vittoria approach is to fill the tube with sealant, so that any puncture up to $5/32$ of an inch will seal without loss of air, provided the wheel is in motion. Both makes of tire come with two-piece detachable Presta valves, which permit adding sealant and replacement of a broken valve tip.

Selecting Tubulars

There is a wide selection of tubulars for the racing cyclist. There are tires for rainy days, for off-the-road cyclo-cross racing, and for sprints. The type of tread design will be determined by the type of race and the conditions under which it will be run. Table 9-3 gives a selection of tubulars for various types of racing and racing conditions. There are many more tubulars available; those in the table will give you an idea as to types, weights and prices.

Tubular tubes are either of butyl rubber or natural gum rubber. The latter is somewhat permeable to air and will require pumping up every day on a tour. Make it a ritual; as you get ready to leave the campsite, your final chore should be pumping up the old tubes. Lately tubulars have been coming in butyl, which are not so permeable and will hold their pressure for at least a week or two. I agree with Gene Portuesi, the former Olympic bicycle team coach, that butyl tubes in tubular tires are "a contradiction; the proper procedure for long tubular life is to deflate them from extreme pressure after a long ride." Gene agrees that tubulars can stretch and thus be damaged if not deflated for storage or even overnight. Furthermore, the purpose of cycling is primarily exercise and enjoyment. Why boggle at a little exercise in pumping up the tires, for as Portuesi notes, the pumping up of a tubular can be done in twenty strokes or so, and this exercise is a good warm-up procedure. So butyl tubes merely add weight, decrease the opportunity for exercise and shorten the life of tubulars by inviting you not to deflate them after each ride. Muscles of the upper torso are needed in cycling, and the few minutes of pumping action can help strengthen them.

Care of Tubulars

If you do a lot of racing and/or like touring with tubulars, I advise you to stock up a year in advance and age them for longer life. Aging is necessary because new "raw" tubulars, whether the casing is cotton, silk, polyester or nylon, are latex impregnated and the latex is soft when new. As time passes, the latex bonding with casing fibers toughens. If you ride with new tubulars you are much more prone to flats and the tread may separate from the casing, which you definitely do not want to happen to your good $30 silks. The best way to age tubulars is to mount them on old rims, hang them up in a cool, dark, dry place for six months. A year would be better. In the off-season, never leave the bicycle with tubulars on the ground; hand the bike from the ceiling so the tubulars won't take a "set."

With age, tubular casings tend to dry out, become brittle and crack or show "craze" marks. The rubber coating actually evaporates. You can avoid or at least delay this deterioration by applying a latex solution on sidewalls, over sidewall cuts and use it to glue down the base tape onto the tubular casing after repairing (see below). If your bike shop does not have this sealant, order from Palo Alto Bicycles, P.O. Box 1276, Palo Alto, California 94302 for $1.50 for a four-ounce container.

You should, of course, always carry a spare tubular even on day trips. There's where tubulars have a real advantage over tires: You can change a tubular in two minutes or less, even on the back wheel, but replacing a tire takes upwards of ten or fifteen minutes, at least. (It's when you get home that all the time is used in repairing the punctured tubular. But at least on the road, if you're with a group, you won't hold anyone up for long if all you have to do is strip off the punctured tubular and roll on a good one.)

Do not leave spares folded on bicycles longer than two weeks. Remove the spare, inflate lightly, let it stand overnight, deflate, and reroll. This prevents spares from taking a "set" on the folds. In refolding, fold the opposite way so that the part that was on the inside is now on the outside. However, always fold so that the tread is on the outside. When folded, mount the spare so that it cannot rub or chafe anywhere. Ideally, you should carry it in a plastic bag.

Valves should be protected against dirt with a light plastic dust cap. Remember to close the valve on the spare. Open, it can be easily bent.

Extra spares should always be stored lightly inflated, in a warm, dry place. Be very careful not to store tubulars that have become wet, unless you inflate them so they can dry out.

For safety, particular if you do a lot of riding, check rim cement frequently. If you are on a tour, check rim cement at least weekly, because this cement can dry out and flake off. Rim cement is absolutely essential to keep tires from creeping and crawling.

On the road, protect spare tubulars against road dirt with plastic cloth. *And before you leave on a long trip, check rim cement to make sure it hasn't dried out.* Try to pry the tubular off with your fingers. If it lifts easily, the cement is dry. Remove tubular, old cement, and recement. Do try to keep rim cement off side walls; that makes for a fast, skidding stop every time, and it's messy, besides.

If you carry your bicycle, be careful not to let the tires rub on any metal or wooden parts. Check the placement of wheels against car seats, carrying racks, toe straps, and tie-down straps.

Never let oil, grease, kerosene, gasoline, rubber cement or any other kind of solvent touch your tubulars. Solvents will eventually eat right through your tubular.

When you're car-carrying tubulars, partially deflate them so the hot sun won't heat the air inside the tube, causing a blow-out. Keep tubulars from rubbing anything; preferable use a cover. You can make a cover out of an old 27 x 1¼-inch tire casing by removing its wire bead.

Don't fill tubulars with CO_2 because it leaks out even faster than air. If you use a pressure cartridge, use nitrogen.

If you realign your rim, remember that retensioning spokes can cause spoke heads to protrude and puncture the tube. Remove the tubular, and check and file off any protruding spoke heads.

On an airplane trip, if you bring your bicycle, remember to half deflate your tubulars (or tires); because if your bicycle is stored in an unpressurized or partly pressurized baggage compartment, the low pressures at high altitudes may permit the high pressures inside the tube to cause a blowout.

Tire Savers

Experienced cyclists have learned to rub a gloved hand over the tire every so often during a trip, or whenever they think the tire has rolled over something that might puncture it. Quite often you can remove tiny sharp items this way, before they've had a chance to work their way through the casing and the tube. This applies to all tires, but especially to tubulars and the new lightweight tires.

Sometimes it's difficult or impossible to reach tires when panniers or a handlebar bag are in the way, and if you're not careful, it's not too difficult to get your hand caught between the tire and the brake bridge, which can be a painful experience at best and cause a spill at worst. Which is why I strongly urge you to cycle only with double thick palm cool bike gloves (Fig. 9-32) which cost about $8.50 in any good bike

Table 9-3 Tubular Selections

Make and Model	Weight (Grams)	Casing Material	Width (mm)	Tube	Vulcanized	Cold Processed	Applications*	Cost
Clement No. 3 Pista Seta	145	Silk	20	Gum		Yes	Track. For flat, smooth surfaces	$30
Clement No. 1 Pista Seta	175	Silk	20	Gum		Yes	Track. For flat, smooth surfaces	22
Hutchinson Special Seta	180	Silk	23	Gum		Yes	Track, flat, rough surfaces	25
Clement Sie Giorni 8 BIS	190	Cotton	21	Gum		Yes	Track, flat, rough surfaces	22
Clement Criterium 1 BIS	195	Silk	24	Gum		Yes	Criterium, road, time trials, flat, rough surfaces	30
Hutchinson Krono	210	Cotton	22	Gum		Yes	Same	21
Clement Criterium 6	220	Silk	24.5	Gum		Yes	Criterium, road, time trials, light use, flat and rough surfaces	29
Hutchinson Super Corsa	250	Cotton	24	Gum		Yes	Same	20
Clement 12BIS	260	Cotton	25	Gum		Yes	Road racing or touring	22
Hutchinson Corsa Leggero	270	Cotton	25	Gum		Yes	Racing or touring. Long life	18
Michelin Nibbio	275	Cotton	26	Butyl	Yes		Racing or touring	12
Hutchinson 80 GTX	290	Cotton	24	Butyl	Yes		Touring, training	11
Clement Campionato del Mundo 13	310	Silk	29	Butyl		Yes	Touring, distance riding. The old reliable	30
Michelin Falco	320	Cotton	28	Butyl	Yes		Touring, general purpose, training	10
Hutchinson Cross TR	380	Cotton	28	Butyl	Yes		Touring, all surfaces	11
Clement Veltro 21	370	Cotton	26	Butyl	Yes		All-rounder, touring, training	12
Clement Elvezia 24	440	Cotton	28	Butyl	Yes		All terrain, touring, very tough	11

*Treads vary depending on application. Track tubulars should be inflated from 120 to 140 psi; road racing from 100 to 130 psi; heavier road racing, training and touring, to 120 psi; and general use up to 120 psi.

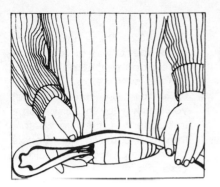
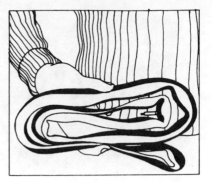

Fig. 9-29: Fold a spare tubular as shown. Valve should be located as indicated at right, where it cannot chafe the tubular.

Fig. 9-30: Carry a spare tubular, folded, under the saddle. Tire carrier shown is made by Vittoria. You can also use a pedal strap.

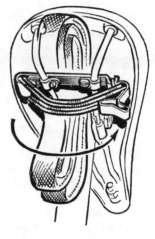

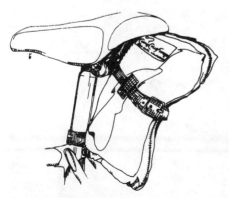

Fig. 9-31: It's a good idea to carry spare tubulars in a pouch to protect them from ultraviolet-ray and heat damage from the sun, and from road dust and water. This waterproof nylon pouch will hold up to two spare tubulars (or foldable tires) and a few other small items such as a patch kit. *(Palo Alto Bicycles)*

Fig. 9-32: These gloves are made specially for bicyclists. They have a double-thick palm so you can rub over tires as you pedal, to remove any foreign objects you think may have become imbedded in the tire, before they can cause a flat. Double palm also protects your palm in case of a fall.

store. These gloves can also save a lot of skin on the palm of your hand in the event of a fall.

Back to tire savers. You can also mount a pair of tire savers (Fig. 9-33) onto brake bolts, and adjust them to rub lightly over the tires. Use them on tubulars and tires. They cost around $1.50 a pair and are cheap insurance against punctures. At least they help scrape off stuff you do not notice as you ride.

Fig. 9-33: These "tire savers" can be used for both tubulars and conventional tires. They fasten onto brake-mounting bolts, rub lightly over tire treads to scrape off any small pieces of glass, nails and other objects that would work their way through the tread and casing into the tube. The tire savers do not work well on heavier tires because puncture-causing objects can lodge in the deeper tread indentations where the savers can't reach them. Use savers only on tubulars and on the lightest high-pressure tires.

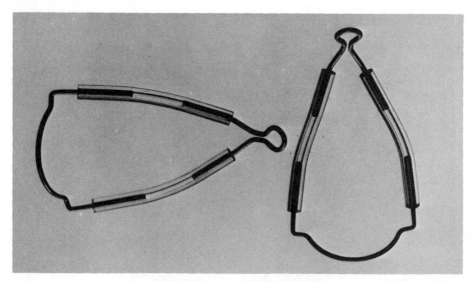

Rims for Tubulars

The lighter the rim, the less rolling and braking resistance, other things being equal. If you're using tubulars for touring or training, though, you want a rim that will stand up under road shock, minor bumps and the pressure of a load of camping gear. You may elect for the lightest rim you think you can get away with, and that's okay, as long as you stick to road rims and don't try to tour with rims designed only for racing. The racing cyclist is generally going to be riding fast on a fairly smooth surface, not carrying anything but himself and perhaps a water bottle and so is putting less stress on the wheels than you will if you tour with a gear-laden bicycle. Because wheels generally hit first in an accident, they deform first, and absorb much of the impact. If you use a forty-eight spoked steel rim on the front wheel you will have a very strong wheel, indeed, but there will be very little energy-absorbing deflection in a normal collision. As a matter of fact, if you have time to think about it and know it's unavoidable, try to hit whatever you must wheel-first.

I learned about the strength of a wheel the hard way, by running into the back of a black Cadillac on a dark street on a January night. I was traveling at about 15 miles per hour, not paying enough attention, obviously, to what was ahead and creamed this car wheel-first. I hit hard enough to bend the steering tube of a double-butted Reynolds '531' tubing lugged frame. But the aluminum alloy, tubular-equipped rim never even went out of true. I am using it to this day, and that was in 1963.

Hi-E Engineering, Inc.; 1247 School Lane, Nashville, Tennessee 37217 makes a unique line of aluminum rims that are the lightest or nearly the lightest on the market at 250 grams for the heavy-duty version. This is only 9 ounces. Their rims are made of 2024 T 4 aluminum sheet, doubled on the inside for greater strength at spoke holes, which are formed with hollow rivets in the center of the rim. This location of spoke holes permits a wide variety of spoke configurations. The lighter-weight Hi-E rim, for light duty, weighs in at only 199 grams (7 ounces). Model 240 is available with 28, 32, 36 and 40 spoke holes, weighs 199 grams and is anodized a silvery finish. Use this rim primarily for time trials or for general-purpose racing if you weigh less than 150 pounds. You can use this rim with up to 180 pounds, but expect a shorter rim life. This rim costs $14.50. The heavier-duty Hi-E Model 241 costs $14.50 also, with the same drilling options.

For training and heavier riders, the Super Champion 350 gram rim is 21.5 millimeters wide, in 36-spoke hole drilling only, and is an economical rim at $9.90. This is an alloy rim.

An excellent all-purpose road rim is the Super Champion Arc-en Ciel at 330 grams, 36 spoke holes, 20-millimeter width, at $10.98.

Another excellent all-purpose rim, with smooth sides, is the Fiamme Red Label at 360 grams, 36 holes, smooth side walls, at $9.98.

A fine road or criterium racing rim is the Fiamme Ergal yellow label smooth-sided rim at 290 grams, 36 holes, at $14.98.

For heavy riders, rough use or where an extremely strong but light-weight rim is required, I can recommend the rather expensive Super Champion Performance tubular rim at 265 grams, 36 holes. It's made of alloys specially hardened in a time-consuming tempering process. Cost: $49.98.

For smooth surfaces such as tracks, and for lighter riders, the Super Champion Medaille d'Or at 260 grams and a choice of 28, 32 and 36 spoke hole drillings, costs $13.98.

In general, use rims from 390 to 420 grams for the heavier rider, such as the Super Champion Etoile at 390 grams, 20 millimeters width, 36 spoke holes, at $11.75.

Lighter rims from 340 to 370 grams are fine for heavier riders or for training. Track racing rims generally weigh from 270 to 285 grams for such events as match sprints, six-day races and team races. The really flyweight rims, from 195 to 230 or so grams are basically used where flywheel effect, inertia and rolling resistance must be at an absolute minimum, where the riding surface is smooth and the ultimate in lightness is sought.

How to Repair Tubular Tires

To repair tubular tires, you will have to cut a few stitches in the area where the puncture is located, repair the puncture, and restitch the tire. To repair tubulars, follow this procedure:

STEP ONE: You will need a patch set (Fig. 9-34) consisting of:

- Special thin tube patches (such as the ones made by Dunlop)
- A triangular-pointed hand-sewing needle
- Tubular tire linen thread
- Rubber cement
- A small tube of talc powder
- A small piece of yellow chalk
- A small screwdriver
- A sharp knife or razor blade
- A small square of fine sandpaper

Most of the bicycle mail-order houses sell a tubular tire repair kit with most of the above items. The reason for the extra-thin tube patches is that tubulars have a very thin tube. An ordinary tire patch is far too thick for this tube and would cause a lump inside the tubular which would thump as you ride. Thin patches are especially needed for the lighter track-racing tubulars, which are generally handmade from silk cord and rubber latex. An old piece of tubular tube will do in an emergency.

Fig. 9-34: Here is a tubular-tire surgical repair kit, everything you need to repair the tubular—scalpel, needle, suture thread, pincers, patches, scrapers, compounds. Not shown is shellac, used only on nonrubberized base strip of track tubulars.

STEP TWO: If you have an old rim, mount the tubular on the rim, inflate it to sixty or seventy pounds of air pressure, and set the tire and rim in a half-filled washtub. Or simply remove the tubular from the wheel, inflate as above, and put it, a bit at a time, into the washtub. If you can see no puncture, you could have a loose or torn valve or a puncture at the valve area (Fig. 9-35).

Fig. 9-35: Step Three in tubular repair: Dunk tubular in water to find location of leak before cutting base-strip threads.

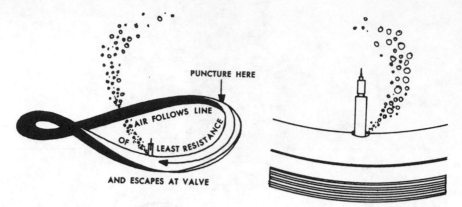

Fig. 9-36: Sometimes you can get a false reading on the location of the leak because air follows the path of least resistance and escapes around valve. Never accept bubbles at the valve as prima facie evidence; keep checking for another air-bubble location.

STEP THREE: As you insert the tubular into the tub of water, you will notice that a lot of air seems to be bubbling up from around the valve stem first (Fig. 9-36). The tubular is sewn and has a rubber-cemented strip over the sewing, so this is about the only place air *can* escape, except through the puncture itself.

Rotate the tubular slowly until you come to the spot where air is seeping out through a small puncture in the tire casing. With a piece of yellow chalk, mark this area; it is also the location of the tube puncture. Deflate the tubular and remove it from the rim.

STEP FOUR: With the small screwdriver or another flat (but not sharp!) tool, carefully pry about two-and-a-half inches of the tape on both sides of the puncture away from the inner circumference of the tire (Fig. 9-37).

STEP FIVE: With the razor or small sharp knife, carefully cut the stitching about two inches on either side of the puncture. Do not cut down *into* the tire, but insert the knife edge under the stitching and cut upward to avoid cutting into the tube, which lies just under the stitching (Figs. 9-38 and 9-39).

STEP SIX: Pull about four inches of the tube out gently and, with a hand pump, inflate the tube enough to find the puncture (Fig. 9-40). With the yellow chalk, outline the puncture, centering it in a chalked circle about the size of a quarter. A simple way to find the puncture is to hold the tube near your lips and rotate it slowly. You should be able to feel the flow of air from the puncture. If you can't find the puncture this way, put a drop of liquid soap in a glass, fill it with warm water, and place this mixture on the tube until you find a bubble marking the location of the puncture.

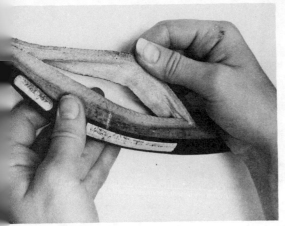

Fig. 9-37: Step Four: Pull away base strip.

Fig. 9-38: Step Five: Cut base stitching.

Fig. 9-39: Step Five: Remove old stitching.

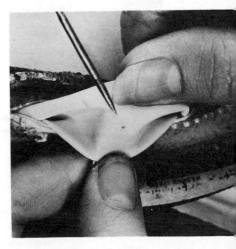

Fig. 9-40: Step Six: Pull out tube, locate puncture.

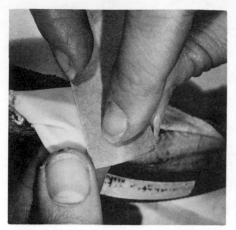

Fig. 9-41: Step Seven: Abrade tube lightly.

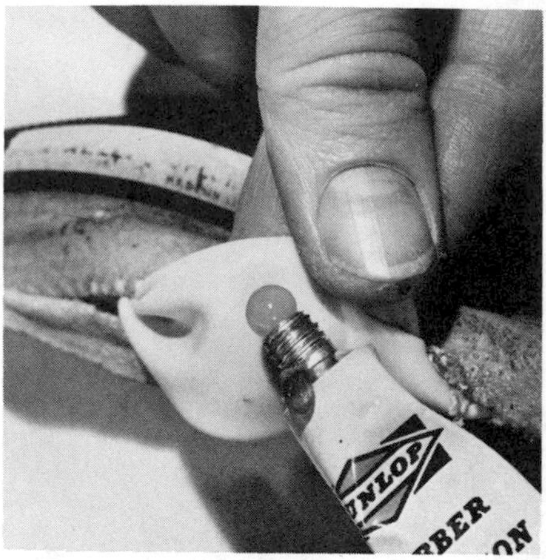

Fig. 9-42: Step Eight: Apply rubber cement, let dry till tacky.

Fig. 9-43: Step Nine: Apply patch.

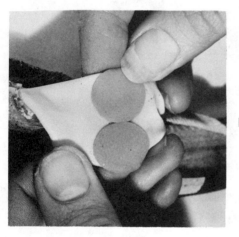

Fig. 9-44: Step Ten: Push tube back in casing.

STEP SEVEN: Dry the tube thoroughly, if you have wet it. With the sandpaper, abrade lightly the area you have marked off around the puncture, putting a small, solid object under the tube to support it as you rub it with the sandpaper (Fig. 9-41).

STEP EIGHT: Apply several light coatings of rubber cement to the area abraded. Let each coating dry to a hard glaze (Fig. 9-42).

STEP NINE: Apply a patch of finest-grade thin rubber to the tube over the puncture. Dust with talcum powder to prevent the tube from sticking to the casing. Note that two patches have been applied to this tube. This is because whatever caused the flat often goes through *both sides* of the tube, so you should check the other side of the tube from where you found the first puncture to make sure *that* side also hasn't been penetrated (Figs. 9-43 and 9-44).

STEP TEN: Reinflate the tube slightly with the hand pump. Check the area for further punctures. Deflate the tube.

STEP ELEVEN: Inspect the tire casing for damage, such as bruises, gouges, rips, tears and the rare manufacturing defect (Figs. 9-45 and 9-46). If the tire casing itself is damaged, I recommend relegating the tire to the spare-use-only category, because although the casing damage can be patched with a thin piece of canvas applied with rubber cement, if the bruise or hole is small, even this patch will bulge and cause the tire to "thump" annoyingly, especially at high speeds. Tubular-tire repair kits do come with a special piece of canvas for this purpose, but I recommend its use for emergency situations only. Patched tires can, of course, serve ideally as spares.

STEP TWELVE: Sew up the tire, using the triangular-pointed needle and doubled thread. In an emergency, a twelve-pound-test linen thread or double thread *silk* fishing line will do. Nylon line won't serve the purpose; it cuts into the tire. Start by sewing back about a half inch over the cut stitching. Use a simple overhand stitch to finish the stitching, running the thread about a half inch through *existing* holes left from the manufacturer's original stitching. Don't make new holes. Pull stitches firmly, but don't overdo it or you'll cut the tire casing (Fig. 9-47).

STEP THIRTEEN: Apply rubber cement over the area revealed when you peeled back the protective tape over the stitching and on the tape itself (Fig. 9-48). Let dry. Carefully lay tape back in position.

STEP FOURTEEN: Mount the tire, inflate to riding pressure, and check again for leaks. Leave inflated so rubber cement has a chance to dry thoroughly.

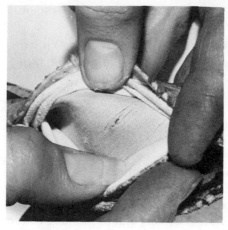

Fig. 9-45: Step Eleven: Reinstall tube cover.

Fig. 9-46: Step Eleven: Make sure tube cover is smooth, like a bed sheet.

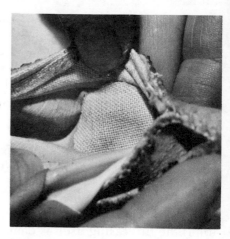

Fig. 9-47: Step Twelve: Begin cross-over stitching.

Fig. 9-48: Step Thirteen: With dilute solution of rim cement, replace base strip. Use shellac on track tubulars.

Fig. 9-49: Step Fourteen: Inflate, check for leaks.

STEP FIFTEEN: Fill in any cuts in the tread with black rubber cement (*not* patch cement) that comes with your patch kit, or with black plastic rubber cement you can buy in a hardware store (Fig. 9-49).

For Track Tubulars

If you are fastening track tubulars you should always use shellac. Track tires have a cotton or silk nonrubberized base tape which is best cemented with shellac. Road tires have a rubberized base tape, and these are secured best on the rim with a rubber solution such as Clement. More about road tires later.

If the track rim is new it should be scored with a rough file so that the smooth bed is roughened for better adhesion. The lighter silks may puncture just from pressure over the nipple holes, so if you wish, these may be filled with tight-fitting corks which should then be filed flush with the rim base so as to present a smooth, unbroken surface.

Don't apply one thick coat of shellac. It's far better to apply two or three coats to the rim, allowing each coat to dry thoroughly before applying the next coat. Drying time depends on temperature and humidity. What we are looking for is a smooth bed of shellac on the rim. Any shellac which has strayed over onto the rim sides should be carefully scraped away.

Now that the rim is prepared, let's work on the tire. Inflate the tire so it is just beginning to feel firm, with around five or six strokes of the pump. Remove any rubber solution which may have adhered to the base tape in the manufacturing process. Thin out the shellac solution and brush it carefully on the base tape and allow it to dry. What we want to do here is fill the cotton- or silk-weave base tape with shellac for proper adhesion. This is an important step, because otherwise the base tape will not adhere firmly to the shellac on the rim.

At this point, go back to the rim and give it one final coat of shellac and let it dry for ten to forty minutes, depending on the temperature, until it gets tacky, or a bit less than tacky.

Adhering Road Tires

Road tires should be stuck on the rim with mastic, a form of rubber cement. Look for Tubasti, Vittoria, or Pastali glue.

If this is not a new rim, remove all old glue (this applies also to track rim shellac) with a paint remover or Bullshot Rimstrip. Apply Rimstrip to the rim, wait for a couple of hours, then wipe the rim clean. Follow with a hot soap and water bath to remove the Rimstrip completely. If the rim is new or has not been scored, do so with a rough file for maximum adhesion.

If the road tubular has a nonrubberized cotton base tape, fill the base tape weave with a thinned-out solution of rim cement, using one of the brands noted above. Some of the base tapes of this type of tubular are sort of fluffy, and unless filled with a thin solution of rim cement, adhesion will not be secure. If the road tubular has a rubberized base tape, you need only apply the rim cement to the rim (Fig. 9-50). In either case, do not wait for the cement to dry on the rim or the tubular, but fit the tubular right on the rim as soon as possible. Wipe or scrap any rim cement that may have slopped over onto the rim sides. Now follow these steps in putting the tubular on the rim:

STEP ONE: Deflate tubular almost completely, leaving just enough air to give the tire a little body. Hold wheel in an upright position and insert valve through the valve hole in the rim (Fig. 9-51).

STEP TWO: With the valve at the top of the wheel and the wheel on a soft pad on the floor, stand behind the wheel and with both hands push the tubular downward onto the rim, finishing on the side opposite the valve (Fig. 9-52). Hold the rim away from your body while you're doing this—or wear old clothes.

STEP THREE: With the tubular on the rim as far as possible, force the remainder of the tubular onto the rim with both thumbs (Fig. 9-53).

STEP FOUR: True up the tubular with your fingers (Fig. 9-54) so that it sits evenly all the way around the rim and tension is even all the way around. Inflate the tubular partially and inspect it to make sure that it is seated evenly. Leave the tubular inflated for a few hours, if possible, before using it, to give the rim cement time to dry and become fixed.

Road Tubular Replacement

So now you are on the road, in a race or just touring, and your tubular punctures. Obviously, you aren't going to sit around for a couple of hours while the rim cement dries. If you're in a race you should have someone

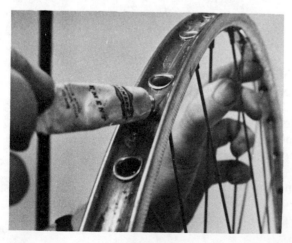

Fig. 9-50: Use thin layer of rim cement for road tubes, shellac for track tubes.

Fig. 9-51: Step One: With valve in rim, start placing tube on rim, pushing from both sides of valve evenly and alternately.

Fig. 9-52: Step Two: Continue pushing tube on rim.

Fig. 9-53: Step Three: Using thumbs and palm of hands, finish placing tube on rim.

Fig. 9-54: Step Four: If tubular is more to one side of rim, move it so both sides are even, as shown.

along with a replacement wheel, no fussing with changing tires. On tour, you won't want to leave the group, let them go ahead, while you sit glumly by the side of the road waiting for cement to adhere tubular to rim. What I do is use sticky tape, a special tape made for mounting tubulars on rims. I keep this tape in a sealed plastic bag, the kind used to store food with a self-sealing top. The tape is messy, to be sure, but it works and it will get you home or to your destination. Rim tape loses some of its adhesiveness in the rain, so take it easy on cornering and high-speed downhill runs in the rain. Another solution is to coat the tubular base tape, if rubberized, with a thin solution of rim cement and let it dry. Then I fold the tubular as noted earlier, for a spare, fasten it in this position with rubber bands or a strap, put it in a plastic bag and put the bag in a saddle carrier. There will be enough residual molecular adhesion between the thin layer of rim cement on the base tape and the rim cement still on the rim under the punctured tubular for fair adhesion, good enough for the day's run or to get you home but not good enough for a tough race situation. That's when you need a tire that will adhere to the rim as well as man can make it stick. If in doubt, try to roll the tubular off the rim. If it comes off easily, you have poor adhesion and you will very likely have a tubular roll off the rim in a race, and very possibly cause an accident involving not only you but others.

How to Use a Pump

On any valve, whether it be Presta or Schraeder, there is a correct way to use a pump. Presta valves, being longer and skinnier, are far easier to break off with improper application of the pump. Figure 9-55 shows how easy it is to break off the top half of a Presta valve. The valve core, when the valve tube is broken like that, cannot be threaded down, so the tire or tubular tends to leak, something like a slow leak. The newer Presta valve comes in two pieces, at least on the better tubulars, so if it breaks, you can replace the top half. I haven't seen any tire Presta valve tubes with two-piece valves, and I don't think I'll hold my breath till they come.

Fig. 9-55: If you wiggle a Presta valve pump as you pump air you can easily break off the valve tube, as shown. Hold pump steady so this doesn't occur.

Fig. 9-56: Remove pump with a sharp downward thump with the base of the hand, as shown. Don't wiggle pump off valve or you may damage valve tube.

To pump a Presta valve properly, first open the valve by turning the core counterclockwise (otherwise you can't pump air in). Then, holding the pump with thumb on top of the tubular (or tire), and holding the pump in place so it does not wiggle from side to side as you pump, shove the pump handle in and out until the tubular is filled to your satisfaction. Wiggling the pump from side to side is a sure way to break off the valve tube. When you are finished pumping, knock the pump off the valve with a firm downward blow (Fig. 9-56). Don't try to wiggle the pump off. That breaks valve tubes.

Now that we have covered the subject of tires and tubulars, rims and repairs, let's go on to the important subject of brakes, how to select them, which kinds are best for you, how much they cost and how to use them to stop effectively and safely.

All brakes will stop your bicycle, eventually. If properly adjusted and used, most brakes will stop you in time to avoid an accident, if you apply them soon enough. Some brakes on the very cheapest five- and ten-speed bikes (as on the bikes from Taiwan) can be lethally inadequate. So how can you tell whether the brakes on your bike are safe? To illustrate, let me tell you about an actual case history of brake failure that did result in a fatality.

A woman had received a bicycle as a premium for opening a savings account in a bank. The bike was assembled in a bike store, and was made in Taiwan. Two of her teenage children tried the bike out and discovered that the brakes simply would not work well. The "safety" levers (Fig. 10-1) could be pulled right down against the handlebar and the bike would not stop on a downhill run. The brake levers could also be pulled flat against the curve of the handlebars, and you could, eventually, stop this bike and if you were an expert cyclist you could have survived what happened to this woman. But the kids never told her about the poor brakes, and when she got on the bike she went down a 5-percent grade hill outside her house and let speed build up before beginning to apply the brakes. She yelled to her daughter, who was on foot, that the brakes did not work, would not stop, having tried both the

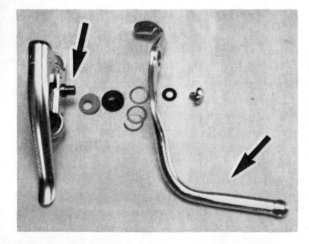

Fig. 10-1: These so-called "safety" or extension levers are actually dangerous because they have a much shorter distance of travel than main handlebar levers and so can "bottom out" if you make a panic stop. If you come to rely on the extensions, they might very well not stop you in time. I recommend removing them. Arrow at left points to longer brake-lever pivot. A shorter pivot can be installed so the end does not stick out to hurt your hand. Arrow at right points to extension lever.

extension "safety" levers and the main levers. She was going, I would judge about fifteen to twenty miles an hour when she came to a right-angle turn at the bottom of the hill, which she never made and indeed, at that speed I would not have made it either, with those brakes. Instead she went into a yard, hit a bump or a boulder, flew off the bars and as she landed was impaled on a stake and died a short time later. A subsequent lawsuit was settled for something like $250,000. I saw the hill, saw the bicycle and saw another bike of the same make, also a bank premium. These were brand-new bicycles. The combination of cable stretch and "give" in the brake stirrups combined to provide very poor braking power. The stirrups are the two lever arms of the brakes, and in this case they were center-pull design.

Now there's nothing wrong with center-pull brakes per se. In fact, they stop just as well as side-pull brakes, if properly made, adjusted and used. Let's get back to testing the braking system.

If you're buying a new bike, one good test is to squeeze the brake lever hard. If the levers go all the way to the handlebars, either they aren't adjusted properly, that is, there is too much cable slack, or the brakes themselves will distort and bend. Watch the stirrups as you grasp the brake levers tightly. As pressure builds up, do the stirrups bend? If so, these are dangerous brakes. If you can push the bike forward while grasping the brakes tightly, that is, if either wheel will turn (try one at a time) with the brake lever tightly grasped, obviously something is wrong. Let go of the brakes and check to see how far from the rim the brake shoe is now located. Ideally the shoe should be about one-eighth inch from the rim (Fig. 10-2). If the rim is out of true, that one-eighth inch may not be enough clearance, so whoever assembled the bike adjusted the brakes for clearance accordingly. The proper procedure would

Fig. 10-2: Correct adjustment of brake shoes, about 1/16 to 1/8 inch from rim flats on both sides. Tire was removed to allow better view of brake shoes.

have been to true the rim, then adjust the brakes. If, with rim trued and shoes one-eighth inch away from the rim, you can still bring the levers all the way to the handlebar, you have a pair of brakes far too flexible for safety. This degree of brake component flex is a characteristic of some center-pull brakes on cheaper bikes.

Safety Levers are not Safe

The so-called "safety" levers or extension levers are never found on better bicycles, they are almost always on mid-priced and less expensive bicycles. I suppose the reason they are installed is to allay any fears the novice rider might have about being able to reach the brake levers on the handlebars. Women, with shorter arms and fingers, and less powerful musculature, seem more concerned about being able to reach these main levers. The extension levers, just under the flat of the handlebars, may seem to be a comforting addition. The fact is that these levers do not offer nearly the stopping power that the main levers offer. This is mainly because the extension levers do not have the distance of travel that the main levers do. On a new bike the brake cables stretch quite a bit until broken in. You will probably find that the extension levers on a new bike, if the brakes are adjusted properly as noted earlier, will stop you well enough if there is no emergency and you are easing up to a stoplight or simply are stopping at a selected place. But in an emergency situation, if you have become habituated to using the extension levers, you will most likely not be able to stop in time. You may then switch to the main levers, and if you have time, will be able to stop, if the brakes are adjusted and do not have too much flex. But in switching from the extension to the main levers you lose precious seconds and come that much closer to disaster. My advice is to remove the extension levers. It's easy. All you do is remove the lever axle and substitute a shorter axle available from your bike store. The lever axle or pull-up stud is shown in Figure 10-3.

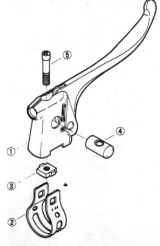

Fig. 10-3: Low-cost brake lever, without "safety lever." Lever spindle "4" can be obtained in a shorter size, as shown, so the longer spindle used on brakes with extension or "safety" levers won't project out and hurt your hand, once extension lever is removed. In other words, in removing extension lever, you need a shorter spindle.

TYPES OF BRAKES

There are six types of bicycle brakes:

Center-pull caliper brakes (Fig. 10-4): My experience with these brakes, over many thousands of miles of use, is that in general they offer some-what better ultimate stopping power than side-pull brakes of equal qual-ity, but that they give less *controlling* stopping power. If you could run a curve comparing the stopping power of center-pulls versus side-pulls, my own empirical riding experience tells me that braking power builds up quicker with center-pulls but that unless you are careful you can go into a sliding skid as wheels lock up. With side-pulls you can apply braking power much more evenly and stop just as well. That's why the high-priced bikes, and those used by road racing cyclists, use side-pulls; they are much more graduated in braking control. This is not to say that side-pulls won't work as well as center-pulls in an emergency, other things being equal. Not at all. I am saying that center-pulls seem to concentrate stopping power more quickly than side-pulls. I prefer side-pulls. I am discussing only the higher-quality brakes of both designs. See Table 10-1.

Side-pull caliper brakes (Fig. 10-5): These are less flexible than center-pulls, in general, and as far as I am concerned are more "forgiving" in maintaining stopping power if the rim is out of line. Going back to center-pulls for a moment, you will notice that there is an extra short cable attached to both stirrups (Fig. 10-4) which can also stretch. (Later

Fig. 10-4: Mafac center-pull brake offers excellent stopping power. Note that brake shoes or pads can be moved up and down the slotted opening in brake stirrups, to adjust brake shoes to fit against rim flats for different size rims and/or frames. Some frames have longer clearances between rim flats and brake-pivot mounting bolt.

Fig. 10-5: Campagnolo side-pull brake is one of the best brakes made any-where.

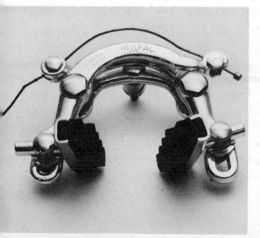

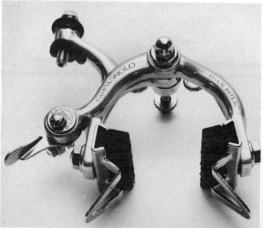

Fig. 10-6: Shimano disc brake, designed for the juvenile market. Not strong enough for adult use, especially on tandems: (A) brake cable; (B) brake disc; (C) brake body; (D) brake adjustment.

on in this chapter I will offer suggestions about how to stop safely on the flats and how to control speed on fast downhill runs.)

Disc brakes: There are two types of disc brakes, those made for children's bicycles, (Fig. 10-6) where the slight similarity to automotive or motorcycle disc brakes is a marketing feature . . . and the high-quality, much lighter-weight disc brakes (Fig. 10-7) designed primarily for tandems, where the extra stopping power is required. I will describe these brakes in more detail later on in this chapter. For now, I can say that they stop better in wet weather than caliper brakes but that they are heavier.

Drum brakes (Fig. 10-8): These are internally expanding brakes, and operate just like those on a car. An internal brake shoe, when braking is applied, presses against the brake drum. Because working parts are internal, drum brakes are less affected by water than any other type of bike brakes, and offer excellent stopping power. But because they are far heavier than the high-performance, lighter, more expensive disc brakes, drum brakes are going out of style for general use and for tandems.

Fig. 10-7: The excellent Phil Wood disc brake mounted on the rear wheel of a Schwinn Paramount tandem, on which these brakes are now standard equipment.

Nowadays you seldom see them on new bikes. I might add that you need a special hub for either disc or drum brakes—and that because friction-generated heat is absorbed by the brake lining and dissipated to the air, either disc or drum brakes do not heat up the rim. Caliper brakes, on the other hand, do heat up the rim because brake shoes rub on rims, and friction heat is transferred to the rims. On a fast downhill run, therefore, rims can get hot enough to soften the cement that holds on tubulars. When this occurs, tubulars slide around rims and can tear off the valve and cause a blowout or sudden flat, and loss of control of the bicycle. And on conventional tires, rims can get hot enough to blow out tubes, although this is a far less likely occurrence than the cement-melting problem of tubulars. More about downhill braking later.

Fig. 10-8: Phil Wood disc brakes on the front wheel of the Schwinn Paramount tandem. Notice straight-in approach of the cable in both this illustration and in Figure 10-7.

Fig. 10-9: Typical internal expanding hub brake: (A) brake shoes; (B) brake shoe cam; (C) cam spring; (D) bearings; (E) actuating arm; (F) axle; (G) brake drum; (H) hub spoke holes. This hub brake is made by Jonas Oglaend, Sandnes, Norway, and is on some of the models this firm exports to the U.S.A. Advantages of hub brakes are: They do not heat up rim; there is less "fade"; they have excellent wet-weather stopping power. Although they are heavy compared with alloy caliper brakes, they are needed on heavy tandems.

Fig. 10-10: Hub brake installed. Notice clip at bottom center, removable so wheel is easy to take off; and adjustment barrel to take up cable stretch and brake-shoe wear.

Fig. 10-11: Cantilever brakes on the author's Alex Singer touring bicycle. Note that Matthauser shoes are installed. You sharp-eyed experts will notice two items in this photo. The brakes look as though they are touching the fork blades, due to camera angle. I can assure you that they are not; this is **my** bike. The fixing bolt on the right hand lever is not the original, which fell on the floor and, as in all such incidents, immediately and, apparently permanently, disappeared from view. The replacement is temporary. Also there's some paint off the fork crown, where the Singer front-carrier fits. Well, this bike has thousands of miles on it, and has earned a few nicks and scratches. I'm considering awarding it a Purple Heart.

Cantilever brakes (Fig. 10-11): In Paris to attend the Bicycle Convention and Exhibit held there each year, I fell in love with an Alex Singer touring bike displayed in their booth, and ordered one made for me. The model I saw had cantilever brakes. I felt, when I saw them, that the leverage that could be exerted by the longer arms would offer greater stopping power, with less braking effort on my part, than the center-pull or side-pull caliper brakes I had been used to. Eventually the bike arrived, and I set off on a tour of Vermont and Cape Cod. How did the brakes work? Well, all I can tell you is that I am disappointed. These brakes are mounted on special fittings which are brazed on to seat stays and fork blades. Everything I had ever read about cantilever brakes, and discussed with other experienced cyclists, told me that in fact they would be more powerful with less effort exerted at the levers. Not so. These brakes take a lot of effort to work, and they don't let you stop any better than any other brakes I have ever used . . . in fact I suspect they don't stop as well. But they do *look* unusual and expensive and powerful, as they should on a bike that costs today over $1,500. For myself, I would never specify cantilevers on any custom bike. Strangely, though, to be fair, I have found that the shorter-lever cantilevers on the new Raleigh Rampar Tourist 14-speed bicycle do work very well, certainly as well as the excellent Mafac Competition center-pulls, and with less effort at the levers. My Singer is six years old, however, so perhaps the Raleigh Japanese made cantilevers represent engineering advances.

Coaster brakes (Fig. 10-12): These are also internal brakes, located in the rear hub, and on some bicycles, notably the single-speed models, this is the only brake on the bike. You stop by backpedaling. Because all working parts are internal, they stop better in wet weather than any of the three types of caliper brakes. But for two-wheel brakes you still need a caliper brake up front, and some of the bikes, mostly the three-speed models, have a coaster brake rear and a caliper up front. Coaster brake hubs are okay for utility use, but too heavy for touring. Even the five-speed coaster brake hubs do not offer anything like the range of gear ratios available in a ten-speed derailleur system. Coaster-brake hubs also

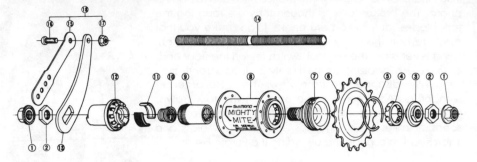

Fig. 10-12: Detailed view of a single-speed coaster brake hub. Part No. 11 is the brake shoe, which under back pedal pressure is forced against the inner perimeter of the brake cone, No. 12, by the clutch cone, No. 9. Coaster brakes are great for children, who have short, weak fingers and so should not have to grasp caliper-brake levers. A foot exerting hard back pressure on the pedal is easier for them to manage.

do not permit you to kick the pedals around so that one of them is at the two-o'clock position, ready for takeoff. For children I like a coaster-brake hub rear and caliper front. The coaster brake lets the child use his weight to stop by backpedaling, although kids will lock brakes and skid just for the fun of it. "Laying a patch" is a fun thing to do, but not a safe maneuver as the rear of the bike skids to one side as the wheel locks up. More about coaster brakes in Chapter 12.

BRAKE SELECTIONS

There are something like eighty or ninety models of side-pull and center-pull brakes that are available and used on new bicycles today. In general, the less expensive bikes use less expensive Weinmann or Shimano side- or center-pull brakes, and if you see a bike with these names on the brake, be assured the brakes are okay. In this discussion, I prefer to stick to the more expensive models of these brakes—and of all brakes, for that matter. Less costly Weinmann, Schwinn-approved or Shimano brakes will, other things being equal, stop you about as well as the best brakes. The difference is weight, controllability in terms of being able to apply minute braking effort instead of big chunks of it to control speed, and in appearance and ease of maintenance. The better brakes, described in detail below, are those I have used and can report on from my own experience and testing. Controllability is important because if you overapply braking power, you slow down more than you need to and so lose forward momentum more than is necessary, and therefore have to work harder to build up speed again. So high-quality brakes actually make cycling a lot more enjoyable and for that reason are well worth the extra cost. Table 10-1 compares various makes of better brakes in terms of price and weight.

Fig. 10-13: Rear center-pull brake, showing quick-release and cable-slack take-up mechanism.

   A. Take-up barrel. Turn counterclockwise to remove cable slack.
   B. Take-up barrel locknut. Turn clockwise till it tightens down on brake fitting below it.
   C. Brake quick-release. Flip up to move brake shoes farther out so wheel can be removed.
   D. Brake cable locknut. Loosen to take up cable slack when cable has stretched so far take-up barrel (A) won't take out slack. First, though, screw barrel (A) all the way clockwise. Pull excess cable through locknut (D) and retighten.

A quick-release (Fig. 10-13) is desirable because it permits you to spread the brake stirrups and get the brake shoes farther away from the rim so you can get the wheel out to repair a puncture. If brake shoes are the correct distance away from the rim, the tire will be too fat to get by the shoes easily. You can do it, but it's a slight struggle. Some quick-releases, on side-pulls, are on the stirrup (Fig. 10-14). On centerpulls, they usually appear on the brake levers as a small lever which you slide sideways to permit the brake lever to separate further, thereby moving the brake shoes farther away from the rim. Just be sure you release the quick-release before pedaling off again.

In selecting a new set of brakes, you should make sure that those you purchase will have enough "reach" so the brake shoes can be adjusted to rub on the flats of the rims (*not on the tires!*) Some brake stirrups are not long enough for some bike sizes. To make sure that new brakes will fit, measure the distance from the centerline of the brake mounting hole in the brake bridge on the seat stays (rear) and of the same hole in the

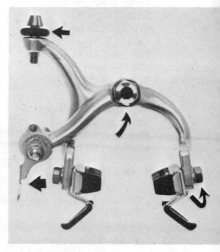

Fig. 10-14: Dia-Compe's excellent top-line Gran-Compe side-pull brake. Arrow at top points to cable slack take-up; rubber bumper protects frame finish if fork bangs against frame. Bottom left: quick-release which permits brake shoes to move back for easier removal of wheel. Lets fatter tire move past shoes. Top center: pivot bolt. Right: U-shaped arrow points to brake-shoe adjusting nut. Shoe can travel vertically up and down slot on stirrup to permit shoe-adjustment compensation for varying size tires, rims and frame clearance. If you switch from tubulars to 27-inch tires, for example, you will have to move brake shoes up because the 27-inch tires have a larger diameter than the 700-centimeter tubulars. If you switch to 700-centimeter tires, brake shoes can stay put.

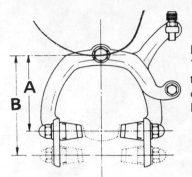

Fig. 10-15: This drawing shows how brake stirrup "reach" is calculated. You need to know the distance from centerline of brake pivot bolt, top, to centerline of rim and select a brake with stirrups long enough, or short enough, to fit.

fork (front) to the centerline of the rim (Fig. 10-15). You may find that the rear brake stirrups should be longer than the front, or vice versa, depending on the frame builder. If, for example, your bike was designed for fender clearance, so that there is considerable space between the brake mounting hole and the rim centerline, you will need a longer brake reach. Some models of the same brake come in various reaches. For example, from Table 10-1 you will notice that Shimano DuraAce brakes come with minimum/maximum reaches of 39/49 and 47/57 millimeters respectively. Some brakes come in only one reach. If you have a bike with very little clearance between the fork and rim, be sure you buy a brake that will fit.

Table 10-1   High-Quality Brake Selections

Make and Model	Q/R *	Weight †	Min/Max Reach ‡	Type §	Cost ''
Campagnolo record	Yes	22	49/52	SP	$89.95
Universal CX	Yes	19.08	NA	SP	74.98
Galli Ti	Yes	15.87	NA	SP	74.98
Dia-Compe 400	Yes	19.50	40/50	SP	66.00
Dia-Compe 450	Yes	19.75	45/57	CP	66.00
SunTour Superbe	Yes	19.50	39/50	SP	NA
Galli 75	Yes	17.64	NA	SP	54.90
Shimano DuraAce EX CS-49	Yes	19.90	39/49	SP	87.75
Shimano DuraAce EX CS-57	Yes	19.90	47/57	SP	87.75
Shimano 600-BB-300	Yes	18.50	43/47	SP	35.00
Shimano 600 BB-400	Yes	20	47/62	SP	35.00
Shimano 600 cc-75	No	20.45	57/75	SP	35.00
Shimano 600 BB 330	Yes	18.5	43/57	SP	35.00

* Quick release.

† In ounces.

‡ Minimum/maximum brake reach, in millimeters (translates to inches by multiplying by .03937).

§ SP = side-pull; CP = center-pull.

'' Approximate retail list price.

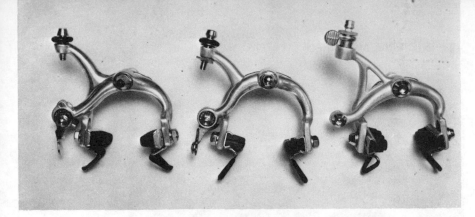

Fig. 10-16: These three top-grade, expensive side-pull brakes look pretty much alike, on the surface. Left to right, they are Campagnolo Record, Dia Compe 400 and Shimano DuraAce. It's when you take them apart that you begin to notice that the Campagnolo has superior features, higher precision machining that make close, even minute, braking control possible. The other two brakes have comparable stopping power, but not the minute control or the durability of the Campy line. Campy brakes are nearly twice as expensive, however.

BRAKE REVIEW, DETAILS

Finish: Most of the brakes in Table 10-1 are more highly polished than the Campagnolo Record (Fig. 10-16). But cosmetics are far from the whole story.

Lever Design: The Campy lever, for example, has an intricately cast body in which the pivot pin is held in the body by a fixing bolt (Fig. 10-17) so that this pin is separated from the lever mounting bolt and fitting. Other brakes, such as the Shimano DuraAce (Fig. 10-18) have a simple alloy shell in which the brake lever pivot bolt goes through the brake lever mounting bolt, so that when the mounting bolt is tightened, to hold the brake lever on the handlebar, some pressure is put on the lever pivot bolt. Confused? Don't blame you. Take a look at the drawing in Figure 10-20. You will see in this close-up view of a Dia-Compe lever that the

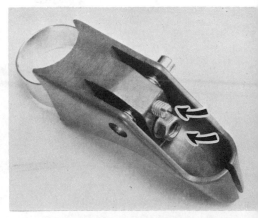

Fig. 10-17: Precisely machined body of the Campagnolo Record brake lever is what you see when you peel away the rubber hood. The major difference between the Campy and most other side-pull top-grade brakes is that the brake-pivot bolt, or spindle, is separated from the brake-lever mounting clamp bolt. Arrow at top points to brake-lever spindle retaining bolt; arrow at bottom points to brake-lever handlebar clamp bolt and nut. Since these are separated, there is no pressure exerted on the lever spindle as the clamp is tightened against the handlebar.

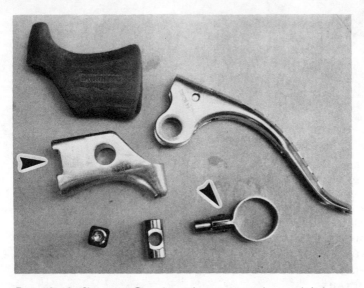

Fig. 10-18: Shimano DuraAce, their top-grade model, has a brake lever with simple parts. Arrow at left points to brake body. At right, arrow points to brake-lever clamp. Clamp-bolt end goes through spindle hole, center, so clamp and spindle are held on by the same fitting.

Fig. 10-19: Like the Shimano brake lever, this Dia-Compe combines the brake-lever spindle with the lever clamp. Lever clamp is shown by the top arrow, spindle by bottom arrow.

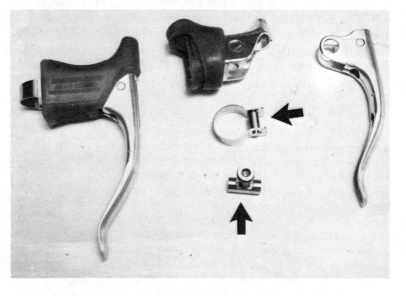

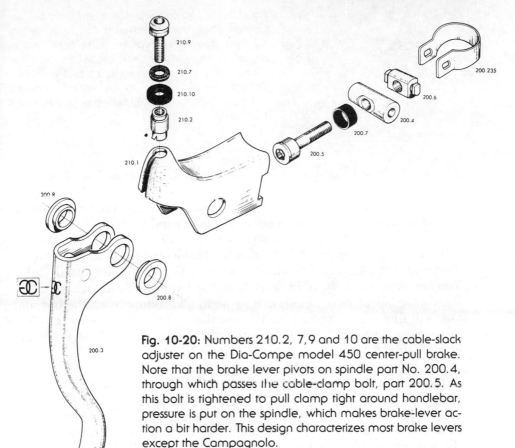

Fig. 10-20: Numbers 210.2, 7,9 and 10 are the cable-slack adjuster on the Dia-Compe model 450 center-pull brake. Note that the brake lever pivots on spindle part No. 200.4, through which passes the cable-clamp bolt, part 200.5. As this bolt is tightened to pull clamp tight around handlebar, pressure is put on the spindle, which makes brake-lever action a bit harder. This design characterizes most brake levers except the Campagnolo.

lever pivot pin, part 200.4, the axle on which the brake lever rotates, is held in place by the bolt no. 200.5, which in turn threads into part 200.6, which in *its* turn fits into the clamp part no. 200.235. As my statistics instructor used to say so infuriatingly, "It should be perfectly obvious . . ." that as the clamp bolt 200.5 is tightened so as to draw clamp 200.235 up tight, there will also be some pressure put on the pivot pin part 200.4 and that this pressure will bind the pin somewhat and make it that much more difficult to pull the brake lever. I have found the Campy brakes the smoothest of any I have tested in operation.

Campy is also the only brake I have used that has knurled ends on the cable nipple holder spindle, Fig. 10-21, which makes it easy to use your fingers to move the nipple holder when threading the nipple into the holder. This can be an exasperating operation, something like threading fine silk thread into a small needle, and the knurling helps a lot in aligning the spindle and keeping it in position (with fingers). None of the other brakes have this feature except the Galli Ti, which is an almost exact duplication of the Campy with not quite the finish, but pretty close.

Fig. 10-21: Top arrow points to the flats on the Campy pivot bolt, which you can hold with a 13-mm. open wrench as the bolt is tightened in place in the fork or rear brake bridge. This makes aligning or centering of brake easier. Bottom arrow points to two-sided serrated washer which helps hold brake in place, once tightened.

Center Bolt: The Campy center bolt has a deeply serrated washer (Fig. 10-21) with serrations on both sides, which help hold the brake centered over the rim. Galli comes close to this feature, and the others use merely a locking type of washer serrated on the edges only.

The Campy center bolt also has flats (Fig. 10-21) which accept a 13-millimeter open-end wrench to align the brake over the rim. This feature is shared by Galli, SunTour and Dia-Compe Gran-Compe 400 sidepulls. You can center the brake by loosening the fixing bolt nut on the end of the center bolt, moving the brake by hand and retightening the nut, but you will find that in tightening the nut the brake will move out of position again. The proper way to align the brake is to adjust it by the centerbolt flat, if there is one, as in Figure 10-21.

Cable Attachment: The Campy, Galli, and SunTour Superbe brakes lock the end of the brake cable with a fixing clamp. There's no need to thread a cable through a tiny hole, as in the Shimano DuraAce and Dia-Compe brakes. You can attach a frayed cable to the clamp type, but not through the latter type. If you wish, for example, to remove brakes for cleaning, and the cable end is frayed, you won't have to replace a perfectly good cable when you reattach the brake. Of course, you can avoid this situation by soldering cable ends before snipping them off after installing a new cable, so you won't have frayed ends on your cables. Just apply a half inch or so of solder, shake off excess solder, and cut the cable midway between the soldered area. Figure 10-22 shows the hole-in-locking-bolt type of cable end attachment. Personally, I applaud the clamp type;

Fig. 10-22: Center arrow points to cable-end fixing bolt. Note the hole in the bolt, through which cable is to pass. An Allen wrench at other end of bolt is tightened to clamp cable end in place. It is not possible to get a stranded cable end through this small hole, so that if just the end of the cable is stranded, entire cable must be replaced if cable is removed, as for lubrication.

it's so much easier to use. And if just one cable thread is loose, this is the one that won't go through the bolt hole.

Matthauser: While I'm on the subject of brake shoes, I would like to point out that there is an American-made shoe that, although quite expensive, is considerably better in terms of wet and dry stopping power than any shoe I have tested, including the Campagnolo. This is the Matthauser brake housing and shoe (Fig. 10-23). Various models are available for all the popular makes of brakes, including Mafac cantilever brakes. These brakes are curved, following the contour of the rim, and in this manner making for a longer brake shoe. Otherwise, a brake shoe of this length would extend slightly beyond the curvature of the rim, and the part that did not touch the rim would of course be useless.

Tests show that the finned design dissipates heat away from the rim, so that in high-speed downhill braking, Matthauser shoes will not heat up the rim nearly to the degree that conventional brake shoes do. Further, the friction material itself is bonded to the housing, very much like automobile brakes (rivets went out some years ago). The bonding transmits friction-generated heat to the fins much more efficiently than pressed shoes of other brakes, which means that shoes should last longer because they won't heat up as much. There is no insulating air space between the shoe and the housing in the Matthauser shoe, so heat conductivity is at a maximum. The housing itself is aluminum, a much better heat conductor, and dissipator, then the steel used on conventional housings. When ordering Matthauser brake shoes, you will need to specify what kind of brake it is to be used with. Also, Matthauser wants to know whether your rims are angled or straight. (Some rim flats are slightly angled and there is a Matthauser shoe for them.) If your dealer does not have them, ask him to order them from Scott/Matthauser Corp., Box 1333, Sun Valley, Idaho 83353. Around $15 for four. They have vastly improved the performance of the Mafac cantilevers on my Alex Singer. However, I found that the Matthauser shoes are so long that, with normal cantilever clearances, the shoes hit the fork blades and seat stays. I got around this problem by adjusting the shoes closer to the rim so that in the hands-off position the shoes did not touch the bike tubes. This is not

Fig. 10-23: Matthauser brake shoes upgrade any brake with better wet and dry stopping power. Ribbed alloy housing dissipates heat better than conventional brake shoes. Matthauser shoes are also bonded to the housing, so insulating air space between alloy housing and shoe is removed for maximum heat transfer from shoe to finned housing.

an entirely satisfactory solution, however, because the levers are brought out farther than I like them; that is, there is less lever travel. This is highly desirable on other types of brakes, but cantilever brakes don't work the same way as other brakes. Torque is transmitted much faster to cantilever brakes, so there can be more lever travel in relationship to how far away shoes are from the rim. Just be aware of the problem. Know that Matthauser shoes are 5.3 millimeters long, versus 4.55 millimeters for Mafac shoes and 4 millimeters for Campagnolo shoes. Make sure this extra length of the Matthauser shoes won't involve their hitting any member or component of the bike frame. Remember too that Matthauser shoes *must* be toed slightly in at the front so the foremost part of the brake hits the rim first.

Brake Shoes: I find the various makes of brakes to have shoes with about equal stopping power (Matthauser excepted). I tested all the shoes on one make of brake, and they all performed about the same. The SunTour shoes were a bit softer than the others and would therefore probably not wear as long. The Campy, Shimano DuraAce and Galli blocks are open on one end, making it possible for a new set of shoes to be pressed in without buying an entire new set of shoe holders. For example, Campy blocks alone are $2.25 *each.* With holders, make that around $4.50 to $5 each. Other brake shoes and holders are less, but you get the picture. If both ends of the shoe housing are closed, as with the Dia-Compe and SunTour, at least if you get the housing in backward there's no danger of the shoe sliding out of the housing. This can easily happen with open-ended housings. Try it. First time you grab the brakes the shoe will fly out ahead of you as the rim is grabbed. *The end that's open must always face toward the rear of the bike!* See Figure 10-24.

Attaching Points: Here's where some of the other brakes have an advantage to some extent over Campy. The Campy 8-millimeter T wrench (socket end), which costs around $5 but which is equivalent to a thin wall socket, will fit the Campy Lever mounting nut, the one that locks the clamp section on the handlebars and the cable end attaching nut on the stirrup. If you don't have this wrench, you will have some difficulty using a standard socket, at least on the lever clamp nut. I find so many

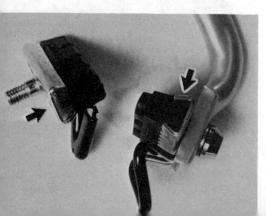

Fig. 10-24: Left, this brake-shoe housing is closed at both ends. Right, housing is open at one end, which must face toward rear of bike so shoe won't be forced out of housing when brake is applied. Right-hand shoe is easier to replace, but also easier to install backward. Be careful!

Fig. 10-25: Campagnolo brake cable thicker, stronger, better made than other bike cables, is the cable at bottom. Campy cable is soldered for about two inches from the end so cable ends won't fray. If you trim off excess cable-end length, be sure to apply solder for one inch on either side of your intended cut. Soldered cable ends are much easier to deal with when removing cable later on for servicing and lubrication.

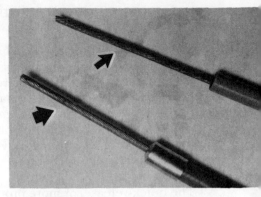

parts on a bike that this 8-millimeter wrench will fit that I would suggest you buy one, even though it's grossly overpriced. My initials are etched on mine.

Brake housing mounting nuts on the Shimano take an 8-millimeter Allen wrench (the "T" end of a Campy wrench will fit), as does the cable attaching nut on this brake, and the brake lever clamp nut.

The brake lever clamp nut on Dia-Compe levers take a 5-millimeter Allen wrench, a major convenience in mounting and demounting these levers, as when, for example, you need to change handlebar tape or reposition the levers.

Cables: All brakes, sold as a set, also come with cables. There's a vast difference, though, in cables. For example, the Campagnolo cables (Fig. 10-25) are considerably thicker than other makes, are soldered up to a couple of inches from the end, and are made with an outer shell or core which is reverse wrapped around an inner core. This construction is both stronger and less conducive to fraying at the cut end. The Campy housing is slightly oversized to permit the cable to slide freely. Because the free end of the cable is soldered to prevent fraying, as noted, it may be just a tad thicker at that point and so bind a bit as you shove it through lever tops, cable guides and hole-in-bolt clamps. If this is a problem, pull the cable end through medium coarse sandpaper a few times. You might also check out the Buffalo brand cable housing if your bike shop carries it. This is a Teflon-lined housing that helps cables slide easier. Of course, the Teflon coating will wear eventually and, like all cables, will need to be greased to prevent binding and even rust. Further, cables last much longer when lubricated. If dry, they can fray, and if just one strand breaks inside the cable-housing spaghetti, you could have a cable that binds and works hard. And a hard-working or binding cable could negatively affect the stopping power of the best brakes.

Brake "Reach"

Table 10-1 has a column entitled "reach" which we discussed earlier and which refers to the minimum/maximum length the shoes can be adjusted to the centerline of the rims. Put another way, it is the distance from the centerline of the brake pivot bolt mounting hole in the fork and rear brake bridge to the centerline of the rim (Fig. 10-15).

If for some reason you can't find the brakes you want (or can afford) that will have enough reach, or if you have bought them and perhaps are stuck with them, you can increase the reach by using a special brake pivot bolt that is dog-legged shaped or dropped. It drops the brake about five millimeters below its normal position if the stock pivot bolt were used. Be sure to buy the pivot bolt that fits your make and model brake, though. Pivot bolts are not universal, by any means.

Quick-Release

The quick-release, or more properly called, the cable release, is a device that adds slack to the brake cables so brake stirrup arms can spread wider to permit easy removal of the rim. The quick-release on the Campagnolo brakes (Fig. 10-26) is the best I checked. The nice thing about this feature is that it stays put in any position, so you can have a choice of brake shoe openings. This could be a helpful assist if you bust a spoke and have to wobble home. You would, in this situation, be able to pull the brake shoe just far enough away from the wobbly rim for some effective braking yet not have the rim dragging on the brake shoe. This is the only quick-release that works this well of any brake that offers this function.

The quick-release of the other brakes is either 100 percent on or 100 percent off, without any choice of intermediate position. The quick-release on the Dia-Compe Model 400 side-pulls does offer some intermediate stop positions, however.

Cable Slack Adjustment

Again, the Campagnolo brakes offer the neatest adjustment for taking up cable stretch. This is done via a cam-type of screw adjuster—to quote from a recent Campy ad that puts it as well as I could—"that maintains constant tension on the cable and prevents vibration from changing this adjustment." A rubber bumper on the adjuster also prevents damage to the frame paint if the fork is swung around to where the right brake stirrup could bump the frame and nick the finish. The Dia-Compe 400 side-pulls also have a similar adjuster that works the same way.

Fig. 10-26: The quick-release on Campagnolo brakes will hold brake in any open position at which you set release lever—a help in case you break a spoke and want to set shoes just back far enough to clear rim wobble at broken spoke.

To Sum Up

There's no question that from a standpoint of cosmetics, all the brakes mentioned look better than the Campagnolo models. But none are built better, work better, offer more precise braking control or work as well under all conditions including wet weather. There's a lot to be said in favor of Campy design, quality and performance that's not apparent on the surface. But dissect these brakes and you will find beauty that's a lot more than skin deep. Perhaps something like a Mercedes-Benz. They look pretty ordinary, but under the paint and the surface chrome there's an awful lot of quality. Sure Campy stuff costs more. But it's worth it.

Okay, so I haven't mentioned the second-line brakes, which are in many respects excellent as far as stopping ability is concerned. Among these are Weinmann center- and side-pulls, all models, and Mafac center-pulls, all models. These brakes cost a small fraction of the price you dish out for Campy equipment, but for budget stoppers they offer a lot for the money. The Shimano DuraAce line is excellent, their 600 line less well made, less well finished. The Altus and other Shimano brakes are for less expensive bikes and/or children's bikes.

ABOUT OTHER BRAKES—A CAPSULE REVIEW

Here are some other excellent brakes, also noted in Table 10-1. *Galli Ti* is almost an exact duplicate of the Campy brake and uses a titanium center or pivot bolt and ergal nuts to get weight down to 15.87 ounces, a 38-percent weight reduction or a weight differential of 6.13 ounces. It comes in a midnight blue finish for $74.98. The same brake, without the titanium and ergal parts, is *Model 75* for $54.98.

Universal makes three excellent brakes. The CX model does not offer quite the overall quality of the Campy line but looks better because it is more highly polished. The CX is also easier to work with because the levers use a five-millimeter Allen wrench to tighten the handlebar clamp, although the Campy T wrench (Fig. 10-27) is really just as con-

Fig. 10-27: The Campy "T" wrench is a very useful tool. Socket end is 8 mm., Allen ends of "T" are 6 mm. If you have Campy components, carry this wrench on your cycletours.

venient if you don't mind spending the money for one, which, as noted earlier is around $5. This little wrench is so useful I recommend that every bike owner buy one. The T handle is actually a six-millimeter Allen wrench, the socket is eight millimeters although I'm hanged if I can figure out why Campy did not take this opportunity to make one of the "T" arms a five- or a seven-millimeter Allen wrench—or why Campy does not go to Allen nut fittings on all its parts. Sure would save a lot of hassle, and carrying around of extra tools. It would be nice if component manufacturers got together and settled on, say, seven- or eight-millimeter Allen nuts for everything on the bike that is held by a threaded nut and bolt. Well, I'd settle for two sizes, five and eight millimeters. *Universal's Model 77* is virtually a clone of their higher-priced CX model, but at a much lower price. Not Campy quality but well worth the money. *Universal Model 68* is a budget-priced side-pull that works well. Model 51 is the same except for lower calipers (stirrup arms). Table 10-1 has prices.

DISC BRAKES

Disc brakes, as noted earlier in this chapter, are made either for children's bicycles, or for the high-priced bike for the serious owner who wants the ultimate in stopping power. I see no need for a disc brake or brakes on a single-rider bicycle, unless perhaps we're dealing here with a 250-pound rider, a heavily laden touring bicycle and a lot of up- and downhill riding. Certainly the heavier rider does need greater stopping power, the laws of physics will see to that. And perhaps one can make a case for a disc brake in this situation. But disc brakes really come into their own on a tandem application. There we have a situation where two riders, with a combined weight of, say, 300 pounds, plus a 42-pound tandem, plus 45 or 50 pounds of camping gear, total up to nearly 400 pounds. That amount of kinetic energy, tearing down a steep hill, is well beyond the safe stopping ability and range of any brakes I know of except a good disc brake, or set of brakes. Schwinn knows this, and that's why they equip their new Paramount high-grade tandems with disc brakes.

There is only one really high-quality disc brake on the market, and that is the Phil Wood Duopar, Figure 10-7. This is an all-weather disc brake with tremendous stopping power. To use it you will have to scrap your old hubs because the Phil Wood disc brakes require their own special hub. This brake uses a parallelogram action—two, in fact, that transmits braking torque to the wheel. I can highly recommend this brake. I have two on my own Paramount tandem and feel a lot safer on downhill runs, believe me, than I did, even with Campy brakes. For the ultimate in stopping power, leave your caliper (or install) brakes in place, move levers to rear bars, mount disc-brake levers (you will need new ones because Phil Wood does not supply them with his brakes) on front handlebars. Now you have backup brakes for those long downhill descents.

Phil Wood disc brakes feature:

- Quick-disconnect for brake cable so wheel can be removed quickly.
- No tools needed to move brake from one wheel to another. Brake action is done without servo action so brakes are fairly impervious to water and have no tendency to lock up, which could cause a skid.

The Phil Wood disc brakes cost around $145 *each,* so we're talking about a tab of $290 for two brakes, one for each wheel. You could save by using a caliper on the front and a Phil Wood on the rear. But no dealer will break up a pair of caliper brakes, so unless you have an old set, I'd go the whole Phil Wood route and use two. Now you have to add in the cost of Phil Wood sealed-bearing hubs, made for these brakes, because you must use these special hubs to mount the brakes. A front Phil Wood sealed bearing hub with a hollow axle for a quick-release skewer sells for around $40, minus the skewer. Any make of front-wheel skewer will fit. A bolt-on Phil Wood sealed-bearing hub costs around $45 for the front wheel. I prefer bolt-on hubs for a tandem; they are a lot safer because they are much less likely to accidentally come off. You can kick or hit a quick-release skewer and not notice that you've pushed it to the open or partially open position until the bike hits a good hard bump, at which point the wheel can pop right out of the dropout; and because you can't pull a wheely with a tandem, you are just not going to be comfortable very long with only the rear wheel to hold you up. That's my cheery way of saying you could get killed this way. A Phil Wood rear hub goes for around $50. Let's add all this up. Two brakes, $290. Two hubs, $95. Total, $385. That's about 25 percent of the total price of a good tandem these days. But it's awfully good insurance in case you need to stop suddenly, control downhill descents without heating up rims and have general overall good controllability of a tandem, especially one gear-laden with camping equipment.

With the hub, the Phil Wood disc brake weighs 26 ounces, only 4 ounces more than a pair of Campy brakes with levers. Two Phil Wood disc brakes with hubs weigh in, then, at 42 ounces, or 2.625 pounds, or 1190.7 grams.

Shimano makes a very fine disc brake, but not for distribution in the U.S.A. because of lack of demand. Shimano is geared for high-volume production and Phil Wood is more of a cottage industry, content with making very high-quality components at fairly high prices. There is a good market for Shimano disc brakes in Europe and Japan but not in this country, at least not in volume. Shimano is coming out with a hydraulic disc brake soon, but, again, not for this country. The Shimano disc brake, their C-type model (Fig. 10-6) is okay for light duty, on tandems of the heavy, "putzing around" kind; but it definitely does not have the stopping power for touring tandems, and I cannot recommend it at all for this application. This brake is not even in Shimano's 1979 catalog, but there may still be some in bike shops.

DRUM BRAKES

Before the Phil Wood disc brake, the only other decent tandem brake was the drum brake, such as the one made by Jonas Oglaend Bicycle Co., Sandnes, Norway (Fig. 10-9). This is, or was, an internal expanding brake, just like the brake on the car that carried dear old Dad. This isn't such a bad brake, it's just very heavy and cumbersome, and impractical for the high-performing tandems we like so well in this country. The only drum brake imported into this country is Shimano's Radiax Fin drum brake, and that is designed for children's bicycles and not at all suitable for anything else. This brake weighs 20.8 ounces, and with the steel hub you have to use with it, comes to a massive total of almost 2½ pounds.

Now, before I get into brake adjustment and maintenance, just a word about how to apply brakes safely, because the best brakes in the world won't save your skin if you do not use them properly.

BRAKING TECHNIQUES

If you're riding a pannier-laden bike on a camping trip, remember that for every pound you add you decrease effective stopping distance. It may take you longer to get going, but it will also take longer to stop, so be careful, anticipate stopping situations and begin to apply brakes earlier than you have been used to doing with an unladen bike.

On fast downhill runs, don't let speed build up to where you are barely under control. You don't really know what's around the bend, and at high speed you just may not make the turn. And will you be able to stop if there's a trailer truck on its side just around the bend or, as happened to me once, a runaway bull from a nearby slaughterhouse picking its way down the center strip? As you brake, apply the front and rear brakes alternately to give the rims a chance to cool, so as to avoid brake fade or a blowout from heat buildup or a tubular sliding around the rim as heat melts the cement that holds it on the rim. If you're riding a tandem, remember that you can build up to some pretty terrific speeds very quickly, and that even the best of disc brakes can fade if they get hot enough. There's no guarantee that *any* brake won't fade away, even the most expensive. I know it's tempting to see how fast you can go if there's a five-mile coast on a straight road, but resist the temptation and keep speed under control. If you're a skilled racing cyclist, go, man, go. But if you're a tourist out on a cycle camping trip and on a loaded-down tandem, better keep the speed to where you can stop if you have to.

When cornering, it's better not to brake as you make the turn, but slow down well before you begin to steer around the curve. The greater the turn angle, the slower you should approach it. Braking as you turn puts an extra sideway stress on wheels and, if you hit a sandy spot at the same time, that's when you're likely to spill. I might note that beginning cyclists usually do not corner well. The idea is to look as far ahead as you can as you make the turn, and not just at the next ten feet in front of you. You need to know what's ahead as soon as possible. After a while you learn how far you can lean, how sharply you can turn, how fast you can make the turn and still stay upright. Not that speed in cornering is vital to the casual rider or the touring cyclist. It's just that you know what you can handle in terms of safe cornering speed.

When commuting in traffic or on bike lanes and trails that I have to share with children, skaters and joggers, I keep my hands close to the brake levers at all times. You just never know what will be coming at you or from what direction and you need to be able to stop quickly.

In a panic stop, ease your buttocks as far back on the saddle as possible to spread weight evenly over both wheels. Otherwise, if you bend far forward and throw more weight over the front wheel, the rear wheel will not have as much road-gripping stopping power as the front wheel. I prefer to apply the rear brake first, just slightly ahead of the front wheel, because I have found that if I grab the front brake first I have difficulty in controlling steering accurately. And in a panic stop I really want to be able to steer away from danger. One thing you don't need in an emergency is a situation where the bike wants to go where you don't want to be. Be careful about applying brakes for a controlled emergency stop. If the wheels lock and skid (and this is more likely to occur with a coaster brake or with a good center-pull brake than with side-pulls) you certainly are not stopping. What you want is maintained wheel contact with the ground so that the force applied by brake shoes to brake rim is transmitted to tires and the road, *without skidding.*

ADJUSTMENT AND MAINTENANCE OF CALIPER BRAKES

First. let's talk about lubrication. Caliper brakes need periodic lubrication—not, of course, on the brake shoes. I know you know better than that. But caliper brakes all have a pair of springs, or one spring with two arms, that hold the caliper arms apart so they won't drag on the rim until you pull on the brake levers. The place to apply a little grease is the point where the spring arms press against the back of the caliper arms or stirrups (let's call them "stirrups" from now on). Lubriplate is fine. You can buy it in most hardware stores, and it can be used on all bike bearings as well. Figure 10-28 shows where lubrication should be applied. Rub off old grease and accumulated dirt with a cloth before applying clean grease. Lightly oil pivot bolts and stirrup cable of center-pull brakes.

At least once a year you should remove brake cables, check them for wear and frayed strands and replace any cable that has a broken strand. If the inside of the cable cover, the spaghetti tubing through which the cable itself runs, is frayed, replace it. Rust inside a cable tube is a sign of

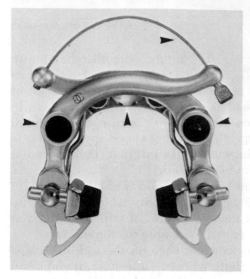

Fig. 10-28: Arrows point to lubrication spots on a Dia-Compe center-pull brake. Top, the stirrup cable should be lightly greased where it passes through yoke. Apply small amount of light oil at stirrup pivot bolts, right and left arrows, and at brake pivot bolt, center arrow. Put a dab of grease on spring ends where they rub on stirrups (not shown, location is on rear of brakes).

neglect, such as having left the bike out in the rain a lot. If you do a lot of commuting, you really need brakes that respond fast to your touch of brake levers. Rusty, frayed or lube-dry cables will delay and make brake action that much harder, so they are a definite safety hazard. Remember, brake shoes should be about one-eight inch from rims, as noted earlier. As I will point out later, this is so important, because the farther shoes are from the rim the slower the brake reaction time, and the farther brake levers will have to travel to bring the shoes to the rim. If shoes are too far away, as in an effort to keep a crooked rim from hitting a shoe, the levers may, in a panic stop, travel all the way tightly against the handlebar, and still not stop you. There is a finite relationship between brake-lever travel, cable stretch or slack, shoe wear and distance of shoes from the rim. Unless all these factors are taken into consideration in adjusting brakes, you can have brakes considerably under par in terms of stopping power—yes, even Campagnolo brakes. Any brakes.

TOOLS YOU WILL NEED (OR SHOULD HAVE) FOR BRAKE MAINTENANCE

Depending on the make of brake, you will need a five-, six-, seven- or eight-millimeter Allen wrench or a six-, seven-, eight- or nine-millimeter box or open-end wrench. You should also have a "third hand" to hold brake stirrups closed while you take up cable slack when installing new brake cables or reinstalling old ones after lubricating them. (Fig. 10-29).

If you commute to work on your bike and leave it out in all sorts of weather, cable lubrication is especially important: first, because the cables are far more likely to run dry of grease and even rust when the bike is out all day; and second, lube-dry or rusty cables or cable tubing makes braking harder and slower, and robs you of braking torque by absorbing some of what should go to the brakes. If you commute you are most likely cycling through city traffic, and your brakes should be in top-notch condition at all times. To remove and replace cables, follow these steps:

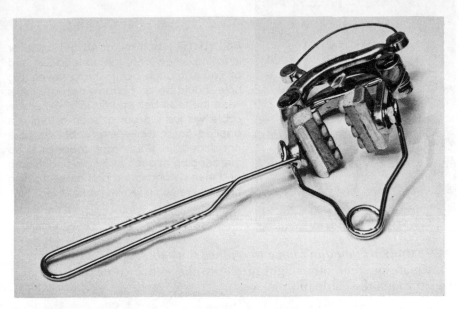

Fig. 10-29: Brake "third hand" tool holds brake shoes close to rim to make take-up of cable slack easier. You apply tool, pull cable end through cable clamp at brake end, tighten clamp, remove tool.

STEP ONE: *Loosen cable holding or fixing bolt nut* (Fig. 10-30) and pull the end of the cable through. If the cable end is frayed and the cable end fixing bolt is the kind with a hole in it, discard the cable, because you will never get the frayed cable end back through the tiny bolt hole (Fig. 10-22).

STEP TWO: *Shove the cable back through the cable tubing* until the bell end comes slightly out of the slotted hole in the brake lever (Fig. 10-31). Or, simply push the cable out at the brake end until enough of the cable shows at the brake lever so you can pull the cable entirely through.

Fig. 10-30: Dia-Compe brakes. Pencil at left points to where grease should be applied to make brakes work smoothly. Arrow at upper right shows cable-adjusting barrel. To remove slack so as to keep shoes about ⅛ inch from rim flats, turn rubber bumper counterclockwise. Bottom right, arrow points to clamp-type cable gripper and quick-release unit.

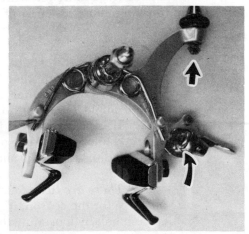

Fig. 10-31: When replacing old cable or installing a new one, thread lead bell end of cable through slot in brake lever. Big hole should be on bottom, because this is what the lead bell end fits into. Otherwise cable will just slip out as soon as brake is applied. Some brake-lever cable studs are not slotted, in which case cable must be threaded up through stud from underneath and then up and into top of brake-housing hole where cable leaves brake lever.

STEP THREE: *If you don't have to replace the cable,* apply a thin layer of Lubriplate or some other light grease to the entire cable and thread it back through the cable tubing.

STEP FOUR: *Fit the bell end of the cable* into the slot in the brake lever.

STEP FIVE: *Apply the "third hand" tool* (Fig. 10-29) to keep brake stirrups closed.

STEP SIX: *Pull brake cable all the way through.* Holding the brake end, pull on the brake lever to make sure the bell end of the cable is firmly inside the slotted hole. The small end of the hole slot must be on top. If the cable is not properly inside the slotted hole, this is when the bell end will pop out. Once the bell end is in place, fasten the other end to the brake-cable-end fixing bolt and tighten its fixing-bolt nut. Solder cable end so ends won't fray.

STEP SEVEN: *Release the "third hand" tool,* check to make sure brake shoes are about one-eighth inch from both sides of the wheel rim flats and that shoes are aligned with the rim. No part of the shoe should touch the tire nor should any part of the shoe be below the inner edge of the rim.

STEP EIGHT: Spin the wheel, watching the shoes. If the rim is out of alignment, it will rub on the shoe wherever it is out of line. Align the rim as described in Chapter 15. Again check to make sure the brake shoes have about one-eighth-inch distance from the rim flat on *both* sides (Fig. 10-32). If you have installed a new cable, squeeze the brake levers tightly to take out some of the cable stretch that new cables always have, and readjust the brake shoes again.

STEP NINE: *There are two places to adjust brake shoes.* If you are tuning up your bike for the season, it's best to remove cable slack at the brake-cable fixing bolt by loosening the fixing-bolt nut and pulling excess cable

Fig. 10-32: An older model of the excellent Dia-Compe 450 center-pull brake. Note that tire is wider than shoe adjustment, so to remove wheel easily, the quick-release is opened to spread shoes back farther from the rim flat, to allow fatter tire to pass through. Parts are:

A. Brake-cable locknut. Loosen to pull cable through.

B. Stirrup cable

C. Cable yoke pulley. Makes brakes work easier.

D. Brake-shoe locknut. Loosen to move shoe up or down, or tilt until shoe is accurately aligned on rim flat. **Must not touch tire!**

through, with the "third hand" in place. This way you will have plenty of adjustment room left in the cable-adjusting barrel. On side-pull brakes the adjusting barrel is on one of the stirrups (Fig. 10-33). On center-pull brakes the adjusting barrel can be on the front yoke (Fig. 10-34), the rear yoke (Fig. 10-35) or on the brake lever itself (Fig. 10-36). In either location, to take out cable-stretch slack, just loosen the barrel locknut (Fig. 10-34), and turn the barrel counterclockwise. (Make sure that if you have a quick-release it is closed before adjusting.) This pulls the cable up and removes slack. Brake shoes also wear, and some of the slack can be caused by worn shoes. Replacing shoes is simple enough; just unscrew the brake-shoe-housing fixing nut, remove it and replace with either a new housing and shoe or the shoe alone. Squeeze the worn shoe out of the housing and squeeze a new one in. You can best do this with a vise. *You must reinstall housings with the open end, if it has one, toward the rear of the bike.*

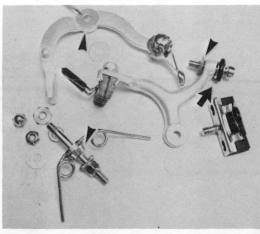

Fig. 10-33: Campy brakes dissected. Top arrow shows precise machining of stirrup-pivot-bolt area. Arrow at bottom points to 13-mm. flats on pivot bolt which make it easier to hold brake in position while tightening pivot-bolt fixing nut. Washer, top-right arrow, helps hold cable take-up adjuster in place, under vibration of bicycle riding. Pencil at top also points to pivot flat where light oil should be applied from time to time.

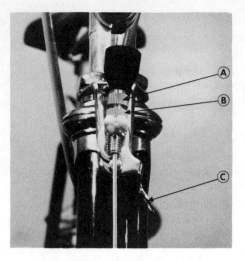

Fig. 10-34: This cable-slack take-up barrel is located on front cable yoke of center-pull brake. Note threaded end of barrel, at bottom.

    A. Take-up barrel. Turn counterclockwise to remove cable slack.

    B. Barrel locknut. Turn clockwise to tighten after adjusting barrel.

    C. Quick-release lever.

Fig. 10-35: Cable-slack remover, arrow is on rear center-pull brake yoke. Bottom arrow points to cable-clamp locknut on stirrup. This type of yoke can move up or down, tighten or loosen brake, if saddle-fixing bolt is adjusted. When adjusting saddle, hold brake yoke so cable comes out of barrel in line with the barrel. In this photo, the yoke is tilted too far down, so cable rubs on top of barrel opening. Note also that a quick-release is part of this yoke.

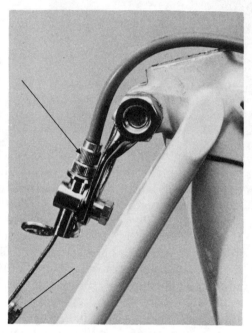

Fig. 10-36: Dia-Compe new Model 450 center-pull brake has cable-slack adjusting barrel located at top of brake lever (arrow), a more convenient location.

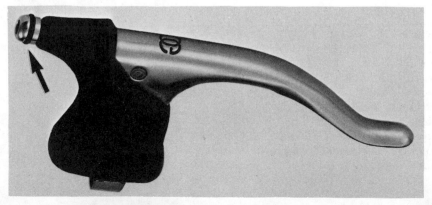

BRAKE TROUBLESHOOTING

- *If Campagnolo brake shoes drag on one side or the other,* first make sure the pivot-bolt fixing nut is tight. Then, with a thirteen-millimeter open-end wrench, grasp the pivot bolt just behind the stirrups (Fig. 10-37 and 10-21) and move the brake so the rim is centered between them. Shimano and other side-pull brakes can be adjusted the same way.
- *If brakes squeal,* check shoes for imbedded glass or small stones or other foreign material. Old, hardened brake shoes will also squeal. Brake shoes should slightly "toe-in" at the front. To toe-in, bend the stirrup arms slightly with a crescent wrench. Be careful not to overdo the bending process, so you don't break the stirrup arms.
- *Hand levers on handlebars bind:* Check to find the exact location of the binding. If sides of brake lever rub abainst the lever body, use a thin screwdriver to gently pry the lever inward (or bend the lever slightly inward). Check to make sure the cables aren't binding and that the cable housings (the spaghetti tubing through which the cables run) curve gradually from the levers to the frame and from the frame to the brakes without "kinks" at any point.

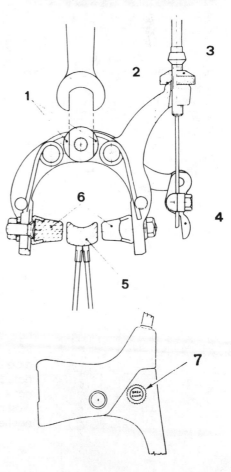

Fig. 10-37: Drawing of Campagnolo brake showing:

1. 13-mm. pivot-bolt flats where pivot bolt can be held from rotating while pivot-bolt fixing nut is tightened. Helps keep brakes aligned while tightening this nut.

2. Rubber bumper on adjusting barrel protects paint finish if fork swings too far.

3. The adjusting nut has a semispheric shape which wedges in the lever to keep it in place under vibrations of cycling.

4. Quick-release lever

5. Rim

6. Brake shoes

7. Knurled cable spindle makes it easier to keep the slotted end in place while you insert cable. You just hold the exterior knurls with fingers.

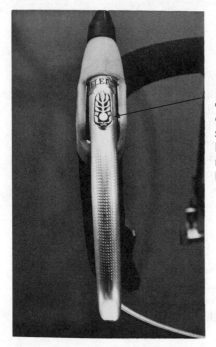

10-38: Yet another location for quick-release on brakes, this one is on brake lever, arrow. To actuate quick release, depress brake lever, slide quick-release lever sideways, release lever. With quick-release sideways, brake-stirrup spring will spread shoes wider, push brake-lever handle up farther.

Fig. 10-39. Front Campagnolo brake.
1. Pivot bolt flats for 13-mm. wrench.
2. Fork
3. Serrated washers hold brake alignment, keep brake centered.

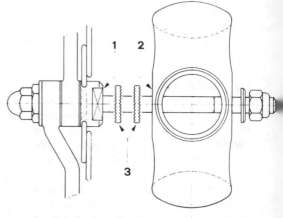

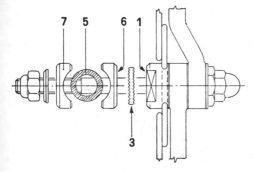

Fig. 10-40: Rear Campagnolo brake mounted on round brake cross tube (bridge) between seat stays. Serrated washer (3) fits between flat side of concave washer (6) and flat inner surface of pivot bolt to hold brake centered. Concave washer (7) fits around outside of round cross tube. If the cross tube is not round, washers (6) and (7) are eliminated; however, in this case, the cross tube must not be shorter than 14.5 mm. or the serrated washer (3), which is 14.4 mm. in diameter, will not keep brake centered.

- *Center-pull brake arms do not pivot freely on trunnions (center bolt):* If the center bolt or trunnion fits too tightly, ream out a small hole in the arm with a drill. Or sand the trunnion to a smaller diameter. If the arms are too thick, file at the pivot area so that the pivot bolt sits against the trunnion without binding the arm. Loosen the pivot bolt; if the arm moves freely, the arm is too thick.
- *Uneven braking:* Check for out-of-round or dented rims. Sometimes the brakes will grab unevenly and, at the same time, "shudder" or "judder." Juddering means that the entire brake assembly is loose on the trunnion bolt holding it to the frame. The brake assembly must be rigid. Loosen the locknut, take up on the adjusting nut and retighten the locknut. The brakes should have no front-to-rear play; they should pivot freely but not loosely. If the brakes still "judder," check the head bearing play on the front fork, and readjust (see Chapter 14).

Hubs and Freewheels That Make Your Wheels Go Faster—or Slower: a Critical Look at Today's Hubs and How to Maintain Them

Hubs are right down there near the ground. Dirt, dust or sand are thrown up at them pretty much all the time and a lot hits the hub some of the time. And when it rains it pours all over the hubs. Tires kick up dirt and pick up water. In connection with hubs, I well remember one bicycle camping trip in Vermont. We had pulled into Calvin Coolidge State Park, off that notorious 15-percent grade backbreaker of Route 101A. I felt, subconsciously, that something was amiss with my rear hub. When we settled in and got the tents up and the panniers unpacked, I pulled off the rear wheel and twirled the axle between thumb and forefinger. There it was. I could *feel* as well as *hear* the grains of sand wearing down my expensive Campagnolo hub bearings and beautifully ground and precision-polished and -honed cones and races. Fortunately I had a pair of hub wrenches along for this very eventuality, along with a small tube of grease. I cleaned out hub and bearings and repacked with Lubri-plate grease. Took about fifteen minutes all told.

In this chapter we will go into hub maintenance in some detail and evaluate, in terms of their strengths and weaknesses, the more popular hubs you can buy today.

Not all hubs have the same friction-free rolling ability. Some have more friction built into them by virtue of their less precise machining tolerances and sloppy thread cutting, among other reasons. Cheap hubs use low-quality steel and bearings. Lapping and polishing them is a waste of time: You can't make a silk purse out of these sow's ears, if for no other reason than as soon as you put them back together the poorly cut threads will cause moving parts to assume a different relationship, probably somewhat cocked to one side, so you will literally wind up with hubs in a bind, as before.[1] The only think to do with cheap hubs is to put them on your wheelbarrow, or cheap bikes, which is where they came from in the first place.

In this book our emphasis is on utility, but we like our utility tempered with fun, if not enjoyment. Good hubs are easy to find, so why not use them and make cycling easier and more enjoyable.

[1] And they weigh a ton. A cheap steel rear hub, without freewheel and solid axle nuts, will depress the scale (and me) over 484 grams, versus 225 grams for a Phil Wood rear hub or 291 grams for a Campy rear hub. Remember, an ounce of weight off the wheel is worth two off the frame.

The better bicycles, say those over $250 and up, will very likely come with fairly decent hubs. But if they do not have the better hubs described in detail in this chapter, then I would urge you seriously to consider spending the $50 or so per pair it takes to upgrade your cycling fun. The difference between good hubs and poor, high-friction hubs is really enormous in terms of rolling resistance. You won't notice it at first, perhaps, but on a long trip poor hubs can be a real drag.

CHOOSING A NEW HUB

High Flange Versus Low Flange

Back in the early 1970s when the bike boom began and a lot of European bikes were imported to fill the demand in this country, most of them had high-flange hubs because they looked sporty and racy. In fact, with high flange hubs you use shorter spokes. Shorter spokes make for a more rigid wheel, which is fine for a road racing cyclist who wants maximum efficiency in getting his energy into forward movement. But for a touring cyclist, the less resilient high-flange wheel offers a harder ride.

That's why I prefer low-flange hubs. They help make your wheels a bit more resilient. If, however, you have a problem with spokes breaking, due to your size and strength, you might want to go to a 40- or a 44-spoke wheel, in which case, I would recommend a high-flange hub, because all those holes drilled in the flange of a small-flange hub are awfully close together and weaken the hub. This would be particularly true in a tandem. See Table 11-1 for hubs with these drillings.

Checking for Width

Dropout distances (distance between the inner surface of both dropouts) on both fork and rear dropouts come in different widths so you should measure these widths and select a hub with correct width to fit. For example, front dropouts, measured from the inside surface, (Fig. 11-27) can be 90, 100 or 110 millimeters (3.937 in. or 4.3307 in.). Rear-dropout distances can be 120, 125, 126 or 127 millimeters. The wider distances are designed for six- or seven-speed freewheel clearances. Tables 11-3 and 11-4 recap these dimensions.

A HUB PATHOLOGIST'S DISSECTION REPORT

Before I get into the clinical pathology of bicycle hubs, I would like to review, quickly, the pros and cons of sealed-bearing versus non-sealed-bearing hubs. A good example of the former are Campagnolo hubs (Fig. 11-1), in all their glory, and Durham or Phil Wood hubs (Fig. 11-2).

Table 11-1 Comparative Specifications of Hubs

Make and Model	Front	Rear	Flange	Speed	Locknut to Locknut (mm)	Spoke Holes	Weight* (grams)	Threading†	Cost (Per Hub)‡
Campagnolo Hubs									
Record 1034/A Road	x		Low	—	100	24,28,32,36,40	227	—	$35.00
Record 1034/B Road		x	Low	5	120	Same	291	A,B,C	40.00
Record 1034/P Road		x	Low	6	125	Same	299	Same	43.00
Record 1035/A Road	x		High	—	100	Same	263	—	45.00
Record 1035/P		x	Same	5	120	Same	326	Same	51.00
Record 1035/P		x	Same	6	125	Same	331	Same	53.00
Record 1036/A Track	x		High	—	100	24,28,32,36	226	—	45.00
Record 1036/P Track		x	High	—	120	Same	336	Same	51.00
Nuovo Tipo 1264 Road	x		Low	—	100	Same	227	—	23.00
Nuovo Tipo 1265 Road		x	Low	5	120	Same	291	Same	26.00
Nuovo Tipo 1266 Road	x		High	—	100	Same	251	—	27.00
Nuovo Tipo 1267 Road		x	High	5	120	Same	326	Same	29.00
Shimano Road Hubs									
DuraAce HA-100	x		Low	—	100	28,32,36	220	A,B	31.00
Same		x	Low	5	120	Same	305	Same	35.00
Same		x	Low	6	125	Same	310	Same	38.00
DuraAce HA-200	x		High	—	100	Same	260	Same	30.00
Same		x	High	5	120	Same	330	Same	33.00
Same		x	High	6	125	Same	335	Same	37.00
600 HB-100	x		High	—	100	36	275	—	23.00
Same		x	High	5	120	36	350	A	25.00
Same		x	High	6	125	36	355	A	26.00
600 HB-200	x		Low	—	100	36	235	—	22.00
Same		x	Low	5	120	36	340	A	24.00
Same		x	Low	6	125	36	355	A	25.00

(See Table 11-2 for Shimano Freehub specifications)

Model	F	R	High/Low	Speeds	Width	Holes	Weight	A	Price
Shimano Track Hubs									
DuraAce HA310	x		High	—	100	28,32,36	225	—	28.50
DuraAce HA310		x	High	—	110 or 120	Same	295	—	32.50
DuraAce HA300	x		High	—	100	Same	240	—	21.00
DuraAce HA300		x	High	—	110 or 120	Same	313	—	23.50
Hi-E Road Hubs									
201	x		High	—	100	28,32,36,40	170	—	34.50
2282 (Tandem)	x		High	—	110	Same	210	—	28.50
232		x	Low	5	120	Same	227	A	26.00
233 (Heavy Duty)		x	Low	5	120	Same	245	A	28.00
Normandy Road Hubs									
H3F Sport	x		High	—	100	36	270	—	7.00
H3R		x	High	5	120	36	355	A	8.00
Sanshin Road Hubs									
HPA 101	x		Low	—	100	36	241	—	15.00
HPA 102		x	Low	5	120	36	327	A	16.00
HPA 103	x		High	—	100	36	270	—	16.00
HPA 104		x	High	5	120	36	344	A	17.00
SunTour Road Hubs (Maeda)									
Superbe RH 2000	x		High	—	100	28,32,36	236	—	25.00
Superbe RH 2000		x	High	5	120	Same	341	A	27.00
Superbe RH 2000		x	High	6	125	Same	346	A	29.00
Superbe RH 1000	x		Low	—	100	Same	278	—	23.00
Superbe RH 1000		x	Low	5	120	Same	354	A	25.00
Superbe RH 1000		x	Low	6	125	Same	362	A	26.00

Table 11-1 Comparative Specifications of Hubs

Make and Model	Front	Rear	Flange	Speed	Locknut to Locknut (mm)	Spoke Holes	Weight* (grams)	Threading†	Cost (Per Hub)‡
Phil Wood Hubs (1)									
Standard (Road)	x		Med.	—	90,100 or 108	20 to 48	170	—	26.00
Standard (Road)		x	Med.	5 or 6	120 or 127	Same	225	A	35.00
Brake Hub	x		Med.	—	90,100 or 108	Same	210	—	35.00
Brake Hub§		x	Med.	5 or 6	120,125,130, 135,140	Same	354 to 378	A	48.00
Track§	x		Med.	—	100,105,110	Same	170	—	35.00
Track§		x	Med.	—	115 or 120	Same	265	—	42.00
BMX Motocross	x		Med.	—	90 or 100	Same	170	—	26.00
BMX Motocross		x	Med.	—	100,105,110, 115,120	Same	225	—	35.00
Zeus Road Hubs §									
81	x		Low	—	NA	24,28,30,32,36,40	230	—	NA
81		x	Low	5	NA	Same	305	A,B,C	NA
81		x	Low	6	NA	Same	321	A,B,C	NA
81	x		High	—	NA	Same	241	—	NA
81		x	High	5	NA	Same	340	A,B,C	NA
81		x	High	6	NA	Same	353	A,B,C	NA
Zeus Criterium 80-1	x		Low	—	NA	Same	210	—	NA
80-1		x	Low	5	NA	Same	310	A,B,C	NA
80-1			Low	6	NA	Same	353	A,B,C	NA
Road Titanium	x		Low	—	NA	Same	180	—	NA
Road Titanium		x	Low	5	NA	Same	290	A,B,C	NA

Avocet Road Hubs

Model I	x	Low	—	100	36	202	—	16.50
Same	x	Low	5	120	36	310	A	23.50
Same	x	Low	6	125	36	319	A	25.00
Model I	x	High	—	100	36	212	—	18.50
Same	x	High	5	120	36	346	A	25.50
Same	x	High	6	125	36	351	A	27.50
Model II	x	Low	—	100	28,32,36	198	—	21.50
Same	x	Low	5	120	Same	252	A	28.00
Same	x	Low	6	125	Same	258	A	31.50
Same	x	High	—	100	Same	205	—	23.50
Same	x	High	5	120	Same	295	A	31.50
Same	x	High	6	125	Same	310	A	34.50
Model III	x	Low	—	100	Same	110	—	53.50
Same	x	Low	5	120	Same	285	A	72.00
Same	x	Low	6	125	Same	295	A	76.00

Durham Hubs

Bullseye	x	Low	—	110	28,32,36,40	170	—	34.50
Same	x	Low	5	120	Same	230	A	40.50
Same	x	Low	6	125	Same	242	A	42.50

* Less skewers but with dropout lock nuts where provided.

† A = English (1.370 inch x 24 TPI [threads per inch] BSC). B = French or metric (34.70mm x 1mm). C = Italian (35mm x 24 TPI).

‡ Pairs of hubs will be priced slightly less than single hubs. Zeus prices and components sizes about the same as Campagnolo, but varies considerably from dealer to dealer. Shop around.

§ Bolt on only. Bolt on road axles available at slight extra cost.

Fig. 11-1: Here is a conventional, loose-ball-bearing hub, and a very fine one at that, made by Campagnolo. This is a low-flange Record front hub. Arrow points to quick-release skewer.

All of these hubs are made to the finest of precision machining tolerances and finishes. They all offer about as low a rolling resistance as can be expected by today's technology, provided they are properly adjusted (an area we will cover later on in this chapter).

The non-sealed-bearing hubs such as the Campagnolo, DuraAce, SunTour Superbe are easy to disassemble, clean and put back together, as I did on my Vermont tour. You would need to take these hubs apart, clean out all old grease and dirt, repack and reassemble about once a year, depending on how much you bicycle.

The sealed-bearing hubs, such as Phil Wood, Avocet Models II and III and Durham, will go for years without requiring disassembly, cleaning and repacking with grease. I have been riding on Phil Wood hubs for about four years and they show absolutely no sign of needing lubricant or of being infiltrated with any abrasive substance such as fine sand. Occasionally, during shore rides along an ocean or Lake Michigan, I will ride over fine sand blown upon the bike trail from the beach. It's unavoidable so long as I am out on the trail; there will always be a thin, virtually invisible layer of beach sand on the bike trail near any beach. So far, the Phil Woods are doing fine.

Fig. 11-2: This hub, made by Phil Wood, has sealed bearings that last for thousands of miles without requiring maintenance. Note that you can use a quick-release skewer, or bolt the hub on with the Allen bolts furnished and shown on the hub. Spacer also has serrated detents which help hold it where you put it.

Sealed-bearing hubs are just that. They use a set of precision bearings fitted with neoprene or similar material (capillary or labyrinth shields) that are effective dirt and water stoppers. Figure 11-12 shows a Durham hub dissected, with parts laid out. At the left is a complete, intact sealed bearing, also at the left, a sealed bearing with seal removed. Later on we will show how to take one of these hubs apart, step by step, and reassemble it. For now, in terms of maintenance, the Durham is the only one of the three that can be so maintained without special tools. In fact, Phil Wood has designed his hubs so you *can't* take them apart because he would prefer to do that himself. In over five years of making many thousands of these hubs, Phil reports that only a handful have been returned for bearing work. The Avocet hubs you can take apart as far as the bearing by removing the two locknuts on one end and pulling the shaft out. But then there is no place to grip the bearings to pull them out, and you can only get at one side of the bearing to remove the seal for relube. But if it's only a matter of having to replace the grease, which, although it may last for five years, will ultimately need to be replaced, I don't see this as any great drawback. The sealed bearings are not sealed between sides. There is room between the balls in their races to force grease through to the other side, so even though you can't get at the other seal, on the inside of the bearing, you can still get some grease through by pushing it into the openings around the balls. In fact, you can easily lift off the outside grease seal on any of these sealed bearing hubs, dunk the entire hub in a grease-removing solvent such as Carbo-Chlor (1,1,1,-Trichloroethane) available in your hardware store, and repack from one side only. Now this is not the method I would recommend. It's much better to remove the entire bearing, both seals and repack that way. But if you are about to go on a trip and your sealed bearings are dry, or you think they are, just pry off the outer seal and inspect. If they need lubricant, add a dab, force through and replace the seal.

SEALED-BEARING HUBS PREFERRED

For touring, the obvious advantages of maintenance-free sealed bearings are the major selling point for their use in hubs. I like the idea that I can take off and never have to worry about dirt, fine sand or, in a downpour, water getting into my hub bearings and abrading polished cone surfaces, or water washing grease away. It's a happy feeling to leave a campsite on a lovely morning with the certain knowledge that all is well with my hubs. I might also point out here that I like sealed-bearing everything, including pedals, bottom brackets and headset; these we will review later on in other chapters. If there were such a thing as a sealed-bearing chain, you can bet I'd have one on my touring bike.

The better non-sealed-bearing hubs have, as noted, beautifully finished cones and races. The cheaper hubs have bearing races machined out of the same steel of which the hub is made, and you know that steel is not going to be anything like the inserts of polished alloy steel metal

Fig. 11-3: A high-quality hub race, showing the ground, lapped, honed and polished race surface. This cup is a high-quality steel insert in the aluminum-alloy hub body.

Fig. 11-4: This is an inexpensive steel hub, showing the race, arrow. The race is actually machined right out of the hub metal, and is not an insert, so the cup and race are not of high-quality steel. Arrow points to slight defect.

used in aluminum alloy hubs. For example, Figure 11-3 shows the ground, lapped and polished bearing race of a Campagnolo hub. Figure 11-4 shows the roughly machined race of a cheap steel hub. The Campy hub has a steel insert for the race, but the cheap steel hub race is made out of the same steel used for the entire hub. These two photos do not really do justice to the enormous differences between the two hubs, but you will get the picture. The arrow in Figure 11-4 points to a corroded spot in the cheap hub.

Another fairly major problem with cheap hubs is, as I stated earlier, the roughness of axle, cone and locknut thread cutting. There's so much slop in these that you have to be really careful in reassembling them. As you will note later on, when I get into more detail on hub assembly in this chapter, in tightening cone nuts you do it until you feel tightness (tightening by hand, never by wrench). As the cone snugs up to the bearings, back the cone off a half turn. Then insert any spacers and the locknut, and tighten the locknut. You should have a barely perceptible amount of sideplay in the hub axle. Now, if you tighten the quick-release skewer (arrow in Figure 11-1) on a cheap hub, slop in threads will force the cone tightly against the hub balls and, in short order, will score and gall the balls and races and make a poor hub even worse. Even on a fine hub as in Figure 11-1, you have to be really careful in hub-cone adjustment. Due to machining variations, no two hubs are really *exactly* alike, so you have to judge for yourself how tight the cone nut should be, how much play to leave in the hub, before tightening down on the locknut. Remember, the play or looseness between cone-race surface and balls will be taken up to some extent as you tighten down on the locknut, and to an additional extent as you tighten down on the quick-release lever or axle nuts. *Ideally there should be no sideplay in the hub after tightening the quick-release skewer or axle bolts, yet the wheel should spin freely.* How free is free? One way to tell if the wheel hub is binding is to spin the axle between thumb and forefinger before inserting the wheel into the dropout (end of fork or rear stays). You can tell right away if there is any roughness. The axle should rotate with a feeling of silky softness, like mist sliding over the land on a damp morning. When the wheel is back in the dropouts, tighten down on the quick-release skewer or axle bolts and turn the wheel until the valve is at the one-o'clock position and stop the rim at this point. As you let go, the wheel should turn by itself; the weight of the valve should pull it down. A properly adjusted hub will, if started at one o'clock, continue to spin on past six o'clock to about nine o'clock, back to four o'clock and oscillate more slowly back to between five and seven o'clock, with axle quick-release or axle bolts tightened. If the wheel does not show this degree of freeness, with *no* sideplay, you are putting way too much pressure on cones, balls and races and will have a fairly short-lived hub. Eventually, if not sooner, you will notice a wear spot, galling, around the hub race where excess pressures are forcing balls into the race metal.

Sealed-Bearing Adjustment

There are no cone nuts, as such, on sealed bearings. But there are flat nuts followed by locknuts on the Avocet hubs (Fig. 11-5). If these are taken up too tightly, excess side load is placed on the sealed bearings and they will bind, turn tightly. Figure 11-6 shows the axle removed from an Avocet Model II sealed bearing. Figure 11-7 shows a seal removed from one of the bearings. When (or if) you remove the axle and look inside the Avocet hub you will notice two long spacers inside the hub itself. There's about a quarter-inch space between the outer edge of the spacers and the inner edge of the bearing, room enough for a small

Fig. 11-5: Avocet sealed-bearing hubs, showing one of the bearings removed. Left is the rear hub.

Fig. 11-6: This is as far as you can go in disassembling the Avocet hub without special tools to remove the bearing. But you can remove the axle, should it need replacing if it gets bent. The bearing outer seal can also be removed, and one of them is shown at bottom left. This is a thin brass and neoprene seal, easily damaged; so if you remove, be careful not to force or bend it. See text for details.

driver to be placed and an attempt made to carefully punch out the bearing at the opposite end. No go. The bearing is in the hub in a very tight press fit. I don't recommend any attempt at replacing these bearings. Send any bad hubs back to Avocet, they will be glad to replace them. For subsequent lubrication, if ever needed, prying off the outer seal should enable you to force enough light grease into the bearing for another 5,000 miles or so. As Figure 11-7 shows—and this is a factory-fresh hub—there isn't much grease in a new hub anyway, and what there is is almost the consistency of oil. In prying off the seal, the best way, and this applies to all such seals, is to insert the point of a small knife blade behind the outer edge of the seal, and carefully pry upward and outward. The seal should lift off easily, and be as easily replaced by two fingers. It sort of snaps back into a groove just below the rim of the bearing.

I felt that the lubrication in Avocet hubs was so light that this in part accounted for the ease with which the axle could be spun between thumb and forefinger. I also feel that this very light grease or oil is not adequate lubrication for the stresses of a loaded-down bicycle on a long camping tour, although I am sure that the factory supplied the bearings to Avocet this way. I removed seals from both bearings and packed them with Lubriplate. Now the axle does not spin so freely. In fact, it does not

Fig. 11-7: The Avocet hub with seal removed. Note that you can force grease through the bearing into the other side; but go easy so you don't push off the seal on the inside where you can't get at it. But sealed bearings are easy to regrease because the seal comes off so readily.

Fig. 11-8: To do any hub maintenance you will need these thin but strong hub-cone wrenches. I recommend two of each because you will need to hold the cone while you tighten the locknut. Any bike shop will have them.

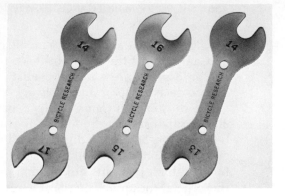

spin nearly as freely as a properly adjusted non-sealed bearing Campagnolo hub, packed with the same grease. Sealed bearings in the Durham hub are packed with a grease similar to the viscosity of Lubriplate, yet the axle spins very freely.[2] To remove locknuts from the Avocet hubs you will need two thin cone wrenches (spanners), (Fig. 11-8) as for all hubs, available from your local bike shop for about $3 each. The Avocet takes two 13-millimeter cone wrenches, one to hold the inner nut, one to turn the outer nut while you hold the inner nut from turning.

Grease is more viscous, heavier, than oil and will of course reduce

Fig. 11-9: Campagnolo Record hub dissected. This hub, like all rear Campy hubs, takes a total of sixteen ¼-inch balls, eight to a side. The two grease seals are shown at top left and at right. (Campy does not make this hi-lo combination at this time).

[2] To be fair to Avocet, I may have overpacked the bearings, in turn causing friction between the grease and the seals.

rolling resistance. That's why racing cyclists use oil in bearings, and why on Campy hubs there's an oil hole in the hub, covered by a black clip. But unless you are a racing cyclist, oil instead of grease on a tour will lead to disaster, to prematurely aged bearings.

The dust cap on Campy hubs is pretty good, (arrows in Fig. 11-9), fits closely against the axle but is not as good a seal as on sealed, precision-bearing sets. Some fine dust can still get into conventional loose ball and cup hubs. Spoke holes on Avocet hubs are not generously radiused. That is, they don't cup outward enough, in my opinion, to support spokes at this crucial location. The point where spokes bend through flange holes is an area of high stress where spokes are most likely to break.

Phil Wood Sealed-Bearing Hubs

The most popular sealed-bearing hub in this country is the one that's made here and has been around the longest, the Phil Wood hub (Fig. 11-2). There are a number of excellent features designed into this hub. First, I have never been able to get it to bind, no matter how tightly I squeeze the quick-release lever. Hubs always run freely. So there's no problem in excessive side loading. The flanges angle in slightly, instead of being straight up and down as in conventional hubs, including the Campagnolo front hub in Figure 11-1. Figure 11-2 does not show this slight angle, but it's enough to lead spokes at a less stressful angle, which, combined with the generous radiusing or cupping of flange spoke holes which *is* shown in Figure 11-2, leads to longer spoke life and less likelihood of spoke breakage. The hub in Figure 11-2 happens to be a bolt-on, with more convenient Allen nuts. You will also note the serrated end of the spacer, which helps hold the hub where you want it. The axle is hollow, so you can use a quick-release if you wish. And here is as good a place as any to take a breather and talk for a moment about bolt-on versus quick-release hubs.

To Bolt or Not to Bolt

If you understand the genesis, the development of the high-performance touring bicycle we Americans love so well, you can understand how it came to pass that we see most of these machines with quick-release hubs. The modern high-performance touring bicycle is descended from the high-performance road-racing bicycle popular in Europe. When the bike boom hit America in the late 1960s and early 1970s, the only decent bikes were actually modified road-racing bikes with, for the most part, minor concessions to touring, such as fenders and conventional tires. But the best bikes most of us bought were short-wheelbase, short-fork-rake racing machines, with tubular tires, and high-flange hubs with quick-release skewers. The quick-release is a fairly heavy device. The quick-release in Figure 11-10 weighs 70.875 grams (around 2.5 oz.) and

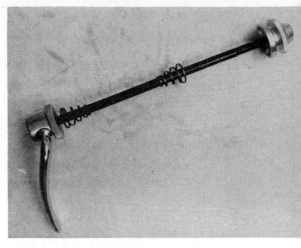

Fig. 11-10: Typical quick-release skewer. Note correct position of springs, small end facing toward hub. As you remove skewer from hub, be ready to catch the spring, because if you drop it on the floor it will bounce right to a terrific hiding place. I must have a dozen such lurking around my basement, destined never to be found.

that's the shorter front-hub unit. A longer, heavier rear-wheel quick-release skewer weighs 87.885 grams or a tad over 3 ounces. Compare these measurements, a combined weight of 158.76 grams, with the 57.7 grams (2 oz.) of the axle bolts of the Durham hubs, or about the same weight for axle nuts, and you will see there is a considerable savings in weight when you bolt the axle and do not use a quick-release. Remember, an ounce off the wheel is worth two off the frame.

The only reason for the quick-release is to be able to change wheels in a hurry. That's why quick-releases are universally used by road-racing cyclists, both professionals and amateurs. But tourists are not road racers, and you don't need to be able to tear a wheel from a bike and stick on a new one in seconds. You have time, if you get a flat, to leisurely sit down and curse out the situation, then repair the puncture, in most instances without even removing the wheel. Quick-release skewers can be accidentally loosened, so that when you hit a bump, the wheel can pop out of the dropouts and cause an accident. Or, if you push hard on the pedals, you can pull the rear wheel to one side so it rubs on the stay. If you bolt the wheels on, however, they are in place to stay, and you need not worry that leaning the bike against a tree or bumping into something as you wheel the bike has loosened the skewer lever. And bolted-on wheels are a bit harder to steal. A quick-release invites wheel theft. True, bolted-on wheels are the hallmark of cheap bikes, with heavy threaded solid axles. But anyone who can't tell your good bike from an el cheapo, with or without quick releases, is not someone you need to impress anyhow.

On tour, take along one lightweight wrench that will fit hub nuts so you can remove the wheel from the bike if you have to. If you are touring with friends, only one of you need carry a tool kit if you include enough sizes to fit everybody's bike. You don't need ten sets of tools for ten bikes. Just make sure that any odd-size Allen wrenches, for instance, are in the tool kit.

Durham Sealed-Bearing Hubs

You can buy the more popular Phil Wood hubs in most bike stores, but you may have to order Durham hubs from the manufacturer because these are so new. Major specifications and prices are in Table 11-1. The Durham people are: Durham Bicycles, 3944 Marathon Street, Los Angeles, California 90029. Phone: 213/664-4534.

The Durham sealed-bearing hubs are the only ones of this type that you can easily and quickly take apart, including removal of the bearings. This is a convenience because you don't need to return hubs to the factory if, after 5,000 miles or whenever, the bearing develops roughness. Any roughness in a sealed, precision bearing means that it should be replaced. This is unlike a conventional loose-ball hub, since these can develop some roughness which usually only indicates the presence of dirt. A quick disassembly, cleaning, repacking with grease, readjusting of cones and you're on your way. Durham uses Conrad type of bearings, as do all sealed-bearing hubs, which, when properly greased and seated, have substantially less friction than loose-ball hubs, sometimes as much as 30 percent less.

I have tried to side-load a Durham hub with both axle nuts and quick-releases, and it just can't be done, because bearings have end clearance between them and the internal spacer. The Durham hubs use NTN #6001-LLB bearings, available from bearing supply houses. A cross-reference check will discover other makes of bearings that will fit.

To disassemble Durham hubs:

STEP ONE: Loosen Allen bolt with small Allen wrench provided with hub (Fig. 11-11).

STEP TWO: Pull axle out through one of the bearings (Fig. 11-11).

STEP THREE: Look inside, through one of the bearings, You will see a central spacer that has dropped off to one side, like the Leaning Tower of Pisa. With the end of the axle, push lightly and the bearing at the other end will drop out. Bearings are held in the hub by a hand-pressure fit, snug but not very tight. This takes accurate machining, because you want just enough tightness to keep the outer circumference of the bearing from spinning under a load but enough looseness so bearings can be removed without special tools, and replaced the same way.

Fig. 11-11: Durham sealed-bearing hub. Spacer comes with Allen bolt and Allen wrench to fit.

Fig. 11-12: Durham hub dissected. Note that the seal at top left is slightly damaged and will have to be carefully straightened before installation so it won't rub on bearing. This is the only sealed-bearing hub on the market you can easily disassemble yourself. All it takes is the tiny Allen wrench furnished with the hub. Bolts are furnished if you do not wish to use a quick-release skewer. I prefer the bolts. Saves a lot of weight, makes for greater security and peace of mind. Internal spacer is at top of photo.

STEP FOUR: Remove the other bearing, following Step 3.

STEP FIVE: With the sharp edge of a knife, press down at the edge of the seal and slightly outward, lifting the seal carefully out of the bearing. The seal has a thin brass shell that's easily dented and, once dented, difficult to straighten. If not straightened, though, the seal can rub internally on the bearing and cause a slight amount of drag—enough to bother you, or at least me. Figure 11-12 shows a bent seal arrow (the one at the top).

STEP SIX: Clean and repack bearings, both sides, with a light grease such as Lubriplate or the grease Phil Wood sells through bike shops in tubes.

STEP SEVEN: Replace seals, being careful to get them into the groove around the inner edge of the bearing, pressing all around until well seated.

STEP EIGHT: Replace center spacer. Push in both bearings with the palm of your hand. If they do not go in easily, push around the edges. Try to seat them in evenly so they don't get cocked to one side as you insert them.

STEP NINE: Replace end bushings (spacers) and tighten Allen bolts.

NOTE: The rear hub has two one-millimeter spacers on the left side and one on the right, or freewheel, side. If you use a freewheel that is so wide that the high gear is too close to the chainstay, so the chain binds on the stay, you need to move the hub to the left. On the Durham, you just use the old Allen wrench, remove both spacers, and move a washer (Fig. 11-14) from the left to the right side. So you can calculate the amount of "dish" you will need when lacing up the hub and rim (see

Fig. 11-13: Durham hub has flats on axle (arrows) which distribute the load to the axle more efficiently than if the axle were round, as on other hubs.

Chapter 15) it's a good idea to screw the freewheel onto the hub and put it into the rear dropout, making sure there is enough room for the chain between the small high gear and the chainstay (please refer to Appendix for an illustrated glossary of bicycle terms). Do not use washers on the right unless you have to, to keep "dishing" at a minimum. The greater the dish, the weaker the wheel construction. We'll talk more about wheel dishing in Chapter 15, and when we discuss the new Shimano Freehubs later on in this chapter.

Internally generated friction is low in Durham hubs. One reason for this is the noncontact labyrinth seals, which seal without touching inner races. If you plan to ride in rough, open country where you will meet a lot of dust and dirt, Durham can provide heavy-duty contact seals, but expect greater friction.

Durham, in their literature, claims that a wheel used for six months with their hub was released, with valve stem around the 2-o'clock position, and the wheel oscillated back and forth sixty-four times before stopping! I tried it on my own bike, and although not exactly hitting that world's record, I did pretty well at fifty-one small oscillations, on a hub with about ten miles on it. By oscillations I mean the valve moving back and forth past the six-o'clock mark. I know I've given Durham hubs a lot more space in this book than any other hub. This does not imply that good sealed-bearing hubs such as the Phil Wood or Avocet are any worse . . . or better, but simply that Roger Durham, the engineer who designs and builds those hubs, is a very verbal type who loves to furnish scads of detailed data, a small part of which I have used.

A few more points. Durham bearings can carry 885 pounds each, a total of 3,540 pounds, which is a bit more than I recommend you carry on a bike touring trip! But you can peak out at a fairly hefty load if you hit a pothole, and cheap hubs bend axles fairly easily under such conditions. Durham axles are machined flat where they fit onto dropouts (Fig. 11-13), which is a more efficient way to transmit the wheel load to the frame. The load is spread over a wider area in the flattened axle than on the smaller area of the conventional rounded axle. Also, if you totally

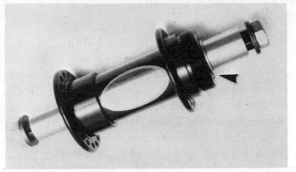

Fig. 11-14: Durham rear hub. Note longer spacers. Arrow points to washers that can be moved from one side of hub to the other to improve chainline.

strip the alloy threads of the freewheel boss, you can have it replaced at the factory, so you can salvage the hub. The Phil Wood hubs are great, but because you can't remove the bearings except at the factory, something of a mystery. That they work and are durable cannot be denied. I've traveled thousands of miles on them. Durham hubs, though, are newer. I've traveled hundreds, not thousands, of miles on *them* and like them as well as the Phil Woods. And I feel a bit more independent knowing that I can take the Durhams apart and fix them myself with no more tools than a fifty-cent Allen wrench that comes with the hub.

Hi-E Sealed-Bearing Hubs

There's one more make of sealed-bearing hub on the market, made and designed by that innovative aircraft engineer and bicycle racer, Harlan Byrne, president of Hi-E Engineering, Inc. Harlan sells most of his products by mail and can be reached at 1247 School Lane, Nashville, Tennessee 37217, 615/361-1312.

Harlan makes road and track hubs (Fig. 11-15), and some of these are

Fig. 11-15: Lightweight Hi-E Engineering, Inc., sealed-bearing hub weighs only 3.1 ounces, can go around 1,500 miles before requiring hub maintenance.

the lightest in the world (see Table 11-1). I can testify to the strength of these hubs, paper light as they are, because in my own inimitable fashion I put the front hub, traditionally the weaker of the two hubs because it's smaller, to the total-destruct test. I hit the expansion crack in a long bridge at about 30 miles per hour. (The going was downhill, the wind was at my back. I normally travel at a more sedate speed with a loaded bike.) The bike broke in half at the steering head tube. I was injured but the hub stood up fine and I use it to this day on my lightest frame, which is handy when impressing bike novices with how light a bike can get (this one is around eighteen pounds) but strictly for day touring. I don't race, and to tour on this super lightweight would be not only a travesty of use but would probably hurt this poor light baby.

Hi-E hubs, like all such, use precision-sealed bearings, they're rated as ABEC-1 in the Hi-E hub, which means they are very high precision. You can't remove these bearings without special tools, and Harlan asks you to return them if they get rough. You also have to be careful not to overtighten the quick-release so as to prevent undue sideload on the bearings. Harlan goes for lightness and low rolling friction in his designs, as witnessed in probably the world's lightest front hub, his Number 202 time-trial hub which weighs in at a flyweight 114 grams (4 ounces). The Hi-E heavy-duty front hub is what you should tour on, though, and this weighs 156 grams, or 5.5 ounces, still among the world's lightest, although Zeus's titanium front hub reaches down there at 180 grams (Table 11-1).

Hi-E bearings can only be replaced at the factory unless you have a machine shop with arbor press and are careful to pack up the hub area to prevent damage. Harlan uses Santotrac HT-2 grease to repack his hubs. This is an excellent waterproof, light-viscosity grease which should be obtainable at your local bearing supply house. Repacking should include replacing bearing capillary seals.

CONVENTIONAL HUBS

There's a lot to be said for the old tried and true conventional loose-ball hubs; however, you will find that if you should drop one of the balls as you take them apart, it instantly disappears—forever. You can clean the basement floor till it shines, but you will still never, ever, find that bearing. Quicksilver rolls more slowly. Campagnolo hubs are in my judgment the winner and still champion among quality loose-ball hubs. (If this nomenclature is too anthropomorphic for you, just think of these hubs as Campy types, at least until Campy comes out with a sealed-bearing model.) Campagnolo hubs have high-precision races, ground, honed, lapped and polished to a fare-thee-well, and no other hub is better in this department. Sunshine, Shimano DuraAce (Fig. 11-16 and 11-17) SunTour Superbe and Zeus, not in that order necessarily, are close seconds.

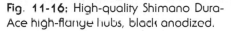

Fig. 11-16: High-quality Shimano Dura-Ace high-flange hubs, black anodized.

Fig. 11-17: Shimano DuraAce black anodized low-flange hubs.

Which brings us to Shimano's newest creation, the one and only Free-hub. This is so different from anything on the market that we will need an entire subhead for it.

The Shimano Freehub

The Shimano Freehub, in both DuraAce, the next lower priced 600 EX, and the Altus models in the lower price range, incorporates the free-wheel as part of the hub. In weighing the Shimano freewheel, with six-speed cogs installed and quick-release skewer in place, I came up on my scales with a weight of 666.5 grams (23.5 ounces). Weighing a Campagnolo hub with a much bigger freewheel, also six speeds but with larger cogs, I came up with a weight of 694.5 grams (24.5 ounces), only a 4 percent difference in weight between the two. With a Regina Titall seven-speed freewheel, the Campy rear hub with quick-release weighed only 567 grams (20 ounces).

However, the freehub does offer advantages, other than weight savings, over conventional hubs with separate freewheel. First, the free-wheel cogs come in a cassette (Fig. 11-18) held together by three four-millimeter bolts. In Figure 11-18 the bolts are painted white so you can see them. It is possible to make up different gear combinations (see

Fig. 11-18: Shimano freewheel cassette for the Freehub. Cassette slides into the splined Freehub body, is tightened by the last (high-gear) cog using the cog tool (Fig. 10-19). Arrow points to 4-mm. cassette bolt. There are three. To change individual cogs, remove all three bolts.

Table 11-2) and carry them along with you on tour. To change gears, all you do is unscrew the high-gear cog, the one farthest on the right, remove it and pull off the remaining four or five teeth (depending on whether you use five or six gears). Shimano says you can switch from five to six gears without redishing the wheel or changing the bike frame, but in their literature I notice that whereas zero dish (see Chapter 15) is required for the 110-millimeter locknut-to-locknut hub, 2.95 millimeters are required for the five-speed 120-millimeter hub and 7.8 millimeters of dish are required for the six-speed 120-millimeter rear hub, so some redishing will be necessary in switching from the five- to the six-speed combination. As of this writing, you can only get up to a low gear of 26 teeth on the DuraAce freehub, which is not enough for your author, who likes a "Granny" gear combination of 32 or 34 teeth plus a 24- or 26-tooth chainwheel for a low, low, low hill-climbing gear. You could walk up the hill faster, but riding is easier and more elegant. But the Shimano people tell me that they are working on a wider gear range for the freewheel hub. Back to the cassette system. I suppose this would appeal to you if you were a real fanatic and wanted just that perfect combination of gears for each and every flat or hill and didn't mind stopping every few miles to change the cassette. To do this, though, you would need to carry along a fairly heavy tool (Fig. 11-19) that weighs nearly one pound

Fig. 11-19: Cog remover (and tightener). Tool is shown on a Shimano cassette. But use this tool the same way on any freewheel to remove cogs, removing always the high-gear cog first. You can hold freewheel gears in a special holder that grips them without damage, or put the freewheel between two pieces of wood in the jaws of a vise, or if the freewheel is on a hub, put the opposite-side locknut in a vise. In all cases, turn the cog remover **clockwise** to remove a cog. In reassembling cogs, hold the low-gear cog in a freewheel and with the cog tool, tighten the cog down lightly. Pedal action will take care of the rest. Just make sure that the cogs are seated as far as they can go before you pedal away.

Table 11-2 Shimano Freehubs*

Model No.	Speeds	Flange	Weight* (grams)	Locknut-to-Locknut Dimensions (mm)†	High-Gear Selections (threaded cog)	Low-Gear Selections	Cost‡
DuraAce EX							
HF-100	6	Low	398	120	11,12,13,14	12,13,14,15,16,17,18,19,20,21, 22,23,24	$42.50
Same	6	Low	403	126	Same	Same	45.00
HF-110	5	Low	393	120	Same	Same	41.50
600 EX §							
HF 350	6	Low	403	120	12,13,14,15	13,14,15,16,17,18,19,20,21,22, 23,24,28	27.00
HF 360	5	Low	395	120	Same	Combinations of above in five speeds	25.00
HF 370	6	High	405	120	Same	Same in six-speed selection	28.00
HF 380	5	High	413	120	Same	Same in five-speed selection	25.00

* For conversion to ounces, see Appendix. Weight is less cogs.

† Combination freewheel and hub in one unit. Use only with EX derailleur.

‡ Costs are approximate and subject to change without notice. Dealers have different markups; shop around.

§ Also available in 124- and 126-millimeter locknut-to-locknut widths. Weights will be a bit greater.

(around 440 grams), not a terribly practical touring tool to lug around. If you race, have a sagwagon on the road and it's a long, long stage race, you would find the cassette sprocket interchange system handy, though. You can also tear down individual freewheels, with the tool shown in Figure 11-19, and swap cogs around, although the freewheel cassette system is more convenient. If you leave out the cassette bolts (Fig. 11-18) and forget about the cogs as a cassette, you can carry individual cogs and change them with the cog-removal tool.

If, with a freehub, you break a spoke on the freewheel side, you will have to remove the cogs so you can install a new spoke. This also applies to the conventional hub and separate freewheel system, except that in this case all you need do is remove the entire freewheel with a free-wheel removal tool, which is a lot lighter and smaller than the cog remover in Figure 11-19. Figures 11-20 and 11-21 show a number of these tools, and you will note that they are different, so on tour be sure to carry the one that fits your freewheel. The splined freewheel and matching tool are the easier combination to use. Figure 11-22 shows a Shimano Altus freehub with cassette gear cluster removed. The Shimano DuraAce, or 600 EX series freehubs, *must be* used with an EX series rear derailleur. This is the type of derailleur that has an open cage on the inner or left side (Fig. 11-23). This type of derailleur must be used because the freewheel unit is so close to the right-hub flange that it would run against the flange when the chain is shifted onto the low gear. There's nothing new about this type of "broken" cage derailleur; Sun-Tour has had them for years. They do offer the additional advantage of being able to lift the chain out of the freewheel entirely, without having to use a rivet remover to take the chain apart. This is handy when all you want to do is remove the derailleur for cleaning. Of course, if you really

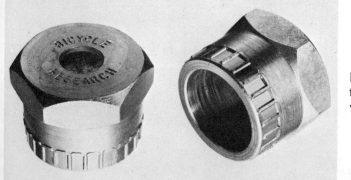

Fig. 11-22: Shimano Altus freehub. Freewheel is an integral part of the hub. Cogs fit on splines, except high-gear cog, which threads on.

Fig. 11-23: You can only use a derailleur with the top inner case, or most of it, missing, with Shimano freehubs, because the full cage would rub on the low-gear cogs. Arrow points to area where inner cage has been eliminated except for small guide. In this design the chain can also be lifted off so derailleur can be removed without "breaking" chain.

Fig. 11-24: This is the kind of derailleur you **cannot** use with a Shimano freehub. Arrow points to inner cage that would rub on low-gear cogs.

need to clean the derailleur, the chain undoubtedly needs cleaning too and should be removed, cleaned and relubed as explained in Chapter 13. The type of derailleur shown in Figure 11-24 cannot be used with the freehub because here, as shown, the cage is not "broken" and extends around the derailleur cage and would run on the Shimano Freehub right flange when in the low gear. This explains in part why the freehub only goes to 26 teeth—because the Shimano Crane GS wide-range derailleur with extra-long cage, similar to the one in Figure 11-24, does not have a "broken" cage and so a cog with more than 28 teeth requiring a wide-range derailleur could not be used. This poses no terrible technical problem and I expect to see it solved fairly soon, probably by the time this book is off the press.

Let's look now at problems involved with the Shimano DuraAce freehub and similar Shimano freehub designs. To take the DuraAce version apart you need a 14-millimeter cone wrench for the cone nut and a 13-millimeter cone wrench for the locknut over the cone. You also need a special Shimano tool to remove the freewheel unit, (indicated with an asterisk in Fig. 11-25, which also shows the entire freehub dismantled).

Dismantle following these steps:

STEP ONE: Remove quick-release skewer by holding the lever in one hand and unscrewing the skewer nut at the other end. Be careful to catch the two small springs as you pull the skewer through the hollow axle.

Fig. 11-25: Shimano DuraAce Freehub dissected. Arrow points to threading on the freewheel body that fits into matching threads inside the hub itself. Asterisk is next to special freewheel remover.

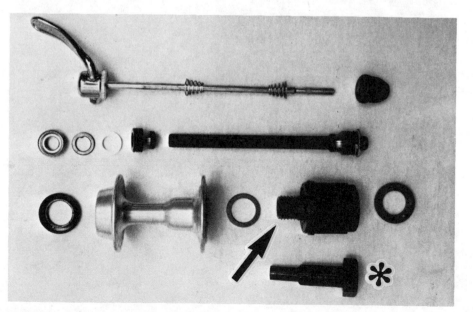

Figure 11-10 shows a skewer. Note that the smaller part of each spring always faces toward the hub.

STEP TWO: With a 14-millimeter cone wrench holding the cone, loosen the locknut on the left side (facing forward) of the hub. Remove splined washer and spacer. Remove the cone. Now carefully pull the axle out through the freewheel side, catching all loose balls (and they will be loose) in a rag on the workbench or table. If you drop a ball on the floor, you may never find it, as I noted earlier in this chapter. If you lose a ball, don't worry about measuring another one. Just take one of the remaining balls to the bike shop where they can find you a duplicate. The freehub uses nine quarter-inch (6.35-mm.) balls per side.

STEP THREE: Insert the special freehub removal tool (arrow, Fig. 11-25) and turn it counterclockwise. The freehub threads out of the hub shell, and if you look closely at Figure 11-25 you will see the threads. Note that there is a washer or spacer between the freehub and the hub shell which must be replaced when you reassemble the freehub. The round black things at both sides of the freehub are plastic dust seals.

There is a layer of grease between the freewheel and the hub. Figure 11-26 shows the bored-out hole into which the freehub is threaded, and you can see deeper inside the hub some of the threads for the freehub.

STEP FOUR: Clean out all old grease and dirt, repack with grease and reassemble, reversing the above instructions. As you begin to adjust the left-side hub cone, however, be very careful about taking up on it. Leave just a smidgen of sideplay so that when you tighten the locknut the freewheel turns freely. I have found that just a touch too tight an adjustment on the cone and locknut will cause the freewheel to rub and bind against the hub. You can have acceptable smoothness in axle rotation but still have tightness in the freewheel rotation. As you tighten the quick-release, again check to make sure *both* axle and freewheel turn freely and that there is no sideplay in the axle.

I do not recommend taking the freewheel apart. There are about fifteen million tiny little ball bearings plus springs and ratchets. Every-

Fig. 11-26: This is the part of the hub where the freewheel (Shimano Dura-Ace hub) fits. Arrow points to threads inside hub body where freewheel threads. Note layer of grease in outer hub flange, where end of freewheel rotates. There is a spacer that must be used between the freewheel and the hub, shown above. Freewheel must not be overtightened or it will bind and rub on hub body.

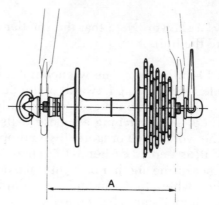

Fig. 11-27: Hubs come with varying locknut-to-locknut widths, as do the spacings between the inner surface of front and rear dropouts. To make sure a new hub will fit in your bicycle, measure distance (A) between dropouts and the same distance between inner surface of dropouts. Both measurements should be the same, or at least within one millimeter of each other. Add or remove thin spacers if necessary. But before buying a new set of hubs, specify correct locknut-to-locknut distance.

thing you need to do will be covered later on in this chapter, in more detail, and I will disassemble a typical freewheel and lay the parts out on a table and show you what you will be faced with. Then, if you're brave, go ahead. You may have a broken ratchet, or a stuck one in your good freewheel, or want to replace worn cogs and save the freewheel body, and we'll get into that later.

Conventional Hub Maintenance

Earlier in this chapter we reviewed the problem of conventional loose-bearing hub-cone adjustment, which is the one most overlooked. It's easy to say to yourself, "Well, I've had this bike now for four years and I have never looked at the wheel bearings. Maybe I better do it before I go on tour." Tour or no, you really should remove the wheel every six months or so, spin the axle between thumb and forefinger and feel and listen for signs of roughness and dirt. Once a year you should disassemble hubs (Fig. 11-28) clean out old grease, repack with fresh light grease and readjust hub cones. I have already reviewed maintenance of sealed bearings and the Shimano freewheel hub. Since most of us still have the conventional loose-ball hub, let's now review maintenance of this excellent hub design, with emphasis on cone adjustment.

STEP ONE: Remove wheel from bike. Remove freewheel. You will need a freewheel remover that fits your freewheel. If you have a freewheel that takes a serrated tool (Fig. 11-21) you're lucky, because all you need do is remove the quick-release skewer or axle bolt, insert the freewheel remover in the freewheel, turn the wheel over, holding the tool in place,

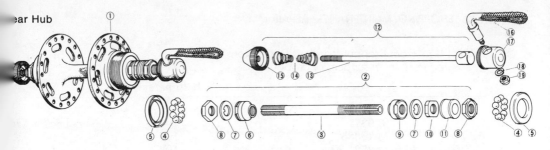

Fig. 11-28: Detailed view of a typical good-to-excellent conventional rear high-flange aluminum alloy hub. Parts are: (1) complete hub; (2) complete axle; (3) axle; (4) ¼-in. steel balls; (5) dust cap; (6) cone nut; (7) keyed washer; (8) locknut; (9) cone nut; (10) locknut (two on freewheel side on this particular hub); (11) spacer; (12) complete quick-release skewer assembly; (13) skewer axle (mounting stud); (14) volute springs; (15) nut for mounting stud; (16) quick-release lever; (17) lever body; (18) spring washer; (19) cap nut on lever.

and clamp the tool in a vise. Then just twist the wheel counterclockwise. The freewheel will be very tight, so you will need a little muscle, both hands on the tire. If the freewheel tool won't fit over the locknut, then remove it. You might also have to remove any washers and spacers under the locknut. If you do not have the serrated kind of freewheel, but one with two indents, you will need a freewheel-removing tool like that in Figure 11-30.

STEP TWO: With one cone wrench (Fig. 11-29) on the inner cone, holding it so it can't turn, loosen the left locknut. Figure 11-28 shows a close-up

Fig. 11-29: Thin cone wrenches are needed to disassemble hub. One, bottom, holds cone nut from turning while the upper wrench loosens locknut.

Fig. 11-30: Freewheel remover for Regina BRP freewheels

Table 11-3 Front Dropout Standard Dimensions*
(Measured from inner surfaces of dropouts)

Inches	Millimeters
3.5433	90
3.937	100
4.13385	105
4.252	108
4.3307	110

* There may be differences of plus or minus one or two millimeters but these are negligible. See also Figure 11-27 for measuring hub size to fit the dimensions in this table.

Table 11-4 Rear Dropout Standard Dimensions*
(Measured from inner surfaces of dropouts)

Number of Freewheel Cogs	Inches	Millimeters
5	4.7244	120
6	4.9125	125
6	4.9999	127 †
6 or 7	5.1181	130 †
6 or 7	5.31495	135 †
6 or 7	5.5118	140 †

* There may be differences of plus or minus one or two millimeters, but these are negligible. Use spacing washers. See also Figure 11-27 for measuring hub size to fit dimensions in this table.
† This size hub available from Phil Wood.

of a rear-wheel hub. One cone wrench should hold the cone, number 6 in Figure 11-28; the other cone wrench should turn the locknut, part number 8. If the hub has never been apart, the locknut may be pretty tight due to factory assembly. If this is the case, you can put two pieces of hard wood in the jaws of a vise and the freewheel side locknut in between the wood, and clamp down on that locknut. You will still need to hold the cone nut on the left side as you put leverage on its locknut with the cone wrench.

STEP THREE: With the locknut loose, you should be able to back it off the axle by hand. If not, use the cone wrench. Remove the locknut. Now stop and make a note about the location of the washer and the spacer, if any. You will see next to the locknut a washer with a tiny raised portion on the inside circumference, which fits into a slot machined in the axle. This is part 7 in Figure 11-28. The reason for this washer is to keep the spacer and the cone nut from turning as you tighten up the locknut. This doesn't always work and you will need to hold the cone with the cone wrench to keep it from turning. Now remove the spacer if there is one. At this point, put the wheel and hub on the workbench, so the freewheel side of the axle is resting on the bench. This is so the axle won't fall out when you remove the cone nut.

STEP FOUR: Remove the cone nut from the left side of the hub (you've just removed the locknut, washer and spacer). Pop out the grease seal (number 5 in Fig. 11-28). The axle, with its freewheel end resting on the bench, will stay in the hub when the cone is removed. A rag should be under the hub to catch balls as they fall out of the hub. We all have different ways of preventing hub balls from dropping on the floor. Mine is to try to remove as many balls as I can reach from the top, then lift the wheel, remove the axle slowly from underneath to keep the balls from dropping out, and put the hub, with axle removed, back down on the bench over a rag. Then, with a small screwdriver, I push the top set of balls, those that have rolled down the shaft of the hub axle, out the other side and lift the others out of the race by hand or with the edge of the small screwdriver. Usually there's enough grease left in the hub to hold the balls in the race—but don't count on it. Now turn the hub over carefully, with a hand all ready on the other side, to catch any balls that will fall out at this point. With the hub turned over, remove the rest of the balls, and the grease seal.

STEP FIVE: Clean out all old grease and dirt with kerosene (don't get kerosene on the tire!), clean balls and cones and axle. This is also a good time to clean the outside of the hub, the spokes and to polish the rim of the wheel.

STEP SIX: With cones and balls now clean, inspect them for damage. Look for a galled spot, an area around the hub cone that's obviously different from the other polished surfaces of the cone. If the galled spot (caused by excessive pressure from cone and locknuts that are screwed too tight) is so deep you can feel it with your fingernail, I would suggest you need a new hub. Check the cone for the same condition. You may only need a new set of cone nuts. Your dealer will need to know the make of your hub or, better, that plus the old cone nut, for a replacement. Do not mix other makes of cone nuts with your own, because the radii may be different, and you can wind up with a ruined hub! Further, some hubs use 7/32-inch balls, and to use a cone machined for ¼-inch balls is going to concentrate wear points and lead to early cone failure. A word at this point about nomenclature: I think I've been remiss in using the word "race" too freely, and you may have the impression that a "race" is one thing and a cone another. Actually the part inside the hub into which the balls fit and around which they turn is more properly called a "cup" and it is in fact cup shaped. The cone is the threaded part with a highly machined surface, which threads on the shaft or axle and fits on the outside of the balls. The "race" is that part of both the cup and the cone against which the balls rotate. When I mention galled spots I refer specifically to rough sections of the races, either or both on the cup or cone race.

STEP SEVEN: Now that the races are okay and the balls look good, devoid of any cracks, rust or galled spots, or have been replaced, let's reassemble the hub. First, put a dab of grease on a rag and roll the clean, shiny balls around in the grease. This makes the balls much easier to pick up. Put a layer of grease in the cup and on the cone race surfaces. To make ball placement easier, put the axle back through the hub, ignoring the fact that there are no balls in place. You may have the right-side cone, assorted spacers and washer and locknut also in place on the axle. Now slide the axle in from the freewheel side. Then drop the balls in place on the left side, around the axle, and tamp some grease on top of the balls. They should now stay in place while you withdraw the axle and reverse it in the hub, and follow the same procedure as above. Then reverse the axle again and insert it through the hub. Another way is simply to lay the balls carefully in the freewheel-side of the cup and depend on the grease to hold them in place; then put the axle back in the hub. Now comes the tricky part.

STEP EIGHT: Here is where all your good work can go down the drain unless you are very careful. As I discussed in some detail earlier, hub-cone adjustment is a fine art, almost. Every brand of hub has just slightly different slop in the threads cut into the cone nut and axle. You can't depend on generalizations such as "take up the cone until it is finger tight, then tighten down the locknut," because with those instructions you could wind up with a hub that will wear out in nothing flat if you have too much side pressure on the cones and balls and races. Try this procedure. Take up or tighten the cone nut by hand, until it's snug, and won't turn anymore. Back it off a half turn. Holding the cone nut with the cone wrench, tighten the locknut (having, of course, replaced the spacer, if any, and the washer). Then spin the axle by hand. There should be no feeling of tightness, the axle should spin silky free and smooth. Then move the axle from side to side. There may be just a bit of sideplay. Very little. Very, very little. Put the wheel in the dropout, install the quick-release skewer and tighten it. Now put the wheel so the valve is at two o'clock and let it go. The wheel should move by the weight of the valve alone, and swing past the six-o'clock position. The valve should oscillate back and forth over the six-o'clock position at least fifteen or twenty times, moving more slowly all the time with each oscillation. If your wheel has a reflector, put it at the two-o'clock position because it's a lot heavier than the valve. Now, with your fingertips, check the wheel for sideplay by trying to move the tire from side to side. There should be no sideplay, if you're lucky, or very experienced, or, indeed, both. And the initial adjustment on the cone nut that will work for some will not work on others. You need a bit of sideplay at first, and this you get by backing off the cone nut from the initial finger snug position about a half turn. Of course, thread slop may call for a full turn, or a quarter turn. The important fact to remember is that getting the wheel to spin freely *before* you clamp down on the quick-release lever is not the final criterion of a correctly adjusted set of hub bearings. The final judgment depends on what happens *after* you tighten down the quick-release or axle bolts, and that's what a lot of people do not realize. Now we come to the freewheel (of course, ignore any statements about the freewheel if you're doing the front hub, but all other instructions apply).

FREEWHEEL MAINTENANCE

With the freewheel removed from the hub, as discussed above, you should do basic maintenance on it. With a toothbrush and kerosene, remove all old, accumulated, caked-on grease and dirt from the cogs. Then dunk the freewheel in *clean* kerosene and shake vigorously to get dirt out of its innards. If the freewheel has seals, you can skip the dunking step.

Then squirt on a *very* light oil, such as Chainlube (but do not use any aerosol lubricant that comes out depositing a layer of grease). Inside the freewheel (Fig. 11-31) are dozens of tiny balls that must rotate freely, and a layer of grease could cause them to bind. Further, the pawls must

Fig. 11-31: Detailed view of the new SunTour Ultra-7 seven-speed freewheel. Parts are: (1) raceways on inner and outer ends; (2) ratcheted pawl is heat treated to withstand stress of reverse rotation when pedal torque is applied; (3) heat-treated body; (4) sprocket teeth are slant cut to help smoother, more precise chain shift from one cog to another; (5) adjusting cone nut (Note that this freewheel has **two** adjusting nuts [most have one] the cone nut and the locknut with lock washer.); (6) inner freewheel body with grooves for removal tool (Use SunTour tool designed for this freewheel.); (7) a 12-tooth high-gear cog is available for racing. Please also take note of the many small ball bearings that must be tucked back in place without benefit of grease to hold them. Disassembly of any freewheel requires a watchmaker's patience and dexterity.

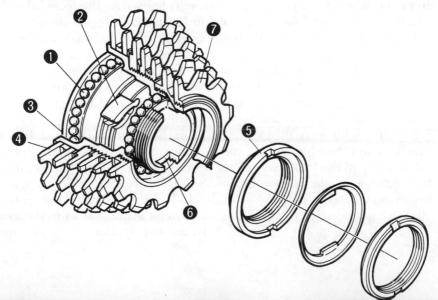

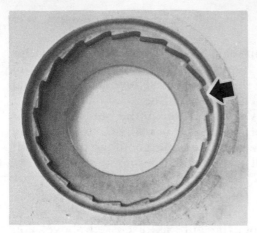

Fig. 11-32: Ratcheted teeth against which spring-loaded pawls open to keep freewheel from turning when you pedal, let the hub turn when you coast.

be free to turn or at least move (Fig. 11-31) so as to ratchet against the freewheel body ratchet gear (Fig. 11-32).

Sometimes, fairly rarely, you will start pedaling and nothing will happen. Pedals will spin but the bike stays put. What has happened, once you are sure the chain is on the cogs and not broken, is that a piece of dirt has gotten between the pawls and the ratchet body, so that the pawls are held closed. This lets the freewheel spin around uselessly. The purpose of the pawls is to let the freewheel turn in one direction, as when you are coasting, but not in the other direction, as when you are pedaling. If you are on the road and the pawls get stuck, causing this to happen, bum some kerosene or some sort of nonflammable solvent (well, I guess Listerine would work although it has alcohol in it, which makes it flammable, so be careful) and flush out the freewheel. Don't get any on the tire. I know I mentioned this earlier, but it bears repeating. Spin the freewheel as you dunk it until the pawls work free and catch. If they don't work free, you may have a broken pawl spring. Some freewheels have only one spring, others have a tiny phosphor bronze spring behind each pawl. In any case, now you will need a replacement freewheel, if on the road, since it's unlikely you will find a replacement set of springs in the boonies. But if you are near a town of any size, the local bike shop can fix the freewheel for you or, of course, furnish a replacement.

I don't like freewheels with seals; they are almost always a drag, until worn in, at least. But on the other hand the seals do keep out dirt from the pawl mechanism, so perhaps the drag is worth the protection. I prefer freewheels with tightly fitting components so seals aren't all that necessary. Regina, SunTour, Atom, Normandy, are a few of the makes that come to mind that are top-grade freewheels. Of those with wide gear ratios with cogs that go from 13 or 14 up to 34 teeth, I like the SunTour and the Shimano alternate-tooth sprocket type, in which every other tooth on the two lower gears is missing to make the chain jump to this extreme angle more efficient. Shimano also has a new approach involving what they call a "UniGlide" freewheel, on which the teeth are slightly twisted so as to guide the chain more accurately onto the gears. My experience with this model freewheel is that it works quite smoothly, is a bit quieter with shifting (less gear grind if you don't shift accurately the first time because the chain tends to go to a cog and not hang up in between) and a bit easier shifting to a lower gear if you forget and don't shift until the pedaling gets hard. You should always shift down before you have to, though. It's easier on the chain, chainwheel, derailleurs and your nerves. The UniGlide as of this writing goes to 32 teeth on the low-gear side.

Sprocket combinations for the FG-100 UniGlide freewheel are:

Type	Standard Sprocket Combinations (Teeth)				
5DS	15	17	19	21	24
5DW	14	17	20	24	28
5DUW	14	17	21	26	32

Sprocket combinations for the Alternate-Tooth Sprocket freewheel are:

Type	Standard Sprocket Combinations (Teeth)				
5AW	14	17	20	24	28*
5AUW	14	17	21	26*	32*
5AUS	14	17	22	28*	34*

* Alternate-tooth sprocket

You may have noticed that I have refrained from giving instructions about disassembling freewheels. To do so you will need special tools, an awful lot of patience sticking all those little balls back in without benefit of grease to hold them, and no reason outside of curiosity to undertake the project. If the pawls stick, you know how to clean them. If a pawl spring breaks, you won't be able to replace it on the road and so should buy a new freewheel. In all the thousands of miles I have traveled in this country and in Europe I have yet to have a pawl spring break on me. So this is a fairly remote possibility. All you need do is clean out the freewheel itself, and spray a little *light* oil on it every month or so. Aim oil delivery at the bearing area, on both sides.

ABOUT OTHER FREEWHEELS

Regina makes a very interesting close-ratio seven-speed freewheel, the Titall, that requires 140 millimeters, well, perhaps 136 millimeters will fit if you have the right frame, between dropouts, and a correspondingly long locknut-to-locknut hub. The new freewheel weighs only 10.5 ounces, (297.7 grams), has cogs of 13, 14, 15, 16, 18, 19 and 21 teeth. The first three cogs are titanium, the last three are aluminum, hence the name Titall. The first three cogs are threaded on, the rest fit over the splined body of the freewheel. You can also get 12-to-6-tooth cogs. The cost: $210 or so, depending on dealer markup.

Cog-to-cog width is 32 millimeters, so cogs are a little more closely spaced than a more conventional freewheel. I would recommend you use the Regina Record chain with maximum width at the rivets of 7.9 millimeters or the SunTour 7.3-millimeter Ultra 6 chain. Other chains can run to 9.5 or even 1 millimeter at the rivet, and could rub between cogs on this freewheel. The Titall requires a special remover, so buy one when you buy the unit.

If you change to any wider freewheel body, say going from a five- to a six- or seven-speed freewheel, you will have to re-dish the wheel slightly, as I noted earlier. This is because the rim must be centered between the locknuts (locknut-to-locknut distance) *not between the hub flanges.* (See Chapter 15 on wheel truing.) In other words, the rim, to be centered in the bicycle, must be centered between the dropout inside dimension or the locknut to locknut distance, which should be the same dimension. See Chapter 15 for dishing instructions, and Fig. 11-27 for locknut-to-locknut measurement. "Dishing" means pulling the wheel slightly to the right by tightening spoke nipples of the spokes on the right side, leading from hub flange to rim.

SunTour has a new freewheel, the Ultra Six, and, as noted above, a new narrower chain to go with it. Their six-speed freewheel will fit on a normal 120-millimeter locknut-to-locknut hub, made for a five-speed freewheel. This means you can switch over to a six-speed cluster with this freewheel without having to change to a longer axle, assuming of course that your dropouts will handle the longer width. Bikes built for five speeds have 120 millimeters between the inner surfaces of the dropouts. Frames built for six speeds have 125- or 126-millimeter spacing, and frames built for seven-speed freewheels have a still wider distance, from 130 to 140 millimeters. These newer, narrower freewheel-and-chain combinations now let you increase your choice of gears without having to buy a new frame. If you have a long touring frame you usually won't have to be concerned about chain clearance between the chain when on the high gear and the inside of the chainstay. On some bikes, the chainstay is rounded and not flattened, which will probably cause chain rub on the small (high-speed) cog. You can sometimes get by with a spacer: You simply remove the spacer from between the left side locknut washer and cone nut, and move it over to the freewheel side on the axle. If adding spacers to the axle means you have to force the stays apart so the axle will fit in, don't do it if you have a fine frame. And don't let anyone else do it. If the chainstay is flattened where the high gear cog rotates, (a very slight flattening) you will probably have clearance for the wider freewheel with more cogs. The SunTour Ultra-Six freewheel is 26.5 millimeters between cogs, and this is a six-speed freewheel, remember, so it will fit onto a 120-millimeter axle where your five-speed freewheel now resides. The Ultra-Six weighs 510 grams (18 oz.) and has

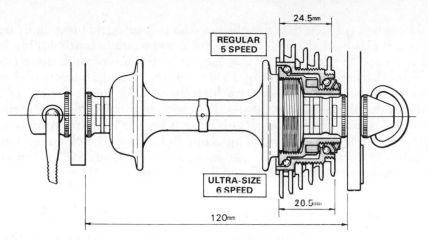

Fig. 11-33: SunTour's new Ultra-6 freewheel fits onto a five-speed hub, as shown.

cogs from 14 to 32 teeth. The model I tested has cogs of 13, 15, 17, 21, 26 and 32 teeth. Figure 11-33 shows that the six-speed freewheel fits nicely on the five-speed hub, with only a 2-millimeter greater width than the five-speed; plenty of space for the chain.

If you have a six-speed hub and chainstay clearance to match an axle of 126 millimeters you can now go to a seven-speed freewheel without concern about chain clearance. The normal six-speed freewheel requires a 126-millimeter locknut-to-locknut distance. As Figure 11-34 shows, the Ultra Seven-speed will fit the six-speed hub without adding more than

Fig. 11-34: SunTour's new Ultra-7 **seven**-speed hub fits onto a six-speed hub. Now, if you have a triple chainwheel, you can be the only one in town with a 21-speed bicycle.

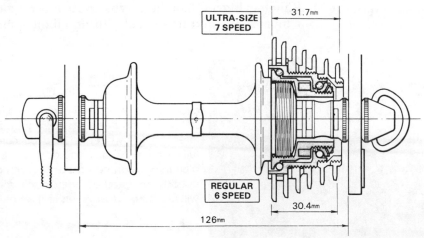

1.3 millimeters of width to the cluster, which should and most likely will give you plenty of chain clearance. For the close-ratio buff with big leg muscles and the cardiovascular system of a sixteen-year-old, these free-wheels also come with cogs of 13, 14, 15, 16, 17 and 18 teeth, and the seven-speed model can accept a high gear of 12 teeth. Figure 11-31 shows a detailed view of a close-ratio version of the seven-speed model. See the caption for further details. Teeth on the new freewheels are "slant cut" which, according to SunTour, helps move the chain from one gear to another more smoothly and accurately. Shimano has a similar and more pronounced slant on a few of their freewheels.

A Warning About Threading Freewheels

From the footnote in Table 11-1, you will note the threading specifica-tions for hubs threaded English, Italian and French. When you purchase a freewheel to mount on your good aluminum alloy hub, you need to remember two things. First, the hub boss, where the threads are located, is aluminum (see Fig. 11-35). Again, I repeat, these threads are a-l-u-m-i-n-u-m. They are very soft compared to the hardened steel of the free-wheel body. If when you thread the freewheel, it's cocked at even a very slight angle you may strip the threads on the hub. So be careful to thread the freewheel on straight.

About Interchangeability

From Table 11-1, you will note that the English-threaded hubs are 1.370 inches by 24 threads per inch, and that the Italian-threaded hubs are 35 millimeters by 24 threads per inch (TPI). Now if you multiply 1.370 x 25.4 to transform the English to metric, you come up with an English hub in metric terms of 34.799 millimeters, very close to the 35 millime-ters of the Italian hub threading. Because the TPI is the same, but the Italian hub is 0.201 millimeters bigger than the English hub, it is reason-able to assume that an Italian-threaded freewheel will fit, albeit some-

Fig. 11-35: Threads on an aluminum alloy hub, even forged alloy, are a lot softer than the steel of a freewheel. So thread a freewheel on and off care-fully, and make sure you don't use En-glish threads on one piece and French threads on another. They don't mix, will ruin hub. Arrow points to threads.

what loosely, on the 0.201-millimeter smaller English threaded hub. But it will fit and work okay.

Going the other way, if you bought an Italian bike on your last trip to Milan, and the *hub* is threaded Italian, and now you want to put an *English*-threaded freewheel on that hub, will it fit? The answer is, maybe. It's yes if you are terribly careful not to start threading the freewheel on cocked but get it on straight. You will have some slight forcing to do, because you will be cutting 0.201-millimeter deeper threads on the softer aluminum Italian-threaded hub with the hard steel of the slightly smaller English-threaded freewheel, but you can do it. I don't recommend the practice, but this is out of sheer perfectionism, not because it isn't fairly easy to do.

Worn Cogs and New Chains Don't Mix (and Vice Versa)

If you ride enough, eventually friction will wear freewheel and chainwheel cog teeth so they start to develop a slight "hangover," like a small inverted "L"—a tiny "lip" at the top of the tooth. This alone will cause the chain to be hard to shift or to jump from cog to cog. Even if the teeth are not worn down this far, though, a more subtle problem occurs when you install a new freewheel set of cogs (you can keep the old body, just change the cogs. We humans should be so lucky). The chain will have stretched and become worn, and with the new cogs, you can have the chain jumping from one freewheel cog to another, with a pronounced and very annoying jerk, especially when you strain on the pedals. I recommend you install a new chain when you change cogs. After all, if the cogs are worn, it stands to reason the chain is worn and stretched also, other things being equal.

How to Remove Your Freewheel

If you break a spoke on the freewheel side, you will need to remove your freewheel and dunk it in a solvent to clean dirt away from sticking pawls. To remove a freewheel, follow these steps:

STEP ONE: Make sure you have the proper tool for your freewheel. The bike shop will need to know the make and model. Don't use a tool that has the two teeth chewed up. The tool must fit exactly and snugly into the two notches of the freewheel. If you round off one of the gripping edges on the tool, file it down flat or, using a sharp chisel, with the tool in a vise, try chipping the gripping edges off square. Or buy a new tool. Figure 11-36 shows just some of the great variety of freewheel removers. There's no standardization at all between freewheel manufacturers in this respect. If the tool won't fit over the lockring, remove the lockring.

STEP TWO: Insert the remover jaws in the freewheel, insert the quick-release skewer (or axle nuts) and tighten down the freewheel. Back off

Fig. 11-36: A few of the many styles of freewheel removers. Arrow points to the thin-walled Phil Wood splined remover that removes freewheels without having to remove the locknut on the freewheel side.

about a one-quarter turn so that as you turn the wrench (Fig. 11-37), you will have room for the freewheel body to turn. With the wrench on the remover, turn counterclockwise until the freewheel is loose. You will have to turn hard. Then loosen the quick-release just a bit more, turn the remover and by now you should be able to remove the skewer and turn the tool by hand. Be careful as you approach the end of the hub freewheel boss threads. At this point, hold the freewheel weight in your hands so that as you unscrew those last two or three delicate aluminum threads on the boss, you don't damage them.

About Fitting a Freewheel

The arrow in Figure 11-36 points to a Phil Wood splined freewheel remover that fits mating splines in freewheels such as the splined Regina, Shimano and Zeus 2000. This is a neat tool, it's thin enough to fit right into the freewheel without having to remove the locknut on the freewheel side. Also, you don't have to use the quick-release to hold it down. Just stick the remover in a vise, put the freewheel down over it, grasp the tire and twist counterclockwise; and off it comes.

I found out the hard way never to put a freewheel on a hub unless I was sure I could get it off. Because once you pedal, you really tighten

Fig. 11-37: To remove freewheel (nonsplined type) in insert tool, hold in place with slightly loose quick-release, with other end in vise or cogs between wood in vise, and turn wrench counterclockwise.

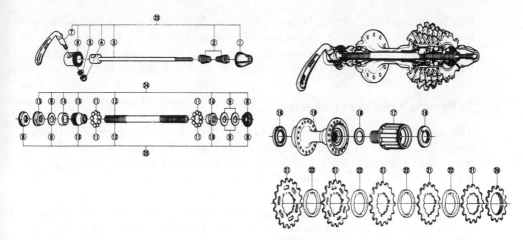

Fig. 11-38: Detailed view of a Shimano DuraAce Freehub. Parts are: (16) seal; (17) freewheel body assembly; (18) stopper; (19) hub; (20) sprocket (lock ring type); (21) sprockets; (22) sprocket spacers; (23) quick-release skewer, complete; (24 and 25) axle assembly, complete.

down on the freewheel where it threads onto the hub boss. For example, I blithely screwed a splined freewheel onto a Hi-E hub. Clearances are so tight between that hub's spacer and the inside of the freewheel that I could not get a remover in there. I had to dismantle the freewheel, remove everything, balls and all, right down to the basic freewheel shell, to get that baby off that hub. Never again! Now I check first to make sure I can get a tool in there to get the freewheel off, before I go about threading it on tight. By the way, Figure 11-39 shows what happens to a remover that doesn't fit or is allowed to get too loose. You can also mangle the indents in the freewheel.

You also have to make sure that the freewheel will clear the shoulder of the hub flange. Some flange bosses have wider or deeper shoulders (the raised part just behind the threads) than others, and when you tighten down the freewheel it rubs on the shoulder, sometimes so tightly

Fig. 11-39: Here's a damaged freewheel remover. Damage can occur in two ways: (1) use of the wrong tool; (2) tool not held firmly enough by quick-release so it can pop out and tear off teeth. Freewheel can also be damaged the same way, except that if this happens you will have to tear down the freewheel all the way to the basic shell and remove it with a pipe wrench over cloth. If you go this route, do it over a large cloth to catch the tiny balls that will come spilling out of the freewheel.

the freewheel can't turn. In any case, the freewheel *must* rotate freely and not rub on anything. Some combinations of freewheels and hubs just won't work for this reason. I can't give you particular combinations, there are too many; just be aware that the problem does exist.

To Remove Cogs from Freewheel

The cog remover in Figure 11-19 is simply a long piece of metal with about six inches of chain fastened at one end. To remove cogs from a freewheel mounted on a hub laced in a wheel, just put the left side of the hub, with the quick-release skewer removed, in a vise around the locknut. Use the tool, as shown in Figure 11-19, on the small (high-gear) cog, rotating it *clockwise* to remove the cog. On some freewheels the rest of the cogs fit onto a spline of the freewheel body and can be slid off after the first cog is removed. Others require unscrewing two or even *all* of the cogs. Keep track of any spacers between cogs; they must go back in the way they came out so the correct distance between cogs is maintained. Otherwise the chain will hang up on any cog that's too close to the next one.

Three-Speed and Coaster-Brake Hubs

There are four makes and a wide variety of one-, two-, three-, and five-speed integral rear hubs in common use on bicycles in this country. There is even an adapter kit to convert multi-speed integral rear hubs into a six- or nine-speed machine, using a derailleur. A Japanese manufacturer makes a twelve-speed combination rear hub and derailleur which, if used with a double front chainwheel, will give you twenty-four speeds, and with a triple front chainwheel, thirty-six speeds. I don't know what you'd do with more than twelve or fifteen speeds, but if you want them, they're available. More on these combinations later in this chapter.

I am not going to attempt to give you detailed take-apart and assembly instructions for all these hubs; there are simply too many makes and models to make this practical. Hubs are a rather complicated assemblage of gears and mechanisms. (If Fig. 12-1 doesn't scare you off, nothing will!) Many require special tools to assemble or disassemble, and the majority of bicycle dealers are competent to deal with most of them.

This chapter, therefore, will be limited to routine hub maintenance, adjustment, and tips on correct usage. If you follow these instructions, your hub should last the life of the bicycle and seldom, if ever, need to be taken apart. However, if you really want to disassemble your rear hub, either out of curiosity or because you can't find a bicycle mechanic who knows how to fix it, you can obtain step-by-step illustrated assembly and disassembly instructions, complete with a list of spare parts, from the hub manufacturer or the bicycle manufacturer.

BENDIX AUTOMATIC COASTER BRAKES

The Bendix automatic coaster brake is a two-speed unit which contains both coaster brakes and a set of internal gears. This type of hub permits the cyclist to change gears by backpedaling slightly, or to brake by backpedaling, both without removing hands from the handlebars. It is well suited for a young rider, up to age twelve. There is a 32 percent decrease in gear ratio between high and low gears on this hub—enough to enable a young rider to negotiate moderate hills fairly easily.

There are two types of Bendix coaster-brake two-speed hubs. The standard model is marked with three yellow bands around the hub shell.

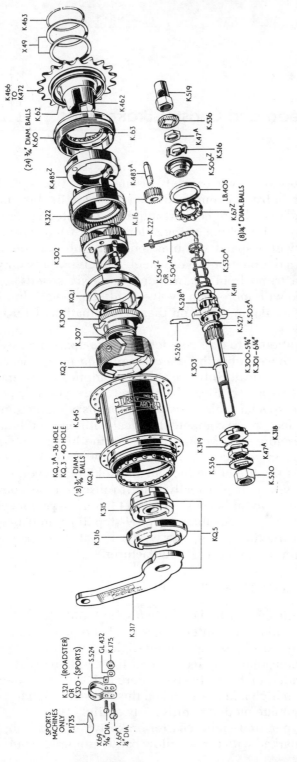

Fig. 12-1: Sturmey-Archer three-speed hub and coaster-brake combination. This drawing is shown here to convince you not to take any three-speed hub apart. Let your bicycle dealer fix these. Of course, if anything mechanical poses a challenge to you, go right ahead and take it apart, but save the pieces.

LEGEND

Part No.	Description
GL432	Shakeproof Washer
K16	Planer Pinion
K47A	Cone Locknut
K60	Right-Hand Ball-Ring
K62	Sprocket Dust Cap
K67Z	Ball Retainer—(8) 1/4" Ball
K175	Nut for X69A Bolt
K227	Locknut
K300	Axle 5¾"
K301	Axle 6¼"
K302	Planet Cage
K303	Axle Circlip
K307	Brake Actuating Spring
K309	Thrust Plate
K315	Left-Hand Cone
K316	(Chromium) Dust Cap for Left-Hand Cone
K317	Brake Arm
K318	Brake Arm Locknut
K319	Lock Washer
K320	Clip for Brake Arm (Sports)
K321	Clip for Brake Arm (Roadster)
K322	Gear Ring
K411	Thrust Washer
K462	Driver
K463	Driver Circlip
K466	Sprocket 16 Teeth
K472	Sprocket 22 Teeth
K483A	Planet Pinion Pin
K485Z	Gear Ring Pawl-Ring
K504Z	Gear Indicator Rod and Coupling. For 5¾" Axle.
K504AZ	Gear Indicator Rod and Coupling. For 6¼" Axle.
K505A	Clutch
K506Z	Cone
K516	Right-Hand Cone Locking-Washer
K519	Right-Hand Axle Nut
K520	Left-Hand Axle Nut
K526	Key
K527	Clutch Sleeve
K528A	Thrust Ring
K530A	Clutch Spring
K536	Serrated Axle Washer
K645	Lubricator
KQ1	Planet Cage Pawl Ring
KQ2	Brake Band
KQ3	40-Hole Shell and Left-Hand Ball Cup Assembly
KQ3A	36-Hole Shell and Left-Hand Ball Cup Assembly
KQ4	Ball Retainer—(18) 3/16" Ball
KQ5	Brake Arm/Left-Hand Cone/and Dust Cap Assembly
LB405	Dustcap
S524	Nut for X 69 Bolt
P1735	Strengthening Pad—For Sports Machines only
X49	Sprocket spacing Washer (1/16")
X69	Clip Screw, 3/16" Diameter
X69A	Clip Screw, 1/4" Diameter

The other, which is marked with three blue bands around the hub shell, is the overdrive automatic unit. This has a direct drive and a high gear with a 47 percent gear ratio increase, which makes cycling a bit easier on hills.

Lubrication

Because all the working parts are inside the hub, these hubs don't require much maintenance, beyond regular lubrication about every month, and after long trips. Use a fairly light oil, equivalent to No. 20 SAE viscosity motor oil. Squirt about a teaspoonful into the hub through the hub hole provided for this purpose.

Also, once a year you should take the bicycle into the dealer and have him disassemble and regrease the hub and check for any worn or broken parts.

Because coaster brakes (*unlike* caliper brakes) need grease for proper operation and for long life, if you've made extensive tours in hilly country involving a lot of braking, it's a good idea to have your dealer disassemble the hub and regrease it when the tour is over, rather than wait until the year is up.

If the hub does not shift properly, makes grinding noises, shifts into low without back-pressure, or if the brakes fail, this means that new internal parts may be necessary. These can be installed by your bicycle dealer.

No routine operating adjustments are required on any Bendix hubs, making them even better for children and more child-proof than other hubs, which have wires attached to them.

All you need to remember, if you remove the rear wheel, is to refasten the coaster-brake clamp arm which clamps onto the rear fork stay.

STURMEY-ARCHER MULTI-SPEED REAR HUBS

Sturmey-Archer multi-speed rear hubs are perhaps the most widely used of all hubs.

There are three- (Fig. 12-1), four-, five-speed and combination coaster-brake and three-speed Sturmey-Archer rear wheel hubs in use today. All of them have a number of things in common, one of which is that proper gear shifting is greatly dependent upon proper adjustment of working parts.

Lubrication is also very important. In fact, oil can evaporate from a hub between the time the bicycle leaves the factory and when you buy it, so be sure to have the dealer add a tablespoonful of *light* oil to the hub before you ride off.

When changing gears with any Sturmey-Archer hub, ease pedal pressure slightly, and change gears quickly.

Sturmey-Archer Troubleshooting

PROBLEM: Gears slip; they won't stay in the gear selected.
SOLUTION: Adjust the indicator rod. Check your hub so you know which type you have, and follow the instruction on the indicator rod adjustment for your particular hub.

TCW, AW, AB, AG, and SW Hub Indicator Rod Adjustment

STEP ONE: Put the gear-shift lever in No. 2 position (or S5 five-speed hubs in third gear) (Fig. 12-2).

STEP TWO: Unscrew the locknut (A, Fig. 12-2).

STEP THREE: Adjust the knurled section of the cable (B, Fig. 12-2) until the end of the indicator rod is exactly level with the end of the axle (B, Fig. 12-3). Check the location of the indicator rod through the "window" in the *right-hand* nut on the axle (B, Fig. 12-2).

STEP FOUR: Tighten the locknut.

STEP FIVE: If you can't obtain enough adjustment with the cable connection at the hub, unscrew the nut and bolt holding the cable on the top tube (X 90, Fig. 12-4) and move the cable forward or rearward, as required. This step is known as "changing the fulcrum point" of the cable.

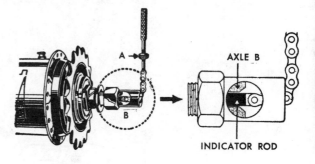

Fig. 12-2: Cable adjustments for SW-TCW hubs, including locknut (A), and knurled section of cable (B). Indicator rod should be where shown for proper hub operation. *(Courtesy of Raleigh Industries, Limited)*

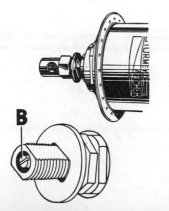

Fig. 12-3: Rod (B) on a Sturmey-Archer hub should line up with end of axle for proper cable adjustment of Sturmey-Archer hubs.

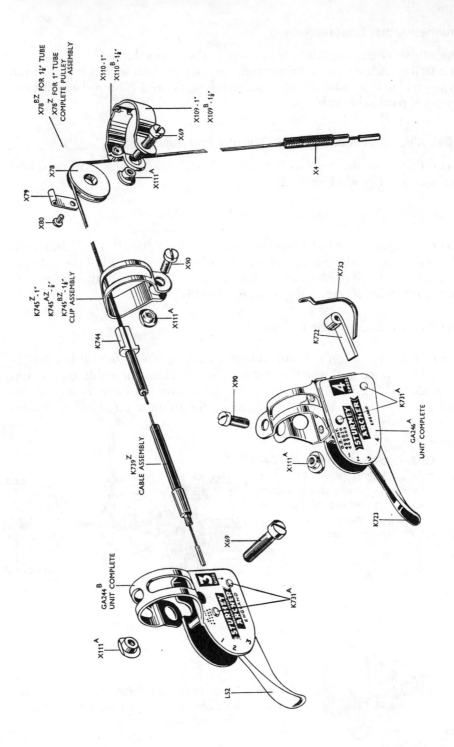

X78 BZ FOR 1¼" TUBE
X78 Z FOR 1" TUBE
COMPLETE PULLEY ASSEMBLY

X110-1"
X110-B-1⅛"

X109-1"
X109-B-1⅛"

X69

X78

X79

X80

X111 A

X4

K745 Z-1"
K745 AZ-⅞"
K745 BZ-1¼"
CLIP ASSEMBLY

X90

X111 A

K744

K733

K722

X90

K731 A

STURMEY ARCHER
ENGLAND

GA246 A
UNIT COMPLETE

X111 A

K723

K739 Z
CABLE ASSEMBLY

X69

GA244 B
UNIT COMPLETE

K731 A

STURMEY ARCHER
ENGLAND

X111 A

L52

Fig. 12-4: Trigger control gear-shift lever for three- and four-speed Sturmey-Archer hubs. If you cannot get enough adjustment with the cable locknuts at the hub, loosen nut X90 and slide clip assembly further forward about a half inch, and retighten.

Code No.	Description
K739Z	Trigger cable assembly—give length of both inner and outer cable
K744	Fulcrum sleeve
K745Z	Fulcrum clip complete 1" diameter
K745AZ	Fulcrum clip complete ⅞" diameter
K745BZ	Fulcrum clip complete 1⅛" diameter
X90	Clip screw
X78Z	Pulley complete for 1" tube
X78BZ	Pulley complete for 1⅛" tube
X69	Clip screw
X78	Pulley wheel only
X79	Pulley arm
X80	Pulley arm screw
X110BZ	Clip with pulley stud (1⅛" tube)
X109B	Half clip (1⅛" tube)

3-Speed Unit	4-Speed Unit	Description
GC3B	GC4A	Trigger control complete less pulley
GA244B	GA246A	Trigger unit
L52	K723	Trigger lever
K731A	K731A	Pivot pin
L55	K722	Trigger pawl
L56	K738	Trigger spring
X69	X69	Clip screw
X111A	X111A	Clip screw, ¼" diameter

AM, ASC, and AC Sturmey-Archer Hub Indicator Rod Adjustment

The only difference between indicator rod adjustment for these hubs and other Sturmey-Archer hubs lies in the location of the indicator rod adjustment indicator. On AM, ASC, and AC hubs, the indicator rod is in the correct position when the end of the rod is level with the end of the axle on the *left-hand* side of the hub. This is the side opposite the chain, or left side as you face the front of the bicycle.

Adjustment of the indicator rod should be made as shown above.

If gears still slip or change noisily after the indicator rod has been adjusted, wear on the internal parts in the hub is indicated. Take the bicycle to your dealer for repairs, or, if you with to make them yourself, write to the bicycle manufacturer or see your dealer for assembly and disassembly instructions and the special tools that are needed.

Cable Change on Sturmey-Archer "Sportshift"

Sturmey-Archer also makes a gear-shift mechanism for their three-speed hubs, which is mounted on the top tube. Follow these steps to change cables:

STEP ONE: Loosen the locknut on the hub cable at the hub, and unscrew the knurled ferrule until the cable is free at the hub end.

STEP TWO: Remove the center screw from the control unit (gear-shift unit) and remove the cover from the plastic cover plate.

STEP THREE: Push the control lever to the No. 3 position, and remove the old cable. Pull the old cable through the slot of the cable anchorage and over the pulley wheel to remove the entire cable.

STEP FOUR: Readjust the cable by moving the lever to the No. 2 position and adjusting the cable ferrule at the hub end until the indicator rod is in the correct location for the type of Sturmey-Archer hub involved. (TCW, AW, AG, AB, and SW hubs have a different adjustment from AM, ASC, the AC Sturmey-Archer hubs.)

Here are common symptoms of Sturmey-Archer hub problems, their causes and their solutions. If hub needs disassembly, I recommend you let your bicycle shop do it.

PROBLEM: Sluggish gear change.
CAUSE: Cable binding or worn toggle link chain.
SOLUTION: Lubricate or replace cables. Lubricate gear-shift unit.

PROBLEM: No gear at all; pedals turn, wheel doesn't.
CAUSE: Internal pawls stuck or held in place by too heavy oil.

SOLUTION: Add light oil. If this does not free up, dismantle hub. Clean parts. Reassemble and oil again.

CAUSE: Bent axle.
SOLUTION: Dismantle hub. Replace axle.

CAUSE: Distorted axle spring.
SOLUTION: Replace spring (requires hub disassembly).

PROBLEM: Hub runs stiffly, drags on pedals when free-wheeling, wheel seems to "bind."
CAUSE: Chain stay ends not parallel. When the axle nuts are tightened, this causes the axle to be "sprung" out of true, which, in turn, makes the internal hub parts "bind."
SOLUTION: Straighten the chain stay ends, or add packing washers on the left-hand side to align. You may also need a new axle.

CAUSE: Corrosion of hub working parts due to nonlubrication.
SOLUTION: Disassemble the hub. Check and replace worn parts. Re-lubricate. Follow lubrication instructions above.

PROBLEM: Slips in any gear.
CAUSE: On S5 hubs, this could be a kinked gear cable. On other hubs, internal parts are worn or incorrectly installed.
SOLUTION: Replace cable or reassemble hub with new parts as needed.

PROBLEM: On TCW (coaster-brake and three-speed) hub combinations *only*, brakes are noisy or "shudder" when applied.
CAUSE: Loose brake arm clip.
SOLUTION: Tighten clip nuts and bolts.

PROBLEM: On TCW hubs only, internal brakes in hub "grab" on application.
CAUSE: Lack of oil in rear hub.
SOLUTION: Add good quality *thin* oil, SAE 20 or thinner.

General Instructions

Sometimes even when you take the steps to correct any of the problems listed above, you will still not have corrected them. If this happens to you, there is probably wear in the internal parts of the hub. I do not recommend that the average bicycle owner attempt to replace any of the interior parts of these hubs. But, if you want to anyway, troubleshooting charts and hub-assembly data can be obtained from the manufacturers.

In any case, do not attempt to adjust the rear wheel cones on multi-speed hubs. If the wheel binds, or shows side-play, and you think that cone adjustment is the answer, let your dealer do it. Some hubs have factory-adjusted cones, and you can ruin the hubs if you try to adjust them yourself, without following a detailed instruction manual.

Sturmey-Archer Trigger (Gear-Shift) Control Maintenance

There isn't much that can go wrong with a gear shift (Fig. 12-5) unless you bend it accidentally. If you do, it should be replaced.

Cables do fray, wear, and break, however, and you should know how to replace the gear-shift cable (or cables, on an S5 five-speed hub).

Trigger Control Cable Replacement, Three- and Four-Speed Hubs

STEP ONE: (Note: You do not have to remove the control mechanism from the handlebars if you can pull the lever back far enough to permit the cable nipple to pass between the pawl and ratchet plate.) Remove the inner wire from the indicator chain at the hub.

STEP TWO: Remove the outer wire casing (the spaghetti tube) from the fulcrum clip on the top tube (or, if it is a woman's model, from the top of the two downtubes.)

STEP THREE: Pull the cable ferrule upward (so that the metal sleeve is entering the gear shift) until the ferrule screw (which you can't see because it's in the control casing) engages the control casing. Then, unscrew the ferrule.

STEP FOUR: Pull the control lever back beyond the bottom gear position as far as it can go. Push the cable (inner wire) through so you can remove the cable nipple (leaded end) from the ratchet plate, then pull the wire out between the pawl and ratchet and through the threaded hole.

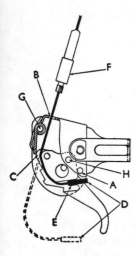

Fig. 12-5: Typical Sturmey-Archer gear shift. To remove control wire, it is not necessary to remove control from handlebar if the lever can be pulled back far enough to allow cable nipple to pass between pawl and ratchet plate. Procedure is (1) detach inner wire from indicator chain at hub, and (2) outer casing from fulcrum clip. Pull cable ferrule (F) upward until screw engages that of control casing at (B), then unscrew ferrule. Pull lever right back beyond bottom gear position to stop (A), push inner wire through to detach nipple from ratchet plate, then pull wire out between pawl and ratchet at (C) and finally through threaded hole (B).

To fit control wire, pull lever right back beyond bottom gear position to stop (A) and insert wire through threaded hole (B) and between pawl and ratchet plate at (C). Wire nipple (D) is then fitted into notch (E) and cable ferrule (F) screwed into (B) until it rotates freely. Keeping tension on wire, push lever forward into top gear position. Control is then ready for reconnection.

STEP FIVE: To replace an old cable with a new one, reverse Steps One through Four, above.

Fitting Gear-Shift Cable to Frame (Sturmey-Archer)

When you install a new cable and its spaghetti cover on the bicycle frame, be sure to have the cable and cover long enough so you can turn the handlebars through their full movement in both directions. But do not overdo it. Make it just long enough for adequate handlebar movement.

Standard control wire length for most bicycles with Sturmey-Archer multispeed hubs and handlebar controls is 54½ inches with a spaghetti cover length of 17½ inches. For controls mounted on the top tube, standard lengths are thirty-two, thirty-four, and thirty-six inches.

For Sturmey-Archer Five-Speed Hubs

When installing new cables on Sturmey-Archer five-speed rear hubs (Fig. 12-6), follow this procedure:

STEP ONE: For the right-hand gear-shift lever, follow the same procedure as for standard handlebar flick control. Screw down the locknut (Fig. 12-6).

STEP TWO: For the left-hand lever, push the left-hand lever to the forward position, screw the cable connector to the bellcrank (the metal connecting piece between the cable and axle, held onto the axle by a nut). Screw the cable connector (1) to the bellcrank just two or three turns, no more.

STEP THREE: Push the left-hand lever to the backward position, and screw the cable connector until all cable slackness is eliminated.

STEP FOUR: With light pressure, push the bellcrank arm forward and, at

Fig. 12-6: Right- and left-hand gear-shift cables for Sturmey-Archer five-speed hubs.

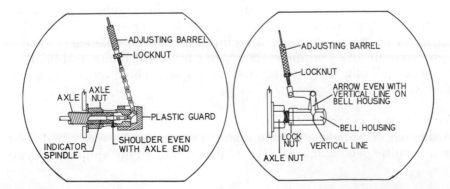

the same time, turn the wheel backward or forward. If the gears are not fully engaged, the bellcrank arm will move farther forward.

STEP FIVE: Screw the cable connector as far as possible, and secure with the locknut.

GENERAL INSTRUCTIONS ON MAINTENANCE, ADJUSTMENT, AND ALIGNMENT OF HUBS

Sturmey-Archer Hubs

For efficient cycling with minimum effort, as well as for proper operation of the rear hub, it is important that the rear sprocket of any rear hub, whether coaster brake or multi-speed, line up with the front chainwheel.

For more information on alignment, see the discussion in the section on derailleurs.

To align Sturmey-Archer rear hubs, all you need do is change the rear sprocket a little, which is easy. You have an alignment adjustment of between 1½ inches and 1¾ inches in ⅟₁₆-inch increments. To change alignments simply follow these steps:

STEP ONE: Pry off the locknut (circlip) with a small screwdriver. (This is the round springlike clip that fits into a groove around the sprocket side of the hub—outboard of the sprocket.) Snap this ring out.

STEP TWO: Slide the sprocket off the hub, along with the washers on either side of the sprocket. To change alignment, you have a number of choices:

1. Face the concave side of the sprocket toward the outside of the hub. Put all the washers on one side or the other, or one washer on each side.
2. Put concave side toward the hub, washers as above. This gives you a total of six adjustments.

Incidentally, if you with to change the gear ratio, up or down, on any Sturmey-Archer hub, simply ask your bicycle dealer to send to Raleigh of America in Boston for the sprocket with the number of teeth you desire. A larger sprocket with more teeth will give you a larger ratio (less speed in all gears but more hill-climbing ability), whereas a smaller sprocket will give you more speed, but hills will be more difficult to negotiate (all other factors, such as your physical condition, being equal, that is).

Shimano Multi-speed Hubs

A number of American bicycle manufacturers use Japanese-made Shimano multi-speed rear hubs. The Shimano hub, in my opinion, is every bit as good as any American or European multi-speed hub and is a good deal easier to repair. If you plan to remove this hub, and disassemble and reassemble it, you will, however, need two special tools—a split snap ring remover and a ballcup remover—which you will have to order through your bicycle store.

The Shimano 3.3.3. three-speed hub is the most widely used of the Shimano units. Shimano publishes well-illustrated, easily understood, step-by-step disassembly, repair and reassembly instructions. Repair parts are available in this country. Lubrication is very important. Use a light oil, adding about a teaspoonful every thirty days and after each long ride.

There are two types of Shimano gear-shift levers for this hub, both positive "click-stop" types. The first is a handlebar "twistgrip" similar to a motorcycle speed control, and the second is a lever, usually mounted on the top tube.

To remove a frayed wire from the handlebar twistgrip:

STEP ONE: Loosen the locknut on the handlebar twistgrip and remove the ferrule and wire.

STEP TWO: Remove the cable cover from the fulcrum stopper on the top tube.

STEP THREE: Unscrew the locknut on the bellcrank on the rear wheel and unscrew the knurled cable nut from the bellcrank lever. At this point, the cable and cable cover should be removable from the bicycle. Install the new cable and cover, reversing Steps One, Two, and Three.

STEP FOUR: The adjustment for both the twistgrip and the lever-type control should start with the shift in the "N" position. At this position, the red "N" on the bellcrank should be centered in the "window" of the bellcrank or, on older models of this hub, the arrow indicator should be centered over the indicating line on the bellcrank.

STEP FIVE: If the centering in Step Four cannot be made, move the fulcrum stop on the top tube forward or backward, as necessary, to make more or less cable slack as needed; then readjust at the bellcrank end by loosening the cable locknut and screwing the cable ferrule in or out as required. This step applies for both twistgrip and lever-type controls.

NOTE: Wire cables on any bicycle will stretch in time, so you will find it necessary to readjust the shift cable from time to time, as per Step Five.

PROBLEM: In the "H" shift position, the pedal skips or won't turn.
CAUSE: Pawl is worn or installed backward.
SOLUTION: Disassemble the hub and install new pawl and pawl spring (a job for the bicycle mechanic).

PROBLEM: Pedal skips at "N" position.
CAUSE: Planet cage pawl worn or broken, or pawl spring broken.
SOLUTION: Disassemble hub and replace defective parts (a job for the bicycle mechanic.)

PROBLEM: Gears are stuck or do not change smoothly.
CAUSE: Broken parts are caught up in hub mechanism.
SOLUTION: Complete hub overhaul (a job for the bicycle mechanic).

PROBLEM: Hub is noisy.
CAUSE: Rusty mechanism due to lack of oil.
SOLUTION: If rust has proceeded far enough, a new hub may have to be installed. Try oiling the hub first. If this doesn't work, disassemble the hub and look for rusted part. Install new parts as needed (a job for the bicycle mechanic).

PROBLEM: Erratic shifting.
CAUSE: Control cable not set correctly.
SOLUTION: Adjust as described under Steps Four and Five above.

The Shimano click-stop shift lever is used on a number of 20- and 24-inch-wheel bicycles, as well as on 26-inch-wheel machines. To change the cables on the "stick" shift, follow these steps.

STEP ONE: Pry out the plastic dust cover on the round section at the bottom of the lever, which will reveal a screw in the center of the space.

STEP TWO: Remove the lever hub screw. The factory has this screw down rather tight, so use a good screwdriver and apply some elbow grease. Be careful not to lose the spacing washers under the nut, and to replace them in the same order.

STEP THREE: With the lever screw removed, the lever handle and wire will come off the lever slip in one piece. Remove the metal dust cover. Remove the cable nipple (leaded end) from its seat in the lever handle, and remove the cable and cable cover, replacing them with the new cable and cover by reversing the above steps.

The Shimano Combi-12 uses a combination four-speed derailleur and three-speed rear hub, for a total of twelve gear changes (twenty-four gear changes if a double chainwheel is used, thirty-six if a triple chainwheel is used).

Full instructions on the care, adjustment and alignment of derailleurs are given in Chapter 13. Because the three-speed section of the Combi-12 is identical to the standard Shimano 3.3.3. three-speed hub, maintenance and adjustment instructions already given in this section for this hub apply to the Combi-12 hub unit. Cable-changing procedures for both lever gear shifts have already been described.

There is, however, a difference between the derailleur lever on the Combi-12 and the conventional derailleur gear-shift levers. Standard levers have no click stops. The rider must adjust the lever position so that the derailleur is not pushing the chain part way off a cog and causing a grinding noise from the rear wheel while underway. The Shimano lever has click stops, so fine adjustment of the lever cannot be made to prevent the chain from running part way off a cog and causing a grinding noise.

The Shimano click-stop lever shift is a real boon for the adult who has to fix his child's bicycle. Once the cable adjustments are properly made so the click stops and you move the derailleur to the correct position for each hub external gear, you don't have to make any further adjustment of the lever. All you have to do is watch out for later stretching of the cable. When it stretched—and it will—you'll need to readjust the cable positions as follows:

STEP ONE: A stretched wire will cause an inaccurate setting of the click stop on the three-speed hub. Put the gear-shift lever in *top* position. If speed change cannot then be made to the *second* position, readjust by loosening the wire-adjusting nut at the bellcrank and loosen or tighten the knurled ferrule on the cable as necessary. Then retighten the lock-nut.

STEP TWO: Make sure the indicator on the bellcrank is pointing directly to the red indicator line, with the three-speed lever in the "N" position.

To adjust the derailleur wire:

STEP ONE: Put lever in *top* position. If the cable is not tight (taut), cable tension is correct.

STEP TWO: Now move the pedals (the bicycle should be upside down or hung from the ceiling) and change the gears through the four gear changes. Make sure the derailleur moves the chain from highest to lowest gear and back, smoothly.

STEP THREE: If the lever cannot be put into the *second* position easily, tighten the wire by loosening the locknut at the clamp on the seat stay and adjusting the knurled ferrule as necessary. Retighten the locknut.

STEP FOUR: Check adjustment by moving the lever to *top* position, as you turn the pedals. If the lever won't go into *top* position easily, loosen the wire slightly. Now, move the lever through all the gear ranges and adjust the cable as needed, if there is any noise in any of the gear-click stops.

Torpedo Duomatic Hubs

Some American and imported bicycles are fitted with a West German–made two-speed hub with a foot-operated gear change and backpedaling brake. This hub, which is called a Torpedo Duomatic, is similar in design to the Bendix automatic two-speed hub with coaster brake, and requires the same type of maintenance. Just follow the same instructions as for the Bendix unit.

I do not recommend your trying to dismantle this hub, unless you make sure you have complete step-by-step illustrated instructions, which can be obtained through your bicycle dealer.

Torpedo also makes a two-speed hub without the coaster brake, for use with caliper-brake-equipped bicycles. Maintenance instructions for this hub are the same as for the Bendix automatic hub; just feed it some light oil once a month after long trips, and if any strange sounds come from it, rush the bicycle to the nearest bicycle shop. If your mechanic can't (or won't) fix the hub, write to the Torpedo distributor or the bicycle manufacturer for the name of the closest *bicycle store* (not discount or department store) that can do this work.

As on most of the multi-speed rear hubs used on bicycles in this country, the sprocket on the Torpedo hub can be easily changed to one with more teeth for touring in hilly country, or to one with fewer teeth for faster riding where the going is flat and easy. If you do change sprockets, remember that you must order the same make of sprocket as your hub, because sprockets are not interchangeable from one make of hub to the other.

Apropos of changing parts, parts from different makes of bicycles and bicycle components are more likely *not* to be interchangeable, except for mundane things such as tires, seats, and spokes. Be careful about ordering everything else!

A Word of Warning

Before you take your multi-speed rear hub to a bicycle shop, phone the shop to make sure it has the parts on hand or can assure you it is willing to go to the trouble to order them for you from its wholesaler. The problem is that hardly any bicycle shop can afford to carry the tremendous number of parts it would take to be able to service all American, English, and Japanese hubs that are popularly used in this country.

A related problem is that not all wholesalers carry all parts, and if the bike shop proprietor can't find what he needs from his own wholesaler, the chances are very good that he'll tell you they aren't available. If this happens to you, keep calling dealers until you find one who says he can and does repair the type and make of hub you have.

All About Derailleurs, Bottom Brackets,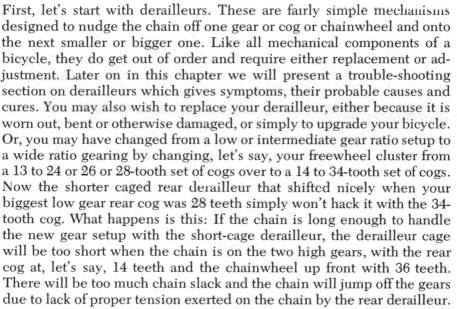
Cranksets and Chains

First, let's start with derailleurs. These are fairly simple mechanisms designed to nudge the chain off one gear or cog or chainwheel and onto the next smaller or bigger one. Like all mechanical components of a bicycle, they do get out of order and require either replacement or adjustment. Later on in this chapter we will present a trouble-shooting section on derailleurs which gives symptoms, their probable causes and cures. You may also wish to replace your derailleur, either because it is worn out, bent or otherwise damaged, or simply to upgrade your bicycle. Or, you may have changed from a low or intermediate gear ratio setup to a wide ratio gearing by changing, let's say, your freewheel cluster from a 13 to 24 or 26 or 28-tooth set of cogs over to a 14 to 34-tooth set of cogs. Now the shorter caged rear derailleur that shifted nicely when your biggest low gear rear cog was 28 teeth simply won't hack it with the 34-tooth cog. What happens is this: If the chain is long enough to handle the new gear setup with the short-cage derailleur, the derailleur cage will be too short when the chain is on the two high gears, with the rear cog at, let's say, 14 teeth and the chainwheel up front with 36 teeth. There will be too much chain slack and the chain will jump off the gears due to lack of proper tension exerted on the chain by the rear derailleur.

From Table 13-1 you will note that some derailleurs have longer cage lengths (column 2 in table) than others. For example, the Campagnolo Rally, SunTour Cyclone, SunTour VX wide range, all have long cages and will handle up to 34 teeth on the freewheel. The other derailleurs have shorter cages and can handle only up to 28 teeth on the freewheel, except the Shimano Altus, which goes to 30 teeth. So if you're replacing your rear derailleur, be sure to select one that will handle the chain wrap-around you need and at the same time maintain chain tension in all gear ratios.

Super wide range "Granny" gears are going to have to be a compromise. If you want a rear cog with 36 teeth and a chainwheel up front with 26 teeth, then you're very likely to find that you can't use the low-gear rear cog and the high-gear or big chainwheel, for two reasons. First I'm assuming that you don't want to drop from a 52- to a 26-tooth chainwheel, that there's a triple chainset involved, which there should be. So the wider chainset, with three chainwheels, means that when the chain is on the far-left big cog in the rear and on the far-right chainwheel up front, the chain is going to be at an extreme angle. It's possible that the new Shimano DuraAce front derailleur with a cage width of 14.6 millimeters will handle this extreme angle without chain rub on the wider front derailleur cage, and without having to move the front derailleur so as to avoid chain rub. I have this combination and it works for me. But if the chain is long enough for wrapping around these big cogs, then the chain will be too long when you're going in the opposite direction, let's say when the chain is on the high-gear cog (smallest) and low-gear chainwheel (smallest). Now even the widest-range rear derailleur is going to have trouble winding up far enough to maintain sufficient chain tension to keep the chain from jumping off the cog or chainwheel. So if you want a super "Granny" gear like mine, you're going to find, as I have, that two of the gear combinations are not really usable or practical—that is, combinations of the two largest and two smallest cogs and freewheels. I have recently switched to a SunTour six-speed freewheel on my Alex Singer, keeping the 30, 40 and 48 triple chainset up front. Theoretically I now have (6 x 3) an 18-speed setup. In practice, I have at best a 16-speed setup. I prefer this arrangement for two reasons. I don't mind sacrificing the two combinations noted above so long as I wind up with my good old "Granny" hill-climbing low low gear. Second, jumps between gear ratios are reasonable, so I am not constantly changing gears. At any rate I am happy, and that's what counts. You may want bigger gaps between gears, or smaller gaps, depending on your physical condition and the type of riding you do.

Table 13-1 Specifications, Selected Rear Derailleurs

Make and Model	Distance of Travel (mm)*	Cage Length (mm)†	Capacity ‡	Weight (grams)	Cost
Campagnolo Super Record	47.9	45.5	28T	214.33	$61.98
Campagnolo Nuovo Record	47.9	45.5	28T	242.51	37.98
Campagnolo Nuovo Gran Sport	47.9	45.5	28T	258.00	24.50
Campagnolo Rally	34.2	74.3	34T	286.34	28.50
SunTour Cyclone	42.2	65.9	34T	190.00	20.98
Shimano DuraAce	45.3	45.0	26T	175.00	NA
Shimano Crane GS	36.7	75.2	34T	226.80	NA
SunTour VX (Wide Range)	52.0	67.6	34T	243.80	11.50
SunTour VX-S	49.0	61.5	28T	243.80	10.98
Shimano 600 EX	45.3	45.0	28T	190.00	NA
Shimano Altus	45.3	45.0	30T	262.00	NA

* Distance between inner and outer stops, with both stops wide open.
† As measured between centerline of the jockey and tension wheels.
‡ Number of teeth in largest rear sprocket (cog) derailleur will handle.

HOW TO INSTALL A REAR DERAILLEUR

Hanging a derailleur on the rear dropout is a fairly simple procedure. First, let's remove the old one:

STEP ONE: Unless you have a derailleur with a two-piece cage on the left side, such as the SunTour Cyclone (Fig. 13-1) or the Shimano 600 EX (Fig. 13-2), you will need to "break" the chain with a rivet remover. Later on in the section in this chapter on chains, you will see that there are derailleur chains that can be "broken" without tools, or with a simple Allen wrench. If you have, or think you have, that kind of chain, I suggest you refer to the chain section of this chapter, before proceeding further.

STEP TWO: With the chain removed or slipped over the two-piece inner cage plate, unscrew the cable stop bolt (A in Fig. 13-3) and pull the cable through and away from the derailleur.

STEP THREE: Most derailleur bolts take a six-millimeter Allen wrench. The Campagnolo derailleur shown in Figure 13-3 is no exception. With the Allen wrench, turn the fixing bolt, "B" in Figure 13-3, counterclockwise and remove the derailleur.

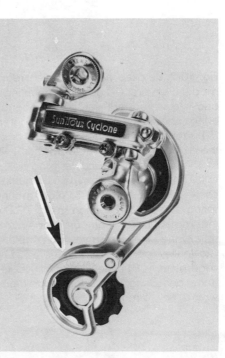

Fig. 13-1: This SunTour top-line derailleur has a left-side cage in two pieces, which permits removal of the derailleur without having to "break" the chain with a rivet remover.

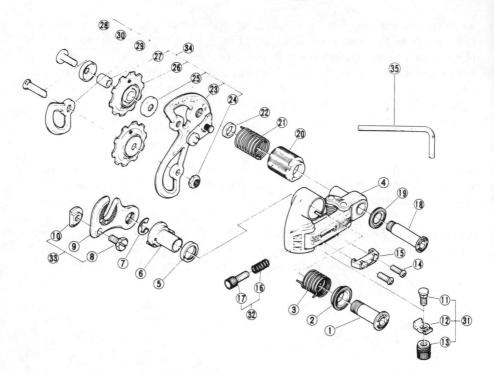

Fig. 13-2: Detailed view of a typical rear derailleur, the Shimano 600EX second-line model. Parts are: (1) adapter-mounting bolt; (2) adapter-mounting collar (bolt will also fit into threaded "ear" of Campagnolo dropout); (3) B-tension spring; (4) mechanism assembly; (5) sleeve; (6) adapter bushing; (7) stop ring; (8) adapter screw; (9) adapter (all this adapter stuff is for cheaper bikes without a threaded "ear" on the dropout to receive the derailleur. I will never understand the economics of this); (10) adapter nut; (11) cable-fixing bolt; (12) cable-fixing washer; (13) cable-fixing nut; (14) adjusting screw; (15) adjusting plate; (16) cable-adjusting spring; (17) cable-adjusting barrel; (18) plate-mounting bolt; (19) plate-mounting collar; (20) spring cover; (21) P-tension spring; (22) plate bushing; (23) inner cage plate (note that most of us call it an **outer** cage plate because it faces toward the outer or right side of the bike. Just so you don't get confused); (24) pulley nut; (25) pulley cap; (26) pulley (also known as wheel); (27) pulley bushing; (28) pulley bolt; (29) outer cage plate; (30) pulley bolt; (31) cable fixing bolt assembly; (32) cable adjusting barrel and spring; (33) adapter screw and nut; (34) pulley plate assembly; (35) hex wrench key, 6 mm.

Fig. 13-3: Campagnolo Nuovo Record derailleur. Basic parts are: (A) cable fixing bolt; (B) attaching bolt (screws into threaded dropout "ear," none of this adapter-plate monkey business; (C) high-gear limit stop (keeps derailleur from going off the high end, pushing chain too far to the right so it jams between chainstay (CG) and freewheel); (D) low-gear travel limit stop (adjusts to keep the derailler from kicking the chain too far to the left where it can jam between freewheel low gear and spokes); (E) flimsy screw that is supposed to keep wheel aligned accurately in dropouts (soon bends and breaks off unless you are very careful); (F) freewheel; (HH) brazed-on cable stop on chainstay.

TO INSTALL A NEW REAR DERAILLEUR

STEP ONE: Figure 13-3 shows a derailleur installed in a threaded "ear" which is part of the dropout. Less expensive bicycles do not have such an "ear" but use a mounting bracket ("A" in Fig. 13-4) that is bolted into the dropout itself and through which the hub axle fits. If your new derailleur does not have one supplied with it, you can buy a mounting bracket from the bike store. Screw the derailleur fixing bolt either into the dropout "ear" or the mounting bracket, turning the fixing bolt clockwise. Make sure the limit stop on the derailleur body fits into the matching limit stop on the dropout "ear" or mounting brackets (Fig. 13-5). Some derailleurs, such as the SunTour Cyclone, have an adjustable stop (Fig. 13-6). Figure 13-7 shows the derailleur fixing or mounting bolt being tightened.

Fig. 13-4: Campagnolo Rally wide-range derailleur for those low, low gears. "A" points to adapter plate so you can mount this derailleur (or any other) onto less expensive bikes without a threaded "ear" on dropout.

Fig. 13-5: Looking at a derailleur as it would appear if you were standing on the left side of the bike, if you had X-ray vision and could see through the hub and freewheel. I took this picture to show that there is a stop machined onto all derailleurs where they mount on the drop-out threaded ear or the adapter plate. The stop keeps the derailleur from rotating so it loses spring tension that keeps the chain under constant tension regardless of which gear the chain is in. If you have a French bicycle you may not be able to use anything but a French derailleur, particularly if the dropout is a Simplex, designed for a Simplex derailleur.

Fig. 13-6: SunTour has a better idea, an adjustable stop so you can adjust the derailleur to keep its wheels (pulleys) as close to the freewheel as possible, without jamming them, for snappier, more accurate shifting. Arrow points to adjusting screw.

Fig. 13-7: In case you are wondering where the low-gear and high-gear adjustments are on a derailleur, keep this rule of thumb in mind. The low-gear adjustment is always the one closest to the freewheel. "A°" shows the derailleur angle adjuster on this SunTour topline derailleur. Note that the left-side cage is in two pieces so chain can be lifted off without taking the chain apart.

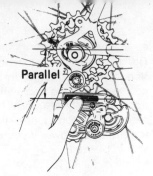

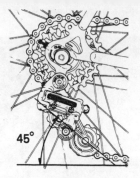

Fig. 13-8: The derailleur body should be adjusted so it is parallel to the chainstays, as shown. *(SunTour)*

Fig. 13-9: Derailleur wheels at the proper 45-degree angle to keep chain tension in all gears. *(SunTour)*

STEP TWO: Ideally, the derailleur body should be parallel to the chainstay. The chainstay is the frame tube marked "G-G" in Figure 13-3. If the derailleur has an adjustable stop, adjust it until the derailleur body is at the correct angle (Fig. 13-8).

STEP THREE: If you have installed new gears, say a low gear with more teeth, as in going from a 28-tooth rear cog to a 34-tooth rear cog, you will now need a longer chain. If you went to a smaller rear cog, say from a 28- to a 23-tooth low gear, you will need less chain. In either case, put the chain on the low (biggest) rear cog and high (biggest chainwheel) front gear. Add or remove chain links as necessary to bring the tension pulley to around a 45-degree angle to the ground (Fig. 13-9). If after shifting to the two high gears, you find you do not have enough chain tension to keep the chain engaged and the chain tends to jump off the gear, particularly the rear gear, try removing another chain link so that with the chain on the low-gear rear and high-gear front, the derailleur pulleys are at the angle shown in Figure 13-10, parallel and in line with

Fig. 13-10: This is the angle the derailleur should assume when the chain is on the low gear in the rear and on the high gear in the front. With all tension the chain will not jump off the cogs in higher gears in the rear. The idea is to keep the chain under as much tension as possible when it is on the two biggest gears, so that as you shift up to higher gears in the rear or down to a smaller chainwheel, the chain will be kept under enough tension so it won't jump off the cog.

Fig. 13-11: To check for chain tension when the chain is on the big cog rear and big chainwheel up front, give it the "pinch" test by seeing if you can squeeze two links together, as shown. If you can, all should be well.

the chain. Another way to check for correct chain length is to pinch together two links (Fig. 13-11). If you can't do that, the chain is too short and you need to add one or two more links. Please also note that there are differences between makes of derailleurs. For example, the Campagnolo Nuovo Record short-cage derailleur should have the cage and pulleys parallel or close to parallel to the chain when the chain is on the two largest (most number of teeth) gears. SunTour and most long-cage derailleurs should, with the chain in this position, be at around a 45-degree angle to the ground. None of these instructions are really absolute but are intended as a guide to correct chain length. But you will get pretty close to accurate chain-length fit with these instructions. Although you probably will never (and I would add, *should not*) use the low-gear and high-front gears together, if you have enough chain wraparound to do so and in this position can pinch two chain links together, you should still have enough chain tension (from the derailleur) to keep the chain on the high-rear and low-front gears without chain jump.

STEP FOUR: Put the chain on the low rear gear (biggest cog) and adjust the low-gear travel stop on the derailleur until the derailleur pulleys are in line with the cog. Figure 13-3 shows the low-gear travel stop on a Campagnolo derailleur, "D". The low-gear stop is always the stop closest to the freewheel, on any derailleur I know of. You should move the chain by hand, because we have yet to install the cable. Move the chain to the high gear (smallest freewheel cog) and adjust the high-gear stop so the derailleur pulleys are in line with this gear (Fig. 13-12). Figure 13-13 shows derailleur pulleys lined up with both high and low gears.

STEP FIVE: With the chain on either the biggest or the smallest rear cog, check to make sure the derailleur pulleys are not only centered on the freewheel cog but also that they are in line laterally with the cog. Sometimes, when the derailleur body is bent, as from an accident, the dropout "ear" is bent or the dropout is bent slightly out of line, so that the derailleur is slightly cockeyed with respect to the freewheel cogs. You should be able to eyeball this alignment. If the derailleur itself is

Fig. 13-12: When installing a new derailleur, even before you attach the cable, move the chain over by hand to the high-gear rear cog and adjust that stop so the derailleur wheels are in line with that cog, as shown.

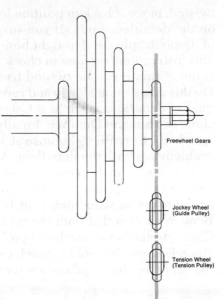

Freewheel Gears

Jockey Wheel
(Guide Pulley)

Tension Wheel
(Tension Pulley)

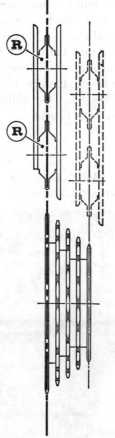

Fig. 13-13: The derailleur wheels should also line up with the low-gear cog.

twisted, move it back in position by using an adjustable crescent wrench on the derailleur body. If you suspect the problem lies with alignment of dropouts, please stop right here and go to Chapter 16 where you will find instructions on how to check for dropout alignment. If the dropout is out of line it can be twisted back to true with the adjustable wrench. Do this adjustment slowly and carefully. If you are installing a new high-quality derailleur, such as a Campagnolo Nuovo Record, SunTour Cyclone or Shimano DuraAce, I really do not advise you to twist the derailleur body to realign, because it is highly unlikely that the alignment problem lies with the derailleur. All I want you to note is that the derailleur pulleys can be centered on the cog by adjustment, but that the pulleys and cogs must also line up laterally or you will have chain jump, an annoying unscheduled shift from one gear to another as you pedal. Remember also that both the cable and the chain will stretch with use. Chain stretch is not much of a problem unless the stretch is such that the chain is worn. But cable stretch can mean that you will have to readjust the cable tension, a procedure we will discuss in installing the cable.

STEP SIX: I am going to assume that you want a new cable, either because the old one has become frayed, so that you can't thread the end through the spaghetti tubing, or you are going on a trip and quite correctly want a new cable for breakdown insurance. Installing a cable on a rear derailleur is fairly straightforward. If you install a new cable I also recommend new spaghetti tubing. Thread the cable into the shift lever, making sure the lead ball is seated all the way in the lever. Figure 13-14 shows the cable end correctly seated, Figure 13-15 shows the other side of the levers, with cable under the guide in the correct location.

Fig. 13-14: Arrow shows proper insertion of cable.

Fig. 13-15: Derailleur cable threads under guide, arrow.

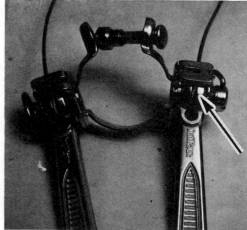

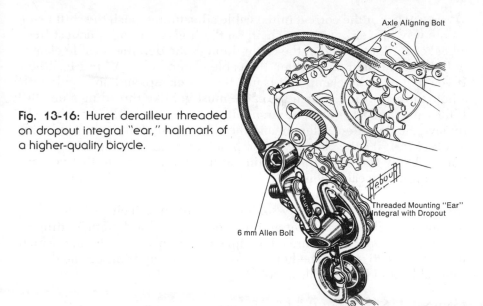

Fig. 13-16: Huret derailleur threaded on dropout integral "ear," hallmark of a higher-quality bicycle.

STEP SEVEN: Cut off enough length of derailleur-cable spaghetti tubing so that you have the kind of curve shown in Figures 13-3 and 13-16. The length of the tubing will depend on the make of derailleur. In measuring tubing, the chain should be on the low rear cog so the derailleur is at its maximum travel. When cutting tubing, check ends to make sure they are not partially cut, leaving a piece that either obstructs the tubing exits or has sharp edges at this location. I grind off the ends on a bench grinder to eliminate burrs that would hamper cable travel and possibly cut the cable strands. Thread the cable through the cable guides brazed or clamped onto the frame. Brazed-on cable guides are shown in Figures 13-3(HH) and 13-17.

Fig. 13-17: Some custom-built bikes have cable guides underneath the bottom bracket, arrows.

STEP EIGHT: For the correct initial cable adjustment, push the shift lever all the way forward, with the chain on the high-gear cog (smallest free-wheel cog). Put the end of the cable through the derailleur cable clamp, pull the cable tight and tighten the cable clamp bolt ("A" in Fig. 13-3). If you're lucky, the clamp bolt is just that—a clamp, and not a bolt with a hole through it into which the cable must go, like threading a needle. If the cable end frays just one strand, it means a new cable if you have to remove the derailleur later on, and the cable clamp bolt is the kind with a hole in it. If it's the clamp type, no problem, so long as the cable end is not too badly frayed. I am assuming at this point, though, that you are installing a new cable which has its free end dipped in solder to prevent fraying. Lightly sand the cable from a location about one to two inches from the derailleur and apply solder along this one-inch section. When the solder cools, you can cut and trim off extra cable length, cutting in the middle of your solder area. I use an electrician's wire trimmer, which has various size holes. The hole marked 4–40 nicely trims off the derailleur cable (and brake cables, too).

STEP NINE: Now hang the bike from pipes in the basement (I prefer hanging the bike, using coated "U" hooks, to standing it. Bike work-stands that clamp good tubing and mar the finish are not for me. Besides, you can make two coated hooks for practically nothing; a bike work-stand costs upwards of $50 or more.) Twiddle the pedals, move the rear derailleur lever so the derailleur goes through all its gears and make sure it shifts smoothly, without chain override on the high or low gears. At this juncture I would like to add that I *hate* those metal pie plates that are supposed to keep the chain from tangling in the spokes on the high-gear side. If you keep the derailleur properly adjusted, the chain will never jump over the gear and land between it and the spokes. Pie plates are ugly and add unecessary weight; I suggest you remove the freewheel (see Chapter 11) and pull off that hunk of metal. I don't even like plastic pie plates. I know Uncle Sam has in his infinite wisdom decreed them. But if I want to take one off my very own bike, by golly, I am going to.

If you added a new freewheel that's wider, say from a five- to a seven-speed freewheel, you may need to add a spacer on the freewheel side of the hub axle so the chain won't rub or jam on the seat stay when it's on the high-gear cog. Chapter 11 has details on axle length. You may also have to re-dish the wheel (see Chapter 15).

INSTALLING A FRONT DERAILLEUR

In selecting a front derailleur, make sure it will handle whatever gears you have up front. Table 13-2 gives front-derailleur specifications and capacities, where this data is available from the manufacturer. For example, and here I am assuming you have a bottom-bracket spindle of the

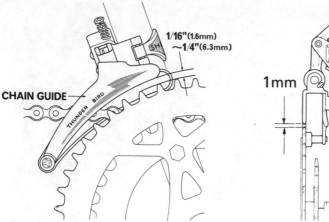
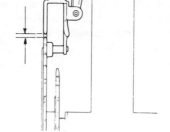

Fig. 13-18: Align front derailleur cage in line with chainwheel and about ⅟₁₆ to ¼ inch above outer (high-gear) chainwheel.

Fig. 13-19: Chainwheel cage should be in line with chainwheels. *(SunTour)*

correct length and not one that's too long (see discussion of bottom brackets later on in this chapter) so the chainwheel is not too far away from the seat tube for the front derailleur to be able to move the chain to the biggest chainwheel. If you have a triple chainwheel you need a derailleur with a wide travel, such as the SunTour Cyclone which will move through 21 millimeters, or the Campagnolo Nuovo Record which will go through 24 millimeters. I have the most success and satisfaction with the Campagnolo front derailleur, which handles my triple chainset nicely. To install a front derailleur, follow these fairly uncomplicated steps:

STEP ONE: Assuming the old derailleur has been removed, clamp the new one around the seat tube so that the cage is parallel to and about ⅟₁₆th inch above the biggest chainwheel (Figs. 13-18 and 13-19).

STEP TWO: The spring action of most front derailleurs is such that the cage is always at the left when the shift lever is all the way forward. Adjust the left, or smallest, chainwheel derailleur travel stop screw so that the cage is centered over the small chainwheel (left chainwheel). In front derailleurs where the spring action pulls the cage to the right, over the largest chainwheel, adjust the high-gear stop, at right, so the chainwheel is centered in the derailleur chain cage. Figure 13-20 shows the gear stops. The low-gear stop, which limits how far the derailleur cage will move to the left, is always located closest to the seat tube. The front derailleur where spring action keeps the cage at the right is typified by the SunTour Model NSL.

STEP THREE: Insert the cable through the shift lever (Figs. 13-14 and 13-15) and through the cable guides, and fasten the end to the cable clamp of the derailleur, with the shift lever all the way forward, in the low-gear

Fig. 13-20: Low- and high-gear stops on a front derailleur. Note that low-gear adjustment stop is closest to seat tube, which is where most of the low-gear stops are located on front derailleurs.

position. Pull the cable taut to remove cable slack, tighten cable clamp bolt. There is very little uniformity among derailleurs, in terms of bolt and nut sizes. For example, the excellent SunTour front derailleur is clamped to the seat tube with a 4-millimeter Allen bolt, its cable clamp is an 8-millimeter bolt and the adjusting screws (travel stops) are Philips head which can take, however, a standard screwdriver. Campy uses 8-millimeter bolts for the tube and cable clamps. Shimano uses, on the 600EX, 6-millimeter bolts on tube and cable clamps. In installing the cable, remember that you may need spaghetti tubing between the cable guide and the derailleur so the cable will not rub on the downtube.

STEP FOUR: Move the shift lever back as you twirl the pedals (with bike suspended from the ceiling, on a stand or upside down) to get the chain onto the largest front chainwheel. Adjust the high-gear stop so the derailleur cage is centered over the chainwheel, with the chain on the middle rear freewheel cog. Now run the gears through all speeds. You will note that as you shift from one freewheel cog to another, without changing adjustment of the chainwheel shift lever, that the chain will tend to rub on the cage as it assumes steeper angles going up and down the gears of the freewheel. This is as good a point as any to get into chain alignment, because it is related to the problem of readjustment of the front derailleur when you shift fron one rear cog to another.

THE PROBLEM OF CHAIN RUB, FRONT DERAILLEUR

The novice ten-speed cyclist will wonder why, with all parts properly adjusted as instructed so far, the chain makes an annoying sound as it rubs on the inside of the front-derailleur cage when shifting from one rear cog to another. What you have to get used to is making minor adjustments of the front-derailleur shift lever so as to move the front-derailleur cage slightly one way or the other, depending on whether you are shifting up or down on the rear cogs.

For example, take a look at Figure 13-21. Here is the gear setup that most of you will have, a simple five-speed freewheel rear and a double chainwheel up front. In this drawing, the chain "A" is on the smaller chainwheel. Now you shift down to the low gear (the one with the most teeth) on the freewheel. You will see that the chain "B" has assumed an angle that brings it so close to the left side of the front-derailleur cage that it rubs, making a metallic sound as you pedal. To correct this rub, you now have to reshift the front lever, moving it forward so that the cage moves slightly to the left. If you have adjusted the cage so it can't move far enough to the left for chain clearance with the cage with the chain in this position, now is the time to readjust the front-derailleur stop so it can move over more to the left. Now you have climbed the hill that caused you to shift to the low rear cog, and you are on a slight downgrade, so you can shift over to the high rear cog (the one with the smallest teeth). As you can see from Figure 13-21, the chain "C" position is such that the opposite angle from chain "A" is taken and if you have moved the cage left to compensate for chain angle in position "A" you will surely have rub in position "C" and so must again make a minor adjustment of the front-derailleur cage, pulling the shift lever slightly upward. Don't worry, after a few hundred miles this minor reshifting will become automatic, and you will instinctively reach for the front lever right after shifting a rear cog, to make this slight adjustment.

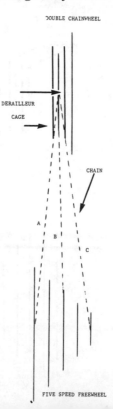

Fig. 13-21: As you shift from one rear cog to the other but don't shift to another front chainwheel, the chain assumes an ever-increasing angle. Here, with the chain on the low front gear it begins to rub on the front derailleur cage as it approaches the low rear cog. And with chain in the "C" position the chain again rubs on the derailleur cage. All this means is that you need to readjust the front derailleur slightly so the chain won't rub on its cage as you shift from one gear to the other. In the "B" position the chain will not rub on the front cage.

Now if you have become a cycle-touring enthusiast you will perhaps want a triple chainwheel so you can have a super low "Granny" gear for those steep 10- and 15-percent grades, without sacrificing an intermediate chainwheel. The Granny gear can be 30 or 34 teeth, the chainwheel 40 teeth, the high-gear chainwheel 48 teeth. You may also want a wider gear spread, so you have gone to a six- or seven-speed freewheel. The extreme would be a triple chainset with a seven-speed rear cluster (Fig. 13-22). Now you will have chain rub for sure as you shift through the various gear combinations, and to keep the chain from rubbing on the derailleur cage up front you will need to make these slight adjustments with the front derailleur shift lever. You won't have chain rub in all gear combinations, of course, but as the chain approaches extreme angles, your ears will tell you that the front derailleur cage and the chain are in pain.

The new Shimano front derailleurs have a wider cage than other makes, as noted in Table 13-2. For example, the 600 model has a cage width of 14.6 millimeters, 3 millimeters wider than the Campagnolo Nuovo Record. The wider cage minimizes but does not eliminate all problems of chain rub up front. You will also note from Table 13-1 that front-derailleur capacity is a function of the difference in the number of teeth between the smallest and the largest chainwheel. My Alex Singer has a 30 small and 48 large chainwheel, a difference of 18 teeth. Campy does not give capacity but it handles this range nicely. The DuraAce should also handle this range, although Shimano rates it at 16 teeth.

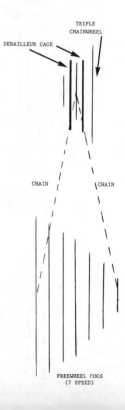

Fig. 13-22: Chain rub can be especially acute with a seven-speed freewheel and triple chainwheel.

Table 13-2 Specifications, Front Derailleurs

Make and Model	Travel * (Milli- meters)	Weight (Grams)	Capacity † (No. Teeth)	Cage Width ‡ (Milli- meters)	Cage Length §
SunTour Cyclone	21.0	99.23	NA	12.5	118.5
SunTour NSL	17.3	113.4	NA	12.5	95.0
SunTour VX	23.0	116.24	NA	11.7	104.0
Campagnolo Nuovo Record	24.0	99.24	NA	11.6	104.5
Shimano 600	18.5	113.40	14 or less	14.6	107.8
Shimano DuraAce	18.5	108.00	16 or less	14.6	107.8
Shimano Altus	21.0	127.60	14 or less	14.9	108.0

* Maximum cage travel with high and low stops wide open.

† Difference between number of teeth on both chainwheels, or largest and smallest chainwheel. For example, small chainwheel has 36 teeth, big one has 52 teeth. Difference is 16 teeth.

‡ Measured from center width of inner surface of cage plates.

§ A measure of longest (right) cage plate from tip to tip.

With the wider cage you would think that you would have to shift through a great lateral movement to get the chain to move from one chainwheel to another. Shimano seems to have solved this problem by incorporating a trapezoidal motion (Fig. 13-23) which Shimano claims lifts the chain up and deposits it squarely on the chainwheel teeth, providing a shorter-stroke cage movement, and permitting the wider cage. Looking at other front derailleur movements, they all seem about the same to me, but the Shimano design does work well and that's what counts.

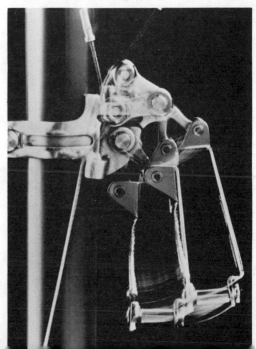

Fig. 13-23: Shimano's new front derailleur has a wider cage which minimizes the need for adjustment as you shift, and the trapeze swing movement helps smooth shifting.

CHAINLINE ALIGNMENT

To keep the chain from assuming too great an angle, and to divide the chain angles that do occur as evenly as possible between the gears, the bottom bracket and, therefore, the chainwheels and, to some extent, the freewheel cluster, should be aligned as follows:

Single chainwheel and five-speed freewheel (five-speed setup) should have the chainwheel in line with the third freewheel gear, as shown in Figure 13-24.

Double chainwheel, five-speed rear cluster should have the centerline *between* the chainwheels in line with the third rear gear, as shown in Figure 13-25.

Triple chainwheel and five-speed freewheel should have the center chainwheel in line with the center (third) rear cog (Fig. 13-26).

Double chainwheel and six-speed freewheel. Here the centerline *between* the chainwheels should be in line with the centerline *between* the third and fourth rear cogs (Fig. 13-27).

Triple chainwheel and six-speed freewheel should have the center chainwheel in line *between* the third and fourth rear cogs (Fig. 13-28).

Double chainwheel and seven-speed freewheel should have the centerline *between* the chainwheels in line with the fourth rear cog (Fig. 13-29).

Triple chainwheel and seven-speed freewheel should have the center chainwheel in line with the fourth rear cog (Fig. 13-30).

ALIGNMENT ADJUSTMENTS ARE:

Adding or removing spacers on the rear hub. This is most practical with the Durham Bullseye hub. The wheel should be re-dished in this case. See Chapter 15.

Using a shorter or long bottom-bracket axle (spindle). There is a limit to how short the axle can be to avoid chainwheel rub on the chainstay. See discussion of bottom brackets and spindle lengths later on in this chapter.

Adjusting a Phil Wood bottom bracket. As you will see when we discuss bottom brackets, it is possible to make a small adjustment on these units, which would move the chainwheel laterally a few millimeters.

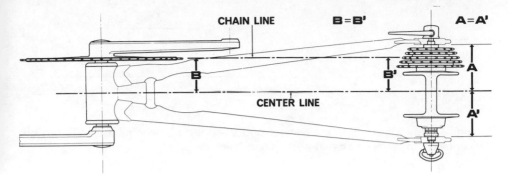

Fig. 13-24: Chainline adjustment for a single chainwheel and five-speed freewheel. Chain should line up with third-gear cog.

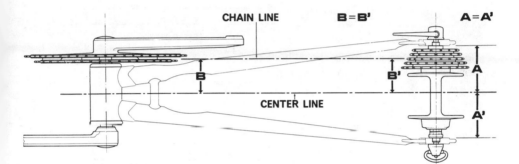

Fig. 13-25: For double chainwheel and five-speed freewheel, chain should line up **between** chainwheels and on third rear cog.

Fig. 13-26: With a triple chainwheel and five-speed freewheel, chain should line up with center freewheel and third rear cog.

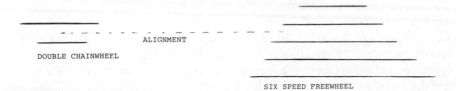

Fig. 13-27: With a double chainwheel and six-speed freewheel, chain should line up centered between chainwheels and between third and fourth cogs.

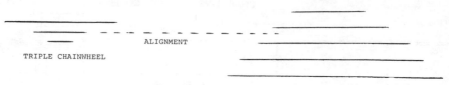

Fig. 13-28: With a triple chainwheel and six-speed freewheel, line up chain on center chainwheel and between third and fourth cogs.

Fig. 13-29: With a double chainwheel and seven-speed freewheel, center chain between chainwheels and on fourth cog.

Fig. 13-30: With a triple chainwheel and seven-speed freewheel, line up chain on center chainwheel and fourth cog.

Adjusting a Durham Bullseye bottom bracket. There is considerably more adjustment possible with this bottom bracket spindle set than with the Phil Wood or any other make bottom bracket arrangement. You can move the spindle until the cranks rub—in either direction. For more details, see the discussion in this chapter on bottom brackets.

LOCATING THE SHIFT LEVERS

Less expensive bicycles often come with shift levers mounted on the handlebar stem (Fig. 13-31). You should not have shift levers in this location. If you were to hit something, such as a bad bump, or a rut, or get the front wheel caught in a bridge expansion joint, as I have, you will go flying over the handlebars. With shift levers in the location shown in Figure 13-31, men are in fair danger of getting hurt in a testicular spot,

Fig. 13-31: Shift levers mounted on stem should at least have lever tops below handlebars. This photo shows levers above handlebars, where you could get hurt in an accident. Sudden bike stops almost always mean you are propelled over the handlebars. I prefer shift levers on the downtube or handlebar ends.

and women can get gouged the same way. I would move the shift levers to some other place.

The more common location is on the downtube (Fig. 13-32). Better bikes have a small "pip" brazed on the downtube that keeps the downtube shifters from sliding down the tube. Clamping shift levers onto the tube will usually hold them, but sometimes vibration works them loose, and the pull of both front and rear derailleur springs on the cables can pull the shift levers downward. When this happens all the derailleur adjustments, front and rear, go out the window, at least in the higher-gear front and lower-gear rear, because the cable will be too slack to pull the derailleurs over.

The only other problem with downtube shifters is that the shift lever lock bolt works loose under constant shifting. That's why the better shift levers, like the one shown in Figure 13-33, have a wire grip on the bolt so you can bend over as you cycle to tighten the lever down. You can

Fig. 13-32: Shift levers can clamp on downtube. To keep them from moving or sliding down the tube, better bikes have a "pip" brazed on the downtube against which the shift-lever clamp can seat.

Fig. 13-33: Better shift levers have a turn grip so you can tighten the shift-lever mounting bolts, which will work loose eventually. Other makes may require a screwdriver, or a dime. If gears shift unasked, check this adjustment.

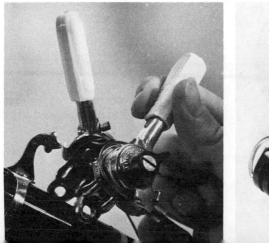

tell when your lever bolt has worked loose because the gears shift by themselves. There are other causes for this phenomenon, such as a worn chain or cog or too long a chain causing low tension and chain jump. But your first check should be the shift lever bolt. In fact, you should make a habit of twisting this bolt every day if you ride a lot. Less expensive downtube shifters require a screwdriver but sometimes a dime will work. Even the best of levers will have loosened retaining bolts eventually.

My favorite place to put the shift lever is at the tip end of the handlebars. We have already discussed the safety aspects of stem-mounted shift levers. As for downtube shifters, the problem here is that you have to bend down slightly to reach them, which can be a safety hazard because you are momentarily unbalanced, and because you have to remove one hand from the handlebars to use the lever. With the shifters located at the ends of the handlebar, you can shift with both hands on the bars, without having to lean over sideways, or without having to take your eyes off the road ahead; however, bar-end shifters (Fig. 13-34) are a separate piece of equipment from downtube shifters and are not interchangeable. You can also use both hands to shift as you go through the gears, without taking your hands off the bars. As I have mentioned before and will bring up again, you need to readjust the front derailleur slightly to compensate for changing chain angle as you shift through the gears, in order to keep the chain from rubbing on the inside of the front derailleur cage. With downtube-mounted shift levers you can only use one hand at a time, so you will find yourself reaching down with the right hand to move to a different rear sprocket, then bringing that hand back to the bars while you bend over the left side and reach down with the left hand to readjust the front derailleur. The bar-end shifters are *much* more convenient.

Here is a pictorial step-by-step method for changing to handlebar shift

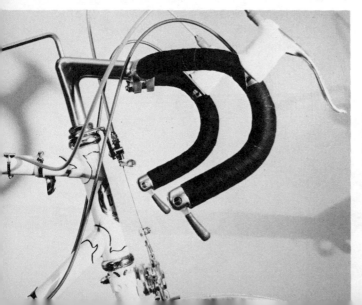

Fig. 13-34: Bar-end shifters, located at handlebar ends, as shown here, are a lot safer than levers located anywhere else because you can shift without removing your hands from the bars.

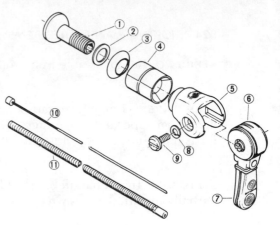

Fig. 13-35: Detailed view of Shimano bar-end controls. (1) anchor bolt; (2) plastic washer; (3) tapered washer; (4) segment assembly with spring; (5) body; (6) lever assembly with lever cap; (7) lever cap; (8) spring washer; (9) lever fixing bolt; (10) front inner cable, rear inner cable; (11) lever-end outer casing, front derailleur outer casing, rear derailleur outer casing.

levers. First, though, a word about which lever system to change to. Handlebar shifters are made by Campagnolo, Shimano, SunTour, Huret, and Simplex, among others. I prefer the Shimano (Fig. 13-35) levers because they have internal spring tension, which compensates for derailleur spring tension, making shifting easier. Next I prefer the Sun-Tour, which has a ratchet mechanism to hold the gear where you shifted. I don't like the Campagnolo bar levers because they are hard to shift and won't stay in place; it's easy for the rear gear to shift by itself. Construction details among the various makes of handlebar shifters vary slightly, but basic principles are the same. If you can master one, you can install any of them. Tools and materials· you will need are: Campagnolo "T" wrench or 6-millimeter Allen wrench; medium-sized screwdriver; new handlebar tape, preferably the cloth type; extra-long derailleur cables for handlebar-end shifters (if yours did not come with them); ⅛-inch or ³⁄₁₆-inch inside-diameter clear plastic tubing (from a chemical supply or hobby store, to keep cable tubing from rubbing on head tube); 6- or 8-millimeter socket wrench or adjustable wrench to remove old cable and install new cable on derailleurs.

STEP ONE: Become acquainted with the basic parts of handlebar shifters. (A) shift lever-axle bolt; (B) housing barrel; (C) lever housing; (D) cable (extra long); (E) lever; (F) lever-axle nut; (G) lever-axle locknut. (H) is not a part of the shifters; it is the 6-millimeter Allen wrench you will need to tighten the barrel in the handlebar end (Fig. 13-36).

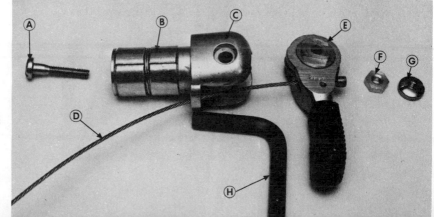

Fig. 13-36:
Step One

STEP TWO: Remove cable from front derailleur (Fig. 13-37).

STEP THREE: Remove derailleur shift levers and cable, and remove handlebar tape and end plugs. If tape can be reused, remove only as far as brake-lever body (Fig. 13-38).

STEP FOUR: Insert handlebar shift barrel into handlebar end, with cable partially installed as shown (Figure 13-39).

STEP FIVE: Insert 6-millimeter Allen wrench into barrel and tighten counterclockwise, making sure axle holes are level as shown (Fig. 13-40).

Fig. 13-37: Step Two

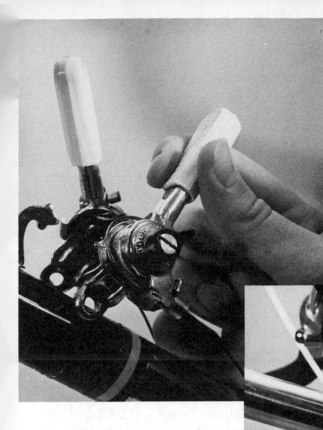

Fig. 13-38: Step Three

Fig. 13-39: Step Four

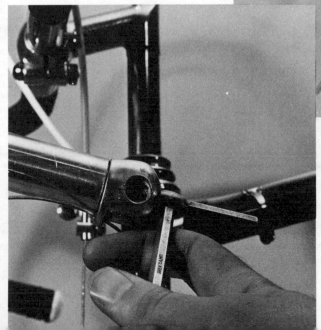

Fig. 13-40: Step Five

STEP SIX: Slide shift lever into milled section of housing. Note that flat lever flange fits into milled section of housing (Fig. 13-41).

STEP SEVEN: Insert lever-axle bolt into round countersunk hole in lever housing (*not* into square shank hole; see Step Eight) (Fig. 13-42).

STEP EIGHT: Insert lever-axle nut on axle and thread down into octagonal-shaped hole that holds this bolt in place. Tighten lever-axle-nut from other side with screwdriver (Fig. 13-43).

STEP NINE: Thread on and tighten lever-axle locknut, using screwdriver. Slide steel tubing sheath over cables, and enough ⅛- or 3⁄16-inch clear plastic tubing over sheath so that sheath won't rub on head tube (Fig. 13-44). Fish tank air pump tubing works fine.

STEP TEN: Install cable sheath stop on downtube. Leave enough cable out so handlebars can turn unimpeded. Bring cable through metal sheath and cable stop, and install ends in front and rear derailleurs (Fig. 13-45). Check adjustment of derailleurs.

STEP ELEVEN: Retape handlebars. You can either stop tape over derailleur cable sheathing just before you reach brake levers and let sheathing flop loose at this point, continuing beyond levers to top of bar without going over cable sheathing; or continue over cable sheathing till cable is covered up to near end of bars near stem. The latter method keeps cables from flopping around and looks a lot neater, but makes it difficult or impossible to remove handlebars when you bring your bike on an airplane, as some airlines request.

Fig. 13-41: Step Six

Fig. 13-42: Step Seven

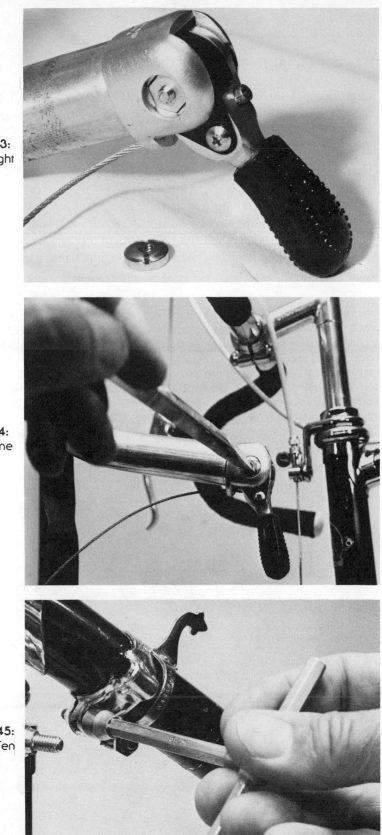

Fig. 13-43:
Step Eight

Fig. 13-44:
Step Nine

Fig. 13-45:
Step Ten

DERAILLEUR ADJUSTMENT TROUBLESHOOTING

Before we get into details on troubleshooting, you might take a look at Figures 13-46, a close-up view of a Shimano DuraAce rear derailleur, 13-47, the same for a DuraAce front derailleur, and 13-48, downtube shifters. Figure 13-49 shows in detail a Campagnolo second line derailleur, the Gran Sport.

1. PROBLEM: Gear changes while riding.
   CAUSE: Gear-shift control lever too loose.
   SOLUTION: Tighten gear-control-lever thumbscrew (wing nut), or use a screwdriver on nut type. Caution: Tighten just enough so lever feels slightly tight. Do not tighten so hard that shifting becomes difficult.

Fig. 13-46: Shimano DuraAce rear derailleur. Parts are: (1) plate-mounting bolt; (2) plate-mounting collar; (3) P-tension spring; (4) adapter-mounting bolt; (5) adapter-mounting collar; (6) B-tension spring; (7) adjusting screw; (8) cable-fixing nut; (9) cable-fixing bolt; (10) adjusting plate; (11) cable-adjusting plate; (12) cable-adjusting barrel; (13) mechanism assembly; (14) adapter-mounting sleeve; (15) adapter bushing assembly; (16) stop ring; (17) plate-mounting sleeve; (18) plate bushing; (19) stopper pin; (20) pulley bolt; (21) inner cage plate; (22) plate mounting nut; (23) pulley cap; (24) pulley bushing; (25) pulley; (26) outer cage plate; (27) pulley plate assembly; (28) hex wrench keys, 3 mm. and 6 mm. (1/8" and 1/4").

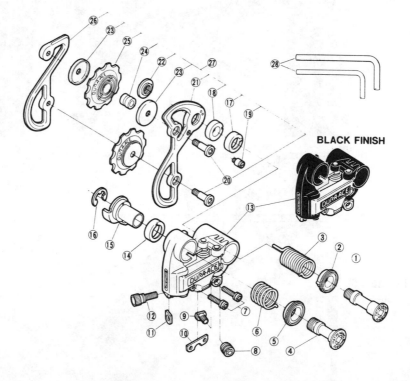

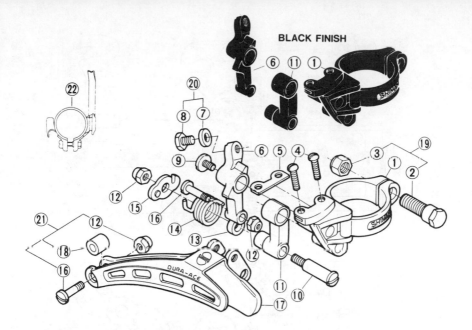

Fig. 13-47: Shimano DuraAce front derailleur. Parts are: (1) clamp assembly; (2) clamp bolt; (3) clamp nut; (4) stroke-adjusting screw; (5) stroke-adjusting plate; (6) outer link; (7) cable-fixing plate; (8) cable-fixing bolt; (9) fixing screw; (10) axle screw B; (11) inner link; (12) nut; (13) spring collar; (14) return spring; (15) spring plate; (16) screw A; (17) chain guide assembly; (18) roller; (19) clamp bolt and nut; (20) cable-fixing plate and bolt; (21) roller fixing screw assembly; (22) cable guide.

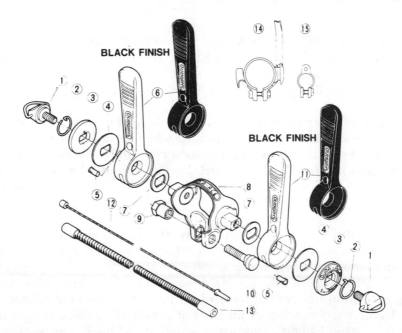

Fig. 13-48: Shimano downtube shift levers. Parts are: (1) lever fixing bolt; (2) clutch spring; (3) cap; (4) spring washer; (5) stopper pin; (6) front shifter lever; (7) washer; (8) lever clamp, goes on downtube; (9) clamp nut; (10) clamp bolt; (11) rear-derailleur lever; (12) inner cable (2); (13) cable housing (2); (14) cable guide; (15) outer stopper.

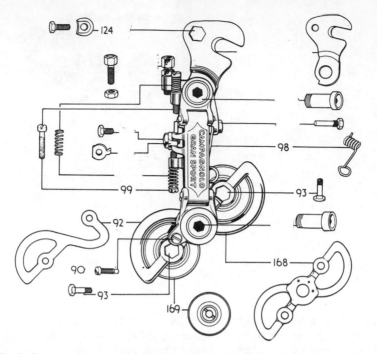

Fig. 13-49: Typical derailleur mechanism, in this case the Campagnolo "Gran Sport" unit. Parts are as follows (major ones only): (90) peg stop; (92) inner roller plate; (93) bolt to jockey roller; (98) traverse spring; (99) limit stop adjuster bolts (top bolt is for low or larger gear limit travel, lower bolt is for high or smaller gear limit travel); (124) chainstay bolt; (168) outer roller plate; (169) tension roller.

2. PROBLEM: Difficulty in shifting to front high-gear chainwheel.
   CAUSE: Front-derailleur right-hand control stop needs readjusting.
   SOLUTION: Readjust so front-derailleur cage can travel far enough to the right to lift chain up onto front high-gear chainwheel.

   CAUSE: Bottom-bracket spindle too long. For example, you may have changed to a longer spindle when installing a new bottom-bracket set. Just one or two millimeters too long a spindle will do it.
   SOLUTION: Install the correct length spindle for your bottom-bracket shell width. See discussion of bottom-bracket dimensions later on in this chapter.

3. PROBLEM: Gear changes erratically, slowly and noisily.
   CAUSE: Derailleur jockey and tension sprockets are not lined up in the same plane as rear gears.
   SOLUTION: Turn bike upside down. (Note: I prefer to hang the bicycle from the ceiling by hooks attached to the saddle [seat] and handlebars, which puts all parts at eye level or close to it or use a bike stand.) Sight along a vertical line to check that tension and jockey wheels are parallel to rear hub gears, as discussed earlier in this chapter.

A good reason for having everything in correct alignment on derailleur mechanisms, aside from the noise and extra wear and tear caused by misalignment, is that a good deal of energy-wasting friction can also result from such misalignment.

4. PROBLEM: Chain keeps riding up on the rear low gear sprocket (the largest rear gear). This can cause the chain to bind in the spokes, with disastrous results.
   CAUSE: The low-gear derailleur adjustment screw needs readjustment (Fig. 13-50).
   SOLUTION: Make this adjustment.

5. PROBLEM: Chain runs off high-gear (small) sprocket.
   CAUSE: High-gear adjusting screw is moved out of place because of vibration.
   SOLUTION: Readjust the high-gear adjusting screw. Turn wheel so that the chain is on the large front chainwheel and small rear gear. If the chain has jammed between seat stay and gear, be careful that in pulling it out you don't bend it or the derailleur. If necessary, loosen the quick-release skewer or axle nuts and push the wheel forward, or rotate it gently backward. Turn the high-gear adjusting screw until the chain will not slip off high gear. On Huret Allvit derail-

Fig. 13-50: Low-gear adjustment screws on three popular Campagnolo rear derailleurs (arrows). Left to right: Super Record; Rally (wide ratio); Gran Sport (bargain basement).

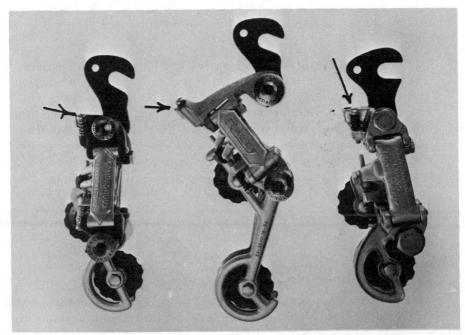

leurs, the high-gear adjusting screw is the small screw about two-thirds of the way down the outside face of the main housing bracket, recessed into a small hole in the bracket. On Campagnolo derailleurs, the high-gear adjusting screw is located about halfway down, at the rear of the main housing casting, and points toward the bottom. And on the Shimano "Skylark," it is at the bottom of the two Phillips-head screws at the center rear of the derailleur.

Note: Every time your bicycle is knocked over on the derailleur side, you should check high- and low-gear stops on the rear derailleur. If you've parked (and locked) your bicycle where people can get at it, curious passersby may have played with the gear shifters. If this is the case, look at the position of the gear-shift handle, move it back about where it was when you parked, and start off by pedaling very gently, while, at the same time, adjusting the gear-shift levers. Otherwise, if you take off with the chain on one gear and the lever in position for another, you can catch the chain between gears and damage the derailleur. This goes for the front (chainwheel) derailleur too.

If you've had your bicycle for some time (six months or so), or you've ridden on sandy or dusty roads, sand or dirt can get into the derailleur linkage arms and clog up the derailleur. It is a good idea to clean the mechanism about every hundred miles, and relubricate pivot points and linkage with light oil.

6. PROBLEM: Chain skips while pedaling, usually in high gear.
   CAUSE: Insufficient chain tension.
   SOLUTION: Varies with type of derailleur.

   HURET ALLVIT DERAILLEUR: Move the chain tension spring back a notch.

   SIMPLEX DERAILLEUR: For more spring tension on a Simplex derailleur, remove the screw and dust cap from the bottom pivot bolt, and insert a metric Allen wrench in the hole you'll now see. Then, while you hold the locknut between the pivot bolt and the cage (the bracket with two half-moons holding the two small derailleur wheels), with a wrench (metric), turn the Allen wrench toward the rear of the bicycle for more chain tension, or toward the front for less tension. (Note: Use as little tension as possible to reduce drag, wear and tear, and make pedaling easier. This applies to all derailleurs.)

   CAMPAGNOLO DERAILLEUR: To increase chain tension on a Campagnolo rear derailleur, remove the chain cage stop-bolt (the thin bolt with a small round head that looks like a water tower lying on the ground, and that keeps the cage from rotating too far clockwise). Let the cage unwind until no more spring tension can be felt. Then, with an Allen wrench, remove the cage pivot bolt (the bolt that holds cage to derailleur), located at the bottom of the derailleur, and re-

Fig. 13-51: This is how the chain goes on. Starting at top, the chain goes around the freewheel (it's easier if you shift to high gear, small cog), in front of the top derailleur pulley and down and around the rear of the bottom pulley, then forward and around the small front chainwheel, going up from underneath. It doesn't really matter which way you start, just so long as you wind up with the chain in the above position. People who have difficulty visualizing things three-dimensionally should find this photo a big help. If you are wondering what became of the wheel, well, I used a sample hub without rim or spokes so you can see what gives.

move the cage from the spring end. Turn the cage slightly forward until the end of the spring fits into the next of the three holes. Replace the pivot bolt and cage assembly and tighten the pivot bolt. Wind the cage assembly counterclockwise one-half to one-and-a-half turns, hold it in this position and reinstall the cage stop-bolt. (Make sure the cage assembly is right side up by checking that the top roller is the one that has the inner side exposed. The bottom roller has the cage on both sides of the wheel, the top wheel has the cage on the outer side only.)

Replace the chain (with rear wheel in place) and check the shifting while pedaling. (Finally check the bicycle on the road, not hanging from the ceiling.) Be sure to check high- and low-gear adjustment screws.

CAUSE: Burrs on teeth of freewheel gear.
SOLUTION: File or grind burrs off.

CAUSE: A chain link too tight or binding.
SOLUTION: If you've removed and reinstalled the chain, check the link involved. Or check *all* the chain links. If a link binds or is tight (when you move it up and down), twist the chain gently from side to side. Of course, if your chain is rusty, don't bother with this procedure; simply install a new chain.

CAUSE: Excessive wear in chain or gears.
SOLUTION: Chains and gears do wear, and old chains stretch as a result of wear. Always replace worn loose chains (an old chain always breaks when you're miles from a bike shop). Do not replace an old chain and leave worn gears. Replace both at the same time. Old gears are identifiable by a slight hook on the inner lip of the gear teeth, which can catch the chain and make it "skip." Check the most-used gears first, using your fingernail. Removing a gear from the freewheel is not difficult, but you will need a special tool. Therefore, I will describe this procedure later.

CHECK CHAINWHEEL TEETH: Chainwheel teeth can also wear. They show this wear on the "lands" of the teeth; that is, by wearing away the face of the curvature of the gear teeth on the side toward the rear of the bicycle, away from the direction of rotation of the chainwheel. If the chainwheel is worn this much, it should be discarded and replaced with a new one, to avoid rough pedaling and erratic drive. Also, a worn chainwheel will soon wear out a new chain. If you're in doubt about chainwheel wear, check the chainwheel as follows: wrap a chain around the chainwheel and pull the chain down into the teeth by holding the ends of the chain snugly together. If the chain links fit tightly into the chainwheel teeth and cannot be picked away from the wheel at any gear, the wheel is in good shape. But if the chain climbs up on the teeth without being lifted up by you, mark this point of climb. Then try a new chain and repeat the procedure. If the new chain comes up at the same point, the gear is worn and should be replaced; however, if the new chain fits nicely, the old chain is shot and should be replaced.

Remember that a chain doesn't actually "stretch," but because the parts wear and "give," it acts as though it *has* stretched. It takes only a few thousandths of an inch of wear on each of the rivets to make the chain stretch a half-inch. (This is why frequent cleaning and lubrication are important in chain maintenance.)

Another check for the chainwheel and chain fit is to put the chain you intend to use on the chainwheel, already installed on the bicycle, and watch how the chain flows over the chainwheel teeth. There should be no "lifting" or sticking of the chain to the chainwheel teeth. Hang the bike for this test and hand-turn the pedals.

CAUSE: Chain is too long.
SOLUTION: Remove extra links. See earlier discussion in this chapter on chain length.

7. PROBLEM: Gear won't shift all the way into low (onto rear, large sprocket).
CAUSE: Low-gear adjusting screw is out of adjustment.
SOLUTION: Readjust as per instructions in this chapter.

CAUSE: Cable has stretched, or has slipped in the cable pivot bolt (where it is fastened to derailleur).
SOLUTION: Shift derailleur into high gear while turning pedals. Cable should have small amount of slack. If too loose, take up slack by turning the adjusting barrel on the derailleur, or, if there is no barrel on your machine (many good bicycles don't have one), put shift lever in high-gear position, all the way toward the front of the bicycle, loosen the cable pivot bolt-nut, pull some of the cable slack through, and retighten.

If the gear-shift cable breaks while you are on a trip, you can at least avoid having to pedal all the way home in high gear by adjusting the high-gear stop screw to keep the chain on the first or second gear up from the highest (small-sprocket) gear.

8. PROBLEM: Chain slips off small front chainwheel sprocket.
CAUSE: Low-gear limit screw is out of adjustment.
SOLUTION: Turn pedals and shift front derailleur to small chainwheel. Readjust low-gear limit screw. On most front derailleurs, the low-gear adjusting screw is the inner (closest to seat tube) screw, just forward of the cable anchor screw. Remember, the function of

the chain guard is to derail or move the chain from one chainwheel sprocket to the other. There is no tension adjustment to the front derailleur; this is taken care of by the rear derailleur.

9. PROBLEM: Chain won't stay on large chainwheel (front derailleur).
CAUSE: High-gear adjusting screw is out of adjustment.
SOLUTION: Because there are only two adjusting screws on front derailleurs (chainwheels), and we have already told you where the low-gear adjustment screw is on all popular front derailleurs, all you need do is shift the front derailleur lever to the high position (toward the rear of the bicycle), while turning the pedals, and adjust the chain guide over the large chainwheel with the high-gear adjusting screw. If shifting from small to large chainwheel after this adjustment is hard, bend the upper front corner of the inner part of the chain guide (cage) slightly inward, toward the chainwheel. If, however, the chain tends to jump off the chainwheel toward the outside (away from the bicycle), bend the upper front corner of the outer chain guide slightly toward the chainwheel. To find the exact spot where you bend the chainwheel guide, turn the pedals (cranks) by hand while the bicycle is off the ground and move the front shift lever until the chain just starts to lift off the chainwheel teeth. The part of the chain guide (cage) to be bent is touching the chain at this point.

10. PROBLEM: Chain won't shift onto large front chainwheel.
CAUSE: High-gear adjusting screw is out of adjustment.
SOLUTION: Readjust screw so chain guide will push chain up onto large front chainwheel.

CAUSE: Cable has stretched.
SOLUTION: Push front derailleur control lever all the way forward while turning pedals (cranks). Cable should be nearly tight. If it is loose, move shift lever all the way forward, unscrew cable bolt (the bolt that holds the cable to the front-derailleur shifting mechanism), pull cable through, and retighten cable bolt.

11. PROBLEM: Front-derailleur chain cage rubs on chain. Chain rattles.
CAUSE: Low- or high-gear adjustment screws have vibrated out of adjustment.
SOLUTION: Readjust screws.

CAUSE: Front-derailleur mechanism not aligned so chain cage is parallel with chainwheel.
SOLUTION: Loosen the two bolts that hold the front derailleur mechanism to seat tube (frame) and turn the derailleur mechanism left or

right to align the chain cage parallel to the chainwheel. While you've got the mechanism loose, make sure it is as close (low) to the chainwheel as possible, so that the outer plate of the chain cage just clears the teeth of the large chainwheel.

CAUSE: Crooked or wavy chainwheel. Chain rattles.
SOLUTION: Straighten chainwheel by prying it back into position with a long, square-shanked screwdriver. To avoid bending the chainwheel more than you want to, use as fulcrum (levering) points the bottom bracket cup (holding chainwheel axle in frame bottom), inside the right crank and chain-ring mounting bolts, with chain on large chainwheel. To judge which way to bend the chainwheel, sight through the front derailleur chain cage, and use the inside plane of the chain cage as a guide.

Another good way to straighten a chainwheel is to use the rear stay as a guide, turn the chainwheel, and mark the high and low spots (near and far distances from chain stay) on the chainwheel with a china-marking pencil or a piece of chalk. If a high and low spot are opposite each other (directly across the chainwheel), using adjustable wrenches and pulling on the low point and pushing on the high point will usually bring the chainwheel back into true.

To protect chrome plating or finish on the chainwheel, use a piece of rag between the jaws of the wrench. Take it easy as you push—don't overdo it. It is far better to make too slight a push than to give it all you've got and shove the chainwheel out of true in the other direction.

If, however, there are two high points opposite each other, and two low points opposite each other, all you need do is push the two high points inward toward the frame simultaneously.

If the chainwheel is wavy, the straightening job is going to be tougher. Use an adjustable wrench at the point where the wave peaks or bottoms out and press gently in the required direction. Move around the wheel and adjust all waves or bends in this manner. If you can't bring the wheel back into true, you'd better buy and install a new chainwheel. Find out what rough treatment bent the chainwheel in the first place so this won't happen again. (If you have to replace it with a new chainwheel, see page 560 for instructions on removing and installing chainwheels.)

12. PROBLEM: Pedals turn, crank turns, chain turns, freewheel turns, but the wheel doesn't turn.
CAUSE: Pawls inside the freewheel mechanism are stuck open by a piece of dirt or by the use of too heavy a lubricating oil in the freewheel.

SOLUTION: Remove the freewheel and soak it in kerosene to remove dirt and/or heavy oil. Oil again with a light oil such as No. 5 SAE.

Note: If the spacing washers in the rear wheel on the freewheel side are too narrow or too wide, the freewheel gears will not be aligned correctly with the chainwheel and you will have chain rub front or rear, as well as loss of power due to rub. Please see section on alignment, pages 676–88 for this alignment check and solution.

13. PROBLEM: Chain won't shift to combination of largest front chainwheel and next-to-largest and largest rear gears.
    CAUSE: Chain is too short.
    SOLUTION: Add one or two links. See instructions earlier in this chapter for finding correct chain length.

14. PROBLEM: Chain won't shift to small rear gear, or rubs on chainstay when in this position.
    CAUSE: Too little clearance between small gear and chainstay.
    SOLUTION: Add clearance by removing washer from left side of axle and adding one or two washers to right side of axle under lock nut. This will move freewheel far enough to the left to allow chain clearance.

    CAUSE: You have too long a bolt head holding the carrier onto the frame. Replace with a shorter bolt or file the bolt head flat so it projects as little as possible on the inside of the seat stays, and clears the chain.

To help you locate the high- and low-gear and cable-clamp bolts on some of the popular makes of front and rear derailleurs, Figures 13-53 through 13-60 show these locations. You will note that in every case the *low*-gear adjustment screw is located closest to the nearest frame tube. In the front derailleurs, the low-gear adjuster is closest to the seat tube; in rear derailleurs, the low gear adjuster is closest to the dropout or chainstay.

CHAIN OVERSHIFTING

One other derailleur problem I should mention is that of chain overshift or overshooting the gear you select. You may, for example, be shifting up from a low to a higher gear and instead of the chain landing on the next higher gear, which you want to do, it goes over an extra gear, so you are pedaling harder and slower than you, or your knees, want to. The major cause of overshift is either the wrong derailleur or the derailleur's not being at the correct angle. If, for example, you have a close ratio freewheel, say a 26-tooth low cog, and you have a wide-range derailleur

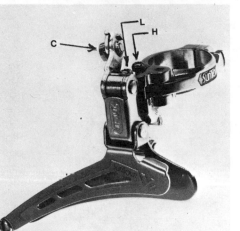

Fig. 13-52: SunTour front derailleur: (C) cable clamp; (L) low-gear (small chainwheel) adjustment; (H) high-gear adjustment. These stops keep chain from being moved too far laterally.

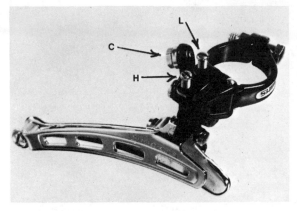

Fig. 13-53: Shimano Dura-Ace derailleur: (C) cable clamp; (L) low-gear adjustment; (H) high-gear adjustment.

Fig. 13-54: Another view of Campy Rally derailleur: (L) low gear; (H) high gear; (C) cable clamp.

Fig. 13-55: A closer view of the Campy Gran Sport, with a very good view of the derailleur travel stops. The low-gear stop, "L," prevents the derailleur from overtraveling the chain so it jams between the low gear and spokes. High-gear adjustment stops derailleur from pushing chain off high gear so it jams between high-gear cog and chainstay. "C" is the cable clamp.

Fig. 13-56: The old standby and probably the best derailleur made, Campagnolo Super Record, has low-gear adjuster at top (L); high-gear adjuster at bottom (H); and cable stop center (C).

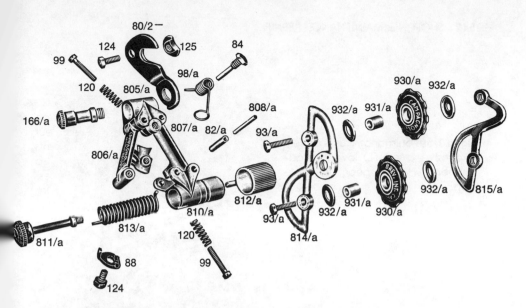

Fig. 13-57: Campagnolo Nuovo Record detailed view, rear derailleur. Parts are:

80/2	**Gear** fixing plate		806/a	**Front** arm
82/a	**Body** ferrule		807/a	**Inner** arm
84	**Spring** screw		808/a	**Spindle**
88	**Clamp** washer		810/a	**Spring** cage
93	**Sprocket** bolt		811/a	**Gear** spring bolt
98/a	**Gear** return spring		812/a	**Spring** cage cover
99	**Gear** adjusting screw		813/a	**Tension** spring
120	**Safety** spring		814/a	**Outer** cage plate
124	**Fixing** screw		815/a	**Inner** cage plate
125	**Clamp** nut		930/a	**Roller**
166/a	**Upper** pivot bolt		931/a	**Roller** bush
805/a	**Rear** body		932/a	**Roller** dust cover

Fig. 13-58: Shimano Crane close ratio derailleur. Low gear stop, "L," is nearest dropout fixing bolt. High gear stop, "H," is outboard of "L" and "C" is cable clamp.

Fig. 13-59: Shimano Altus is on less expensive bikes: (L) low-gear adjustment; (H) high gear; (C) cable stop.

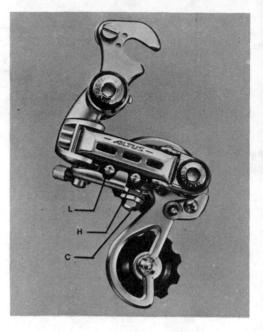

Fig. 13-60: Adjustments are in slightly different locations on different makes of derailleurs. Here's a Triplex with low-speed adjustment (L) at left and high-gear adjustment at right. You can clearly see where adjustment screws hit travel stops, as at bottom or left side of screw (H).

Fig. 13-61: Shimano Crane wide-range derailleur, with longer cage, has adjustments in same place as the close-ratio model.

such as the Campagnolo Rally, SunTour Cyclone GT or the Shimano Crane GS (Fig. 13-61) then the jockey wheel is going to be so far from the cog as to shift at a smaller angle than if it were closer. Figure 13-62 illustrates my point.

In Figure 13-62 you will note that the derailléur at the left is closer to the cog "C" than the long-cage derailleur at the right is to cog "CC." As the jockey wheel "J" attempts to move the chain from cog "C" to cog "D" it assumes the characteristic angle best suited to crisp shifting. Now look at cog "CC." You will notice that the jockey wheel "JJ" of the rear long-cage derailleur, is at a narrower angle than chain "E." In other words, at the same point, chain "E" is at a greater angle than chain "EE." Thus chain "EE" shifts less precisely and is more likely to over-shoot than chain "E" because it is the greater angle of chain attack by the jockey wheel that contributes to precise shifting.

Fig. 13-62: Which derailleur, the one with jockey wheel "J" or "JJ," will give you the snap-piest, most accurate shifting? "J" will because the acuter angle between "J" and the cog "C" moves chain faster, more accurately.

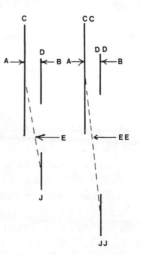

Even with a short-cage derailleur, the jockey wheel can be too far away from the cog for precise shifting if the chain is too long. As noted earlier in this chapter, the derailleur body should be at about a 45-degree angle, when the chain is on the low-gear cog in the rear and the high-gear chainwheel up front. If necessary, remove links from the chain but not so many that there is "play" or upward movement left in the derailleur body.

Only one maker of derailleurs, at this writing, provides a fine adjustment for tuning derailleur angle, and that is the SunTour Cyclone, both the short- and the long-cage (GT) models. Figure 13-63 shows this adjustment, which is very convenient when you are off only a half link in chain length. Another point. Look again at Figure 13-62. You will note that to get jockey wheel "JJ" to assume the same angle as jockey wheel "J," you will have to move the derailleur farther. This can contribute to chain overshoot also. That is, to get the chain at a steep enough angle to move the chain, the derailleur with jockey wheel farthest from the cog has to move farther.

Another way to adjust chain tension to move the jockey wheel closer to the cogs is to move the rear wheel forward in the dropout slot (provided of course you do not have vertical dropouts, which are a rarity).

A WORD ABOUT DERAILLEUR CAPACITY

Earlier in this chapter I discussed briefly what is meant by derailleur capacity. Now I will amplify this discussion a bit. To determine derailleur capacity, you subtract the number of teeth in the high-gear rear cog from the number of teeth in the low-gear rear cog—subtract the number of teeth in the low-gear front chainwheel from the number of teeth in the high-gear front chainwheel and add up the two numbers. For example, my Alex Singer touring bike has (as of now) a 14–32 rear cluster and a 30–48 front chainwheel. Well, actually, the front chainwheel is 30–38–48 at the moment. Subtracting the rear cogs: 32 minus 14 = 18. From the front, 48 minus 30 = 18. That the two numbers are the same is pure coincidence and entirely irrelevant. So we have 18 plus 18 = 36 teeth. One of these days I am going to change to a 26-tooth front low gear and a 34-tooth rear gear, so I will need a rear derailleur with a capacity of 48

— 26 + 34 — 14 = 42T. Then I'll really be able to see just how far these wide-range derailleurs will stretch. I can predict the results. I won't be able to use the combination of both high-rear-low-front and low-rear and high-front, but boy, will I have a super duper "Granny" gear for that mean old 15-percent climb into Vermont's Calvin Coolidge State Park and other roads of that disposition.

I think there's an awful lot of undue mysticism about derailleur capacity anyhow. Look at Table 13-1, for example. You will note that most of the derailleurs have a maximum extension or travel (lateral distance the jockey wheel will move) (the average) of 45.1 millimeters. The widest travel is the SunTour VX wide range with 52 millimeters, smallest in the Campagnolo Rally wide range at 34.2 millimeters. I would agree that these measurements may be somewhat unrealistic in that with the low-gear stop wide open you might have the cage enmeshed in the spokes. But allowing 10 full millimeters to keep the cage away from the spokes, you would still have 35 to 39 millimeters of useful travel. The new $200 Regina Titall aluminum/titanium seven-speed freewheel has a maximum tooth-to-tooth width between high and low gears of 32 millimeters, so I would certainly expect any rear derailleur with a useful travel of 39 millimeters to handle it easily. You need a derailleur that will swing the width of the freewheel and then some, that will maintain correct chain tension through all gears for snappy, precision gear changes and that will resist wear and tear at least for five or six thousand miles.

Frankly, I like the Campagnolo derailleurs for high-quality construction. I think the ultimate, as Campy calls it, in close-ratio (up to 28 teeth) rear derailleurs is their Super Record. It has a prelubed titatium pivot bolt (spring loaded), inner and outer arms of hot-forged aluminum alloy, replaceable brass bushing on body arms (replaceable, sure, but did you ever try to buy a tiny Campy derailleur part in a bike store?), removable stop so you can take the lower pivot joint apart for maintenance and spring-tension adjustment. The lower pivot spring is adjustable, which is necessary because the spring will lose tension as time goes on. Cage plates, the sea horse-shaped pieces that hold the jockey and idler wheels, are of cold forged alloy that resists flex when shifting, and these wheels roll on a sintered bronze bushing.

The top line Shimano DuraAce, Huret DuoPar and SunTour Cyclone series are also top-grade derailleurs, front as well as rear, with many of the same features as the Campy at considerably less cost. But if you want the best, Campy is the winner and still champion.

SEALED-BEARING DERAILLEUR WHEELS

None of the rear derailleurs I have dissected recently have ball bearing idler and jockey wheels. Earlier Campy models had them but in recent years Campy has gone to the sintered bronze solid bushing or axle, upon which the wheels turn. Naturally there is more friction generated with this type of loading than with ball bearings. The difference may be hard to detect, of course, given the small amount of rolling resistance even in the cheapest, most recalcitrant of derailleur wheel bearings. But rolling resistance isn't the whole story. Derailleurs are right down there where the dirt is, are very vulnerable to being coated with gunk, sand, all sorts of road debris that can wear out the metal and add friction. So it is with some enthusiasm that I, a sealed-bearing buff, welcome Roger Durham's brainchild: sealed-bearing rear derailleur wheels (Fig. 13-67). Here you will see one of his wheels with a bearing seal removed. Compare it with the plain shaft bushing of the average derailleur wheel. Roger sells his wheels for $14.50 a pair, and guarantees they will fit any derailleur; they come with adapters for many makes of derailleurs. The price is a bit steep, but the piece of mind on a long tour is worth it. Roger sells through bike stores or directly. (Durham Bicycles, Los Angeles, California 90029 (213/664-4534)).

TO SWING, OR NOT TO SWING

Some derailleurs, such as the SunTour, pivot freely on the mounting bolt that threads into the rear dropout or into the adapter bracket. This permits you to pull the derailleur back out of the way when removing the rear wheel. Without a spring in the mounting bolt, or rather attached to it, it's easier to pull the derailleur body back out of the way. Some rear derailleurs, such as the Campagnolo and some of the Shimano models, have the mounting bolt spring loaded, so this spring tension helps the main spring in the derailleur body maintain chain tension, which in turn helps keep the chain on the gear you have selected, and makes for somewhat snappier changes. You can tell whether or not the mounting pivot bolt is spring loaded simply by looking at the thickness of the derailleur body through which the mounting bolt goes. Figure 13-64 shows the difference.

Which works the best, the spring-loaded or non-spring-loaded pivot bolt? There are advantages and disadvantages both ways. Obviously the spring-loaded pivot-bolt design, which also has a main spring in the

Fig. 13-64: Derailleur at left has no spring in mounting bolt; the one at right does.

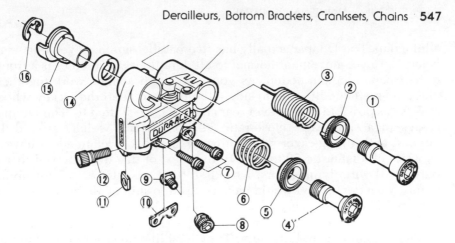

Fig. 13-65: Spring-loaded mounting bolt type of derailleur, the Shimano DuraAce. We are concerned here only with part No. 6, the spring that keeps the derailleur on back pressure to aid in chain-tension control.

body pivot point (as shown in Fig. 13-65) puts more tension on the chain. My experience has been that the double-spring models have a wider range and greater capacity than single-spring models (no spring on the pivot bolt) of equal cage length. The disadvantage of the spring-loaded pivot-bolt design is that this spring pulls the derailleur back at all times. Thus, as you shift up to smaller cogs, the spring-loaded pivot-bolt model take up the chain tension nicely, but in the process, pulls back so far that there is less chain wraparound on the smaller (higher gear) cogs. Figure 13-66 shows the free pivoting bolt at left and the spring-loaded pivot bolt at right. This is not an actual working demo, just a setup on my workbench table to help you get the point. On balance, I opt for the spring-loaded pivot bolt.

Speaking of the necessity of keeping the jockey wheel as close as possible to the rear cogs for precise, snappy gear shifting (you do remember, don't you, about Figure 13-62? If not, please check it out), a few years ago Huret introduced a derailleur that pretty well solves this problem. The Huret Duopar uses an interesting variation on the normal par-

Fig. 13-66: Spring-loaded mounting or pivot bolt does provide, in some gears, less chain wraparound (right cog) than the free nonloaded pivot bolt, left.

allelogram. The Duopar actually has *two* parallelogram movements, one is lateral travel movement normal to all derailleurs. The other is a front-to-rear parallelogram action. As you shift, both actions work together, one to move laterally, side to side—the other to keep the jockey wheel as close as possible to whatever rear cog you have shifted to. The Duopar comes in a short-cage, close-ratio version, which weighs around 10 ounces, and a long-cage, wide-ratio version that is claimed to have a capacity of a fantastic 50 teeth. My own test of this unit showed that it performed with flying colors. I tried shifting too late, on a hard uphill climb. Most derailleurs would have refused to shift at all, or would have overshifted or even mangled the derailleur. Not so with the Duopar; it shifted even under this rather severe, stressful torque. Both models are made of aluminum and titanium. They look like no other derailleur you have ever seen, but they sure do work well.

MORE ON SHIFTING GEARS

Shifting gears on a five-, ten-, fifteen- or eighteen- or twenty-one-speed bicycle may not be a fine art, but the procedure has something of the esoteric about it. Something like climbing Mt. Everest, or swimming the English Channel. It's always a heroic effort to be able, precisely, to select just the right gear that matches your physical condition of the moment with the forces of the wind, the gradient of the road and your own desire to proceed slowly so as to savor the wild beauty of the land-scape (that's my excuse) or to move from point to point as rapidly as possible (that's madness for a touring cyclist). See Chapter 2 for a de-tailed discussion on gear shifting.

No matter what your need, there is one salient point you must never forget and, if you are a novice cyclist, you ignore at the peril of your new steed. That is: *Never shift a derailleur bicycle unless you are pedaling!* If you try to shift without pedaling, you can wind up with a mangled derailleur, even a bent rear axle and, at worst, a nasty spill and the chain and derailleur tangled, perhaps locking the wheel if the chain and spokes decide to mate.

A WORD ABOUT LUBRICATION AND SEALED BEARINGS

On headsets (see details on chain lubrication later on in this chapter) and bottom brackets, pedal bearings, and hub bearings *only* use a light grease, preferably a waterproof type that will not turn to the consistency of chewing gum in cold weather or run at the first sign of hot weather. I like Phil Wood's grease, which you can buy in a tube or in a small can, or Lubriplate's cold-weather grease, the kind used on snowmobiles; an alternative would be Lubriplate's marine grease which resists being replaced by water—not the best lubricant in the world. In fact water may be the *worst*.

In Chapter 11 I went into considerable detail on sealed-bearing hubs and how to get at them to grease them. The same applies to Durham sealed-bearing derailleur wheels (Fig. 13-67) (pulleys, rollers). There is just one trick about removing the seal on any sealed bearing, and I learned it the hard way, by bending up a seal. First of all, remember that the seal is a very, very thin brass sheet covered with a thin layer of nylon or some other plastic. If you dab at it with a screwdriver you are going to dent the thin seal metal and will have a tough time restoring it to something resembling the original. The seal also fits into a tiny groove inside the bearing shell. It sort of *snaps* back in place, and you can feel it pop back in as you press gently with your finger all around the edges until it is seated. But to remove it, I have the best success with the end of a sharp penknife blade or an X-acto knife. I slip it carefully but firmly straightdown between the outer edge of the seal and the bearing housing, and once the tip of the knife has gone past the seal, I pry upward, gently. I might repeat the process in another location if the seal does not pop out at the first try. There's no secret to it, but you do have to go gently to avoid damaging the seal. You should remove the wheels from the derailleur if you are going to grease them, and here I refer to Durham sealed bearings only. Other derailleurs need only a dab of the same lubricant you use on the chain, applied as often as you spray the chain. As you spray, it's important to keep lubricant off the tires; many lubricants have solvents that can eat away your tires and weaken side walls. This applies in double spades and aces to tubular tires, especially hand-

Fig. 13-67: Top row, Durham sealed-ball-bearing derailleur wheels. Left to right, top row: (A) wheel with seal in place; (B) wheel with seal removed to show bearings; and (C) seal. Bottom row, Campagnolo pulley, left to right: (D) cap seal; (F) bolt; (G) sleeve or journal bushing; (E) wheel. Durham wheels will fit any derailleur.

sewn silks. We have already covered lubrication of brake pivot points in Chapter 10.

BOTTOM BRACKETS—SELECTION AND MAINTENANCE

I think we need to clarify some nomenclature at this point. A bottom-bracket shell is the part of your bicycle frame at the bottom, where almost all the tubes are brazed on. The downtube, the seat tube and the chainstays are all brazed onto the bottom-bracket shell, as shown in Figure 13-68.

Inside the bottom bracket you will find the bottom-bracket set, consisting of the spindle (you might call it an axle, but we bikies call it a spindle) the bearings, the adjustable cup on the left side and the fixed cup on the right side, all as shown in Figure 13-69. There's also a lock ring, (Fig. 13-70) which locks the adjustable cup in place after you have adjusted it to eliminate end or sideplay and, if it's a cotterless crank, the washers and crank lock bolts. Figure 13-69 shows a typical cotterless crankset, in this instance a Shimano set. I have identified the parts for you, as you will see in the caption.

Attached to the bottom-bracket spindle are the left and right cranks

Fig. 13-68: The parts we are concerned with here are the seat tube, downtube and stays, all brazed to the bottom-bracket shell.

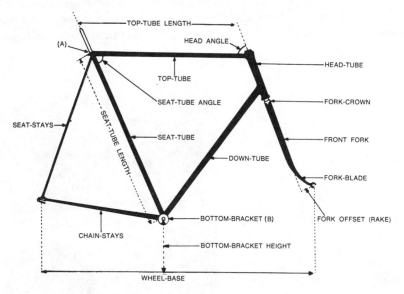

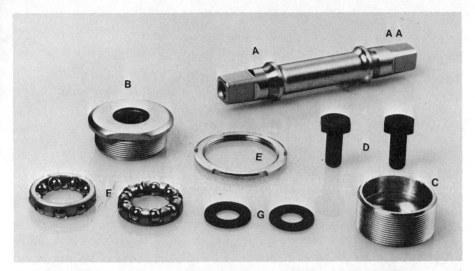

Fig. 13-69: Typical bottom-bracket set assembly. (A) spindle, showing left side; (AA) right (chainwheel) side, note that it is longer to provide space for the chainwheel; (B) fixed cup, goes on right side of bottom-bracket shell; (C) adjustable cup; (D) crank fixing bolts; (E) lockring, goes on adjustable cup (C); (F) bearings in races; and (G) crank fixing bolt washers, go under bolt heads.

Fig. 13-70: Adjustable cup lockring, shown removed from adjustable cup.

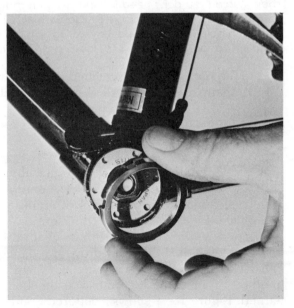

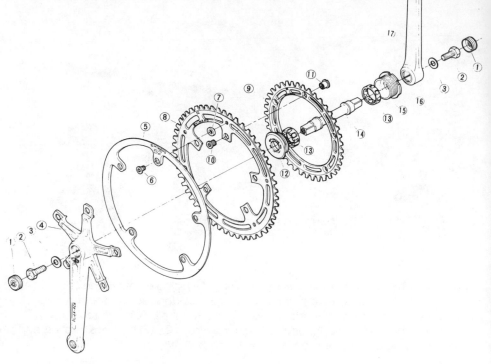

Fig. 13-71: Complete crankset, this one a Shimano DuraAce design. Going over the parts, they are: (1) dust cap; (2) crank-fixing bolt; (3) washer; (4) right crank; (5) chain guard (you don't need it and I would remove it); (6) chain-guard bolt; (7) chainwheel mounting bushing; (8) chainwheel; (9) chainwheel; (10) chainwheel mounting bolt; (11) chainwheel mounting nut; (12) fixed cup; (13) bearings; (14) spindle; (15) adjustable cup; (16) lockring; (17) left crank.

and to the right crank are attached the chainwheels, as shown in Figure 13-71. Again, this is a cotterless aluminum alloy crankset.

TYPES OF CRANKSETS

For convenience I am going to forget about bottom brackets and just talk about cranksets, and include in cranksets their associated bottom brackets. There are three types of cranksets—cottered, cotterless and one-piece. First, the cottered crankset.

When the safety bicycle, with its chain drive and two small wheels of more or less equal diameter drove the dangerous antique high wheeler (also called a "Penny Farthing" or "Ordinary") off the market, the method of attaching the cranks to the bottom-bracket spindle was retained. Figure 13-72 shows a cottered crank of an antique high wheeler, where the cranks are fastened to the spindle by a sort of wedge, or as we call it today, a cotter or key. Fig. 13-73 shows a cross section of a cottered crankset and Fig. 13-74 shows an actual crankset. Note in Figure 13-74 that in order to remove the cotter pin or wedge, you should support the

Fig. 13-72: Early form of cottered crank design on a high wheeler of the 1880s.

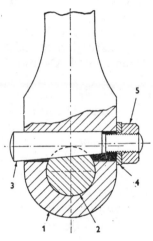

Fig. 13-73: Cross section of cottered crank: (1) crank; (2) spindle; (3) cotter pin; (4) washer; (5) nut. *(Temple Press)*

Fig. 13-74: Cottered crank. Chainwheel is steel. Note that to remove this crank the crank base is laid over a notched 2-by-4 and supported at points "B" and "C." The cotter pin nut (A) is loosened a few turns and hit squarely with a mallet to drive pin down into notch. This way you avoid damage to bearings because hammer shock is absorbed at base of crank and by the 2-by-4. Remember, the nut on a cottered crank is **not** intended to pull the pin up tight; the pin must be hammered back in. You just turn the crank around until the top of the pin is over the notch, the reverse of the position it is in in this photo. A special (expensive) shop tool is available for pin.

crank over a notched-out piece of 2-by-4 lumber, loosen the cotter bolt about three turns, and tap smartly straight down on the bolt with a ball peen hammer. The wood brace absorbs the shock of the hammer and keeps it from harming the spindle bearings. Installing the cotter is just the reverse process; you turn the cotter so its top is where the nut is in Figure 13-74 and smack it firmly down into the wedge. As Figure 13-73 shows, the wedge or cotter fits into a slot in the spindle. The slot is at an angle that matches the cotter, and the crank is held onto the spindle shaft by the drive fit between the spindle, the cotter and the crank. Most cottered cranksets (and their chainwheels) are made of steel, as is the one shown in Figure 13-72. Up until 1973 or 1974, most of the inexpensive bicycles had such cranksets. They are heavy, difficult to remove and re-attach and, as far as I am concerned, are totally without merit when compared with even the cheapest cotterless crankset. If you have a bicycle with which you are inordinately in love, and it has a steel cotterless crankset, I urge you to substitute one of the less expensive lightweight aluminum alloy cotterless cranksets, such as the Shimano 600EX—about which, more later.

You have already become somewhat acquainted with the cotterless crankset, so all I need add at this point is that the cranks fit onto the tapered ends of the bottom bracket spindle. The taper, usually around three to three and a half degrees, matches a similar taper inside the crank arm. The crank is then forced up the spindle taper by the locking bolt. Note that the washer fits under the locking bolt. More about taper and maintenance later, except that other than methods of attaching the cranks, all maintenance of bottom brackets involves similar steps—dismantling, removing and cleaning bearings, and reassembling all parts and adjusting for zero play and free movement.

Oh yes. Were it not for innovative Japanese component manufacturers, whose lead was followed by old-line European suppliers, we would still be stuck with cottered cranks on less expensive bikes. But Japanese manufacturers such as Shimano, Sugino, SunTour and Sakae began to introduce low-cost aluminum alloy, cotterless cranksets in high volume around 1974, and today even low-cost bikes can boast cotterless cranks, once the hallmark of only the most costly two-wheelers. True, the cheaper alloy cranksets are not as strong or as highly polished and beautifully machined as the more expensive designs such as Campagnolo and the top lines of the Japanese and other manufacturers overseas. The less expensive cotterless cranks have teeth with a hardness of around 55 to 59 on the Rockwell "B" scale, and the top-line cranksets of special aluminum alloy such as the Campagnolo and Avocet have teeth hardness of 88 on the Rockwell "B" scale. As you have undoubtedly guessed by now, the harder the teeth, the longer the wear. Cranksets are expensive, and the chainwheels alone, just the rings, can range in price from $28 for a Campagnolo ring to $7.98 for the 59 Rockwell TC Cyclotouriste rings. The chainrings are what the chain goes around. Ah well, I know you know that.

Fig. 13-75: One-piece crank-set (arrow) on balloon-tire Schwinn bike of the 1930s.

Later on in this chapter I will review each major make of crankset—again, crankset includes all the parts of the bottom-bracket set, although you can buy any part of the total ensemble from any good bicycle store. You can buy different-sized chainrings—which you might want to do to get a very low "Granny" gear, for example—a new spindle, new cups, new bearings, new cranks, a new lock ring. Some chainwheels and spindles are interchangeable with other makes, but be careful to buy only parts that will mate. I have attempted, later on in the section on interchangeability, to chart those parts that will mate, but manufacturers' specifications and machining tolerances change from time to time. Even machining tolerances can change between production runs. So any interchangeability guide can only be just that, a general guide as to what fit when we tried it.

The third and final type of crankset I will mention here is the so-called Ashtabula or one-piece crank, shown in Figure 13-75, on an old balloon-tire Schwinn, circa 1930, and a modern version on a Monarch-Crescent (Swedish) bicycle (Fig. 13-76). These cranks are solid, one-piece steel.

Fig. 13-76: Modern version of one-piece crank

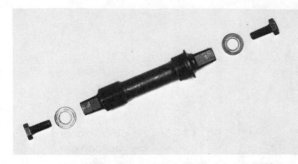

Fig. 13-77: Conversion unit, to convert one-piece crankset to cotterless alloy crankset. Spindle threads fit one-piece cups, old bearings are used.

The cranks and the chainwheel are all one piece of steel, and the left crank is pulled out through the bottom bracket to disassemble it, as detailed later on in this chapter. Schwinn sells a replacement spindle (Fig. 13-77) that turns a one-piece crankset into a cotterless crank. You buy the spindle and the cranks and chainwheels separately. You use the old bearings. The replacement spindle costs around $35. But I'm hanged if I can figure out why you would want to spend any money on the type of bicycle that comes with an ungainly, heavy, ugly one-piece crankset and have to replace that crankset with a lightweight aluminum alloy crankset. Well, there is one bike I know of that *is* worth the changeover and that's the old Schwinn SuperSport, which has a fine, lugless, high chrome moly steel frame. If you have a SuperSport, by all means make the conversion. Then you will have a bike the equal of some of the $400 or even $600 models being sold these days. I'd add aluminum alloy 700-centimeter rims, Shimano DuraAce side-pull brakes and hubs to totally upgrade the SuperSport, though. If you have an otherwise good BMX bicycle, you might also want to go to a cotterless crankset. A supplier of sealed bearing replacements is Durham Bicycles, who make a unit that clamps into the bottom-bracket shell (Fig. 13-78). Now let's get into bottom-bracket maintenance, because I imagine most people will want to know how to do this important procedure, after which we will cover the selection of bottom brackets or cranksets and the features of major makes.

Fig. 13-78: Sealed-bearing bottom-bracket set to convert one-piece cranks to cotterless cranks: (A) long bolt and nut holds this unit in place (three supplied); (B) end pieces fit bottom-bracket shell. (C) thrust collars have Allen bolts that permit movement of spindle to adjust it for correct chainline (lateral movement). *(Durham Bicycles)*

MAINTENANCE OF BOTTOM BRACKETS AND CRANKSETS

Let's break this section down into four parts: (1) new bicycle checks; (2) cotterless crankset maintenance; (3) cottered crankset maintenance; and (4) one-piece crankset maintenance. Starting with a new bicycle . . .

Before you wheel the bike out of the shop, I strongly recommend you check, among other things, adjustment of the bottom-bracket spindle left-hand adjustable cup. Do this by having the shop put the bike on a bike stand so the wheels are free to rotate. Grasp each pedal with your hands and rock the cranks from side to side. There should be no side play. Hold the cranks by the top, just above the pedals. Then slip the chain off the chainwheels and spin the cranks. The cranks should rotate freely, without evidence of binding. If you spin the cranks and they come to rest with a sort of sudden stop as they slow down, that's binding. If the stop or slowdown is very gradual, that's okay. Have the shop adjust the left hand-cup as needed.

On a new bike, remove the dust cap (Fig. 13-79) (Campy dust caps take a five-mm Allen wrench, e.g.) and tighten down the spindle locking bolt every 50 miles or so for the first 200 miles (Fig. 13-80) with 215 to 240 inch pounds of torque (18–20 ft. lbs.) using an automotive type torque wrench (or enough muscle to move the bolt slightly). Depending on the make, bottom bracket bolts take a 14-, 15- or 16-millimeter wrench. Most common metric sockets will be too thick to fit into the crank opening to get at the pedal, so you will need a special wrench, such as the Campagnolo spanner shown at the bottom of Figure 13-81,

Fig. 13-79: Dust cap on cotterless crankset

Fig. 13-80: Fixing bolt forces tapered crank up onto taper of spindle.

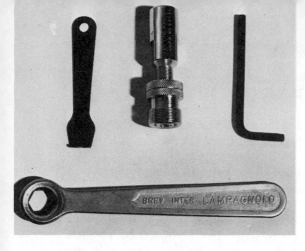

Fig. 13-81: Some of the tools you will need to remove and reinstall cotterless cranksets. Top row, left to right: chainwheel fixing nut tool; crank puller; Allen wrench to fit chainwheel fixing bolt. Bottom, crank fixing bolt tool (also shown in Fig. 13-80).

or the four-in-one wrench made by Park Tool Company (Fig. 13-82), which has 14-, 15- and 16-millimeter ends plus a 5-millimeter Allen pip for dust caps (available in Schwinn bike stores, among others). Remember, the spindle-tapered shank is hardened steel . . . the crank is relatively soft aluminum. If the crank is not firmly pushed up on the tapered shank it will be loose, and just a few miles of pedaling with the crank hanging loose will destroy the tight tapered fit, and you will never be able to get the crank to fit properly again on the spindle . . . you will then need a new crank ranging from $10 to around $28.

Also on a new bike check the mounting bolts holding the double or triple chainwheel set together (Fig. 13-83) with the special pronged tool shown at top left of Figure 13-81 and an Allen wrench, usually 5 millimeters. Hold the inside (left) bolt with the pronged tool (bushed nut wrench) while you tighten with the Allen wrench. These and other tools you will need are available at your bicycle store.

I have a very good reason for asking you to check the tightness of the chainwheel bushed bolts occasionally, especially on a new bike. I was

Fig. 13-82: Three-in-one Park crank bolt removing wrench fits all popular makes of crank bolts (and they are different sizes, believe me). Comes in 13 mm., 14 mm. and 15 mm.

Fig. 13-83: Here's how the chainwheel fixing bolt tools shown in Figure 13-81 look in use. Use them to tighten this bolt every few months, and to remove chainwheel if necessary.

test riding some new bikes for one of the consumer testing magazines some years ago and on a hard uphill climb, the chain suddenly slipped off the inner chainwheel and in between the two chainwheels. Looking down I discovered that the inner ring was distorted, wavy, which had thrown the chain off. The reason for the distortion was that one of the bushed bolts had come loose and had fallen out somewhere along the road, and the other bolts were about to do the same. From now on I check these bolts on every new bike I test ride. And I can tell you that, with the exception of Campy equipment, I have found many chain-wheels with bushed bolts that, although not exactly loose, could be taken up from a half to a quarter turn, and that's incipient trouble up the road. I do check all chainwheels, regardless of make, and although Campy equipment has been tight so far, I still check them just to make sure. I would check *all* chainwheel sets at least twice annually because vibration from road shock can loosen these bolts eventually. The few minutes you spend going over them can save downtime on the road or the cost of a new chainwheel. Here are steps in complete cotterless crank maintenance:

STEP ONE: Remove dust cap as previously discussed (Fig. 13-79).

STEP TWO: Remove crank mounting bolt with the crank bolt wrench (Figs. 13-80 and 13-82). Remove the washer behind the bolt head (don't lose it).

STEP THREE: Now you will need a crank puller. This is the type of tool shown in the top center of Figure 13-81. This particular tool is made to fit Shimano cranks but it will also fit Campagnolo cranks, although a bit loosely. Far better than this type of crank puller is the multiple crank puller that fits French, Italian and Japanese cranks, Fig. 13-84. The smaller threaded section fits Campagnolo, Sugino, Shimano and Sun-Tour cranks; the larger section fits Stronglight, T.A. Cyclotouriste and other French chainwheels. To use any of these crank pullers, you will note first that there are actually two threaded sections, the larger one

Fig. 13-84: A more convenient, easy-to-use crank puller than the one in the top center of Figure 13-81, this Park tool has its own handle. The tool threads into crank dust cap threads. This part is reversible to fit Stronglight and T.A. cranks as well as Campagnolo, Shimano, SunTour and other makes.

threading over a central threaded shaft. Turn the larger section counter-clockwise until the end of the inner section is flush with it, as shown in Figure 13-81. Here the larger section of the crank puller (top, center) has been screwed forward until it is flush with the end of the inner section. Now insert the larger, outer section into the threaded part of the crank, the part where you have removed the dust cap. Be sure to get the crank tool *all the way inside the crank,* because, to pull the crank off the tapered spindle, the tool depends on the threads of the aluminum crank to hold it while the center section is turned to exert backing force on the end of the spindle. With the puller in the crank, turn the center section with a wrench clockwise (the Park puller [Fig. 13-84] has its own wrench handle). If you can't get the crank to budge, tap the end of the puller smartly with a ball peen hammer (not too hard) two or three times to help loosen it. Then turn some more, tap some more and finally you should be able to pull the crank off the spindle (Fig. 13-85). Remove the right-hand crank complete with chainwheel.

STEP FOUR: Now remove the left-hand adjustable cup lockring. Figure 13-86 shows a Campagnolo lockring wrench; but I prefer the new Shimano lockring wrench (Fig. 13-87) because it has a crescent plate or guide over the jaws of the wrench which help keep it from slipping off the narrow lockring, which is only around 3.5 millimeters thick (or thin). If the wrench were to slip, you could mangle the lockring indents, which would make it more difficult to remove; and/or you could ruin the paint finish on the tubes just behind it, and your knuckles. The lockring threads off counterclockwise. *Unless you are going to replace the entire bottom-bracket set, there is no need to remove the right-hand, or fixed, cup, which I will discuss later.*

STEP FIVE: With a pin wrench (Fig. 13-88) remove the adjustable cup (threads off counterclockwise, as shown in Fig. 13-90). Shimano makes a fixed-pin wrench (Fig. 13-90) which fits their own and Campagnolo

Fig. 13-85: When puller has loosened crank, it comes off tool and all.

Fig. 13-86: Lockring remover

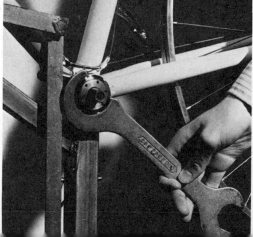

Fig. 13-87: Shimano lockring remover is a better tool because it has a shield that helps keep it from slipping off the narrow lockring.

Fig. 13-88: Adjustable pin wrench fits holes in adjustable cup.

Fig. 13-89: Adjustable cup removed. Spindle lies on bottom-bracket shell. Bike is upside down.

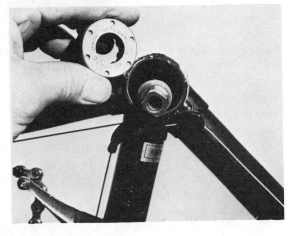

Fig. 13-90: Shimano makes a very nice pin wrench that fits their adjustable cups. This is not an adjustable pin wrench; pins are fixed.

adjustable cups, and which has a 32-millimeter wrench on the other end. If you have an older bike, the ball bearings may be loose, not in a race, so be prepared to catch them. You might have the bike, with wheels removed for convenience, lying on its side on the workbench, with a rag underneath the bottom-bracket shell to catch loose balls. Pull the spindle out. Remove all balls. If balls are in races (Fig. 13-91), remove the left-hand set, reach in and remove the right-hand set, after you pull out any dust shields. Some dust shields, such as the Campy, are in two sections.

I *do* recommend a dust shield (Fig. 13-92) over the spindle inside the bottom-bracket shell, because dust and dirt and water can drift down onto the precisely machined surfaces of cups and bearings from the tubes. You can make your own dust shield from an old beer can. But whatever you do, do not succumb to temptation and make a dust shield out of paper or cardboard! Cardboard dust shields crumple at the first sign of moisture or water, and the resulting gunky mess will clog bearings, absorb and so rob bearings of grease.

STEP SIX: Clean bearings and cups of all old grease, with a solvent such as Carbo-Chlor, available from your local hardware store. *Do not use gasoline or any other flammable, explosive liquid!* When using any other solvent, even kerosene, try to have plenty of ventilation around you, such as an open window or, better still, the great outdoors. Wipe out the inside of the bottom-bracket shell thoroughly and take this opportunity to inspect the inside of the tubes for signs of rust. If you spot rust inside the tubes, remove it with fine sandpaper and, with a small brush, coat with two or three layers of aluminum paint. With a rag on the end of a coat hangar wire, coat the tubes with grease as far up as you can reach. You may have to remove the saddle to get at the seat tube from the top. Squirt oil into any small "breather" holes in the seat or chainstays.

STEP SEVEN: If you have loose bearings, loose balls, replace them by first dabbing a layer of grease on the right-hand fixed cup. With the bike on its side, lay in all the balls, replace the spindle, making sure the long end goes in first, because this is the end the crank/chainwheel fits onto. If you will go back and look carefully at the spindle in Figure 13-69, you will see that the right side, "AA," is longer than the left side, "A." Side "AA" goes in first. Of course, if you have bearings in a cage, the cage should go in first. Remember, there is a convex side (outward curving) and a concave side (inward curving, like the inside half of a tennis ball) to the caged bearing set. The convex side faces toward the cups, the concave side toward the concave side of the spindle. Figure 13-93 shows the correct position of the caged bearing and spindle; for example, you will note that the outwardly curving portion (convex) of the spindle faces the inwardly curving portion (concave) of the caged-bearing set. I am not going to take any chances that the instinctive mechanical ability of most of us will automatically ensure that we get these bearings in

Fig. 13-91: Adjustable cup removed, showing bearings set in race. Some bikes have loose bearings, so be ready to catch them as you remove cup. Pull spindle out carefully, with bike lying on right side, if you have loose bearings, so you don't lose them up the tubes or on the floor.

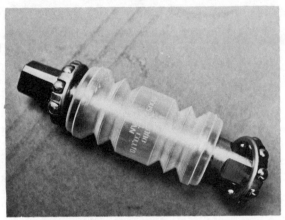

Fig. 13-92: Plastic dust shield keeps dust from bearings.

Fig. 13-93: Correct positioning of bearing races toward curvature of cups.

straight. It's just too easy not to, and too expensive if you do it wrong. Okay, now you have either coated fixed and adjustable cups with grease for loose balls, or filled the now clean and empty cavities of the caged bearing sets with some good waterproof grease such as Lubriplate or Phil Wood grease lubricant, added a dab more on both sides and moved the right set of bearings into position; and slid the spindle, long end in first, into the bottom bracket and out the right-hand side, through the bearings. Now insert the dust cover.

The left set of bearings should be in the adjustable cup. If loose, it should be held there by grease; if a caged set, you should slide it onto the spindle. Now you can thread on the adjustable cup.

STEP EIGHT: Thread the adjustable cup all the way, by hand, and then with the pin wrench, tighten up very slowly and carefully until just snug, no more, and back off half a turn.

STEP NINE: Thread on the lock ring by hand till snug. Holding the adjustable cup in place with the pin wrench, tighten the lock ring. Use some muscle on it. Now grasp the spindle at both ends and move up and down to check or feel for too much "play" or looseness. If the spindle moves vertically, it's too loose. If the spindle feels tight when spun between thumb and forefinger, it's too tight, especially if you feel a metallic sort of grittiness as you spin it. Loosen the lock ring, holding the cup with the pin wrench, and either tighten the cup slightly or loosen it, as needed; then, holding it with the pin wrench, tighten the lock ring down. Remember, you will probably have to make one or two more minute adjustments, unless you work in a bike shop and do this all day.

STEP TEN: Install the cranks. *Do not grease the taper on the spindle or the inside of the crank!* If you add grease here, you can force the soft aluminum alloy crank too far up on the spindle and ruin the crank. The spindle taper ends should be clean and dry and free of grease, as should the matching taper of the inside of the crank. After you slide the crank on by hand, install the washer, then the locking bolt, and tighten the locking bolt 215 to 240-inch pounds (18–20-ft. lbs.) or with moderate to strong muscle until snug. Then, with a piece of wood such as a one-foot length of 2-by-4, using a ball peen hammer over the wood, tap the crank smartly; then tighten the locking bolt once again. Remember, from now on tighten up the locking bolt every 50 miles for the next 200 miles.

STEP ELEVEN: With both cranks installed (I hope in the right direction, perpendicular to each other) grasp the end of each crank and move laterally—sideways—to feel for looseness. Spin, and listen for tightness and feel for tightness. Readjust adjustable cup as necessary. There should be no sideplay or tightness or binding. If in the future you have trouble getting the spindle just right, you might try installing the right-side crank all the way, as in Step Ten; then install the left-side crank just tight enough, with the locking bolt in place, so as to remove looseness from the crank arm; then check for proper cup adjustment. That way the left crank won't be on so tightly that you have trouble backing it off to make cup adjustments with crank removed.

Cottered Crank Maintenance

We have already discussed removal and reassembly of cottered cranks. The rest of the steps are exactly the same as for cotterless cranksets.

Maintenance of One-Piece Cranksets

Unlike the other two types of cranks, on one-piece cranks you will have to remove both pedals for complete disassembly. All you need remember for pedal removal is that the right-side pedal threads on clockwise and the left-side pedal, counterclockwise; and that for removal, the reverse applies. The rule here is that pedals *always* thread on in the direction of crank rotation, but because the crank rotates clockwise when you look at it from the right and counterclockwise when you look at it from the left, the same applies to pedals.

With pedals removed, just remove the lock ring and adjustable cup, and pull the entire one-piece crank assembly through from the right side. Clean bearings and the chainwheel(s), and reassemble.

A Final Word About Adjustment

Inexpensive bikes may have the bottom bracket out of alignment with the stays and dropouts. Or the face of the bracket shell may not be accurately machined. Or the less expensive bike may have been dropped on its side so the bottom-bracket shell or its spindle became misaligned upon impact. Also the bottom-bracket threads on these less expensive bikes are not as precisely machined as the threads on the better bicycles. There is going to be a lot more slop in these threaded part fits. So what may seem to be proper alignment when the adjustable cup is threaded down and backed off a half turn may well turn out to be so tight as to greatly shorten the life of bearing surfaces. *Any* bearing surfaces, no matter how expensive the bike, will have a far shorter life if too tight, not to mention the fact that pedaling will be a lot harder when bearings are too tight. So bear in mind that when you tighten up on the lockring you will, unless you hold the cup in place, also move the cup so bearings will be too tight. If you do hold the cup in place, tightening the lockring can move the cup slightly in, so what was just right before is now too tight. Sideplay in a bottom bracket can flatten bearings and score the cups because it tends to concentrate instead of spread the load among all the bearings.

HOW TO SELECT A BOTTOM-BRACKET SET OR CRANKSET

If you have a good frame you may want to upgrade the bottom-bracket set or the entire crankset. Or you may want to change from a double to a triple crankset, which will require a longer bottom-bracket spindle to accommodate a third chainwheel. I think the best reason of all to change bottom-bracket sets, though, is to go to a sealed, precision-bearing bottom-bracket setup, such as the Phil Wood, Durham or Avocet designs. These sealed-bearing sets end for years the hassle of bottom-bracket maintenance and adjustment. If your chainwheel is worn to the point where the chain jumps off, you will of course need a replacement. Check chainwheel teeth, look for wear that causes them to come to a point, to have a hook at the trailing edge or to be thinner at the top than a new chainwheel of the same make. If you change chainwheels, you should also change the chain, unless it's new. Check for chain wear as described under the section on chains later on in this chapter.

To select a new bottom-bracket assembly of the right size, first measure the end-to-end distance of your bottom bracket, as shown in Figure 13-94. If you are going to another double chainwheel and your bottom-bracket shell is anywhere between 67 and 69 millimeters, it takes a 68-millimeter spindle. The problem is that you can't really *measure* the 68 millimeters on the spindle; there is no reference point where, with a metric caliper ruler, you can measure off 68 millimeters and have it make any sense with reference to end of bearing lands, or any other point. All the 68 millimeters means is that the bearing lands will be such that when you screw home the adjustable cup there will be room for the lockring, as shown in Figure 13-95. Here I have set the metric caliper ruler at 68 millimeters with the cups removed. You can see it applies to nothing seeable on the spindle. With cups in place (Fig. 13-96) you can see there is room (I count five threads) for the lockring. So that's what the 68 millimeters means—you get a spindle long enough between bearing lands (the convex part where the bearings ride) to allow room for the lockring on the adjustable cone side. Which, by the way, is one good reason never to interchange different makes of cups. Cups have different widths, and if you switch to a narrower (thinner) set of cups, the adjustable cup is going to screw all the way flush with the left side of the bottom-bracket shell, leaving you no room for the lockring. Without the lockring, the adjustable cup can move as you pedal, and change adjustment, because it will be quite loose; need I say, after all the preceding, that such movement will be an unmitigated, expensive disaster? Figures 13-97 and 13-98 show the difference in width, for example, between Shimano and Campagnolo adjustable and fixed cups. I also would not advise changing or interchanging makes of bearing sets in cages. It's okay to change individual *ball bearings*, as long as they are the same size. By the way, apropos of nothing at all except measurement, you can

Fig. 13-94: To determine correct size of bottom-bracket spindle, measure length of bottom-bracket shell. This one measures 68 mm. (2.68 in.)

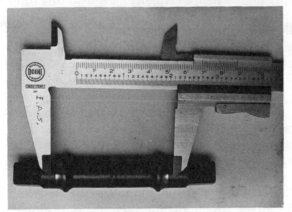

Fig. 13-95: The "invisible" measurement of a 68-mm. spindle is simply to specify that a 68-mm. bottom-bracket shell will not "swallow" the adjustable cup so all the threads go inside the bottom-bracket shell with no room for the lockring; you **must** use the lockring.

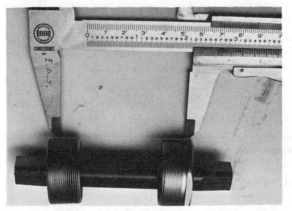

Fig. 13-96: At 68 mm. wide, the adjustable cup leaves four or five threads for the lockring.

Fig. 13-97: Left, Shimano adjustable cup. Right, Campagnolo adjustable cup.

Fig. 13-98: Left, Campagnolo fixed cup. Right, Shimano fixed cup.

buy an inexpensive metric caliper ruler from a local hardware store or from a metric specialty supply house such as Ametric. To read this ruler (Fig. 13-99) which measures inside diameter (A), outside (B) and depth (C) in both inches and millimeters, put the jaws or the depth gauge on whatever you want to measure. For example, let's say that what you measure reads 69 plus someplace between 69 and 70. Each large number at the top of the scale is 10 millimeters, each of the smaller divisions represents one millimeter. So if the end of the vernier (Fig. 13-99) is at 6 plus 9 and a fraction, which totals 69 millimeters plus a fraction of a millimeter, now we have to find out what that fraction represents. This is where we turn to the vernier scale on this ruler (Fig. 13-100). The vernier (A) is not numbered, but is divided into ten major divisions and two smaller divisions between each of the major divisions. Each of the major divisions represents one additional decimal point to the right and each of the smaller divisions an additional decimal point. For example, in Figure 13-100, the left side of the vernier is just above 69. To read the additional fraction, go to the vernier division closest to being aligned with the division in the main metric scale underneath it. In Figure 13-100, the division in the vernier main scale is 3½ vernier divisions . . . that is three major divisions plus a half division. So the closest we can come to an accurate reading with this vernier metric caliper ruler is 69.35 millimeters. Got it? No? Ah, well, I tried. Buy yourself a vernier metric ruler anyhow—they come with instructions and you'll get a real feeling of accomplishment by using it. Unless, of course, you are a machinist or an engineer, in which case this description is strictly ho-humsville, and I don't blame you for thinking so. Now back to bottom-bracket selection. Important dimensions of the spindle are shown in Figure 13-101. Note that dimension (A) is longer than dimension (B); this is because (A) is the chainwheel side of the spindle. On the spindle body in the dimension (B) section is stamped 68 and 112, which means that the spindle is for a 68-millimeter bottom-bracket shell and that the total spindle length is 112 millimeters. All of which is fine, but you still

Fig. 13-99: Vernier caliper ruler is a very handy tool for quite precise measurements in both millimeters and inches. (A) measures inside diameters; (B) measures outside; (C) measures depth.

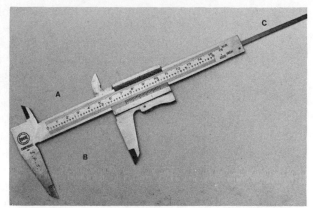

Fig. 13-100: Close-up of vernier scale section. Read measurement where vernier line comes closest to mm. line below it. Vernier scale is in 100th of a mm., each major vernier scale is ⅒ of a mm. So if the major scale below is, say, 69 mm., and vernier lines up with the third major vernier line plus one, over the major scale, the reading would be 69.35 mm.

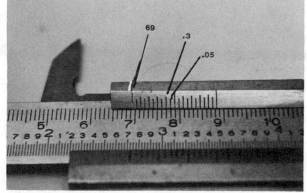

Fig. 13-101: Important measurements of a bottom-bracket spindle. Although you can read the manufacturer's marking on the spindle as 68 W 112, which means that the spindle will fit a 68-mm. bottom-bracket shell and the 112 is the spindle length, there really is no measurable place on the spindle that you can say is 68 mm. Dimension (A) shows the length of the right side, for the chainwheel side; (B) is bearing surface to bearing surface; (C) is left side of spindle; (D) is spindle diameter; (E) is overall spindle length and taper° is just that (most spindles have a 2° taper, the way we measure it).

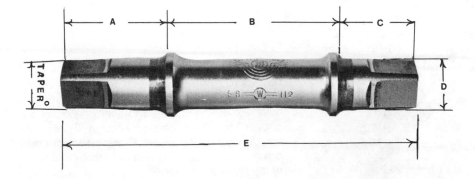

have to have room for the chainwheel to clear the stays. You need a good healthy 10-millimeter clearance between the inner chainring and the chainstay to avoid chain rub in low gear. With the conventional bottom-bracket set consisting of balls loose or in a race, a fixed cup and an adjustable cup with lockring, you have absolutely no way to change the clearance between the chainring and the chainstay. This is a fixed dimension depending directly on spindle length. If you are going from a double to a triple chainwheel, keep the cups and bearings, and change to a longer spindle to accommodate the triple chainwheel set. For example, Campagnolo's double-plateau chainwheel uses a spindle with an (A) dimension (Fig. 13-101) of 31 millimeters, but this dimension goes to 35 millimeters for their triple chainwheel. Of course the triple chainwheel is now longer by the 4-millimeter difference between the two (A) dimensions; the double-chainwheel spindle is a total of 112 millimeters long and the triple is 116 millimeters long. But both will fit a 68-millimeter bottom bracket; the only difference is the (A) dimension, which is longer for the triple chainwheel.

It's risky to interchange cranks. For example, you can count on Campagnolo cranks and spindles to be up to specs, the taper cut to 3½ degrees exactly. But other cranks may have a specified 3½-degree taper but be slightly off that mark, or even be cut to 3 degrees. Also, you will find the tapered end of the spindle to be longer on some makes than on others, as shown in Figure 13-101. This means that it may be possible to force the crank too far up onto the spindle so that the shoulder of the crank abuts the inner rise of the spindle taper, as shown in Fig. 13-102. Here I have placed a Shimano 600 crank on a Campagnolo spindle. The tapered opening in the Shimano crank is enough larger than the Campy shank that the Shimano crank is actually loose. The fit between the crank and the spindle should be a press fit, so tightening the spindle bolt will force the crank tightly up onto the spindle's tapered end. You will note in Figure 13-102 that the crank is so far up onto the spindle that you can't even see the shoulder of the tapered end. You can tighten down on the spindle locking bolt, sure, and the crank will now *feel* tight. But believe me, that tightness is not good—there's an awful lot of air be-

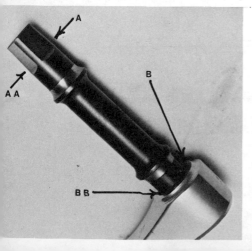

Fig. 13-102: If the crank can be pressed by the crank fixing bolt so far up the spindle taper so it butts against the spindle shoulder, the crank is a poor fit and will not be tight enough. This is a sure way to destroy the crank. Crank is too far up at points (B) and (BB). (A) and (AA) show that some of the taper should show.

Fig. 13-103: Crank end is about right distance from end of spindle. If spindle protrudes beyond inside flat of crank, fixing bolt can't tighten so crank will be too loose and will be ruined.

tween most of the inside of the crank and the spindle, so that the crank is hanging onto the spindle by just a fraction of its body. It won't take very many miles of pedaling before this type of crank-to-spindle fit will shear off the insides of the crank and leave you with a nice, freewheeling crank that can only be repaired by buying and installing a new, properly fitted and mated crank. If in doubt about the crank-to-spindle fit when buying a new crank, bring along your old spindle to the bike shop, put the new crank on it, and tighten it down to check the fit before you leave the store. You'll know, right away, if the fit works or not. In some fits, the end of the spindle is flush, or close to being flush with the bottom of the crank-puller hole. After tightening the bolt, remove it and check to make sure that you have a clearance of at least ⅟₁₆th to ⅛th inch between the end of the spindle and the inside surface of the squared end of the crank, as shown in Figure 13-103. If the crank is closer than that, or flush with the spindle end, the bolt is tightening against itself and not against the crank. If the bolt tightens on itself, further tightening will only shear off the bolt and not bring the crank tight enough up on the spindle. If you don't shear the bolt off, you will also have a loosened crank eventually, and because the spindle is steel and the crank softer aluminum, the result can be a ruined crank.

As another example of spindle length for double versus triple cranks, Stronglight's double has an (A) dimension (see Fig. 13-101) of 32.5 millimeters and the triple has an (A) dimension of 39.5 millimeters—a difference of 7 millimeters. Overall length (Fig. 13-101) (E) dimension for the double is 118.5 millimeters, for the triple, 125.5 millimeters, a difference of 7 millimeters. So the difference is in the longer crank end, dimensions (B) (C) and (D) remain the same, and if one fits a 68-millimeter bottom-bracket shell, the other will also fit it.

National Differences

The threads that are cut into the bottom-bracket shell, into which are threaded the adjustable and fixed cups, are not the same for all bottom brackets. Would, indeed, that they were. As it is, the national differences

Table 13-3 Phil Wood Bottom-Bracket Sizes

Campagnolo and copies	TA or Stronglight	Phil Wood Part Number	Spindle Length (millimeters)
Single	—	1	108 (4.25″)
Double	Single	2	113 (4⁷⁄₁₆″)
Triple	Double	3	119 (4¹¹⁄₁₆″)
—	Triple	4	125 (4¹⁵⁄₁₆″)

make bottom-bracket set selection a real mess. As a guide, *if your bicycle was made in the U.S.A., England or Japan,* it is most likely to have the bottom-bracket threads of 1.370 x 24 threads per inch, which is British Standard Coarse. *The adjustable cup will have right-hand threads* and so will thread on clockwise, as will its lockring. *The fixed cup will have left-hand thread* and so will thread on counterclockwise. The crank will be threaded ⁹⁄₁₆ x 20F for pedal threads with those dimensions. *The bottom bracket will most likely be 68 millimeters wide.*

If your bicycle was made in France or Belgium, the bottom-bracket threads will be 35 millimeters x 1.00 millimeters and the pedals will be threaded 14 x 1.25 millimeters. Because it is difficult to find pedals with this thread cutting, any good bike shop can chase these threads out to the more standard ⁹⁄₁₆ x 20F in a few minutes—and don't hestitate to do it if it's necessary. The bottom bracket will most likely be 68 millimeters wide from edge to edge (Fig. 13-94). The fixed and adjustable cups will be right-hand threaded (threads on clockwise).

If your bicycle was made in Italy the bottom-bracket threads will be 36 millimeters x 24 threads per inch, and pedal threads will most likely be ⁹⁄₁₆ by 24 threads per inch. The bottom bracket will probably be 70 millimeters, which means you will need a 70-millimeter spindle (that's the nondimension I noted above and illustrated in Figure 13-95. Both fixed and adjustable cups will be right-hand threaded (threads on clockwise). Figure 13-104 shows the difference between right- and left-hand threads, in case there is any doubt. Note that the right-hand thread (which is normal thread direction found on most bolts and nuts) slopes to the left, and left-hand threads slope to the right. On finely cut threads you will need a magnifying glass to tell the difference.

If, God help you, *your bicycle was made in Switzerland,* your bottom-bracket threads will be a cross between English and Italian, and will be 35 millimeters x 1 millimeter pitch and the fixed cup may be left-hand threaded. Or, it *may* be right-hand threaded. You never know, and you will need to make a visual check (Fig. 13-104). If the fixed cup is

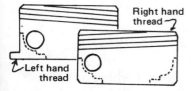

Right hand thread

Left hand thread

Fig. 13-104: Difference between left- and right-hand threads can usually be determined by inspection. Here's what to look for. Left-hand threads are "normal," spin on clockwise. Right hand threads are on British, American and Japanese fixed cups, spin on counterclockwise.

Table 13-4 Bottom-Bracket Spindle Dimensions (See Fig. 13-97)

Make	Type	"A"	"B"	"C"	"D"	"E"	Taper*	Axle Marking
				Dimensions (millimeters)				
Campagnolo	Double	31	54	27	13.5	112	3.5°	68 SS 120 †
Campagnolo	Triple	35	54	27	13.5	116	3.5°	68 SS 120 X 3
Campagnolo	CycloCross	31	54	30	13.5	115	3.5°	68 SS
Campagnolo	Double SR (Titanium)	34	54	30	13.5	118	3.5°	68 SL 120
Campagnolo	Track	28	54	27	13.5	109	3.5°	68 P 120
Stronglight	Double	32.5	56	30	13.5	118.5	3.5°	113
Stronglight	Triple	39.5	56	30	13.5	125.5	3.5°	125
Stronglight	Double Long	34.5	56	30	13.5	120.5	3.5°	120
Stronglight	Double X Long	38	56	30	13.5	124.0	3.5°	124
Sugino	Double	34	50	29	13.5	113	3.5°	MW 68
Sugino	Track	29.5	50	28.5	13.5	108	3.5°	MS 68
TA	Double	32	56	26	14.0	114	3.5°	344
TA	Triple	36	56	26	14.0	118	3.5°	374

* This chart was taken in part from manufacturers, and I wish to note that the taper measurement is controversial in that Sutherland and Phil Wood measure of these spindle tapers is 2 degrees and not 3.5 degrees. The variance may be due to how the taper is measured, that is, whether from the centerline of the spindle to either end of the taper, or from the difference between the tapers. I fail to see how this major a difference can exist, however. I am inclined to stick with Sutherland and Phil Wood, because my own measurements indicate closer to 2 degrees than to 3.5 degrees.

† For Campy only, the code means 68 (for 68-millimeter bottom bracket); 120 means recommended rear-hub axle length for accurate chainline.

right-hand threaded, the bottom bracket will accept the French bottom-bracket sets. But if the fixed cup is left-hand threaded, then your replacement is going to be a problem, and may have to come from a Swiss source. Good luck!

Table 13-4 shows basic spindle dimensions of common makes of bottom-bracket spindles. Table 13-5 shows chainring interchangeabili-

Table 13-5 Chainring Interchangeability

Make	Number of Chainwheels	Model	Crankarm Type	Interchangeable With
Stronglight	Double	49 D	5 pin	TA
Stronglight	Double	93	5 arm	—
Stronglight	Double	Criterium	5 pin	—
Sugino	Double	Mighty Compe MCD	5 arm	Campy Rec. S
Sugino	Double	Mighty Custom MCC	5 arm	Campy Rec. S
Campagnolo	Double	Super Record S	5 arm	Super Record P Avocet
Campagnolo	Double	Super Record P	5 arm	Super Record S Avocet
Campagnolo	Double	Record S	5 arm	Sugino
Avocet	Double	Racing/Touring	5 arm	Campy Rec. S & P

Table 13-6 Chainring and Crank Length Availability

Make	Model	Inner Center Outer (Number of Teeth, Minimum/Maximum)			Type	Crank Lengths (In millimeters
Campagnolo	Nuovo Record	42–52*		53–57	Double	165,170,177.5
Campagnolo	Nuovo Record	(any combination of above)			Triple	Same
Shimano	DuraAce	Inner and Outer rings are interchangeable with teeth from 39 to 55			Double	165,170,172.5,17₄
Avocet	Racing/ Touring	24–40	41–54	41–54	Triple	170,172.5,175
Sugino	Maxi 2	Comb. of 32–57			Double	165,171
Sugino	Mighty Comp.	Comb. of 42–54			Double or Triple	165,168,171,175
Sugino	Maxy 5	Comb. of 32–57			Double	165,171
Sugino	Mighty Tour	34–45	40–52		Double	
Sugino	Mighty Tour	34–45	34–45	40–52	as Triple	165,171
SunTour	Superbe CW-1000	42–47		47–54	Double	167.5,170,172.5, 175
SunTour	Road VX	34–48		48–53	Double	165,170
TA Cyclo-Touriste	W1690 Pro	26 to 68 as one to triple			Single, Double, Triple	160,162.5 165,167.5 170,172.5 175,177.5 180

* Interchangeable as inner or outer chainrings

ties. Table 13-6 shows chainring-teeth availabilities. For example, from Table 13-6 you will note that TA makes a low-gear inner ring for a triple chainset of only 26 teeth, which can be fitted to a Stronglight triple chainwheel set to replace their low of only 38 teeth.

Most of the bottom-bracket chainsets on the market come in both English, French and Italian thread specifications. If in doubt, check with your bicycle shop, because availabilities change fairly frequently.

About that Fixed Cup

You may be under the impression that I am avoiding the subject of how to remove the fixed cup. I really am not, honest. For one thing, there's no reason why you should *ever* remove a fixed cup unless it is worn out or unless you are changing over to another brand of bottom-bracket set or to a sealed-bearing bottom-bracket set (yes, I recognize the redundancy). To remove the fixed cup, which you might think is *welded* on the bottom bracket because it's so tight, first think through which direction you should turn it. If your bike was made in England, France, the U.S.A. or Japan, it's 99.9999 percent likely you have a left-hand-threaded fixed cup, *which means it unthreads clockwise.* If your bike was made

Fig. 13-105: Shimano fixed-cup wrench is a terrific tool. If you change bottom-bracket sets and wish to remove the fixed cup, I would advise you to buy one. Fits 36-mm. fixed cups.

in France or Italy, the bottom bracket is most likely to be right-hand threaded and will thread off counterclockwise. If your bike was made in Switzerland, the fixed cup could be right- or left-hand threaded. Try it counterclockwise first.

If the flats on your fixed cup measure 36 millimeters, you are lucky, because you can use a Shimano 36-millimeter fixed-cup wrench (Fig. 13-105). If your fixed cup is some other size, you can have a problem without a special wrench, because the *shoulder* of the fixed cup is only 3.5 millimeters wide, tapering to 3 millimeters at the ends, and the bottom-bracket shell is right next to the flats, so it's virtually impossible to get a good enough grip to turn the fixed cup with, say, a monkey wrench or adjustable crescent wrench. One way I have removed fixed cups is by removing both wheels and holding the bike up over a large machinist's vise and tightening down the vise on the fixed-cup flats; then I twist the whole bike. Remember that if the cup is right-hand threaded the bike must twist clockwise, vice versa if left-hand threaded. If the vise jaws are not mangled and you have tightened them down fair and hard, you can usually unscrew the fixed cup at the first try. But resign yourself to scraping paint off the edge of the bottom-bracket shell. It's hard to avoid when you use the bench vise method.

SEALED-BEARING BOTTOM BRACKETS

At this writing there are three makes of sealed-bearing bottom-bracket sets on the market, available either in bicycle stores or directly from the manufacturer. The manufacturers use commercially available sealed precision bearing sets which are replaceable but which should give you at least 5,000 miles before requiring relubrication. You can, on all of them, pry the outer dust seal off if you are careful. Do it with the point of a sharp knife inserted *underneath* (not into!) the seal, between it and the bearing, and pry up and out. With the seal removed you can visually inspect the bearing for lubrication, clean it if necessary with a small brush and solvent such as Carbo-Chlor and force a mild grease such as Phil Wood or Lubriplate into the cage. Be careful not to overforce the grease or you might push out the seal on the other side. Some bottom-sealed sets cannot be taken apart except at the factory, so if you push in the inner seal, you won't be able to replace it. I would like to review the three makes in some detail at this point.

Phil Wood Bottom Brackets

I mention Phil's bottom brackets first because he's the granddad of sealed bicycle components with precision bearings in the U.S.A. Two other firms make them now, but Phil Wood was the first, outside of a few machinists/cum/bicyclists or bicyclists/cum/machinists in Detroit and California whose production is extremely limited. You can buy one of these elegant bottom-bracket sets for around $45 in your local bike store, or should be able to. If not, write Phil Wood directly at 153 W. Julian St., San Jose, California 95110 or phone 408/298-1540. Phil makes his bottom-bracket spindles with a 2-degree taper (see first note, Table 13-4) so you should have no problems with fitting your old cranks on the spindle. Just make sure they don't bottom out. Here are the sizes available:

Phil's bottom brackets are available in British, Italian, French, Swiss, Raleigh Super Course, 1.370 x 26 right adjustable cup, left-hand fixed cup; and Chater Lee, 1.450 x 26 right adjustable cup and left-hand threaded fixed cup. You will need to order the cups that fit your bicycle. Specify which one.

You will need special tools to install Phil Wood bottom brackets. Figure 13-106 shows a shop version of this tool, which costs around $10; however, there's a much less expensive version, suitable for home use, for around $3.50 (Fig. 13-107). Figure 13-108 shows one end of an installed Phil Wood bottom bracket, Figure 13-109 shows a close-up of one of the "cups."

As you might guess, there is considerable leeway in moving the spindle laterally by adjusting both cups. You can move the spindle to one side or the other at least five millimeters (0.197 in.) for correct chainline (which we discussed earlier). You can tighten up both cups without causing binding pressure on bearings, so lateral adjustment is no problem. Just be sure to leave two thirds of the threads inside the bottom-bracket shell.

To install Phil Wood bottom brackets, disassemble the old set as per previous instructions, thoroughly clean bottom-bracket shell threads with a nonoily solvent and dry off. Insert the bearing cartridge in the shell, long side of the spindle first, toward the right side of the bike (No. 1 model will have both spindle sides the same length). Apply mounting compound to ring threads (supplied) and screw both rings in by hand. Rings must have the plain or nonserrated end facing toward the center of the bottom-bracket shell (arrow in Fig. 13-109). Adjusting them so that both rings are about centered or screwed in the same amount, hold one ring with one of the tools (you should have two) and tighten up the other to about 25 foot pounds. Tighten the remaining one the same way. If you

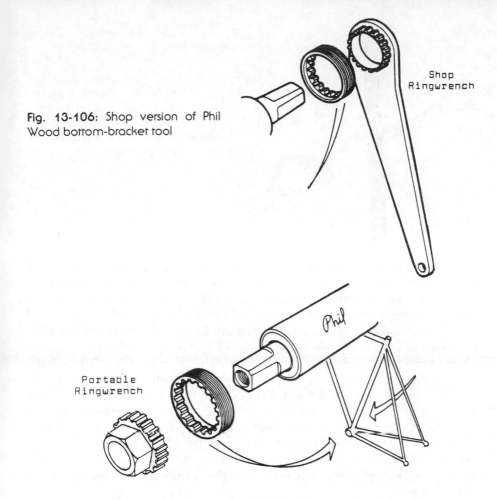

Fig. 13-106: Shop version of Phil Wood bottom-bracket tool

Shop Ringwrench

Portable Ringwrench

Phil

Fig. 13-107: Home version of Phil Wood bottom-bracket tool

Fig. 13-108: One end of Phil Wood bottom-bracket adjustable bearing retainer

Fig. 13-109: Phil Wood bearing retainer. Nonserrated end goes in first.

Fig. 13-110: Phil Wood bottom-bracket shell child adapter for tandems. Shell clamps on seat tube. Requires Phil Wood bottom-bracket set, an extra purchase.

are using the British thread on the right-hand cup, the cup or ring will be marked by a red-painted face on the inside of the ring. Remember to thread this one in counterclockwise since it will be left-hand threaded. Make chainline lateral adjustments before tightening shells.

Phil also makes a youth adapter bottom bracket for your small child, say from five to ten years of age, whose legs would otherwise be too short to reach the pedals on your tandem. The adapter (Fig. 13-110) bolt/clamps onto the seat tube. The adapter was mentioned in Chapter 3. You're looking at around $30 for this unit. It fits either a 1⅛-inch seat tube or a 28-millimeter (slightly smaller) seat tube. A neoprene liner is provided to protect the paint. This is *not* the complete unit. You still have to install a bottom-bracket set, and the adapter will (of course) accept one of Phil's bottom-bracket cartridges. Or you can use an old bottom-bracket set, if you have one, and the cranks and chainwheel from another bike.

Crank Shorteners

If you have one leg shorter than the other, it's a lot easier to pedal if one of the cranks is shorter than the other one. They bolt to crank arms. If the right leg is the problem, you will have to dispense with the right or outer chainwheel, to make room for the adapter (Fig. 13-111). They run around $30 each.

Fig. 13-111: Phil Wood crank shortener, for people with orthopedic requirements

Durham Bottom Brackets

Roger Durham, engineer and cyclist, has come up with a dandy bottom-bracket set (Fig. 13-112) that mates well with your old cotterless crank spindle length. Roger's spindle lengths are: 114 millimeters (4.5 in.), 127 millimeters (5 in.) and 140 millimeters (5.5 in.). English, Italian or French threadings for bearing carriers (replace adjustable and fixed cups). The spindle is 15.9 millimeters versus 15.06 millimeters for the Phil Wood bottom-bracket diameter, so there is a mite of added strength here. I have never had a bottom-bracket spindle break, or even bend, but then my cycling torque is far below that of a road racing athlete. Roger uses four sets of bearings. In the description that follows, please refer to the keyed number in Figure 13-112. Number 1 is of course the spindle. Number 2 are the aluminum bearing carriers, one on each side of the spindle. Number 3 are the caged roller bearings carried inside the bearing carriers (Fig. 13-113). These bearings sets are rated at 2,000-pounds capacity *each* so the total capacity of the two of them is two tons. In the center of the set is an aluminum thrust collar (4) (see also Fig. 13-114) which is held on the shaft by two socket set screws (Allen wrench provided with the set). This thrust collar can be loosened and moved laterally on the spindle for chainline adjustment. I found I could get 7 millimeters (a bit over ¼-inch) lateral adjustment by moving the thrust collar on the spindle and still have the bearing carriers threaded far enough inside the bottom bracket for comfort. Between the bearing carriers are hardened steel thrust washers (7) which are on either side of a pair of retainer-type thrust bearings (6). The thrust bearings take up lateral thrust (Fig. 13-114). Finally, there is an internal sealing sleeve (8), consisting of a hollow tube of aluminum which protects thrust bear-

Fig. 13-112: Durham bottom-bracket sealed-bearing set. Parts are: (1) spindle; (2) bearing retainer or holder; (3) needle bearings in sealed races; (4) thrust collar can be adjusted by loosening Allen screws (5) to allow lateral movement of spindle for chainline alignment (Lateral movement can be as much as needed till chain-wheel rubs on tubes.); (6) thrust ball bearings in race; (7) machined, hardened flat washers; (8) an aluminum shell that is precisely machined so you can't overtighten bearing holders (2) with pin wrench. Shell is a spacer.

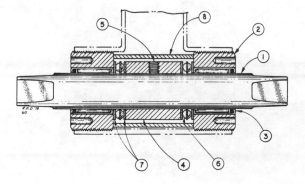

Fig. 13-113: Durham bearing retainer, showing needle bearings.

ings from being end-loaded by the bearing carriers and which also provides precise bearing clearance. The sleeve prevents you from tightening the threaded bearing carriers in the bottom-bracket shell so tightly that you cause the spindle to bind. The sleeve also seals bearings from contaminants such as water or rust in the frame and keeps bearings from loosening.

To install: Remove old bottom-bracket set as previously instructed. Clean threads in bottom bracket. Screw in right-side bearing carrier by hand. Make sure there is a washer next to the thrust collar, followed by thrust bearings, followed by another washer (Fig. 13-113). Reverse this sequence on the left side. The thrust collar Allen screws should be tight and the collar in about the center of the spindle. Now thread in the left-hand bearing carrier by hand. If you have a bracket set of the right size,

Fig. 13-114: Bottom, Durham spindle with machined flat washer (A); thrust bearings (B); and thrust collar (C) above is conventional spindle.

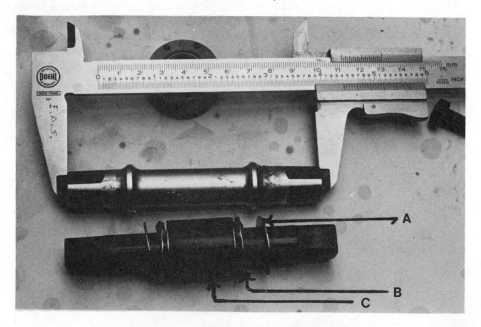

you should have the carriers pretty nearly flush with the ends of the bottom-bracket shell. Tighten both carriers with an *adjustable pin wrench* (the Shimano fixed-pin wrench won't fit). Now check for end play by trying to move the spindle up and down. If you find play, remove the left-hand carrier, make a paper washer out of a business card, and locate it between the carrier and the flat washer. If one of these paper shims does not take out play, use two. I used three in my installation. This is a bit of extra trouble, but not much, and it is certainly worthwhile, considering how well the bracket set works. The sealed bearings add very little friction; in fact, my set showed none worth mentioning, compared with the old conventional set. As you have guessed by now, I am sure, the bearings are easily get-attable, and simple to remove and replace if necessary. All bearings are the standard commercial precision type available either from Durham or from a bearing supply house.

Now check chainline. Please review chainline specifications for your gear setup given earlier in this chapter. One easy way to arrive at a reasonable approximation of correct chainline (eyeballing won't do, and it's difficult to get a straightedge on the chainset and freewheel cogs due to their location and size) is to measure the distance between the freewheel cog that you are using as the chainline reference point and the wheel rim. I hope you have the wheel in the dropouts straight and that the rim is accurately trued. If you have a five-speed freewheel and a double chainwheel, correct alignment is when the centerline *between* the chainwheels lines up with the number-three rear cog (Fig. 13-25). If you knot a piece of string around the chainwheel bushing, between the two chainwheels, and bring it back and tie it to the seat stay, you will have a reference point to check chainline. You should have the same distance between the rim flat closest to the chainwheel and the string as between the rim flat farthest to the rear of the bike and the chainwheel; and the rear part of the string should be lined up with the number-three cog of the freewheel. Measuring in both locations gave me 29 millimeters; and, because I had the chainring end of the string close to the centerline between the chainwheels, and right over number 3 rear cog, it indicated that the chainline was pretty surely on the mark. This is a rough gauge of chainline, but unless you are a racing cyclist, it is good enough. If the chainline is off, you can unscrew the Durham left-side bearing carrier, pull out the spindle (watch that you don't lose the washers) and move the thrust collar as needed.

You will note that the spindle is threaded for a bolt and that the bolt and a washer are supplied to replace your old crank bolt. Your old crank bolt will *not* fit the Durham spindle because it's not metric thread, but $\frac{5}{16}$ by 24 TPI. The bolt also takes a ½-inch socket, so it's small enough to permit entry of the socket into the crank, which is a real convenience, because the tight fit of the larger bolts that came with the crankset makes it easy for the wrench to slip off; and I clearly remember skinned knuckles, once on the chainwheel teeth. The Durham set sells for around $40.

Fig. 13-115: Avocet sealed-bearing bottom-bracket set

Avocet Sealed-Bottom-Bracket Set

The Avocet version of a sealed bottom bracket (Fig. 13-115) is a new introduction to American bicyclists, and should be available in volume in early 1980. The design is substantially different from the Phil Wood, but similar to the Durham in that the bearings are inside threaded holders. There is a lockring for both the left and right side of the spindle, and some lateral adjustment for the chainline is available. The set can replace most high-quality conventional bottom bracket sets such as Campy, Sugino, T.A. and Stronglight, and is available in English, French, Italian and Swiss threadings. Complete weight is 260 grams (9.17 oz). Cost, around $33. Installation is straightforward, the only tool you need is an adjustable pin wrench.

CHAINWHEELS

We have already covered chainwheel interchangeability. I would only like to add a word about some of the new developments in chainwheel design. For example, Shimano has a new line of what they refer to as

Fig. 13-116: Cross section, Avocet sealed-bearing bottom-bracket set

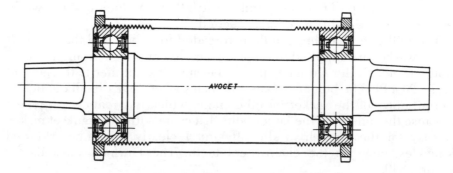

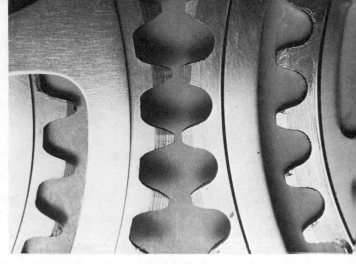

Fig. 13-117: Shimano "W" cut chainwheel teeth, left, versus Campagnolo chainwheel teeth, right.

"W" cut gear teeth on their chainwheels. Figure 13-117 compares their chainwheel with Campagnolo, to give you an idea of the differences. In addition to the wider "W" cut, Shimano has shortened the two teeth just behind the crank and the two on the opposite side of the chainwheel from the crank. The theory is that it is at these two points that chain stress is greatest; so the shorter teeth means that the chain does not have to lift as far to be nudged by the derailleur cage from one chainwheel to the other. However, the difference in teeth height is only one millimeter (about ⁴⁄₁₀ inch). I found no noticeable difference in shiftability between the Shimano chainwheel with these four shorter teeth. The wider spacing at the base of the teeth has nothing to do with ease of shifting, but is better designed to accommodate the Shimano UniGlide chain, about which, more later.

Shimano has one new development which I applaud, and that is their one key-release mechanism on cranks (Fig. 13-118) that takes only a 5-inch-long, 6-millimeter Allen wrench (supplied), both to tighten the crank onto the spindle-tapered shaft, and the same Allen wrench, turned counterclockwise, to pull it off. Turn the wrench clockwise to fasten the crank on the spindle; counterclockwise, the crank comes off the spindle. When the crank comes loose you have to give four or five more turns to unscrew the fixing bolt. This mechanism is on the top line of DuraAce cranks, as well as the special DuraAce pedal. I'll discuss these pedals in

Fig. 13-118: New Shimano crank showing Allen wrench crank-fixing bolt that also is a crank puller, all integral with the crank.

Fig. 13-119: Conventional crank, left, and new Shimano crank, right, for their new pedals. Note pedal end has much larger diameter opening.

detail in Chapter 14, coming right up. Figure 13-119 shoes a conventional crank-pedal threading and the new DuraAce pedal crank. Obviously you have to buy the whole shebang if you want these excellent pedals. Clearly this product is for the original-equipment market, because you are not buying just a pedal, you're buying a system of mated, designed-together components that will, for the most part, only work with each other. The new Shimano UG chain, which I will review later on in this chapter, for example, will not work well except with Shimano matching freewheel cogs and derailleurs. If you install the DuraAce freehub you must use Shimano's rear derailleur with a hatch plate (half inner plate so you can slide the chain out and remove the freewheel without removing the chain, and without "breaking" the chain with a rivet remover). To "break" the Shimano chain with its fatter bowed plates you should use a special Shimano rivet remover in order to avoid bending the plates flat again, or else be darned careful when you use a conventional rivet remover, which I have used on these chains successfully. And so on . . . You need to select Shimano components, at least the newer ones, with great care to be sure that what you buy will fit what you have unless you buy the entire system, freehub or hub and freewheel, chainset, bottom-bracket set, chain and rear derailleur.

To digress a moment, I will say that the Shimano Crane GS derailleur is the best wide-range derailleur on the market that I have tested, and that it can be used on any system or combination of components. The DuraAce derailleur line is usable anywhere as is the excellent DuraAce front derailleur. I merely wish to note that when it comes to Shimano, be aware that in the third-line component series especially (Altus, for example) you need matched components. True, most of Shimano's DuraAce conventional line such as the chainwheels, derailleurs, and hubs, are standard and can be used with equipment of other makes, except that Shimano chainwheels are not interchangeable with any other make, at least as of this writing.

I'm not going to get into the minutiae of comparing the five or six top lines of cranks. I will say that Campagnolo equipment is polished and machined to a fare-thee-well, and every time I look at their components I am reminded of my old Irish grandmother. She used to make me sweep *behind* the couch, even though no one could see back there, and when I balked at this unnecessary labor she would always say, "Yes, but God can see back there and *he* knows." Campy polishes and hones their parts on all sides, even where you can't see. For example, the taper squares

Fig. 13-120: SunTour Road VZ chainwheel set   **Fig. 13-121:** Avocet triple chainwheel set

on the spindle are finely machined to a shiny flat surface, whereas the same section on other makes is much more roughly machined. Yet the spindle taper shanks are inside the crank, where you can't see them. The fine grinding job just makes for a better fit, and a better fit is a tighter fit and a tighter fit means a longer lasting crank that won't come loose and wear its insides to a frazzle rubbing against the hard steel spindle. I might point out that highly *polished* finishes are not what I'm talking about here . . . I mean highly *machined* surfaces of great *consistent* precision. All that glitters is not precision, by any means. And sometimes vice versa. I can recommend SunTour's top line, the Superbe group of chainwheels, and their second line, the Road VX (Fig. 13-120). The Superbe models are equal to the Shimano DuraAce and the Road VX compare well with the Shimano 600EX line of chainwheels. TA CycloTouriste offers a low triple chainwheel of 26 teeth, but Avocet (Fig. 13-121) goes down to 24 teeth and their line is better made and harder and so should last longer. Stronglight cranks and chainwheels are excellent quality but harder to find and not as well distributed in the U.S.A. as Campy, SunTour, Avocet or Shimano equipment.

For BMX-ers

A tough, lexan or similar plastic chainwheel (Fig. 13-122) is now on the market for $80 a pair. That's a lot of money, but the result is a cog that will give good results in the mud, dirt and dust of the BMX race course.

Fig. 13-122: Plastic chainwheel

THE GREAT CRANK-LENGTH CONTROVERSY

A few years ago a fellow who owned a foundry made some extra-long cranks and a frame with higher ground clearance so the cranks would not hit the ground and a longer frame so pedals would not hit the front wheel on a turn, and he set off up a mountain. He claimed a new world record for that particular peak, which, he said, could only have been made with those extra-long cranks. I don't recall the exact length of the cranks, but they were substantially longer than any commercially available size, probably over 200 millimeters. But when other cyclists in good condition attacked that same mountain with conventional-length cranks they found this "record" easy to beat: The original speed and record time had been attained some forty or fifty years before the long crank "record," when bikes were not as efficient as they are today.

Still, there seems to be rather a lot of controversy over crank length. Theoretically, from the simple standpoint of the lever (Archimedes said something like "Give me a lever long enough and I will move the world" but he never said where he would stand, and he knew nothing about bicycles) the longer lever would appear to give you more torque, but at the expense of crank rpm capability. There's always a trade-off, always a penalty. Nevertheless, the theory is that the longer the crank (lever), the higher the gear that can be used without undue fatigue. Somewhere there is a point where the longer gear impedes smooth pedaling action (the French have a nice, silky sounding smooth word for this action which is *suplesse*) and crank rpm and therefore speed. The problem, then, is really not whether the crank is too long or too short, but what the correct crank length (Fig. 13-123 shows a variety of crank lengths) is for your particular leg length and physical stamina and gear ratios available on your bike. Another limiting point is how far your bottom bracket is above ground and the pedal clearance from the front wheel. Also on short-wheelbase road-racing type of bikes there is going to be a minimum front-wheel clearance at best, so before you change to longer cranks turn the front wheel until it is at its closest point to the toe clips or pedal, measure that distance and decide whether you can go, say, from 6½-inch cranks (165 mm.) to 7-inch cranks (178 mm.). Of course, there are smaller gradations between available crank lengths, as shown in Table 13-6. The widest range of cranks are made by T.A., and go from 160 millimeters (6.3 in.) in 2½-millimeter increments all the way to 180 millimeters (7.1 in.).

Let's see if we can come to some rational method of deciding upon the correct crank length for you. We have already mentioned two limiting factors, bottom-bracket-to-ground clearance and wheelbase. Apropros of ground clearance, I'm not worried so much about bottom-bracket-to-ground clearance while the bike is upright. The problem is when you bank for a turn, because then the pedal comes much closer to the ground. You also need to consider leg action as well as leg length as measured

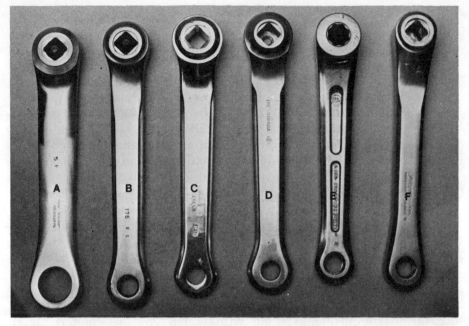

Fig. 13-123: Selection of various crank lengths. Left to right: (A) Shimano DuraAce with new pedal threading and integral crank puller, 170 mm.; (B) Shimano DuraAce conventional crank but with integral puller, 175 mm.; (C) SunTour Road VX 170 mm. crank; (D) Campagnolo Strada 170 mm. (notice beautiful machined finish); (E) Shimano Selecta with octagonal female joint to fit their octagonal spindle on this less expensive crankset, 165 mm., and (F) Shimano 600EX crank, 170 mm.

on the inside (inseam). What you want is a pedal action that simulates, as closely as possible, the natural action of the knee. A pedal that's too long or too short exaggerates this natural action, which can lead to knee problems as well as decrease pedaling efficiency. If you are doing a lot of hill climbing, as long a crank as will fit you is going to give you more leverage. I might note here that the difference between 160 millimeters, the shortest crank available commercially at this writing, and 180 millimeters, the longest crank available, is 20 millimeters, which is .7874 inches (call it ¾ of an inch). I might also note that the 160-millimeter crank available from T.A. is on their single chainwheel. I mention this only to let you know its availability.

Some experienced cyclists advocate determination of crank-length formula as one-tenth of the overall body height. To me this makes no sense at all because, as we discussed in Chapter 2, there are people with long torsos and short legs and short torsos with long legs and all gradations in between.

Another formula, which makes a lot of sense to me, has been derived after extensive study of the physiology of pedaling by three doctors in France, as reported in a cycling journal from that country. The formula is that the crank length should be around 20 to 21 percent of the inseam measurement. You measure your inseam in stocking feet from the floor to the crotch. Thus if your inseam measurement is 32 inches, 32 x .2 = 6.4″ you would use a 6.4-inch crank, which converted to millimeters (6.4 x 25.4) = 162.56 mm. Call it 162.5 millimeters, because T.A. makes a single chainwheel crank this short. I would go to the 21-percent end of the scale, which gives us .21 x 32 inches (my inseam measurement) = 6.72 inches x 25.4 = 170.688 mm. For the same inseam measurement, that's a difference of around eight mm., which is only around 5 percent, or .31496 inches (8 x .03937), or a tad over ¼ inch. I'm not trying to minimize the importance of the ¼-inch+ difference, because this can be fairly major if it means going beyond your natural pedaling action of the knee and associated bones and tendons and joints and musculature. But the longer crank gives more leverage on uphill climbs.

Another way to look at selection of crank lengths is more experiential, but based on the following factors: How fast do you routinely "spin" the cranks? If your normal pedal cadence is 80 rpm, I suggest you use as long a crank as is comfortable for you. The reason for this is that the longer cranks give you more leverage. If, however, you twirl along at, say, 90 or 100 or greater crank rpm, then you can use shorter cranks which facilitate faster rotation. This would be true particularly if you are a strong rider. If you are heavy plus strong, but pedal slower, I would use the maximum crank length with which you are comfortable. I changed from 165-millimeter to 170-millimeter cranks and found that my own pedaling was smoother and that I had more power to climb hills. I also found my normal cadence to be unaffected by the longer cranks; I still crawl along at 72 to 80 rpm. I have what pants manufacturers call a statistically normal relationship of inseam to overall height. The waist relationship I would rather not discuss. That is, I am just average in terms of inseam to height. Among other things. I won't bore you with a recitation of what all the experts in racing, physiology and cycling in general have had to say about crank length. Needless to say, there is no magic formula for determining crank length that is hard and fast and works for everybody. My own conclusion is that the 20-to-21-percent formula of crank length to inseam measurement is a good starting point. At least you won't subject your knees to damaging abnormal stresses from too short or too long a set of cranks. On the other hand, it's expensive to buy a lot of cranks just to experiment to see which length is best for you, under widely varying conditions of cycling such as cadence rpm's, cycling on the flats and on different percentages of road grade and your own physical condition which can change from day to day. Figure 13-111 shows Phil Wood crank shorteners, which sell for around $30; but that, too, is a fairly costly investment unless you have an orthopedic reason to use them. On the other hand, if you have invested $600 or more in a really fine bicycle, you might want to go the one step further and experiment with different crank lengths. You don't have to buy new chainwheels, because you will only need the cranks and can transfer the chainwheels from one to the other if you can find a bike store that will

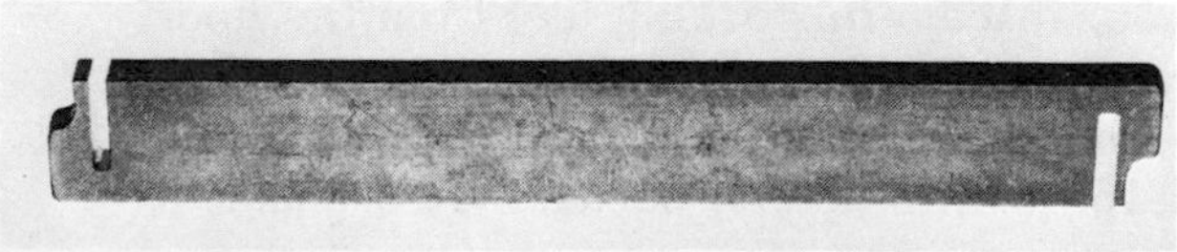

Fig. 13-124: Shop chainwheel straightener

sell you the naked right-side crank. Or, you might borrow cranks of a different length from a friend (does anyone have that good a friend?).

ABOUT ELLIPTICAL CHAINWHEELS

Before leaving cranks and chainwheels, I would like to discuss, briefly, the elliptical chainwheel, a Roger Durham design shown in Figure 13-125. I hasten to add that although Roger makes a modern version, the elliptical chainwheel has been around since the late 1890s and has varied from a plus or minus ovality of 8 percent to the Durham version of plus or minus 25 percent. I have used the Durham model and can report that it does smooth out my power stroke on hill climbing, if the hills are moderate. But if you will look at the chainwheel in Figure 13-125 you will quickly see that you can't use a front derailleur with it because the top of the ellipse would hit the derailleur cage. To shift into the lower-gear chainwheel you have to stop and move it over by hand, ideally lifting up the rear wheel, twirling the pedals and shoving the chain over. But since I do not have three hands, my preferred way is to use the heel of my foot as the derailleur (I have grease marks on my right shoe) to move it over, while pedaling with my left foot. This is not the safest procedure in the world and *must* be done before approaching the hill, unless you are strong enough to hill climb with one leg. I did not find the elliptical chainwheel to be any substitute for the lower gear possible with the inner, smaller chainwheel. But I did find that the ellipse design made cycling on the flats smoother. I don't think I would want to tour any great distance with the Durham design, though, because I need the instant availability of all my gears, particularly my low, low "Granny" gear on steep hills. But for around town and on the flats, the elliptical chainwheel is a real eye-catching conversation starter, and it is somewhat helpful in eliminating the dead spots in crank rotation. To see what I mean at this point, I suggest you go to your bike (or do it mentally if you are good at three dimensional visualization), and put a crank at the 12-o'clock position. The other crank will of course be at the 6-o'clock position. Here you now have zero torque on the pedals. Torque in-

Fig. 13-125: Durham elliptical chain-wheel

creases with the angle of pedal and falls off rapidly as you approach the noon position with one crank. If you look at Figure 13-125 you can see that as the pedal approaches the noon position the chainwheel becomes smaller, which in effect gives you a lower gear automatically. Conversely, as your pedal swings past noon the ellipse begins to pick up more teeth, creating a bigger chainwheel effect, and you swing automatically into a higher gear.

You might think that the switch from the big to the small portion of the chainwheel will be beyond the capacity of the rear derailleur, but not so, any more than the difference between a 42 and 52 dual chainwheel and a 14-to-28-tooth freewheel would be. Of course if you have a 14-to-34-tooth freewheel, you will be using a longer cage wide ratio derailleur, so again I see no problem. Except that as the chain swings over the oval chainwheel, the derailleur will move back and forth, so derailleur bushings wear a lot faster.

ABOUT CHAINS

Earlier in this chapter I pretty thoroughly covered how to obtain the correct length of chain for your bicycle's wheelbase and gear setup. Now I would like briefly to describe how to detect chain stretch and the proper procedure for chain cleaning and lubrication, and to review new developments in chain technology.

First, chain stretch. Eventually, like all things, chains wear out. Most of the wear is detected by stretch. A chain can stretch as much as one inch, and when it does you will have the chain jumping from one gear to the next inadvertently, or "skipping" over gears, which means chain side plates are hanging up on the cog teeth, creating a feeling of chain roughness as you pedal. A stretched chain should be junked and replaced immediately, because it can cause undue wear on cog teeth, particularly on the softer aluminum alloy teeth of chainwheels (unless chainwheels are steel, of course, and on the small freewheel cog.

At least once a year, more often if you ride a lot, and certainly before the start of each new spring riding season, check chain stretch. With the chain on the bicycle and with a ruler, measure exactly twenty-four chain links, from center of rivet to center of rivet, or from edge of outer plate to edge of outer plate. If either distance is more than $\frac{1}{16}$th inch over 12 inches, you have a worn chain which should be replaced. In fact, don't keep it around—dump it; because you might forget later on and use some of the worn links with a newer chain.

To remove the chain, you will need a rivet remover or, as some call it, a "chain breaker," a name akin to a baggage smasher at airports. I prefer the more genteel name of "rivet remover." To use the rivet remover (Fig. 13-126) you need first to take some precautions to avoid damage to the chain side plate. First, check the tool point, the part that pushes the

Fig. 13-126: Chain rivet remover. To use, line up tool point with chain rivet, turn handle five times to leave a bit of rivet still in chain side plate for easier reassembly.

rivet out of the chain. The point must be absolutely straight. If others have been using the tool, the point could be slightly bent. If you screw this crooked point into the rivet it won't go in straight and part of it will hit the side plate, enlarging the rivet hole. Figure 13-127 shows such a damaged plate. If you put this chain back together the chain will come apart, usually when you are miles from nowhere and you have forgotten your rivet tool. This happened to me once, in the wilds of central Wisconsin. I was lucky. I found a nail and a rock in the road and with some time, some patience, a lot of cussing and even more luck, was able to pound out the damaged link and pull the chain up another link and pound the rivet back into place. I do not recommend this procedure, believe me. You'll save yourself a lot of trouble if you remember to take your rivet tool with you on any long bike trip.

Okay. To use the rivet remover, make sure the rivet pushing end of the tool is lined up exactly on the rivet, so you don't damage the side plate. Screw down the handle until the rivet end just touches the rivet and note where the end of the handle lies—what o'clock position it has assumed. Then, with that position as a reference point, turn the handle exactly five times up to that reference point. Now you should be able to

Fig. 13-127: Damaged side plate caused by improper use of chain rivet remover tool. Tool point was not accurately lined up with rivet. (*R.L.L. Limited*)

back off the tool, put it down, take the chain between the fingers of both hands, one hand on each side of the rivet you have pushed out, and twist the chain sideways, until the chain comes apart. If you will look at what's left of the rivet inside the plate you will see perhaps ⅟₃₂-inch of the rivet still visible. This is just right, because when you reassemble the chain (I am assuming here that you are not replacing the chain, just removing it for cleaning) you will have that little bit to hold the chain together. All you do is snap the chain back together—the little bit of rivet showing will hold it until you can get the rivet tool back on it to push it in again. Make sure that the rivet is in as far as the other rivets, but no farther.

One further point about chain removal and reinstallation. When you push the rivet through, the rivet is now protruding from the left side of the chain, where it is hard to get at to replace. The temptation is to reinstall the chain with this rivet facing outward, toward you, where you can get at it. And for most of us it's a matter of sheer chance which side of the chain goes back on. If you reverse chain direction and the top and bottom, both, you could have some chain chatter, because it will have worn in the opposite direction. To avoid this, I suggest you push out the rivet on the left side (rear of bike) of the handiest side plate. Now the end of the chain on your right (toward front of bike) will be free and will be the end without the protruding rivet. Remove the chain, sliding it out of the derailleur wheels, over the rear cogs and the front derailleur cage. To reinstall the same way, start with the protruding rivet facing away from you, with that end of the chain toward the rear end of the bike. Take the other end and pull it over the chainring, down through the front derailleur cage, over the smallest (high gear) rear cog and through the derailleur pulleys (see Fig. 13-51). If you have done all this right, when you snap the chain together (it's easier if the chain is off the chainwheels and lying on the bottom-bracket shell) you should have put the chain back just the way it was before you removed it. The rivet will be facing toward the left side of the bike, which will make it a bit more difficult to use the rivet tool, but you can do it. I hang the bike from the ceiling and work on the chain with the tool from the left side.

There are two makes of instant come-apart links, one made by Shimano (Fig. 13-128) and one by RLL Limited, Box 296, River Forest,

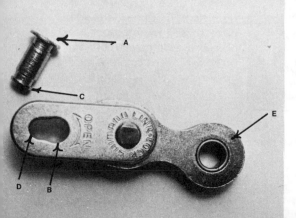

Fig. 13-128: Shimano quick-link eliminates need for chain rivet tool. Parts are: (A) Bushing, showing wide end and (C) showing smaller end that fits in to hole (B) in side plate and when chain is in use slides into (D) area of side plate. (E) is conventional chain bushing that fits into your chain (rivet goes through).

Fig. 13-129: R.L.L. Limited Super Link which uses either a tiny Allen wrench bolt and nut or screwdriver and bolt and nut instead of a rivet. Also eliminates need for rivet remover.

Illinois 60305 (Fig. 13-129). The Shimano version does not require any tools, once you have installed it with your rivet tool on one link. It simply pushes together. You twist the chain up and together so as to force the special little rivet (A) (Fig. 13-128) back into the enlarged section of hole (B). Then you push the small end of the rivet (C) out and, presto, the chain is apart. If you're lucky, you did not drop the tiny rivet on the floor where it was promptly lost to view forever. Just be careful to cup your hand under the chain to catch it. To reassemble, reverse the process and check to make sure the rivet (A) now rests securely in the small end of the plate hole (D). The quick-release end (E) is where it fits into your chain. This system is a very good idea, unless you lose the special rivet, because now you can take your chain apart on the road without having to carry a heavy rivet remover. I hope Shimano makes it possible to buy extras of these special rivets; I'd be much happier away on the road with a couple of extra ones stowed in my handlebar bag, wrapped in a small plastic bag.

The other RLL quick-release uses either a tiny screw, which takes a tiny screwdriver, or a 1-millimeter Allen wrench. I'd opt for the screwdriver, because the 1-millimeter Allen wrench is so tiny it's easy to lose; you can at least use the point of a pocket knife if you lose the screwdriver. One or the other is furnished with the RLL master link. Like the Shimano master link, you also run the risk of dropping both the link and its attaching screw, which, if dropped, will disappear. Well, you can always take the chain up one more link to get home, if you have also brought along a rivet tool. At this point I feel that I am leaving the impression with you that I drop things a lot. That's a slanderous, libelous and fairly accurate conclusion. I drop teensy, itsy, bitsy things easily and permanently lose them—which is why I surround myself with so many itsy, bitsy parts such as ball bearings and microscopic sizes of bolts and nuts. Saves a lot of running around looking for spares.

Now, about chain lubrication. I know I recommended that you throw away old chains so you don't use them for spare links. I keep mine because I have been testing a lot of different lubricants on my chains over the years. I have an odometer on my bike, so I know how many miles I travel, and because I test bike components, I keep track of mileage and other things such as how long the chain lasts before it stretches to the replacement point. I've used just one lubricant on each chain until the chain stretched too far. After trying a zillion lubricants, and without boring you with the hundreds of chicken scratchings on my record pads, I can tell you that the lubricant that made my chains last longest, with least stretch, is a heavy-gear oil with a viscosity of around 140 SAE, which is something like cold molasses. You can buy such an oil in any auto-supply store; just ask for gear lube. This oil is so heavy you have to heat it to get it thin enough to penetrate into the chain parts. I use a hot plate, an old pot (stolen from the kitchen) and soak the chain in the warm oil overnight. The hot plate has a thermostat which I set to low. Don't try this method unless you are in a room with lots of ventilation or outdoors, and keep the heat low and on long. Spray-type lubricants such as those sold in motorcycle stores will work, but they are not good enough to prevent chain wear from occurring fairly quickly. In fact, I found that my chains, lubed with the heavy gear oil (well, you can use 85 or even 80 SAE viscosity thickness and still get good results) lasted up to five or six times as long as the chains lubricated with the spray lubricants. The one drawback to the heavier oil is that it does attract more dust. I simply relube after every trip, or once a month, as necessary, and wipe off all extra oil before remounting the chain. I didn't dream up this method of chain lubrication, by the way; it's been practiced by experienced cyclists for at least fifty years.

Now let's look at some of the newer chains that have been introduced recently. Probably the most controversial is the new Shimano UltraGlide chain (UG) (Fig. 13-130). As you can see in this picture, the UG chain has widened or bowed-out outer chainplates. The theory is that with conventional chains, the chain roller (See "A" in Fig. 13-131) hits the teeth of the larger gear when shifting to a lower gear, before outer chain-

Fig. 13-130: Shimano UltraGlide (UG) chain has bowed-out side plates.

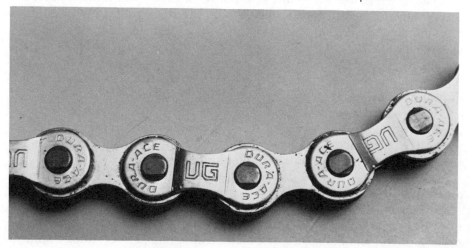

Fig. 13-131: Dissected chain showing parts: (A) roller; (B) outer side plate; (C) inner side plate; (D) rivet; (E) bushing. This is a SunTour New Winner chain. Note chamfered inside of outer plate which reduces overall chain weight.

plates can engage that gear. According to Shimano, this creates friction, and can cause overshifting. Shimano claims that the increased width between the outer plates makes shifting easier and more accurate. I measured the widest point between the two Shimano UG outer plates as 5.5 millimeters. The widest point between the new Ultra-Six SunTour outer plates is 4.5 millimeters and between these plates of a Regina chain the measurement is 5 millimeters. I used the Shimano UG chain and found little difference between it and conventional chains when used with a conventional freewheel. But when used with Shimano's new freewheels which have cogs twisted at an angle, I found shifting to be snappier and more precise. Therefore I suggest the UG chain be used with Shimano freewheels. With this combination I also discovered that shifting under high pedal torque while hill climbing was much easier, although I still recommend that you shift down before the hill grade forces you to do so. I feel that the Shimano UG chain and twisted-tooth freewheel cogs (UniGlide freewheel) should be used together on a tandem, where torque is at a maximum. At this writing these cogs go up only to 28 teeth, but I hear Shimano will eventually go to 32 or 34 teeth for the wider range you need on a touring tandem. As noted earlier, you should use a special chain-rivet tool to avoid bending the bowed out-plates, although with care you can use your old tool. Because the plates are bowed out, my survey of bicycle mechanics in the Chicago area as to their experience with these chains reveals that they are concerned about undue chain stretch. This is contrary to Shimano's claim that the UG chain will stretch half as much and last twice as long as the conventional chain. We will just have to wait and see. At the moment I am neutral.

Fig. 13-132: Regina chain is one of the most reliable I have used, and after five years on one chain, I have yet to have it break. Of course I cleaned and relubricated it regularly.

SunTour has come up with a nice chain which works well with their freewheels. It's the Ultra-Six model which has thinner side plates and smaller roller pins. Say, let's stop here for just a moment and look at the parts of a chain link. It's a legitimate detour because my illustration is a SunTour link. Going from the outside in, we have, in Figure 13-131: (A) the outer side plates; (B) the inner side plates; (C) the bearing surface on which (D) the roller rotates; and (E) the rivet that goes through the bearing surface, the inner side plate and the facing side plate to hold the whole shebang together. Wear points of a chain are inside surfaces of plates, the roller and the roller journal. Stretch is due to internal rearrangement of molecules in chain plates and wear on rollers, bearing surface and rivets. You will note, I hope, that the Ultra-Six outer plate has a slight bevel to the inside. This has the effect mainly of lightening the chain, an effect enhanced by the narrower, smaller rollers. The Ultra-Six works on a variety of makes of freewheel cogs as well as on Sun-Tour's new line of freewheels with slightly narrower space between rear cogs. I would not recommend using the Shimano UG chain on the Sun-tour New Winner freewheels, because spacing is narrower on this freewheel and the Shimano UG plates are a half millimeter wider than the Regina and one millimeter wider than the SunTour Ultra-Six side plates. Eyeballing the clearance, I would say there is darned little between the wider side plates of the Shimano UG chain and the adjoining cogs of the SunTour New Winner freewheel.

When all is said and done, however, my favorite is still the old faithful, the Regina line of chains (Fig. 13-132). These have the hardest plates and the best metallurgy of any chain I have tested. They have given me many thousands of miles of good and faithful service, and they work well on the more conventional components. Now to the next chapter, on pedals and headsets.

What You Need to Know About Pedals, Headsets, Stems, Handlebars and Seat Posts 14

This chapter will take you from top (headsets) to bottom (pedals) and a few places in between. Let's start with pedals.

Pedals are small. They use small ball bearings (most require ⁵⁄₃₂-in. balls) which take an awful lot of pressure and abuse for their small size. Pedals are right down there near the ground where they are exposed to considerable amounts of sand, dust and dirt, not to mention water.

Fortunately, pedals are quite simple in design and easy to take apart, clean, lubricate and reassemble. On a scheduled basis I recommend taking pedals down for maintenance at least once a year, more often if you ride a lot and certainly after every long tour.

The only way to avoid routine maintenance, aside from brushing off accumulated gunk from the outside, would be to use sealed-bearing pedals such as Hi-E, Phil Wood or Berthet which run from $85 to $100 a pair. Nonsealed, high-quality pedals often run you $50 or more a pair (a lot more if you go in for super lightweight parts, such as titanium pedals which list up to $108.98). Table 14-1 gives comparative specifications on most of the popular, available makes of pedals. What kind of pedals do I use? Well, I like maintenance-free bicycling, insofar as technology has it in its power to give it to me, so I use sealed-bearing pedals. I have Phil Woods on one bike, Hi-E on another. For roadracing, the high-grade nonsealed bearings are preferable because they use titanium components and are much lighter in weight.

Because most bikes have conventional nonsealed ball-bearing pedals, and I imagine you would like to know how to maintain them, I'll cover this aspect first and then get into details on sealed-bearing and other exotic makes and designs of pedals.

As a starter, please look at Figure 14-1, a disassembled pedal with all the parts laid out on the table. Note that the tapered end of the spindle goes into the body of the pedal, from the crank side. You won't really have to worry about which way the spindle goes in; you can only do it the right way for the pedal to screw back into the crank. Note that the washer (E) has a little tang. This is so the washer won't turn while you tighten the lock nut (F). The washer tang fits into a groove cut into the spindle. Most pedals have twelve balls. They are loose. As you take the pedal apart, please follow the sequence below so you don't lose one or two. If one falls on the floor it will most likely never be found again, as

Table 14-1 Pedal Specifications

Make and Model	Pair Weight (grams)	Body	Spindle	Sealed Bearings	Precision Bearings	Price Pair
Campagnolo Record Road 1037	454	Steel	Steel	No	Yes	$ 46.98
Campagnolo Record Track 1038	404	Steel	Steel	No	Yes	46.98
Campagnolo Super Record Road	206	Alloy	Titanium	No	Yes	108.98
East Rochester Tool & Die Titanium	240	Alloy	Titanium	Yes	Yes	87.50
East Rochester Tool & Die	290	Alloy	Steel	Yes	Yes	62.50
Phil Wood	325	Alloy	Steel	Yes	Yes	51.00
KKT Pro Ace	460	Alloy	Steel	No	Yes	31.50
Hi-E	284	Alloy	Steel	Yes	Yes	41.00
KKT Pro Ace Track	431	Alloy	Steel	No	Yes	21.50
Barelli SS	410	Alloy	Steel	Yes	Yes	NA
Barelli B-10	NA	Alloy	Steel	Yes	Yes	NA
Shimano DD LA 100	346	Alloy	Steel	No	Yes	NA
SunTour PL 3000	335	Alloy	Steel	No	Yes	NA
SunTour PL 1000	353	Alloy	Steel	No	Yes	NA
SunTour Road VX	390	Alloy	Steel	No	Yes	NA
Lyotard 23	367	Steel	Steel	No	Yes	10.98
Lyotard 460D	325	Steel	Steel	No	No	5.98
Barelli SS	470	Stainless	Steel	Yes	Yes	54.50
Barelli B-10	350	Alloy	Steel	Yes	Yes	65.90

I have pointed out earlier in this book. Take heart, however. Every bike shop worthy of the name stocks new ones.

PEDAL MAINTENANCE—STEP BY STEP

STEP ONE: *Remove pedals.* The left pedal threads off clockwise as you face it; the right threads off counterclockwise. The rule of thumb here is that pedals *always* go *on* the crank in the direction of crank rotation; *off;* opposite the direction of crank rotation. Here are pedal markings, if you are installing new ones, to tell you which is the left and right pedal:

Italian pedals: D is right side: D stands for "Destro," or right.
 S is left side: S stands for "Sinistro," or left.

French pedals: D is right side: D stands for "Droit," or right.
 G is left side: G stands for "Gauche," or left.

Spanish pedals: D is right side: D stands for "Derecho," or right.
 I is left side: I stands for "Izquierdo," or left.

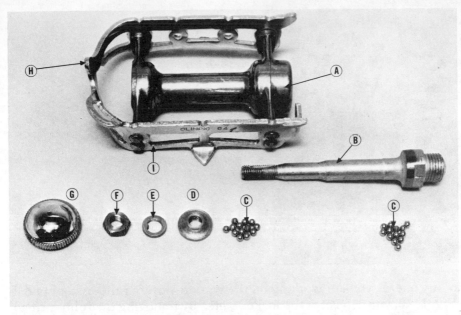

Fig. 14-1: Here are pedal parts: (A) body; (B) spindle; (C) bearings; (D) screwed race; (E) tanged washer; (F) locknut; (G) dust cap; (H) quill; (I) front plate.

And now for a word about pedal thread sizes. English and Italian pedal threads are ⁹⁄₁₆ x 20 Threads Per Inch (TPI). Italian thread is just a wee bit different from the English, however, so although it will fit English cut crank threads labeled ⁹⁄₁₆ x 20, it will be a little tight, so you will have to use a little muscle. French cranks and pedals will probably be marked 14 mm. x 12.5 mm., which is what they are. French threads can be easily tapped out to the English ⁹⁄₁₆ x 20 TPI, so don't hesitate to have this done, because the English threads are becoming standard. Some French bikes are even arriving in this country with cranks tapped the ⁹⁄₁₆ x 20 TPI and pedals to match. But if you have a one-piece crank, be advised that the threads will be ½ inch by 20 TPI and the good-quality pedals are not available in this size. But then you would not install high-quality pedals on a one-piece crankset in any case.

Most pedals take a 15-millimeter thin steel wrench, long enough to exert some force, because pedals are going to be threaded in fairly tightly due to the fact that pedal rotation is in the same direction as the threads, and you will need muscle to remove them.

STEP TWO: Put the pedal in a vise (Fig. 14-2), gripping the *flats* of the axle sides on the crank side with dust cap end up. The pencil points to a dust cap. Don't grip the threads in the vise. Turn the dust cap with a small screwdriver using the rattrap opening as a fulcrum, similar to where the pencil is located above. Be careful in removing the cap, so that you don't damage the knurled edges. There is a special wrench for dust cap removal; if you have a lot of bicycles to maintain it would pay

Fig. 14-2: Step Two

to buy one. If you are working on the garden-variety rubber-steel pedal (Fig. 14-3), you can get at the locknut, etc., by removing the rubber-tread locknuts on the crank side and pulling off the entire rubber pedal assembly, after which follow the steps above and below, except the rubber treads should be replaced as above.

STEP THREE: Remove the locknut, to which the pencil points in the photograph. On many pedals an 8-millimeter socket wrench will do the job; for others you will need a 9- or 10-millimeter wrench, or a small adjustable crescent wrench. I prefer wrenches that fit the nuts I am working on (Fig. 14-4).

STEP FOUR: Remove the splined washer (Fig. 14-5).

Fig. 14-3: Left, rattrap style of pedal with toe clip and strap. Right, conventional rubber-tread pedal. Pencil on rubber-tread pedal points to rubber-tread nut which must be removed from each tread so you can get at the bearings for maintenance.

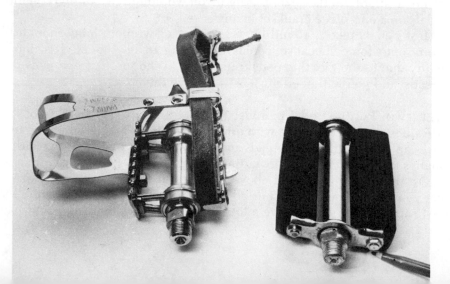

Fig. 14-4: Step Three

Fig. 14-5: Step Four

Fig. 14-6: Step Five

STEP FIVE: Remove the cone nut with a screwdriver. Count the balls so you have the proper number to put back (Fig. 14-6).

STEP SIX: Holding the threaded portion of the pedal axle, loosen the vise and carefully pull the entire pedal out of the vise and hold it over a cloth rag on the bench top. If you are careful, you can remove the axle and leave the bearings in the races, and let them spill out on the cloth (Fig. 14-7).

Fig. 14-7: Step Six

STEP SEVEN: Clean the bearings, races, and axle in kerosene. Remove the toe strap from the toe clip, dunk the pedal body in kerosene, and clean off all road dirt, stuck-on tar, etc.

STEP EIGHT: Check the balls and races for cracks and rust. Replace balls as necessary.

STEP NINE: Put a light layer of grease, such as Lubriplate Type A (from auto supply stores) or Marine Lube grease (from boat stores), on races, and roll bearings around in a dab of grease till they're coated and clump together. Stick bearings back in the crank side of the pedal first. Make sure you have the correct count (see Step Five).

STEP TEN: Insert axle, threaded end first, into the crank side of the pedal; insert the remaining ball bearings in the dust-cap side; screw on the cone nut with a screwdriver until it's snug against the bearings (not tight), and back off about a quarter turn. Push on the splined washer and thread on the locknut. Put the pedal back in the vise, gripping the axle flats on the crank side as in Step One. Tighten the locknut. Remove from the vise and twirl the axle between thumb and forefinger to check for binding. Hold the pedal firmly and push the axle from side to side to check for looseness. If it is binding, loosen the locknut, back off the cone nut an eighth of a turn, retighten the locknut, and check again for binding. Repeat as necessary. If it is too loose so that you have sideplay, loosen the locknut, take up on cone nut an eighth of a turn, retighten the locknut, check again for sideplay, and repeat as necessary.

STEP ELEVEN: Put the pedals back on the cranks. Be careful to get the correct pedal on the correct crank, because the right side is threaded differently from the left, and if you're threading into a softer aluminum alloy crank you can strip threads easily. Also, be sure to thread on straight, using a drop or two of lube oil on threads. Don't get started cross-threaded. Alloy cranks are costly.

Remember that it has been estimated that most of us can easily exert 16 to 30 pounds of pressure on pedals, and if we learn how to lift up with one foot as we press down with the other (requires toe clips and straps) we can add another 25 pounds or so of pressure. If you are "honking" up a hill, you can add even more pressure, and if you are a trained athlete you can go up to 300 pounds.

The pedal is also vulnerable to damage if the bike falls or is knocked over. If your own bike is dumped, always check pedals for a bent spindle. Cranks are easily bent, too. You might also keep in mind that cheaper pedals do not have precision-ground races, so that they will have greater rotational friction, which makes pedaling a bit harder. Even the balls used in these pedals can be inferior.

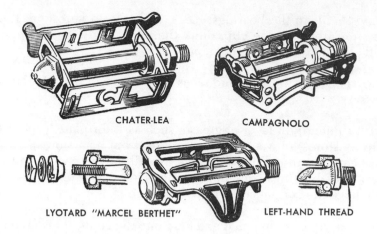

Fig. 14-8: Three types of rattrap pedals. The Chater-Lea at top left is pretty well obsolete. The Campagnolo pedal is a high-quality, popular brand and the Lyotard at bottom center is a platform type you can use with ordinary street shoes and still use toe clips and straps.

ABOUT TOE CLIPS AND STRAPS

Various tests have been made pedaling with and without toe straps and toe clips. As I mentioned in Chapter 2, most of the test results show that with toe clips and straps (Fig. 14-9) you increase pedaling efficiency about 40 percent. My own experience bears this out. But just because you have toe clips and straps, and even cleats (Fig. 14-10) on your shoes (which you must have to achieve this added efficiency) you are by no means guaranteed this improved efficiency. Clips and straps alone, even

Fig. 14-9: This is how the toe strap is threaded into a rattrap pedal with toe clip. Note that the strap adjuster is out-board of the pedal and far enough from clip top so it does not interfere with pe-daling or rub on side of shoes.

Fig. 14-10: Underneath part of shoe, showing leather shoe cleat nailed to bottom, with a tunnel or groove that fits over the shoe plate. Notice also the twist of the strap, which keeps it in place.

with cleats, will do little for you unless you learn to pedal correctly, so that you pull *up* with one foot as you press *down* with the other. We discussed efficient "ankling" in Chapter 2, and I suggest you review those recommendations. All clips, straps and cleats do for you is lock your feet in the pedals so you can exert pedal action pretty nearly around the clock, except of course for the dead spots at 12 o'clock and 6 o'clock. There is a wide variety of shoe cleats on the market. I prefer leather ones because you can more or less walk on them without scratching anybody's floor or making a clanking sound. One problem with shoe cleats is getting them nailed onto bicycling shoes in the right location. The best rule I can give you is that you should cycle *without* them for at least 50 miles, and preferably 100 to 150 miles. This will give you time to find out what location your feet naturally assume on the pedals. There will be a mark on your shoe soles made by the metal plate; this is the toe-to-heel location for the centerline of the tunnel of the shoe cleat. To determine how far inboard the cleat should be, center the cleat on the pedal (have someone hold it there) and place your shoe on the cleat. (Have the bike next to a wall so you can hold yourself up.) The cleat tunnel should be right on the imprint made by the pedal on the sole of your shoe. Let your foot now assume the normal pedaling position, and have your helper then draw a line around the cleat with a white or other visible marker. Now you have the cleat more or less properly located, subject to later change if you find you are uncomfortable with this location of the cleat. Wherever I mention "shoes" I am assuming all along that they are cycling shoes such as those made by Detto Pietro or by some other high-quality supplier of leather cycling shoes.

A better way to position pedals is to use shoes that already come with cleats that are adjustable as to location, but already fastened onto the shoes, such as the new Detto Pietro shoes from Italy. These cleats are adjustable laterally and lengthwise. As to clips, I like the good old Christophe, or the newer Avocet Mod III, the latter of which cost $5.98 a pair and come in three sizes, small, medium and large.

Cleats come with nails, which never hold. I take mine to an Italian shoemaker who seems to understand these things, and I advise you to do the same. Then they will last. And, in the city, leave straps loose so you can get feet out fast. Tighten straps down only in the country, but loosen them if a dog appears.

Basic to this discussion of clips, straps and cleats is the proper size of toe clip. These clips come in small, medium and large lengths, as noted in Chapter 2; and you should get the size that gives you a little space, about ¼ inch at most, between the end of your shoe and the clip. A new pedal comes with an adjustable toe clip. This is the Shimano DuraAce EX Model VA-100. As you can see in Figures 14-11 and 14-12, there are three Phillips screws which, when loosened, permit the clip to move forward or backward. Maximum travel adjustment is 10 millimeters.

These Shimano pedals have precision bearings and do not require a wrench to install. Instead you use a 6-millimeter Allen wrench, which

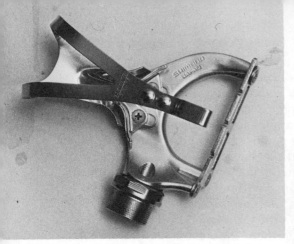

Fig. 14-11: The new Shimano pedal has a built-in toe clip that's adjustable fore and aft.

Fig. 14-12: Close-up of the new Shimano pedal, showing the three Phillips head screws which permit adjustment of the toe clip.

simplifies life considerably. I should note, however, that to use the new Shimano pedals requires that you install a new set of cranks on both sides, because the diameter of the spindle thread is 25 millimeters, versus 14 millimeters for conventional pedals. Chapter 13 compares these two cranks. I have used these pedals and find them quite comfortable. Bearings are sealed but easy to get at for maintenance, with very low friction. Figure 14-13 shows a detailed view.

Fig. 14-13: Detailed drawing of the unique new Shimano pedal, Model VA-100. Parts are: (1) dust cap; (2) cone; (3) 5/32-in. balls; (4) housing; (5) pedal body; (6) washer; (7) lock bolt; (8) side plate; (9) strap guide; (10) screw; (11) toe clip (comes in medium and large sizes); (12) front plate; (13) strap clip; (14) strap band.

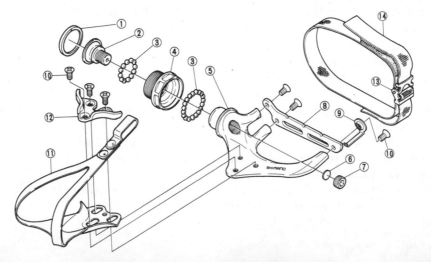

DISASSEMBLING THE NEW SHIMANO PEDAL

Disassembling the new Shimano pedal is a fairly tedious operation; at least I found it so, compared with conventional pedals. However, this pedal does run exceptionally smoothly, and the design has a seal that, although not as tightly fitting as on a conventional precision-sealed bearing, still will keep out a lot of fine, sandy, bearing-wearing stuff, without adding friction drag via the seal fit, so relubing need not be done as often as on conventional pedals. Now, here's how to disassemble the Shimano DD pedals.

STEP ONE: Remove the strap. Remove the toe clips by unscrewing the three Phillips head screws. There is just no way you are going to take this pedal apart conveniently without these steps. Figure 14-14 shows the toe clip removed.

STEP TWO: Remove the pedal from the crank with a 30-millimeter wrench (Fig. 14-14). (You can install the pedal with the Allen wrench, but do not remove it with that wrench.)

STEP THREE: Before I forget, I counted 14 $\frac{5}{32}$-inch (2.5 mm.) balls in the inner cone and 18 in the outer cone. In case you lose one (or two or three). With a 5-millimeter Allen wrench in the locknut (refer to Fig. 14-13) and a 6-millimeter Allen wrench holding the cone (outer side), turn the locknut clockwise and remove it. Catch the tiny spacing washer (part 6 in Fig. 14-13) as the locknut comes out. Don't lose it, your dealer will have a tough time replacing it until Shimano stocks build up on this new pedal. If you do lose it, it will help if you ask for Shimano part number 461 0800.

Fig. 14-14: Removing Shimano pedal from crank

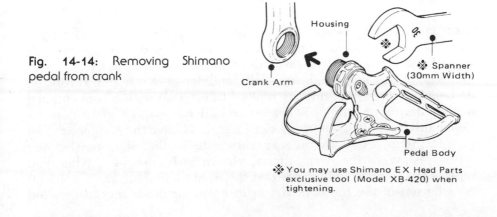

Housing

Crank Arm

❉ Spanner (30mm Width)

Pedal Body

❉ You may use Shimano E X Head Parts exclusive tool (Model XB-420) when tightening.

STEP FOUR: The locknut, part 2 in Figure 14-13, holds the whole she-bang together. Holding the cone with the 6-millimeter Allen wrench, turn the locknut counterclockwise one or two turns, just enough to take pressure off the cone threads (no. 4 in Fig. 14-13). Figure 14-15 illustrates the position of the two Allen wrenches. The locknut is going to be really tight, believe me, so use some muscle on it. You may have to put the 6-millimeter wrench in a vise. Once the locknut is loose, back out on the cone with the 6-millimeter Allen wrench, and the works will come apart (Fig. 14-16). Be ready to catch balls. Clean and regrease.

STEP FIVE: Stick balls back in a layer of grease in the right-side housing, (part 4, Fig. 14-13). Now, you may think you can do the same with the left side of the housing, but you can't because the cone won't go in that way. You have to stick the balls back in a layer of grease on the cone itself and reassemble as follows:

STEP ONE: Refer to Figure 14-13 and to the set of fourteen balls at the left, next to the cone, part 4. These are the balls you have to stick on the cone. Okay, now we have balls inside the housing and on the cone. Fourteen on the cone, eighteen in the housing. Now, holding the pedal body (platform) in one hand (left hand if you are right-handed), put the left-side housing back onto the right-side housing, holding pedal upright with your other hand. Still holding the pedal, take the cone with balls held by grease, and with the flat washer on the end, held with grease, and put it inside the housing (part 4) and gently, by hand, turn the cone clockwise until it is hand tightened. With the Allen wrench (6 mm.) tighten the cone so that it is just snug. Then tighten the locknut. Check for binding or looseness. *Adjustment of the cone does not depend on adjustment of the lockbolt!* Adjust cone to remove binding or looseness, then tighten lockbolt. Shimano recommends tightening it to 55 to 77 feet pounds. No wonder it was so hard to get loose! The lockbolt holds whatever adjustment you have made on the cone. Reinstall toe clip.

STEP TWO: Install the toe strap. Figure 14-23 shows how. The strap should have its Velcro fixing system facing outward. Now, about this strap: I don't like it. There are kinder ways to say this, but I want to get to the point. It's hell to adjust, is stiff, and does not stay put. It rubs on the crank as the crank turns. I replaced this strap with a conventional leather strap with proper adjusting and all was well. I grant that the Velcro theory is nice, but in practice I just don't have the patience to fool with it. Figure 14-10, by the way, shows the leather strap twisted one turn. This avoids the strap "droop" shown in Figure 14-9. When you replace the top clip, remember that the front plate (part 12, Fig. 14-13) goes on top of the toe clip. If you lose one of these special beveled

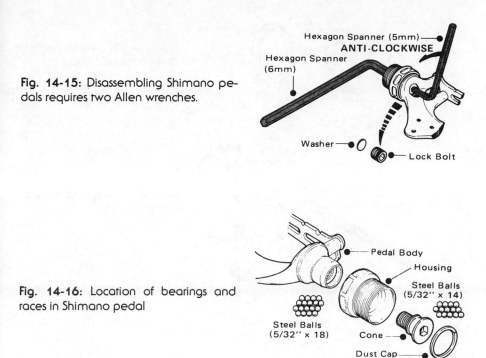

Fig. 14-15: Disassembling Shimano pedals requires two Allen wrenches.

Fig. 14-16: Location of bearings and races in Shimano pedal

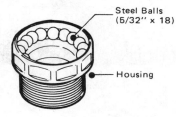

Fig. 14-17: Housing of Shimano pedal goes on inboard side of pedal.

Fig. 14-18: Check housing for binding on Shimano pedal.

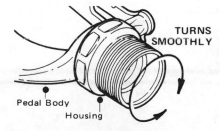

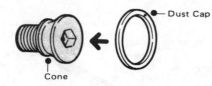

Fig. **14-19**: Installation of outer cone and dust cap.

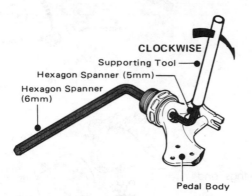

Fig. **14-20**: Adjusting races on Shimano pedal.

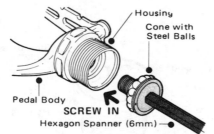

Fig. **14-21**: Installing right-hand (outboard) race requires that balls be held in place by grease on race, so race can be installed in housing.

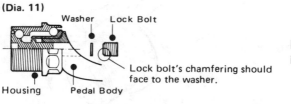

Fig. **14-22**: Installing lockbolt in Shimano pedal

• Strap Use

1. Position the strap as shown in diagram. (Dia. 1)
   Ensure the "velcro" fixing system is facing outwards. (Dia. 2)

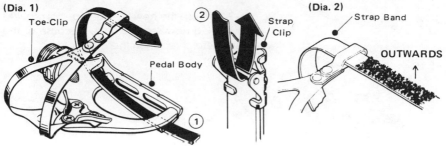

Fig. 14-23: Installation of strap in Shimano pedal

screws, reference to Shimano part number 000 1900 will help your dealer order more. Figures 14-14 to 14-23 illustrate major steps in assembly and disassembly. A final word about bearing adjustment: If you have binding or looseness, you have to back off on the lockbolt before making any adjustments. Then retighten the lockbolt.

Pedal Review

We have already discussed the new Shimano pedal, to some extent. Here is further data. First, consider where your foot goes on the conventional pedal. In Figure 14-9 you can see that the body of the pedal is *above* the spindle. This means that as you pedal and "ankle," your foot is always above the spindle. Now if you look at Figure 14-13 you can see that the body of the Shimano pedal is *below* the spindle, and that your foot on this pedal would be at or near the centerline of the spindle bearings. This location will give smoother pedaling action and ankling, as I discovered when I used this pedal. The *shape* of the DD pedal, the plate (part 8 in Fig. 14-13) is also angled for a better grip if you use shoe cleats. The lower location of the spindle also means that the saddle can be lowered as much as 3 centimeters, according to Shimano. Three centimeters is 300 millimeters, or about 1⅛ inches, which seems like a lot since the pedal is not *that* much lower than the conventional pedal below the spindle. Well, I can see 200 centimeters, though. I did not change my saddle location when I switched to the DD's, and felt okay, so maybe my saddle was a mite low. The bike I was using was new to me and I always ride at least fifteen miles before changing saddle height. I was also using Bata shoes with thicker soles, which I hadn't used in some time, so I believe that made the difference and accounted for the fact that I did not notice the difference in pedal-spindle location. I will say the DD's felt mighty comfortable, just like an old shoe, in fact. Shimano also claims the DD's are aerodynamically more streamlined, but I doubt you could tell the difference at the speed even a racing cyclist

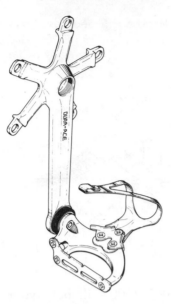

Fig. 14-24: To use the new Shimano pedal requires that you buy a new set of cranks, because of the wider diameter threads on these pedals.

will go. Figure 14-24 shows the Shimano DD pedal on the chainwheel crank. This drawing clearly shows the front plate at an angle, a feature Shimano claims gives more natural and greater pedaling efficiency. It worked for me, at least to the extent that my feet felt a bit more "normal," that is, there seemed to be less strain and a better connection between my feet and the pedal. When it comes to efficiency, I can use all the help I can get.

Here are a few observations about other pedals. If you cycle to work, you may not want to use cleated shoes. With ordinary street shoes the plates on conventional rattrap pedals such as the Campagnolo in the upper right of Figure 14-8 can cause pain. I commute with Lyotard platform pedals, like those at the bottom of Figure 14-8. Phil Wood pedals are also platform design, as you can see in Figure 14-25, but here you will note that the front plate is raised enough so you might have some discomfort with street shoes. Bicycle shoes, remember, at least European bicycle shoes, have a stiffener, usually a steel plate, in the sole, plus sometimes a double-thick sole, which absorbs the concentrated pressure of the plates. Pedal plates are the front and back raised pieces. The front plate is the part that fits in the tunnel of a shoe cleat. Table 14-1 gives prices and weights and specifications on most popular makes and price categories of pedals. As for specifics . . .

Fig. 14-25: Phil Wood sealed-bearing pedals use both ball and roller bearings.

Fig. 14-26: Phil Wood pedal fitted with toe clip and strap. Reflectors are built-in.

Phil Wood Pedals

These pedals take any standard toe clips and straps. The unique design uses both ball and roller bearings for high-load capacity and reliable performance. Bearings are claimed to be permanently lubricated. The platform is of high-strength aluminum alloy, the spindle of heat-treated aircraft-quality steel. Fasteners and other small parts are stainless steel. Spindle threading is $\%_{16}$ x 20 TPI. Reflectors are built-in and standard equipment. I have toured extensively with these pedals, both in the U.S.A. and in Europe and can report sterling results. Riding in heavy rainstorms did not affect these pedals one iota; the seals held and water penetration was, as far as I could tell, nil.

Campagnolo Pedals

Although the bearings are conventional ball and cup, and are not sealed, Campy pedals are very precisely machined and designed, and have withstood the test of time for more years than I care to remember. Road and track pedals come in either plain, or anodized black for ten bucks more. The black model is dural (light alloy), and the plain have steel bodies, hence the extra $10. The Super Record black has a titanium spindle and is superlight (see Table 14-1). All spindles have a knurled section that imparts reverse spin to rotation, helps keep out foreign matter and helps throw off water. (Fig. 14-27, arrow, shows this knurling.) Figure 14-28 shows the road type of pedal, which has a "quill," a raised section that helps keep the shoe from sliding off the side. Figure 14-29 shows a Campy road pedal; Figure 14-30 shows a Campy track pedal, which is narrower and lighter than the road version.

Fig. 14-27: Campagnolo pedal spindle. Arrow points to reverse-thread seal, which helps throw off dirt, dust and, to some extent, water.

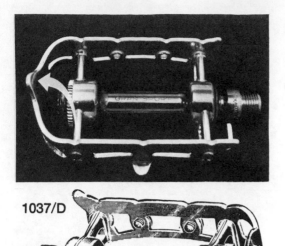

Fig. 14-28: Conventional rattrap pedal; arrow points to quill.

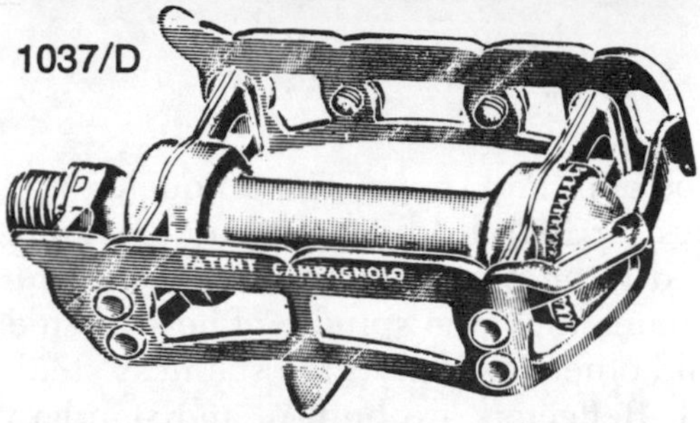

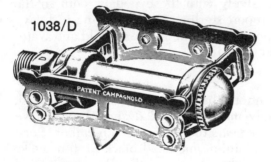

Fig. 14-29: Campagnolo road pedal

Fig. 14-30: Campagnolo track pedal. Note that this pedal is narrower than the road pedal in Figure 14-29.

Lyotard Pedals

Lyotard has been making pedals almost since the bicycle began. The firm is not an innovator, but the basic parts of the pedal are of reasonably high quality and over the years have proved to be reliable. My own feeling is that for the price (see Table 14-3) Lyotard pedals represent the best value for the money of all pedals made. If your bike has inexpensive German or Japanese pedals and they have a lot of wear, I would certainly opt for Lyotard as a replacement. Certainly Lyotard has long since recovered tooling and design costs, thus the low prices today. Type 23 platform design is, as noted earlier, a great pedal if you don't use bike shoes with cleats, although there is a cleat plate.

Hi-E Pedals

Hi-E pedals (Fig. 14-31) preceded the Shimano DD pedals by three or four years, and both are similar in design. Hi-E pedals also lower the rider's shoe and put it in the same plane as the direction of rotation. Hi-E uses just one large single-sealed bearing, and the design of the pedal is such that the foot is lower than on standard pedals by about three-

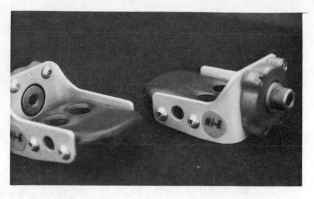

Fig. 14-31: Hi-E sealed-bearing pedals use one large sealed bearing. Note that they are similar in design to the Shimano pedal in that the foot is placed below the centerline of the pedal spindle.

quarters of an inch. This lowered position lowers the center of gravity and increases the effective leverage of the crank. This design also helps keep feet on pedals at the top and bottom of the stroke, an important asset, because the tendency is for the foot to roll over the top when the pedals are at the bottom or top of the stroke. Hi-E bearings are sealed precision design, with balls in a retainer. Unlike with the Phil Wood pedals, you can disassemble the Hi-E pedals. Available from Hi-E, 1247 School Lane, Nashville, Tennessee 37217, or your bike shop.

Cinelli

Cinelli, a premium bicycle manufacturer, 20134 Milano, via egidio folli, 45 Italy, makes a very fine pair of pedals indeed. But to use them you also need their shoes, which are equipped with special cleats. The idea is that the cleats slide into a slot in the pedals. So the shoe is either all the way into the pedal or all the way out. There's no middle ground, so you can't use this pedal-and-cleat combination in the city for casual cycling, because you won't be able to get your feet out quickly. There are no toe clips or straps; the cleat and pedal work as a team. Fine for the racing cyclist but not, in my judgment, for the touring cyclist.

SunTour

The SunTour (Maeda) Superbe pedals, Model PL-1000, come as close as any make to Campagnolo quality. This model is 60 millimeters wide, does not use a sealed bearing but is precision machined throughout and has an alloy body and chrome moly high-quality steel spindle. Unlike some other pedals, you can order Superbe in either English (⁹⁄₁₆ x 20) or French (14 x 1.25) spindle threads. This is a quill type of pedal, designed for the tourist. The track version, PL-3000, does not have a quill and is a bit lighter than the PL-1000 (see Table 14-1). A less expensive model is the Road VX model PL-1500 (Fig. 14-32).

Barelli

An Italian name but an English company, here is yet another platform type of pedal, but not one that gets the foot down to or below the centerline of the crank pedal threads. These pedals have sealed radial bearings that can tolerate any load, and then some, which might be imposed by any human being, or a gorilla, for that matter. The Supreme model has a

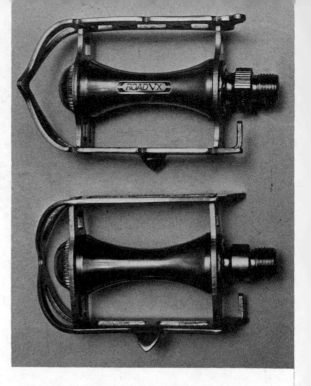

Fig. 14-32: A pair of SunTour Road VX pedals, typical of moderately priced pedals but still well designed.

stainless steel platform and, in another version, an alloy platform. And Model B-10 is like the Cinelli in that it uses a special cleat which fits into a matching fitting on the pedal flat. Platforms are replaceable.

East Rochester Tool and Die

This is an unlikely name for the manufacturer of a very high-quality set of pedals, but it is, in fact, their name. East Rochester Tool and Die makes pedals even Campagnolo could be proud of. Their titanium spindle pedals weigh only 233 grams, and cost about 35 to 40 percent less than the comparable titanium spindle Campagnolo pedals, yet they are every bit as well made, in my opinion. You can buy these pedals directly from the manufacturer, East Rochester Tool & Die Corp., 1841 Ridge Road East, Rochester, New York 14622. The same pedals in 4041 hardened steel alloy spindle, also with alloy body, cost only $60 a pair. Both models use precision-sealed ball bearings with neoprene seals. Visually these pedals resemble Campy pedals. The difference is in the price and in the sealed bearings. Bearings can be field replaced, but the manufacturer requests you send the pedals back so they can check your workmanship . . . or let them do the job.

ALL ABOUT HEADSETS

Like pedals, headsets take a terrific beating. Like pedals, most headsets use small ball bearings, $5/32$ inch, and lots of them, usually 22 or 25 to a set. I think the most important requirement of a headset is that it be properly adjusted. *There should be absolutely no looseness in the head-*

set! To check for looseness, straddle the bike, lock the front brake, grab
the handlebars and move them up and down and back and forth. If the
headset is too loose, you will feel a slight looseness in the handlebars. If
you have down-turned bars, grab them on the drops—the lower part—
and twist that part up and down (not side to side). The reason you can't
have looseness in the headset is that any "play" in the bearings will
quickly flatten the bearings and gall the races, particularly the bottom
set. Take a look at Figure 14-33. Reviewing the nomenclature, in Figure
14-33, parts are: (A) locknut; (B) washer (notice "tang" in the left side of
washer); (C) screwed race; (D) upper pressed race; (E) lower pressed
race; (F) upper bearings; (G) crown race; and (H) lower bearings (interchangeable with upper bearings). If you have "play" in the headset, the
bearings, as noted, will take a terrific beating as you pound over the
road. I might note here that when you disassemble the headset it's a
good idea to replace these bearings anyhow, because they are bound to
be somewhat distorted—if so, it will be difficult to get the silky smooth
adjustment you deserve from a high-quality headset such as the Campagnolo or Shimano DuraAce designs. During the past few years component
manufacturers have begun to furnish headset balls in retainers ("F" and
"G" in Fig. 14-33). If you have an older bike, say, one made around 1973

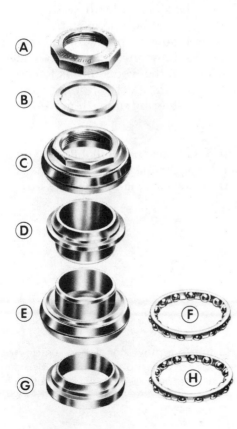

Fig. 14-33: Basic headset parts are: (A)
locknut; (B) tanged washer; (C) screwed
race; (D) top-pressed race; (E) bottom-
pressed race; (F) bearings (in retainer);
(G) crown race; and (H) bearings (in retainer).

Fig. 14-34: Some headsets come with loose balls, which offer greater support than bearings in a cage or retainer. This is how loose bearings should look when inserted back into the screwed race, held in place with grease.

or before, your headset bearings will probably be loose, as in Figure 14-34, which shoes how these bearings should look when packed back in the race.

You really should clean and repack with grease the headset of any bike that has seen much use during the year. Here are the steps:

STEP ONE: Remove the stem (Fig. 14-35). If your stem has a recessed Allen bolt, it will probably take a 6-millimeter Allen wrench. When the bolt is turned enough so that it feels loose, the stem will still be tight in the steering tube, because this is a wedge type of bolt. Loosen the bolt enough to raise it about ¼-inch and then tap it down gently with a plastic mallet to loosen the wedge nut. Figure 14-36 shows the wedge nut (A) at the bottom of the stem. As you tighten the bolt, the wedge nut is forced up into the stem, where it expands the slit in the skirt (B) of the stem and holds it tightly against the inside of the steering tube. Remove the front wheel.

STEP TWO: Remove the headset locknut. Please use a tool that fits so you don't round off the edges. The latest model of Campagnolo locknut takes a 32-millimeter wrench; Shimano has their own special tool (Fig. 14-37) for their new headsets.

Fig. 14-35: To remove handlebars, unscrew binder bolt, at top, tap it down with plastic mallet to unseat wedge nut, pull bars out.

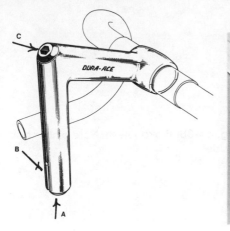

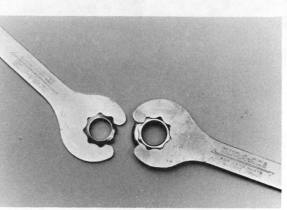

Fig. 14-36: Another version of stem binder bolt, arrow, uses an Allen wrench: (A) points to wedge nut; (B) to stem slit; (C) to binder bolt head.

Fig. 14-37: Shimano requires two special wrenches to remove, reinstall and adjust their new DuraAce headset.

STEP THREE: Remove washer.

STEP FOUR: Remove the screwed cup, pull out the fork, discard the bearings or take them to your bike shop for a new, matching set. Do not replace old bearings, as noted above.

STEP FIVE: Clean and inspect top and bottom races. Look for galled spots, indicated by grooves or roughness. Replace any galled races with same make. In fact, if races are seriously damaged or worn, I would advise you not to try to replace them yourself. It's easy enough to drive the old bottom race out of the steering head tube with a drift, and to knock off the crown race, but replacing them is another matter. They must fit accurately, and there are special tools for this job that are costly and not practical as an investment. Take the fork and bike down to a good bike shop, the kind that specializes in high-priced bikes, and have their mechanic fit on a new headset. You can reassemble the headset yourself, after the races are fitted, of course. Here's how:

STEP SIX: Install new bearings in crown race and on upper pressed race and insert steering head from underneath. Bearings should be well greased with a good-quality lubricant such as Lubriplate.

STEP SEVEN: Screw on the screwed race by hand until tight. Replace washer. Washer tang (protuberance) should fit groove in steering tube. Some washers have a flat instead of a tang and slide over a ground flat on the steering tube.

STEP EIGHT: Screw on the locknut tightly. Turn fork to check for binding. Pull handlebars up and down to check for looseness. If the fork feels tight, or binds, loosen locknut and back off on screwed race about one-

Fig. 14-38: Broken stem. Note binder bolt inside.

quarter turn, tighten locknut and check again. If the fork is too loose, and can be moved up and down by the handlebars, loosen locknut, tighten screwed race one-quarter turn, tighten locknut and check again. Repeat until there is zero play and the fork turns smoothly through 360 degrees.

STEP NINE: Reinstall the stem. Make sure the stem is in the steering tube so that at least two inches of the stem *above the split skirt* are in the steering tube. Newer bikes have stems with a mark that shows how high the stem can be. Never bring the stem up so high that the mark is above the locknut. Some stems have an angle cutoff at the bottom and the wedge nut is cut to a matching angle so that as you tighten the stem bolt, the nut rides up on the stem bottom and wedges between it and the inside of the steering tube. If you bring the stem up too high above the two-inch limit, it can break off. You'd be mighty embarrassed to be barreling up a hill, honking on the bars, pulling the bars as you pedal and have the handlebars suddenly come off in your hands. Not the safest thing that could happen to you. Figure 14-38 shows a stem that did break off. This rider was lucky, I happen to know, because at least the bottom wedge bolt held and he could brake to a stop, although he did lose control and went into a ditch. But he braked as he went so that he was not injured by the impact.

Headset Troubleshooting

If after you have gone through all the bearing adjustments above and still can't get the fork to turn smoothly, here are some suggestions:

Fork Binds
- Too many balls (if loose balls are installed).
- Caged bearings in wrong-side-up. Retainer concave surface faces concave race, and should be vice versa, with concave retainer mating to convex curvature of race.

- Fork could be bent, so that crown race is out of alignment and binds on the lower pressed race.
- Steering tube or head tube could be bent so that they rub on each other or force races out of alignment.
- Headset adjusted properly but binds after handlebar is installed. This is because after tightening, the binder bolt expanding nut forces the stem out very slightly, and minutely alters the fit between bearings and races by "tilting" one side of the steering tube a thousandth or so of an inch. Just loosen the locknut and back off on the screwed race ⅛th turn, retighten locknut and all should be well. But check to make sure, and readjust screwed race as necessary.

Fork too Loose
- If you can't adjust screwed cup to eliminate looseness, check for enough balls in bearing races (if balls are loose, not in retainers). Check also to make sure you are using mated parts that work together.

Headset Selection . . . Notes

The better headsets, such as the Campagnolo and Shimano DuraAce, have precisely mated races that fit very closely. Figure 14-39 shows a bicycle fitted with a Campagnolo headset, and the arrows show that the screwed race plus the upper pressed race, and the lower pressed race and crown race, fit so that the top section fits over the bottom section. That is, the screwed race at the top projects down over the upper pressed race. This type of fit helps keep foreign matter out of the bearings.

Fig. 14-39: Better headsets, such as the Campagnolo installed on this bicycle, have the screwed race and the bottom pressed race overlapping to keep dust and dirt out of bearings.

If you do install your own headset, be aware of the national differences in threads. The English and Japanese steering heads are threaded 1 inch by 24 threads per inch. The French are threaded 24 x 1M and the Italian, 25.4 x 24F. Because the Italian thread diameter of 25.4 millimeters is equal to .999998 inch, and the threads per inch are the same, you might think they are interchangeable with English threads. Well, they are, almost, but I don't recommend forcing the two to mate. Italian threads are cut with a 5-degree pitch difference, from English threads, so the fit won't be accurate and you could have trouble adjusting the screwed race for a smooth fit. Also be aware of the locknut differences. The English will most likely have a 22.2-millimeter locknut; the French, a 22-millimeter locknut. Japanese bikes after 1975 will probably have a .833-inch locknut, which is 21.1582 millimeters and won't fit either the French or English steering head. Check your stem engraving to see if it's marked with a size. The measurements above refer to the I.D. (inside dimension) of the locknut.

Headset Evaluation

Campagnolo headsets still top my list (Fig. 14-40). The Campagnolo Super Record set is in alloy with a satin finish and with steel insert races. Not cheap at $41.98 but definitely a top-quality unit. Campy's conventional all-steel Record road set is also great, and costs $27.98. Both models are available in English, Italian and French threads. Figure 14-41 shows the Record road set; Figure 14-42, the track set, model 1040. Campy headsets for road come with ³⁄₁₆-inch balls; for track, with ⁵⁄₃₂-inch balls, both in retainers.

Shimano Headsets are another high-quality component priced somewhat lower than Campy models. The finish is anodized, with steel inserts in aluminum alloy races (Fig. 14-43). Figure 14-44 shows a detailed view of the DuraAce headset. Remember, the locknut and upper race take a special wrench (Fig. 14-37) shown earlier. You should have two wrenches. You're looking at around $24.50 for the DuraAce headset, $15 for the 600EX.

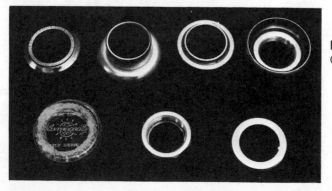

Fig. 14-40: Top-quality Campagnolo headset.

Fig. 14-41: Road type of Campagnolo headset. Parts are: (681) locknut; (682) tanged washer; (683) screwed race; (684) top pressed race; (685) bottom pressed race and (686) crown race.

Fig. 14-42: Campy track headset. Parts are in same sequence as in Figure 14-41.

Fig. 14-43: Shimano DuraAce headset

Fig. 14-44: Shimano DuraAce headset, detailed view. Parts are in same sequence as Figure 14-41, except for bearings.

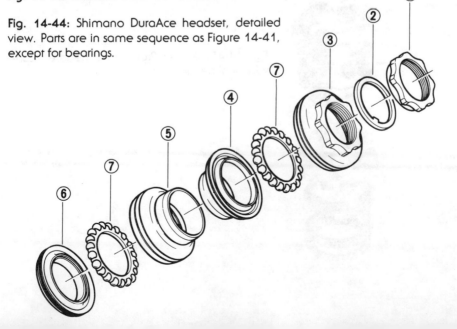

Stronglight headsets are well known, have been proved in use over these many years. The V4 Competition model is available in French and English thread only, costs around $15.

Tange Levin headsets are modeled closely on Campagnolo designs, are chrome-plated steel, come in English thread, have an inside locknut diameter of 22.2 millimeters to fit a wide range of stems, cost around $10.

Avocet makes two headsets. One is a good-quality unit, the Professional, that uses the conventional caged set of bearings and standard precision-ground races. The model is threaded for English, Italian and French threads, weighs 190 grams, costs around $18.90 (Fig. 14-45.)

Another Avocet headset is brand new and as of this writing has not been put on the market. I have been using a test set and can report excellent results. This model (Fig. 14-46) is a sealed-bearing unit that comes with a lifetime guarantee if properly installed. The unit is designed to take the heavy radial and lateral loads on headsets due to road shock, and should never require maintenance, according to Avocet. I have about 250 miles on my sample, which is very little mileage to indicate durability, but a tear-down after this mileage shows the unit to be in the same condition it arrived in—in other words, like brand new. The entire headset, which uses alloy races and sealed bearings, is only 190 grams (6.7 oz.), which makes it one of the lightest on the market.

Fig. 14-45: Avocet Professional headset, conventional design

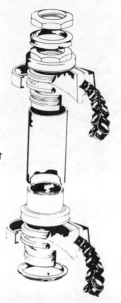

Fig. 14-46: Avocet sealed-bearing headset

To install the new Avocet sealed-bearing headset, you will, of course, have to remove the old one on your current bike. Just follow the steps above as far as getting out the bearings is concerned, and add these steps:

- With a drift (tapered metal bar with a flat end), punch out the upper and lower pressed races.
- Invert the fork and tap off the crown race, moving the drift around as you tap.

To install the Avocet, all you do is push down the small flanged seal (see Fig. 14-46) where the crown race was located, and on top of that press down the bottom-bearing set. The tricky part here is that you must exert pressure *only on the inner part of the bearing* and be careful that whatever tool you are using you don't let it slip and hit the bearing seal, which could ruin it. Ideally you should use a Campy or VAR tool, which bike shops use. In discussing this problem with Avocet I suggested they supply a simple piece of pipe of the right diameter to fit over the steering tube and contact the inner-bearing race of the sealed-bearing set. Then pushing the bearing, which is a light drive fit, down over the steering tube, would be a simple matter. Because steering tubes have an outside diameter of 25.4 millimeters if English, 25 millimeters if French, or 25.4 millimeters if Italian or American, a piece of straight pipe that's a bit bigger, say 1 inch, should do it. Twelve inches of 1-inch inside diameter of any kind of pipe of ferrous metal, say gas pipe, would do just fine. Or, you can buy a crown race seating tool for about $5 (Fig. 14-47) from Phil Wood, made by Bicycle Research Products, which should work fine. That way, you can't hurt the bearing by banging on the outer retainer, the bearings themselves or the seal. The rest of the installation, according to Avocet and my own experience with this headset, simply involves

Fig. 14-47: This crown-race seating tool can also be used to install the Avocet sealed bearing in place of the crown race. The tool costs around $5 from Phil Wood.

putting the rest of the stack in place—the lower and upper pressed fittings and the top bearing on the steering tube, and tightening down on the screwed race to drive fit the lower pieces. This set costs, at the moment, around $49.95, but it could go up, as all prices seem to be doing these days. Tightening down on the locknut completes the installation of this sealed-bearing headset. Now, with sealed hubs, pedals, rear derailleur wheels and this new headset, the only unsealed component on your bike that requires maintenance would be the chain. Well, there is the saddle: If it's leather, it may need help from time to time, and I will get into that later on in this chapter.

SunTour (Maeda) makes a pair of excellent, high-quality headsets—one for track, Model HS-300, and one for road, Model HS-100. The track model is entirely of chrome-plated steel that takes loose balls and weighs 145 grams (5⅛ oz.); the road model is the same basic design but weighs 172 grams (6 oz.).

A Swiss company, *Edouard & Cie, S.A.,* CH-2108 Couvet, Switzerland, has introduced their line of Edco competition headsets in light alloy.

Replace Caged Bearings with Loose Ones

You can add two more balls to the races at each end if you discard the caged set and use just loose balls. The extra balls add considerably greater shock resistance than the fewer balls in the caged set. Just be careful to use balls of the same size as in the caged set (retainer). With loose balls your headset will last a lot longer.

More About Cone Fit

Although poor fit of the crown cone seems to be a plague of the less expensive bike, it should not be ruled out as a cause of steering assembly looseness, or tightness in a better bike either. Seating of the crown race is extremely critical, and if it's too loose, you can have a case of the "shakes" on a downhill run—the handlebars develop an uncontrollable "shimmy" that gets worse by the millisecond and will cause you to spill if you don't stop immediately. This type of front-wheel wobble can also be caused by loose front-wheel bearings and/or a bent fork. But the cone race must be seated very precisely in order to align the rest of the steering races and bearings. This race must seat perfectly square in the steeering tube, and the lower and upper pressed races must also be exactly square with their mating crown race. It's easy to drive off the old parts, but darned difficult, without experience and costly shop tools, to get new parts in just exactly right. If you remove the fork and look at the races, you may find, particularly when caged bearings in a retainer are used, a series of symmetrically spaced dents in the raceways, corresponding to bearing location. If you see this condition, you must scrap the headset entirely, and chalk the cost of a new headset up to experience and to the certain knowledge that you will henceforth keep the headset properly adjusted. Or switch to the Avocet sealed set. The dented race term, if you should speak to an engineer about this, is "brinell" or "brinelling," which is a sort of peened effect you would get if you pounded a flat piece of steel plate with the rounded edge of a ball peen hammer.

As you check headset bearing raceways, I advise you to use a good magnifying glass, such as a jeweler's loup, and look for tiny, hairline cracks and for grooves cut into the raceways, either of which is cause for scrapping the headset. Remember, the road shock forces that impact on these small bearings can be on the order of thousands of pounds. On any day trip, if loose, the headset can receive a great many thousands of such blows, spread out among the bearings that absorb them. If the headset is adjusted for zero end play, the shock will be minimized.

ABOUT STEMS

The stem is that "L"-shaped component, one leg of which goes into the steering tube, the other end of which holds the handlebars.

Stems come in a variety of lengths to suit different body, arm and torso sizes. I won't repeat how to select the correct length stem for your body dimensions, or the sizes available, because I have already covered this subject in Chapter 2. I do want to review some of the newer stem designs, just briefly, in case you are thinking of changing to a different stem.

The cheaper stems have bolts with protruding bolt heads that usually take a 10-millimeter wrench; and the market has been flooded in recent years with inexpensive imitations of high-quality European stems with recessed Allen bolts. So the mere presence of an Allen bolt does not necessarily guarantee that the stem is a high-quality, strong forged alloy one. Some cheaper stems are made of steel and are, of course, a lot

Fig. 14-48: Cinelli stem. Note the location of binder bolt at handlebar end.

Fig. 14-49: Cinelli stem, showing binder-bolt wedge that fits into stem head.

heavier than alloy stems. The relatively new *Cinelli road stem,* Model 1/Record (Fig. 14-48) has a hidden expanding binder bolt arrangement that grips the handlebars via an internal expansion sleeve (Fig. 14-48). Figure 14-49 is a front view of this stem. Note the slotted skirt, bottom. Both the hidden and the top binder bolts take a 6-millimeter Allen wrench. This stem comes in lengths of 10, 11, 12, 13 and 14 centimeters (smaller sizes not available because the internal expansion sleeve would interfere). To find inches, multiply the centimeter figure by the conversion factor .3937. Figure 14-50 shows a cross-section drawing of this stem. This stem weighs 287 grams in the 10-centimeter size, slightly more in longer sizes, and costs $29.50. The 1/Record comes in a 22-millimeter diameter, which will fit steering tubes with a 22-millimeter inside diameter.

Fig. 14-50: Cross section of Cinelli stem. Left drawing shows binder bolt loose, and internal expanding wedge drawn back from handlebar. Right drawing shows binder bolt tight, expanding wedge firmly tight against handlebar.

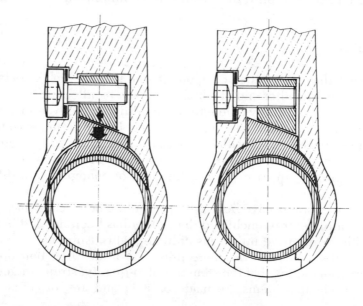

Before you order any stem, you should measure the inside diameter of your steering tube. Most English and Italian bikes take a 22.2-millimeter stem, French bikes a 21.9-millimeter stem and Japanese bikes a 21.15-millimeter stem. The difference between the 22.2- and 21.15-millimeter stems is 1.05 millimeters, which is about ⅟₁₆th of an inch, which is just too much slop to deal with for the tightly fitting stem you should have. After all, you don't want suddenly to wrench the handlebar one way and to find the bike does not respond though the bars turn. The difference of .2 millimeters between 22 and 22.2 millimeters is only around 8 thousandths of an inch, so the 22-millimeter stem would probably work in a 22.2 millimeter but not the other way around. I prefer a stem that fits exactly. Cinelli road stems model 1/A are in 22.2-centimeter widths and in lengths from 7 to 13 centimeters in half-centimeter increments and in lengths of 13 and 14 centimeters, and in the 22-millimeter French diameter in one-centimeter increments from 7- to 14-centimeter lengths. Both are $19.50; and the 10-centimeter size weighs 300 grams.

The SR Extra Super Light Stem. If you are a weight freak (like me) you will like this stem. It uses a titanium binder bolt and expander nut and is, in addition, bored out internally to arrive at a 210-gram weight in the 10-centimer size. It has a 22.2-millimeter diameter in lengths of 7, 9, 11 and 13 centimeters. Not an especially wide choice of lengths, but if one of these sizes fits you and you want lightness with some sacrifice of strength, it's yours for around $29.98.

Another SR Stem, the Super Light, weighs 300 grams in the 10-centimeter size, comes in the 22.2-millimeter diameter and in lengths of 7, 9, 11 and 12 centimeters for $16.98.

Shimano makes a stem (Fig. 14-36) that is virtually a duplicate of the Cinelli 1/Record, also with hidden binder bolt and internal expansion sleeve. This unit is so new, as of this writing, that I have not had a chance to check it out; but it it's up to Shimano's DuraAce quality, the new DuraAce Handle stem should rank somewhere near the Cinelli clone.

Figure 14-51 shows an Allen head stem, with external wedge nut at right, and a stem with standard binder bolt and internal expanding bolt, right.

A unique stem, recently introduced, can permit you to move your handlebars up or down a few inches, and to bring them a bit closer to you, or farther away. This "universal" device fits into 21-millimeter ID steering tubes, and accepts 21-millimeter stems. In other words, this adapter requires use of your old stem, and fits into the steering tube. It's pretty heavy, though—weighs about 16.5 ounces (on my scales, or 468 grams). Add the 300 or so grams of your standard stem and you have a combination that weighs 768 grams or 27.08 ounces. That's a lot of extra weight, but if you have an orthopedic problem, say, a bad back that

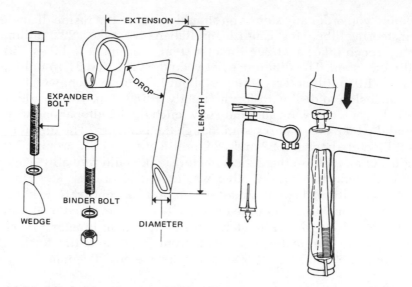

Fig. 14-51: Left, parts of high-quality stem. Right, lower-quality stem has standard bolt head. Stem at left uses external wedge on expander bolt; at right, this stem uses internal wedge.

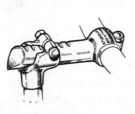

Fig. 14-52: Stems come in a wide range of sizes to suit varying arm and torso lengths. Stem at left is adjustable. The smaller the bike frame, the shorter the stem usually.

requires alternating handlebar settings, this unit could work for you. I don't have a price, but it looks as though it should sell for around $10. It's cast alloy, rather roughly finished, made by Bel-Mar Corporation, Madison, Wisconsin. Should be available through your bike store.

A SOFT SADDLE IS GOOD TO FIND

Sooner or later, as you gain experience in bicycling, you will most likely find yourself, after a hard day's ride, with a sore bottom. If you're a woman, the chances are better than even that you will wind up with such a problem. Before we offer any solutions, let's first take a look at types of seats—or saddles—on the market.

What kinds of saddles are there and what should you know about them? Well, before the bike boom of the early 1970s most bikes sold to adults in America had saddles that I can only classify as awful, horrible and terrible. They were (and still are on some bikes) heavy, so wide the inside of your thighs scraped on them (Fig. 14-53) and with so many springs and so much foam rubber that a substantial percentage of your pedaling action went into depressing the mattress of a saddle instead of turning the cranks and the wheels of the bike. The saddle in Figure 14-53 is fine if all you do is coast downhill, but for an active sport this saddle is just plain awful. Stronger words come to mind, but this is a family book, after all.

The spring saddle in Figure 14-54, at the left, begins to approach the

Fig. 14-53: This saddle is too wide for comfort; the inner thighs scrape on it and it is very heavy. Great for downhill coasting.

Fig. 14-54: Standard saddle types: left, spring type; center, narrow touring design; right, narrower road-racing type.

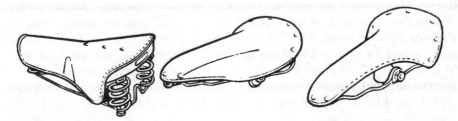

Fig. 14-55: Spring-type saddles use up energy that should go into pedals.

Fig. 14-56: Coil-spring saddle also absorbs pedal power.

Fig. 14-57: Combination spring and "mattress" saddle is another energy stealer.

narrower configuration that lets the muscles of the thigh ripple into action without scraping the saddle, but the springs, again, absorb pedal action and so, again, this type of saddle has to go. There is a similar saddle, euphemistically called a "mattress" saddle, that has longitudinal, lengthwise springs running fore and aft, instead of coil springs. The theory here is that the springs are springier than a coil-spring saddle, so the mattress design will conform to the shape of . . . you. So will Jello. But you don't want to ride on a saddle of Jello—you lose contact with the road, and you wind up pumping a lot of energy into the Jello instead of into the wheels. For some real Jello types of saddles, take a look at Figures 14-55 through 14-57. The saddle in Figure 14-55 is a real springer; the one in Figure 14-56 has heavier springs at the rear; and the one in Figure 14-57 combines the mattress with the coil springs. Can't you just *see* and *feel* yourself bouncing jauntily down the street, while others with honest bike saddles career by you? The saddle on the bike being

Fig. 14-58: A saddle is a saddle, whether on a horse or a bicycle. At least the horse's saddle does not have springs, although there are times when on a horse I think it would have helped.

held by the equestrienne in Figure 14-58 is not only a spring version but is tilted at an angle guaranteed to cause pain. I include this photo, though, to emphasize the action aspect of the word "saddle," a better one of which, suited for the purpose, is on the horse. One more chamber-of-horrors kind of saddle is the "banana" design (Fig. 14-59), on so many children's bikes. This design at least has the virtue of narrowness, but it's hard as a rock, will never break in and furthermore invites the addition of a passenger. This bicycle is further cursed by the embellishment of "high rise" handlebars which put the child's arms in an unnatural posture and which thereby contribute to imprecise steering and balance.

So now we come to the definition of a real working saddle for the bicyclist. A reasonable approximation of such a saddle is in Figure 14-60. This is a Brooks Professional top-grain all-leather saddle on a Schwinn Paramount road bike—one of the finest saddles ever made. It

Fig. 14-59: Banana saddles tempt children to ride "two-up" which is hazardous. The high-rise handlebars also make steering difficult and so also can be dangerous.

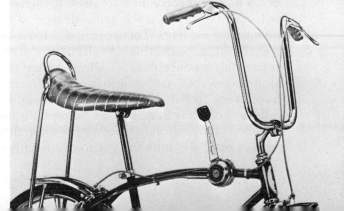

Fig. 14-60: A fine all-leather Brooks Professional saddle

is also one of the most butt-wearying saddles you can buy, until it is broken in; but once shaped to fit you, it is comfort supreme. Efforts to break in these saddles range from beating them to death every day for a couple of months with a baseball bat, after overnight soaking each night in an oil such as neat's-foot, to an automatic saddle beater which pounds them into resilient submission. I recently gave such a saddle to a friend who has been beating on it for ten days and it still looks up at him with as hard a face as it came with.

My own Brooks Pro has seen about 50,000 miles and I would not part with it for anything short of its weight in gold . . . and that was when gold was $25 an ounce. Now, I'm not so sure. Seriously, though, this saddle of mine has a kind of cockeyed, perhaps crooked, appearance, because due to a childhood football injury to my knee (I went to a Catholic grade school and I think we tended to take our guilt out on the football field) I pump harder with the left leg than the right. Also this saddle has been on five bikes now and has traveled extensively upside down on my bike carrier, where the saddle was free to bump up and down all day on the carrier wood, being transported upside down. The saddle is extremely comfortable, so much so that I would propose a variation of the old saw to read: "It fits him like an old saddle."

So top-grade all-leather saddles will break in, eventually, and when they do they are really great. The two top-grade Brooks saddles and the Ideale (French) top-line saddle are the best you can buy of the old-fashioned, all-leather genre. You can buy expensive saddles made of plastic or nylon, but with few exceptions, this kind of saddle will *never* break in, never accommodate itself to the configuration of your posterior, will always give you the same degree of comfort as the day you first mounted it . . . hard. These saddles I leave to the racing fraternity, who want nothing, but nothing, to absorb pedal torque but the wheels. These super athletes have muscles where I have cheeky cushions, so bouncing around on a rock-hard saddle is something they can absorb. Well, I really have found that if, due to bad weather and my disinclination to ride the rollers at times, I have laid off riding for a month or two, the supportive muscles in my rear end offer more spring than support, and I tend to hit bottom until the muscles get tougher with use, from cycling. So don't condemn a fine saddle to the scrap pile until you have broken it in or until you have some muscles down there instead of flab to absorb road shock.

A Hard Saddle is Bad to Find

From 1971 through 1979 I estimate, with the help of industry statistics, that some 96 million bicycles were bought by the American public. Of these I would say at *least* five million were reasonably good bicycles— at 7 on a scale of 0 to 10 in quality. That's five million bottoms bouncing up and down on serious long-distance cycle camping and touring. It's no wonder, then, that the medical profession has, for the first time in the history of bicycling, taken a long, serious look at the nether end of the body and the saddle it sits on.

You will find, for example, cheap leather saddles that have caved in on the sides, like the cheeks of toothless cadavers. Sometimes all that's left of the saddle is a narrow hump on top, an instrument of pain more appropriate to a medieval torture chamber. And you will see nylon saddles tilted up to hurt where it counts. A lot of people have complained about aching crotches, sore bottons, and some of us suspect (I use the word "us" editorially, because I am not a doctor) that some saddle designs contribute to prostate problems, or at least exacerbate them.

Women have a special problem. Even the most comfortable (to men), the most thoroughly broken-in conventional high-grade all-leather saddles can give a woman problems. The reason is that a woman has a bottom (and here I must choose my words with some exactitude, if not care) that's about one inch wider between the hip bones (medically, between the ischial tuberosities). Conventional saddles are too narrow to support this wider bottom, and the hip bones of women tend to ride or land closer to the metal brackets or supports of the saddle, not a location conducive to comfort. Even most slim-hipped women can find the ordinary saddle just too narrow for comfort. Women are also longer in the crotch, and therefore tend to come in uncomfortable contact with the nose of the saddle. Tipping the saddle downward a few degrees helps because it throws more weight on the wider rear part of the saddle, and forces the woman rider to absorb more weight and therefore more road shock with her arms. This is how I have my saddle adjusted, and it works fine for me, so forward tilt is good for men, too.

Sometimes a leather, or even a plastic, saddle will stretch and so become swaybacked, and the saddle will have a lot of bounce, sometimes so much that you will hit the saddle supports. In that case, the better saddles have an adjustment in the nose bolt that takes out this stretch. Figure 14-61, arrow, shows the stretch adjustment on my well-broken-in Brooks Pro saddle. The other arrow shows the saddle-tilt adjustment.

One other disadvantage of nylon shell saddles is that they don't "breathe." On a hot day your own body moisture can cause you to slide around on these saddles, even if they are padded. Lambertini makes a

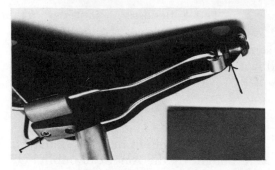

Fig. 14-61: Better saddles have a stretch adjustment, arrow.

padded leather saddle, but the underneath is still a nylon molding that does not break in. Cinelli's best, the Buffalo model, is still basically a nylon shell covered with water-buffalo hide that sells for around $35. The Brooks Professional saddle is around the same price and is all leather. A similar saddle, the Ideale 90TB, is around $35 also and is all leather and is claimed to be "preconditioned," whatever that means. It still requires a thousand-mile break-in period, like all fine leather saddles.

A New Approach to Saddle Design

As I said, my favorite is my broken-in Brooks leather saddle. But I'm also interested in a new approach to saddle design, based on anatomical principles (in this case hindsight is better than foresight), which offers a good compromise between the comfort of a broken-in leather saddle and the inconvenience of having to spend time breaking in a new saddle. I refer to the new line of Avocet saddles. This saddle is basically a nylon shell, but it is a shell with a difference. First, thickness varies throughout, so that the nylon shell is thinner and so more resilient in the rear areas where the pelvic bones rest. For women, the saddle is also thinner and lowered up front to permit extra padding in that area, plus being wider in the rear area with anatomically correct location of support padded bumps. All saddles are leather covered.

As you can see when comparing an Avocet man's saddle (Fig. 14-62) with an Avocet woman's saddle (Fig. 14-63), the woman's model is

Fig. 14-62: An orthopedic approach to saddle design, this Avocet men's saddle offers excellent support and comfort.

Fig. 14-63: Women's version of the Avocet saddle is wider and a bit shorter to conform to female anatomy.

wider. Avocet saddles are really quite comfortable; I've used them. My female test riders, who substituted the women's Avocet saddle for the nylon saddle that came with their bikes, report a vast improvement in support and comfort. The Touring I costs around $19 and has a softer shell with more padding, so it may be better for distance touring. The Touring II costs $27, has a better-quality shell and is a bit firmer but still comfortable. I can recommend it for the distance tourist who knows how to ride the bumps by getting up off the saddle and taking the shock with feet, legs and arms (which you should learn to do with *any* saddle because it's easier on you and distributes the shock more evenly between wheels). The men's Touring III model can be used for touring and racing, is lighter and costs $38. The Touring WI women's saddle costs $20; a better version, the Touring WII, costs $28.

Saddle Frame Considerations

If you have an older bicycle, I suggest, before buying a new saddle, that you check the width of your seat-post mounting, whether that seat post is the more deluxe design (Fig. 14-64) or the el cheapo in Figure 14-65, the clamp type. Most saddles these days come with the wire frame about 48 millimeters as measured on the outside of the frame members, and so most seat posts, such as the one in Figure 14-64, will accommodate this width. But if you have an older bike, say one made around 1974 or earlier, better check the width of the seat-post clamp to make sure a new saddle will fit it. And vice versa with a new saddle.

A different approach to saddle comfort is the "Bummer," a wide leather affair fastened to a pivoting cradle slung between what looks like a small handlebar that fastens in the seat tube. I haven't tried a Bummer due to lack of time, but a proctologist friend of mine has one and says he

Fig. 14-64: Measure a new seat post where shown to make sure a new saddle cradle will fit it. Most saddles today have 48-millimeter wide cradles, or close to that dimension. This is an Avocet seat post.

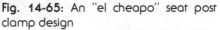

Fig. 14-65: An "el cheapo" seat post clamp design

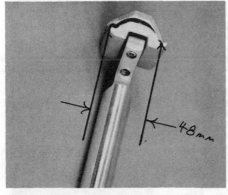

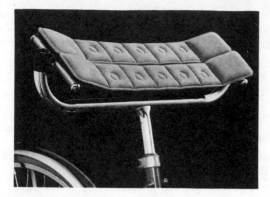

Fig. 14-66: The "Bummer" saddle also tilts

likes it. Figure 14-66 shows a close-up of a Bummer, which is 17 inches wide, made of nylon safety seat webbing and covered with suede-finished Naugahyde. The manufacturer says "the patented action permits it to move and flex with each stroke of the leg while cradling you across the full width of your bottom." On my scale, the whole rig weighs almost 2¾ pounds, but that would include the seat post as well. Still, a Brooks Pro saddle with Campagnolo Super Record fluted seat post together weigh 1.67 pounds, which is a lot less than the Bummer. What weight comfort? And the Bummer costs around $25, from HMC Products, 56849 Grand River Road, New Hudson, Michigan 48165. Figure 14-67 shows a nice Bummer. The seat post of the Bummer is only 21 millimeters in diameter, so you will need to order a bushing, supplied

Fig. 14-67: Another view of the "Bummer"

Fig. 14-68: Procover can be laced over saddle to absorb moisture, soften ride.

with the unit; you will need to give the diameter (I.D.) of your seat tube, or old seat post, to get the right size bushing to fit your seat tube.

Other approaches: If you don't want to turn in your old saddle, you can buy a seat cover such as the Procover, which you tie on the saddle, made from a double-wall fabric (Fig. 14-68). It costs $9.95 from Comfort Products, Inc., P.O. Box 9200, Aspen, Colorado 81611. Softer tie-on covers are made by Grab-on Products, and should be available from your local bike store.

SEAT-POST SELECTION

First, the mechanics of seat-post sizing. There's an incredible array of tubing used by bike manufacturers worldwide. The inside diameter can range anywhere between 26.2 and 27.2 millimeters, in 2-millimeter increments. If you try to stuff a 26.8-millimeter seat post down the throat of a 26.4 or 26.2 millimeter seat tube, you will have nothing but trouble. You'll get it down maybe one inch, just past the seat-tube binder-bolt slot, and then the post will jam and you won't be able to back it out without cutting it in pieces with a special hacksaw—a tedious process, indeed. Not to mention the possibility of cutting into the seat tube itself. *So don't guess*, especially if you order by mail. Know the inside diameter of your seat tube by measuring it. Sometimes you will find the seat-post diameter stamped on the post, and if you are changing posts and your old one fits, that's the new size to order.

If your bike was made in England, chances are the seat tube will be 27, 27.2, 26.2 or 26.8 millimeters. If the bike is from Italy, the seat tube I.D. can be 26.2, 26.8, 27 or 27.2. If from France, the seat tube will most likely be either 26.2, 26.6, 26.8 or 26.4. Good luck and measure accurately! See the metric conversion table to get to inches, in the Appendix.

Until fairly recently, the best seat posts were made by Campagnolo, and even these seat posts were a real nuisance to adjust, even though the adjustments were micro-tilt. The reason? You had to reach up under the saddle (Fig. 14-69) and with a 10-millimeter wrench adjust the fore

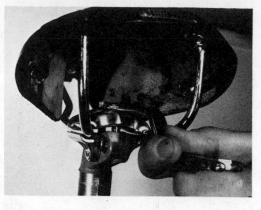

Fig. 14-69: On older model Campagnolo seat-post binder bolts microadjustments are hard to make because bolts are located under the saddle.

and aft bolts to put the saddle at the distance desired from the handlebars and the saddle at the tilt you wanted. Figure 14-70 shows another view of this adjustment. The bolts were very hard to reach, and if you had a tough leather saddle, pushing the side of the saddle away was not easy. Today Campagnolo has come out with a beautiful fluted seat post with an Allen binder bolt you can easily reach from under the seat-post mounting bracket (Fig. 14-71), which weighs only 8½ ounces (241 grams) versus 11.5 ounces (326 grams) for the old version (Fig. 14-69). As Figure 14-71 shows, the tilt and lock binder bolt is readily accessible, with a 13-millimeter wrench. One reason, fluting and bracket aside, for the lighter weight is the thinner gauge of the post tube, as shown in Figure 14-72. The old post is on the left. The new Campy post costs around $37, comes in 25, 25.8 through 27.4 millimeters in .2-millimeter increments and is 180 millimeters long.

Zeus makes an elegant seat post, model 51, (Fig. 14-73), which weighs 280 grams; and their model 52, very much like the older Campy post (Fig. 14-74), weighs 310 grams. Prices are not available on Zeus equipment.

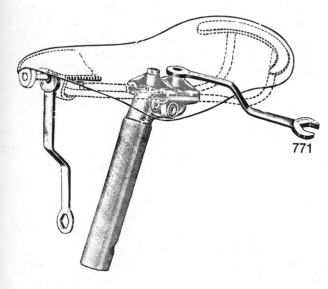

Fig. 14-70: Campy seat-post micro-tilt adjuster bolts, another view. Note saddle stretch bolt in nose of saddle.

771

Fig. 14-71: New Campagnolo Super Record seat-post tilt can be adjusted with a conveniently located, easy-to-reach adjustment bolt under the seat-post head, arrow.

Fig. 14-72: Old Campy seat post tube, left, is thicker walled, heavier. New Super Record seat post is thinner, lighter, as shown at right.

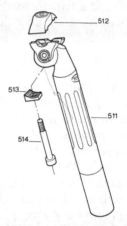

Fig. 14-73: Zeus Model 51 fluted seat post has adjustment from underneath.

Fig. 14-74: This Zeus Model 52 seat post is a clone, almost, of the old model Campy seat post. Adjustment is made from under the saddle, which is a more difficult place to reach than under the seat-post head as in Figure 14-73.

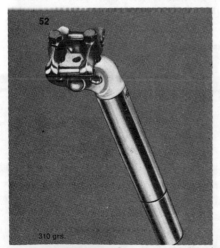

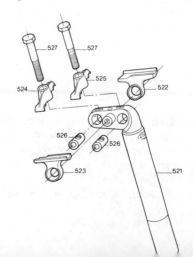

Fig. 14-75: Sketch of new Shimano DuraAce fluted seat post. Adjustment is from underneath seat-post head, with an Allen adjust bolt.

Avocet has a handsome seat post that can also be reached under the mounting bracket with an Allen wrench, which is more convenient than a conventional wrench, and lighter so it's more practical to take the wrench on a trip to readjust the seat angle just the way you want it. Comes in 25, 25.4, 25.8 through 27.4 millimeters in .2-millimeter increments. It costs $21.95, weighs around 235 grams and is 180 millimeters long.

At this writing, Shimano is about ready to introduce *their* version of the under bracket binder-bolt adjustment seat post (Fig. 14-75). I am reasonably sure this simple sketch by no means does justice to the quality and finish of the new Shimano effort at producing a high-grade seat post. No price available.

SunTour also makes a fine seat post, their model SP-1000 Superbe, weighs only 230 grams, and has the added safety factor of 200 millimeters length. Diameter lengths are limited to 26.8 millimeters, which they claim will fit a 27-millimeter seat tube, which is okay, I am sure. But you can't go the other way, as I noted earlier, and fit a 27-millimeter seat post into a 26.8-millimeter seat tube. The post is also available in a 27.2-millimeter diameter. No price available, but it should be competitive with Avocet and Shimano.

Let me emphasize something I have said before: *You must have at least 2½ inches of the seat post (Fig. 14-76) inside the seat tube!* Otherwise the seat tube can break off under the stress of riding, and you could be hurt.

Fig. 14-76: **Always** leave at least 2½ inches of the seat post inside the seat tube, for safety. If you have to get the seat post up higher, you need a bike with a bigger frame. You could also buy a longer seat post, say 200 millimeters.

Table 14-2 Standard Seat-Post Diameters

Metric	Inches (decimal)	Inches Fraction (approx.)
25	.98437	63⁄64
25.8	1.01562	1 1⁄64
26	1.03125	1 1⁄32
26.2	1.03911	1 1⁄32
26.4	1.04687	1 3⁄64
26.6	1.05473	1 3⁄64
26.8	1.06250	1 1⁄16
27	1.07036	1 1⁄16
27.2	1.07812	1 5⁄64
27.4	1.08598	1 5⁄64

One final seat post. That's the Gipiemmi, which goes from 25 to 27.2 millimeters and is 180 millimeters long. This is a handsome seat post also adjusted from underneath. If you need a seat post, I suggest you check your dealer to see if he has a Gipiemmi. It might just appeal to you. Now, about those handlebars.

CHOOSING HANDLEBARS

There are many configurations of handlebars and design, and they all have their devotees. For example, many tourists swear by Randonneur shaped handlebars (left, Fig. 14-77), which have a slight upward bend toward the sides. The theory is that the upsweep gives you more places to put your hands, which varies the pressure points on the hands. During the course of a long day's cycle, the ulnar nerve, which is somewhere in the middle of the palm of your hand, can hurt, a lot, if pressure is constant on it. If you can move your hand around so as to relieve the pressure at one point on the ulnar nerve, you will have a lot less pain and, in fact, little or none if you shift hands around. There are old, experienced cyclists who would never tour on anything but Randonneurs. For me, I prefer the flatter bar because I find the rise at the ends somehow contorts my shoulders, and I just don't like the shifting effect on my skeleton and

Fig. 14-77: Three basic handlebar shapes: at left, a Randonneur bar with the top bar rising slightly at the outer section, favored by touring cyclists; center, the more conventional dropped bar with flat top tube; and right, track bars with more area for that bent over, streamlined position and a bigger drop.

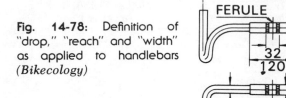

Fig. 14-78: Definition of "drop," "reach" and "width" as applied to handlebars (*Bikecology*)

muscles, such as they are, of the Randonneur. I would never suggest you not try a Randonneur, however, particularly if you have pain in the palm of your hands as you ride. For you, Randonneur design bars could be the answer. We are all built so differently, with such widely varying bone structures, that I hesitate to offer steel engraved recommendations about handlebars. Going on from the Randonneur, we have the bars with flat tops, the various trade names meaning little because they all come out pretty much the same. I really see little difference other than drop and reach and width, between makes of the same basic design. This may be heresy, but so be it. Then we have the track handlebars, such as the one at the right of Figure 14-77 with radical sweeping bend from the stem to the drops. Definitely not for touring, track bars have a long "reach" (see Fig. 14-78 for a description of "reach," "width" and "drop"). How radical the bend of the track bar is is a function of the track racer's fancy, or need. Bikecology, in their catalog, show a track bar with a very radical bend, with just about two inches of flat on either side of the ferrule. The ferrule is the thicker flat part in the center of the top of the handlebar (Fig. 14-78). Figure 14-79 shows a variety of bends, all pretty much the

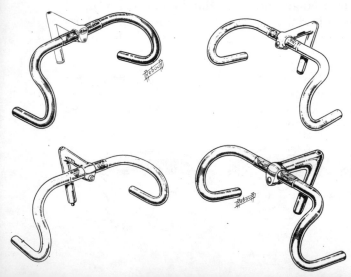

Fig. 14-79: All these bars have fancy European names but they really are all alike except for the reach, width and drop. For example, the bar at upper right has much less drop and reach than the bar at lower left.

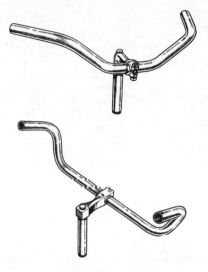

Fig. 14-80: Top, gently rising bars and, below, a more extreme version, tend to force you to sit up straighter than downturned bars. The upright position compresses spinal segments and is harder on the back when you hit bumps. Downturned bars let you bend over a bit to expand cartilage between spinal segments, which can then act as a shock absorber. Also, bent-over position lets you absorb more road shock with your arms.

same, except for variances in the reach, width and drop. Figure 14-80 shows two types of more or less flat bars, which I would hope you would not use. We need the downturned bars to throw more weight forward and to stretch the spine, to absorb road shock, and to let you bend forward a little bit to ease wind resistance. The sit-up-straight school is hell on the spine, because road shock travels straight up from the saddle. Also the downturned bars let you use your arms and shoulder and chest muscles to transmit torque to the pedals, along with legs. On steep hills you can literally almost pull yourself along by grabbing farther down on the drops of the bars and "honking" up hill. So whether you call conventional downturned bars Campione Del Mondo, Giro d'Italia, Maes, or whatever, these fancy, racy European names are nothing more than the manufacturers' designations for the same bar but with different width, drop and reach. Unless, of course, you're talking about track bars, which are another design entirely.

Now, you quite properly ask, what reach, drop and width bars should I use? The width should be about the same width as the width of your shoulders, so that if you have shoulders 15 inches across (38.1 cm.) you should use handlebars with about that width. The better handlebars come in widths from 38 to 40 centimeters, and the model 66 Cinelli comes in a 42-centimeter width. (The conversion factor to translate centimeters to inches is .3937; and to convert inches to centimeters multiply by 2.54.)

If you have big hands you need a longer reach and possibly a deeper drop. If you have long arms you will need a longer reach, particularly if you like to ride on the drops. Most touring cyclists seldom seem to use the drops anyway (the bottom part of the handlebar) except perhaps going downhill when you need to steady the bike steering. You also need a greater drop if you have a wide hand. I realize you can't buy a lot

Table 14-3 Compatability Table

Stem	Bar	Fits
ttt	ttt (all)	Good
	Cinelli	Good
SR	SR (all)	Good
Cinelli	ttt (all)	Good
	Cinelli	Good
	SR (all)	Good
SR	ttt (all)	No
	Cinelli	No
	SR Randonneur	Good
Gran Compe	ttt (all)	No
	Cinelli	No
	SR Randonneur	OK

of handlebars to determine which one you should have—thus these general guidelines, which will at least steer you in the right direction.

There is one further dimension to be aware of on handlebars and that is the outside diameter of the ferrule (Fig. 14-78). There is little uniformity between makes of stems and the overall dimensions of bar ferrules, and unless you are careful you could wind up with a stem you can't tighten down enough to grip the handlebars, so they don't turn in the stem, or so small you can't get the bar ferrule through it without almost spreading the stem expander section apart so far you are in danger of breaking off part of the stem, and of having to use a longer binder bolt. I am indebted to Bikecology for Table 14-3, which lists good, indifferent and no-go fits between stems and handlebars.

Taping Handlebars

The conventional canvas or cotton tape is okay, if you don't mind a fairly hard grip surface that can hurt your ulnar nerve. Certainly racing cyclists need that kind of a firm, unyielding gripping surface. The rest of us could surely use a more comfortable grip, and some suppliers have tried to bring us just that. For example, the Grab-On people have come up with a sponge type of bar cover that works well for me. To mount it you have to remove *all* the old tape and *all* the old tape-glue residue on the handlebars. I removed my old glue stuff with paint remover, being careful, of course, not to drop any on the frame finish. To slide the Grab-Ons on, it helps to whip up a soapy mixture of liquid dish detergent and water and pour some inside the Grab-On and put some on the handlebars. You also have to remove the brake levers. Figure 14-81 shows the finished job. For flat bars, you can replace the rubber grips with Grab-Ons, as shown in Figure 14-82. You can also buy a tape something like the leather tape used on tennis rackets, which is elegant, expensive, sweat absorbing, good gripping but not very spongy. On my own favorite Alex Singer touring bike I wound thin sections of sponge rubber around

Fig. 14-81: Any kind of padding, such as the Grab-On sponge type, helps alleviate or prevent ulnar-nerve pain in the palm of your hand.

the bars, and held them in place with rubber cement, while I wrapped overlapping rubber tape with raised middle sections (Fig. 14-83) available in bike stores. Another less expensive solution to softer bars is to go down to your hardware store and buy the kind of pipe insulation used to keep basement pipes from dripping. It installs and looks and feels much like Grab-On. Measure the overall·dimension of your bars to make sure you get the insulation tape that will slide over; not too big so it slides around; not too small so it won't fit on.

If you prefer conventional tape, start at the top, work down and tape around the brake levers as shown in Figure 14-84 (which does not show brake-lever rubber covers, but you can raise the skirts of these enough to get the tape under them as shown) and leave an inch or so extra and tuck that extra into the ends of the drops, and push in the bar end plugs over the tape, as shown in the rear drop in this illustration. If you use bar-end shift levers, though, start taping from the bottom, just behind the levers, using tape with adhesive backing, and wind up at the ferrule. It's not considered good form to cover the ferrule, especially if it has fancy engraving, as do Cinelli bars, for example. The bumpy kind of rubber tape mentioned and shown in Figure 14-83 is made by Bailey.

Fig. 14-82: This type of padding, by Grab-On, fits on end of flat bars.

Fig. 14-83: Or you can use Bailey II tape over sponge-rubber segments.

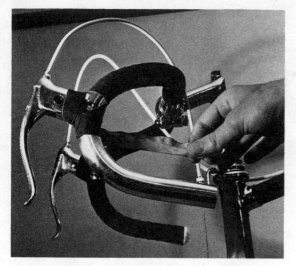

Fig. 14-84: Conventional canvas tape goes on as shown. Brake-lever rubbers are removed to show how tape goes around lever body. You can life the rubber cover to get the same effect. End of tape is tucked into bar-end plugs.

FAIRING FOR BICYCLES

Jim Blackburn Designs, who make those beautiful aluminum carriers we liked so well in Chapter 4, has come up with a fairing, or windscreen, for bicycles. This is a lightweight unit that costs around $20, mounts on the handlebars and presents a smooth face to the wind, which is said to improve the rough treatment you get aerodynamically. This in turn claims to cut cycling effort, and in truth, I found it to be so. I mounted Jim Blackburn's Windfoiler fairing, headed off into a stiff 18-mile-per-hour wind with the fairing, removed it and found the going demonstrably tougher. The fairing also does a good job of keeping out rain; and if the wind at high speed, say going flat out downhill, brings tears to your eyes, the fairing will offer good eye protection as well. It's made from tough, shatterproof plastic, alloys and stainless steel and can be mounted or removed in minutes by spinning two wingnuts. It should be available at your bike shop. Or write Jim Blackburn Designs, 2071 Rosswood Drive, San Jose, California 95124.

Zzipper is the name of a new fairing just out by Zzip Designs, 458 Thayer Road, Bonny Doon, California 95060, which is said to reduce drag 20 percent. It weighs but 14 ounces and costs around $25.

Wheel Lacing and Truing 15

For any of a number of reasons, you may want to "lace" up a wheel. Your rim may develop a flat spot after a hard jolt and rotate with an annoying "thump, thump, thump." You may wish to upgrade your wheels, change from steel to aluminum rims, change hubs, replace spokes or simply build up a new set of wheels. You may want tubular tires for local touring over good roads, and another set of wired-on tired wheels for long-distance touring over a variety of good and bad road conditions. So if you already have either a set of wired-ons or tubulars, you can buy a pair of rims for one or the other, a set of good hubs, enough spokes and nipples and build your own wheels.

If you have a bike shop build your wheels, you'll pay from $15 to $30 for lacing and truing to commercial standards, exclusive of parts. For a more exacting job to professional European road-racing standards, you'll pay more, because to lace and true to those requirements takes at least three hours. Bicycle shops that cater to the racing trade in this country charge around $40 for labor alone just to lace and true a set of racing wheels. It would, of course, be courting disaster for a racing cyclist, especially one who in Europe depends on his equipment for his livelihood (as much as $150,000 a year), to have anything but the most painstakingly accurately laced and trued wheels. In fact, there is at least one reported instance of a professional wheel builder in England taking forty hours to build a pair of wheels for European racing! I will say, categorically, and this is going to raise a lot of eyebrows, that any bike mechanic who claims he can build and true a wheel in fifteen minutes, and some do, can't possibly be doing anything more than a minimum job. That's the kind of wheel building that will buy you wheels that go untrue quickly, cause permanent flat spots in the rim and ultimate spoke breakage. I urge you to learn how to lace and true your own wheels, then you can be as finicky as you please, take all the time you want and come up with wheels that will stay "true" to you indefinitely, with perhaps minor touching up after the first 200 miles.

We will discuss wheel lacing or building (they're synonymous terms) and truing, after which we will take up more exotic wheel building such as radial spoking, tying and soldering spokes and various spoking arrangements.

Wheel building seems difficult, but once you get the hang of it, it's really quite simple. I still recall the time I saw a math prof busy with compass, protractor and slide rule, figuring out all the spoke angles so he could lace a wheel; he computed spoke angles, but not how to lace. Then I recall the time I was taught by an old-timer (who was taught by *his* grandfather) to lace a wheel. The lesson took exactly ten minutes. I have taught a twelve-year-old boy to lace a wheel in ten minutes, and *he* can still lace a wheel. Remember just one thing while you're learning. Forget about the maze and mess of loose spokes flopping around you as you lace, and learn to concentrate *only* on the spoke you're working with and its preceding spoke.

WHAT SPOKES TO USE

I've nothing against other makes, but I prefer French-made Robergel spokes because they're stronger and used by racing cyclists in this country and abroad. You can buy Robergel spokes from Bikecology if you can't find them locally (see Appendix for addresses). Robergel spokes come in three types: *Etoile,* of stainless steel, plain gauge (not thicker or "butted" at the ends). Etoile spokes have a tensile strength of 14,930 to 16,360 pounds per square inch. Robergel Sport spokes are butted stainless steel with a tensile strength of 19,900 to 21,300 lbs./sq. in. (Table 15-1). Trois Etoiles spokes are butted stainless chrome nickel, with a tensile strength of 17,068 to 18,500 lbs./sq. in. The Trois Etoiles spokes will stay better looking longer, but the Sport spokes are stronger and I prefer them. Other good spokes are Berg-Union, made in Germany.

I don't recommend mixing makes of spokes in the same wheel. Spokes of different makes are made of different metals. High-quality spokes are of high-tensile-strength stainless steels; cheap spokes are little better than drawn wire. Mixing makes of spokes means that there will be variations in "modulus of elasticity" (stretch) and tensile strength at random places in your wheel, so it will be next to impossible to adjust spokes to keep wheel rim in perfect alignment, and even to keep the weaker spokes from breaking. And spoke nipples aren't always interchangeable either.

Table 15-1 Robergel Spoke Lengths

Inches	Millimeters
10¹⁵⁄₁₆	278
11	280
11⅛	282
11⅝	295
11¾	298
11¹³⁄₁₆	300
11⅞	302
12	305
12¹⁄₁₆	306
12⅛	308

If you change to a low- from a high-flange hub, you may need longer spokes, unless you lace three cross, for example.

Table 15-2 gives spoke size in relation to hub size and whether spokes are crossed two, three or four. This table is fairly accurate. The problem of the accurate selection of spoke size will never be solved by any table, however, because there are dozens of makes of hubs, and even so-called standard high- and low-flange hubs do not have spoke holes spaced the same distance from the hub-axle housing. The problem isn't particularly great, though, because so long as you can get at least half the spoke threads in the nipple, the spoke can be made to fit. I just want you to know that this table is more of a reasonable indication than an exact specification as to which length of spoke to order to lace your particular combination of rim and hub. For example, ferruled rims may take a slightly shorter spoke than a nonferruled rim using a washer over the spoke hole (see discussion of these rims below).

A wood-filled rim, such as a Milremo Weltmeister, uses a spoke about an eighth of an inch longer than a non-wood-filled rim, given the same hub; so you'd add an eighth of an inch to the spoke regardless of the number of spoke holes and crossing. This is because the nipple head seats on the rim section just underneath the tire, instead of in the center section of the rim (Fig. 15-1). Also, you will notice that the chart breaks

Fig. 15-1: As you look at a rim, you will note that every other spoke hole is near one side of the rim, as shown here. Some rims (very few) have spoke holes drilled at an angle, so nipples can follow spokes in tangential (cross 1, 2, 3 or 4) lacing, minimizing stress and the potential of spoke breakage. If rims don't have angle nipple holes, you can angle them yourself, if you're careful. Also some rims have first hole to right of valve hole on top, others on bottom. The direction in which you twist the rim after the first nine spokes depends on location of first hole to right of valve hole. The objective is to twist the rim so as to keep the valve **between** groups of four spokes instead of in between a group, where the valve will be harder to get at with a pump or air hose. But if you have laced up a wheel with the valve inside a group of four spokes, I would not relace, because the valve won't be **that** hard to get at. Experts can tell at a glance you goofed, but 99 percent of bike riders won't know (until they get this far in this book).

Table 15-2   Spoke Length Selection Chart

Rim (in.)		Hub	Holes	Cross	Spoke Length (in.) Front	Rear
Tubular Tires	27 x 1⅛	Hi*	24	2	11⅝	11⅝
and 700C		Hi*	28	3	12	12
wired-on tires		Hi	28	3	12	$11\frac{15}{16}$
		Hi	32	3	$11\frac{13}{16}$	11¾
		Hi	36	3	11⅝	11½
		Hi	36	4	12	12
		Hi*	36	4	$12\frac{1}{16}$	$12\frac{1}{16}$
		Lo	28	3	$12\frac{1}{16}$	$12\frac{1}{16}$
		Lo	32	3	$11\frac{13}{16}$	11¾
		Lo	36	3	11⅝	11½
		Lo	36	4	$12\frac{1}{16}$	$12\frac{1}{16}$
		Lo	40	4	11⅞	$11\frac{13}{16}$
Tires,	26 x 1⅜		36	3	11	11
English Sizes	26 x 1¼		36	4	11¼	11¼
			40	4	—	11⅛
			36	3	$11\frac{3}{16}$	$11\frac{3}{16}$
			32	3	$11\frac{13}{16}$	—
			40	4	—	11⅜
			36	3	11¼	11¼
			36	4	11½	11½
			40	3	—	11¼
			40	4	$11\frac{7}{16}$	$11\frac{7}{16}$
Tires,	27 x 1¼	Hi	28	3	$12\frac{1}{16}$	12
Lightweight,		Hi	32	3	11⅞	$11\frac{13}{16}$
Hi-Pressure		Hi	36	3	$11\frac{3}{16}$	11¾
		Hi	36	4	12⅛	12⅛
		Hi	40	3	11⅝	11⅝
		Hi	40	4	12	12
		Lo	28	3	12⅛	12⅛
		Lo	32	3	$12\frac{1}{16}$	12
		Lo	36	3	12	11⅞
		Lo	36	4	12⅛	12⅛
		Lo	40	3	$11\frac{13}{16}$	$11\frac{13}{16}$
		Lo	40	4	$12\frac{1}{16}$	$12\frac{1}{16}$
Tires,	26 x 2.125	CB	36	3	10	10
U.S.A. Sizes		CB	36	4	10⅝	10⅝
		3S	36	3	10	10
		3S	36	4	10⅝	10⅝
	26 x 1.35	3S				
		CB	36	4	$11\frac{7}{16}$	$11\frac{7}{16}$
	26 x 1⅜	3S				
		CB	36	4	10⅞	10⅞
	26 x 1.75	3S	36	3	10⅝	10⅝
		CB	36	4	10⅞	10⅞
	26½ x 1½	3S/				
		CB	36	4	11⅛	11⅛

* Track rims: Hi = Hi Flange; Lo = Lo Flange.
3S is Three Speed; CB is Coaster Brake.

down rims and hubs by country. Rims and hubs given for the U.S.A. are the common garden-variety all-steel rims and low-flange hubs used on one-, two-, and three-speed hubs with and without coaster brakes. The 27-inch wheels are, however, presented first because these are, I hope, the sizes you are mostly involved with. In addition, if by some quirk of the manufacturer, your spokes are too short or too long, Table 15-1 gives the size range of Robergel spokes in inches and millimeters so you can go up or down one size, as you need. If, as is the case in the smaller wheel sizes, you must use other than Robergel spokes, I suggest Berg-Union or Torrington. I have left out wheels smaller than twenty-six inches since they would be mostly for the juvenile market.

STRENGTH OF WHEELS

Properly laced wheels, even the light tubular-tire rim type, are very strong. I ran into a parked car head-on at about twelve miles an hour once, and the front wheel never even varied from true, yet I hit with sufficient force to bend a very strong Reynolds butted '531' tubing fork. (I varied from "true" for about ten minutes.)

A 40-spoke wheel weighing only 27 ounces was tested for maximum axle loading. The wheel sustained an axle load of more then 1,200 pounds, after which the wheel showed a permanent slight buckle. Since the buckling occurred at a pressure more than 700 times the weight of the wheel, it can be said that this wheel can safely sustain a working load of about 700 pounds at smooth riding conditions. Because the *average* cyclist weighs certainly no more than 180 pounds, we can assume this wheel is amply strong enough for racing on smooth roads and for touring even on fairly rough roads, such as cobblestone streets. But don't count on not putting a permanent crimp in your rim if you hit a pothole! In the section on safety where I discuss crash helmets I mention two of my own accidents, one in which I hit a crack in a bridge and the other in which I hit a parked car once again. Both times I used the same 3½-ounce Hi-E aluminum alloy hub, 32 spokes crossed 3 with an alloy rim. The second accident did put a crimp in the rim but the hub held up fine (I wish I had).

WHEEL LACING STEPS

Let's start wheel building with a few basic observations about rims and hubs. First, to make life complicated, rims and hubs have spoke holes drilled off-center. Figure 15-1 shows that rim spoke holes are drilled so that every other hole is closer to one side of the rim than to the other side. Please keep that in mind as we proceed, because we'll come back to it. Next, study Figure 15-2; note that hub holes are also drilled off-center; that is, the hubs in one flange are offset from the holes in the

Fig. 15-2: All wheel hubs have holes drilled off-center with respect to holes in top and bottom flanges, as shown by spoke (A), which falls between spoke holes (B) and (C) below; and spoke (D), which falls midway between holes (E) and (F). Note also every other hole on **both** sides of the hub is countersunk. Spoke head goes in noncountersunk hole. Countersinking minimizes spoke breakage by spreading stress at spoke head bend over greater area, instead of at sharp right angle. See Figure 15-3.

facing flange. If you poke a spoke down a hub hole from the top flange, straight up and down, it will land *between* the spokes in the bottom flange of the hub. Check this for yourself and bury it in your memory. Finally, and this is also important, pick up your hub and look at the spoke holes closely. You'll notice, as in Figure 15-2, that if you have a fine hub such as a Campagnolo alloy Record, Phil Wood, or Hi-E, every other hub hole is countersunk. This countersinking is to permit the spoke to bend gradually and to eliminate a sharp corner that would stress the spoke at this point, and contribute to premature spoke breakage. At first, though, because we're used to putting screw heads in countersunk holes, you may believe spoke heads should go into hub countersunk holes. Believe me, it's not so! You can bury spoke heads in countersunk holes for a sexier-looking hub, but you'll have busted spokes on the road if you do! Figure 15-3 illustrates this point. (Some hubs have *all* spoke holes countersunk.)

Fig. 15-3: Left, wrong way to put spoke in wheel hub, which stresses spoke at sharp noncountersunk hole. Right, correct way to insert spoke so that head is flush against rim and spoke shaft angles out against countersunk side of hole, which reduces stress and breakage at this point.

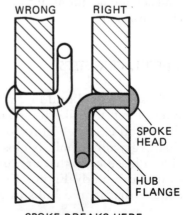

WRONG   RIGHT

SPOKE HEAD

HUB FLANGE

SPOKE BREAKS HERE AT SHARP TURN ANGLE

Before you start bulding a wheel, first make sure you have the right length of spoke. Refer to the spoke chart in this chapter if you're not sure. Also, remove the freewheel gear cluster from rear wheels; you can't poke spokes in the rear hub with the freewheel in the way (which is why you should take a freewheel-removing tool as well as spare spokes on trips). You may also find it difficult or next to impossible to poke spokes through hub holes if they are drilled too small to accommodate the spoke. Most dealers, if they stock Robergel Sport spokes, only have them in .080-.072 gauge. This means the butted ends are .080, and the rest of the spoke is .072 inches. The nearest fraction equivalent to .080 is ⁵⁄₃₂-inch (or 2.032 millimeters). So you would drill out a too-small hole with a ⁵⁄₃₂-inch drill. Actually, I'd rather see you use a metric drill, 2.05 millimeters, to be exact, which gives you a snugger-fitting hole only .018 millimeters larger than the butted section of the spoke. Be sure to drill straight, and remember, once you've drilled out your hub, always replace spokes with ones of the same diameter. If you use a smaller-gauge spoke you will invite spoke breakage, as the spoke bounces around the larger spoke hole under stress. If you have a drill press you should recountersink holes, or countersink every other one on both sides if not already so countersunk. If you can't find metric drills locally (see Appendix), you can get them from either of the two metric mail-order supply houses listed in the Appendix.

A few definitions, so we're talking in the same language:

- *Rim* is the round steel or alloy part that the tire goes on.
- *Spoke head* is the section of the spoke with the curved area and flat head (flat on the bottom). The other end of the spoke is threaded.
- *Spoke nipple* is the short, tubular, internally threaded piece that holds the spoke on the rim and threads onto the spoke.
- *"Spoke head up"* means that in referring to the hub, the spoke head faces up, as shown in the Step One drawing (Fig. 15-4).
- *"Top rim hole"* means rim hole closest to upper edge of rim.

Before you start, you might consider drilling a one-inch hole in your wooden workbench to fit the axle of the hub so the hub assembly will stay put as you stick spokes in the wheel. And, while I'm thinking of it and before you despair, remember that, as I said, lacing a wheel is simple. It just *seems* difficult; it surely is hard to write about how to do it so that it comes out sounding as easy as it really is.

Since most wheels on ten-speed bikes have 36 spokes front and rear, I'll assume this is what you're about to lace. You have a naked hub and rim, and a fistful of spokes and nipples of the right diameter and length. You can get fancy later on and lace up 24-, 28-, 33-, or 40-spoked rims and hubs, and lace them radically or 3 or 4 cross as your heart desires. For now, we'll stick to 36 holes, crossed 4.

STEP ONE: Grab 9 spokes, threaded ends down. Hold the hub in one hand, the spokes in the other, and stuff a spoke down every other hole.

The spoke head must be on the now countersunk side of the hub flange. Do the same for the bottom flange, with the hub in the same position as when you started. You should now have a hub that looks like the drawing below (Fig. 15-4).

STEP TWO: Sweep up all the spokes on both flanges into two bundles, hold them so they don't fall out, turn the hub over and repeat Step One. When you're through, the hub will have all 36 spokes in it, with every other spoke head alternating, on each side of both hub flanges as shown in Figure 15-5.

STEP THREE: Sweep all the spokes as far away from the spoke hole as possible. Take any head-up spoke from the top flange (spoke head up means the spoke head is facing upward, on top of the flange) and put it in the first hole to the *right* of the valve hole. This rim hole must be a top rim hole (a top rim hole is the hole closest to the top of the rim); however, some rims are drilled so that the first hole to the right of the valve is a bottom rim hole (hole closest to the bottom of the rim). If so, start lacing with the first hole to the *left* of the valve hole. On this spoke and from here on thread a nipple four turns on each spoke as you lace it into the rim (Fig. 15-6).

STEP FOUR: Count off five spokes to the right (not counting the valve hole), including the hole you spoked in Step Three. This must also be a top rim hole. Into this hole put the next head-up spoke to the right of the one you spoked in Step Three. Continue this sequence until you have laced all head-up spokes in the top hub flange. The wheel will now look like Figure 15-7, with three holes between each spoke, the center of the three empty holes being a rim-top hole, the other two, rim-bottom holes. (This happens to be a 32-hole rim and hub so only 8 spokes are showing. You should show 9 spokes.)

STEP FIVE: This is a critical step, so take it slowly and repeat it if you don't get it at first. Take the partially spoked rim and hub, and, keeping the same side up, *twist* the rim so the spokes are at an acute angle, just grazing the outside of their adjacent spoke holes. Depending on how the rim has been drilled, twist the rim either left or right, just so no spoke crosses over the valve hole (Figs. 15-8 and 15-1). Hold the hub as you twist the rim.

Fig. 15-4: Step One.   **Fig. 15-5:** Step Two

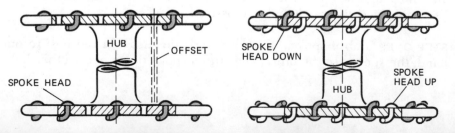

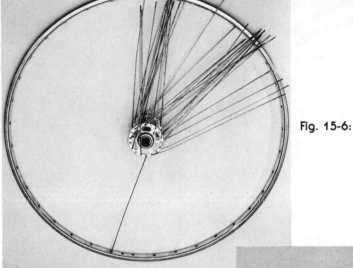

Fig. 15-6: Step Three

Fig. 15-7: Step Four

Fig. 15-8: Step Five

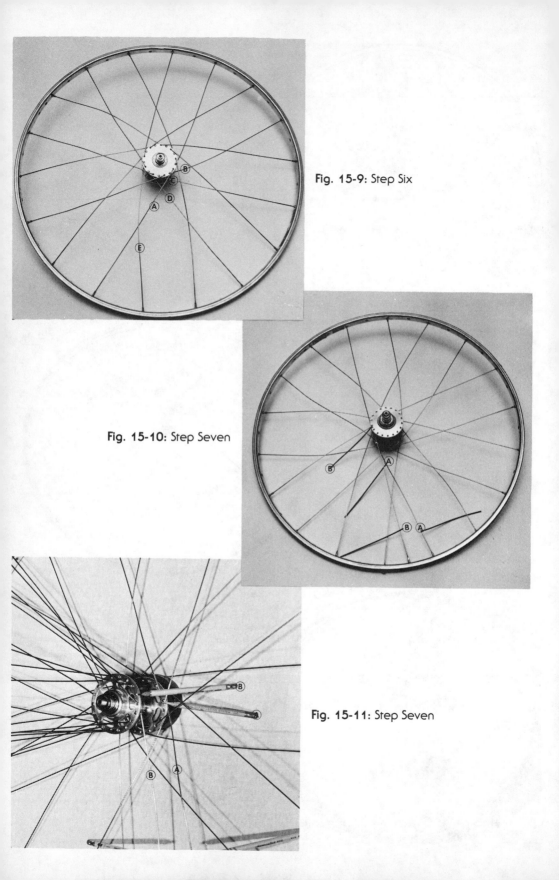

Fig. 15-9: Step Six

Fig. 15-10: Step Seven

Fig. 15-11: Step Seven

STEP SIX: Another critical step. Take any head-down spoke from the top-hub flange (the wheel should still be in the same position as when you started) and, going in the *opposite direction* from the spokes laced so far, cross *over* three and *under* the fourth spoke, as shown above, then stick it in the rim and thread on a nipple four turns. Remember Step Four? You had three empty spoke holes between each spoke. Right? I hope you did, anyway. If not, stop now and go over the preceding steps to check what you did wrong. Let's assume all is well. The spoke we are lacing in Step Six should go into a center-rim hole (top rim hole) (Fig. 15-9). You are lacing spoke "A." Note that it crosses *over* spokes "B," "C," "D" and *under* "E," and winds up in a top-rim hole. Continue lacing all head-down spokes in the top flange, cross *over* three and *under* the fourth spoke, as above. When you are finished, spokes will be in groups of two, with one bottom-rim spoke between each group of two. (If you wish to lace in a "cross three" pattern, pass the spoke *over* two and *under* the third spoke. A three-cross pattern uses shorter spokes.)

STEP SEVEN: This is a most critical step. Turn the wheel over, with all unlaced spokes in the top flange. Straighten spokes out, sweep all but one out of your way. Take an old spoke, put it straight up alongside any head-up spoke in the top flange, with the threaded end resting on the bottom flange facing you. Notice that just to the left of this trial spoke is another head-up spoke, offset, to the left (naturally) in the bottom flange (see Fig. 15-2). We will call the bottom reference spoke in the bottom flange Spoke "A" and the spoke above and to its right, Spoke "B." Referring to the photo at left, bring spoke "B" parallel but angled to the left of spoke "A" below it. Refer to Figure 15-10. Put spoke "B" in the first empty rim hole to the left of spoke "A," thread on a nipple. Now you will have (you'd *better* have) your first group of three spokes, with one empty spoke hole on either side. Step Seven is so critical I have taken extra photos from various angles to demonstrate it. Figure 15-11 shows a close-up of the hub, with key spoke "A" at the bottom on the hub and key spoke "B" at the top of the hub. Figure 15-12 shows key spokes "A" and "B" as they enter the rim. Figure 15-13 is another view of Step Seven, with pencils on spokes "A" and "B." An important point to remember is that spoke "B" is parallel to spoke "A," is offset to it, and goes next to it in the rim, just above (to the left of) spoke "A."

STEP EIGHT: Now, if all is well so far, the rest is simple. Just take the next head-up spoke, count off two *empty* (*EMPTY*) spoke holes to the

Fig. 15-12: Step Seven

left (*LEFT*), stick this spoke into *that* top rim hole and thread on nipple four turns. Repeat until all head-up spokes are in the rim with nipples on. Now you will have all spokes in groups of three (Fig. 15-14) and are ready for the final step.

STEP NINE: Take any one of the remaining spokes (they will all be head down, with heads *under* the top flange) and bring it around to the right, crossing *over* three and *under* the fourth spoke and stick it in the only hole it will fit into. If you're not sure which hole this is, please repeat Step Seven, only with head-down spokes, referencing a head-down spoke in the bottom flange and being sure that the parallel head-down spoke in the top flange also goes in a direction opposite to *its* reference spoke below. Confused? Well, actually I don't blame you. Let's take it from the top. First, find any head-down spoke in the bottom flange. Then find the first head-down spoke in the top flange offset to the right (counterclockwise) of your reference head-down spoke below, and put it in the first empty spoke hole to the right (counterclockwise) of spoke "A." Refer to the drawing of Step Six to refresh your memory as to what crossing over three and under four is all about. Continue as above, lacing up the remaining head-down spokes. Now the wheel is laced, spokes are in groups of four as shown above, and we are ready for the exacting job of "truing" the rim. Finished wheel is shown in Figure 15-15.

Varieties of Wheels

As you will note from Table 15-2, wheels can be laced with various spoking configurations. You can buy tubular tire rims and hubs drilled in multiples of 4, from 24 to 40 holes. And spokes can be crossed over three or even two, or not crossed tangentially at all but spoked radially, that is, straight up and down. They can even be laced tangentially on the driving side (the freewheel side) and radially on the other side; some racing cyclists prefer this combination, with 24 spokes, although it's rare in this country.

Wheels can also be tied and soldered, with 40 or 50 turns of thin steel wire wrapped around spoke intersections, and the wire soldered. Tying spokes in this manner makes a stiffer wheel and reduces spoke breakage by cutting spoke "whip" under stress.

Radial Lacing

Some cyclists prefer a radially laced front wheel and a tangentially (conventionally) laced rear wheel. Because radial spoking offers little resistance to forward power thrust, it's not practical for rear wheels. Radial spoking does offer less wind resistance because the spokes are in line behind each other, whereas tangentially laced spokes angle out more and so offer greater wind resistance. Radial spoking gives you a strong, rigid wheel for a front wheel only.

Fig. 15-13: Step Seven

Fig. 15-14: Step Eight

Step 15-15: Step Nine. **Voila!**

Crossing three instead of four spokes means that spokes are shorter and, again, offer a stiffer ride on any wheel.

High-Versus Low-Flange Hubs

High-flange hubs provide a stiffer ride than low-flange hubs because they take shorter spokes. There's less spoke to absorb road shock. But I do not recommend using a 40-hole lacing with low-flange hubs, because this would put holes too close together and make a weaker hub. But that's my opinion, and if you wish to lace up a 40-hole rim and low-flange hub, by all means try it out. If you're a 200-pounder carrying 26 or 30 pounds of gear on tour over rough roads, I definitely would use a 40-hole rear wheel with *high*-flange hub, and a 36-hole *low*-flange front wheel and hub. If you're lighter, say from 150 to 180 pounds, on tour with normal camping gear of about 30-35 pounds, I'd stick to a 36-hole high-flange rear and a 36-hole low-flange front arrangement. If you're lighter, a 32-hole front and rear low-flange hub should hold up. This assumes all the wheels recommended above are cross four. If you're a real lightweight, say 100 to 115 pounds, you may get by with a 28-hole, crossed-four, low-flange hub front, and a 32-hole, crossed-four, low-flange hub rear. Spoke breakage isn't all just spoke configuration, though. It's also how even spoke tension is, and how much tension is applied. Too little tension permits excessive spoke play in the hub, and whipsawing can break spokes at the bend near the hub hole. If you're lacing a 36-hole rim, cross four, in a low-flange hub, and *rim* holes are not drilled at an acute enough angle to permit the nipple to follow the spoke line, you will have stress and possible breakage at the nipple. If, as you apply tension, the spoke winds up with a twist, you can have spoke breakage at the twist. As you apply spoke tension in truing, watch that spokes stay put. If not, hold spokes with a smooth-jawed pair of pliers as you tighten the nipple.

Speaking of nipples, use short nipples for lightweight rims and long nipples for heavier rims, such as wired-on-tires and touring tubular rims.

Here is a rather general recommendation for wheel-lacing configuration, subject to modification as personal experience warrants, and as to weight and style of riding:

Table 15-3 Wheel-Lacing Configuration

Type of Riding	Front Wheel	Rear Wheel
Massed-Start Racing	28	36
Track Sprints	36 or 32	36
Distance Time Trials	36	36
Short Time Trials	28 or 32	28 or 32
Pursuit	28 or 32	28 or 32
General Riding	36	36
Touring, Heavy Rider, With Luggage	36	40

Remember, as one final observation, that reliability is more important than lightness, particularly when it comes to racing.

HOW TO "TRUE" A WHEEL

When we finished instructions for wheel lacing, you were left with spokes hanging loose. An accurately trued and tensioned wheel is vital to spoke life, for all the reasons noted above. You should also know how to true a wheel that has come untrue, because continued riding of an out-of-line wheel can put a permanent crimp or flat spot in the rim, and you will need a new rim. Braking is also safer with true rims because brake shoes can grab the rim evenly all the way around, and because brake shoes can be adjusted closer to the rim for minimum brake-lever travel and maximum stopping power. In other words, never ride very far with untrue rims; they're bound to be unfaithful.

Tools you will need for truing a wheel are shown in Figure 15-16. They are: "A," truing stand; "B," vernier caliper gauge; "C," spoke wrench; "D," ratchet screwdriver; and, "E," rim-centering gauge.

Fig. 15-16: Tools for truing include: (A) wheel-truing stand; (B) inch-metric vernier caliper and depth gauge; (C) spoke wrench; (D) ratchet screwdriver; and (E) rim-centering gauge.

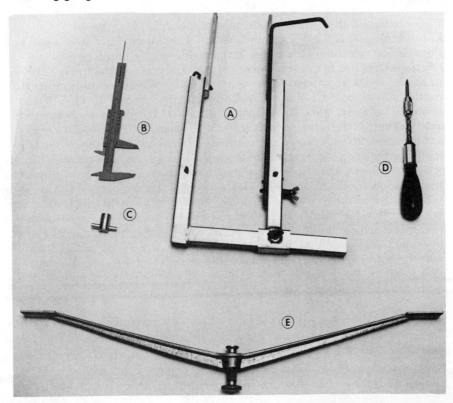

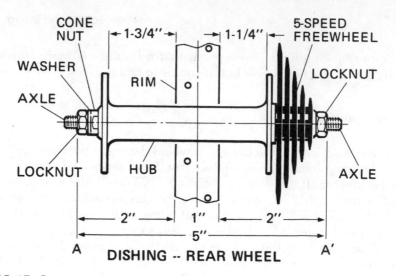

CONE NUT |← 1-3/4" →| →| 1-1/4" |←   5-SPEED FREEWHEEL

WASHER   RIM   LOCKNUT

AXLE

LOCKNUT   HUB   AXLE

|← 2" →| 1" |← 2" →|

5"

A   **DISHING -- REAR WHEEL**   A'

Fig. 15-17: Rear wheel must be "dished," or moved to the right, so the rim is centered over the axle locknuts, as shown. Note that the distance on both sides of **rim** is equal (2 inches), yet hub is 1¾ inches on left and 1¼ on right side of rim. Rear wheel left-side spokes will be about ⅛th inch (2 mm. or so) longer than spokes on right (freewheel) side.

It will be helpful before starting step-by-step truing instructions to establish a common vocabulary of truing terms, so we all talk the same language:

- *Concentricity* is the degree to which the wheel is perfectly round.
- *Lateral trueness* is the degree to which the wheel is centered over a point on the axle and remains on that point, with no side-to-side untrueness.
- *"Dishing"* applies to the rear wheel only, and means that the rim is "dished" or moved to the right so as to be centered *between* axle locknuts rather than on the hub alone. "Dishing" is well illustrated in Figure 15-17. The rim is centered between A and A', and you will notice that the space between the axle locknuts is the same on *both* sides of the rim. Notice also that the rim is *not* centered on the hub alone, as evidenced by the fact that more of the hub is on the left than on the right side of the rim. "Dishing" is vital not only to rear-wheel alignment, but also to the alignment of the rear wheel with respect to the frame and to the front wheel. Please study Figure 15-17 until you are sure you understand the concept of "dishing." Remember that dishing is necessary because the extra width of the freewheel gear cluster adds a dimension to the rear wheel which the front wheel doesn't have; and so the rim must be centered on the total dimension, which *includes* the freewheel, just as the front wheel must be centered on *its* total width, which includes only the hub and axle locknuts. However, the new Shimano "free-hub" designs are said to require little or no dishing. Measure just to make sure.

- *"Centering"* is what you do to the front wheel; although, of course, it's done to the rear wheel too, only we use the word "dishing" for the latter to stress that the rim is moved to the right side of the hub. The front wheel is centered on its hub. See Figure 15-18; note that the rim is centered on the hub.
- *"Tension"* is the degree to which spokes are tightened. Too much tension can

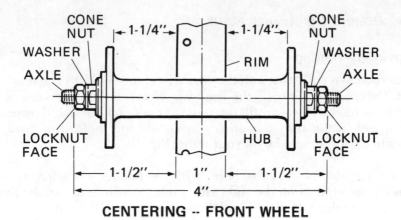

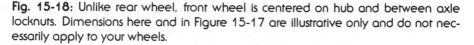

CENTERING -- FRONT WHEEL

Fig. 15-18: Unlike rear wheel, front wheel is centered on hub and between axle locknuts. Dimensions here and in Figure 15-17 are illustrative only and do not necessarily apply to your wheels.

cause broken spokes; so can too little. Tension of *front*-wheel spokes should be equal on all spokes; on *rear* wheels, tension of right-side spokes is a bit more than left side because the rim is pulled (dished) over to the right.

- *The rim gauge* (see Fig. 15-16) helps you center the rim, or "dish" it accurately.
- *Direction of rim movement* is which way the rim moves (left or right, up or down, with respect to the hub centerline) as you tighten or loosen a spoke nipple. Please study Figure 15-19 until you understand in which direction the rim will move as you tighten a particular spoke nipple. Remember that the rim will move the opposite way as you *loosen* a spoke nipple.

Fig. 15-19: Arrows show which way rim moves as spokes are tightened. Rim moves opposite way if spokes are loosened. Note that to remove out-of-roundness, **two** spokes must be tightened, spokes "A" and "B." If spoke "A" alone is tightened, rim moves to left. If spoke "B" is tightened, rim moves to right. If both spokes "A" and "B" are tightened to the same degree, rim moves only downward.

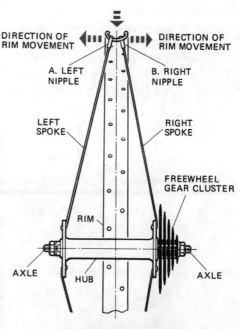

DIRECTION OF RIM MOVEMENT

Steps in Wheel Truing

STEP ONE: We will start with the rear wheel, because it's the most difficult. Except for "dishing," the front wheel is trued up the same way as the rear wheel. If they're still on, remove the quick-release skewers. Put the wheel in the truing stand (or in an old fork held in a vise). The freewheel side should be on your right (Fig. 15-20).

STEP TWO: Start at the valve hole. With the ratchet screwdriver, speed-turn all the nipples on the right side down to where the spoke threads disappear under the nipple, and stop. Screw down the left-side nipples until the last four threads are visible on the spoke, under the nipple. When you do the front wheel, screw down all the nipples until the threads are just covered.

STEP THREE: Measure the distance beween axle locknuts. Now is when we learn to use the rim-centering gauge. Please study Figure 15-17 again. (Dimensions are illustrative only, and do not necessarily apply to your rim.) You will see that the measurement between axle locknuts is 5 inches. The rim is 1 inch wide. There are 2 inches on either side of the rim, between the locknut faces and the edges of the rim. Two plus 2 plus 1 equals 5 inches. So you can see the rim is *not* centered between the hub flanges, because there are 1¾ inches between the left hub flange and the left rim edge, and only 1¼ inches between the right rim edge and the right hub flange. The rear wheel is "dished" to the right. To adjust the rim-centering gauge to your rear wheel, measure the distance between axle locknuts with the vernier calipers. You can buy a surpris-

Fig. 15-20: Step One

Fig. 15-21: Step Two

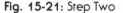

ingly accurate pair of these calipers for around $3.50 from one of the metric supply houses listed in the Appendix. I prefer the one from Ametric. They are inside, outside, and depth vernier calipers, in both inch and metric. Metric measurements are so much easier to use that I also urge you to convert your thinking to that system. Let's say the distance between locknut faces is 120.3 millimeters (for inch comparison, see Step Five).

STEP FOUR: Measure the width of the rim with the vernier gauge. Let's say it's 19.4 millimeters wide.

STEP FIVE: Subtract the first measurement from the second and divide the answer by 2. For example:

Table 15-4 Measuring Hub Width

	Millimeters	Inches, Fraction	Inches, Decimal
Locknut to locknut width:	120.3	4¾	4.750
Hub width:	− 19.4	−⁴⁹⁄₆₄	− .76242
Subtracting:	100.9	3⁶³⁄₆₄	3.988
Dividing by two:	50.45	1¹²⁷⁄₁₂₈	1.994

As you can see, the metric system is much easier to work with and more accurate. Good bikes are almost all made to metric measurements. A reminder: The measurements above are hypothetical, and may or may not apply to your wheel and hub. You will have to measure the ones you are working with.

STEP SIX: Put a reasonably flat strip over the rim-centering gauge, and with the vernier depth gauge set to 50.45 millimeters (or 1¹²⁷⁄₁₂₈ in.) adjust the rim-gauge centering screw to 50.45 millimeters. If you can't find a flat metal strip, set the gauge on a flat surface and look at the setting, as in Figure 15-22. (Remember, we are using hypothetical measurements as an example. You should use the actual measurements of your hub locknut to locknut distance and rim width.)

STEP SEVEN: Put the rim gauge on *both* sides of the rim to check how far off you are on dishing the rim to the right. Remove the wheel from the truing stand for checking, and then put it back. The rim-gauge screw is hollow, so it fits over the axle and axle locknut and permits the rim-gauge set screw flat to rest on the axle locknut face (Fig. 15-23).

STEP EIGHT: Set the lateral-movement indicator on the truing stand so it touches the worst bump on the left side of the rim. (Or, if you're using an old fork, anything that will stay still and indicate will do, such as a pipe cleaner wrapped around the fork blade.) When you find the worst left-side bump, stop there and find the spoke nipple just to the *right* of

Fig. 15-22: Step Six

Fig. 15-23: Step Seven

the bump. (Also at this point, study Figure 15-19 to review rim-direction movement. Note that when spoke "B" is tightened, the rim moves to the right, and vice versa when spoke "A" is tightened.) Tighten this spoke nipple one turn to pull rim to the right. Then find the next worst bump and tighten the spoke nipple to the right of *that* bump one turn. Repeat this process once around the left side of the rim. Fine truing will come later.

STEP NINE: Move the indicator so it touches the right side of the rim, and repeat Step Eight. Continue uniil you have removed all the right-side bumps.

STEP TEN: Check rim centering with the rim gauge, as in Step Seven. If the rim is too far to the left, tighten *all* the spoke nipples, on the *right* side one-half turn; if the rim is too far to the right, tighten all the spoke nipples on the left side one-half turn (Fig. 15-24). You may have to loosen opposite side spokes a half-turn or so.

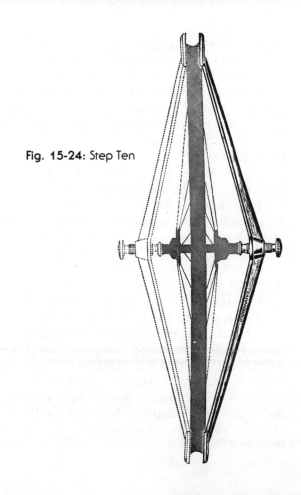

Fig. 15-24: Step Ten

STEP ELEVEN: With wheel in truing stand, repeat Steps Eight and Nine, except this time turn the spoke nipples one-quarter turn as you continue to pull out major lateral untrueness once around; one-quarter turn the second time around; one-eighth turn succeeding times around.

STEP TWELVE: Now, with the wheel back in the truing stand, move the indicator so it touches the *outside circumference of the rim*, so we can remove out-of-roundness. Referring again to Figure 15-19, notice that when spokes "A" *and* "B" are tightened, the rim moves toward the hub; this is also true when spokes "C" *and* "D" are tightened. In other words, in removing concentric untrueness, *both* spokes at the points of major concentric highs must be tightened to pull the rim down. Rotate the rim, watch the indicator till you find the highest out-of-round spot, and tighten both left and right spokes at that spot one-half turn the first time; one-quarter turn the second time around; one-eighth turn third and succeeding times around.

STEP THIRTEEN: Repeat Step Seven, except turn the nipples one-eighth turn.

STEP FOURTEEN: Remove the wheel from the truing stand, and put the axle end on a wooden bench, holding the rim with both hands on either side of the rim. Press the rim sharply and hard down on the bench, to stress the rim, and seat in the spoke heads and nipples. You may hear popping sounds as spokes seat in. Rotate rim one-quarter turn, change grip, repeat rim press, and go around the rim twice.

STEP FIFTEEN: With the wheel in truing stand, touch up lateral and concentric untrueness, turning nipples one-eighth turn. If you can't move a nipple, loosen the spoke nipple on the *opposite* side. Example 1: If you find a small lateral bump on the left side, and the right-side nipple is too tight to move, *loosen* the left-side nipple at the bump one-eighth turn. Example 2: You have a concentric high bump and both nipples at the bump can't be tightened any more. Instead, loosen both nipples at the point on the rim *opposite* the bump one-eighth turn (on the other side of the rim). On a rear wheel, as stated earlier, right-side spokes should all be slightly tighter than left-side spokes. Spokes on each side should show the same tension as other spokes on the same side. Don't try to pull a high or low spot out by tightening a nipple all at once; you'll have a highly stressed spoke that will very likely be short-lived, perhaps breaking when you're careening downhill. Later, as you ride on your trued wheels, you may hear "twanging" sounds as the spokes seat in more. Or you'll likely hear that sound on a new bicycle, no matter what the price. Your rims will need touch-up truing for each 50 miles until you hit about 150 miles, after which rims should remain true, barring accident.

Fig. 15-25: This is a fairly expensive wheel-truing device that is very popular with expert wheel builders in Europe and is even used in bicycle factories overseas. It costs around $600, is made in Belgium by Preci-Ray and I swear by it. But it's not practical for home use. There are any number of practical wheel-truing devices, however, such as the simple truing stand available at Palo Alto Bicycles for $12 (see mail order section in Appendix), or the TL WT wheel-truing jig with precision calipers for $50 from Bikecology, or any number of other wheel-truing fixtures from your local bike shop. Another unit I like very much, and which I have used, is the Dial-O-Meter, which uses two digital depth type of gauges, which give you an extremely accurate readout of concentric and lateral trueness, to the thousandth of an inch on dial gauges. This unit is made by Dial-O-Meter, 2376 Pacheco Boulevard, Martinez, California, and costs around $95.

Fig. 15-26: Another view of the Preci-Ray wheel truer, this one in a class on bicycle maintenance taught by your author. Yes, you **can** learn to lace and true wheels.

Fig. 15-27: Close-up of wheel-truing unit. All such units have some sort of indicator which tells you how far off you are from perfect roundness and perfect side-to-side trueness. Well, perfect may be too strong a word . . . let's just say "accurate" or "on the button."

Fig. 15-28: If your good wheel has hit a pothole and is dented, do not despair. Your bike shop should have a tool something like the one shown here to pull out wheel dents, if they aren't too bad. This would be a good tool for a bike club to own.

Fig. 15-29: If you have ever run out of a spoke of just the right length, or can't find one, or have 500 spokes too long (say you're changing to 700-centimeter rims and have 27¼-inch rim spokes) and want to thread down to a smaller length spoke (after cutting off long ones) this little machine is a dandy tool. Costs about $15 without rolling heads, which are extra ($10 each). Made in England by Cyclo Gear Co., and available through Raleigh dealers (who will have to order from Raleigh) or from The Third Hand, P.O. Box 2, Markleeville, California 96120. Rolling heads are available for 12-, 13-, 14- and 15-gauge spoke wire and in 1.8-millimeter pitch, at $12 per head.

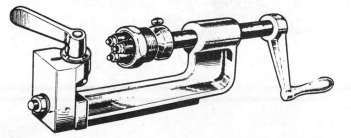

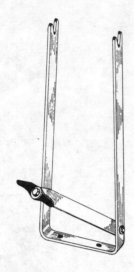

Fig. 15-30: Here is an inexpensive truing stand, made by Park Tool Company and available through Schwinn dealers for about $13.50.

Fig. 15-31: You will also need a set of spoke wrenches, for $7.50 a set, which will fit, as a set of four, 80-gauge Union and Torrington spokes, 80-gauge Japanese spokes, 105- and 120-gauge spokes.

Fig. 15-32: Campagnolo tools cost an arm and a leg. Here's a wheel-alignment tool made by Park Tool Company, which only costs $10 from any Schwinn dealer, who will have to special-order it for you, most likely. You can check rear-wheel dish without removing wheel from bike. You can also tell, if dish is okay but wheel is not aligned in frame, that frame is bent out of alignment.

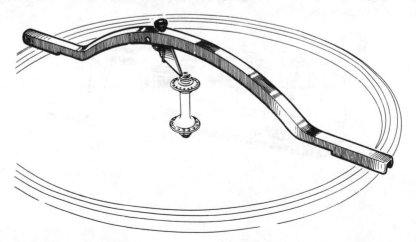

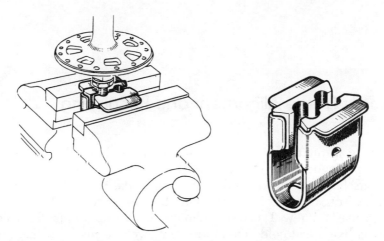

Fig. 15-33: If you wish to hold a hub in a vise, you can damage spindle threads if you are not careful to block with wood. Or, you can use this axle vise from Park Tool that costs around $6 from a Schwinn dealer.

Fig. 15-34: Another rim saver is this $15 tool from Bicycle Research Products (sold by Phil Wood) which removes rim dents. Might almost be worth buying one if you are rim-dent prone . . . or, a good buy for a bicycle-club toolbox.

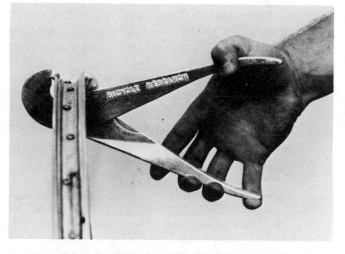

It's a lovely spring day in the south of Austria, and you're going lickety-split, full tilt, wide open, down a winding mountain road. Suddenly, the handlebars begin to shake, and with each shake the bars swing wider and faster. You are out of control. This happened to me. I was able to stop because I knew I had no choice. This dangerous front-wheel shimmy is like a bad cold: There are so many reasons for it that almost anything could cause it, such as an unbalanced load, loose head or wheel bearings . . . or a slightly bent fork blade. The latter proved to be the case, thanks to the tender ministrations of the Austrian airline that transported it. Sometimes the fork blade can be so minutely bent out of line as to be almost undetectable to the naked eye; certainly it won't be seen at a casual glance—which is one good reason to block dropouts with a dummy spindle or piece of wood when shipping a bike with wheels removed.

I guess what I'm saying here is that an out-of-line bike frame can be a dangerous thing . . . a bike that can whip into a frenzy of front-wheel shimmy at high speed . . . a bike that will steer inaccurately and waste pedaling energy . . . a bike that in many instances can be saved through judicious application of muscle at the right tube member. Let's review how to check your frame for accurate alignment, and what to do about a misalignment of any of the tubes. First, if you are not familiar with bicycle frame terminology, please check the photo on page 708 in the Appendix.

STEP ONE: *Check wheel tracking.* I use a five- or six-foot length of steel angle as a straightedge, which comes straight as stocked in a hardware store. Lay this straightedge (Fig. 16-1) against the front- and rear-wheel rim flats (remove tire if necessary). Both wheels should be in the drop-outs straight and should have been trued (see Chapter 15 for wheel-truing instructions). Wheels should track straight, with no more than a millimeter or so (1/16-to-1/8, inch max) difference. Try riding no hands and see if the bike pulls to one side or the other. If it does, or if the wheels are not tracking, go through the entire sequence of frame-alignment checks that follow.

STEP TWO: *Rim centering check.* Check to make sure both wheels track true between frame members. Check rear wheel against *both* seat stays

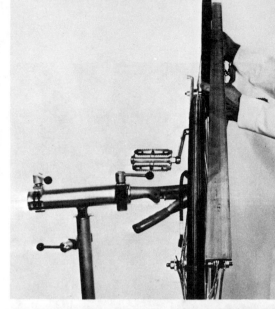

Fig. 16-1: Step One: Wheel-tracking alignment *(Schwinn Bicycle Company)*

(Fig. 16-2) and chainstays (Fig. 16-3) and front wheel against both sides of fork (Fig. 16-4). Wheels should be equidistant from frame members. I'm unhappy with a one-millimeter difference, but I can live with it. I'd rather see the rims absolutely centered. This test won't work unless the wheels are trued and the rear wheel correctly dished (see Chapter 15). If the rear wheel is consistently too far to one side as measured on both sides from both seat and chainstays, it is incorrectly dished. Go to Step Three.

Fig. 16-2: Step Two: Wheel-centering check, rear wheel

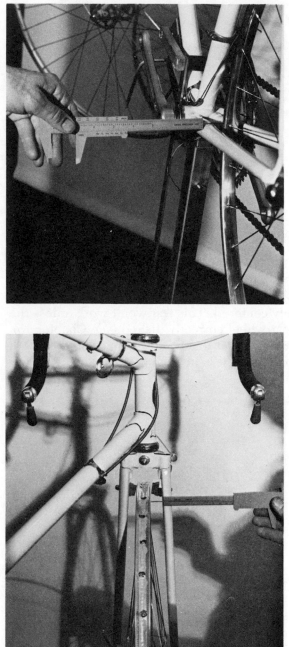

Fig. 16-3: Step Two: Wheel-centering check, rear wheel

Fig. 16-4: Step Two: Wheel-centering check, front wheel

Fig. 16-5: Step Three: Check rear wheel dish. *(Schwinn Bicycle Company)*

STEP THREE: *Check rear-wheel dish* with a wheel-dishing gauge, such as the one shown in Figure 16-5. If the rim is not centered or dished accurately between axle locknuts, remove wheel and re-dish, following truing instructions in Chapter 15. If, however, the rear wheel *is* correctly dished, then we have a frame problem such as bent stays, bent dropouts, unparalleled dropouts, buckled main frame tube. So now . . .

STEP FOUR: *Check alignment of rear dropouts and stays.* Put a straightedge between steering head tube, seat tube and against the dropout (Fig. 16-6). You will have, if the straightedge is on the right side, a clearance between the right side of the straightedge and the dropout. Measure this distance. Now move the straightedge to the *left* side of the tubes and measure that clearance from the left side of the straightedge to the dropout. Both measurements should be the same. If not, the chainstay or seat stay could be bent, or the dropouts might not be parallel.

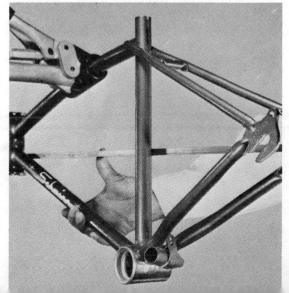

Fig. 16-6: Step Four: Check alignment of rear dropouts and stays. *(Schwinn Bicycle Company)*

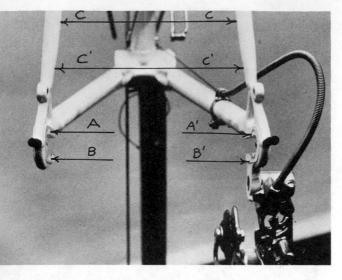

Fig. 16-7: Step Four: Check alignment of dropouts and stays.

STEP FIVE: *Check dropouts for parallel alignment* with seat or head tube and with each other. Measure distance between dropouts in several places. Measurements should be the same (Fig. 16-7). Also measure dropouts between points "A" and "A¹" and "B" and "B¹"; measurements should be the same if dropouts are parallel. Also check seat stays at points "C" and "C¹"—the difference between the tube angles should be the same on both sides. Another way to check dropouts is to put a straightedge on both sides, as in Figure 16-8, and measure the distance in several places on the straightedge. The measurements should be the same. This is going to take a helper, of course, because three hands are needed, or four. If the dropouts are not parallel, straighten, as shown in Figure 16-9, or by using a large crescent wrench on the dropout. Sometimes a framestay or chainstay can be bent. If so, straighten by using a hollowed-out block of steel or wood over the bent portion (Fig. 16-10) and tapping gently and carefully with a hammer. Wrap the stay to prevent damage to finish. Dropouts on less expensive bikes (Fig. 16-11), are just stamped pieces of metal and can easily be bent. The dropouts in Figure 16-7 are high-grade forged steel, and are much sturdier.

Fig. 16-8: Step Five: Check dropout parallel alignment. (*Schwinn Bicycle Company*)

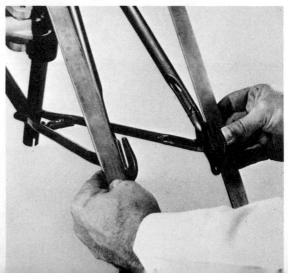

Fig. 16-9: Step Five: Straighten dropouts if not parallel, or if stays are bent. *(Schwinn Bicycle Company)*

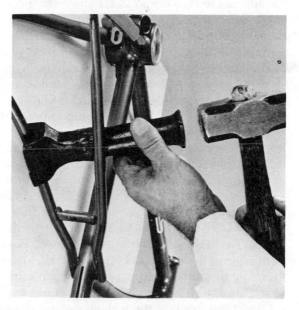

Fig. 16-10: Step Five: Remove kinks from stays if necessary. *(Schwinn Bicycle Company)*

Fig. 16-11: Step Five: These dropouts, of stamped steel, are easier to bend.

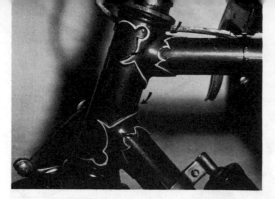

STEP SIX: *Check fork-blade alignment.* The fork is right up there where it or the steering head and head tube it fits into can easily be bent in an accident. First, though, if you have been in an accident, visually check the area around where the top and downtubes join the steering head (Fig. 16-12). Look for wrinkled paint, indicating stress, particularly at the top of the downtube lug and where the top-tube lug joins the steering head. I'm not sure if the printed version of this photo shows the damage, but this is the bike I hit a Cadillac rear bumper with, at about 16 miles an hour. (The Caddy was black, parked on the forbidden side of the street; it was dark and streetlights were dim. So was I.) The fork steering tube was bent and straightened cold, but you can see some paint wrinkling at these two spots if you look closely. Figure 16-13 is a nonlugged frame, undamaged, brand new, but the arrows point to where to look if damage is suspected. By the way, with neither of these excellent frames will you be able to detect whether or not the frame tubes are mitered so they fit snugly against the rounded surface of the tube they fit or lie next to. Figure 16-14 shows a drawing of an unmitered joint. The flat edges of the tube leave a lot of air, and only a small part of the tube actually lies against the adjoining tube (arrow). The black section shows where a fillet of brass was put to disguise the unmitered tube joints. This is a very weak joint indeed. Figure 16-15 shows a mitered joint where the tube butts up more securely, with greater surface against the adjoining tube. A filleted joint is shown in Figure 16-16, and another in Figure 16-17, although the latter is not well finished.

Okay, now back to the fork-alignment check. This is to check the fork blades. Put a straightedge along the rim flat of the *trued* front wheel and the steering head and eyeball the clearance, or measure it. The clearance should not change from top to bottom. This will show a bent steering

Fig. 16-13: Step Six: On a nonlugged frame, look for paint wrinkling at locations where tubes join, as at arrows.

Fig. 16-14: Step Six: An unmitered joint is weaker.

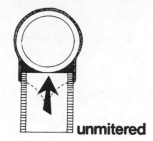

unmitered

mitered

Fig. 16-15: Step Six: A mitered joint is stronger.

Fig. 16-16: Step Six: Filleting can hide an unmitered joint or strengthen a mitered one.

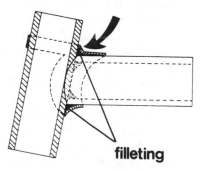

filleting

Fig. 16-17: Step Six: A filleted joint, not beautiful but at least strong. Arrows point to filleted areas.

Fig. 16-18: Step Six: Checking fork align-ment

tube or steering head, or twisted steering head (Fig. 16-18). To check fork blades really requires a special jig, but another way to check blades requires removal of the fork. Lay the fork down on a flat surface and with a carpenter's bubble level, check alignment by moving the level from dropouts to crown. If you start level, the bubble should not have moved when you reach the crown. A rougher check is simply to lean the bike against the wall, squat down and eyeball the blade closest to you against the adjacent blade; you will pick up a gross misalignment that way. If fork blades are out of alignment, remove the fork and straighten them cold. Or buy a new fork if the old one is badly bent. Cold straightening is for *minor* misalignment *only*.

STEP SEVEN: *Check alignment of steering head.* Take a ten-foot-long piece of string. Tie one end to a rear dropout. Run the string around the steering head back to the other dropout and tie in the same place on *that* dropout as on the facing dropout. There will be clearance between the string and the seat tube (Fig. 16-19). Measure that clearance between the string on *both* sides of the seat tube. Both measurements should be alike. Figure 16-20 shows another view of this measurement technique. If the measurement is not the same, straighten cold as in Figure 16-21.

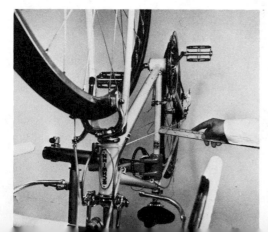

Fig. 16-19: Step Seven: Check steering-head alignment.
(*Schwinn Bicycle Company*)

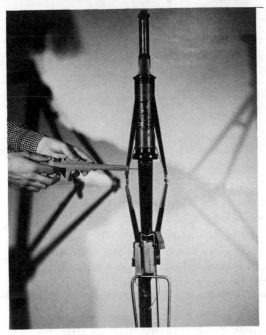

Fig. 16-20: Step Seven: Checking steering-head alignment, front view

Fig. 16-21: Step Seven: Straighten steering head as necessary. (*Schwinn Bicycle Company*)

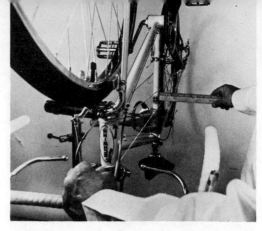

STEP EIGHT: *Check for steering-head twist.* Leaving string in place as in Figure 16-19, move it to the bottom of the steering head and then to the top of the steering head and measure distance from seat tube to the string on both sides when the string is in each position. Figure 16-22 shows the string in *both* positions. This check involves four measurements, all of which should show the same clearance on both sides of the seat tube. If the steering head has been twisted, realign as in Figure 16-21 or 16-23.

STEP NINE: *Check for steering-head centering* by placing straightedge against the side of the bottom bracket and steering head. Measure from the center of the steering head to the straightedge (Fig. 16-24) and repeat the same measurement on other side of the steering head. Both should be the same.

STEP TEN: *Check alignment of seat tube.* Put the straightedge against the bottom-bracket shell and parallel to the seat tube. Measure at top and bottom of clearances between the seat tube and the straightedge (Fig. 16-25). Measurements must be the same. You can align the seat tube, if you're lucky, without undue damage by straightening cold as shown in Figure 16-26.

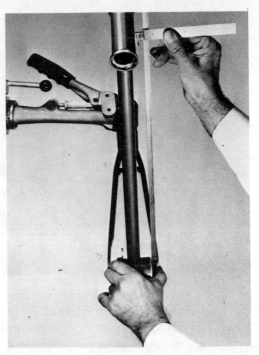

Fig. 16-24: Step Nine: Check steering-head centering. *(Schwinn Bicycle Company)*

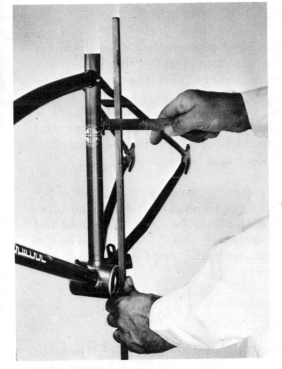

Fig. 16-25: Step Ten: Check alignment of seat tube. *(Schwinn Bicycle Company)*

Fig. 16-26: Step Ten: Straighten seat tube as necessary. *(Schwinn Bicycle Company)*

Fig. 16-27: Step Eleven: Check chainline.

Just a word of caution: The alignment procedures you see in these photos are being made on an inexpensive frameset. You should carefully wrap all tools so as to prevent damage to finish, and if you use a vise be sure you use copper plates in the jaws. If you straighten cold, do it ⅟₆₄th of an inch at a time, or less, and recheck alignment as you go. *Do not use a torch* under any circumstances unless you are willing to ruin the paint finish and risk removing the heat treatment or temper in the tube, and so weaken that tube. A torch is for expert frame builders only.

STEP ELEVEN: *Check gear alignment* by putting the straightedge between the appropriate gears. See Chapter 13 for chainline for your bike. The straightedge should lie flat (Fig. 16-27) on the appropriate front and rear gears (e.g., on a ten-speed, flat against the No. 3 rear cog and on the centerline between the two front chainwheels). See Chapter 13 for instructions on how to adjust chainline.

FRAME TOUCH-UP AND PAINTING

If you have a really fine bicycle, it will pain you to see the finish become nicked, scratched and marred. Unless you keep your bicycle wrapped in cotton batting, in your bedroom, nicks, scratches or mars are the inevitable concomitants of use. Perhaps you will feel better if we call these indications of healthy use "battle scars." And I know you will feel a lot better if these flaws on your beautiful, peerless machine can be removed and the finish brought back to perfection.

Removing scratches and nicks in the finish of a bicycle is virtually a fine art, and one, I must quickly admit, I am congenitally unsuited to and find difficult to do. I have, however, followed the instructions of experts and, with a great deal of internal stress and many mistakes, suceeded eventually in removing battle scars from my good bikes. But then I am not good at fine digital movements . . . I have always hated building tiny little things such as airplane models out of balsa, or ships in a bottle, things like that. If it were not for the sneers of my more artistic friends, and their twinges of real pain as they view my bike's battle scars, I would probably be content to daub something approximating the original color over them, just to keep the rust away. But you, I am sure, have the fine digital touch, the artistic taste and the desire to bring your two-wheeled steed back to its original state. For the following instructions on scratch removal and frame finishing, I am indebted to Otis Childress, of Los Angeles, and to that highly recommended magazine *Bike World* in which the following material appeared in the October 1977 and January 1979 issues. These data are from Mr. Childress's articles in those issues, reprinted by permission of both Mr. Childress and *Bike World*.

Before quoting from these articles, however, let me note that matching paint on your bike is going to be a problem, unless it is a Schwinn, Raleigh or Nishiki. Puch furnishes a small bottle of finish with their top-line models. Otherwise, my solution is to wheel my bike into a large auto-supply store, right up to the display of pressure cans of touch-up paint, and try to select one from either the color on the top of the can (not always a reliable indication of what's inside) or from a color chart sometimes available and hanging on the rack next to the paint cans. My color-matching reliability is around 3 on a scale of 0 to 10, so I always ask a clerk or another shopper for help, and the consensus determines the can I buy. But I have never really ever precisely matched colors this way, although the match is close enough for my low-grade taste. Okay, Otis, the rest is all yours. I won't put it in quotes because it isn't necessary.

Scratch Removal and Refinishing

For a "quicky" repair of scratches so they won't show at a distance, at least, follow these steps:

STEP 1. Clean scratch with soap and water and grade "000" steel wool to remove loosened bits of clinging paint.

STEP 2. If bare metal shows, apply a layer or two of primer and let it dry between coats for at least one hour. Brush in direction of scratch.

STEP 3. Find matching paint. Schwinn bike stores market spray paints, as do Raleigh and bike stores selling Nishiki bikes. You can spray a small amount of paint into a clean small container or onto a small piece of lint-free paper, first shaking the can.

Then, with a small artist's brush, brush in the color coats. If it's just a spot dent, dab in a little paint. If the scratch is tiny, you can dabble some primer and color in it. You can also use paint sticks (Fig. 16-28) such as the ones marketed by Schwinn, rubbing the paint into the groove and then smoothing it out. Paint sticks are easier to use if softened with a match flame first. They won't work on a flat scrape where there is no groove to fill in.

Larger Scrapes—Blending In

You can fill in and blend larger scrapes with a technique known as vignetting and feathering. If you have darkroom experience you will recall how this is done to shade off areas in order to avoid abrupt changes in tone in the finished print.

You can mask off the damaged area with newspaper or masking tape. But

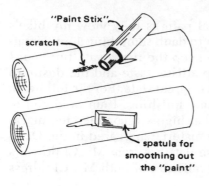

Fig. 16-28: Filling in small scratches

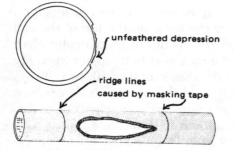

Fig. 16-29: Ridge lines can form around edges of masking tape.

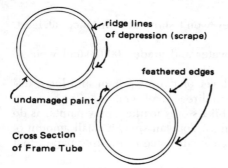

Fig. 16-30: Vignette shields can prevent ridge lines.

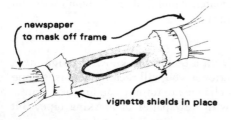

unless you follow these steps you will have an abrupt ridge line (Fig. 16-29) where the paint repair ends and the tape starts. These can be removed by 400-grade sandpaper or "000" steel wool and rubbing compound, but ridge lines may still show. Here are steps that will do the job:

STEP 1. Sand the scraped area to eliminate the abrupt paint break or depression ridge; feather out the edges as shown in Figure 16-30. Use wet or dry sandpaper of a grade appropriate to the hardness and toughness of the old paint (grade 280 or 320), progressing to finer sandpaper, (400 or 600). Final sand with the paper wet to reduce its abrasive action. After final sanding, wash away all residue with clear water.

STEP 2. Mask off the area of the scrape and the rest of the bike to protect it from paint overspray. Don't follow the outline of the scrape. Instead, place one or two layers of masking tape around the frame tube, perpendicular to the tube axis and two or three inches from the edges of the scrape.

Use masking tape because it works well, is not so adhesive it pulls off the paint when you remove it, yet holds well enough to prevent paint seepage under the edges of the tape.

STEP 3. Build a "platform" around the masking tape already in place. Either wrap extra layers of tape or wrap a folded piece of paper around the tape, holding in place with a separate piece of tape. This platform should be ¼ to ½ inch thick.

STEP 4. Tear a piece of paper so it has an uneven and ragged edge, which then serves as a vignette shield. The shield should be long enough to encircle the frame tube, and should overlap about ½ inch. Use paper that is lint free and clean.

STEP 5. With the ragged edge toward the scrape, wrap the shield around the platform and secure it with a piece of tape as shown in Figure 16-30.

If the shields are placed too close to the frame surface (a low platform), the paint may not be fully vignetted, thus leaving a light paint line (though easily removed with steel wool). To be discussed later, but worth noting now, are such variables as paint temperature and spraying distance, which also can cause paint lines and paint "runs."

STEP 6. If bare metal is visible, apply two or three light coats of primer from a spray can. If only a small spot of metal is exposed, it may be covered by using a small brush. Spray, however, leaves a much smoother and more even surface.

After the last primer coat has completely dried, sand lightly with grade 400 or 600 wet-type sandpaper. Steel wool (grade "0000") may be used instead of sandpaper. After sanding or steel wooling, clean the area with a clear water solution.

You may find it easier to sand and clean the area with the vignette shields removed. In this way you are assured of clearing away all sanding residue and completely drying all traces of water before applying the color coats. Do not forget to reposition the vignette shields if you do remove them. Also, you may wish to sand each, or every other, primer coat instead of only the last.

STEP 7. If the original paint finish had an undercoat (which gives tone and depth to the outer color coats) apply two or three layers of an appropriately colored undercoat. This step with assure the fidelity of the final color coat with the original color. (To eliminate this step, especially with a large patching, would result in the repaired area being of a noticeably different shade, something that can still result if the original finish is badly weathered.) Sand or steel wool each layer of undercoat or only the last as instructed in Step 6.

Sanding a previous coat is necessary if it dries rough, even slightly so, as the next coat may amplify the roughness.

STEP 8. Spray on the outer color coats (four or so light ones). To assure a smooth final color coat, each previous coat should be wet-sanded (grade 400 or 600) or steel wool (grade "0000"). The final color coat is, of course, left unsanded.

Spray paints generally function best at room temperature. Submerge spray cans into warm water for 10 minutes or so if necessary. If the paint temperature is too low, the spray will be relatively thick or instead of a spray, the paint will stream out; in either case, the paint will tend to run. The spray nozzle should be held 8-12 inches from the paint surface.

The closer to room temperature the spray is, the closer to the paint surface the nozzle may be held. This is particularly important when "shooting" tight spots in which the nozzle must be held very close to the surface, such as around the seat cluster.

When selecting paint, match it not only by color, but also by type: lacquer on lacquer, or enamel on enamel. Lacquer painted over enamel will lift the enamel off; enamel, however, can be painted over lacquer without damage.

STEP 9. After the final color coat has dried, remove all the shieldings, masking tape and so forth from the bike. After a few days to a week, and especially if the patched area shows any "powdered" or lightly rough spots, go over the area with steel wool (grade "0000") saturated with water. If the area is gone over with dry steel wool, the gloss of the area will be removed and even waxing will not return it to a gloss matching the rest of the frame. You may want to try rubbing compound instead of steel wool. At any rate, such rubbing should be at a minimum.

STEP 10. After the paint has completely dried (three weeks), apply wax.

If paint is not allowed to dry completely and equipment is clamped on, the clamps will make an imprint into the thickness of the paint leaving it to dry not flat and smooth, but bunched up. The reader will do well to consider that a frameset completely refinished requires not less than a month to dry before waxing or clamping on components. Paint may surely be dry to the touch within an hour or two, but only to the touch; it will not be thoroughly dry, nor will it be durable.

An alternate method of vignetting paint is to use a hand-held vignette shield (made by tearing an opening into a small piece of paper). The opening should be slightly larger than the size of the scrape and follow the general outline of the scrape.

In using, hold the shield half an inch to an inch away from the scrape to be repaired and spray with sweeping motions across the openings. This method is applicable to any flat, curving or irregular surface such as around the bottom bracket shell.

An example of using a hand-held vignette shield is in repairing a deep scratch. Using touch-up paint and brush, fill in and build up the scratch above the level of the undamaged paint surface. Carefully sand until level down to the undamaged paint. Finally, after washing away the sanding residue, use the hand-held shield and spray across its opening.

Do not stop spraying while within the opening of the hand-held or taped-on vignette shield or you risk the paint running. Also, thick layering of paint into a deep scratch may take several days to build up to allow each lower layer to dry. Do not sand paint that is not dry or you will literally roll layers of paint off the area and create a gorge in the still-wet, dry-to-the-touch paint. Finally, by placing a strip of masking tape on the opposite side of the frame tube, opposite the scrape, this unprotected area would then be protected against any paint overspray. The result of overspray, when dry, is a rough texture.

Chrome Forks and Stays

The second use of vignetting techniques is in the refinishing of chrome forks and stays (if the frame as a whole is being refinished).

First, if chrome is to be painted, it must be sanded, the standard preparation for painting any surface, but especially important with chromed surfaces. Secondly, a primer coat is a particular necessity prior to any color coat.

Paint will absolutely not "take" to a shiny chrome surface, even one clean of wax. In such a case, the paint easily can be removed with the lightest grade of steel wool, or literally peeled off as you might peel an orange. Yet sanding need not be too harsh. In fact, the chrome under some factory-finished forks is so undamaged that with a little buffing and polishing you can have an all-chrome fork or at least one with more chrome and less paint, like a Raleigh Pro.

Basically, the same problem exists with masking tape in refinishing chrome forks and stays as in repairing scrapes and scratches: a piling up of paint into a ridge at the end of the tape. More importantly, in refinishing a frame more layers of paint are used, causing a tendency for the paint to "sheet-over" the edge of the masking tape, forming a continuous layer (or sheet) of paint. When the paint dries and the masking tape is removed, the effect is one like tearing a sheet of paper, leaving a torn and ragged edge (Fig. 16-31). Vignetting puts a stop to such problems before they start.

The following describes the refinishing of chrome forks and stays (for simplicity only one seat-stay is described and illustrated).

STEP 1. Measure off the amount of chrome to be painted (or not to be painted) by using a taut line anchored equidistant between the stays or fork blades. The brake anchor-bolt hole is suitable for this, unless the stays or fork blades are badly misaligned (Fig. 16-32). Pen or pencil is used to mark off the distance.

Fig. 16-31: Platform of masking tape at edge and paper shield over platform

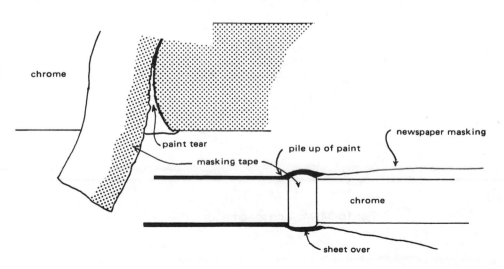

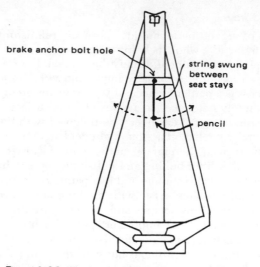

brake anchor bolt hole

string swung
between
seat stays

pencil

Fig. 16-32: Measuring chrome to be painted

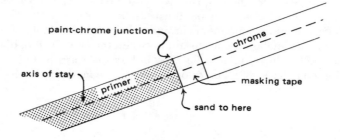

paint-chrome junction

chrome

axis of stay

primer

masking tape

sand to here

Fig. 16-33: Masking stays

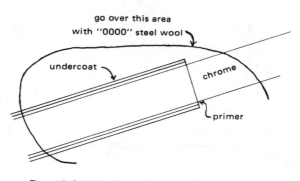

go over this area
with "0000" steel wool

undercoat

chrome

primer

Fig. 16-34: Masking spearheads

If the stays are misaligned, have them properly re-aligned (there are tools for this) before chroming, or if already chromed, before painting. Besides an ill-tracking and ill-handling bike, the misalignment may throw the above measurements off (however, unnoticeably so).

If you are a bit daring, you might consider having chrome only on the right, drive-side chain-stay, or the drive-side chain and seat-stays with the left side drop-out only showing chrome. Asymmetry, if well-balanced and thought out (in this case, using a dark color, particularly black) can have an unusual sort of attractiveness.

STEP 2. Using masking tape, encircle each stay. Now, with grade 400 or 320 wet or dry paper (dry), sand the stays to the edge of the masking tape (to the paint-chrome juncture line, (Fig. 16-33).

STEP 3. After sanding, remove and replace the tape with new tape. Using no more than three encirclements of tape around each stay, be certain that the tape is straight (perpendicular to the axis of the stay, Fig. 16–34). Using newspaper, mask off the chrome that is not to be painted. Mask off each stay individually, as the masking tape will be removed and replaced several times.

With modification, the same procedures are used to create "spearheads" (Fig. 16-34). Masking tape is flexible enough to conform to tapering stays and chain-wheel indentations.

STEP 4. Prime the complete frame (four or so light coats). After the last primer coat has dried, remove the masking tape and go over the immediate area of the juncture line with "0000" steel wool in addition to wet-sanding (grade 400 or 600) the rest of the frame.

Do not sand in the area of the juncture line, or you may remove too much edge paint and scratch the chrome. If you continually sand through paint to bare metal when sanding the frame in general, you might want to try "steel wooling" the frame with grade "000" or "0000" steel wool instead of sanding it.

STEP 5. Replace the masking tape (from Step 4) with a new strip. Apply an undercoating (three or so coats) to the frame if you have decided to use one over the primer coat. After the last undercoating has dried, remove the masking tape and steel wool the area of the juncture line (as in Step 4) to remove any hint of paint buildup as you sand the rest of the frame.

If at any time you suspect paint seepage under the masking tape, remove the tape and clear away the excess paint with steel wool.

STEP 6. Replace the masking tape (from Step 5) with new tape, but this time place it about one millimeter away from the juncture line (Fig. 16-35 top two figures).

Now, build a platform of masking tape or folded paper behind the strip of tape already in place (Fig. 16-35).

STEP 7. Make a vignette shield from torn paper and shield off the juncture line about half an inch (Fig. 16-35).

STEP 8. Using your chosen finish color, spray the frame. The finish coats will be lightly layered (vignetted) under the vignette shield.

Before spraying the last two color coats, remove the shield permanently, but leave the masking tape in place (or replace it with new tape, still with one-millimeter gap). The final two coats, sprayed with the shields removed, will cover the drop-off at each paint-chrome juncture.

When the frame is completely dry (about a month) apply wax.

After wet-sanding each color coat, it may be necessary to remove the shields in order to effectively clear away any sanding residue and water that may have

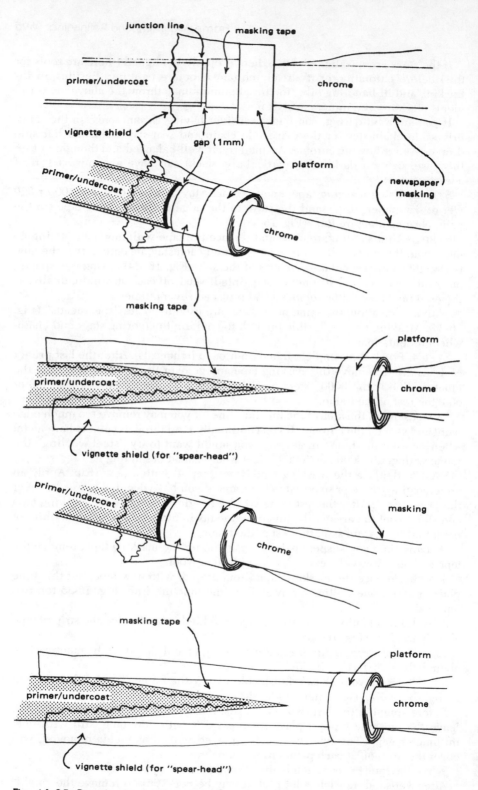

Fig. 16-35: Details of masking on stays and spearheads

"rolled" under the shields (to prevent fouling the next applied coat). This would also, with the shields removed, be a good time to smooth out the area of the juncture line with steel wool. Remember to replace the shields.

To vary the amount of spray being vignetted under a vignette shield, alter the shield's height above the paint surface or the amount that it overlaps the juncture line.

The number of coats suggested is simply that, a suggestion. Three or four coats may just as easily be five or eight light coats (but definitely no less than three). Vignette shields can be used with each coat of paint (from the first primer to the last color coat), or only with every second or third coat (be sure to remove paint buildup between coats).

An extra degree of protection may be added to the paint-chrome juncture by lining it with clear lacquer or enamel. First, using "000" steel wool, go over the juncture line (about one-eighth inch of paint and an equal amount of chrome). Next, using an artist's brush, trim the juncture line with two or three thin layers of the "clear" (which will "take" sufficiently to the chrome and be durable).

The value of all of this seemingly unnecessary concern and preparation is in the results: smooth and sharply defined juncture lines, unlike some assembly line paint jobs that require a contrasting trim color to hide (unsuccessfully) hurried workmanship.

Color Contrasting

The third use of vignetting is in color contrasting the head-tube with the frame color (as the complete frame is being refinished).

The preliminary steps are no different from painting the frame in general— apply primer, then an undercoat. Next, select a color that is contrasting to the chosen frame color. For illustration, orange will be the frame color with gray as the head-tube color.

Step 1. (After the primer and undercoatings are applied and completely dried.) Mask off the frame, using masking tape and newspaper, about two or three inches from the lugs on the head-tube.

Remove the headset before painting the frame. This will allow the inside of the head-tube to be cleaned thoroughly, particularly of rust. Secondly, if the headset is not removed, paint may seep into the thin gap between the headset and the head-tube and remain "wet" for quite a while. Finally, painting is easier with non-essentials removed.

STEP 2. Place vignette shields about the upper and about the lower lugs. The opening between the shields and the lugs should be about half an inch.

STEP 3. Spray about four light coats of the chosen contrast color (gray) onto the head-tube. (Always spray with a sweeping motion, horizontally or vertically.) When dry to the touch, remove the shields.

Schwinn aluminum undercoat is a silver-gray, perfect in this case as both an undercoat and a contrast color, thus allowing steps 1, 2 and 3 to be eliminated.

STEP 4. After the head-tube area is completely dry, mask off the head-tube only (leave the lugs unmasked.)

If the head-tube is now allowed to dry completely (one or two weeks depending on the number and thickness of the coats), the masking tape will, when eventually removed, pull off the paint.

While the frame is completely stripped of paint, a "masking" should be made to fit the head-tube perfectly into the area between the lugs. A masking is made by placing overlapping strips of masking tape on a plastic or glass surface and,

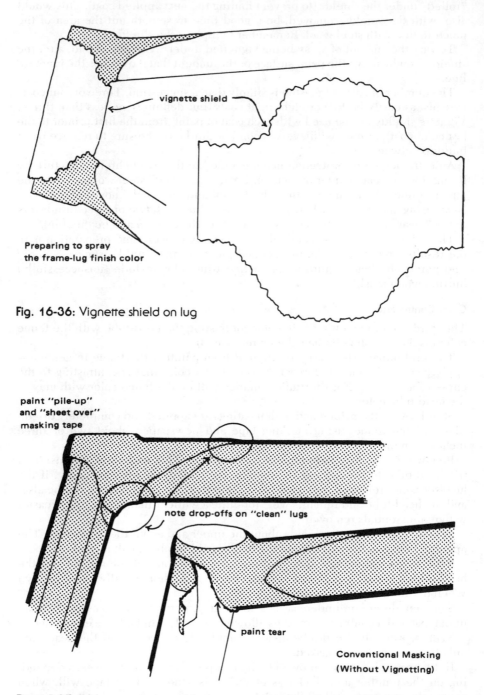

vignette shield

Preparing to spray
the frame-lug finish color

Fig. 16-36: Vignette shield on lug

paint "pile-up"
and "sheet over"
masking tape

note drop-offs on "clean" lugs

paint tear

Conventional Masking
(Without Vignetting)

Fig. 16-37: Without proper masking you can get paint pile-up and paint tear where shown.

using a razor blade, cutting out the masking. This is a trial-and-error proposition. Be sure to get a good fit and make an extra one. (The masking should be only one layer thick except at the overlap.)

Small pieces of tape can be fitted on the head-tube along the lugs if necessary to completely mask off the head-tube. Use a fingernail (or whatever) to shape the masking into a perfect fit along the edge of the lugs where there should be no bunching.

STEP 5. Make a platform one-fourth to one-half inch high of masking tape or folded paper and place around the head-tube.

STEP 6. Make a vignette shield by tearing newspaper to the contour of the head-tube, but about one-fourth of an inch larger.

Place the shield around the full circumference of the head tube, and tape in place. The shield should not only overlap the lugs by at least one-fourth of an inch, but should "stand off" from the head-tube and lugs by the same amount. Some adjustment of the shield may be necessary at the rear of the head-tube (Fig. 16-36).

STEP 7. With the shield in place, apply the frame-color coats (orange). After the last coat is dry to touch, remove the shield, but do not remove the masking.

STEP 8. With the shield removed, examine the lug/head-tube juncture (where the gray and orange colors meet). If the frame paint at the edge of the lugs appears to thin, spray on an extra-light layer or two of the frame color about the lugs (with the shield still off, but with the masking in place).

STEP 9. If satisfied with the results thus far, and after about three days to a week, remove the head-tube masking. After at least a month, wax may be applied to the complete frame.

If contrasting the head-tube is an after-thought (after the frame has been painted one color), it may be necessary to sand away some of the paint from the lugs and head-tube before beginning Step 1. If not done, the extra paint of the contrast color on the head-tube and the extra frame paint applied to the lugs may be so thick that it would be difficult to distinguish the lug drop-off from the head-tube proper, especially with lugs thinned and tapered at the edges (Fig. 16-37).

As extra protection and as a "leveler," before waxing, you might want to line the lug/head-tube juncture with a clear lacquer or enamel using a small artist's brush.

If only the head-tube masking were used (without the vignette shield), the expected piling up and "sheeting-over" of paint at the lug/head-tube juncture would occur. The masking would, when removed, pull and tear the lug paint leaving a ragged edge (Fig. 16-37).

Attempting to smooth out ragged edges by sanding is frustrating at best, as it is easy to sand through to bare metal. Of course, the juncture line can be trimmed or lined with a third color and so, to a degree, can hide poor workmanship. Yet, steady hand or not, the trim line would just be a tacky reflection of tacky workmanship.

Tips to Inexpensive Frame Painting

More often than not, experience is acquired through costly mistakes and wasted time, often only to learn a few tips, a couple of shortcuts and several do's and don'ts. This holds true in the painting of your frame.

If you have decided to repair your frame this winter, but are without experience, the following may help guide you through inexpensively. Each set of tips has been placed under appropriate headings for easy reference.

Solvents (Removers)

You should apply semi-paste solvents with a paintbrush. Then, use coarse-grade steel wool to remove the solvent-loosened paint from the frame. Before rinsing the frame clean of solvent, however (in fact, before applying the solvent), plug up the bottom bracket shell and the head tube by tightly stuffing them with newspaper to keep water out of the frame tubes.

Keep in mind that newer paint generally dissolves more quickly and easily than older (cured) paint. Also, remember that warm, ambient temperatures will speed the dissolving action of solvents. Solvents burn, so cover exposed skin areas and have water nearby for rinsing off. Be careful. Although the fingertips may be somewhat insensitive to the "burning" of solvents, the sinuses, insides of the wrists and the eyes are not.

Use paint and lacquer thinners only secondarily, as they are not primary paint removers.

Preparing the Frame

Strip off all the old paint, or at least repair all scratches, chips and scrapes. Consider well that the original paint can hide the "carelessness" of a frame builder. If it needs to be repainted, then it needs to be stripped.

File off all excess brazing material (which was hiding under the original paint). If necessary, reshape the dropouts and the dropout derailleur-attaching "lug" (or "boss"), and make any needed frame realignments before painting or chroming.

Remove all nonessentials (such as the headset) for ease and completeness in preparing the frame for painting and in the actual painting. Optionally, you may wish to remove the builder's head tube "marque," replacing it later with rivets, or leaving it off and filling in the rivet holes with a filler such as one of the commercially available "liquid metals."

Forget about liquid "etchers." Sandpaper the bare frame to a smooth, but not slick finish. Use coarse or medium-grade emery cloth followed by "180" or "220" Wet-or-Dry sandpaper. (As you sand, remember to do it always in one direction.) If you sandblast the old paint, be sure to use the proper grade of blasting material and mask all chrome and repaint immediately. Sandblasted frames begin to rust *very* quickly. *Do not touch frame with bare hands.*

You will need to look for, and remove, rust. Many times it hides in areas such as inside the seat tube.

Mask all threads before painting. Shove rolled-up newspaper into, and sticking out both ends of, the bottom bracket shell and head tube. Removing paint from bottom bracket threads, without damaging the outside frame finish, is not always easy. In addition, the front fork can and should be refinished separately from the main frame.

Painting Conditions

If you are painting indoors, you should open all windows, clear the room of furniture (or cover everything with newspaper, including the floor) and close all closets. It might be wise to wear a "respirator"-type mask or breathe through a wet face towel held over your mouth and nose. Paint overspray should not be allowed to enter your lungs.

Use well-diffused lighting. In addition to opened window curtains, use ceiling

Fig. 16-38: This W.R. Brown Co. combination of small compressor and spray gun works well for small paint jobs. I have also used their sand blaster, which looks very much like the spray unit at left with with a hardened steel nozzle. Use fine grit, spray in an old bike box, wear protective goggles and filter mask over mouth and nose.

lights, repositioned table lamps (with the shades removed), and a hand-held flashlight for checking tight areas.

Remove all dust from the frame between coat applications. A clean paint brush is adaptable for this purpose, because rags rarely are lint- or static-free. Dust particles caught under layers of paint will show through as paint "blisters."

Do not create static charges by rubbing the frame tubes unnecessarily, as this tends to attract dust particles. Besides, there is no such thing as clean, oil-free hands, so hands off between coats.

Do not spray onto a cold/damp frame or on cold/damp days. Water (dampness) will bubble up or blister the paint, as I have sadly and expensively learned from personal experience. Spraying on a cold/damp night can cause the paint to dry to a dull, "frosty" finish even though a "glossy" finish color is used. Maintain spraying conditions as constantly as possible from one spraying session to the next, especially if respraying only a small section of the frame. Note such spraying instructions as ". . . material and surface temperature 65-95 degrees . . . relative humidity 85% . . . recoat at 70 degrees. . . ." Keep in mind that instructions may vary between paint brands.

When cleaning up paint overspray, use a vacuum cleaner and a damp dusting cloth. Sweeping with a hand broom only will cause the overspray to become

Fig. 16-39: Sanding frame prior to painting

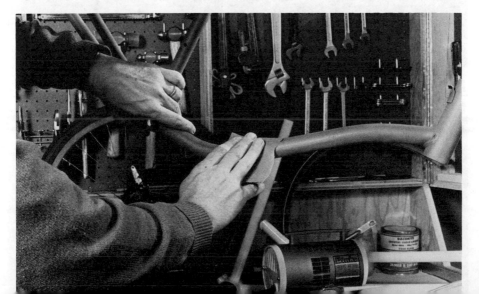

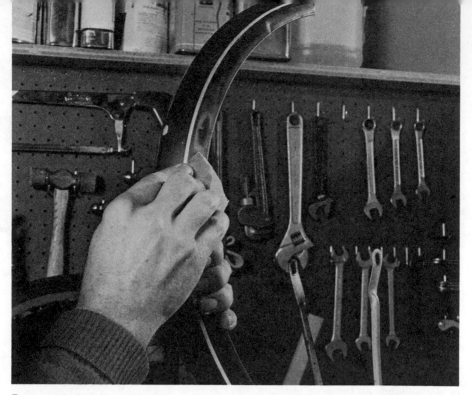

Fig. 16-40: Sanding small area. Note that sanding is "feathered" at the edges.

Fig. 16-41: Masking around area to be refinished

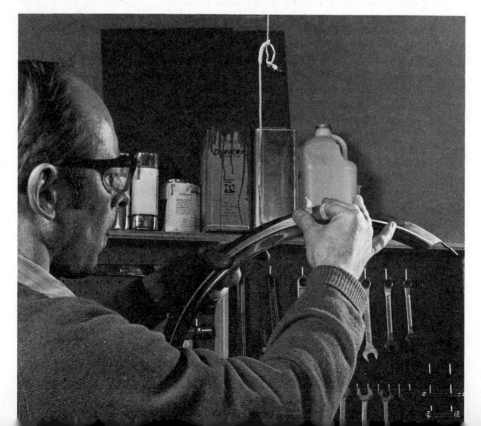

airborne and settle or resettle on furniture, shelves and you, and even worse, in your lungs.

When you finally are ready to start painting, practice on something first. Learn the spray characteristics of each spray can, and read all label instructions.

Hang the frame so that you easily can get to and spray all areas of it. A pipe, one end supported in a stable base and the other end inserted into the frame's seat tube (at about waist or head high), is even better. The frame should be easily rotatable on its "paint stand."

Always spray with sweeping motions, except when spraying tight areas or very small spots, which are "shot" with quick bursts of spray. Lightly spray hard-to-get-to areas before spraying the frame in general, assuring that easily missed areas such as the undersides of the frame tubes and around the seat and head tube lugs are fully covered. Some manufacturers miss these areas, or the paint is so thinly applied that Comet cleanser, a dish towel and very little "elbow grease" are enough to rub away the finish completely. (Use a nonabrasive cleaner for cleaning the frame.) Additionally, extra paint also should be applied to the underside of the down tube and the backside of the seat tube as extra protection against kicked-up road gravel.

Shake the spray can often to keep the paint ingredients well-mixed. Never start spraying directly onto the frame, as this may cause a paint "run." Begin spraying first into the air, then with a sweeping motion move onto the frame. Conversely, stop spraying by first sweeping from the frame into the air before releasing the spray nozzle.

At some point before applying the first color coat (preferably before the first primer coat), coat the insides of the frame tubes, chainstays and bottom bracket shell with a rust inhibitor ("Penetrol" or "Rust-oleum" primer) to protect from the effects of rain and condensation. Plug up one end of a frame tube and, using a funnel, fill completely with the rust inhibitor and then empty. Do the same with the other tubes. Alternately, you might want to try using a sponge brush with a long, flexible handle.

The first two or so coats of primer, undercoat and color coats should be "misted" or "dusted" onto the frame. They will dry slightly rough, but with successive coats and with sanding, the coats will be smoothed out. Use grade "400" or "600" Wet-or-Dry paper.

A painting tip to remember is that several thin, light coats are better than one thick coat. However, spread the coat applications over time (one or two weeks). Each coat of paint will reflect the quality of the previous coat. So, prepare each coat for the next one.

Do not try to stop paint runs by wiping with a rag. Runs can be stopped by the following methods: soaking them up with a finger wrapped in a rag; by turning the frame over to reverse the run; by using quick sweeps of spray, undercutting the run (but without feeding it much more paint), thus sweeping and spreading out the run; or by blowing on the run to spread it out and prevent its running farther. (For a stream of "air" without paint, turn the spray can upside-down, aim just below the run and depress the nozzle.)

If all else fails, allow the run to dry completely, then sand and repaint. To lessen the time needed for a thick run to dry, cut away part of it (when partially dry) with a razor blade. Do not attempt to sand wet paint, as you will only create a gorge in the thickness of the paint surface. *Do not sand a wet paint run.*

A coat of paint being applied over a previously applied coat may rewet the previous coat, thus effectively acting as a solvent. This is one reason for not

Fig. 16-42: Spraying with Binks "Wren" air gun. This small air gun comes with different nozzles and is ideal for small jobs such as bicycle frames. It gives very little overspray and can be aimed at very small areas.

Fig. 16-43: Spraying fork with Binks "Wren" air gun

wiping away a paint run. You may wipe through the rewetted previous coat of paint to expose bare metal.

If your touch is too light, or the spray nozzle is held too far from the frame, the paint will "dust-on," creating a rough or "powdered" texture. To smooth it out, use "0000" steel wool. Keep your technique controlled.

Do not apply lacquer over enamel, as the former will lift off the latter. Enamel can be applied safely over lacquer without damage, but why confuse yourself? Stick with one or the other throughout.

If you are painting outdoors, do so on ideally windless, dry and warm days and in the shade. If you can outlast family objections, it is preferable to paint indoors in an empty, well-ventilated room in which control of dust and other conditions can be maintained.

If a bug lands on wet paint, remove it with a pin or needle. If the removal messes up the paint, allow the surface to dry, then sand and respray the area without masking it off.

If only a small amount of paint remains in the can, or if the nozzle is clogged, the paint will tend to spurt out, creating large paint globs ("toad skin") on the frame. Either throw away these cans, or use only with an artist brush for small touch-up jobs. Besides, the "last" of the paint is never quite the same quality as the "first" of it. Clear the spray nozzle/siphon tube by turning the spray can upside down and depressing the nozzle. The nozzle itself also can be cleared by reaming it out with a pin or needle. Occasionally wipe clean the outside of the nozzle with a rag.

EPOXIES AND EXOTICS

"Exotics" such as epoxies and the like are up to you, but learn their limitations, special preparation and so forth. Again, practice on something first. Remember that if you choose an unusual frame color, and later must repair a large paint scrape, you may have difficulty in matching that color.

Clear lacquer (or enamel) applied over the frame color coat will give it a heightened gloss and, to a certain extent, act as a protective coat. However, a clear coat is not in the least bit necessary, and if improperly applied, may prove disastrous. If you do use a "clear," practice on something before applying it to the frame.

"Levelers," "surfacers" and rubbing compound all have the same basic function of smoothing out scratches in the primer and finish coats. These refinishing accessories are not especially necessary, however, and you can do just as well without them. You may, however, want to try rubbing compound on the finish coats.

Enamels require a different application procedure from lacquers, despite the fact that some manufacturers use the same label instructions regardless of whether the paint is lacquer or enamel.

Find and stay with one supplier who has a good, "no-hassle" refund policy and who is knowledgeable (a salesperson who gets all of his or her information by reading the back label of the spray can is not knowledgeable). Finally, do not lose that receipt.

CHROMING TIPS

The surface to be chromed must be absolutely smooth. Chrome plating does not fill in nor does it smooth out scratches (large, small or tiny), it just plates them. Sand out all scratches (grade 400 or 600 Wet-or-Dry paper).

Those parts of the frame not to be chromed should be masked with plastic electrician's tape, which will conform to just about any irregular shape. It may be to your advantage to mask the frame yourself, as the plater may charge you extra (a lot extra) for masking the frame himself. Talk to the plater first.

Even if you want only a few inches of the lower blades chromed, have the complete front fork chromed (chrome, properly sanded, can be painted). If chroming the rear stays, chrome each stay completely, from the dropout to the seat lug or bottom bracket shell—in general, to any point where there is a bend or turn. Do so even if only partially chromed stays are desired, otherwise the chrome plating may form a "ridge" at the edge of the electrician's tape (depending on the thickness of the plating). Partially chromed stays (and forks) of commercially produced frames actually are completely chromed.

There are a few tight areas on a bike frame that are difficult for the plater to polish properly (a prerequisite to plating "bright" chrome). The result is that if you have these areas or the complete frame chromed, they may not be as bright as other areas of chrome.

Mask all threads. In general, mask anything in which a dimensional enlargement would cause a component "misfit" (such as the headset lower race platform, or shoulder, or the fork crown). Chrome plating is not at all easy to file off, so do not put it where it is not wanted.

Chrome plating has its disadvantages, such as the corrosive actions of the plating process (for example, rust forming on the insides of the frame tubes). Hydrogen embrittlement, another bugaboo of the plating process, is caused when hydrogen diffuses into the metal being plated during the chroming operation. Oven baking at a prescribed temperature/time setting will relieve the hydrogen. However, some platers will not do this, do not want to be bothered with it and simply do not care. The question is, do you? Some cyclists are very wary about riding with front forks weakened or made brittle by the plating process.

As soon as the frame is chromed, get it back from the plater and remove the rust formed during the plating process. Do not allow the frame to remain in the plater's shop longer than necessary.

The disadvantages of chroming (real, imagined or simply exaggerated) are enough to discourage many from having any frame part plated. It is your choice. If the plater becomes lazy during one of the steps of the plating process, you easily may end up with a shoddy plating job.

One plater, who assured me that he had experience in plating bike frames, returned a front fork to me that literally peeled. Yes, I was able to peel much of the chrome plating off the fork (just as you would peel the foil wrapping from a candy bar), exposing the copper base, or "under-plating." Collective opinion suggested that one probable cause was the plater's failure to keep the fork, while handling it, clean of dirt and/or grease. In any case, it was a shoddy job.

A verbal guarantee is just another way of saying, "maybe, but probably not." Get it in writing, and hang on to that payment receipt. A final consideration, for chromed (as with unchromed) frames is to coat the insides of the tubes with a rust inhibitor/preventative.

Admittedly, the foregoing is less than complete. But with experience, you will no doubt add several tips of your own. In the meanwhile, the usual, but avoidable, "blunders of inexperience" hopefully will be minimized.

Appendices

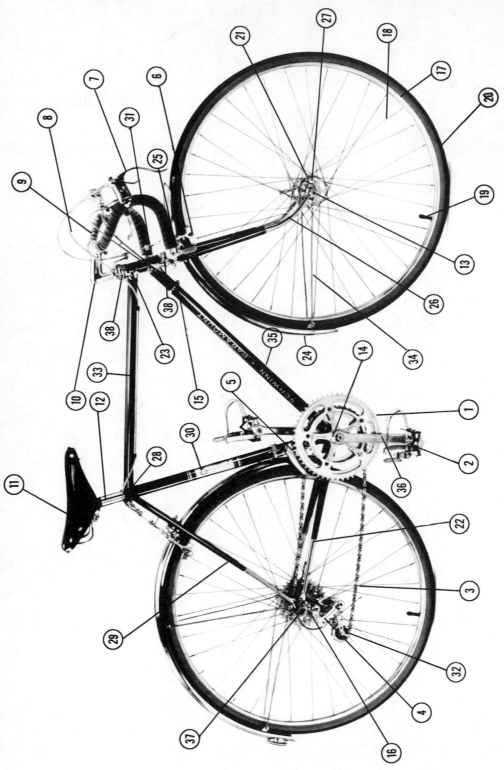

Fig. 325: Key to Bicycle Parts

1. Chainwheel
2. Pedal
3. Chain
4. Rear derailleur
5. Front derailleur
6. Caliper brake
7. Brake lever
8. Brake cable
9. Handlebars
10. Handlebar stem
11. Seat (saddle)
12. Seat post
13. Quick-release skewer (for instant wheel removal)
14. Bottom bracket
15. Gear-shift lever for rear derailleur
16. Freewheel gear cluster
17. Rim
18. Spoke
19. Valve
20. Tire
21. Hub (high-flange type)
22. Chainstay
23. Lug
24. Fender
25. Fork crown
26. Fork
27. Front wheel dropout
28. Seat cluster lug
29. Seat stay
30. Seat tube
31. Head tube
32. Tension roller, rear derailleur
33. Top tube
34. Fender brace
35. Downtube
36. Cotterless crank
37. Rear wheel dropout
38. Headset (top and bottom)

A Cycling Dictionary of Terms

Alignment Applies basically to bicycle frame. Dropouts should be parallel; fork blades and stays parallel to top tube; top tube centered between stays; head tube parallel to fork blades; fork blades parallel to each other; stays parallel to each other; seat tube parallel to bottom-bracket sides, for example.

Ankling Technique of pedaling, in which the foot follows through 180 degrees or more.

Bottom-Bracket Assembly Spindle, bearings, right fixed cone, left adjustable cone, adjustable cone locknut.

Bottom-Bracket Hangar Short round tube, usually from 68 to 72 mm. long, to which is welded or brazed the seat and downtubes and chainstays, and which accommodates the bottom-bracket assembly.

Brake Levers Levers mounted on handlebars to actuate caliper brakes.

Cable Wire to brakes or derailleur gears for controlling their movement.

Caliper Brakes Hand brakes. Actuated by handlebar-mounted levers.

Chain Articulated drive unit which transmits power from chainwheel to rear wheel.

Chain Stays Section of frame from bottom bracket to rear wheel dropout.

Chainwheel Large wheel with gear teeth on right crank, which delivers power from crank, through chain, to rear wheel. Chainwheel can be single, double, or triple wheel.

Coaster Brakes Footpedal-activated internal hub rear brakes.

Cotterpin Holds cranks on bottom-bracket axle in cottered crank designs.

Crank Steel or dural member, one end of which is threaded to receive pedal, other end of which is fastened to bottom-bracket spindle. Right-hand crank (facing forward) also is fitted with chainwheel.

Cyclometer Bicycle odometer for measuring mileage. Mounts on lower front fork.

Derailleur From the French "to derail." A mechanism to derail or move chain from one gear to another on either rear wheel or chainwheel.

Derailleur Cage Holds rear derailleur idler and jockey wheels.

Downtube Part of frame extending from steering head to bottom bracket.

Dishing Truing rear wheel so rim is centered exactly between outer faces of cone locknuts; necessary because of added width of freewheel. In dishing, rear rim is more toward right of hub centerline, whereas front-wheel rim is centered on hub centerline.

Fork Crown Flat or slightly sloping part at top of fork, just under steering head.

Front Fork Part holding front wheel dropouts, which is turned by handlebars to steer bicycle. Included in this unit is steering head (inside head tube of frame), fork blades (round or oval depending on whether a track or road bike), and fork tips.

Front Dropout Lug brazed to front fork bottom tips into which front wheel axle fits.

Handlebar Stem Steel or dural piece, top section of which holds handlebars, bottom part of which fits into top of fork.

Head Tube Large-diameter tube holding front fork and fork bearings, into which is brazed or welded top and downtubes.

Hub Front or rear wheel unit drilled to receive spokes and machined to hold axle and bearings.

Jockey Sprocket The top of the two rear derailleur idler wheels. This wheel moves the chain from one rear-wheel gear to another.

Mudguards Fenders.

Mudguard Stays Fender braces.

Pannier Saddlebag for mounting on rear of bicycle, usually in pairs for balance. Smaller units may also be mounted on the front of bicycle.

Quick-Release Skewer Mechanism to permit removal of front or rear wheels in seconds.

Rattrap Pedals Steel or aluminum alloy body, steel axle, cones, and bearings of open design. For racing or touring, usually with toe clips and straps to hold foot in place and permit 360-degree pressure on pedals.

Rear Dropout Lug brazed or welded to seat stays and chainstays into which rear-wheel axle fits.

Rim Wheel, less spokes and hub.

Saddle Seat.

Seat Cluster A three-way lug into which is brazed or welded top and seat tubes and seat stays.

Seat Post A hollow cylinder made of dural or steel, the top end of which holds seat, the bottom section of which fits into seat tube.

Seat Stays Part of frame extending from just under seat to rear wheel dropout.

Seat Tube Part of frame in which seat is placed and which extends from under seat to bottom bracket.

Steering Head That part of fork just above crown. Threaded to receive headset locknuts and splined or flattened on one side to receive headset washer.

Tension Roller Bottom of the two rear derailleur idler wheels. This wheel keeps correct tension on the chain.

Tires, Tubular Ultralightweight track- or road-racing tires. "Sew-ups" with tube sewn in all around inner periphery of tire.

Tires, Wired-On Conventional tire, with wire bead that holds tire seated on rim section. Open so tube can be easily removed.

Toe Clips Cage on pedals, to hold feet in position, keep them from sliding off pedals.

Top Tube Horizontal frame member between seat tube and head tube.

Truing Also "centering" of rim between axle locknuts. Also concentric (roundness) and lateral (side-to-side) alignment of rim.

Valve Where air is put into tire.

Variable Gear Hub Rear hub containing two, three, or five internal gears and as many gear ratios, shiftable from external gear lever mounted on handlebars or top tube.

BICYCLING MAGAZINES

American Bicyclist and Motorcyclist
461 Eighth Ave.
New York, New York 10001

Of little interest to the general cycling fan, unless he wants to start a bike store. Mainly for the bike dealer. Subscription: $28 per year, monthly.

Bicycle Journal
4915 W. Freeway
Fort Worth, Texas 76107

For the bike dealer exclusively. Subscription $7 per year, monthly. $1 first copy.

Bicycle Motocross Action
5222 Arvada St.
Torrance, California 90503

For the young BMXer and for the dealer interested in BMX products, this covers racing and new equipment. Subscription: $4.50 per year, bi-monthly.

Bicycle Paper
(formerly the Great Bicycle Conspiracy)
Box 842
Seattle, Washington 98111

Subscription: $3 per year, seven issues.

Bicycling
33 E. Minor St.
Emmaus, Pennsylvania 18049

One of the two major cycling magazines, this is for the entire biking public. Subscription: $10 per year, monthly.

Canadian Cyclist
333 River Rd.
Vanier City, Ontario
K1L 8B9 Canada

Published by the Canadian Cycling Association.

Cycling
161-166 Fleet St.
London, E.C. 4
England

Primarily for the cycle-racing enthusiast, although it contains excellent articles on touring in England, Ireland and on the continent. Subscription: $33.80 per year. Published every Thursday.

Cycle Touring
69 Meadrow
Godalming, Surrey
England

Free to members of the Cyclist's Touring Club (same address as the publication). Subscription: $4 for six yearly issues, postage paid. Published in December, February, April, June, August and October. Well worth the money if you plan to cycle abroad on your own.

The Hosteler
American Youth Hostels, Inc.
Delaplane, Virginia 22025

You have to join your local AYH chapter in order to receive this publication, but you get it free of charge once you do. Carries articles on outings, cycling in general, and other AYH outdoor activities.

The LAW Bulletin
League of American Wheelmen publication
Box 988
Baltimore, Maryland 21203

You get this publication free when you join the local chapter. It is an excellent guide for cycle touring and for preventive maintenance for your bicycle.

Minicycle/BMX Action
7950 Deering Ave.
Canoga Park, California 91304

Another BMX racing magazine. Subscription: $13.50 per year, monthly.

Velo-News
Box 1257
67 Main St.
Brattleboro, Vermont 05301

Comprehensive coverage of the bike racing scene both here and abroad, a must for the serious racing cyclist. Subscription: $9 for 18 issues.

The Wheelmen
% G. Donald Adams
214 Maywinn Rd.
Defiance, Ohio 43512

The Wheelmen is an organization devoted to the restoration and riding of early bicycles, and to the "encouragement of cycling as a part of modern living." Published twice a year. You get the magazine when you pay dues to the organization. Join by writing Mrs. Donald Cottrell, 6239 Anavista Dr., Flint, Michigan 48507.

BICYCLE SUPPLY SOURCES

L. L. Bean, Inc.
Freeport, Maine 04032

The old standby. High-quality camping equipment at quite reasonable prices.

Bellwether
1161 Mission
San Francisco, California 94103

Free catalog for panniers, bags, sleeping bags, etc.

Big Wheel, Ltd.
Dept. K, 340 Holly St.
Denver, Colorado 80220

Send $3 for catalog.

Bike Warehouse
215 Main St. B1
New Middleton, Ohio 44442

Send 50 cents for general catalog.

Bikecology Bike Shops, Inc.
1515 Wilshire Blvd. W.
P.O. Box 1880
Santa Monica, California 90406

Excellent, free 96-page catalog, a mine of information on what is available and some technical data.

The Handbook of Cycl-ology
2735 Hennepin Ave. So.
Minneapolis, Minnesota 55408

$4.00 for a 200-page catalog.

Camp-7
802 S. Sherman
Longmont, Colorado 80501

Free catalog on sleeping bags.

Camp Trails
P.O. Box 23155
Phoenix, Arizona 85002

Free catalog for various camping gear.

Cyclopedia
311 N. Mitchell St.
Cadillac, Michigan 49601

$3.00 for valuable catalog, bikes to bags.

Early Winters, Ltd.
110 Prefontaine Place South
Seattle, Washington 98104

Terrific collection of camping gear, outdoor clothing and related equipment. Send for handsome, beautifully illustrated catalog.

Freewheeler
P.O. Box 851
Metuchen, New Jersey 08840

$1.50 for catalog on components, framesets.

Frostline
Dept. C, 452 Burbank
Broomfield, Colorado 80020

Sew it yourself bike bags and camping equipment.

Great Outdoors Trading Co.
109 Second St., Dept. B303
Sausalito, California 94965

For various outdoor stuff.

Handbook of Cycling
Flying Dutchman, Ltd.
Dept. K, P.O. Box 20352
Denver, Colorado 80220

Send $2 for catalog on road and track bikes.

Hartley Alley's Touring Cyclist Shop
P.O. Box 4009B
Boulder, Colorado 80306

Send 35 cents.

International Pro Bike Shop
1400 Beaverton Dr.
Kettering, Ohio 45429

Send $2 for catalog on all components, frames.

Jones Cycle Wear
24 Brown Ave.
Lunenburg, Massachusetts 01462

Send a quarter for catalog on custom-made wear.

Kirtland Tour Pak
Box 4059 B
Boulder, Colorado 80306

Panniers, etc. Free catalog.

Malibu Cyclery
22524 Pacific Coast Highway
Malibu, California 90265

Free catalog.

Palo Alto Bicycles
P.O. Box 1276
Palo Alto, California 94302

Another free one.

Redwood Cycling Apparel
1593 A St.
Arcata, California 95521

A quarter for catalog.

Sierra Specialties
P.O. Box 6094
Reno, Nevada 89503

Tires, hubs.

The Source
2300 Central Ave.
Boulder, Colorado 80301

All about touring, an excellent source. 35 cents for catalog.

Wares
2656 N. 76th St.
Milwaukee, Wisconsin 53213

Racing and touring bikes, plus accessories.

Wilshire West
11841 Wilshire Blvd.
Los Angeles, California 90025

$1 for catalog on bikes and components.

Zeus
11 Stone St.
New York, New York 10004

Send $2 for components catalog.

FOR METRIC SUPPLIES

Both firms below supply, on mail-order basis, just about every hard-to-find-size metric nut, bolt, measuring tool, drills, wrenches, cutting and reaming tools, fasteners and thread inserts. There's also British stuff, the British Standard Whitworth thread you'll find on some English bicycles. Especially useful is a caliper vernier inside, outside, and depth gauge of plastic for measuring bike parts, and a metric screw gauge, to make sure you get the right size replacements.

Ametric Supply Co.
2461 N. Clybourne Ave.
Chicago, Illinois 60614

Metric Multistandard Components Corp.
198 Saw Mill River Road
Elmsford, New York 10523

Metric to American Conversion Table

Multiply	by	to obtain
(Linear)		
Millimeters (mm)	.03937	Inches
Millimeters (mm)	.00328	Feet
Centimeters (cm)	.3937	Inches
Centimeters (cm)	.0328	Feet
(Distance)		
Meters (m)	39.37	Inches
Meters (m)	3.28	Feet
Kilometers (km)	3281	Feet
Kilometers (km)	.6214	Miles
(Area)		
Square Centimeters (cm²)	.155	Square Inches
Square Centimeters (cm²)	.001076	Square Feet
Square Meters (m²)	10.76	Square Feet
(Volume)		
Cubic Centimeters (cc)	.06102	Cubic Inches
Liters (1)	61.02	Cubic Inches
(Liquid Capacity)		
Liters (1)	2.113	Pints
Liters (1)	1.057	Quarts
Liters (1)	.2642	Gallons
Cubic Centimeters (cc)	.0338	Fluid Ounces
U.S. Gallons	1.2	Imperial gals.
Imperial Gallons	4.537	Liters
Imperial Gallons	277,274	cu. in.
(Weight)		
Grams (gm)	.03527	Ounces
Kilograms (kg)	2.205	Pounds

American to Metric Conversion Table

Multiply	by	to obtain
(Linear)		
Inches (in.)	25.4	Millimeters
Inches (in.)	2.54	Centimeters
Feet (ft.)	304.8	Millimeters
Feet (ft.)	30.48	Centimeters
(Distance)		
Inches (in.)	.0254	Meters
Feet (ft.)	.3048	Meters
Miles (mi.)	1.609	Kilometers
(Area)		
Square Inches (in.²)	6.452	Square Centim.
Square Feet (sq. ft.)	929	Square Centim.
(Volume)		
Cubic Inches (cu. in.)	16.39	Cubic Centimet.
Cubic Inches (cu. in.)	.01639	Liters
(Liquid Capacity)		
Pints (pt.)	.4732	Liters
Quarts (qt.)	.9463	Liters
Gallons (gal.)	3.785	Liters
Fluid Ounces (fl. oz.)	29.58	Cubic Centimet.
U.S. Gallons	1.2	Imperial gals.
Imperial Gallons	4.537	Liters
Imperial Gallons	277.274	cu. in.
(Weight)		
Ounces (oz.)	28.35	Grams
Pounds (lb.)	.4536	Kilograms

CUSTOM FRAME BUILDERS

Europe

Harry Hall Cycles
30 Cathedral St.
Manchester 4
England

Rene Herse
12, Rue de President Wilson
92 Levallois-Perret
France

I can especially recommend the builders marked with an asterisk because I am personally acquainted with their work. This is not to say, of course, that the others are not builders of fine bicycles . . . simply that I have not seen their products but know that they do build framesets.

Bob Jackson
148 Harehills Lane, Leeds LS8 5BD
England

† Alex Singer
53, Rue Victor Hugo
92-Levallois
France

United States and Canada

Advanced Bicycle Engineering
75 Glenville Ave.
Allston, Massachusetts 02134

F. H. Appel Co.
100 West 35th
Suite "G"
National City, California 92050

Aquila Cycles
2909 Fascination
Colorado Springs, Colorado 80917

* F. M. Assenmacher
104 E. May
Mt. Pleasant, Michigan 48858

* Behringer Co.
4204 Mavelle Dr.
Edina, Minnesota 55435

Gus Betat
819 N. Broad Ave.
New Orleans, Louisiana 70119

Bike Warehouse
6187 West Blvd.
Youngstown, Ohio 44512

Bouquet-Coole-Richman
1826 West Ave.
Santa Rosa, California 95401

William Boston
505 Lakeview Dr.
Swedesboro, New Jersey 08085

Sam Braxton
2100 South Ave. West
Missoula, Montana 59801

Theodore De Capiteau
1201 N. Frederik St.
Arlington, Virginia 22205

† Terrific touring bikes!

Colorado Bicycle Co.
P.O. Box 15452
Denver, Colorado 80215

Bob Cox
9755 Durham Dr.
St. Louis, Missouri 63137

* Albert Eisentraut
910 81st Ave.
Oakland, California 94621

Hugh Enochs
1585 La Honda Rd.
Woodside, California 94062

* Fastab Cycles
2706 S. Glenbrook
Garland, Texas 75041

Fernwood Cycle Works
20024 Valley View Dr.
Topanga, California 90290

Griffon Cycles
% Wilshire West Bike Shop
11841 Wilshire Blvd.
Los Angeles, California 90025

Roger R. Jansen
Worcester, Vermont 05682

Peter Johnson
230 Erica Way
Menlo Park, California 94025

* Klein Bicycle Corp.
1305 Maple Ave.
San Martin, California 95046

* Colin Laing
% Pickering Cycles
3454 N. 1st Ave.
Tucson, Arizona 85719

* Pepi Limongi
% Paris-Sport
186 Main St.
Ridgefield Park, New Jersey 07660

Masi Bicycle Co.
6106 Avenida Encinas
Carlsbad, California 92008

Medallion Bicycles
(William Lagna)
11209 Sandyville Rd.
Bradshaw, Maryland 21021

James Redcay
82 George St.
Lambertville, New Jersey 08530

Tom Ritchey
914 Moreno Ave.
Palo Alto, California 94303

* Angel Rodriguez
5267 University Way NE
Seattle, Washington 98105

* Romic, Inc.
4434 Steffani Lane
Houston, Texas 77041

* RRB Cycles
562 Greenbay Road
Kenilworth, Illinois 60043

Dwight Safter
% Turin-Chicago
1932 N. Clark St.
Chicago, Illinois 60614

Ben Serota
% Cycle Imports
P.O. Box 235
Cornish, Maine 04020

* Schwinn Bicycle Co. Paramount Division
1805 N. Kostner
Chicago, Illinois 60639

Sparrow Frames (The Cyclist)
523 S. Higgins
Missoula, Montana 59801

Frank Spicer
1310 6th Ave. East
Kalispell, Montana 59901

Stout Cycles
% Transition Cyclery
201 South 13th East
Salt Lake City, Utah 84102

* Talbot Frames (Rick Green)
3237 Kingsway
Vancouver, BC Canada V5R-5K3

William Vetter
RFD Greensboro
Bend, Vermont

Witts Bicycle Shop
22138 Mission Blvd.
Hayward, California 94541

BICYCLE TOURS

The following are the major organizations that put on tours of the United States and abroad. This is not a complete list of all touring groups; there are, in addition, many fine small groups which tour specific regions of the United States and Canada. These small, independent tour groups change from year to year, and the easiest way to keep track of them is through the bicycling magazines or your local American Youth Hostel or League of American Wheelmen chapter.

American Youth Hostels: The AYH tours are run by the local chapters. The AYH is a nonprofit organization which sponsors bike tours, backpacking and other outdoor trips, usually stopping at hostels, or homes converted into inns, where you share cooking and cleaning duties in exchange for very inexpensive lodgings. AYH is for the young and the young at heart, which includes many middle-aged persons and older on average trips. Contact local AYH chapter or national organization, AYH, Delaplane, Virginia 22025. June–August tours.

Bikecentennial: Various tours follow historic routes established for the bicentennial, all of them tried and true by this date. One tour follows the Lewis and Clark expedition from Missoula, Montana to Astoria, Oregon. Many good western tours. The Bikecentennial also publishes booklets about the routes, with detailed maps. Write P.O. Box 8308, Missoula, Montana 59807. May–September tours.

Bike Dream Tours: Tours of faraway places in Europe and the American continent. Stops at hotels with good food, as opposed to the more spartan AYH tours. These can also be a lot more expensive. Many different tours, with different emphases. Write P.O. Box 20653, Houston, Texas 77025. May–September tours.

Bike Tour France: Longer tours, up to 1½ months, with emphasis on history, culture, museums. Geared to the experienced, in-shape cyclist. Tours go to Amsterdam, Paris, Brussels, Munich and Geneva. Write P.O. Box 32815, Charlotte, North Carolina 28232. May–September tours.

Biking Expedition: Varied tours in the U.S., Canada and British Isles. Moderately priced since you share some of the cooking, geared to the young. Write Biking Expedition, Inc., Hall Ave., Henniker, New Hampshire 03242. June–August tours.

Britain Cycling: Varied tour with days off for meeting local people and detailed look at localities such as London, Edinburgh, Stratford-on-Avon. Traditionally for students, but open to all comers. Hiking side trips, and much theater thrown in. Write Suite 95, 1050 2nd Ave., New York, New York 10022. Only July 25–August 17 tour.

Country Cycling Tours: Most of the tours are in the Berkshires and Southern Vermont. Delaware River tour includes rafting and canoeing. One-day to week-long tours. Contact 410 W. 24th St., New York, New York. June–September tours.

Euro-Bike Tours: Northwest France, Germany, England, Switzerland. These are organized tours where you do the touring on your own during the day but must get in by dark. There are bilingual tour guides to help you, though. Stops include some days off for more detailed look at area, with buses from area to area. 1805

Margaret Lane, Dekalb, Illinois 60115. June–August tours.

International Bicycle Touring Society: For a membership fee, you can get in on the most comprehensive touring organization around. Dr. Clifford Graves, noted cycling-touring expert, leads many tours. Group goes to places all over the world, various times of the year. Called the Huff n' Puff tours, they range from southern America to British Isles. 846 Prospect St., La Jolla, California 92037.

League of American Wheelmen: The league sponsors tours in member chapters of all sorts. A good way to learn about cycling and about bicycles, because league members are often experts. Contact local chapter or the national organization, which puts out the LAW Bulletin, the cyclist's bulletin board. LAW, Box 988, Baltimore, Maryland 21203.

New England Bicycle Tours: Tours go everywhere in this scenic and pleasant part of the country, and where they do not, this group will custom-make tours. P.O. Box 226, Granby, Connecticut 06035. May–October tours.

Out-Spokin': Fifty tours of the United States, including a coast-to-coast tour that goes from June to August. Special tours for students, family, adults, women, men. Established to provide a Christian encounter through exercise. Box 370, Elkhart, Indiana 46515. January–August tours.

Pacific Adventures: California and Hawaiian tours, in April, May and December. Sponsors backpack, canoe trips as well, and emphasizes experimental learning. P.O. Box 5041, Riverside, California 92517.

Rocky Mountain Cycle Tours: Tours for the novice and the experienced cyclist on some pretty rough and pretty interesting terrain. Trips include bike clinic for those unfamiliar with maintenance and how to cycle. Tent camping. Box 895, Banff, Alberta, Canada.

Sierra Club: Something like the AYH tours, the Sierra Club, a national environmental organization, runs tours through member chapters. Unlike the AYH, however, tours are geared to environmental awareness. Some tours go to Hawaii, to Canada and midwest. Contact local club chapter or the national organization, 530 Bush St., San Francisco, California 94108. June–August tours.

Student Hosteling Program of New England: Tours for ages 13–17, emphasizing learning to cooperate and live with others, so friends and family are discouraged from going on same tour. Actually, tours are of Europe, Canada, western U.S. Write Maple Hill, Rochester, Vermont 05767. June–August tours.

Tamure: Brittany, Loire Valley, Germany, Paris, England tours for students. Many stops at important sites, with stays in cities. Tamure Study Groups, 14613 E. Whittier Blvd., Whittier, California 90605.

Wandervogel: AYH-chartered group which tours mainly California. L. Appleby, Secretary, Wandervogel Bicycle Touring Association, 8145 Woolburn Dr., Huntington Beach, California 92646. Summers.

BICYCLING ORGANIZATIONS

American Bicycling Association
P.O. Box 718
Chandler, Arizona 85224

Governs BMX racing.
American Youth Hostels, Inc.
Delaplane, Virginia 22025

Sponsors bicycle trips and tours in the United States and abroad. Maintains hostels throughout the country, where members can stay at reasonable rates. Provides touring information and maintains a stock of cycling gear sold from its catalog. Holds membership in International Youth Hostel Federation.

Association Cycliste Canadienne
BP 2020 Succersdale D.
Ottawa, Canada (Ontario)

Governing body of competitive cycling in Canada.

Bicycle Manufacturers Association of America
1101 15th St. NW
Washington, DC 20002

British Cycling Federation
26 Park Crescent
London W.1
England

Governs bicycle racing in England, although it also offers assistance to members who wish to cycle-tour by providing itineraries, routes between youth hostels in Europe, maps, accident insurance and general advice.

International Bicycle Touring Society
846 Prospect St.
La Jolla, California 92037

Plans and conducts tours throughout the world. Operates famed "Huff 'n' Puff" tours.

International League for Cycling Touring
700 Avenue des Platanes
Bat. 17 B2 50000 Saint Lo
France

League of American Wheelman
Box 988
Baltimore, Maryland 21203

International organization devoted to all aspects of bicycling, based in this country but with members all over North America and Europe. Local chapters form the basis of this club, with cycle tours, fellowship, maintenance tips and so on. National organization puts out LAW Bulletin, a valuable guide, free with membership. Contact local organization or the national group, which can lead you to a local member or chapter.

National Bicycling Association
P.O. Box 411
Newhall, California 91322

BMX racing exclusively, puts out magazine.

National Bicycle Dealers Association
435 N. Michigan Ave.
Chicago, Illinois 60611

National Bicycling League
3801 N. Federal Highway
Suite 8
Pompano Beach, Florida 33064

Another BMX racing organization.

U.S. Olympic Committee
67 Park Ave.
New York, New York, 10001

United States Cycling Federation
1750 E. Boulder no. 4
Colorado Springs, Colorado 80909

The governing body of bicycle racing in the United States. Allied member of the Amateur Athletic Union of the United States, and of the U.S. Olympic Committee, as well as the Union Cycliste International (the world governing body for cycling).